Peter Gerlich/Krzysztof Glass (Hrsg.)

ZWISCHEN DEN ZEITEN

Verband der wissenschaftlichen Gesellschaften Österreichs
(VWGÖ)

Herausgegeben von: Peter Gerlich und Krzysztof Glass
Mitherausgeber: Österreichische Gesellschaft für Soziologie
Österreichische Gesellschaft für Politikwissenschaft
Institut für Staats- und Politikwissenschaft der Universität Wien

Redaktionskomitee: Peter Gerlich, Krzysztof Glass, Barbara Serloth
Englischlektorat: Maximilian Kudler

Druck und Symposium gefördert durch:
Bundesministerium für Wissenschaft und Forschung
Dr.-Karl-Renner-Institut
Politische Akademie der ÖVP
Kulturabteilung der Stadt Wien
ÖGB, LUGA
Österreichische Forschungsgemeinschaft
ÖVP-Klub
BWK
Verband der wissenschaftlichen Gesellschaften Österreichs (VWGÖ)
auf Antrag der Österreichischen Gesellschaft für Soziologie

Die Deutsche Bibliothek – CIP-Einheitsaufnahme

Zwischen den Zeiten / [Mithrsg.: Österreichische Gesellschaft für Soziologie . . .]. Peter Gerlich ; Krzysztof Glass (Hrsg.). – Wien : Verb. der Wiss. Ges. Österreichs (VWGÖ), 1992
ISBN 3-85369-867-0
NE: Gerlich, Peter [Hrsg.]; Österreichische Gesellschaft für Soziologie

ISBN 3-85369-867-0

1. Auflage
Umschlagentwurf: Krzysztof Glass
Satz/Datenkonvertierung: Laudenbach, A-1070 Wien
Druck: Anton Riegelnik, A-1080 Wien
Umschlagdruck: Lang & Gratzenberger, A-1070 Wien

Inhaltsverzeichnis

IV. Zeitsignale

V. Anhang

I.
Vorworte

Quo vadis Mitteleuropa? Demokratieentwicklung, Konservatismus und Nationalismus

Vorwort von Dr. Heinz Fischer

Das Thema dieser Veranstaltung ruft die Erinnerung an ein Wort von Bert Brecht wach: „Die Mühen der Gebirge liegen hinter uns, vor uns liegen die Mühen der Ebene." Es versinnbildlicht jenen Zyklus in den Gezeiten der politischen Entwicklung, welcher zuletzt von den Höhen eines begeisterten Aufbruches in Osteuropa zum mühsamen Alltag seiner politischen Aufarbeitung führte.

Dem Fortgang politischer Entwicklungen scheinen solche Bewegungen eigen zu sein.

Wenn man etwa die großen revolutionären Prozesse in Europa analysiert, so glaube ich feststellen zu können, daß auf jeden Höhepunkt eine Periode der „Ebene" gefolgt ist. Es gilt dies gleichermaßen für die französische Revolution 1789, für das Revolutionsjahr 1848, für den Umbruch des Jahres 1918, und letztlich kündigt sich ähnliches für die Bewältigung der europäischen Umgestaltung des Jahres 1989 an, auf die jetzt eine Konsolidierungsphase zu folgen scheint, die von Verunsicherung, Instabilität und größter Mühsal gekennzeichnet ist. Das Sprengen des Eispanzers hat zu einer plötzlichen Veränderung und einer darauffolgenden Verlangsamung dieses Prozesses geführt. Was die Inhalte der damit verbundenen gesellschaftlichen Lösungen anlangt, so pendeln diese in solchen Phasen der gesellschaftlichen Entwicklung von einem Extrem ins andere: So folgt etwa auf eine strenge Planwirtschaft der uneingeschränkte Glaube an die Marktwirtschaft.

Bei der Entwicklung der Demokratie in Osteuropa hat in den letzten Jahren eine Dynamik stattgefunden, welche wie im Zeitraffer Prozesse, welche sich im Werden unserer Demokratie in Jahrzehnten vollzogen haben, auf einen kurzen Zeitraum zusammengepreßt hat. Ich darf hier nur an die Entwicklung der Parteienlandschaft in diesen Staaten erinnern, welche sich von Bürgerbewegungen, wie etwa „Solidarność" in Polen, dem „Bürgerforum" und „Öffentlichkeit gegen Gewalt" in der ČSFR, zu einer Vielfalt von Parteien entwickelt haben, die nunmehr in wechselnden Allianzen und Inhalten auf neue Identitäten hinarbeiten und nur schwer in unser herkömmliches Schema des Parteienspektrums eingeordnet werden können.

Besonders deutlich zeigt sich, daß die Qualität einer jungen Demokratie nicht von ihren Institutionen allein abhängt, sondern daß hiefür ein Mindestmaß an Bewältigung der wirtschaftlich und sozialen Rahmenbedingungen und vor allem Gedankenvielfalt mindestens ebenso wichtige Voraussetzungen sind. Die gegenseitige Bedingtheit dieser Bereiche haben vor allem die Erfahrungen in der Sowjetunion erwiesen. Auch dem Auseinanderklaffen zwischen geschriebener Verfassung und Realverfassung wird bei der Beobachtung der Demokratieentwicklung in den jungen Demokratien größtes Augenmerk zu widmen sein.

Die Fragen, die sich dort stellen, sind vielfältig, und wir können nur beschränkt mit unseren Erfahrungen helfen, um so mehr als die Lösung gerade der wichtigsten Probleme Bewußtseinsveränderungen und die Überwindung emotionaler Momente zur Voraussetzung hat. Insoweit aber unsere Institutionen und unser Wissen über den Umgang mit ihnen hilfreich sein kann für die Entwicklung einer demokratischen, sozialen und wirtschaftlich intakten Gesellschaft in den ost- und zentraleuropäischen Staaten, müssen wir diese Erfahrungen, wo immer möglich, weitergeben; ohne jede Überheblichkeit und in dem Bewußtsein, daß man gesellschaftliche Entwicklungen nicht durch den Export von Modellen ersetzen kann. Unserem Parlamentarismus kommt dabei eine besondere Verantwortung zu.

Erhard Busek

Vorwort

„Mitteleuropa is a semantic confusion." Diese Ansicht des amerikanischen Historikers Henry Cord Meyer mag seine Berechtigung haben. Denn eine genaue Bestimmung dessen, was allgemein unter einem zentralen Europa verstanden wird, bereitet einige Mühe. Dennoch – oder gerade deswegen – wird die Frage nach einer mitteleuropäischen Identität oft gestellt. Man fragt nach einer mitteleuropäischen Geographie, nach mitteleuropäischen Nationen oder nach einer mitteleuropäischen Kultur.

Es gibt viele Antworten auf diese Fragen. Die des einen gleicht selten der des anderen. Und doch stimmen wir alle, die in dieser Diskussion das Wort ergreifen, darin überein, daß Mitteleuropa das pulsierende Herz Europas darstellt. Es liegt in der Mitte unseres Kontinents, dessen Aufgabe der spanische Schriftsteller, Philosoph und Diplomat Salvador de Madariaga einst mit den Worten definiert hat:

„Laßt uns ein Europa schaffen, daß sowohl sokratisch wie christlich ist, gleichzeitig voll Zweifel und Glauben, voll Freiheit und Ordnung, voll Vielfalt und Einheit – ein Europa, in dem der Staat vor allem unter der beständigen Wachsamkeit der öffentlichen Meinung gezwungen ist, das Individuum zu achten."

Mit diesen Gedanken erkannte Madariaga das Europa von morgen. Indem es aus den Fehlern seines Gestern und Heute zu lernen sucht, findet es seine Zukunft in konstruktivem Kontrast: in sokratischer Philosophie und christlicher Religion, in gläubigem Zweifel und bezweifeltem Glauben, in geordneter Freiheit und freiheitlicher Ordnung, in Vielfalt aus Einheit und Einheit aus Vielfalt.

Unser Europa ist die Harmonie seiner Himmelsrichtungen. Es darf kein Europa der einen gegen die anderen sein, kein Europa des Westens gegen den Osten, keines des Nordens gegen den Süden. Unser Europa, das wir im dritten Jahrtausend zu vollenden hoffen, hat viele Glieder. Sein Herz freilich ist Mitteleuropa.

Heinrich Neisser

Eröffnung des Seminars „Quo vadis Mitteleuropa"

Es ist offenkundig, daß die Diskussion über Mitteleuropa in Österreich eine bemerkenswerte Tradition besitzt. Lange vor den umwälzenden Ereignissen in Ost- und Mitteleuropa analysierte man in zahlreichen Begegnungen jene besonderen kulturellen, historischen und geistigen Elemente, die den Begriff „Mitteleuropa" charakterisieren, und zwar hinsichtlich ihrer Gemeinsamkeit, aber auch in bezug auf ihre Unterschiedlichkeit. Mitteleuropa wurde dabei nicht als isolierte Kategorie gesehen, sondern immer als verbindendes Element in Europa. Die Frage nach dem weiteren Weg Mitteleuropas ist eingebettet in die Bemühungen um die Gestaltung einer neuen Architektur Europas. Dieser Gestaltungsprozeß erfolgt mit einer verblüffenden Geschwindigkeit und mit ungeahnten Ergebnissen. Westeuropa und die Reformstaaten in Mittel- und Osteuropa erleben einen politischen Prozeß, in dem sich der vom totalitären Kommunismus zusammengehaltene Großraum in ein Gebilde auflöst, dessen Teile mit größeren Schwierigkeiten zu neuen Formen des politischen Zusammenlebens finden müssen. Alte historische Strukturen, wie etwa die Nationalitätenfrage, schaffen neue Abgrenzungsprobleme und erzeugen Rivalitäten. Für manche erscheint die Installierung eines Zentralstaates das probate Mittel zur Überwindung des Nationalstaates. Vorherrschend ist allerdings die Auffassung, daß die neue, sichtbar gewordene Verschiedenheit politisch neu organisiert werden muß und keinen zentralistischen Organismus duldet. Die neuen politischen Systeme Ost- und Mitteleuropas ringen um eine neue Eigenständigkeit im politischen Verbund. Diese Eigenständigkeit kann nicht destruktiver Nationalismus oder Chauvinismus sein, sondern muß auf die Schaffung einer neuen europäischen Gemeinsamkeit hinzielen.

Die unmittelbar nach dem Wechsel der politischen Lage allgemein vorherrschende Euphorie ist in der Zwischenzeit einer sehr realen Einschätzung gewichen. Die neuen demokratischen Systeme in Mittel- und Osteuropa erleben nach kurzer Zeit nicht nur den Wert pluralistischer demokratischer Systeme, sondern auch damit verbundene bedenkliche Erscheinungen und Herausforderungen.

In manchen Ländern macht sich schon kurze Zeit nach dem Erwachen der Demokratie eine Krise derselben breit, Anzeichen einer demokratischen Apathie entstehen und das Vertrauen zur Demokratie und ihren Institutionen wird schütter. In vielen Ländern ist der Weg zu demokratischen und parlamentarischen Systemen noch nicht abgeschlossen. Spannungsfelder, wie sie etwa in Polen zwischen dem Präsidenten und dem Parlament bestehen, werden den Prozeß der Verfassungsentwicklung sicherlich in Zukunft noch stark beeinflussen. Dazu kommt, daß in manchen Ländern die Parteienlandschaft durch eine übermäßig große Zahl von politischen Parteien unübersichtlich wird, die Regierbarkeit in diesen Systemen steht auf dem Prüfstand. Beispiele sind die ČSFR und Polen. Es ist bemerkenswert, daß vor dem Hintergrund dieser politischen Wirklichkeit die Diskussionen manchmal von einer eigenartigen Skepsis geprägt sind. Dies zeigt sich schon in der Semantik; anstatt von politischen und wirtschaftlichen Erfolgen zu reden, spricht man von Altlasten, die Schuldfrage verdeckt in vielen Fragen die Lösungsfrage, und die staatlichen Institutionen, kaum geschaffen, werden in ihrer Wirksamkeit in Frage gestellt.

Ich glaube, daß die heutige Veranstaltung zwei grundsätzliche Aspekte besitzt. Der erste Gesichtspunkt ist die Frage nach der Rolle der Wissenschaft in dem neuen europäischen Gestaltungsprozeß. Die kommunikative Funktion der Wissenschaften spielt in den politischen Veränderungen eine enorme Rolle. Die Wissenschaft hat hiebei nicht nur zu analysieren, sondern vor allem auch Element der Anregung zu sein. Bedeutsam sind hiefür nicht allein die Sozialwissenschaften, sondern auch die Geisteswissenschaften. So haben beispielsweise die historischen Wissenschaften bei der Aufarbeitung des Nationalitätenproblems eine große Verantwortung. Aber auch die Politikwissenschaft ist aufgerufen, in dem Prozeß der Systementwicklung Initiativen zu setzen und Lösungsmodelle anzubieten.

Die zweite Frage, die ich hier erwähnen möchte, konzentriert sich besonders auf Österreich. Man muß die Rolle Österreichs in dem neuen europäischen Zusammenhang realistisch sehen. Das bedeutet allerdings nicht, daß wir unsere Aufgabe unterschätzen sollen, im Gegenteil. Ich glaube, daß Österreich als Diskussionspartner eine große Verantwortung zukommt. Wissenschaftliche Veranstaltungen von der Art, wie sie heute stattfindet, haben nicht nur die Aufgabe, Informationen auszutauschen, sondern sollen einen neuen Geist der Diskussion prägen. Es ist in den letzten zwei Jahren geradezu eine Inflation von Veranstaltungen festzustellen, die sich mit dem Thema Ost- und Mitteleuropa befassen. Viele dieser Begegnungen haben eher rhetorischen Wert. Im Gegensatz dazu sehe ich das heutige Seminar mit hohem wissenschaftlichen Anspruch in seinen Ergebnissen als Bereicherung für den europäischen Prozeß an.

II.
Zeichen des Aufbruchs

Peter Gerlich

Das neue Europa – Chancen und Risken

Es ist bereits ein Schlagwort geworden, aber es ist dennoch wahr: Wir stehen an einer Zeitenwende. Wir stehen an einer Zeitenwende, was die Entwicklungen in Osteuropa betrifft.[1] Wir stehen an einer Zeitenwende, was die Entwicklungen in Westeuropa und im Raum der EG betrifft, und wir stehen auch an einer Zeitenwende im Hinblick auf unser eigenes Land, auf Österreich.

Im Schutze unserer neutralen Position zwischen den beiden Großmächten konnten wir uns lange Jahre hindurch der Illusion der Stabilität, der bestenfalls bloß graduellen Veränderungen hingeben. Aber die Zeiten, in denen Österreich eine Insel der Seligen war, sind schon alleine deshalb vorbei, weil es keine Insel mehr ist. In einem Gespräch mit zwei US-amerikanischen Journalisten antworteten diese mir vor kurzem, als ich ihr Interesse für Österreich relativierte und sie auf die doch viel bemerkenswerteren Entwicklungen in Osteuropa hinwies, mit der Bemerkung, Österreich sei jetzt ganz besonders interessant, da es in gewisser Hinsicht zu einem „Frontstaat" geworden sei. Es sei zu einem Staat geworden, der zwischen die Mühlsteine der Veränderungen in Ost und West geraten ist und in dem wechselseitig diese Veränderungen zunächst auch ihre Auswirkungen finden.

Diese Veränderungen betreffen die drei Aspekte des vorliegenden Symposiums zur generellen Thematik „Quo vadis Mitteleuropa?", nämlich die Frage der Demokratieentwicklung, die sich in Ost und West und auch bei uns stellt, und ebenso die Fragen des neuen oder alten Konservativismus und des neuen oder alten Nationalismus. Auf alle diese Fragen in ihrer Vielschichtigkeit, aber auch faktischen Bedeutsamkeit wird im folgenden Symposium aus der Perspektive von Kollegen aus Polen, der Tschechoslowakei und Österreich eingegangen.

In Vorlesungen versuche ich meinen Studenten immer zu erklären, daß Experimente im sozialen Bereich und daher auch für die Sozialwissenschaften im Unterschied zu den Naturwissenschaften als Mittel der Überprüfung von Theorien entweder nicht möglich oder aus ethischen Gründen problematisch seien, daher im Prinzip nicht stattfinden könnten. Die Entwicklung in Osteuropa falsifiziert diese Aussage. Wir beobachten ein ungeheures Experiment bzw. auf die einzelnen Länder bezogen ungeheure Experimente, allerdings Experimente, die ohne theoretische Grundlage stattfinden, wie Botschafter Bartoszewski in seinen einführenden Bemerkungen sehr richtig bemerkt hat.

Ich finde es auch nicht übertrieben, diese enormen Veränderungen mit dem Bild einer Geburt unter entsprechenden Geburtswehen zu erfassen, wie er es getan hat. Die durch diese Experimente ausgelösten Veränderungen bewirken Chancen, beinhalten aber auch nicht geringe Gefahren, und zwar Chancen und Gefahren zumindest für Europa in seiner Gesamtheit. In der anfänglichen Euphorie des wunderbaren Jahres 1989 schien alles möglich, schien die Geschichte zu

Ende zu sein und zumindest ein mitteleuropäisches Paradies bevorzustehen, und auch heute noch gibt es architektonische und andere Wunschträume über das zukünftige Europa, die sich jeder nach Lust und Liebe selbst ausmalen kann.

Daß dies alles allerdings nicht so einfach sein wird, ist mitunter nach dem Abklingen der ersten Begeisterung vielen auch schon klarer geworden, und mir scheint es besonders wichtig, über mögliche Gefahren zu reflektieren, um möglichst rechtzeitig entsprechende Gegenmaßnahmen setzen zu können. Ein ganz wichtiger Faktor dabei ist das Verhältnis von wirtschaftlicher Entwicklung und demokratischer Entfaltung, worauf Präsident Fischer in seinen Einleitungsbemerkungen so treffend hingewiesen hat. Auch für mich war es eine der wichtigen Lehren, die von einer Persönlichkeit wie Bruno Kreisky aus der politischen Praxis für die politische Theorie übernommen werden konnten, nämlich seine Aussage, daß die beste Demokratiepolitik eine effektive Wirtschaftspolitik ist. Und die wirtschaftliche Entwicklung ist in Zukunft vor allem in Osteuropa keineswegs von vornherein als positiv gesichert anzusehen. Sogar bei relativ guten Entwicklungen ist mit der Gefahr einer gesamteuropäischen Zweidrittelgesellschaft zu rechnen, und daß diese ökonomischen Schwierigkeiten und Ungleichheiten zu politischer Instabilität, zum politischen Abrutschen in nichtdemokratische Regierungsformen in einzelnen Ländern und zu internationalen Spannungen und Konflikten führen können, liegt auf der Hand. Es ist wichtig, daß sich die Wissenschaft mit diesen Fragen auseinandersetzt, und es ist wahrscheinlich noch wichtiger, daß die Politik der westlichen Länder und auch die Politik Österreichs sich auf die Herausforderungen einstellt, die sich aus derartigen Diagnosen ergeben und ergeben müssen.

Wie erwähnt, fehlt es uns an Theorien, um die neuen Prozesse des Wandels wissenschaftlich analysieren und verstehen zu können. Auch ich kann mit solchen Theorien nicht aufwarten. Jedoch gehen mir häufig Metaphern durch den Sinn, die ja, wenn man so will, primitive Formen von Theorien darstellen. Es sind vor allem zwei derartige Bilder, die mich beschäftigen.

Das erste, das das Ost-West-Verhältnis betrifft, ist das Bild der kommunizierenden Gefäße. Ob wir es wollen oder nicht, hängen wir nach der Aufhebung des Eisernen Vorhanges mitt den ehemaligen sozialistischen Ländern zusammen, und dieser Zusammenhang besteht in vielerlei Form, ein Trend zum zumindest ansatzweisen Ausgleich der unterschiedlichen Zustandsformen dieser Länder wird auch nicht von der Hand zu weisen sein. Man wird etwa die Wanderungsbewegungen, die sich als natürliche Konsequenz einer solchen Situation ergeben, kaum durch administrative oder militärische Maßnahmen abstoppen können. Es sei denn, man errichtet einen neuen eisernen Vorhang, diesmal in umgekehrter Richtung.[2]

Das zweite Bild, daß mir zu denken gibt, betrifft den Westen und dessen Verlust eines Gegenübers, das bisher dazu gedient hat, Selbstkritik zu reduzieren. Der alte Eiserne Vorhang war so etwas wie ein Scheinspiegel. Man konnte sich in ihm eitel betrachten und Kritik an den Zuständen in unseren Ländern mit dem Hinweis, die Kritiker mögen sich doch in den Osten begeben, begegnen. Im Kontrast war alles, was bei uns war, immer gut und besser. Dieser Scheinspiegel ist nun zu einem Wahrspiegel geworden. Die nicht mehr bestehende hermetisch abgeriegelte Grenze führt dazu, daß wir uns zunehmend nicht mehr in einem blinden, sondern in einem sehenden Spiegel sehen. Zunehmend wird es für uns die schmerzliche Notwendigkeit der Selbsterkenntnis geben. Der Gegenpol, auf den man sich sozusagen ausreden konnte, ist weggefallen. Das in unseren Ländern nicht alles zum Besten steht, kann niemand bestreiten, und die vielen Nachteile unseres Systems, das im Prinzip nun siegreich erscheint, werden daher in Zukunft sicher intensiver zur Diskussion stehen.

Der Sinn wissenschaftlicher und sonstiger Aussprache zwischen Vertretern der ehemaligen sozialistischen und der anderen europäischen Länder muß darin bestehen, von einander zu lernen und einander zu helfen. Ich bin zutiefst davon überzeugt, daß solches Lernen und solche Hilfen wechselseitig erfolgen können und sollen. Nunmehr steht zwar die Hilfe von West nach Ost im Vordergrund. Es geht um Transfer von Know-how, es geht um ökonomische Hilfen, es geht um politische Hilfen. Aber man sollte auch die Möglichkeit der Hilfe in umgekehrter Richtung, die Möglichkeit im Westen belehrt zu werden und durch Kontrastierung Selbsterkenntnis zu ermöglichen, nicht unterschätzen.

Was den Transfer von Hilfe von West nach Ost betrifft, glaube ich, sollte vor allem – und das betrifft auch uns in diesem Kreise von Sozial- und Politikwissenschaftlern – das politische Know-how zur Diskussion stehen. Es sollte heute also nicht nur um die Mac-Donaldisierung von Mittel- und Osteuropa gehen, sondern auch um die Vermittlung der Erfahrungen der westlichen Demokratie von Rechtsordnung, von Verfassungsformen, von politischer Kultur und Erfahrungen mit politischen Entscheidungsmechanismen. Dabei glaube ich, daß gerade die bei uns in Österreich entwickelte Form etwa der Sozialpartnerschaft und des Korporatismus für die Länder, die nun versuchen, eine Demokratie aufzubauen, von großer Bedeutung sein könnte.[3] Ich sehe keinen Gegensatz darin, daß im Zuge der Veränderungen der Politik in Österreich diese Formen zunehmend überholt wirken.[4] Der Entwicklungsstand in Österreich und in den neuen Demokratien ist eben in demokratiepolitischer Hinsicht unterschiedlich. Ich stimme Klaus von Dohnanyi zu, daß die Mithilfe bei der Übertragung von technischem Know-how nicht zu schüchtern erfolgen sollte.[5] Die politische Entwicklung in den Ländern Ostmitteleuropas betrifft uns alle, und wir sollten zumindest argumentativ jene Kenntnisse und jenes Wissen, über das wir verfügen, einbringen.

Darüber hinaus gibt es sicher auch noch die Möglichkeit, Managerschulungen durchzuführen und anderes technisches Know-how zu vermitteln und nicht zuletzt auch Wirtschaftshilfe zu leisten.[6] Aus meiner Perspektive ist es nicht recht verständlich und auch sehr wenig erfreulich, daß die Idee eines Marshallplanes insbesondere für die Länder der ehemaligen Sowjetunion von den westlichen Staaten offenbar zu früh ad acta gelegt zu sein scheint. Dieses ist um so bedauerlicher, als die Sowjetunion in Zukunft sicher jenes Land sein wird, dessen wirtschaftliche und politische Entwicklung am problematischsten ablaufen könnte und dessen Schwierigkeiten aber dann auch die ganze Region der ehemaligen Satellitenländer beeinflussen wird.

Nicht zuletzt sei auch darauf hingewiesen, und das trifft uns Österreicher wie so vieles schmerzlich und ist auch als eher peinlich anzusehen, daß eine der wichtigsten Hilfen, die der Westen für Ostländer leisten kann, die Öffnung der westlichen Märkte für Waren aus dem Osten sein müßte und daß Österreich selbst hiebei noch einen großen Nachholbedarf hat.

Was die Hilfen von Ost nach West betrifft, glaube ich, könnte es uns nur von Nutzen sein, Teile einer frischen politischen Kultur, die in Entwicklung begriffen ist, zu importieren.[7] Ich bin davon überzeugt, daß sie indirekt über die Massenmedien bereits auf uns einwirkt und daß manche politischen Veränderungen in Österreich und anderen westlichen Ländern als Reflex auf die Entwicklungen im Osten zu verstehen sind.[8] Wenn Menschen in Mittel- und Osteuropa nicht mehr bereit sind, sich der Herrschaft dummer Bürokratien zu unterwerfen, ist es relativ wenig einsichtig, warum das mutatis mutandis für Bürokratien im Westen zuzulassen sein sollte. Vom Osten können wir lernen, daß man Politik ernst nehmen kann, daß man nicht bloß Symbolpolitik betreiben muß, sondern daß es einen echten Willen zur Erneuerung geben kann. Wir können davon lernen, wie eine echte und faktische Demokratisierung gelebt wird, wie sie wirkt, wie sie zu einer ganz anderen aufrichtigeren politischen Haltung führt, wie sie dazu führt, daß man „in Wahrheit lebt".[9] Und wir können auch die Bescheidenheit und Selbstkontrolle bewundern lernen, die wohltuend mit der Arroganz kontrastiert werden kann, die bei uns der übergroße Reichtum und die funktionierende Konsumgesellschaft ausgelöst haben.[10] Insbesondere scheint es mir gerade die Aufgabe der Wissenschaft zu sein – und darauf hat Klubobmann Neisser hingewiesen, und ich stimme ihm darin zu –, daß wir versuchen müssen, einander wechselseitig zu verstehen und zum wechselseitigen Verständnis beizutragen. Es geht darum, nicht nur Informationen über Verhältnisse und Zustände auszutauschen, sondern auch dazu beizutragen, Ressentiments abzubauen. Die Tendenzen des Ethnozentrismus, der Fremdenfeindlichkeit und des Nationalismus sind Folgen des Wandels nicht nur im Osten, sondern auch im Westen. Beim Abbau dieser Tendenzen mitzuwirken war sicher auch mit eine Aufgabe dieses Symposiums.

Die Beiträge, die hier vorgelegt werden, sind einerseits Beiträge zur Zeitdiagnose allgemein, insbesondere zum großen Paradigmenwechsel in der Politik in Richtung auf den neuen Konservativismus. Sie sind aber auch Diagnosen und Berichte zu Zustandsanalysen in den Ländern, die hier betroffen sind: Polen, Tschechoslowakei und Österreich, und sie sind schließlich Berichte und Analysen zu möglichen Strategien angesichts dieser verschiedenen Entwicklungen. Am Beginn konnte man den Referaten unseres Symposiums und den Diskussionen offizieller und inoffizieller Art, die an diese anschlossen, nur mit Interesse entgegensehen. Und dieses Interesse wurde nicht enttäuscht.

Anmerkungen

1 Vgl. Timothy Garton Ash u. a., Osteuropa – Übergang zur Demokratie?, Transit 1, Europäische Revue, Frankfurt 1990.

2 Vgl. dazu allgemein M. Merle, The Sociology of International Relations, Leamington Spa, 1987.

3 Zur Sozialpartnerschaft vgl. nun E. Tálos (Hrsg.), Sozialpartnerschaft, Verbände und Wirtschaftsmacht, in: H. Dachs u. a. (Hrsg.), Handbuch des politischen Systems Österreichs, Wien 1991.
4 Vgl. Peter Gerlich, Österreichische Politik im Wandel, in: SWS Rundschau 1, Wien 1990.
5 Klaus v. Dohnanyi, Harte Arbeit für die Freiheit, Die Zeit 45, Hamburg 1991.
6 Vgl. J. Stankovsky, Österreich, Osteuropa und die EG, in: Wirtschaftspolitische Blätter 5, Wien 1990.
7 Vgl. S. Berglund/J. A. Dellenbrant, The New Democracies in Eastern Europe, London 1991.
8 Vgl. dazu Peter Gerlich, Die Zukunft der Politik, in: Internationales Jahrbuch für Rechtsphilosophie und Gesetzgebung, Wien 1989.
9 Václav Havel, Living in Truth, London 1986.
10 Vgl. z. B. Gerfried Sperl/Michael Steiner (Hrsg.), Wortmacht/Machtwort, was 66, Graz 1991.

Krzysztof Pałecki

The Dynamic of Political Transition: Toward the New Paradigm

1. What is lacking?

The collapse of communism exposed the misery of political theory.[1] At least that important part of it which concerns the political change. What has happened in Central and Eastern Europe in this decade not only had not been predicted – with very few exceptions – but what is much worse, has not been adequately and satisfactorily explained till now.[2]

This situation raises a provocative question as to the capability of existing methods of explanation in political science for the elucidation of such political changes. In spite of numerous works devoted to this task, an unproportionally small step has been made toward our understanding of this historical set of events, labeled sometimes by the internally contradictory term: the peaceful or quiet revolution.

The variety of proposed explanations is somewhat misleading if they are not examined carefully. They are founded on only a few basic schemes of explanation, usually well exploited in previous literature and destined for some specific processes more or less remote from the field of *political change*. Multiplicity of approaches and factors used for elucidation are somehow illusory and there always rests a slight feeling of incompleteness. So, we can find some "fundamental" and rather petrified paradigms of *general social change*; the theory of evolution, revolution or functional change. Farther on, some theories of *convergency* and *modernization* or theories of *economic growth and crisis* are used; sometimes political thinkers are resorting to the concepts of *sovereignty* or *global international relations*.[3] At other times, they resort to the theory of *communication, diffusion of culture* or *uniformisation through mass media*, even some theories of human nature,[5] *conspiracy, innovatory personality of political leaders*[6] or *socio-linguistic*[7] concepts are used in an effort to explain. The eclectic approach, combining some of the listed above "theories" is not exceptional either. But while enumerating all those factors "responsible" for *peaceful revolution*, one may be struck by two points; first – they are always somehow objective or *external* to the political changes they affected; second – the main actors of changes and the main subject of these changes – the *common people* and their *consciousness* – are absent[8]. So, we have been taught about the disastrous effects of a centrally planned economy for communist countries[9], the changes in the international balance of power as a result of the end of the "cold war" and "iron curtain". By the way, I am always confused as to whether this is the result of peaceful revolution or the cause of it. We have also been taught about the decomposing and stimulative role of unlimited mass-access to information, thanks to the new "high-tech" technologies, the inconsistency of the "human nature" with the requirements of communism, about the high ranking apparatchiks and officers who conspired to prepare the whole "revolution", about the role of personality in politics, especially that of Gorbachev, Reagan, and others, the desinformation processes and collapse of the communist propaganda machine as a result of some socio-linguistic phenomena, and many other different but "crucial reasons" causing "the end of communism" in Europe. All those attempts could not help us much to find out what really happened "inside" the *political processes*, and specifically between the political power wielders and subordinated subjects. The whole dynamic of this relation has been routinely reduced to the personal changes, the emergence of new political elites[10], and/or the more democratic way of governing.

From the perspective of the above mentioned concepts, both are only a kind of reaction against the strong impact of one or more combined factors of *political change*, previously marked. What I should like to add, comes from my conviction about the importance of the internal phenomena, which are active inside the political power relations and play, at least, the equally substantial role as an "objective" factors for *the process of political change*. I should like to grasp this specific process as analytically semi-autonomous and generated by some inner forces. Once more, in my opinion what is lacking in analyses we meet in present literature is the factor of *the social consciousness* of those involved in political power relations. Social consciousness is irreducible from the process of social construction and realization of any social relation, and so, indispensable for understanding its dynamic. Paraphrasing the classics of sociological thought, I want to repeat, that what the people are thinking about their political relations is as important for these relations as the material or "objective" conditions in which they occurred.[11]

As I said, most of the ways of thinking about the *peaceful revolution* are primary rooted in a very few basic paradigms of *social change*. Usually some kind of theory of evolution or revolution,[12] theory of conflict, reformative ideas, theory of modernization and structural-functional concepts are used as a base.

Unsatisfactory results which have to come from application of evolutionary paradigm are obvious to many thinkers today but as Gabriel Almond once remarked: ". . . we seem to be falling victim to the same unilinear evolutionary theory, from which we are seeking to escape".[13] In evolutionary terms "change" is more or less synonymous with "progress" and there are enormous difficulties with some periods. For example, with the period of communism in Central and Eastern Europe, in which the progress in many realms has been at least stopped, If not turned back, and now, the restoration of previous socio-economic orders is following.

But what is even more puzzling here, and what could occur in some countries of the former Soviet Block is that some crucial changes of social and economic systems seem to be convertible, may be not only once, and this is not adaptable with evolutionary paradigm anyway. To explain the phenomenon of peaceful revolution as a result of perpetual, gradual, continuous *evolution* (progress) seems to be rather a breakneck venture.

There is also no doubt that *peaceful revolution* has very little in common with *the revolution*, in the real sense of this term. There was no blood in the streets of Poland, no militant fights, no culmination of social or class conflicts, no total destruction of former political apparatus or killing of representatives of former regime in the time of decisive political turn (June 1989).

On the contrary, the round table negotiations are commonly considered to be a breaking-point in the situation. Quite clearly, some political thinkers are using the "revolutionary" terminology as a figure of speech only (e. g. the expression "conservative revolution" used for the description of political changes in Poland, or the expression "velvet revolution" to describe the political events in Prague). The purpose of such a metaphor is to emphasize the scale of changes and to point out the ideological connotations of these changes rather than to undertake a substantive analysis of them.

Taking the *reformative paradigm* as a point of departure is also not very useful. What happened in Central and Eastern Europe could hardly be elucidated in terms of the reformative efforts of political deciders. Much more the changes were caused by the failure of reforms or the lack of reforms, and what is essential to note here, is that it is the predominant opinion among political thinkers; the so-called "real socialism" is in principle irreformative.The concessions which rulers are ready to make, as the price of their survival, have nothing to do with the sanative will of true reformers. The dynamic of this situation is attributed to temporary and partial preservation of political privileges and the cumulation of negative effects of such a give-and-take policy, what, in the end, has to force farther concessions. It is not the dynamic of progress – which is the main goal and principle of any reforms and modernization. It is not the dynamic of regress, either (this could be – of course – described and explained in terms of reformative paradigm). It is the specific dynamic of decline and *transition* of a political system. The analytical and projective categories of above mentioned paradigms are rather incompatible with this case.

The application of the *functionalist model* seems to be also limited. As Randall Collins notes: "Since it is based on an organic analogy, the functionalist model has always been implicitly concerned with *change*, as an analogue to growth".[14] But the concept of growth, usually regarded as better integration, socialization, more efficient use of resources, increasing output of the system, and so on, could rather be seen as desirable results of *peaceful revolution*, its goal rather than a factor of political change, especially in the present situation of countries being in transition. It will be very difficult to analyse the events in Poland, Czecho-Slovakia, GDR, or Baltic Republics using the concept of political change formulated in terms of the performance capabilities of political system, more precisely, such a new quality which decisively improve its capabilities.[15]

Even though to omit the uneasy problem what is a "new" quality or capability of a system, and how much it is the previous quality, to which the communist political systems came back rather than acquired it, e. g. the market economy, we have to take under consideration some obvious fact; it is not the increasing composition and equilibrium which have been generating a new quality of communist regimes in the time when they were quite efficient, integrated and "flourished", and then transformed them, but in contrary, the increasing decomposition, disintegration and disequilibrium promoted the "reforms" and "innovations" of those political systems (usually "the innovations" well known and functioning in a given country before the communism has been established in it).

It is characteristic that the followers of structural-functional theories are likely to view some forms of democracy – for example pluralistic and participatory politics – as functionally related to economic development. In general, they are likely to view politics as a dependent variablel.[16] Nevertheless this has been not the case in Poland, where political and institutional changes, e. g. democratization, somehow outdistanced and evaded the economic reforms, and now, this restored political opportunities are giving the strongest impulse for the changes in the still obsolete economy.

In closing these remarks, some further conclusions come to mind. I am not questioning the explanatory capability of the above mentioned paradigms of social change. Their failure lies in being more *social* than *political*, and as a result something is lacking in their explanation. From the point of view of the political matters, we are left far from satisfied. The interdependencies between political subsystem and the other subsystems of a social system are trivial, though, the ways of thinking about both of them could be, to some extent, independent. What is political has its own semi-autonomous dimension, which should be examined separately.

2. What is "political"?

I do not intend to refer to the whole of the body of literature written on this problem.[17] I just want to propose an approach which seems to be fruitful in analysing the political transition, taken as a specific kind of political change.

The basic unit of everything which can, in all seriousness, be called "political" is the *political relation*[18]. It is amazing how little attention has been paid to this fundamental concept in the theory of political science. For the purpose of this paper, it will be enough to recall the analytical model of social relation, which is a genus Proximum for a political one. The simplest description of social relation should contain – at least – two social subjects, one interaction, one social norm which regulate the course of this interaction and one social value which motivates and rationalizes this interaction. The social subjects have to have some special quality for realizing a social relation; the capability to interact with the other members of a given community. Which means that the actions directed toward them will be *socially valid*. The child does not have the capacity to act in many roles, which are socially "reserved" for adults only. Some adults have more of this capability because of their social position, status or because of roles they play; in some societies, groups, associations, organizations, etc., the people have – in general – more ability to interact, than in others. It is the *social normative order* which prescribes the extent of this capacity, and it is the real social and economic order which is providing the conditions and means for realization of this potential ability. Realizing the social relations people can satisfy their material (economic) and ideal interests.

The normative right, and related to it, real possibility, for independent decision-making and action (interaction) directed to gaining some material or ideal goods, I call the *social agency*.

In other words, it is the normative-real possibility of self-realization of a given social subject (no matter the individual or collective) through interaction with the other social subject. The scope of social agency is not only different for different social subjects, but also never ultimately fixed for any of them. While the normative regulations are usually more static, the real (material) conditions for self-realization could be more changeable. Sometimes both are simultaneously dynamic, not necessarily in concert.

It is also important to underline, that this "objective" (normative-real) possibility of self-realization is not necessarily adequate with its "reprint" in social consciousness, so, with its "subjective" equivalent. More often than not, this is the case.

To distinguish the *political relation* one has to recognize the nature of some specific social relations; not those harmonious and mutually beneficial relations, but the *asymmetrical relations*, which means that one social subject has a privileged position comparing with the other. This privilege consists in the possible use of some part of social agency on the part of a counterpartner in a given social relation, according to the decision of the privileged subject and without the will of deprived one. Briefly, it is a *relation of power*.[19]

In the relation of power one subject can seize from the other, the part of his right to decision about self-realization, and/or the part of being to his disposal material and ideal goods.

This deprivation from social agency does not have an arbitrary character. On the contrary, it is regulated by social norms, so at "the bottom" some order of social values is an acting factor. The privileged subject does not necessarily have to use the seized social agency for its sake, but for the common benefit of subjects linked by a given set of social relations, or even for the advantage of the deprived subjects.

In many cases this deprivation of social agency has not an individual, spontaneous, and temporary character, but a continual, *institutional*, intentionally organized, and procedural.

Then, the material and ideal goods which are the object of deprivation could sometimes qualify as *public goods*, which means that they are not *private* property, they are not at the disposal of individuals or even small, primary groups, e. g. the family, but they are in the hands and under the rule of representatives of some wide community, nation or, typically, society organized in the state. And going farther, the deprived right to decision-making does not enrich the extent of normative privileges of some individuals as such, their personal social agency, taking under consideration its normative dimension only, but is attached to the *public position* of a given person in the social structure.

So, the *political relation* is that kind of social relation which has the normative, institutional and public character in the sense established above.

Bearing in mind the above described model of social relations, it is easier to say now, what the *political* norms, values, interests and actions (behaviours) are.

The political norms are the social rules for seizing social agency. More precisely, they are the rules for gaining power over the rights to decision and/or disposition of public goods; the rules for the wielding of such power, and the rules for prescribing the extent of social agency which can be seized from subordinated subjects. These first rules I call the *rules* (norms) of *political game* (the stake in this game is a higher or lower position in political hierarchy); the second set of rules, the *rules of politics* regulate the ways of realization of obtained political power, usually formulated as a *political program* or in brief, politics. The third, the *rules of political limitation*. Briefly, the rules of limitation determine the normative – not necessary real – scope of political power.

The political values are those which are justifying (legitimating) and motivating the process of seizing the social agency (political process). Limiting the social agency of social subjects is not easy to justify. The most commonly evoked value of such a limitation is the need for social order. Social order requires the resignation from the part of social agency belonging to the members of given community. This is an indispensable condition of any social organization, and further, any coordinated common action. Therefore, the belief that order is better than chaos, is very often the primary cause of social deprivation. Sometimes the value of being secure can be a good *political value*, while the internal and/or external situation of a given community, nation or state is uncertain or dangerous and people are ready to resign some part of their social agency to leaders, in hope of saving the more essential part of it, or preserving some other value (e. g., life).

In this sense any social value could be political while performing the specific function of a rationalization, legitimation and/or motivation for the realization of the political relations.

The political interests are genuinely dialectic. Both sides of political relations have a common interest in maintaining them because of values which they want to attain (preserve, enrich) together. But the subordinated subject wants to achieve this goal at a minimal loss to its social agency and maximum control over the dominated subject. The latter is opposite. The maximization of power and minimalization of the control of the power wielder; these are its "natural interests". Briefly, the political interests consist in expending, limiting or preserving social agency. In a wider sense, everything which can help to further such goals is in the political interest too.

And in the end we can say that any kind of behaviour (action, interaction) is *political* if undertaken as a way of realizing political norms.

So, political behaviours (actions, interactions) are aimed at the bigger scope of social agency for one, and the smaller scope for another.

However, if the political norms are broken by such behaviours, they ceased to be political and become acts of compulsion and/or crime.

3. What is "political change"?

Once more we have to refer to the construction of the political relation. Political change will occur at the micro-level as just a change of one or a few of such relations between the individual social subjects, usually inside some small group; at middle-level it will be a change of a given set of political relations, e. g. in some associations, organizations, local community, and so on. At the macro-level, it will be a change of the whole structure of political relations in a given politically organized society: the state. There is also an interstate scale of political change which concerns the *international political relations*. But regardless of the scale, any political change can be described as one, few or all of following possibilities:

a) as the change of the *political actors*,
b) as the change of the *political behaviours*,
c) as the change of the *political norms and values*,
d) as the change of the *order of political relations*,
e) as the change in the *scope (extent) of social agency*, possessed by the political actors (the subjects of political relations).

It is easy to see that each of the above listed kinds of changes is more or less interdependent with others. But what is, perhaps, not so obvious, is that the less meaning the given change has for the shape or order of the whole political relations, the more it is independent from others. In politically stable democracies the changes of political actors are periodical and may have little or no impact on the other elements of political relations (one can talk about the changes in the *style of politics* rather than in substantive changes). The changes of political behaviours might not be so independent; in most cases, the new (different) political behaviours have an impact or are the indicators of changes in the political norms and values and, of course, the others changes which are connected with those.

The changes of the political norms are, roughly speaking, of two kinds; the procedural or formal, and the substantial. Though, the changes of political procedure are sometimes very important, they might not affect very much the political values, the scope of social agency of political actors or the order of political relations, especially when intended to improve some technical aspects. But the substantial changes in the political norms (the content) are always crucial for the whole political process, and the order of political relations.

The substantive changes of any social norms, so political norms too, are two-dimensional: a) they are changes of validity (the changes of binding force) and b) changes of content. Because the normative vacuum is a rather temporary and exceptional phenomenon; while one political norm or set of norms is loosing its binding force, the other norms are emerging in its place and their validity is growing. This process is simultaneous with the changes of the normative content of political regulation. In some cases, when the political norms are legal as well, the whole process of changes of political norms might have a procedural conduct. But the *social changes* in the validity of political norms (as well as any other social norms) consist of the changes of the *political consciousness* of the people, their knowledge, beliefs, convictions and feelings about what is valid and binding in political relations and what is not. That is why the state of social political consciousness is so important, when one is trying to explain the political dynamic.

The changes in the order of political relations and in the social agency are causes and/or results of every change in any elements which are taking part in the political process. So, they could be barely thought out independently, with the exception of some analytical (model-like) examination. In this sense they are the more general, and the more crucial as well.

The above "catalog" of political changes facilitates the conclusion that the missing elements in the previously mentioned paradigms are, first of all, the state of *political consciousness* of those engaged in political relations (the subjective dimension of social agency) and, to a much lesser extend, the real (objective) state of social agency of them. I shall focus on these elements in my following examination.

4. What is the political transition?

First of all it is the political change at the macro-level but not exclusively. This means that everything from individual political relations up to the general structure (order) of state's political relations has been embraced by the process of change. It means that all elements of political relations are also affected by the process of changes. The main and decisive factor for all political change, which is also a main sphere (field) of those changes is the *social agency* of the citizens.[20] So, anticipating a little, I say that the political transition is the process of mass-changes in the scope (extent) of social agency of political actors (the people engaged in the political power relations). As a result of this process the proportions of rights and conditions for self-realization of political power wielders and subordinates in the whole political systems are essentially changed, in the sense that they become more adapted to the present level of social needs for self-realization (needs for social agency). So, the term "political transition" might designate both, the process of changes of social agency and the effect of such a process.

To describe the process of political transition (rather roughly) I start with the remark that the dynamic of political power relations can be – from a certain point of view – seen as two opposite, mutually dependent actions; one, of political power wielder (decider) who is trying to come into possession of more social agency than he/she actually possesses, which if he/she is successful, automatically means the deprivation of a given "bit" of social agency from the subordinated subject. We can call this the process of deprivation of social agency, but even better, we can call it the objectivization process, because it is resulting in objectifying (instrumentalizing) the subordinate in political power relations (limiting his/her role as an actor in such a relation and puting him into the position of the tool or object of the political decider).

The counter-action of a subordinate is directed toward the reduction of the scale of his/her deprivation, which is possible only by gaining more social agency and become more the actor (subject) of political power relations. This I call the subjectivization process. A relative balance between these two tendencies can also occur, while both sides of political power relation are intending no more than to preserve the actually possessed social agency.

Let us now take on the consideration of the totalitarian state in which, as a matter of principle, the political deciders are trying to seize for themselves as much social agency as possible.[21]

It is not only the scope of social agency they intend to extend, and enlarge but what is crucial, they are trying to centralize the disposition over the seized social agency. The general extention of social agency (political power) is leading to the subordination of all spheres of social activity: economic, cultural, educational, communicative, and so on. It produces the main divine line between deprived citizens (so called: "we") and deprivers (so called: "they"). The attempt to centralize produces several divisions and splits inside the whole political power hierarchy (structure) between those being higher in the political power ranks and those being lower and, as a result, being deprived of some privileges, too.

So, the political transition could mean the very efficient process of instrumentalization of citizens by their political leaders, and, as a result of it, an essential shift of social agency from its original possessors (the people) to the their centralized political deciders. It could be "the road to serfdom" using Hayek's famous expression.[22] There are many possible causes of such a transition; extreme economic crisis, war or the foreign invasion, for example. For a relatively short time, people are ready to justify (legitimate) and accept this situation. They are even ready to cooperate with their deprivers for the sake of "the better future", "the reason of State", "the glory of nation", and so on. Here lays the secret of the initial success of many dictatorships. But any sudden and extreme shift of social agency in one direction (e. g. toward the instrumentalization) has to produce a tremendous impulse in the opposite direction (toward the subjectivization). The political power wielder, while having successes, are following the way of deprivation with the false conviction that there are no limits to their political growth, and one day, the growing asymmetry of political relation must cross the critical line of a society-wide internalized set of values, first of all those associated with the self-realization matters. Then, a series of gradual changes of political consciousness of the people from both sides of political relations will be put in motion.

The way the people perceive the political relations is as important for its realization as any other condition. The social perception of politics can effectively fuel the political activity and, in time, when this perception has been turned to its opposition, can as easily as before set back any actions of political deciders.

When the developing deprivation of social agency arrives at the point at which it is perceived as "the chains of freedom", the first stage of social contestation begins to emerge.

The characteristic feature of it is that people do not question the legitimacy or efficacy of a given political regime, established due to objectivization, but they simply demand more freedom. This fact was well known to Gorbachev when he decided to offer the people of Soviet Union "glasnost" as the first (and added "perestroika" much later).

This first "doubt" about the political relations and the more and more common perception of them as the constraints of personal (citizen's) freedom (the "first stage"), must unavoidably provide the impulse for the others. Analysing, for example, the events of 1976–78 in Poland, one can say that it was the "second stage" of social contestation against the political system, characterized by the growing delegitimation of the political regime. The feelings of unjust limitations and the depleting social consent are leading some of the people from spontaneous struggle to organized forms of struggle against the power, more precisely, against the political privileges of state (ruling party) institutions. Now, with accelerated speed, the political relations are going to be seen not only as limits to freedom and as illegitimate, but ineffective in providing for social needs. In this moment the "third stage" begins; the people start their struggle, not against power but *for power*. Practically, if they succeed, the essential shift of social agency will have been made; the privileges of political deciders have been limited for the sake of more rights for citizens. In other words, the asymmetry of political relations has been reduced to more symmetrical interdependencies between political actors. This dynamic is easy to see while comparing the Polish events of 1956, 1968, 1970, 1980 and at the end of 1989.[23] When the scope of social agency at the disposal of subordinates grew up in such a remarkable fashion, changes to the whole political order can not be avoided.

Summing up, the political transition can take the form of the *objectivization* (instrumentalization) process or the subjectivization process. The decisive factor here is the social perception of political relations and, as a result of it, the state of social political consciousness, which is the motivational force of political activities. These latter can change – under the given conditions – the substance of relations: the proportions of social agency possessed by their performers.
I am not trying to eliminate or ignore the importance of structural, cultural, economic or other factors of social and/or political change. I am fully aware of the complex dependencies between them and the above distinguished factor. What I intend to do is just an analytical separation of the *political* dimension of social dynamics.

5. The pendulum-like paradigm

Social and/or the political changes are very often described by means of an analogy; the evolution has been illustrated by uniform accelerated motion; the revolution has been compared with the eruption of a volcano, an avalanche or some geometrically accelerated motion; some concepts of social change are pictured as "cyclic", "catastrophic", the other as "spiral" or "undirected fluctuation". All those analogies have obviously limited explanatory value. But they can definitely help our imagination to cope with the very complex reality of social change. This is the reason that I am resorting to some analogies.

The political transition is analogous with a pendulum's motion. The state of social agency is continually leaning toward objectivization or subjectivization. When the distance between the scope of social agency of political deciders and that of citizens is small, the potential of the inner dynamic of the whole system is low and its stability relatively high. When this distance is suddenly extented, "the pendulum" of social agency will accelerate its speed and the reach of the motion become wider. Pushing the "pendulum" of social agency up to one of the extremes, one is provoking a mighty counter-move; this is the most visible indicator of political transition. The pendulum I am describing is not moving in some kind of vacuum. The social environment of political transition can accelerate it, stop it for a while or delay it, but can not hinder it entirely or change its direction before some potential for the motion will be exhausted. This potential is the intensity of social will for self-realization which is always rationalized accordingly to the perception of the political relations (political order) and/or to the other elements of the whole social situation.

Using the pendulum analogy, it seems, that Polish society is quite close to one end of the transitional continuum. The electoral apathy may be remarkable for this. If I am right, we can soon expect the political transition toward the redeprivation of social agency. The nostalgia for the more authoritative government – which is expressed by some voices in Poland – may be the first sign of such a turn.

Notes

1 The weakness of political theory has been depicted before by J. G. Gunnell, "The End of Political Theory", in: Between Philosophy and Politics, The Alienation of Political Theory, The University of Massachusetts Press, Amherst,1986, pp. 169–200.

2 These exceptions are, first of all, some statements by Zbigniew Brzeziński made during his lecture at the Jagiellonian University in March 1989. He "gave" the communist regime in Poland no more than 3 month, and his prediction was wonderfully fulfilled. See also Z. Brzeziński, Agonia Komunizmu ("The Agony of Communism"), in: Kultura, 5/500, 1989, Paryż, p. 51. Concerns over the critique of explanations of the so called peaceful revolution or quiet revolution, are expressed in: K. Pałecki,"Problem of Social Agency in Contemporary Countries of East-Central Europe", in: Metamorphosen der Wirklichkeit in der Gegenwart Ost- und Westeuropas, materials from symposium in Kraków, 1990, pub.: Bundesministerium fur Arbeit und Soziales, Wien, June 1991, pp. 13–20.

3 E. g., J. Pajestka, Changes in the Global System and Their Consequences for Poland, pp. 13–60, in: Poland in the Perspective of Global Change, Polish Association for the Club of Rome, Globality versus Locality, Warsow 1991, ed. A. Kukliński.

4 The most exploited in this matter seems to be the work of J. Habermas, Communication and the Evolution of Society, Beacon, Boston 1979.

5 See for example; J. Ch. Davies, The Priority of Human Needs and the Stages of Political Development, in: Human Nature in Politics, ed. J. R. Pennock and J. W. Chapman, Nomos XVII, New York University Press, 1977, pp. 157–193.

6 Let us cite as an example: "In any political system, the personality of leader, his strengths and

weaknesses, and his skills at political infighting play a crucial role. In the hands of such a forceful personality and skilled politician as Gorbachev, and in a system like that of the Soviet Union, with its strong tradition of popular deference to the leadership, the possibility clearly existed for the Congress of People's Deputies and the Supreme Soviet to be subordinated to the chairman, instead of vice versa . . ."; E. Teague and D. Mann: "Gorbachev's Dual Role", Problems of Communism, January/February 1990, p. 3. The same approach, see A. M. Schlesinger Jr.,Democracy and Leadership, in: Dialogue, Nr 79, 1/1988, pp. 20–25.

7 On this matter, see: M. J. Shapiro, Language and Political Understanding, The Politics of Discursive Practices, Yale University Press, New Haven, London, 1981, pp. 165–198.

8 With some remarkable exceptions concerning mostly the problems of *legitimacy*, see for example, S. Bialer, Stalin's Successors: Leadership, Stability and Change in the Soviet Union, Cambridge University Press, 1980, pp. 183–201; P. G. Lewis, Legitimacy and the Polish Communist State, in: States and Societies, ed. D. Hold et al., Basil Blackwell.1983, pp. 431–455; also: F. Eidlin and T. Sasińska-Klas,"The Delegitimation and Relegitimation of Power in Poland", The Materials of Canadian Political Science Association, (Congress in Laval-Quebec, 1–3 June 1989). The other exception: J. Staniszkis, Poland's Self-Limiting Revolution, ed. J. T. Gross, Princeton University Press, Princeton, New Jersey, 1984, pp. 111–115.

9 Let me cite a typical argument: "The disaster of the East-Central European economies has provided the chance for the construction of market economies. (. . .) The economic disaster of the East-Central European countries is a sign of the failure of the old system and its way of wielding power, its ideology, and its management of the economy. This situation caused the disappearance of the illusion that the system could be reformed. It requires transformation: a complete change." (see: Poland, International Economic Report 1990/91, Word Economy Research Institute, Warsaw School of Economics, Warsaw 1991, p. 5).
But an other source is trying to convince us about the opposite dependence; the economic transformation depends, first of all, on "the political credibility" of a regime; see: G. Kolankiewicz, and P. G. Lewis, Poland, Politics, Economics, and Society, Pinter Publishers, London, New York, 1988, p. 133.

10 To compare see: V. Zubek, Wałesa's Leadership and Poland's Transition, Problems of Communism, January/April 1991, pp. 69–83.

11 See especially S. Ossowski, Struktura Klasowa w Społecznej Świadomości (The Class Structure in Social Consciousness), w: Dzieła, t. V, PWN, Warszawa 1968, pp. 89, 115 and others.

12 See for example; R. R. Ludwikowski: "The anti-communist upheaval in Poland was often characterized as 'a peaceful revolution' but it would be, perhaps, more accurate to speak about the series of events or to call the Polish transformation an 'evolution' rather than to present it as a sudden and radical revolutionary change." In: "Searching for a New Constitutional Model for East-Central Europe", Syracuse Journal of International Law and Commerce, Vol. 17, Spring 1991, No. 1, p. 147–148; along the same lines is K. Kloc's "Poland's Political System – Change and Future Scenarios", in: Poland into the 1990s, Economy and Society in Transition, G. Blazyca and R. Rapacki eds., Pinter Publishers, London 1991, pp. 11–19. For the opposite view, see E. Kux: "The great revolution of 1989 which, in my view, was a revolution in all Europe and not just in its eastern part, ushered in a new era in world politics that will endure well into the fast-approaching 21st century. During a few eventful days and weeks of the spring and fall of 1989, (. . .) the people of Poland, Hungary, East Germany, Czechoslovakia, and Bulgaria brought about peacefully a change of power. (. . .) In general terms, the revolution in Eastern Europe appeared to follow the historical dialectic described by Alexis de Tocqueville and Jacob Burckhardt or by the revolutionary strategists Karl Marx and V. I. Lenin.", in: Revolution – East and West?, Problems of Communism, May/June 1991, p. 1, 2.

13 Gabriel A. Almond, Political Systems and Political Change, in: State and Society, Reinhard Bendix ed., Univ. of California Press, Berkeley, Los Angeles, London, 1973, p. 35.

14 Randall Collins, A Comparative Approach to Political Sociology, State and Society, op. cit., p. 45.

15 Gabriel A. Almond, Political Systems and Political Change, in: State and Society, op. cit., pp. 33–35.

16 See, Randall Collins, State and Society . . ., op. cit., p. 46.

17 Very instructive on this point is Charles F. Andrain's Political Life and Social Change, 2nd ed., Duxbury Press, A Division of Wadsworth Publishing Company, Inc., Belmont, California 1974, pp. 12–25, and J. J. Wiatr, Socjologia Stosunków Politycznych (The Sociology of Political Relations), PWN, Warszawa 1980, pp. 13–30 and 124–126, 139–191; see also F. Ryszka, Nauka o Polityce, (The Science of Politics), PWV, Warszawa 1984, pp. 9–37.

18 This view is different of the "classical" approach; for example, see: D. Jaros, L. V. Grant, Political Behavior, Choices and Perspectives, St. Martin's Press, New York, 1974, p. 7.

19 See, K. Pałecki, Prawo-Władza-Polityka (The Law, Politics and Power), COM, Warszawa 1988, p. 39. It is also obvious, that not all political relations are relations of power; some of them could be quite symmetrical, e. g. relations between parties in a democracy, but I should like to emphasize that which is the very *essence of the political dimension* of social life, and this is the reason for such a simplification.

20 I discussed this matter before, see: "Problem of Social Agency in Contemporary Countries of East-Central Europe", in: Metamorphosen der Wirklichkeit in der Gegenwart Ost-und Westeuropas, red. B. Serloth, K. Glass and H. Oberhauser, BMAS, Wien – Kraków, 1991, pp. 13–20.

21 To compare see for example: Ch. F. Andrain, "Totalitarian Systems", in: Political Life and Social Change, 2nd Edition, Duxbury Press, California State University, San Diego, Belmont, 1974, pp. 217–218.

22 F. A. Hayek, The Road to Serfdom, Polish transl. J. Emil, Polish Books and Arts, Inc., New York, London, 1982.

23 The similar conclusions see: K. Z. Sowa, Russia and Poland Predicament in the 20th c. – Polish Peaceful Revolution and the Future of Communism, in: U. S. R. R. in the Perspective of Global Change, Polish Association for the Club of Rome, Warsaw, Rome 1991, p. 64.

Gerhard Jagschitz

Zwischen Weltkultur und Enge. Mitteleuropas schwierige Identität

Umbruch in Osteuropa – historische Dimension – Sieg des Kapitalismus – Zusammenbruch des Kommunismus: das sind Schlagworte, die die europäische Gegenwart bestimmen und durch eine geschwätzige Medienindustrie verbreitet werden. Doch kann man Phasen dynamischerer historischer Prozesse mit Schlagworten abtun, zufrieden sein mit der vordergründigen Begreifbarkeit durch das Mittelmaß, das sich daraus so zahlreich und anscheinend erfolgreich politisches Kleingeld holt? Sollte man nicht vielmehr – und das ist auch ein Aufruf an intellektuelle Kapazitäten angesichts eines wachsenden Populismus – möglichst rasch ein europaweites Gespräch zur Bestimmung unseres gegenwärtigen Standorts beginnen, aus dem Erkenntnisse für unser zukünftiges Handeln gewonnen werden können? Und obwohl man schon von einer Inflation von Tagungen, Symposien und Foren sprechen kann, so scheint doch eine Diskrepanz zwischen der Anzahl und der Substanz zu bestehen.

Denn es ist Illusion zu glauben, man könne an alten Traditionen, Formen und Ideologien einfach anknüpfen, so als wäre das kommunistische System in Osteuropa nur eine historische Verirrung, eine Krankheit, von der Europa nun genesen ist. Zu sehr hat sich die Welt verändert, haben ein bis zwei Generationen unterschiedliche Haltungen und Werte aufgebaut. Wir übersehen zu leicht, daß dem Umbruch in Osteuropa auch ein Umbruch in Westeuropa, ja der gesamten westlichen Welt gegenübersteht. Niemals zuvor in der Geschichte war der Bruch zwischen Generationen größer als in der Gegenwart.

Es scheint, als ob das einzige verbindende Element der osteuropäischen Staaten das Diktat des Aufholens des Wohlstandes des Westens um jeden Preis ist. Diese Unterordnung aller politischen und sozialen Kategorien unter das Streben nach materiellen Vorteilen bedeutet aber ebenso die freiwillige Aufgabe von Kultur wie den Verlust gesellschaftlicher Regelfunktionen und somit auch den Verlust von Identität. Wurzeln in der Geschichte bedeutet für viele osteuropäische Länder auch wurzeln in einer eben erst überwundenen Vergangenheit, in einem System, das man selbst auf mannigfaltige Weise mitgetragen hat. So ist es unmöglich, die letzten Jahrzehnte aus der eigenen Geschichte und der Geschichte eines Volkes zu streichen, vielmehr bedürfte es einer mühsamen Aufarbeitung von oft gewaltsam unterbrochenen Kontinuitäten und Inhalten, der eigenen passiven und aktiven Arrangements und der Ursachen unterlassenen Handelns. Als Beispiel mag etwa die Eliminierung des nichtkommunistischen Widerstandes gegen den Nationalsozialismus aus der gesellschaftlichen Wirklichkeit in Polen gelten, was zugleich die Vernichtung des einzigen modernen gemeinschaftsstiftenden Elements des polnischen Volkes bedeutete.

Der Wegfall alter Ordnungen führte zu einer verbreiteten Orientierungslosigkeit. Auf der Suche nach Lösungen kommen alte Autoritarismen, Nationalismen oder Monarchismen hervor, da die demokratischen Modelle des Westens angesichts der steigenden Verelendung und Bedrohung fragwürdig erscheinen. Doch wäre es kurzsichtig, die Orientierungslosigkeit auf Mittel- und Osteuropa zu beschränken. Die vordergründigen Alltagsprobleme und der westliche Wohlstand verdecken die Tatsache, daß diese Orientierungslosigkeit auch in den westlichen Industrieländern kennzeichnend ist. Es sind ökologische Krisen, Krisen der Worte, Bilder und Beziehungen und nicht zuletzt Krisen des Ethos. Die Revolution in Osteuropa wurde maßgeblich von aus dem Westen gelieferten Fernsehbildern beeinflußt, und es ist eine Farce der Weltgeschichte, daß dort der Kampf für eine Welt erfolgte, die es gar nicht gibt. Denn der „goldene Westen" war dies nur durch die sorgfältige Auslassung von Problemen aus dem Fernseh-Alltag, die verkitschte Präsentation von synthetischen Lebensstilen oder die verharmlosende Niveaulosigkeit breiiger Unterhaltung. Diese Diskrepanz zwischen Bild und Wirklichkeit mag mit zur gegenwärtigen Ernüchterung beigetragen haben.

In den desillusionierten osteuropäischen Gesellschaften bedeutet aber die Diskreditierung von Ideologie die erhöhte Neigung, die entstandene Lücke durch Irrationalismen auszufüllen. Auch schuf der Wegfall des Staatspaternalismus ein nicht zu unterschätzendes Vakuum, in dem eine erhöhte Mobilität neue Identifikationszentren sucht.

So werden zahlreiche Modelle am politischen Jahrmarkt Europas feilgeboten. Ob es die zentralistische Machtstruktur der auf ökonomisches Wachstum ausgerichteten EG ist, der Zusammenschluß von Regionen, die Illusion von Mitteleuropa mit einem Hauch von Habsburg-Nostalgie, die weltumspannende Beglückung wirtschaftlicher Giganten inmitten der noch ständig steigenden Tendenz zu Massenkommunikation und Massenmobilität, immer besteht die Spannung zwischen Weltkultur und Trachtenkapelle, zwischen Globalisierung und Lokalisierung.

Es geht also um die Frage der Orientierung eines Kontinents. Eines Kontinents mit erheblichen historischen Belastungen. Denn der Griff nach der Beherrschung Europas durch das nationalsozialistische Deutschland ist nicht einfach wegwischbar, das zwischen Kroaten und Serben, vor Jahrzehnten geflossene Blut ist gegenwärtige Realität, das Zusammenleben mit den Unterdrückern und Ausbeutern von gestern scheint unmöglich. Die angebotenen Auswege – einerseits neue Weltbilder und weltweite Wertbilder, die in nicht unbedeutendem Maß industriell gefertigt werden, von Konsum diktiert und auf der Armut von Millionen von Menschen aufbauend, andererseits nationale Enge, die die weltweiten komplexen Zusammenhänge ignoriert und auf archaische Begrenzungen zurückfällt – sind jedoch tatsächlich Irrwege. So wie die ausschließlich an ökonomischen Kriterien orientierte Politik – für die die Europäische Gemeinschaft als abschreckendes Beispiel steht – Wohlstand nur einem Teil der Gesellschaft bietet und bieten kann. Wir erleben ja gegenwärtig das beschämende Schauspiel eines westeuropäischen – meist bundesdeutschen DM- – Imperialismus gegenüber Osteuropa, wo es nicht um den Erhalt lebensfähiger Strukturen und Grundlagen für menschliche Existenzen geht, sondern um den billigen Erwerb mit großem Gewinn verwertbarer Güter, Fabriken, Gründe und Häuser. Dies gleicht jener zynischen Situation, in der der Neffe der nach einem Schlaganfall gelähmten Tante die Sparbücher mit den letzten Ersparnissen stiehlt. Gier als Kategorie des Zusammenlebens von Völkern hat noch nie dauerhafte und vor allem menschenwürdige Ordnungen begründet.

Jene Richtung, die eine neue Basis des Zusammenlebens der europäischen Völker bilden kann, muß von Versuchen charakterisiert sein, eine Balance zwischen Offenheit und Beschränkung zu finden. Nicht Entscheidungen in irgendwelchen fernen, bürokratisierten Zentralen, sondern gleichberechtigte Kooperation muß als politisches Prinzip anerkannt werden. Nur Mitbestimmung der Betroffenen in überschaubaren Räumen und Einheiten verhindert die drohende moderne Sklavengesellschaft. Dies bedeutet vor allem ein neues Ethos Westeuropas im Umgang mit den osteuropäischen Ländern.

Die Entwicklung einer europäischen Identität scheint noch in weiter Ferne zu sein, und es erhebt sich überhaupt die Frage, ob man in Europa zu Hause sein kann. Vielmehr scheint es sinnvoll, die eigene ethnische, nationale oder regionale Identität in ein Europa einzubringen. Nicht das uniforme Einheitseuropa, sondern die multikulturelle Koexistenz, nicht der europäische Zentralstaat sondern die vielschichtige Partnerschaft europäischer Völker, Regionen und Menschen ermöglicht spannungsfreies Zusammenleben. Dazu bedarf es wohl der Entwicklung eines neuen Europabegriffs, neuer Inhalte und neuer Regeln. Mitteleuropa kam hier auf dem Boden jahrhundertealter kultureller und ethnischer Vermischungen als Laboratorium für diese Entwicklungen fungieren. Der Geist vertrauter Nachbarschaft ist dabei nicht Sehnsucht nach vergangenen Zeiten und Ordnungen, sondern höchst realistisches Kapital gegenwärtigen Umgangs von Menschen verschiedener historischer Belastungen, Ideologien, Vorstellungen und Wünsche. Dabei ist es notwendig, die Haltung der Selbstaufgabe zu beenden und die Abkehr von der Beglückungsgesellschaft hin zur Selbstverantwortungsgesellschaft vorzunehmen.

Erhard Busek

Das Neue am Konservativismus

„Ein Konservativer ist ein Mensch, der glaubt, daß nichts zum ersten Mal getan werden sollte."
(Alfred Wiggam, 1909–1960, amerikanischer Journalist)

1. Zur Ambivalenz des Wortes selbst

Das Wort „konservativ" geistert heute oft durch die Medien – und geradezu eine Inflation gab es diesbezüglich im Sommer, genauer gesagt im August 1991, als die sogenannten Konservativen in Moskau putschten, um Gorbatschow zu beseitigen.

Ich setze diese Betrachtung ganz bewußt an den Anfang meiner Stellungnahme, weil ich aufzeigen will, daß der Begriff „konservativ" widersprüchlich ist: Ist er beispielsweise im angloamerikanischen Raum durchaus positiv besetzt, wird er bei uns oft abschätzig verwendet – und hier meine ich vor allem demokratischen Sozialismus und Sozialdemokratie, die alles, was rechts von ihnen steht, gern als konservativ bezeichnen.

Die Moskauer Augustrevolution im Sommer 1991 hat uns indes das Phänomen vor Augen geführt, daß nicht nur konservativ sei, wer rechts der demokratischen Linken stehe, sondern auch links davon: So wurde auch aus Janajew ein – „Konservativer".

Natürlich ist es für die demokratische Linke sehr bequem, eine einzige Bezeichnung für den politischen Gegner zu haben, egal auf welcher Seite dieser auch steht. Ob rechts oder links von ihr – er gilt als „konservativ". Daß die Conservative Party einer Margaret Thatcher wohl kaum etwas mit dem doktrinären Flügel der KPdSU eines Igor Ligatschow zu tun hat – darüber sehen demokratischer Sozialismus und Sozialdemokratie gern hinweg.

Ich wundere mich darüber auch nicht. Denn: für die politische Linke ist diese Sicht der Dinge ja sehr angenehm. Allerdings habe ich mich gewundert, daß die Medien eine solche Diktion übernommen haben – und interessanterweise gilt das auch für Blätter, die selbst mit dem Adjektiv „konservativ" umschrieben werden. Haben sie sich nach österreichischer Manier vielleicht gern ins eigene Fleisch geschnitten?

Aber vielleicht stehen wir wirklich an einer semantischen Wende, an einer Wende zur neuen Sprachauslegung, an der Wende zu einem „neuen Konservativismus", der von den Tories bis zum Marxismus-Leninismus reicht. – Glauben wir das aber wirklich?

Ich darf die Antwort selbst geben: Das glauben nur die, welche einer fleißigen Propaganda aufsitzen und nicht den Mut zur kritischen Reflexion haben.

2. Das sogenannte konservative Spektrum: Von den Konservativen bis zu den Christdemokraten

Nachdem wir nun einen vermeintlichen Aspekt des Konservativismus kennengelernt haben, möchte ich mich dem eigentlichen Sinn des Wortes *konservativ* zuwenden. Wir alle wissen, der Begriff stammt aus dem Lateinischen, von *conservare*, und bedeutet *bewahren*. Was aber wird bewahrt?

So gelangen wir zu einer wesentlichen Unterscheidung, zur Unterscheidung zwischen Wertkonservativismus und Strukturkonservativismus.

Strukturkonservativismus, das ist der abwertende Begriff, verwendet vor allem von Parteien der demokratischen Linken für ihre Gegner. Wir haben zuvor davon gesprochen.

Die Parteien, die sich selbst als konservativ bezeichnen, verstehen darunter hingegen die Bewahrung eines bestimmen – meistens moralischen oder materiellen – Wertesystems. Es kommt auf die Tradition der jeweiligen Partei an, welchem Wertesystem, dem moralischen – Stichwort Ehe – oder dem materiellen – Stichwort Leistung –, der Vorrang eingeräumt wird. Parteien, die insbesondere eine moralische Tradition unterstreichen, gehören eher dem christdemokratischen Spektrum an, die anderen eher dem konservativen im engeren Sinn des Wortes.

Die meisten christdemokratischen und konservativen Parteien sind in der IDU zusammengefaßt – und bekennen sich demgemäß nicht nur zu Koalition miteinander, sondern – namentlich – zur Union.

International gesehen, steht der IDU vor allem die Sozialistische Internationale – oder wird Sie demnächst auch zur „sozialdemokratischen" mutieren? – gegenüber. Allein die Bezeichnung läßt den Schluß zu, daß es sich bei der einen um eine weltanschauliche Allianz, bei der anderen aber um eine ideologische handelt.

Was entspricht eher unserer Zeit? – Ich meine, daß spätestens seit den friedlichen Revolutionen der letzten Jahre das Zeitalter der Ideologien endgültig beendet ist. Mehr denn je gilt heute, daß man sich nicht auf die Kollektivierung einer Idee – auf eine Ideologie also – stützen darf, sondern allein auf einen Grundkonsens der Werte – auf eine Weltanschauung.

Das ist eine wichtige Erkenntnis eines neuen Konservativismus: Er ist Ausdruck einer bürgerlichen Weltanschauung und steht einer sozialistischen Ideologie gegenüber. Die Zeit, in der er selbst danach strebte, sich zu ideologisieren, ist vorbei.

3. Konservativ wider progressiv

Lassen Sie mich jedoch zur internationalen Demokratischen Union und zur Unterscheidung im sogenannten konservativen Spektrum zwischen Christdemokraten und Konservativen zurückkehren: Nicht alle Christdemokraten in Europa gehören der IDU an. Und das hängt mit dem Antagonismus zwischen konservativ und progressiv zusammen.

So versteht sich beispielsweise die italienische DC ausdrücklich als progressive und nicht als konservative Partei. Ihre Programme sehen im Christentum den Wegweiser einer fortschrittlichen Demokratie. Bei der DC spiegelt sich die Skepsis gegenüber dem Konservativismus jedoch nicht nur programmatisch wider; auch in der Praxis gibt es einen starken progressiven Flügel, die sogenannte „sinistra democristiana".

Ähnliches gilt – obwohl sie Mitglied der IDU ist – für meine Partei. Das Salzburger Programm bezeichnet sie – und ich zitiere jetzt – als „Partei der fortschrittlichen Mitte". Seither hat es viele Diskussionen gegeben, ob diese Definition zutrifft oder nicht. Sicher gibt es in der ÖVP eher konservativere und eher progressivere Strömungen; vielleicht hat am Anfang der 70er Jahre, als wir uns dieses Programm gegeben haben, auch die fortschrittlichere überwogen.

Dennoch glaube ich, daß bei der Definition *fortschrittliche Mitte* nicht das Adjektiv, sondern das Substantiv im Vordergrund steht: *die Mitte* – und das ist ganz typisch für Christdemokraten, vielleicht weniger für Konservative.

Am Rande möchte ich hier auch Georges Bidault, Ministerpräsident der Vierten französischen Republik, zitieren. Er hat gemeint: „Christdemokrat sein heißt in der Mitte regieren und mit dem Mitteln der Rechten linke Politik betreiben." – Auch dieser Ausspruch ist vom Antagonismus *konservativ – progressiv* bestimmt und versucht *konservativ* als Weg und *progressiv* als Ziel zu definieren. Ist dieser Ansatz einen Versuch wert – stellt auch er die Frage nach einem neuen Konservativismus?

4. Konservativ, liberal und sozial – eine Beziehung

Ich selbst habe mich immer wieder als einen liberalen Konservativen mit christlichen Wurzeln bezeichnet. Scheinbar braucht das Wort *konservativ* eine Ergänzung, Erläuterung und Erklärung – es braucht weitere Eigenschaftswörter wie *liberal*, *sozial* oder *christlich*. Diesen Umstand kann man sowohl als Stärke als auch als Schwäche des Konservativismus auffassen.

Freilich muß ich einschränken, daß konservative Parteien wie die amerikanischen Republikaner in sachlicher Tradition oder die französischen Gaullisten in personeller Tradition die Eigenschaftsworte *liberal* und *sozial* eher vermeiden. Demgegenüber betont die christdemokratische bayerische CSU in ihrem Grundsatzprogramm: „Die CSU ist eine konservative Partei, weil sie sich einer dauerhaften Wertordnung verpflichtet weiß, sie anerkennt Fortschritt auf der Basis des

Bestehenden. Sie ist eine liberale Partei, weil sie für die Grundrechte des Bürgers und seiner Freiheit eintritt. Sie ist eine soziale Partei, weil sie sich für alle Menschen, besonders die Schwächeren, einsetzt. Sie tritt für eine gerechte Gesellschaftsordnung ein."

Innerhalb des sogenannten konservativen Spektrums sind die Christdemokraten also integralistischer. Sie haben den Willen zur Volkspartei, und boshaft könnte man sagen, sie erliegen der Versuchung einer Allerweltspartei. Das trifft auf die konservativen Parteien im engeren Sinn des Wortes weniger zu: Sie vertreten höchstens wirtschaftsliberale Anliegen, soziale aber kaum.

5. Evolution und Revolution

Lassen Sie mich zum Schluß meines Statements zu einer weiteren Haltung des Konservativismus kommen: zu seiner Stellung zu Evolution und Revolution.

Diesbezüglich hat der amerikanische Politologe Clinton Rossiter den boshaften Satz geprägt: „Konservativismus ist die Verehrung toter Revolutionäre." – In der Tat kommt darin die Skepsis des Konservativen gegenüber revolutionären Umstürzen zum Tragen: Er zweifelt an ihnen, weil sie den humanen Drang nach Freiheit und Gerechtigkeit oft pervertieren. Die Evolution – die langsame Veränderung – ist ihm lieber. Wenn überhaupt, anerkennt er Revolutionen erst nach vielen Jahrzehnten – eben dann, wenn deren Träger längst „tot" sind und deren Ziele – nicht deren Wege – selbst zu konservativen Werten, die ja einem ständigen Wandel unterzogen sind, geworden sind. – An dieser Stelle möchte ich noch einmal an das Zitat Alfred Wiggams erinnern, das ich an den Anfang meiner Betrachtungen gestellt habe: ein Konservativer sei ein Mensch, der glaubt, daß nichts zum ersten Mal getan werden sollte.

Nun, diese skeptische Haltung zur Revolution, können wir sie aufrechterhalten? – Sind wir ehrlich: So sehr wir diese Meinung gestern geteilt haben – heute tun wir das nicht mehr. Denn es scheint tatsächlich friedliche Revolutionen zu geben, Revolutionen, die nicht nur das Ziel, sondern auch den Weg vor Augen haben, Revolutionen, die – einem berühmten Satz von Manès Sperber entgegen – nicht nur diese an die Spitze bringen, die „leidenschaftlich die Macht wollen", sondern auch jene, die leidenschaftlich das Recht wollen.

Eine solche Erkenntnis schließlich, die Erfahrung friedlicher Revolutionen, ist vielleicht der wichtigste Punkt eines „neuen Konservativismus"; es handelt sich dabei sozusagen – und damit möchte ich schließen – um eine „sanfte Revolution" im Denken eines „liberalen Konservativen mit christlichen Wurzeln".

Manfred Prisching

Weltbild im Wandel – geistige Strömungen in den westlichen Ländern Mitteleuropas

Von Schlagwörtern, Etiketten und Metaphern soll hier die Rede sein: von jenen Begriffen, welche die Einwohner der westlichen Industriegesellschaften verwenden, sich selbst – zum Zwecke der Selbstverständigung – kenntlich zu machen. Diese markanten Begriffe sollen das vermeintlich Wesentliche, oft auch nur eine Zeitstimmung oder eine Befindlichkeit erfassen. Sie sind aufschlußreich, weil sie als Schlagworte, die Zustimmung finden und sich verbreiten, ausdrücken, wie viele Mitglieder einer Gesellschaft ihr Gemeinwesen sehen. Diese Stimmungslagen werden oft in Büchern – als artikulierte Versionen dieser Befindlichkeit – „verdichtet", und viele von ihnen werden zu Bestsellern, befördern oder formen diese Stimmungslagen mit. Die Schlagworte dringen ein in die Feuilletons, prägen das Bewußtsein der Medienmacher und diffundieren in die Gespräche, Diskussionsrunden und Tagungen der Intellektuellen. Sie klingen uns allen im Ohr.

In einer Zeit, in der den osteuropäischen Ländern angelegentlich empfohlen wird, das erfolgreiche Gesellschaftsmodell des Westens nachzuahmen, ist es angebracht, zu versuchen, dieses Modell in den wichtigsten Dimensionen zu umreißen. Dies soll nicht dadurch geschehen, daß ein weiterer Begriff gefunden wird, der endgültig das Wesen dieses Gemeinwesens ausdrücken soll; und nicht dadurch, daß ein theoretisches Modell dieser Sozialordnung skizziert wird. Es soll vielmehr eine Übersicht der Selbstverständigungsversuche geboten werden: eine Sammlung der Schlagworte, die solche Versuche in den letzten drei Jahrzehnten begleitet haben. Einerseits zeigt sich daran die *Vielfältigkeit*, der Facettenreichtum, die Vielschichtigkeit der in Betracht stehenden Gesellschaftsordnung; andererseits kann gerade die langwierige Auflistung als Zeichen der *Bescheidenheit* verstanden werden – es wird deutlich, vor welchen Schwierigkeiten die Zeitgenossen stehen, das Wesen jener sozialen Ordnung, in der sie leben, auf den Begriff zu bringen.[1] Es ist zudem eine Zeit, in der nicht nur die osteuropäischen Länder nach einer neuen *Identität* suchen, sondern in der dies auch den westlichen Staaten aufgetragen ist, angesichts der Herausforderungen Europas und der Veränderungen der gesamteuropäischen politischen Szenerie, und auch dabei mag ein Rückblick auf vergangene Versuche, sich seiner selbst klar zu werden, hilfreich sein.

I.

In den sechziger Jahren war das Vertrauen in die Zukunft in allen westlichen Industrieländern ungebrochen, man setzte auf Technik, Fortschritt und Wirtschaftswachstum. Gegenwart bedeutete *Fortschritt*, Zukunft die konsequente

Erfüllung der Gegenwart. Energieknappheiten und Umweltprobleme lagen noch jenseits des Erfahrungshorizontes. Die Gesellschaft wurde immer reicher und gebildeter. Für die Reifephase dieser Industriegesellschaften prägte Daniel Bell einen plausiblen Begriff: die *postindustrielle Gesellschaft.*[2]

„Postindustriell" – das bedeutet zunächst einen Wandel in der Beschäftigungsstruktur entwickelter Länder, gemäß dem Modell von Jean Fourastié[3]: eine Verschiebung der Arbeitskräfte vom agrarischen und industriellen Sektor in den tertiären Bereich – kurz: die *Dienstleistungsgesellschaft*[4]. Bells Beschreibung des Postindustrialismus ging aber über den einfachen Sachverhalt restrukturierter Beschäftigungsverhältnisse hinaus. Seine Grundvorstellung war, daß die Zukunftsgesellschaft eine *Bildungsgesellschaft* und eine *Wissensgesellschaft* sein werde. Die akademisch und technisch qualifizierten Berufe nehmen zu; das theoretisch-wissenschaftliche Wissen gewinnt an Bedeutung; es kommt zur Steuerung des technischen Fortschritts und einer sinnvollen Bewertung von neuen Technologien. In dem optimistischen Modell haben die Experten das Sagen.

Die postindustrielle *Fortschrittsgesellschaft* ist eine *technokratische* Gesellschaft. In den fünfziger und sechziger Jahren wurde von vielen die Überzeugung geteilt, daß weltanschauliche Entscheidungen zunehmend von technokratischen Lösungen – und damit auch die Politiker von den Experten – abgelöst würden. So wurde das *Ende der Ideologien* verkündet. Der Imperativ der Sachzwänge triumphiert auf der internationalen Szene über ideologisierte Systemkonfrontationen in der *Konvergenzthese*: Die Systeme der westlichen Marktwirtschaft und der östlichen Planwirtschaft würden in einer postindustriellen Gesellschaft eins werden. Ein zwangsläufig immer stärker regulierter Kapitalismus, ja ein *organisierter Kapitalismus* – um Rudolf Hilferdings[5] Begriff zu verwenden –, unterscheidet sich kaum noch von einem aufgelockerten Planungssystem. Die Sachlogik dominiert.

Zum anderen gilt der Triumph der Sachzwänge auch für politische Entscheidungen innerhalb eines Staates. Selbst demokratische Einrichtungen werden – diesen Vermutungen zufolge – zunehmend obsolet: Parlament und Regierung in der neugeordneten Industriegesellschaft können vernünftigerweise nicht mehr tun als das nachzuvollziehen, was die Experten als Optimallösungen errechnet haben.[6] Politische Ideologie wird von wissenschaftlicher Rationalität abgelöst. Es ist eine *geplante Demokratie*, die ins Auge gefaßt wird – so etwa von Karl Mannheim, der eine freiheitliche Planung, eine Planung des Überflusses, forderte, eine Planung, die den Mechanismen der Massengesellschaft entgegenwirkt und soziale Gerechtigkeit garantiert, eine Planung des kulturellen Niveaus und der Chancen zur Persönlichkeitsentwicklung, kurz: *Planung ohne Reglementierung.*[7] Wie diese detaillierte Planung aller gesellschaftlichen Bereiche mit Demokratie und Freiheit einhergehen soll, hat Mannheim allerdings nicht näher dargelegt.

Diese technokratische Vision entsprach noch in den sechziger Jahren der Perspektive vieler Sozialtechnologen, denen zufolge sich die Gesellschaft in Anbetracht zunehmender sozialwissenschaftlicher Kenntnisse immer besser steuern ließe – mit keynesianischen *fine tuning*, mit der Regulierung des *Golden-age-*

Wachstumspfades, mit bildungsökonomischen Modellen und anderen Instrumentarien aus der Zauberküche moderner Sozialwissenschaftler. Die Überzeugung, daß eine derartige Steuerung möglich sei, wurde quer durch das ganze politische Spektrum geteilt: Es gab also „linke" und „rechte" Sozialtechnokraten. Jene, die an den Schalthebeln des Herrschaftsapparats saßen, meinten, sie hätten die Gesellschaft nun im Griff, und schrieben die Erfolge der historisch außerordentlich dynamischen Wachstumsperiode ihrer eigenen Steuerungskompetenz zu. Die anderen, die darnach verlangten, an diesen Schalthebeln ebenfalls drehen zu dürfen, begehrten zwar nach einer anderen, von kapitalistischen Verwertungszwängen befreiten Gesellschaft, jedoch bestand auch für sie kein Zweifel daran, daß die von ihnen eingeforderte Zukunftsgesellschaft eine durchgeplante, wissenschaftlich gesteuerte Sozialordnung sein werde.

Von dieser Perspektive ist nicht viel übriggeblieben.[8] Zunächst kam die schlichte Gegenreaktion: der von den Akteuren der Studentenbewegung geäußerte allseitige *Ideologieverdacht*. Herbert Marcuse überzeugte sie davon, daß sich hinter dem Schleier technokratischer Rationalität Herrschafts- und Ausbeutungsverhältnisse verbargen[9], und Jürgen Habermas bezeichnete schlechthin *Wissenschaft und Technik als Ideologie*.[10] Auch wenn dies übertriebene Verdächtigungen sind: Das Bewußtsein davon, daß zwar umschreibbare, aus der Geschichte der politischen Parteien bekannte Ideologien zwischen den Fingern zerrinnen, daß aber das politische Handeln nach wie vor unter dem Einfluß von Wertentscheidungen stehe und daß man in Anbetracht dieser fortdauernden Werthaltigkeit politischer Entscheidungen weder der Kompetenz der Experten in ihrem Fachbereich noch der „Sachlichkeit" ihrer Entscheidungen trauen dürfe, wurde durch die Erfahrungen ökologischer Skandale in den siebziger Jahren erst gefestigt. Energieknappheit und Umweltzerstörung haben das entgegengesetzte Gefühl hervorgerufen: daß die Experten allzu wenig im Griff hätten und daß man ihnen nicht über den Weg trauen dürfe. So gehören auch *romantische Strömungen* zu dem Pendelschlag des Bewußtseins, die den Fortschritt der modernen Welt als Verfall deuten – die heile Vormoderne steht der verwunschenen Gegenwart gegenüber.

II.

Allen Krisenbefürchtungen zum Trotz waren die fünfziger und sechziger Jahre ökonomisch erfolgreich. Nach den Zerstörungen des Krieges und den Knappheiten der Nachkriegszeit kam ein gesicherter Prozeß des Wohlstandsanstiegs ins Rollen. Seit den sechziger Jahren begann man, das Gemeinwesen als *Konsumgesellschaft* und als *Überflußgesellschaft*[11] zu kritisieren.

In der Nachkriegszeit mußte man nicht lange nachdenken, um Wünsche und Bedürfnisse festzustellen: Es ging um Wohnungen, Schulen, Straßen, Nahrung, später auch um Autos, Urlaub, Sozialversicherung, Fernsehen. Die *skeptische Generation* der Wiederaufbauphase – wie sie Helmut Schelsky[12] nannte – realisierte das Wirtschaftswunder, und nach langen Jahren harter Entbehrungen begann sie, das Erreichte zu genießen. Die Gesellschaft trat in die letzte Phase des Industrialisierungsprozesses ein, die Walt W. Rostow[13] die *Gesellschaft des Massenkonsums* nennt. Ab den sechziger Jahren wurde aber auch die Kritik an der Konsumgesellschaft laut[14], und rasch zeigte sich, daß der „skeptischen" eine sehr „engagierte" Generation folgte: Am Ende der sechziger Jahre standen die Mitglieder der letzteren auf den Barrikaden, um Werte einzumahnen, die in der Freude und der Rücksichtslosigkeit des Konsumierens auf der Strecke zu bleiben schienen. Sie beanspruchte, *Revolution* zu machen, wollte jedenfalls Reform, möglicherweise auf dem *Marsch durch die Institutionen*: den *Muff aus den Talaren* klopfen. Absplitterungen wanderten später in den *Terrorismus*, mit den Folgewirkungen des *Radikalen-Erlasses* und des *„Berufsverbots"* in der BRD. Die Generation, die ihre Eltern nun beim Wort nahm, war bereits im Reichtum aufgewachsen. Die Kinder der *Wohlstandsgesellschaft* erinnerten sich nicht mehr daran, daß alle die Güter, die sie umgaben, nicht selbstverständlich waren. Ihre Kritik an dem *Konsumterror* – dem Konsumismus als einem neuen Totalitarismus[15] – wendete sich gegen die Wünschbarkeit und gegen die Machbarkeit eines dauerhaft überbordenden Güterverbrauchs. Überflüssige Güter – so Pasolini – machen das Leben überflüssig.

Einer der Angriffspunkte der Kritik waren Technik und Wissenschaft. Sie werden – mit Recht – als Träger des Fortschrittsgeschehens in einer *verwissenschaftlichten Gesellschaft* angesehen. Sie erzeugen jene Produkte, von denen die Konsumgesellschaft sich nährt. Konnten Herman Kahn und Anthony Wiener in ihrer Wissenschaftsvorschau von 1967 bis zum Jahr 2000 noch jubeln *Ihr werdet es erleben*[16], so werden der Wissenschaft seit den siebziger Jahren alle Defizite zugeschrieben, die in dieser modernen, komplexen Welt beobachtet und erfühlt werden – auch wenn es sich oft eher um Defizite der Politik handelt, also nicht um die Eigenarten der Produktion, sondern um jene der Verwendung wissenschaftlich-technischer Erkenntnisse. „Im bloßen Fortschritt liegt das Glück der Menschen nicht", titelt selbst die „Zeit" zu Weihnachten 1980. Eine oft romantisch angehauchte Kritik forcierte tiefe Aversionen gegen Wissenschaft und Technik. Diese Gesellschaft sei eine gigantische *Megamaschine*, sagte beispielsweise Lewis Mumford.[17] Die Megatechnik sei ungeheuer produktiv; deshalb bedürfe die Überflußwirtschaft des Massenkonsums. Sie setze den Wandel von einer streng restriktiven zu einer expansiv-hedonistischen Ökonomie mit wahl- und zügellosem Konsum voraus. Sie ersetze alte Zwänge durch den „Konsumzwang", und dieser führe zu Langeweile, zu einem inhaltsleeren Leben, zu einem Zustand der Bewußtlosigkeit, der noch als einer der Bewußtseinserweiterung verkauft werde, zu Infantilität und Senilität. Zu den psychischen Folgen zählen Demoralisierung, revolutionär-utopische Aufwallungen, Nihilismus, Regressionssymptome und unfruchtbare Subjektivität. – Diese *antimodernistische* Kritik ist fundamental, nicht reformistisch; sie fordert eine gänzlich andere, eine *Anti-Konsumgesellschaft*. Und sie ist wohl nur in einer reichen Gesellschaft möglich, in der die Härten einer Mangelwirtschaft, wie sie in den osteuropäischen Ländern allemal fühlbar waren, nicht mehr bewußt sind.

Jene Fülle zu schaffen, die Konsumkritik möglich macht, setzt Leistung voraus. Tatsächlich wird das Etikett der *Leistungsgesellschaft* benutzt, um ein weiteres Charakteristikum der Moderne zu bezeichnen. Jahrhunderte hat es gedauert, bis Arbeitsdisziplin und Leistungszwänge verinnerlicht wurden[18], und die Länder, die diesen kulturellen Prozeß der Formung eines marktadäquaten Geistes nicht durchlaufen haben, tun sich schwer mit der psychischen Anpassung ihrer Bürger an die Bedingungen der kapitalistischen Gesellschaft. Diese Leistungsbereitschaft hat nicht nur positive Seiten: Die disziplinierenden Lebensbedingungen der modernen Welt verursachen, wie Beobachter meinen, einen derartigen Streß, daß die anthropologische Substanz ihm nur schwer standzuhalten vermag. Das zur Höchstleistung angespannte Individuum darf sich kompensatorisch in einem überbordenden Konsum aalen, um seine Entsagungen und Entbehrungen in der Arbeitswelt zu vergessen. Konsum ist dann ein Versuch zur Kompensation der sozialen Kosten der Moderne. Andere Interpreten der Gegenwartsgesellschaft lassen dem Individuum auch in seiner freien Zeit keine Chance, dem Leistungsdruck zu entrinnen: Sie behaupten, daß sich die Anforderungen der Arbeitswelt so in die Welt des Konsumieren fortsetzen, daß auch dabei Streß-Symptome auftreten – bei der immer hektischeren Verwendung all der Konsumgüter, die in einer beschränkten Freizeit „genutzt" werden sollen.

Der Konsum richtet die Aufmerksamkeit auf das eigene Ich. Der moderne Lebensstil vermittelt deshalb weniger Bindungen, weniger Zugehörigkeiten; er ist mehr auf Chancen, Optionen, Ansprüche und erreichbare Güter gerichtet. Der Wohlstand der Industrieländer ermöglicht einen Lebensstil der Verfügbarkeit: Es ist nicht mehr notwendig, in soziale Zugehörigkeiten eingebunden zu sein, es ist vielmehr eine Vielfalt an Gütern und Chancen jederzeit disponibel. Wo noch Risiken und Gefahren auftauchen, sorgen kollektive Sicherungssysteme, der Staat vor allem, für die Linderung der Folgen. Auch wegen dieser Herauslösung des Individuums aus „selbstverständlichen" Sozialgruppierungen steigen die Selbstverwirklichungsforderungen – dafür bedarf es vermeintlich nur noch des einzelnen, nicht mehr der Gruppe. Es ist eine *egozentrische Gesellschaft*, die manche Beobachter zu erkennen glauben, gar eine *narzißtische Gesellschaft*, wie Christopher Lasch[19] behauptet. Das unmittelbar zwischenmenschliche Potential für Solidarität schwindet, wie viele konstatieren. Die Kategorie der Pflicht wird unzeitgemäß, so wie andere bürgerliche Werte wie Ehre, Höflichkeit, Takt und Treue. Sinnkrise und Wertkrise verbinden sich.

Disziplinierte Leistung in der Arbeitswelt, spontane Konsumbereitschaft in der Freizeit – es stellt sich die Frage, ob sich die Zwiespältigkeit des Lebens, das Nebeneinander divergierender Prinzipien, auf Dauer aufrechterhalten läßt. Daniel Bell hat in einem Buch über die *Zukunft der westlichen Welt*[20], das jenem über die postindustrielle Gesellschaft folgte, die Befürchtung geäußert, daß die hedonistische Stimmungslage der Freizeitgesellschaft jene Rationalität, auf der die moderne Industriegesellschaft gegründet ist, der Erosion preisgebe. Die klassischen puritanischen Tugenden, auf denen die moderne Industriegesellschaft beruht, würden eliminiert, Disziplin, Askese, Entsagung, Triebaufschub, Pünktlichkeit, Leistungswille und Genauigkeit schwänden dahin. „Konsum" bedeutet genau das Gegenteil: Spontaneität, Freude, Lust, Hedonismus, Sich-treiben-lassen, Zupacken, Kaufen. Diese Haltungen beginnen das Gewebe der modernen Welt zu dominieren, und sie untergraben die Selbstdisziplin. Man kann nicht am Tage „korrekt" und „diszipliniert" und am Abend ein „Herumtreiber" sein. So wird die *Krise der Leistungsgesellschaft*[21] ausgerufen und das Aufkommen einer *hedonistischen Gesellschaft* verkündet, die zugleich – als „reine" Konsumgesellschaft – das Ende der modernen Marktgesellschaft – und damit des Konsumierens – bedeutet.

III.

Am Ende aber sind die Menschen gar nicht mehr so materialistisch gesinnt, wie die Kritiker dies unterstellen? Manche – wie Ronald Inglehart[22] – glauben, hinter den wohlstandsglänzenden Fassaden habe sich eine *silent revolution* in durchaus begrüßenswerter Richtung vollzogen: ein Wertewandel von *materialistischen* Orientierungen, von der Betonung materiellen Wohlstands und physischer Sicherheit, hin zu *postmaterialistischen* Orientierungen wie Lebensqualität, Partizipation, Emotionalität, Ökologie und dergleichen. Die materialistisch-puritanische, leistungs- und einkommensbezogene Generation der Nachkriegszeit wird dieser Auffassung zufolge abgelöst durch eine Generation, die neuen Werten verpflichtet ist; diese richten sich auf Persönlichkeitsentfaltung, Umweltschutz, Kommunikation, Humanität, Mitbestimmung, Frieden.

Wenn dies richtig ist, dann hat ein *postmaterialistischer Wertewandel* stattgefunden. Die Bürger der Wohlstandsgesellschaft – und besonders die jüngeren unter ihnen – hören es gerne, wenn man ihnen attestiert, sie verachteten die materiellen Güter und strebten nach Höherem, nach Altruismus, Partizipation und globaler Verantwortung. So hat die These vom Wertwandel raschen Anklang gefunden. Mittlerweile ist sie in empirische Schwierigkeiten geraten. Es häufen sich die Indizien dafür, daß es sich nicht so sehr um einen Wandel als um eine Akkumulation von Werten handelt. Die materiellen Ansprüche werden nicht wirklich zurückgestellt, sondern sie werden durch immaterielle ergänzt, weil dies in einer „reichen" Gesellschaft möglich ist. Man will nicht nur die Sicherheit des Einkommens, sondern einen befriedigenden Arbeitsplatz. Man fordert nicht nur ausreichende Wohnungen, sondern diese größer, ästhetischer und in guter Lage. Die *postmaterialistische* Gesellschaft bleibt eine *materialistische*, nur stellen die wohlstandsverwöhnten Bürger an die Güter, die sie genießen, höhere Ansprüche.[23] Darüber hinaus ist jede einheitliche Etikettierung verfehlt: Es gibt die „Blumenkinder" der sechziger und die „Aussteiger" der siebziger Jahre, es gab die studentische Protestkultur, und es gibt ökotechnokratische Protagonisten einer „grün-alternativen" Lebensweise, es gibt aber auch „Popper" und „Yuppies", Konsumgierige und Karrierewütige.[24]

Der Postmaterialismus ist also möglicherweise ein Konstrukt ideologischer Selbsttäuschung: eine Projektion dessen, was mittelständische Intellektuelle als normatives Ideal verstehen. Die Wahrheit ist nach Auffassung anderer Zeitbeobachter weit düsterer: Keine postmaterialistische, sondern eine *nihilistische Gesellschaft* bildet sich als Ergebnis der vollständigen Desorientierung, und dieser Nihilismus tritt in vielen Formen auf: als bürgerlicher, anarchischer, bürokratischer, individualistischer, materialistischer, hedonistischer, klerikaler, atheistischer, akademischer, ästhetischer, despotischer, resignativer, dogmatischer oder dionysischer Nihilismus – so die Auflistung von Wolfgang Kraus.[25] Gemeinsam ist allen diesen Formen: Das Wertbewußtsein verliert sich, der Glaube an Sinnhaftigkeit schwindet. Viele merken nicht einmal, daß sie in den Nihilismus gleiten.[26]

IV.

Wenn sich auch der Wertewandel nicht so recht dingfest machen läßt, so kann man doch feststellen: Die Verunsicherung über den Wertekanon, die Desorientierung über Ziel und Sinn des Lebens nehmen zu. Aus der Verunsicherung über das, was gilt, läßt sich ein neues Etikett gewinnen: Der Rückzug von der allgemeingültigen Signatur der Zeit nimmt die *neue Unübersichtlichkeit* als neue Zeitsignatur.[27] Dieses Etikett Jürgen Habermas' ist rasch in alle Feuilletons übernommen worden: Die Zukunft ist negativ besetzt, Ratlosigkeit herrscht in Politik und Öffentlichkeit. Die Lage ist objektiv unübersichtlich und subjektiv durch mangdelndes Selbstvertrauen gekennzeichnet. Allein die Geschwindigkeit des Wandels – die Rasanz einer *dromologischen Gesellschaft*[28] – scheint die Menschen zu überfordern. Hermann Lübbe etwa konstatiert einen Vertrautheitsschwund in allen Lebensbereichen, der die Anpassungsfähigkeit der Menschen übersteigt; zu seinen Folgen gehören Erscheinungen der Rehistorisierung, die kompensatorisch Geschichte als Ressource für Identitätsversicherung und -rückgewinnung benutzen.[29] Die moderne Gesellschaft zehrt somit von traditionellen Beständen, und sie ist nicht mehr in der Lage, diese aus sich heraus zu regenerieren. David Riesmans *einsame Masse*[30] wird nur noch von Umweltimpulsen gesteuert, nicht mehr aus einer inneren Wertorientierung. *Gewißheitsverlust, Bindungsverlust, Sinnverlust, Rechtfertigungsverlust:* Sie befindet sich in der *Orientierungskrise*[31]. Das *Unbehagen in der Modernität*[32] macht sich breit, als Verschärfung des Freudschen *Unbehagens in der Kultur*[33] generell. Intellektuelle treten als Sinnstifter auf, ob als *Apokalyptiker* oder *Integrierte*[34], als Gurus, die durch Bildungshäuser wandern und Bestseller schreiben – eine *Priesterherrschaft der Intellektuellen* etabliert sich, wie Helmut Schelsky[35] sagt. Eine Erhellung der Situation ist davon nicht zu erwarten. „In einer *belle époque* wird die Nachdenklichkeit virtuos, die Enttäuschung gelehrt, die Abklärung kompendiös, die Todessehnsucht redselig. Bücher über Untergangsrisiken erleben Nachauflagen, und die dunklen Autoren genießen den Krisenbonus. Wann gab es zuletzt eine solche Koinzidenz von Sekurität und Verunsicherung? Dieses Frösteln in den Villen, wo weiche Individuen auf harte Schläge warten? Solche Schatten über dem kalten

Büffet, an dem Professoren, Therapeuten und Intendanten über Ästhetiken des Abschieds diskutieren?"[36]

Tatsächlich ist es der einheitliche Wertehimmel, der einzustürzen droht. „Unsere westliche Zivilisation", so meint Richard Löwenthal, „ist gekennzeichnet durch eine Synthese von Werten, die einerseits der jüdisch-christlichen Prophetie, andrerseits der griechisch-römischen Antike entstammen. Ohne Anspruch auf Vollständigkeit zu erheben, nenne ich den Glauben an die Autonomie der *Vernunft* als Schlüssel zum Verständnis der Welt; den Glauben an die Einzigartigkeit des *Individuums*, das mit unveräußerlichen Rechten geboren wird; den Glauben an den bindenden Charakter *freiwillig eingegangener* (und nicht nur blutsmäßig gewachsener) *Gemeinschaften*; den Glauben an die Grenzziehung zwischen individuellem Wollen und gemeinschaftlicher Notwendigkeit durch *rechtliche Satzung*; die Wertschätzung der *Arbeit*, auch der körperlichen Arbeit in dieser Welt als Verdienst und Sinnerfüllung des Lebens und nicht nur als notwendiges Übel."[37] Die Gültigkeit dieser Werte ist fraglich geworden; die langfristige *Kulturkrise* zeichnet sich aus durch einen „Weltbildverlust": die Erschütterung des Glaubens an einen erkennbaren Sinn des menschlichen Lebens und der gesellschaftlichen Entwicklung im ganzen, und durch einen „Bindungsverlust": die Erschwerung von Sozialisierung und Identitätsbildung der Heranwachsenden durch die stetig beschleunigte Veränderung der Lebensformen.

Wenn nichts mehr sicher und alles nebeneinander gültig ist, dann ist auch die Moderne, wie manche verkünden, an ihr Ende geraten – abgelöst von der *Postmoderne*.[38] Dies ist – zum mindesten – die Epoche *nach* der Moderne, und ihr zentrales Element ist die Pluralität. Die „Großen Erzählungen", die Rahmenmythen der Moderne, verlieren ihre suggestive Kraft, sie können den Fortschritt, die Wissenschaft, die Rationalität nicht mehr legitimieren. Vorstellungen wie die Emanzipation der Menschheit (in der Aufklärung), die Teleologie des Geistes (im Idealismus), die Hermeneutik des Sinns (im Historismus) und die Beglückung aller Menschen im Reichtum (im Kapitalismus) lösen sich in Einzelteile auf, und die Teile werden selbständig. – Dieser Befund entspricht der Erfahrung der Zeitgenossen, daß sich Erlebnisse und Erfahrungen zu einem Ganzen nicht mehr fügen wollen. Postmoderne Theoretiker wie Lyotard beschreiben diesen Auflösungsprozeß aber nicht als Krise; sie plädieren dafür, ihn als Chance zu begreifen, ihn positiv zu sehen.[39] Dies ist die eigentliche Umwertung, die die Postmoderne vollzieht. Es entsteht eine Vielzahl von „kleinen Erzählungen", Sprachspielen, Minoritätssprachen. Diese unterlaufen die wuchernden Systeme von Rationalität und Bürokratie, sie bieten Pluralismus ohne Anspruch auf Letztbegründung. Es gibt kein Kriterium der Wahrheit oder Gerechtigkeit mehr; keine Metasprache, keinen Sprecher, der sie alle beherrscht. Der Verlust der Ganzheit ist Gewinn, denn Ganzheit ist mit Zwang und Terror verbunden, und erst der Zerfall der Ganzheit setzt Autonomie frei. Was zunächst als „Krise" begriffen wurde, wird als Chance proklamiert.

V.

Der Kapitalismus hat als ökonomisches System gesiegt, daran kann kein Zweifel bestehen, und der Sozialismus, der die Planwirtschaft als großes Gegenmodell angeboten hatte, ist mit unerwarteter Plötzlichkeit dahingeschieden. Karl Marx hat ein letztes Mal recht behalten: Der politisch-ideologische Überbau ist nicht zu halten, wenn es mit der ökonomischen Basis schiefläuft. Insofern bekennen auch Kritiker, daß das *kapitalistische Modell* – der Entwurf einer *besitzindividualistischen Gesellschaft*[40] – als *Wachstumsgesellschaft* erfolgreich war. Im deutschsprachigen Raum hat man Schwierigkeiten mit dem „linken" Etikett einer „kapitalistischen" Gesellschaft; während angelsächsische Theoretiker unbekümmert von *capitalism*[41] als dem erfolgreichsten aller möglichen Systeme – vom „horn of plenty"[42] – sprechen, hält man sich hierzulande eher an Begriffe wie jenen der *Marktwirtschaft*. Auch von der *Unternehmerwirtschaft* ist gerne die Rede, wenn man die Dynamik dieser Wirtschaftsordnung – und das Erfordernis, die Interessen der wahrhaft kreativen Gruppe im Wirtschaftsleben zu wahren – betonen will.

Das Gegenmodell zu diesen Konzeptionen war die marxistische Utopie des zukünftigen Heilsgeschehens, in diffuser oder theoretischer Form. Was Werner Sombart schon in der Zwischenkriegszeit mit dem Begriff der *spätkapitalistischen Gesellschaft* zum Ausdruck gebracht hatte, ist eine marxistisch inspirierte Endzeitstimmung, in der die Industrieländer als letzte Blüten einer sterbenden Gesellschaftsordnung betrachtet werden. Wirtschaftliche Störungen am Ende der sechziger Jahre wurden von vielen bereits als Signal des nunmehr eintretenden Zusammenbruchs gewertet. Doch die Erklärung dafür, daß der Wandel zu einem sozialistischen System auf sich warten ließ, wurde mit der Theorie des *staatsmonopolistischen Kapitalismus* geliefert.[43] Dieser Auffassung zufolge hat sich das Milieu der Privatkapitalisten zu einem der Monopole und multinationalen Konzerne gewandelt. Die Macht der Monopole verschmilzt mit jener des Staates. Der Staat ist jene Agentur, welche die gemeinsamen Interessen des Großkapitals schützt. Dies war die letzte Verteidigungsposition eines orthodoxen Marxismus; reformistische Linke maßen aber weiterhin mit zweierlei Maß. So warnte etwa Roger Garaudy, nachdem er die unübersehbaren Defizite der realsozialistischen Länder zur Kenntnis genommen hatte, davor, den Sozialismus gleich zu verwerfen wie den Kapitalismus: Die „doppelte Verzerrung – das Fehlen der menschlichen Zweckbestimmung und der autoritäre Dualismus (zwischen Regierenden und Produzierenden, M. P.) – ist für den Kapitalismus *seinem Wesen und seiner Substanz nach*, für den Sozialismus *lediglich in dessen Verirrungen* charakteristisch."[44] Entartete, aber doch irgendwie „wahlverwandte" Modelle – auch diese Phase scheint weitgehend vorbei zu sein. Seitdem gibt es nur noch eine „mehr linkische als linke Kapitalismuskritik".[45]

Auch im Westen war man sich des Erfolges des marktwirtschaftlichen Wirtschaftssystems nicht immer so sicher; gerade in den siebziger Jahren – nach der Ölkrise – rätselte man herum, was den plötzlichen Rückfall im Wachstum bewirkt haben könnte. Man befürchtete, in der Talsohle eines vierten oder fünften Kontratiefs – einer „langen Welle" wirtschaftlicher Entwicklung – zu landen, in die Phase einer *Stagnationsgesellschaft* einzutreten und zukünftig mit einer *no-growth-society*[46] leben zu müssen – manche begrüßten diese Aussicht angesichts zunehmender Umweltschäden sogar und hofften, die Stagnation würde den Zerstörungsprozeß wenigstens verlangsamen und Zeit geben zur Restrukturierung der Wachstumsgesellschaft, andere befürchteten eine *Krise des Wohlstands.*[47] Allerdings machte Lester Thurow darauf aufmerksam, daß sich in einer *Null-Summen-Gesellschaft*, in der Verteilungskonflikte nicht durch wirtschaftliches Wachstum besänftigt und Reformmaßnahmen nicht durch zusätzliche Ressourcen finanziert werden könnten, die sozialen Konflikte zuspitzen könnten.[48] Dies erweiterte sich zu einem generellen *Krisenbefund*[49]: Europas Wirtschaft sei in einer *Trendwende.*[50]

Was viele Wanderprediger der wahrhaft liberalen Lehre mit wiedergewonnenem Selbstbewußtsein nun den Ostländern offerieren, ist ein Bild des kapitalistischen Systems, das auch in den westlichen Ländern keine Realisierung gefunden hat: das „reine" Modell eines dynamischen, aber auch ungebremst-brutalen Systems, in dem die Marktlogik alle Verhaltensweisen und Lebensbereiche beherrscht. Eine *wirtschaftsliberale* Gesinnung, welche die Rahmenbedingungen einer *Verfassung der Freiheit* – so der Titel von Friedrich von Hayeks berühmtem Buch[51] – sichert, hat erst seit den siebziger Jahren wieder einen Aufschwung zu verzeichnen; bis dahin wurden liberale Ideen in den westlichen Ländern mit Argwohn betrachtet, in einigen wohlfahrtsverwöhnten Ländern sogar mit Abscheu. Mittlerweile werden *Markt, Effizienz, Unternehmertum, Privatisierung* und ähnliche Begriffe aus dem Wörterbuch des wirtschaftsdynamischen Aufsteigers mit positiven Assoziationen verbunden.

Allerdings täuscht man sich über die Beschaffenheit des Wirtschaftssystems, in dem wir leben, wenn man glaubt, es ist nach den Vorschlägen wirtschaftsliberaler Provenienz durchkonstruiert. Die europäischen Sozialstaaten sind in Wahrheit Ergebnisse eines pragmatisch realisierten *dritten Weges* – solche Modelle sind immer wieder in unterschiedlichen Varianten gehandelt worden. Es handelt sich nicht um liberalkapitalistische, sondern um wohlfahrtsstaatliche Systeme, um eine regulierte Marktgesellschaft, eben um eine *soziale Marktwirtschaft*: Sie verbindet die marktwirtschaftliche Dynamik mit einer Absicherung der wichtigsten Lebensrisiken – Gesundheit, Alter, Unfall und Arbeitslosigkeit, Familienbeihilfen und Fürsorgeleistungen decken ungleiche Belastungen und Notfälle ab. Knapp die Hälfte des erarbeiteten Wertes läuft in den meisten westlichen Industrieländern über die Kassen des Staates, und somit kann der Marktbereich als hinlänglich domestiziert angesehen werden. Redistributive Steuersysteme, mehr aber noch die Transferleistungen des Staates tragen dazu bei, daß auch Kritiker zugeben, daß es sich nicht mehr um *Klassengesellschaften* handle, allenfalls um *Klassengesellschaften im Schmelztiegel* – so Theodor Geigers[52] Begriff –, ja daß sich eine *nivellierte Mittelschichtgesellschaft* – so Helmut Schelsky – bildet, auch wenn Disparitäten der Lebenschancen bestehen bleiben.[53] Es ist zudem eine beschränkt *meritokratische* und eine *mobile Gesellschaft*, in der Auf- und Abstiegsprozesse möglich sind.

Der Aufschwung des liberalen Bewußtseins, dessen erklärtes Ziel es unter anderem ist, zur *Überwindung der Sozialstaatskrise*[54] beizutragen, führt dazu, die Sozialstaatlichkeit mit Argwohn zu betrachten. Die expandierenden Finanzierungserfordernisse sozialstaatlicher Programme lassen ohnehin seit längerem *Dissonanzen der Wohlfahrtsgesellschaft*[55] und *Grenzen des Sozialstaats*[56] vermuten: Ist nicht die mehr oder minder segensreiche Hand des Staates in Bereiche vorgedrungen, wo dies freiheitsbedrohend ist, wo also eine vielleicht durchaus *paternalistisch* gesinnte Sozialbürokratie sich Herrschaftsallüren anmaßt[57]? Manche sprechen in Anbetracht der Abhängigkeit der Bürger von den finanziellen Strömen aus staatlichen Kassen gar von einer *Taschengeldgesellschaft*. Wird nicht die dichte *Reglementierung* bereits schädlich für das Gedeihen wirtschaftlicher Dynamik? Viele konstatieren eine ausufernde Bürokratie, ja eine *Funktionärsgesellschaft*.[58] Der *Steuerstaat*[59] hat manchen Liberalen zufolge ein Ausmaß erreicht, daß Schädigungen des wirtschaftlichen Mechanismus und Bedrohungen der Freiheit zu vermuten sind. Die *Wohlfahrts-Wende* ist angesagt.[60]

Angesichts der überhöhten Begehrlichkeit staatlicher Kassenverwalter wird es weithin als legitim angesehen, staatsfreie Wirtschaftsaktivitäten zu wahren oder einige Geldströme der offiziellen Registrierung zu entziehen: Die *Schattenwirtschaft* blüht, eine *informelle Wirtschaft* und eine *self service economy*[61] werden proklamiert. Modelle der *Selbstorganisation*[62] oder der *Dualwirtschaft*[63] werden als Lösung finanzieller Engpässe in einigen sozialstaatlichen Aufgabenbereichen, aber auch als Wege zu einem bereichernden Leben angeboten. Aber eine *wohlfahrtsstaatliche Geisteshaltung* herrscht vor: Der Staat wird für alle erfolgsungewissen Aufgaben zur ersten Anlaufstelle. Man ruft nach seiner Regulierungsleistung, wo immer Probleme sichtbar werden. Dies geht allerdings zusammen mit einer Rundum-Aversion gegen staatliche Apparate und Vorschreibungen, mit einer diffusen *Verdrossenheit* gegenüber der Sphäre des Politischen. Im Prinzip verlangt man nach einer *Schlankheitskur für den Staat*[64], nach weniger Staat und weniger Steuern; im konkreten Fall aber wird der Staat als willige *Serviceeinrichtung* gefordert.

VI.

Was dem Kapitalismus am häufigsten angekreidet wird, ist seine Unfähigkeit, dauerhaft einen Zustand der Vollbeschäftigung zu sichern. Es sind nicht alle Utopien an ein Ende gelangt, wie die Postmodernen behaupten; es ist – so meinen Jürgen Habermas und Claus Offe – nur eine bestimmte Utopie, nämlich jene der *Arbeitsgesellschaft*.[65] In der modernen Industriegesellschaft waren alle Bereiche geprägt durch eine marktgesteuerte, kapitalistisch verwertete und betriebsförmig organisierte Erwerbsarbeit. Alle Utopien konnten sich daher auf die Befreiung von dieser Form der Arbeit richten, auf die *Selbstbestimmung* im Produktionszusammenhang. Aber die Arbeit verliert, so stellen Habermas und

Offe fest, strukturbildende und gesellschaftsformierende Kraft. Seit der Mitte der siebziger Jahre kommen die Grenzen des sozialstaatlichen Projekts zu Bewußtsein, ohne daß eine Ersatzprogrammatik erkennbar wäre. Die Utopie einer besseren Arbeitsgesellschaft überzeugt nicht mehr.

Die Zustimmung der Öffentlichkeit zu den sozialstaatlichen Programmen ist allerdings in den westlichen Industrieländern ungebrochen. Schlagworte wie die *Arbeitsgesellschaft, der die Arbeit ausgeht*[66], oder *Wenig Arbeit, aber viel zu tun*[67] drücken jedoch die Befürchtung einer langdauernden Beschäftigungskrise aus, und zwar nicht nur wegen eines schwachen Wachstums, sondern auch wegen der immer dynamischeren Rationalisierung und Technisierung der Produktion; aber sie sind in den letzten Jahren leiser geworden. Zum einen hat sich gezeigt, daß die Protestbereitschaft der Arbeitslosen in Zeiten der Beschäftigungskrise niedrig ist[68]; nicht zuletzt aus dem Grund, daß keine plausible Alternative zu einer systemkonformen staatlichen Beschäftigungspolitik angeboten wird. Zum anderen zeichnet sich mittlerweile eher eine drohende Arbeitskräfteknappheit bei einem einigermaßen befriedigenden Wirtschaftswachstum ab. Ähnlich verhält es sich mit dem Schlagwort von der *Zwei-Drittel-Gesellschaft*[69], das kritisch die Befürchtung artikulieren sollte, daß bei steigender Arbeitslosigkeit der größere Teil der Gesellschaft, nämlich die arbeitende Bevölkerung, einen erheblichen Anteil an ausgegrenzten Arbeitslosen erhalten müsse. Dieses Etikett trifft nun eher die Wirklichkeit in manchen osteuropäischen Ländern, nicht aber kapitalistische Systeme in der revolutionsgeschüttelten Endphase ihrer Existenz.

Auch das Arbeitsleben selbst wandelt sich schnell. Neuere Untersuchungen relativieren das traditionelle Bild der *Massenproduktion*. Die modernen Technologien führen zu einer flexiblen Spezialisierung, zu neuen Formen der Betriebsorganisation, zu einer Höherqualifizierung der Arbeitskräfte: Kern und Schumann sehen Tendenzen zu einem *Ende der Arbeitsteilung*, Piore und Sabel zu einem *Ende der Massenproduktion*.[70]

Zur Sicherung der Vollbeschäftigung wurde oft eine mögliche Arbeitszeitverkürzung vorgeschlagen, die das vorhandene Arbeitspotential auf die Arbeitswilligen gleichmäßiger aufteilen sollte.[71] Die Gegner solcher Maßnahmen wiesen auf den Prozeß der Arbeitszeitverkürzung hin, der bereits im Laufe des letzten Jahrhunderts stattgefunden hatte, und sie brachten damit das Etikett der *Freizeitgesellschaft* ins Spiel: Sie meinten damit eine Gesellschaft, in der allein die quantitative Ausdehnung der Freizeit im Verhältnis zur Arbeitszeit eine Forcierung von „Freizeitwerten" und „-haltungen" mit sich brächte, aber sie machten damit auch auf die neu entstehenden Freizeitprobleme in einer nicht mehr „ausgelasteten" Bevölkerung aufmerksam. Wie füllt man (bei einer Lebenserwartung von 80 Jahren) rund 250.000 Stunden Freizeit? Es steigt die Nachfrage nach Freizeitgütern, aber auch nach Lebenssinn und nach Unterhaltung.

VII.

Die westlichen politischen Ordnungen gelten als *Verfassungsstaaten* und als *Grundrechtsdemokratien*: Sie gewährleisten ihren Bürgern den Schutz der Grund- und Freiheitsrechte. Es sind *bürgerliche Staaten* im Sinne einer *civil society* und einer *civic culture*: eines Gemeinwesens, das rational begründet und rechtlich abgesichert ist und in dem die Menschen ihren Interessen frei nachgehen können.[72]

Der Staat empfiehlt sich als *Rechtsstaat*, aber auch als Serviceeinrichtung, als *Leistungsstaat*, der seinen Bürgern als Serviceeinrichtung mannigfache Lebenshilfen offeriert, vorzugsweise angeboten durch funktionale Eliten, die jenseits politischer Unwägbarkeiten das erwünschte Angebot erstellen. Die modernen Demokratien gelten als *Konkurrenzdemokratien*: Politische Gruppierungen wetteifern um Wählerstimmen. Es sind *formale Demokratien*, die sich lange dem Vorwurf ausgesetzt gesehen haben, erst als *soziale Demokratien* den Sinn dieses Wortes Demokratie richtig erfüllen zu können; einige meinten damit den Sozialstaat, andere die unlösbare Verknüpfung von Sozialismus und Demokratie – beide vermischten Form und Inhalt. Nach der Phase der Rekonstituierung demokratischer Systeme nach dem Zweiten Weltkrieg, die eine „ruhige" politische Entwicklung und den Ausbau wohlfahrtsstaatlicher Systeme (und in diesem Sinne „sozialer Demokratien") brachte, wurde im Modernisierungsschub der sechziger Jahre die Forderung nach einer sozialen Demokratie in jene nach einer *Demokratisierung aller Lebensbereiche*[73], nach *Partnerschaft* und *Mitbestimmung* in Gemeinde, Schule, Betrieb und dergleichen umgemünzt; auch staatstragende Parteien schlossen sich diesem Verlangen an und bemühten sich um *Reformpolitik*.

Als Konkurrenzordnungen sind die westlichen Systeme *Parteienstaaten*: Politische Gruppierungen leisten die erforderliche Integration von Meinungen und Interessen. Allerdings ist heute von einer *Parteiengesellschaft im Umbruch* die Rede, von *Parteien unter Streß*, von den *Grenzen des Parteienstaates*[74]: angesichts ihrer Entideologisierung, der Personalisierung des politischen Wettbewerbs, einer Abkoppelung der Bürger vom politischen Geschehen, ja ihrer zunehmenden Verdrossenheit. Huntington vermutet gar, daß die Parteien eine politische Form der Industriegesellschaft gewesen seien, die auf dem Weg in die postindustrielle Gesellschaft absterbe.[75] Ihre traditionellen Wertwelten, gestützt auf die Zurechnung spezifischer sozialer Gruppen, scheinen sich jedenfalls überlebt zu haben: wenn überhaupt, dann wird mit Etiketten wie *Neokonservativismus* oder *Neoliberalismus* hantiert.

In unterschiedlichem Maße handelt es sich bei den westlichen Industrieländern um *korporatistische (sozialpartnerschaftliche) Systeme*[76]: Etablierte Interessengruppen, die von den staatlichen Instanzen unterstützt werden, sind an dem Prozeß des Integrierens und Aushandeln von Maßnahmen im wirtschafts- und sozialpolitischen Bereich beteiligt. Die fragwürdige Stellung dieser Gruppen im Rahmen einer demokratischen Ordnung hat immer wieder zur Kritik am *Verbän-*

destaat Anlaß gegeben[77]; zuweilen wurde befürchtet, der Staat sei *pressure groups* völlig ausgeliefert, er sei nur noch ein „Riese auf tönernen Füßen"[78] oder gar bereits zu einem „demo-autoritären, leistungsfähigen Obrigkeitsstaat in rechtsstaatlicher Charaktermaske"[79] rückgebildet, dann wieder wurde angedeutet, der Staat könne heikle Materien aus dem politischen Entscheidungsprozeß ausgliedern und sich dadurch entlasten – er „instrumentalisiere" damit aber die Interessenverbände für seine Zwecke.

Schließlich handelt es sich bei den modernen Regierungsapparaturen um *bürokratische Staaten*[80]: *Big government* heißt auch *big bureaucracy*. Die expandierenden Verwaltungsapparate haben das Geschäft des Regierens im Detail zu besorgen, und sie haben dies im leistenden Staat mit hoher Effizienz getan. Aber die wuchernden Bürokratien, die auf ihre Eigeninteressen bedacht sind, als arbeitsscheu, umständlich und routineverhaftet angesehen werden und eine *Beamtenherrschaft* zu etablieren beginnen, haben auch Kritik ausgelöst; ob *budget-maximizing*[81] oder *x-ineffizient*[82] – sie stehen nach Auffassung mancher Beobachter dem *verwalteten Bürger* als Bremsklötze gegenüber, sie schaffen am Ende sogar eine *Gesellschaft in Fesseln.*[83]

Politische Gegenbewegungen gegen den Trend der Moderne haben seit den siebziger Jahren die politische Szenerie so verändert, daß man nicht nur von einer *pluralistischen Demokratie*, sondern gar von einer *Bürgerinitiativengesellschaft* spricht.[84] Gruppierungen unterschiedlicher Zielsetzung und Reichweite wollen im außerparlamentarischen Raum wirken; unter den *neuen sozialen Bewegungen* finden sich grün-alternative Gruppen, die den *Bruder Baum* retten wollen, ebenso wie Feministinnen, die gegen die *patriarchalische Gesellschaft* auftreten, Selbsterfahrungsbewegungen, welche die *Körper*-Thematik betonen, Gesundheitsgruppierungen, die *makrobiotisch*, *vegetarisch* oder sonstwie „gesund" leben, Anhänger verschiedener Friedensbewegungen und viele andere. Sie wollen gewöhnlich nicht ihren Beitrag zu jenem Geschehen leisten, das sie als bloße *Akklamationsdemokratie* betrachten, sondern – mit durchaus *fundamentalistischen* Akzenten – das „Richtige" und „Wahre" durchsetzen, dessen sie sich sicher sind, und sie legitimieren dieses Bestreben üblicherweise durch ihre Berufung auf *Basisdemokratie*. *Betroffenheit* wird zum Partizipationskriterium. Die formalen Spielregeln der Mehrheitsdemokratie erachten sie als unzureichend, insbesondere angesichts des Existenzdrucks der Menschheit, und dies ist ihr Konnex zu autoritären Gesellschaftsmodellen; allerdings lassen sich Gründe dafür finden, daß die Industrieländer in Anbetracht bestimmter Probleme tatsächlich vor den *Grenzen der Mehrheitsdemokratie*[85] herkömmlicher Prägung stehen.

Die westliche Demokratie hat sich als ausgezeichnet geeignet erwiesen, den Fortschritt im Sinne der Mehrung materieller Güter und der Absicherung des einzelnen gegen Lebensrisiken zu gewährleisten. Aber der Parteienwettbewerb scheint weniger geeignet zu sein, jene Reformen zu tragen, die durch die ökologischen Notwendigkeiten auferlegt werden. Darüber hinaus ist der Staat so stark unter Druck geraten, daß die problemlose Folgebereitschaft seiner Bürger – auch wenn es um Härten und Opfer geht – nicht mehr vorausgesetzt werden kann[86]:

Es ist ein *nachauratischer Staat*. So wird von den *Grenzen des Regierens*[87] oder gar von der *Unregierbarkeit* gesprochen. Die Konturen des Politischen sind mittlerweile längst unscharf geworden: Der Geist steht nicht mehr links, wie es einst hieß; ob er rechts steht, ist fraglich; am ehesten ist er unpolitisch geworden, sicher aber verdrossen.

VIII.

Die moderne Gesellschaft ist nur als *technisierte Gesellschaft* – und das heißt: als ein verwissenschaftlichtes Unternehmen – möglich. Es ist ein *technisches Zeitalter*[88], in dem wir leben. In Anbetracht aufsehenerregender Großtechnologien verschwimmen die erwartbaren Vorteile aber im Nebel einer verunsicherten Zukunftserwartung, und es wird eher die Risikoproblematik dieser Technologien gesehen.

Das Problem der individuellen und kollektiven Akzeptanz technischer Projekte und ihrer Risiken wird auch von den Befürwortern und Betreibern technischer Anlagen zunehmend als vorrangiges Problem der Durchführung und Durchsetzung ihrer Projekte angesehen. Seitdem in den frühen siebziger Jahren mit dem Beststeller des Club of Rome über die *Grenzen des Wachstums* die *Apokalypse* ausgerufen wurde, haben die einschlägigen Knappheitsthemen rasche Karriere im öffentlichen Bewußtsein gemacht. Das Ressentiment gegen die moderne Naturwissenschaft und Industrie, das nach den Erfahrungen der beiden letzten Jahrzehnte ja nicht unbegründet ist, läßt sich unschwer mit Stichworten aus einem weltweit bekannten Katastrophenkatalog illustrieren: Contergan, Three Miles Island, Seveso, Assuan, Harrisburg, Tschernobyl, DDT, Ölverseuchung, Asbest, Ozonloch, Robbensterben, Algenpest – und viele Begriffe aus dem Wörterbuch des modernen Menschen ließen sich anfügen. Die apokalyptische Landkarte hat globale Dimensionen erhalten, sie erstreckt sich vom brasilianischen Dschungel bis zum antarktischen Eis. Kein Wunder, daß eine lebensphilosophische und ökologische Kritik aufbricht[89], daß auch die empirischen Sozialforscher eine *zweifelnde Gesellschaft* vermessen[90], daß die Einwohner dieser bedrohten Erde generell an die *Fortschrittsmythen*[91] nicht mehr glauben, daß dem vermeintlichen Fortschritt die *Antiquiertheit des Menschen*[92] beschwörend entgegen gehalten wird. Schumachers Parole *small is beautiful* ist in das Bewußtsein gedrungen, Ivan Illichs Thesen über die *Selbstbegrenzung der Technik*, Mumfords Kritik an der *Megamaschine* der Moderne.[93] Ihnen und ihren Anhängern schwebt die Vision einer *ökologischen Gesellschaft* vor. Die moderne Gesellschaft muß radikal beseitigt werden, damit die unterdrückte Natur wieder zu ihrem Recht kommt. – Die Kritik an der Atomenergie hat einen der wirksamsten Ansatzpunkte für Ängste und Proteste geboten. Die Reichweite der Gefährdung – die Gefahr einer globalen Selbstvernichtung der Menschheit, wurde an dieser Technik besonders deutlich. Auch die politischen Konsequenzen des Versuchs, derartige Technologien unangreifbar zu machen, wurden bedacht, und zwar von Alexander Rüstow schon in den fünfziger Jahren[94] und zwei Jahrzehnte später von Robert Jungk in seinem *Atomstaat*.[95]

Technik dieser Größenordnung läßt sich sicherer machen, aber nicht sicher; insofern ist die *Angst des Menschen vor der Technik*[96] nicht unberechtigt. Das hat etwa Charles Perrow in seinem Buch über *Normale Katastrophen*[97] dargelegt: Bestimmte Risiken der Großtechnik sind unvermeidbar. Viele Großtechnologien vereinen zwei Eigenschaften: Komplexität und enge Koppelung. Es gibt eine Tendenz zu Interaktionen zwischen Betriebsstörungen oder Unfällen, Zufälligkeiten, an die vorher niemand gedacht hat; je mehr Sicherungen eingebaut werden, umso größer wird die Möglichkeit zu weiteren unvorhersehbaren Interaktionen. Wenn die Prozesse sehr schnell ablaufen und sich nicht ohne weiteres abschalten lassen, wenn sich die „gestörten" Systemteile nicht von den anderen isolieren lassen, dann breitet sich die Störung aus. Sicherheitssysteme versagen, weil geraume Zeit während des Störungsfalles kein Mensch weiß, worin das Problem eigentlich besteht. Haben diese Systeme zudem ein hohes Zerstörungspotential, so ist eine Katastrophe von Zeit zu Zeit programmiert. Die *komplexe Gesellschaft* ist eine *Risikogesellschaft*. Ulrich Beck[98] hat diesen Begriff verwendet, und er ist mit bemerkenswerter Geschwindigkeit in alle zeitgenössischen Reden eingedrungen.[99]

IX.

Die Wirklichkeitswahrnehmung in der *Informationsgesellschaft* ist immer stärker durch die *Massenmedien*, insbesondere die elektronischen Medien, geprägt. Die „Öffentlichkeit" wird reduziert auf jene technischen Geräte, die Bedeutungen vermitteln: auf die Massenmedien. Man orientiert sich an einfachen Rezepten, an rascher Information, an einer scheinobjektiven Welt der Berichterstattung. Die elektronischen Möglichkeiten einer *verkabelten Welt* im *Satellitenzeitalter* haben ihren Bezugspunkt auch in Utopien wie jenen Orwells um das Jahr *1984* oder jenen Huxleys in einer *schönen, neuen Welt* gefunden: von der *Informationsindustrie* und dem *gläsernen Menschen* ist die Rede[100].

Unsere Kultur, so meint etwa Neil Postman[101], gerate durch die Erziehung zum Fernsehen zum *Panoptikum*. Man resigniert nicht mehr vor dem Leid, sondern nimmt es einfach nicht mehr wahr; der ernsthafte Diskurs wird nicht unterdrückt, sondern er löst sich im Gekichere auf. Was sich nicht in bunten Bildern darstellen läßt, das existiert nicht, oder jedenfalls ist es uninteressant. Die Visualisierung unseres Alltags läßt unsere Fähigkeit verkümmern, andere Formen der Erfahrung, aktives und abstraktes Denken, den Umgang mit einer *Schriftkultur*, überhaupt noch zu aktualisieren; es entwickelt sich eine *Bildkultur*. Es gibt keinen Unterschied mehr zwischen Schein und Wirklichkeit, zwischen den Nachrichten und dem Abendfilm. Die Bilder vermitteln keine Wirklichkeit mehr, sie sind die Wirklichkeit. Die Wirklichkeit wird vor dem Fernseher konsumiert, immer mehr in einer Welt der Verkabelung und der Satelliten. Die Welt wird jede Stunde ins

Haus geholt, und paradoxerweise bedeutet dies: sie verschwindet. *Wir amüsieren uns zu Tode.*[102] Andere Begleiterscheinungen sind etwa die Primitivisierung des sprachlichen Bereichs. „Für andeutungsreiche, beziehungsvolle Denkfiguren", so Arnold Gehlen, „für den Ausdrucksreichtum des Nichtgesagten, für stilistische Feinheiten, für trennscharfe begriffliche Distinktionen mit ihren Obertönen fehlt es heute in sehr weiten Kreisen an Organen, alles muß eingängig, einprägsam und gestanzt geboten werden."[103]

Die Sozialisationseffekte der elektronischen Medien bereiten Sorgen. Angesichts der Konfrontation der jüngeren Gesellschaftsmitglieder mit diesen Medien befürchten Postman und Hentig ein *Verschwinden der Kindheit.*[104] „Mit den Kindern der TV-culture", so befürchtet Hentig, „ist keine Republik mehr zu machen. Sie werden die Apparate mit großer efficiency bedienen; sie werden die Fülle der Angebote 'gut' aushalten; sie werden eine unkomplizierte Wahl treffen; das alles wird ihnen keine Anfechtung bedeuten – und eben das macht sie untauglich für die 'antiquierte Menschheit' mit ihren 'antiquierten Republiken', die auf Anfechtung angewiesen sind, auf Philosophieren." Manche fordern gleich: *Schafft das Fernsehen ab!*[105]

Die Durchdringung der Gesellschaft mit den Medien – die *Industrialisierung des Bewußtseins*[106] – hat Folgen für die Politik. Durch die Dominanz der Medien kommen andere Typen von Politikern an die Macht, und es entsteht eine neue Art, Politik zu treiben. Politiker müssen grundsätzlich auf zwei Gleisen fahren: „einerseits auf der Schiene der publizistischen Macht- und Zustimmungsgewinnung, andererseits auf der realistischen Schiene der kompromißhaften Bewältigung der vorhandenen Konflikte."[107] Jederzeit muß die Wirkung jedes Arguments und jeder Äußerung bedacht werden; das Politische wird damit grundsätzlich zur „veröffentlichten Halbwahrheit" erniedrigt; es entsteht ein öffentliches *Halbdenkertum.* „Wenn Medienpräsenz alles ist, wird Publizität zum politischen Selbstwert", stellt Rudolf Wassermann in seinem Buch über die *Zuschauerdemokratie*[108] fest. Die Scheinwelt der Medien beherrscht die politische Kommunikation, fordert verschleiernde Sprachstrategien und zündende Formeln, gestylte Auftritte und die Beherrschung des journalistischen Code. Die Medien sind auf „strukturelle Neophilie"[109] verpflichtet, und Politik erschöpft sich in Kommunikationsdramaturgie.[110] Politik wird zum *Showgeschäft*[111], zu einem Resonanzboden für geeignete Strategien in einer *populistischen Gesellschaft.*[112]

Damit ist auch eine weitere Dimension angesprochen: die Existenz von *Öffentlichkeit* überhaupt.[113] Das Verständnis dafür scheint verlorengegangen zu sein, daß es einerseits eine Welt der Intimität gibt, in der Wärme, Vertrauen, der offene Ausdruck von Gefühlen herrschen, andererseits eine Welt der Öffentlichkeit, in der es Respekt vor der Privatheit anderer gibt, in der zivilisiertes Verhalten auch als Charaktermaske und Rollenspiel besteht. Die Welt intimer Beziehungen verliert ihre Grenzen, da ihre Prinzipien in die Welt des Öffentlichen übertragen werden; auch dort, wo sie nichts verloren hat, herrscht die Suche nach Empfindung und Authentizität.

X.

Seit dem vorigen Jahrhundert wiederholt sich die Klage, daß der Prozeß der Modernisierung „die Kultur" zerstöre. Die Massengesellschaft, die Stadt, die Technik, das moderne Leben überhaupt vernichte kulturelle Werte.

Jenes Thema, das die Frankfurter Schule entwickeln sollte, hat zunächst Georg Lukacs angeschlagen: Anknüpfend an die deutsche Tradition der Gegenüberstellung von *Kultur und Zivilisation* attackierte er die Zerstörung der Kultur durch die Dynamik der kapitalistischen Marktproduktion.[114] Herbert Marcuse, der über weite Strecken psychoanalytisch argumentiert, beschrieb die geistige und intellektuelle Welt als eine von der materiellen Zivilisation abgetrennte Sphäre. Die *affirmative Kultur* verspricht Freiheit und Glück, aber verlagert diese Ansprüche zugleich in die illusionäre Sphäre und stabilisiert durch Ablenkung den Status quo. Kultur sei unter diesen Bedingungen eine Art „Opium für das Volk". Bei Theodor W. Adorno und Max Horkheimer wird der Vorwurf ähnlich formuliert.[115] Speziell die *Kulturindustrie* werde nicht beherrscht von den Interessen der schöpferischen Individuen, sondern von den Profitinteressen der Produktions- und Verteilungsmaschinerie.[116] Deshalb sei sie einer antiaufklärerischen Haltung der Manipulation verpflichtet, sie sei ein ideologisches Instrument und verbreite bürgerliche Leitbilder. Die Kultur verliere daher ihre innovativ-kritische Potenz, sie stagniere und beschränke sich auf affirmative Klischees. Die *Massenkultur* sei nur noch bewahrend. Sie werde zum Massenbetrug und führt zur *kulturellen Verelendung*. Hochkultur werde durch Trivialkultur verdrängt. Pier Paolo Pasolini ergänzt: Der Zentralismus der Konsumgesellschaft ebnet alle kulturellen Unterschiede ein, es handle sich um die „schlimmste aller Repressionen der Menschheitsgeschichte".

Das ist wohl eine groteske Verzeichnung; aber es stimmt, daß sich das Kunsterleben durch das massenhafte Kulturangebot verändert: Jederzeit stehen die größten künstlerischen Hervorbringungen zur Verfügung; das bewirkt neue Kunsterlebnisse, aber wohl auch Abstumpfung. Die Kunstprodukte verlieren das Außerordentliche, das Besondere, das Schöne, die Aura. Die weltbesten Orchester verkommen zur tagtäglichen Hintergrundmusik. Die „Moderne" – und ihre Kunst besonders – hat nach dem Zweiten Weltkrieg nicht nur ihre Aura, sondern auch ihren provokativen Charakter eingebüßt; vielleicht nicht zuletzt deshalb, weil sie konsumiert wird wie anderes auch. Um auf einem hart umkämpften Markt einen Platz und ein Publikum zu finden, bedarf es besonderer Marketing-Methoden – beispielsweise der Schock-Methode. Aber es ist das Wesen der *Provokationsgesellschaft,* daß die Dosis an „Schocks" fortwährend erhöht werden muß; das liegt in der Natur der Sache. Längst ist die Zeit vorbei, wo man mit Publikumsbeschimpfungen oder Bühnennacktheit provozieren konnte; heute ist man auf die letzten Schamschwellen – religiöse Gefühle und menschliches Blut – verwiesen. Die *Avantgarde* hebt sich selbst auf.[117]

Andere nehmen die *historistischen Tendenzen* auf, welche die postmoderne Mode mit sich bringt, schlüpfen in geschichtliche Verkleidungen und spielen mit

Zitaten aus dem Bildungsgut – am gekonntesten Umberto Eco mit seinem Roman „Der Name der Rose". Nach der Avantgarde, die alle Gültigkeiten vom Tisch wischte, kam die Leere, die Einfallslosigkeit, und in diesem Vakuum bedient man sich aus der Geschichte, verwendete man alle Stilmittel und Ästhetiken. Das Sammelsurium von Rückgriffen soll Bedeutung verleihen. Da aber alles benutzt wird und alles gleich gültig ist, droht auch alles – für die Rezipienten – in dieselbe *Indifferenz* zu geraten.

XI.

Der Prozeß der Aufklärung wurde immer als einer der Entmythifizierung verstanden, als „Striptease" von Mythen[118], bis der Mensch der wissenschaftlichen Zivilisation nackt, aller Mythen entblößt, dasteht. Die Moderne erzeugt eine *entmythifizierte Gesellschaft*, eine *säkularisierte Gesellschaft*.

Säkularisierung gilt schlechthin als Modernisierungsindikator. Das Leiden der etablierten Kirchen in einer *entchristlichten Gesellschaft* läßt sich empirisch vermessen: am Rückgang der Zahl der Gläubigen, der Gottesdienstbesucher, der Priester. Kirchen blühen in einer Industriegesellschaft allenfalls als Bastionen politischer Opposition; mit dem Schwinden des politischen Drucks verschwinden sie in der Indifferenz der „Gläubigen". *Gott ist tot*, so wird vermutet.[119] Theologie scheint nur noch in den Entwicklungsländern zu gedeihen: als *Theologie der Hoffnung* oder *Theologie der Befreiung*.

Allerlei Sekten, Heilsreligionen und abergläubische Praktiken blühen jedoch in den Nischen, gespeist von fernöstlichen Religionen und indianischen Traditionen, im *New Age* oder im *Zeitalter des Wassermanns*. Fritjof Capra ruft die *Wendezeit*[120] aus, andere tanzen den „Lacancan und Derridada".[121] In diesen Ideen geht es um mehr: um die Abdankung des abendländischen Rationalitätsmodells[122], um den Kampf gegen das kartesianisch-newtonianische Denken, um das *Ende der Aufklärung*, um den Gehorsam gegenüber der *Mutter Gaia*. Der *Psycho-Boom* gehört ebenfalls zu diesen Erscheinungen. Sie alle suchen den „natürlichen" Boden des Lebens wiederzugewinnen: *Unter dem Pflaster liegt der Strand*.

Die Entmythifizierung, so meint der Philosoph Odo Marquard in Anbetracht dieser Tendenzen, sei selbst ein Mythos. Der Mythos ist seines Erachtens unsterblich, denn er habe eine wichtige Funktion: Mythen sind Geschichten, die nicht Prothesen oder Vorstufen der Wahrheit sind, also mit ihr konkurrieren; sie bringen die vorhandene Wahrheit in die Reichweite unserer Lebensbegabung. „Eines ist die Wahrheit, ein anderes, wie sich mit der Wahrheit leben läßt: für jene ist – kognitiv – das Wissen, für diese sind – vital – die Geschichten da. Denn das Wissen hat es mit Wahrheit und Irrtum zu tun, die Geschichten mit Glück und Unglück: ihr Pensum ist nicht die Wahrheit, sondern der modus vivendi mit der Wahrheit."[123] Demzufolge bleibt die Gesellschaft eine *mythifizierte*. Die *Polymythophilie*, die den *Abschied vom Prinzipiellen* beklatscht, plädiert – wie die Postmoderne generell – nur für das, was als Trend ohnehin unübersehbar ist: die Aufdröselung der Gemeinschaftskultur, die Erosion gemeinsamer Überzeugungen, die Pluralisierung der Weltsichten. Aber die Vielfalt der Optionen und die freie Wahl zwischen ihnen erzeugt Bedeutungslosigkeit, Indifferenz: Wenn immer alles möglich ist, bedeutet nichts mehr etwas. Und sogar neue *Fundamentalismen* werden beobachtet.[124]

XII.

Das Neuarrangement Europas bringt eine Weltoffenheit mit sich, der Blick weitet sich über die eigenen Grenzen hinaus. Das gilt für jene Länder, denen dieser Blick in den letzten Jahrzehnten bewußt versperrt worden ist, aber auch für die westlichen Staaten.

Osteuropa ist indessen nur eine der Grenzen. In Wahrheit sind die reichen Industrieländer eine Insel des Wohlstands in einem Meer von Armut, Unsicherheit und Tod, eine Oase in unwirtlichem Gelände, ein geschützter Hafen in einer brutalen Welt. Aber um den *Nord-Süd-Dialog* und um die *neue Weltwirtschaftsordnung*[125] ist es wieder ruhig geworden.[126] Nicht nur aus dem Osten, sondern noch mehr aus der *Dritten Welt* rücken immer mehr Menschen heran, um Teil zu haben an diesem Konsumsegen. Die Reichtümer der Oase werden durch die Massenmedien weltweit publik gemacht, bis nach Südamerika, Zentralafrika und die Länder des Fernen Ostens. Überall erzählt man sich die Sage von den reichen Ländern, in denen sogar jene, die nicht arbeiten, ein reichliches Einkommen erhalten. Der Zustrom wird sich deshalb steigern, was jenseits bestimmter Schwellen weder wirtschaftlich noch kulturell zu verkraften sein wird. Im Extremfall kann Europa vor zwei Alternativen stehen: zu einer bewehrten, gegen Ost und Süd abgeschlossenen Festung zu werden oder ökonomisch und kulturell eine Phase seiner Geschichte zu beenden.

Dabei scheint es alle Hände voll zu tun zu haben, seine eigenen Angelegenheiten zu ordnen. Die Staaten des osteuropäischen Raumes haben ihre totalitären Systeme nicht zuletzt aufgrund enttäuschter Konsumerwartungen abgeschüttelt. Die andauernde wirtschaftliche Misere hat ihnen versagt, was die kommunistischen Utopien in glänzenden Farben ausgemalt hatten: einen zufriedenstellenden Lebensstandard, eine freiere Gesellschaft, reichlich Güter für alle. Sie sind bereit, die erfolgreichen Systeme des Westens zu übernehmen. In diesem Übergangsgeschehen sind Illusionen gängig und Enttäuschungen unvermeidbar. Das Beispiel der ehemaligen DDR, der einer der potentesten Zahler der Weltwirtschaft solidarisch zur Seite steht, zeigt, was die anderen osteuropäischen Länder, die über derart leicht zugängliche Ressourcen nicht verfügen, zu gewärtigen haben. Die Gefahr ist nicht von der Hand zu weisen, daß sich ein *gespaltenes Europa* dauerhaft etabliert, mit einem reichen Zentrum und einer zweitklassigen Peripherie auf dem Standard von fortgeschrittenen Dritte-Welt-Ländern.

Die Neuordnung Europas geht nicht ohne Schwierigkeiten vor sich. Neue

Fundamentalismen und Abgrenzungen bilden ein Gegengewicht gegen die Integrationsprozesse. *Identitätsprobleme*[127] führen zum Aufleben *nationalistischer* Strömungen: Sie wachsen aus der Unsicherheit; aus der Frustration über das Ausbleiben der versprochenen Besserung; aus der Hoffnung, als selbständige politische Einheit besser dazustehen; aus dem Drang, historische Rechnungen zu begleichen; aus politisch-opportunistischen Machterlangungsstrategien.

Die Idee *Mitteleuropas* war in der Zwischenkriegszeit für jene Völker, die sich dem Habsburgischen Völkerkerker entronnen wähnten, nicht attraktiv. Erst in den siebziger Jahren fand die Idee einer Gemeinsamkeit der Donaustaaten Resonanz, nicht zuletzt als Bastion gegen die kommunistische Herrschaft. Nach dem Fall der totalitären Systeme ist diese Komponente geschwunden, es bleibt Nachbarschaftspolitik auf unterschiedlichen Ebenen.[128]

Schon in den siebziger Jahren wurde die Modernisierungspolitik westlicher Länder – so auch Österreichs – mit dem Begriff der *Europareife* bedacht. Nun drängen etliche Staaten in die Europäische Gemeinschaft: das *Europa der Zwölf, der Fünfzehn, der Achtzehn, der Vierundzwanzig* – je nach Assoziationsbereich und Zeitdauer – steht vor der Tür. Von einer *neuen Architektur Europas*[129] ist die Rede: Dies aber ist in der derzeitigen Lage nicht viel mehr als die Hoffnung, daß sich aus all den Schwierigkeiten ein geordnetes Zusammenleben ergeben könne. Die EG ist nicht nur eine Wirtschaftsgemeinschaft. Zunehmend mehrt sich die Sorge darüber, wie die europäische Einheit zustande kommen könne, ohne daß die Mitgliedsländer ihre spezifische kulturelle Eigenart verlören. Das *Gemeinsame Haus*, das die *Einheit in der Vielfalt* wahrt; die schlagkräftige politische Kraft, die zugleich ein *Europa der Regionen* repräsentiert; die *multikulturelle Gesellschaft*, die zugleich spezifische Kultur- und Verhaltensmuster fortbestehen läßt – dies sind derzeit nicht viel mehr als tröstende Schlagworte.[130]

Schlußbemerkungen

Wir haben Etiketten gesammelt: Buchtitel, Schlagwörter, Modebegriffe, die in den Essays und Feuilletons der Zeitberichterstatter auftauchen. Dies entspricht – so könnte man ein solches Unternehmen rechtfertigen – den bescheideneren Intentionen einer zurückhaltender gewordenen Sozialwissenschaft, die nicht mehr gesellschaftsumspannende Modelle anbieten will: nur noch *Stichworte zur geistigen Situation der Zeit.*[131]

Die modernen Industrieländer werden durch diese Begriffe in vielerlei Richtung vermessen, es ergibt sich ein widersprüchliches, vielfältiges Muster. Die Komplexität dieses Musters vermittelt eine Ahnung davon, welche komplizierte Aufgabe die osteuropäischen Länder, die sich wagemutig Teile dieser Konstruktion zum Vorbild nehmen, begonnen haben. Die Aufgabe ist um so schwieriger, als wir bekennen müssen, daß wir das Zusammenwirken dieser facettenhaft beleuchteten Teile auch in den westlichen Ländern nicht gut verstehen. Die immer wieder sichtbaren Bemühungen, treffende Etiketten für diese Gesellschaftsordnung zu finden, machen dies deutlich. Vielleicht ist es richtig, was Peter Sloterdijk – auch ein Schlagwortlieferant – sagt: „Wir haben zu viele Wörter für das, was seinen Gang geht – aber es ist kein treffendes darunter."[132]

Anmerkungen

1 Wesentlich breiter angelegt waren die klassischen zeitdiagnostischen Untersuchungen, etwa von Hans Freyer: Theorie des gegenwärtigen Zeitalters, Stuttgart: Deutsche Verlags-Anstalt 1955; Karl Jaspers: Die geistige Situation der Zeit, Berlin – Leipzig 1931; Wilhelm Röpke: Die Gesellschaftskrisis der Gegenwart, 5. Aufl., Erlenbach-Zürich: Eugen Rentsch Verlag, 1948 (erstmals 1942); Pitirim A. Sorokin: Die Krise unserer Zeit. Ihre Entstehung und Überwindung, Frankfurt a. M.: Joachim Henrich Verlag 1950 (engl. Crisis of Our Age, New York 1941); Oswald Spengler: Der Untergang des Abendlandes. Umrisse einer Morphologie der Weltgeschichte, München: dtv, 1972, 5. Aufl. 1979 (erstmals Wien 1918, 1922); Arnold J. Toynbee: A Study of History, London 1934–61, 12 Bde, dt. Eine Untersuchung der Geschichte, 1949.

2 Vgl. Daniel Bell: Die nachindustrielle Gesellschaft, Reinbek. b. H. 1979a (engl. 1970); L. Frank: „Die postindustrielle Gesellschaft und ihre Theorie", Leviattan 3 (1973), 382–407.

3 Vgl. Jean Fourastié: Die große Hoffnung des zwanzigsten Jahrhunderts, 3. Aufl. 1954 (franz. 1949).

4 Vgl. V. R. Fuchs: The Service Economy, New York 1968; R. Lewis: The New Service Society, London 1973.

5 Vgl. Rudolf Hilferding: Das Finanzkapital, Frankfurt 1968 (urspr. 1910).

6 Vgl. Helmut Schelsky: Auf der Suche nach Wirklichkeit. Gesammelte Aufsätze, Düsseldorf – Köln 1965.

7 Vgl. Karl Mannheim: Freiheit und geplante Demokratie, Köln – Opladen 1970, 31 f. (engl. Freedom, Power, and Democratic Planning, 1951).

8 Vgl. Manfred Prisching: „Der Wandel politischer Stimmungslagen – staatliches Handeln in einer ‚unübersichtlichen' Gesellschaft", Wirtschaft und Gesellschaft, 1989, 15, 9–32.

9 Vgl. Herbert Marcuse: One Dimensional Man, London 1972.

10 Vgl. Habermas, Jürgen: Technik und Wissenschaft als „Ideologie", Frankfurt a. M. 1968, 5. Aufl. 1971.

11 Vgl. John K. Galbraith: Gesellschaft im Überfluß, München – Zürich 1959.

12 Vgl. Helmut Schelsky: Wandlungen der deutschen Familie in der Gegenwart, 2. Aufl., Stuttgart 1954; Schelsky, Helmut: Die skeptische Generation. Eine Soziologie der deutschen Jugend, Frankfurt – Berlin – Wien 1975 (erstmals 1957).

13 Vgl. Walt W. Rostow: The Stages of Economic Growth. A Non-Communist Manifesto, Cambridge 1960; Walt W. Rostow: The Economics of Take-off into Sustained Growth, London – New York 1964.

14 Vgl. Colin Campbell: The Romantic Ethic and the Spirit of Modern Consumerism, London – New York 1987.

15 Vgl. Pier Paolo Pasolini: Freibeuterschriften. Aufsätze und Polemiken über die Zerstörung des einzelnen durch die Konsumgesellschaft, Berlin 1978.

16 Vgl. Herman Kahn und Anthony J. Wiener: Ihr werdet es erleben. Voraussagen der Wissenschaft bis zum Jahre 2000, Wien – München – Zürich 1968.

17 Vgl. Lewis Mumford: Mythos der Maschine. Kunst, Technik und Macht, Frankfurt 1966, 1977.

18 Vgl. Edward P. Thompson: Plebejische Kultur und moralische Ökonomie. Aufsätze zur englischen Sozialgeschichte des 18. und 19. Jahrhunderts, Frankfurt – Berlin – Wien 1980.

19 Vgl. Christopher Lasch: The Culture of Narcissism. American Life in an Age of Diminishing Expectations, New York 1978; Häsing, H., et al.: Narziß. Ein neuer Sozialisationstyp? Bensheim 1979.

20 Vgl. Daniel Bell: Die Zukunft der westlichen Welt. Kultur und Technologie im Widerstreit, Frankfurt a. M. 1979b (engl. 1976).

21 Vgl. Karl Otto Hondrich, Jürgen Schumacher u. a.: Krise der Leistungsgesellschaft? Empirische Analysen zum Engagement in Arbeit, Familie und Politik, Opladen 1988; Bertrand de Jouvenel: Jenseits der Leistungsgesellschaft, Freiburg 1970.

22 Vgl. Ronald Inglehart: The Silent Revolution, Changing Values and Political Styles among Western Publics, Princeton 1977; Ronald Inglehart: „Wertwandel in den westlichen Gesellschaften. Politische Konsequenzen von materialistischen und postmaterialistischen Prioritäten", in: Helmut Klages und Peter Kmieciak, Hrsg.: Wertwandel und gesellschaftlicher Wandel, Frankfurt – New York 1979, 279–316.

23 Vgl. Leopold Neuhold: Wertwandel und Christentum, Linz 1988.

24 Vgl. Helmut Klages: Überlasteter Staat – verdrossene Bürger? Zu den Dissonanzen der Wohlfahrtsgesellschaft, Frankfurt – New York 1981; Helmut Klages und Willi Herbert: Wertorientierung und Staatsbezug. Untersuchungen zur politischen Kultur in der Bundesrepublik Deutschland, Frankfurt – New York 1983; Manfred Prisching: „Grenzen des Wertwandels. Kontinuität und Diskontinuität in kulturellen Veränderungsprozessen", Schweizerische Zeitschrift für Soziologie, 1986, 49–70.

25 Vgl. Wolfgang Kraus: Nihilismus heute oder Die Geduld der Weltgeschichte, Frankfurt a. M. 1985.

26 Vgl. auch Wolfgang Kraus: Kultur und Macht. Die Verwandlung der Wünsche, München 1978; Wolfgang Kraus: Die Spuren des Paradieses. Über Ideale, Wien – Hamburg 1985.

27 Vgl. Jürgen Habermas: Die Neue Unübersichtlichkeit, Frankfurt a. M. 1985.

28 Vgl. Paul Virilio: Geschwindigkeit und Politik. Ein Essay zur Dromologie, Berlin 1980.

29 Vgl. Hermann Lübbe: Die Aufdringlichkeit der Geschichte. Herausforderungen der Moderne vom Historismus bis zum Nationalsozialismus, Graz – Wien – Köln 1989; Hermann Lübbe: Zwischen Trend und Tradition. Überfordert uns die Gegenwart? Osnabrück 1981.

30 Vgl. David Riesman, Reuel Denney, Nathan Glazer: Die einsame Masse. Eine Untersuchung der Wandlungen des amerikanischen Charakters, Hamburg 1958 (engl. 1950).

31 Vgl. Jürgen Habermas: Legitimationsprobleme im Spätkapitalismus, Frankfurt a. M. 1973.

32 Vgl. Peter L. Berger, Brigitte Berger, H. Kellner: Das Unbehagen in der Modernität, Frankfurt – New York 1975 (engl. 1974).

33 Vgl. Sigmund Freud: „Das Unbehagen in der Kultur", 1930.

34 Vgl. Umberto Eco: Apokalyptiker und Integrierte, Frankfurt a. M. 1984.

35 Vgl. Helmut Schelsky: Die Arbeit tun die anderen. Klassenkampf und Priesterherrschaft der Intellektuellen, München 1977.

36 Peter Sloterdijk (Hrsg.): Vor der Jahrtausendwende. Berichte zur Lage der Zukunft, 2 Bde, Frankfurt a. M. 1990, 720 f.

37 Vgl. Richard Löwenthal: Gesellschaftswandel und Kulturkrise. Zukunftsprobleme der westlichen Demokratien, Frankfurt a. M. 1979, 26.

38 Vgl. Wolfgang Welsch: Unsere postmoderne Moderne, Weinheim 1987; Wolfgang Welsch, Hrsg.: Wege aus der Moderne. Schlüsseltexte der Postmoderne-Diskussion, Weinheim 1988.

39 Vgl. Jean-Francois Lyotard: Das postmoderne Wissen. Ein Bericht, Graz – Wien 1986 (franz. 1979).

40 Vgl. C. B. Macpherson: Die politische Theorie des Besitzindividualismus. Von Hobbes bis Locke, Frankfurt a. M. 1973.

41 Vgl. etwa Daniel Bell und Irving Kristol (Hrsg.): Kapitalismus heute, Frankfurt – New York 1974; Benjamin A. Rogge: Can Capitalism Survive? Indianapolis 1979.

42 Vgl. Peter L. Berger: The Capitalist Revolution. Fifty Propositions about Prosperity, Equality, and Liberty, New York 1986.

43 Vgl. Paul Baran und Paul Sweezy: Monopoly Capital, 1966; Nicos Poulantzas: Classes in Contemporary Capitalism, 1975; Margaret Wirth: Kapitalismustheorie in der DDR, 1972.

44 Vgl. Roger Garaudy: Die Alternative. Ein neues Modell der Gesellschaft jenseits von Kapitalismus und Kommunismus, Reinbek. b. H. 1974, 78.

45 Wilfried Gottschalch: „Auf zum letzten Gefecht? Romantische Kapitalismuskritik unter roten Fahnen", Freibeuter, 35, 1988, 94–101.

46 Vgl. Olson, Mancur/ Hans. H. Landsberg (Hrsg.): The No-Growth Society, London 1975.

47 Vgl. Ezra J. Mishan: Die Wachstumsdebatte. Wachstum zwischen Wirtschaft und Ökologie, Stuttgart 1980; Klaus von Beyme u. a.: Wirtschaftliches Wachstum als gesellschaftliches Problem, Königstein/Ts. 1978; Burkhard Strümpel: Die Krise des Wohlstands. Das Modell einer humanen Wirtschaft, Stuttgart u. a. 1977; Grete Klingenstein (Hrsg.): Krise des Fortschritts, Wien – Köln – Graz 1984.

48 Vgl. Lester C. Thurow: Die Null-Summen-Gesellschaft. Einkommensverteilung und Möglichkeiten wirtschaftlichen Wandels, München 1981.

49 Vgl. Walter L. Bühl: Krisentheorien. Politik, Wirtschaft und Gesellschaft im Übergang, 2. Aufl., Darmstadt 1988; Manfred Prisching: Krisen. Eine soziologische Analyse, Wien – Köln – Graz 1986.

50 Vgl. Ralf Dahrendorf (Hrsg.): Trendwende. Europas Wirtschaft in der Krise, Wien u. a. 1981.

51 Vgl. Friedrich von Hayek: Die Verfassung der Freiheit, 2. Aufl., Tübingen 1983.

52 Vgl. Theodor Geiger: Die Klassengesellschaft im Schmelztiegel, Köln – Hagen 1949.

53 Vgl. Karl Martin Bolte, Stephan Hradil: Soziale Ungleichheit in der Bundesrepublik Deutschland, Opladen 1984; Anthony Giddens: Die Klassenstruktur fortgeschrittener Gesellschaften, Frankfurt a. M. 1979.

54 Vgl. Philipp Herder-Dorneich, Helmut Klages, Hans-Günther Schlotter (Hrsg.): Überwindung der Sozialstaatskrise. Ordnungspolitische Ansätze, Baden-Baden 1984.

55 Vgl. Helmut Klages: Überlasteter Staat – verdrossene Bürger. Zu den Dissonanzen der Wohlfahrtsgesellschaft, Frankfurt – New York 1981.

56 Vgl. Johano Strasser: Grenzen des Sozialstaats? Soziale Sicherung in der Wachstumskrise, Köln – Frankfurt a. M. 1979; Peter Koslowski, Philipp Kreuzer und Reinhard Löw (Hrsg.): Chancen und Grenzen des Sozialstaats, Tübingen 1983.

57 Vgl. Peter Gross: Die Verheißungen der Dienstleistungsgesellschaft. Soziale Befreiung oder Sozialherrschaft? Opladen 1983.

58 Vgl. Helmut Schelsky: Der selbständige und der betreute Mensch. Politische Schriften und Kommentare, Frankfurt – Berlin – Wien 1978; Helmut Schelsky: Funktionäre. Gefährden sie das Gemeinwohl? Stuttgart – Degerloch 1982.

59 Vgl. Walter Wittmann: Der Steuerstaat. Die Ausbeutung der Fleißigen, München 1986.

60 Vgl. Peter Grottian u. a.: Die Wohlfahrtswende. Der Zauber konservativer Sozialpolitik, München 1988.

61 Vgl. J. I. Gershuny: After Industrial Society? The Emerging Self-Service Economy, London 1978.

62 Vgl. Christoph Badelt: Sozioökonomie der Selbstorganisation. Beispiele zur Bürgerselbsthilfe und ihre wirtschaftliche Bedeutung, Frankfurt – New York 1981.

63 Vgl. Joseph Huber: Die zwei Gesichter der Arbeit. Ungenutzte Möglichkeiten der Dualwirtschaft, Frankfurt a. M. 1984.

64 Vgl. Hubertus Zuber (Hrsg.): Schlankheitskur für den Staat, Stuttgart 1979.

65 Vgl. Jürgen Habermas: Die Neue Unübersichtlichkeit, Frankfurt a. M. 1985; Claus Offe: „Arbeitsgesellschaft". Strukturprobleme und Zukunftsperspektiven, Frankfurt – New York 1984.

66 Vgl. Wolfgang Bonß, Rolf G. Heinze: Arbeitslosigkeit in der Arbeitsgesellschaft, Frankfurt a. M. 1984.

67 Vgl. Meinolf Dierkes, Burkhard Strümpel (Hrsg.): Wenig Arbeit, aber viel zu tun. Neue Wege der Arbeitsmarktpolitik, Opladen 1985.

68 Vgl. Manfred Prisching: Arbeitslosenprotest und Resignation in der Wirtschaftskrise, Frankfurt – New York 1988.

69 Vgl. Ehrenfried Natter, Alois Riedlsperger (Hrsg.): Zweidrittelgesellschaft. Spalten, splittern – oder solidarisieren? Wien 1988.

70 Vgl. Horst Kern, Michael Schumann: Das Ende der Arbeitsteilung? Rationalisierung in der industriellen Produktion, München 1984; Michael J. Piore, Charles F. Sabel: Das Ende der Massenproduktion. Studie über die Requalifizierung der Arbeit und die Rückkehr der Ökonomie in die Gesellschaft, Berlin 1985.

71 Vgl. Thomas Kutsch, Fritz Vilmar (Hrsg.): Arbeitszeitverkürzung. Ein Weg zur Vollbeschäftigung? Opladen 1983.

72 Vgl. Gabriel A. Almond, Sidney Verba: The Civic Culture. Political Attitudes and Democracy in Five Nations, Boston 1963; Gabriel A. Almond, Sidney Verba (Hrsg.): The Civic Culture Revisited, Boston – Toronto 1980.
73 Vgl. Fritz Vilmar: Strategien der Demokratisierung, 2 Bände, Darmstadt – Neuwied 1973.
74 Vgl. Anton Kofler: Parteiengesellschaft im Umbruch. Partizipationsprobleme von Großparteien, Wien – Köln – Graz 1985; Fritz Plasser: Parteien unter Streß. Zur Dynamik der Parteiensysteme in Österreich, der Bundesrepublik Deutschland und den Vereinigten Staaten, Wien – Köln – Graz 1987; Wilhelm Hennis: „Überdehnt und abgekoppelt. An den Grenzen des Parteienstaates", in: Krockow, Christian Graf von (Hrsg.): Brauchen wir ein neues Parteiensystem? Frankfurt a. M. 1983, 28–64.
75 Vgl. Samuel P. Huntington: „The United States", in: Michel J. Crozier, Samuel P. Huntington, Joji Watanuki (eds.): The Crisis of Democracy. Report on the Governability of Democracies to the Trilateral Commission, New York 1975, 59–118.
76 Vgl. Ulrich von Alemann (Hrsg.): Neokorporatismus, Frankfurt a. M. – New York 1981; Gerhard Lehmbruch, Philippe C. Schmitter (Hrsg.): Patterns of Corporatist Policy Making, Beverly Hills- London 1982; Philippe C. Schmitter, Gerhard Lehmbruch (Hrsg.): Trends Toward Corporatist Intermediation, Beverly Hills – London 1979.
77 Vgl. Theodor Eschenburg: Herrschaft der Verbände? Stuttgart 1955; Warnfried Dettling (Hrsg.): Macht der Verbände – Ohnmacht der Demokratie? München 1976.
78 Bernd Guggenberger, Bernd: „Herrschaftslegitimierung und Staatskrise. Zu einigen Problemen der Regierbarkeit des modernen Staates", in: Michael Th. Greven, Bernd Guggenberger/ Johano Strasser: Krise des Staates? Zur Funktionsbestimmung des Staates im Spätkapitalismus, Darmstadt – Neuwied 1975, 9–59.
79 Otwin Massing: Politische Soziologie. Paradigmata einer kritischen Politikwissenschaft, Frankfurt a. M. 1974.
80 Vgl. Theodor Leuenberger: Bürokratisierung und Modernisierung der Gesellschaft, Bern-Stuttgart 1975; Hartmut Häußermann: Die Politik der Bürokratie. Einführung in die Soziologie der staatlichen Verwaltung, Frankfurt – New York 1977; Wolfgang Schluchter: Aspekte bürokratischer Herrschaft. Studien zur Interpretation der fortschreitenden Industriegesellschaft, München 1972.
81 Vgl. William A. Niskanen: Bureaucracy and Representative Government, Chicago 1971.
82 Vgl. Harvey Leibenstein: Beyond Economic Man. A New Foundation for Microeconomics, Cambridge, Mass., – London 1976.
83 Vgl. Geißler, Heiner (Hrsg.): Verwaltete Bürger – Gesellschaft in Fesseln. Bürokratisierung und ihre Folgen für Staat, Wirtschaft und Gesellschaft, Frankfurt a. M. 1978.
84 Vgl. Karl-Werner Brand: Neue soziale Bewegungen. Entstehung, Funktion und Perspektive neuer Protestpotentiale, Opladen 1982; Karl-Werner Brand (Hrsg.): Neue soziale Bewegungen in Westeuropa und den USA. Ein internationaler Vergleich, Frankfurt – New York 1985; Karl-Werner Brand, D. Büsser, D. Rucht: Aufbruch in eine andere Gesellschaft. Neue soziale Bewegungen in der Bundesrepublik, Frankfurt – New York 1983; Bernd Guggenberger: Bürgerinitiativen in der Parteiendemokratie, Stuttgart u. a. 1980.
85 Vgl. Bernd Guggenberger, Claus Offe (Hrsg.): An den Grenzen der Mehrheitsdemokratie. Politik und Soziologie der Mehrheitsregel, Opladen 1984.
86 Vgl. Helmut Willke: Entzauberung des Staates. Überlegungen zu einer sozietalen Steuerungstheorie, Königstein/Ts. 1983.
87 Vgl. Franz Lehner: Grenzen des Regierens. Eine Studie zur Regierungsproblematik hochindustrialisierter Demokratien, Königstein/Ts. 1979.
88 Vgl. Arnold Gehlen: Die Seele im technischen Zeitalter. Sozialpsychologische Probleme in der industriellen Gesellschaft, Hamburg 1957.
89 Vgl. Thomas Kluge: Gesellschaft, Natur, Technik. Zur lebensphilosophischen und ökologischen Kritik von Technik und Gesellschaft, 1985.
90 Vgl. Günther Chaloupek, Joachim Lamel: Die zweifelnde Gesellschaft. Perspektiven des Fortschritts, Wien 1983.
91 Vgl. Ivan Illich: Fortschrittsmythen, Frankfurt a. M. 1983.

92 Vgl. Günther Anders: Die Antiquiertheit des Menschen, 2 Bände, München 1987 (erstmals 1956).
93 Vgl. F. Schumacher: Rückkehr zum menschlichen Maß. Small is beautiful, Hamburg 1977; Ivan Illich: Selbstbegrenzung. Eine politische Kritik der Technik, Hamburg 1975.
94 Vgl. Sieferle, Rolf Peter: Fortschrittsfeinde? Opposition gegen Technik und Industrie von der Romantik bis zur Gegenwart, München 1984, 230.
95 Vgl. Robert Jungk: Der Atomstaat. Vom Fortschritt in die Unmenschlichkeit, München 1977.
96 Vgl. Walter L. Bühl: Die Angst des Menschen vor der Technik. Alternativen im technologischen Wandel, Düsseldorf – Wien 1983.
97 Vgl. Charles Perrow: Normale Katastrophen. Die unvermeidbaren Risiken der Großtechnik, Frankfurt – New York 1989.
98 Vgl. Ulrich Beck: Risikogesellschaft. Auf dem Weg in eine andere Moderne, Frankfurt a. M. 1986.
99 Vgl. auch Mathias Schüz (Hrsg.): Risiko und Wagnis. Die Herausforderung der industriellen Welt, 2 Bde, Neske 1990.
100 Vgl. Marshall McLuhan: Wohin steuert die Welt? Massenmedien und Gesellschaftsstruktur, Wien u. a. 1978; Günther Friedrichs, Adam Schaff (Hrsg.): Auf Gedeih und Verderb. Mikroelektronik und Gesellschaft. Bericht an den Club of Rome, Wien – München – Zürich 1982; Norbert Müller (Hrsg.): Schöne elektronische Welt, Reinbek b. H. 1982.
101 Vgl. Neil Postman: Das Verschwinden der Kindheit, Frankfurt a. M. 1983; Neil Postman: Wir amüsieren uns zu Tode. Urteilsbildung im Zeitalter der Unterhaltungsindustrie, Frankfurt a. M. 1985.
102 Vgl. auch Alois Huter: Zur Ausbreitung von Vergnügung und Belehrung. Fernsehen als Kulturwirklichkeit, Zürich 1988.
103 Vgl. Arnold Gehlen: Die Seele im technischen Zeitalter. Sozialpsychologische Probleme in der industriellen Gesellschaft, Hamburg 1957.
104 Vgl. Harmut von Hentig: Das allmähliche Verschwinden der Kindheit. Ein Pädagoge ermutigt zum Nachdenken über die Neuen Medien, München – Wien 1984, 59 f.
105 Vgl. Jerry Mander: Schafft das Fernsehen ab! Reinbek b. H. 1979.
106 Vgl. Klaus von Bismarck, Günter Gaus, Alexander Kluge, Ferdinand Sieger: Industrialisierung des Bewußtseins. Eine kritische Auseinandersetzung mit den „neuen" Medien, München – Zürich 1985.
107 Vgl. Helmut Schelsky: Politik und Publizität, Stuttgart – Degerloch 1983, 63.
108 Vgl. Rudolf Wassermann: Die Zuschauerdemokratie, München – Zürich 1989.
109 Otto F. Roegele: „Massenmedien und Regierbarkeit", in: Wilhelm Hennis, Peter Graf Kielmansegg, Ulrich Matz (Hrsg.): Regierbarkeit. Studien zu ihrer Problematisierung, 2 Bände, Stuttgart 1977/79.
110 Vgl. Heinrich Oberreuter: Übermacht der Medien. Erstickt die demokratische Kommunikation? 1982; Fritz Plasser/ Peter A. Ulram/ Manfried Welan, Hrsg.: Demokratierituale. Zur politischen Kultur der Informationsgesellschaft, Wien – Köln – Graz 1985.
111 Vgl. Roger-Gerard Schwartzenberg: Politik als Showgeschäft. Moderne Strategien im Kampf um die Macht, Düsseldorf – Wien 1980.
112 Vgl. Helmut Dubiel (Hrsg.): Populismus und Ausklärung, Frankfurt a. M. 1986.
113 Vgl. Richard Sennett: Verfall und Ende des öffentlichen Lebens. Die Tyrannei der Intimität, Frankfurt a. M. 1983.
114 Vgl. Georg Lukacs: Die Zerstörung der Vernunft, Berlin 1954; Georg Lukacs: Geschichte und Klassenbewußtsein, Berlin 1923.
115 Vgl. Theodor W. Adorno, Max Horkheimer (1987): Dialektik der Aufklärung, Frankfurt 1987, urspr. 1944.
116 Vgl. Walter Benjamin: Das Kunstwerk im Zeitalter seiner technischen Reproduzierbarkeit, Frankfurt a. M. 1976.
117 Vgl. Walter Grasskamp: Die unbewältigte Moderne. Kunst und Öffentlichkeit, München 1989.
118 Vgl. Odo Marquard: Abschied vom Prinzipiellen. Philosophische Studien, Stuttgart 1987.

119 Vgl. Dieter Cwienk, Anton Weiss (Hrsg.): Gott? Graz 1983.
120 Vgl. Fritjof Capra: Wendezeit. Bausteine für ein neues Weltbild, 6. Aufl., Bern – München – Wien 1983.
121 Vgl. Klaus Laermann: „Lacancan und Derridada. Über die Frankolatrie in den Geisteswissenschaften", Kursbuch 84, 1986, 34–43.
122 Vgl. Karl Acham: Rechtfertigung der Rationalität, in: politicum 7, Heft 30, 1986, 6–16.
123 Vgl. Odo Marquard: Abschied vom Prinzipiellen. Philosophische Studien, Stuttgart 1987.
124 Vgl. Thomas Meyer: Fundamentalismus. Aufstand gegen die Moderne, Reinbek b. H. 1989; Thomas Meyer (Hrsg.): Fundamentalismus in der modernen Welt. Die Internationale der Unvernunft, Frankfurt a. M. 1989.
125 Vgl. Eike von Hippel: Grundfragen der Weltwirtschaftsordnung, München 1980.
126 Vgl. auch Global 2000. Der Bericht an den Präsidenten, Frankfurt a. M. 1980; OECD (Hrsg.): Interfutures. Facing the Future. Mastering the Probable and Managing the Unpredictable, Paris 1979; W. Leontief u. a.: The Future of the World Economy, New York 1977; A. Herrera, H. Skolnik u. a.: Grenzen des Elends. Das Bariloche-Modell, Frankfurt 1977; etc.
127 Vgl. z. B. Werner Weidenfels (Hrsg.): Die Identität Europas, Bonn 1985.
128 Vgl. Erhard Busek und Emil Brix (Hrsg.): Projekt Mitteleuropa, Wien 1986; Erhard Busek und Gerald Stourzh (Hrsg.): Nationale Vielfalt und gemeinsames Erbe in Mitteleuropa, Wien – München 1990; Erhard Busek und Gerhard Wilflinger (Hrsg.): Aufbruch nach Mitteleuropa. Rekonstruktion eines versunkenen Kontinents, Wien 1986; György Konrad: Antipolitik. Mitteleuropäische Meditationen, Frankfurt a. M. 1985.
129 Vgl. Wolfgang Mantl (Hrsg.): Die neue Architektur Europas. Reflexionen in einer bedrohten Welt, Wien – Köln – Graz 1991.
130 Vgl. Gerd Bacher, Karl Schwarzenberg, Josef Taus (Hrsg.): Standort Österreich. Über Kultur, Wirtschaft und Politik im Wandel, Graz – Wien – Köln 1990.
131 Vgl. Jürgen Habermas (Hrsg.): Stichworte zur „Geistigen Situation der Zeit", 2 Bde, Frankfurt a. M. 1979.
132 Vgl. Sloterdijk 1990, 719.

Barbara Serloth

Zurück in die Gegenwart: Alte und neue Rationalismen

Vorwort

Jahrzehntelang wurde die politische, soziale und kulturelle Wirklichkeit der westlichen Demokratien durch einen ausgeprägten Rationalismus auf der ideellen Ebene und einen gefestigten Pragmatismus auf der Handlungsebene bestimmt. Das Vorherrschen dieser beiden Denk- und Handlungsweisen war kein Zufallsprodukt der Nachkriegsordnung, sondern eine logische Folge des Zusammenbruchs jenes Systems, das im Europa des Völkerbundes in den zwanziger und dreißiger Jahren Wirklichkeit wurde. Letztlich war es die Konsequenz aus dem Abdanken bestimmter totalitärer Ideologien, wie z. B. Faschismus und Nationalsozialismus, die außer pervertierter Herrschaftsstrukturen, einer Sonderbeziehung zu der Frage des Machtmonopols und einer extremen Expansionspolitik den Menschen wenig anbieten konnten.

Was am Anfang der 20er Jahre mit dem verstärkten Auftreten nationalistisch-konservativer Haltungen begann, was nach der Periode der Links-rechts-Polarisierung im geistigen Umfeld des revolutionären Konservatismus keimte, das führte in den meisten europäischen Ländern – früher oder später – zur Demontage der labilen parlamentarischen Systeme und zur Installierung paratotalitärer, oder anders gesagt, präfaschistischer Regierungsformen.

Innerhalb der Strukturen der beiden verwandten totalitären Regime Italiens und Deutschlands war der Irrationalismus die treibende und vorherrschende geistige Kraft, aber nicht die einzige. Im Wesen der beiden westlichen Spielvarianten des Totalitarismus verbargen sich nicht nur irrationale Elemente der Denk- und Handlungsweise, sondern im gleichen Maße ein spezifischer Pragmatismus, der in allen Bereichen der Außen- und Innenpolitik mitprägend war. Genau diesem sehr spezifischen und aus der jeweiligen Tradition erklärbaren Pragmatismus ist – im Falle des Deutschen Reiches – die Rassen- und Vernichtungspolitik „zu verdanken" und die Tatsache, daß die Verwirklichung dieser Politik industrielle und praktisch nachvollziehbare Formen annahm.

Die Durchführung und im beträchtlichen Maße auch die Konzipierung dieser so folgenschweren Politik brauchte eine Antriebskraft, die die Effektivität und praktische Durchsetzbarkeit sichern konnte. Dazu waren der Fortschrittsglaube und die Förderungdes technologischen Komplexes am besten geeignet, trotz der Tatsache, daß diese Sonderbeziehung zur technischen Revolution in einem Widerspruch zu irrationalen Elementen der nationalsozialistischen und faschistischen Ideologie stand.

Die scheinbare Widersprüchlichkeit der rationalen und irrationalen Elemente spiegelte den geistigen Eklektizismus dieser Ideologie und die Inhomogenität der

Beziehung zwischen dem geistigen Überbau und der politisch-rechtlichen Basis wider.

Im Gegensatz zu den Rechtstotalitarismen stand die linke Form einer totalitären Ideologie, d. h. der Kommunismus. Hier wird er bewußt von den extrem rechten Ausformungen abgehoben und entsprechend seinen idealisierenden Inhalten bewertet. Im Unterschied zu einigen Ideologietheoretikern und in der letzten Zeit erfolgten massiven Versuchen, den Kommunismus undifferenziert in einem Atemzug mit Nationalsozialismus und Faschismus zu zitieren, scheint eine differenzierte Sichtweise zielführender zu sein, weil sie am besten für die Objektivierung der Entwicklung geeignet ist. Differenzieren würde bedeuten, daß die Theorie von der Praxis getrennt betrachtet wird und dementsprechend die theoretischen Vorstellungen der geistigen Väter der kommunistischen Ideologie vom praktischen Umgang mit der Macht und den Menschen moderater, d. h. im Widerspruch zum Zeitgeist bewertet wird. Da der Idealismus und Humanismus der Vordenker der kommunistischen Ideologie im krassen Gegensatz sowohl zu späteren Auslegungen und Fälschungen als auch der praktischen Beziehung zur Macht steht, scheint es zielführend zu sein, die beiden Problemebenen, d. h. die ursprünglichen theoretischen Grundzüge und den Alltag des schon arrivierten Systems, getrennt zu analysieren. Deshalb ist das vor allem die Frage eines entemotionalisierten Zugangs und eines maßvollen Urteilens.

1945, nach dem gewaltsamen Abgang der rechtstotalitären Systeme, schien ein neuer Anfang, ein Weg zu einer besseren Welt, in greifbarer Nähe zu sein. Mit der atlantischen Charta sollten die innen- und zwischenstaatlichen Beziehungen auf eine neue Basis der Verständigung gestellt werden. Mit den bürgerlich-demokratischen Idealen sollte faschistischen und nationalsozialistischen Denk- und Handlungsweisen der Boden entzogen werden. Es bestand die berechtigte Hoffnung, daß zum erstenmal in der Geschichte eine friedliche und möglichst gewaltlose Entwicklung ihren Anfang nehmen würde.

Diese Hoffnung blieb unerfüllt, und es kam zu einer Periode der „kalten" Konfrontation mit vielen Ersatz-Kriegsschauplätzen und einer ideologischen Zweiteilung mit globalen Auswirkungen. In den folgenden Jahren war der Kalte Krieg eine gemäßigtere Form des Konkurrenzkampfes der zwei gegensätzlichen Systeme gewichen, wobei ein begrenzter Dialog die anfänglichen Formen der militanten Gegenpropaganda und einer konfrontationsbedingten Sprachlosigkeit ersetzt hatte. Der Fall des Eisernen Vorhangs war ein sichtbares Zeichen der Beendigung der Konfrontation und des Anfangs einer vielschichtigen Zusammenarbeit. Zwar hatte diese Entwicklung im Osten und Westen Europas bestimmte Erwartungen geweckt, aber in keiner Weise die sich schon vorher abzeichnende Wende beeinflußt – eher die negativen Trends der 80er Jahre vertieft. Diese Trends, die inhaltlich durchgehend vom Irrationalismus (oder besser gesagt von Irrationalismen) bestimmt waren und sind, kann man mit größter Wahrscheinlichkeit als die „Nebenprodukte" der Postmoderne bezeichnen.

Bei näherer Betrachtung des breiten Spektrums der irrationalen Denk- und Handlungsweisen drängt sich die Frage auf, was in diesem sehr vielfältigen geistigen Umfeld des Nationalismus und Konservatismus zu den Ablegern des traditionellen Weltverständnisses der relativ geschlossenen Gesellschaft gehört und was neuartige und der Kommunikations- und Konsumgesellschaft verbundene Formen der antirationalen Haltungen aufweist.

Daraus resultiert der erste Part des Mottos dieses Beitrags „Zurück in die Gegenwart", der einerseits die angenommene Wiederkehr restaurativer Tendenzen im soziopolitischen und kulturellen Bereich andeuten soll und andererseits die vermutlichen Verwandtschaften zwischen alten und neuen Irrationalismen zur Diskussion stellt.

Ob das so ist und ob sich im Bewußtsein der Menschen europaweit ein Umdenken im Sinne eines vielfältig artikulierten Irrationalismus einstellte, das ist eine kontroversielle Frage, die mit einem Versuch der Bestandsaufnahme nicht ausreichend behandelt werden kann. Trotzdem sollte dieser Versuch eine brauchbare, wenn auch skizzenhafte Darstellung dieser zeitgenössischen Erscheinungen liefern.

1. Die Schwächen der Demokratie und die Stärken ihrer neu-alten Feinde

Immer öfter sind die Beobachter der soziopolitischen und kulturellen Entwicklungen in den Demokratien des Westens mit Erscheinungen konfrontiert, die in ihrem Wesen eigentlich antidemokratisch sind. Einerseits zeigen sich in diesen Ländern Veränderungen des parlamentarischen Spektrums, die einen Trend zu rechtskonservativen bzw. populistischen Inhalten signalisieren. Das spiegelt sich in den Verschiebungen der politischen Machtverhältnisse zugunsten nationalpartikularer Bewegungen wider. Andererseits brechen Emotionen auf, die aus Urängsten und zeitgemäßen „Sicherheitsbedürfnissen" resultieren. Bemerkenswert ist dabei, daß diese Ängste mitten in einem funktionierenden demokratisch geprägten Gesellschaftssystem auftreten und im krassen Gegensatz zu den Behauptungen über die Beschaffenheit postindustrieller Wertesysteme stehen. Wenn also primäre Sicherheitsbedürfnisse wieder das Hauptinteresse der Menschen an sich ziehen und gleichzeitig die Einrichtungen des sogenannten Sozialstaates noch intakt sind, dann muß überlegt werden, auf welchem Nährboden solche Werteverschiebungen entstehen und in welchem Verhältnis sie sich zur soziopolitischen Realität befinden.

Es ist dabei noch völlig unklar, ob die zeitgenössischen Ausbrüche der Sprache des sogenannten „Volkszorns" nur eine kurzfristige Reaktion auf die Störungen des Arbeitsmarktes und die sich vertiefenden sozialen Kontraste bedeuten oder ob sie eine viel tiefer greifende Abwendung von der Sprache der Vernunft vorausahnen lassen.

Eines scheint die Welle der Ablehnung liberaler, demokratischer Sozialkonzepte zu bestätigen, nämlich die sichtbare krisenhafte Situation des überforderten Staates im allgemeinen und die strukturellen Brüche im Wesen der politischen Kultur im besonderen.

Obwohl in einer modernen Massendemokratie derartige Gegenstimmungen vorprogrammiert sind und man annimmt, daß es im Zeitalter des völlig rational gestalteten Lebens zu regelmäßig erfolgenden Ausbrüchen des Irrationalen kommen muß, stimmt es nachdenklich, daß die Demokratie zur Zeit keine erfolgversprechenden Rezepte zur Lösung der anstehenden Probleme hervorbringt.

Wie gesagt, zur Zeit ist der Zustand der westlichen Demokratie durch ein Aktivitätsdefizit und eine offensichtliche Konzeptlosigkeit charakterisierbar. Dabei wird das Aktivitätsdefizit durch ständiges Reagieren oder durch Anwendung defensiver Strategien ausgeglichen. Das Fehlen brauchbarer Konzepte wird durch populistische Scheinlösungen ersetzt und der demokratischen Öffentlichkeit als das zeitgemäße Krisenmanagement dargestellt.[1]

Bei der vorherrschenden Einigkeit in der Einschätzung der Gefahren, die aus den Mehrheitsregeln resultieren, bleiben einige wichtige Fragen der derzeitigen Entwicklung außerhalb dieser Erklärungsmodelle, also de facto dem Blickwinkel der Demokratietheoretiker „entzogen".

Die Unerfaßbarkeit der Vielfalt der irrationalen Erscheinungen und Artikulationen der letzten Jahre kann zur übereilten Übernahme rechtskonservativer Ansichten und ebensolcher Deutungsversuche des gesellschaftlichen Zustands verführen. Was als ein Produkt des soziokulturellen Wandels oder ein Phänomen des mehrheitlichen Stimmungsumschwungs betrachtet wird, das kann unter bestimmten Voraussetzungen zum Nachteil eines wachsamen Umgangs mit den demokratiegefährdenden Denk- und Handlungsweisen unterschätzt werden. Das Unterschätzen kann zur Begünstigung nicht kontrollierbarer, gefährlicher Entwicklungen führen und außerdem die labilen Gleichgewichtsverhältnisse aufs Spiel setzen. Dem entgegenzuwirken bedeutet, das Bewußtsein der Gesellschaft zu erweitern und das Öffentlichkeits-Gewissen zu sensibilisieren. Beides kann unter bestimmten Voraussetzungen des politischen Dialogs herbeigeführt werden, d. h., die offene Demokratie muß ihre „Feinde" erkennen und gemäß den demokratischen Spielregeln reagieren.

1.1. Die „Rückkehr" des Irrationalen

Wie schon erwähnt wurde, ist die moderne demokratische Kultur ständig von Ausbrüchen des Irrationalen begleitet. Diese periodisch wiederkehrenden Manifestationen der antirationalen Haltungen gehören zur Wechselbeziehung „Aktion – Reaktion" und zu den Ups and Downs des gesellschaftlichen Ablaufs. Und erst dann, wenn der „normale" Rhythmus gestört wird und die antirationalen Haltungen langfristig die Entwicklung verändern, kann die Rede von einem dauerhaften Umschwung zugunsten von z. B. demagogisch-populistischen, das Metaphysische erhebenden Denkweisen sein.

Die letzten Jahre standen im Zeichen einer massiven Rückkehr zu anachronistisch anmutenden Weltauffassungen und Existenzdeutungen. Dieser stete Vormarsch verschiedener fundamentalistischer Strömungen hatte zuletzt prozeßbartige Ausmaße angenommen. Es kann wohl angenommen werden, daß diese Entwicklung tiefgreifender ist, als man es noch vor zwei bis drei Jahren annahm und daß die Fülle der Strömungen bei näherer Betrachtung an Buntheit und irritierender Vielfalt verliert. Was sich offenbart, das ist die vorherrschende, allgemeine Wende zum Irrationalen.

Das Irrationale stellt auch eine folgenschwere Herausforderung für die Überlebensfähigkeit des demokratischen Systems dar. Diese Überlebensfähigkeit wird an der Effektivität und an der Offenheit des politischen Diskurses gemessen – aber nicht nur daran. Theoretisch gesehen sollte der politische Diskurs unter den Prämissen einer rationalen Auseinandersetzung und dem Vernunftprinzip folgenden Entscheidungen stattfinden. In der Realität wird aber jeder politische Diskurs durch den Irrationalismus mitgeprägt. Dieses Faktum wird weniger durch die Neigung der Menschen zum Irrationalen – wie dies die Vertreter des Irrationalismus behaupten –, als durch das Eigenleben und die argumentative Beschaffenheit der politischen Auseinandersetzung verursacht. Einmal aufgetaucht, können die irrationalen Elemente dauerhaft eine politische Auseinandersetzung beeinflussen, weil irrationale Lösungen immer einfacher und bequemer als die rationalen sind. Ihr Einfluß auf die Gesamtheit des demokratischen Diskurses hängt nicht nur von dem Thema der jeweiligen Debatte oder von der Fähigkeit der Gesellschaft, einen rationalen Diskurs zu führen, ab, sondern auch von der Frage, ob der Irrationalismus mehr oder weniger Befürworter in der Gesellschaft findet, d. h., ob er in Mode ist. Die Modeerscheinungen treten, wie wir wissen, wellenartig auf. Derzeit kann man innerhalb der europäischen Gesellschaft ein steigendes Interesse an spirituellen und esoterischen geistigen Strömungen registrieren, wobei die New-Age-Welle eine wichtige Rolle spielt.[2]

Zum Ausdruck des Irrationalen im wissenschaftlichen Bereich gehört der sogenannte „Postmodernismus". Hier in der postmodernistischen Gedankenwelt wird der Mythos aufgewertet und als Allheilmittel gegen die ‚Irrtümer' der Vernunft hochstilisiert. Die Postmodernisten gehen nach dem Motto, daß die Vernunft eo ipso das Einheitliche begünstigt und implizit terroristische Mechanismen bevorzugt.[3] Z. B. verlangt J.-F. Lyotard, der Star der postmodernen Philosophie, das Ende der Kritik, da sie reformistisch sei und nur die bestehenden Autoritätsstrukturen festige.[4] Mit der Forderung nach dem Abgehen von Kritik verlangt er jedoch nichts anderes als die Beendigung des rationalen Diskurses und einer auf Vernunft basierenden Auseinandersetzung der Individuen, die doch vor Denk- und Argumentationsfehlern nicht gefeit sind und nur durch ein kritisches Zweifeln zu rationalen Schlußfolgerungen gelangen können. Das von J.-F. Lyotard verlangte Ende der Kritik könnte für die Demokratie schlicht das Abdanken bedeuten.

Leo Löwenthal macht in seiner Kritik des Postmodernismus auf dessen irrationale und mythologisierende Bestandteile aufmerksam, auf jene Strömungen, „die auch in der nationalsozialistischen Ideologie zu Hause gewesen sind".[5] Auch wenn man diese Kritik nur z. T. als gerecht empfindet, muß doch festgestellt werden, daß die postmodernen Hohepriester der Vernunft (sprich die Philosophen) die Vernunft zu Grabe tragen, daß der Postmodernismus in seinem

Streben nach Erneuerung die Ebene der Rationalität verläßt und sich zur Irrationalität und Mythologie hinwendet. Das alles geschieht im Namen der kontinuierlichen Entwicklung unter dem Zeichen der Moderne.

Diese Wende hat viele Namen und unzählige Gesichter, deren Anzahl einerseits mit der pluralistischen Vielfalt und andererseits mit der Beschaffenheit der modernen Massenkultur konform ist. Sie steht jedoch unter dem dominierenden Einfluß der rationalitätsfeindlichen Kräfte, die auf den Fundamentalismus eingeschworen sind.

Ca. ab der Mitte der 70er Jahre regte sich in gewissen Kreisen der katholischen Kirche Widerstand gegen die scheinbar zu weit gehenden Reformen des Vatikans. Diese Bewegung hat ihren Wortführer – Erzbischof Lefebvre – und das Prädikat einer fundamentalistischen Reaktion. In den 80er Jahren kam es zur Entstehung ähnlicher Strömungen an den „politischen Rändern" der arabischen Welt, die eine der radikalsten Ausformungen des Fundamentalismus, d. h. den islamischen, erlebten und erleben.

Bezüglich der katholischen Kirche bedeutete dies, daß die relative Reformfreundlichkeit des Vatikans erlahmte angesichts der Gefahr der fundamentalistisch bedingten Abspaltungstendenzen. Man suchte darum einen Kompromiß mit „orthodoxen" und konservativen Gruppierungen innerhalb und außerhalb der Amtskirche. Der Versuch eines Ausgleichs zwischen reformfreudigen und traditionalistischen Kräften mündete in einem christlich-katholischen Fundamentalismus.

Thomas Meyer beschreibt den Fundamentalismus als eine Denkweise, die „an die Stelle des Zweifels und der generellen Ungewißheit ein absolutes Wissen (setzt, B. S.), das allem vernünftigen Zweifel enthoben wird".[6] Von diesem „absoluten Wissen" profitieren die, die das Infragestellen, Anzweifeln oder Mit-Skepsis-Begegnen prinzipiell meiden, also die Sekten, die Religionsgemeinschaften oder die großen Weltkirchen.

Von Lefebres Traditionalisten bis zu Opus Dei reicht die Palette der breiten Front der Befürworter der Kirche im altbewährten Stil des Umgangs mit der Macht, mit den Glaubensvorstellungen und mit dem sogenannten Kirchenvolk. In Österreich ist diese Rückkehr zu den fundamentalistischen Werten in der Aufwertung des Opus Dei und der Verbreitung ultrakonservativer Vorstellungen von der Rolle der Kirche in der Gesellschaft sichtbar geworden. Der neue Wind in den Amtsgängen der Diözesen Küngs, Eders oder Krenns bedeutet Antihumanität gegenüber Homosexuellen, Frauen oder allgemein gegen alle „Außenseiter". Da in Österreich der Einfluß der Kanzelpredigt beziehungsweise anderer kirchlicher Stellungnahmen im ländlichen Raum gerade heute nicht unterschätzt werden sollte, ist zu befürchten, daß ihre irrationalistischen Inhalte eine negative Auswirkung auf das geistige Klima des Landes haben werden.

Ein anderer, die Gesellschaft zutiefst beeinflussender Fundamentalismus ist der grün-ökologische. Seine Genese ist eng mit dem massiv geäußerten Mißtrauen gegenüber dem technischen Fortschritt und den Auswüchsen der Zivilisation verbunden. In Österreich und anderswo kann dieser Fundamentalismus mit einem Teil der grünökologischen Bewegung gleichgesetzt werden. Ein beträchtlicher Teil dieses inhomogenen politischen Spektrums entwickelte sich langsam zu einem fundamentalistischen Block, der im Grün-Spiritualismus und Grünmystizismus adäquate Ausdrucksformen fand. Das führte zur Entstehung stärker artikulierter Gegenpositionen innerhalb der Grünalternativen und außerdem – wie bei den nördlichen Nachbarn – zu Flügelkämpfen zwischen Fundis und Realos, d. h. zwischen den Befürwortern der radikalen Verweigerung und der Bereitschaft zum Kompromiß.

Dem Grünspiritualismus und -mystizismus lagen mythologisierende Vorstellungen zugrunde, wie Thomas Meyer meint: „Es sind dies die Mythen der Versöhnung von Mensch und Natur, der Versöhnung der Menschen untereinander, der Versöhnung von Freiheit und Glück und der Mythos des perennierenden Fortschritts ihrer Erfüllung".[7] Obwohl sie aus dem Geist der Aufklärung und dem Sonderhumanismus der europäischen Linken entstanden, waren sie zugleich die Restbestände einer romantischen Weltanschauung. Mit dem Entstehen der ökologischen Bewegung wurden diese Mythen übernommen und zum Teil uminterpretiert. Sie bekamen den romantischen Anstrich des sogenannten „Pioniergeistes" und dienten als argumentativ-geistiger Überbau der Fluchtbewegung aus der technologisch überforderten Umwelt. Die Öko-Fundamentalisten bedienten sich dieser Mythen, um der Ideologie des ungebremsten Wirtschaftswachstums und des grenzenlosen Konsums eine ideell attraktivere Alternative entgegenzusetzen und mit Hilfe einer argumentativen Überzeichnung das drohende ökologische Desaster der Öffentlichkeit bewußt zu machen. Mit der Zeit wurden die romantisch-irrationalen Vorstellungen mit rationalen Werten ausgestaltet und in den Dienst einer Scheinrealität der grünen Bestandsaufnahmen der Umwelt gestellt. Der Erfolg dieser scheinrationalen Denkweisen resultierte einerseits aus der Verunsicherung des größeren Teils der Öffentlichkeit und andererseits aus der Kanalisierung und Reglementierung des Meinungsaustausches. Dabei wurde ein offener Diskurs über die Prioritäten bei der Gestaltung einer ausgeglicheneren Wirtschaftspolitik zum Teil dank des geschickten Wetterns gegen das Spezialistentum unterbunden. Dank der Immobilität der verantwortlichen polit-wirtschaftlichen Eliten, dank der festgefahrenen Lage der Industrienationen, war es möglich gewesen, die argumentative Position der kritischen Opposition zu nützen. Darum konnte man sich auf der Seite der Grünen auf die Mittel der Bekehrung und des Predigens beschränken. Zwar wurden – je nach Bedarf – Versuche unternommen, realisierbare Konzepte vorzulegen, aber erstens waren die Autoren nicht gezwungen, diese zu verwirklichen, und zweitens war das der Öffentlichkeit präsentierte meistens Detailfragen gewidmet.

Zu den positiven Aspekten des grün-ökologischen Aktionismus gehörte erstens die initiierende Rolle in der Diskussion über die brennenden Probleme der Umwelt und zweitens die Beständigkeit in der Öffentlichkeitsarbeit zugunsten eines umweltfreundlicheren Wirtschaftens. Zu den eindeutig negativen Facetten dieser Bewegung gehörten der fundamentalistische Umgang mit der Meinungsvielfalt, ein „hausgemachter" Mystizismus und ein betont irrationales Umfeld.

Die Folgen der grün-fundamentalistischen Anwendung des widersprüchlichen Argumentationsapparats sind in der Vermischung des Rational-Irrationalen und der Maximierung mystisch-fundamentalistischer Auffassungen von der Wirklichkeit zu finden.

Obwohl sich die Grünen als Avantgarde oder Bewegungen des neuen Fortschritts verstehen, ist ihre Nähe zu anderen irrationalen Strömungen unseres Zeitalters wie z. B. des Nationalismus, des Rechtsradikalismus, des Spiritualismus, der Esoterik und des New-Age etc. nicht zu übersehen.

Eigentlich ist die zum Großteil eklektische grün-ökologische Ideologie durch drei Grundhaltungen bestimmt: eine spezifische Existenz- oder Daseinsangst, eine Hilflosigkeit im Umgang mit den Anforderungen einer modernen Gesellschaft und die Furcht vor dem Apokalypse-Syndrom. Alle drei Haltungen zeugen von einem tiefgreifenden Pessimismus innerhalb der zeitgenössischen demokratischen Gemeinschaft, wobei sich die kongruierenden negativen Grundpositionen quer durch verschiedene politische Lager und soziale Gruppen ziehen.

Daß der Großteil dieser Erscheinungen einen Ausdruck des postmodernen Kulturpessimismus darstellt und substantiell zu den restaurativen Strömungen des ausgehenden 20. Jhdts zu rechnen ist, steht außer Zweifel.

Unsicher aber ist, welche Positionen diese Bewegung in der Beziehung zu den anderen antirationalen Strömungen unseres Zeitalters annimmt und ob sie bereit ist, gewisse Koalitionen einzugehen. Hier sind die Versuche eines gemeinsamen Vorgehens gemeint, die aus ähnlichen oder parallelen Vorstellungen von einer praktisch gemeinten Umweltpolitik resultieren. Zwar kann man prinzipiell bestimmte Formen der politischen Kooperation als eine positive Erscheinung bewerten, aber nicht jede Koalition ist politisch vertretbar. In diesem Zusammenhang sollten jene Teile des grünen Spektrums hervorgehoben werden, die auch rechte Optionen in Betracht ziehen, wenn es um die Sache der Umwelt geht.

In der breiten Front der gesellschaftlichen Kräfte, die seit Jahren den Aufstand gegen die Vernunft proben, sind außer den grünen und christlichen Fundamentalisten vor allem die Verfechter nationalistisch-populistischer Ideologien vertreten. Neben der sie verbindenden Sorge um die Erhaltung der Umwelt gibt es eine Reihe konträrer Ansichten über wichtige außen- und innenpolitische Fragen (wie z. B. Flüchtlingspolitik, der Umgang mit Wirtschaftsflüchtlingen, die Frauen- oder Minderheitenpolitik), die aus der Sicht der rechtskonservativen Kräfte nach den alten Vorgangsmustern gelöst werden sollten.

Die geistige Basis der rechtskonservativen Vertreter der populistischen Lösungskonzepte beinhaltet alte und neue Elemente beziehungsweise alte und neue Verwandtschaften. Zu den alten Grundsätzen der biologistisch und rassistisch begründeten Weltanschauung mit dem klassischen Chauvinismus des beginnenden 20. Jhdts kommen neue Elemente hinzu, die nur bedingt als Zeichen einer relativen Modernität der Ewig-Gestrigen verstanden werden können. Zu diesen Elementen gehört die generelle Bejahung der Werte des freien Marktes, der Konsum- und Informationsgesellschaft und außerdem das Konzept der Versöhnung zwischen Ökologie und Technologie.

Das Schlußlicht der populistischen Denk- und Handlungsweise bildet das Problem der Einstellung zur pluralistisch-demokratischen Gesellschaft. Prinzipiell bejahen sie überall dort die demokratischen Einrichtungen, wo sich die gegebenen

Freiräume politisch nutzen lassen. Ihre Akzeptanz dieses Systems ist eine auf Zeit und von der Tatsache abhängig, ob sich unter Anwendung demokratischer Spielregeln das System von innen aushöhlen läßt.[8]

Dieses gestörte Verhältnis, das eine parasitäre Beziehung der Populisten zur Demokratie aufweist, bedeutet – wie uns die Geschichte lehrt – nichts Neues. Gewisse Ähnlichkeiten in der Strategie der Nutzung legaler Mitteln zur Erreichung antidemokratischer Ziele gibt es zwischen den Populisten der 20er und der 90er Jahre. Nihil novi sub soli könnte man sagen – allerdings mit einem aber. Die zeitgenössischen „Volksverführer" agieren im Zeitalter einer prosperierenden Wirtschaft und des Wohlfahrtsstaates mit allen seinen positiven und negativen Nebenerscheinungen. Ihre Strategie ist von Land zu Land verschieden, also den inneren Schwächen der jeweiligen Demokratie entsprechend angepaßt. Aber prinzipiell versuchen sie, in der Öffentlichkeit zu einem Image der „sozial gerechten Erneuerer" zu gelangen. Sie predigen politische Sauberkeit, wirtschaftliche Sparsamkeit und bieten Lösungen an, die einfach und für jedermann verständlich sind. Sie bieten eine – realistisch gesehen – unrealistische Symbiose von Sozialdarwinismus und einer nicht näher definierten sozialen Sicherheit für alle Nicht-Schmarotzer an.

Nach der populistischen Denkweise ist die Frage des Defizitabbaus eine Angelegenheit der konsequenten und restriktiven Fiskalpolitik, d. h. der radikalen Kürzung der Sozialleistungen des Staates. Ähnlich unkompliziert ist für sie das Problem der Bewältigung der Arbeitslosigkeit, wobei in diesem Fall die lancierte Methode aus der Sicht der schweigenden Mehrheit noch effizienter ist. Die schweizerischen, österreichischen und französischen Populisten plädieren für die Schlichtheit im konzeptuellen Bereich. Sie schlagen vor, die Fremd- und Gastarbeiter ihrem kulturellen Raum „zuzuführen" und die – so gewonnenen – Arbeitsplätze den inländischen Arbeitskräften zur Verfügung zu stellen. Einfacher und „effizienter" kann das keine andere politische Kraft bewerkstelligen, wohlgemerkt in einer Demokratie.

Das konsequente Wettern gegen die müden, von Konzeptlosigkeit befallenen „Altparteien", das permanente Trommelschlagen auf der inner- und außerparlamentarischen Ebene und das geschickte Denunzieren der demokratischen Einrichtungen in der politikmüden Öffentlichkeit bringt – wie die Wahlgänge in einigen Demokratien des Westens zeigen – immer mehr Zuspruch, also mehr Stimmen. Schon jetzt scheinen sie im Vorzimmer der Macht zu stehen.[9]

Dieser Vormarsch rechtskonservativer bis populistischer Gruppierungen bleibt nicht ohne Auswirkungen auf die politische Landschaft Europas. Dem Rechnung tragend, sehen sich die demokratischen Parteien gezwungen, populistischen Jargon aufzunehmen und sich indirekt des Fremdenhasses, der Xenophobie zu bedienen.

Unmerklich kam und kommt es zu einer Verschiebung der politischen Positionen weit nach rechts in die Sphären des autoritären und zum Teil rassistischen Gedankengutes. Und weil das schrittweise erfolgt und der Verzicht auf humanistische Werte sich auf schleichende Art und Weise vollzieht, wird die Immunkraft der Gesellschaft allmählich abgebaut. Immer seltener heben sich die Stimmen des Protestes gegen eine zunehmende Rechtsradikalisierung der Gesellschaft. Immer offener treten die Befürworter der biologistisch-rassistischen Strategie der Verteidigung des Okzidents vor Überfremdung auf.

Die konsequente Negation einer universellen Vernunft fällt auf den fruchtbaren Boden des „postindustriellen Mittelalters".

Schlußwort

Im Zeitalter der extremen Gegensätze hat der Mythos – wie Thomas Meyer sagt – eine neue Konjunktur. Seine Renaissance ist das Produkt der Massenreaktion der westlichen Industriegesellschaften auf die Vormachtpositionen der Wissenschaft und die Rationalität der Vorgänge in allen Bereichen des demokratischen Systems. Eine Allianz der Fortschritts- und Demokratiemüden ist im Entstehen, und da die Rationalität einer der Hauptpfeiler der Konsum- und Informationsgesellschaft ist, wird die Negation des Rationalen zum Hauptmotor der Veränderung ausgewählt.

Im fruchtbaren Schoß des wiedererstarkten Nationalismus wachsen die neuen Vorstellungen von einer Gesellschaft, die nicht vom Gespenst der Unregierbarkeit, der Destabilität, der Überfremdung und Arbeitslosigkeit geplagt wird.

Die populistischen Erneuerer versprechen leicht verwirklichbare Lösungen, und die fundamentalistischen Ideen erzeugen den Eindruck des idealen Fluchtweges aus den Zwängen einer meistens überorganisierten Massendemokratie.

So gesehen sind die 90er Jahre eine Zeit des Rückfalls in die Vergangenheit, in die Welt des anti-humanistischen und totalitären Denkens. Aber ebenso scheinen sie die Möglichkeit des Auswegs der Moderne aus der Sackgasse der Wachstumsideologie zu bieten.

Anmerkungen

1 Die einen Demokratietheoretiker, wie Claus Offe, versuchen, das Instabile mit der Entziehung immer zahlreicherer „Entscheidungsgegenstände" des legitimitätsschaffenden Demokratieprinzips zu begründen. Die anderen, wie S. Hungtington, operieren mit dem Begriff der sogenannten „Glaubwürdigkeitslücke" der zeitgenössischen Demokratie, wenn sie in einem Bereich zwischen normativ aufgefaßten Erwartungen der Menschen und institutionellen Realitäten des Systems eine plausible Erklärung suchen.

2 Vgl. Christof Schorsch, „Die Krise der Moderne", in: „Aus Politik und Zeitgeschichte", B 40/89.

3 Vgl. Wolfgang Welsch, „‚Postmoderne'. Genealogie und Bedeutung eines umstrittenen Begriffs", in: Peter Kemper (Hrsg.), „‚Postmoderne' oder Der Kampf um die Zukunft", Frankfurt/Main 1988, S. 10.

4 Vgl. J.-F. Lyotard, „Derive a partir de Marx et Freud", Paris 1973, S. 14.

5 Leo Löwenthal, „Ich will den Traum von Utopie nicht aufgeben", in: Hajo Funke, „Die andere Erinnerung", Frankfurt/Main 1989, S. 181.
Leo Löwenthal bezieht sich in seiner Kritik auf die Artikel in den Zeitschriften „Konkursbuch" und „Tumult" und insbesondere auf das Buch „Zur Kritik der palavernden Aufklärung" von Gerd Bergfleth, in dem u. a. für einen „gesunden Patriotismus" eingetreten wird und in dem

Bergfleth meint, daß der „Universalismus der Juden . . . die Auslöschung des Individuellen" impliziere (zit. nach a. a. O., S. 181).

6 Thomas Meyer, „Fundamentalismus". Aufstand gegen die Moderne", Hamburg 1989, S. 161.

7 Thomas Meyer, a. a. O., S. 52.

8 Vgl. Hans-Georg Betz, „Radikal rechtspopulistische Parteien in Westeuropa", in: „Aus Politik und Zeitgeschichte", B 44/91; Uwe Backes, „Extremismus und Populismus von rechts", in: „Aus Politik und Zeitgeschichte", B 46–47/90.

9 Vgl. Bauer/Niedermayer, „Extrem rechtes Potential in den Ländern der europäischen Gemeinschaft", in: „Aus Politik und Zeitgeschichte", B 46–47/90; Backes/Jesse, „Politischer Extremismus in der Bundesrepublik Deutschland", Köln 1989.

Literatur

Apel, Karl-Otto, „Diskurs und Verantwortung", Frankfurt/Main 1988.
Bohrer, Karl Heinz (Hrsg.), „Mythos und Moderne", Frankfurt/Main 1983.
Habermas, Jürgen, „Der philosophische Diskurs der Moderne", Frankfurt/Main 1989.
Huyssen/Scherpe (Hrsg.), „Postmoderne", Hamburg 1986.
Kemper, Peter (Hrsg.), „‚Postmoderne' oder Der Kampf um die Zukunft", Frankfurt/Main 1988.
Meyer, Thomas, „Fundamentalismus. Aufstand gegen die Moderne", Hamburg 1989.
Popper, Karl R., „Die offene Gesellschaft und ihre Feinde", Bd. 2, Tübingen 1980.
Schiwy, Günther, „Poststrukturalismus und ‚Neue Philosophie'", Hamburg 1985.
Tallert, Harry (Hrsg.), „Die grüne Gegen-Revolution", Frankfurt/Main – Berlin 1980.

III.
Im Strom des Wandels

Maria Borucka-Arctowa

European Integration and National Identity

1. The goal of my report is to provide a view of the process of European Integration from the following perspectives:

a) social changes which are taking place on a world scale which are termed "globalization";

b) the challenge with which the social sciences are confronted in face of these changes and the search for theoretical assumptions and a multilevel approach to these new problems;

c) the transferral of these considerations to the subject of European Integration with a special emphasis on the role of law and cultural factors in the integration process, as well as the dilemma of "unity versus diversity";

d) the aspiration which Central and Eastern European countries have for a rapid entry into the "Common European Home". Advantages, difficulties and dangers linked with these aspirations;

e) "national identity" versus "nationalism" – a conceptual and functional analysis with reference to the concept of "global village" and European Integration;

f) the role of social consciousness of the breakthrough period, the period of transition from one system to another often resulting in incoherent and contradictory opinions.

2. The process of European integration can be regarded from the broader perspective of social changes which are taking place on a world-wide scale, often defined by the term "globalization".

"The key change over the last few decades has been Globalization – a multifaceted process entailing a growing world-wide interconnectedness of structure, culture and agency, and a parallel de-differentiation of traditional boundaries." (M. Archer, 1990, p. 5)[1]

Globalization of economic, political, military and communicative processes (more recently also of environmental protection) meant the emergence of comprehensive wholes as crucial-political and military blocks, economic areas and unions, sometimes of a horizontal structure, but more often of a vertical hierarchical one with clearly delineated centers and gradations of peripheries or dependencies. (P. Sztompka, 1988, p. 211)

During the second half of our century globalization became visible in everyday life. A highly developed network of traffic lines makes possible the exchange of merchandise and people. The mass media, cable TV and satellites carry information around the world. The social systems have grown together with regards to the economy, science and communications, to a world society. (K. Röhl, 1991, p. 2)

What are the consequences for common people living in such a globalized world, what happens to societal meanings, and concepts entertained by them? For some of them the actual experiences, ways of life and social conditions become more alike. For others they remain different, but even for them the knowledge of foreign experiences, ways of life, social conditions, become more accessible through travel, tourism, mass media, personal contacts.

"The similarity of actual experiences, or at least access to information about others experiences, opens up the actual or at least vicarious, possibility of either re-living or imagining a multiplicity and variety of possible social arrangements . . . Even if they still differ in beliefs and interpretations, members of various societies begin to understand each other instead of talking about each other." (P. Sztompka, 1988, p. 212)

3. The challenge for the social sciences and especially sociology vis-a-vis transformations of this subject matter was expressed in the Presidential Address presented by Margaret Archer at the 12th World Congress of Sociology in the following statement: "As we begin to live in One World, this new social reality supplies us with good reason for overhauling our theoretical assumptions and framework." (M. Archer, 1990, p. 5)

The search for theoretical assumptions and the multilevel approach to new problems is a real challenge for the social sciences. One of the most important theses, closely linked with my paper's topic is, that the polarity between "Unity versus Diversity" constitutes a false dichotomy in social theorizing because of changes in the social world itself. M. Archer has strongly underlined this thesis and presented the damage done through the polarization of social theory.

On the one extreme (pole) are found schools of thought which opt for unity, universalism (that is, they assume a unitary process) and therefore above all positivism with its unity of method, universality of laws, and uniformity of practices. Likewise alongside are found currents critical of positivism, and therefore Marxism and neo-Marxism and their different concept of the unity of methods and of the laws of social development. And also there are the current theories of modernity, presenting successive stages through which the transfer of capital, technology and information from the First World will inevitably generate worldwide uniformity (modernistic statements aroused strong criticism due to their unifactoral, ahistorical, and contextless argumentation and the impossibility of explaining the inefficiency of the transferred model in many countries and its success in others). Other theories of development also gravitate towards this pole, such as that of the Post-Industrial Society and of the Information Society, "Presenting the autonomous effect of information technology with deterministic consequences for structure, culture, and agency alike." (M. Archer, 1990, p. 8–9)

On the opposite extreme (pole) M. Archer places those currents, which in an increasing opposition to positivism as a philosophy of social sciences, voice the viewpoint of diversity (primacy of Diversity versus primacy of Unity), placing emphasis on the socio-centric products of "different worlds". Incommensurability over an untranslatability meant that diverse "forms of life" could only be understood in their own terms. All understanding was contextual.

The growing interconnections between different societies rose problems, how "alien" beliefs and practices had to be understood, but even the admission of intelligibility didn't mitigate the approach to Diversity as the key of problem. Intelligibility consisted in the understanding of difference and divergence and was not the same as initiating dialogue, because societal discourse about such different matters were given different settings.

The presented polarity of social theories could not help in the search of theoretical assumptions and frameworks, corresponding to the new social reality and globalization process. The recent challenge for the social sciences is to find a common ground for the new assumptions and frameworks and to avoid the extremities of the old approaches.

"What has changed is that the global processes are now partly constitutive of social reality everywhere and constitute that part which cannot be understood in strictly local terms, for its origins and impact stem from outside localized 'forms of life'" (M. Archer, 199, p. 6)

In no way can we interpret it as a new universalism from the effects of globalization regardless of local contextual variation. The new sources of unity are grounded on the emergence of global structures and agents and their interplay within the diversity of regional structures and agencies. The integration of diversity and the global-regional interplay are the basic conceptions. Local and regional varieties are presented as a combination of tendencies representing different ways, trajectories. The interaction of such trajectories will produce greater variety rather than reducing it, over time. (M. Archer, 1990, p. 14)

4. Let's try to link the considerations made until now with the problem contained in the title of this paper. European integration, just like globalization, is a multilevel process. Integration is very far advanced, when considered in a legal-institutional light. It is expressed in the creation and functioning of such institutions as the Council of Europe, European Community, European Parliament, Commission of Human Rights, and through a broad framework of common European legal and judiciary activity. The law therefore plays a significant part in European Integration. The question nevertheless arises, what exactly is this part? Is there, alongside the laws of the European Community, the formation of other "ways" of transnational and transborder activities as a type of "lex mercatorial" network? Is the law following the technical and economic development with the usual lag, or at least in some areas is it a promoter of globalization? (K. F. Röhl, p. 2) Is this law based on a distinct institutional level "above" the member states or is it an outcome of economic and social transactions and conflict settlements over international frontiers, based more on a lawless informality? Who participates at the present in the European Union decision making process and how does it relate to the legal modelling of these processes? (All these problems were discussed in depth at the workshops and panels dealing with European Community Law during the international conference "Law and Society in the Global Village" Amsterdam, 1991 (see the abstracts and materials of the conference).[2] Theoretical problems that include the practical and empirical findings into a conceptual perspective and model of European Integration also arise. Is the notion "common village" neutral, or is it intentionally used as a "village" with more attention focussed on super-state customs, rules, and not only on the official, positive "state law"?

The question arises, as to whether or not in this European process of integration the law will always tend to do away with borders and barriers between states and regions, or does it by presenting certain conditions which will have to be fulfilled by its current and future members, create barriers? There is a very strong preponderance appearing here, linked with economic activity as well as ways of achieving the European Internal Market in comparatively short time. (The end of 1992 is the target date by when it should be completed.)

A difference of opinion exists as to whether such a strict and precise observance of these conditions creates an incentive, or challenge in those countries aspiring to membership in the European Community to a quick and complete implementation of economic reforms, or wether their being outside of the Common Market has become a factor which is a handicap for reforms toward a free market economy, and to some extent to the possibility of the full realization of human rights.

In the countries of Central and Eastern Europe, where fundamental political and economic changes are taking place, one can detect a very profound tendency to try to enter the "Common European Home" as soon as possible. European integration is considered from its limited territorial and regional viewpoints, which arouses fears of the existence of "two worlds" alongside each other, in spite of the great changes which have taken place on a European, and really, in essence, world-wide scale.

In our considerations on the role of law in European Integration one can't perceive any kind of transnational or global dissemination of legal concepts and knowledge pertaining to law on the local and national level (National Science Foundation 1990). But if we crosscut law making and law implementation, we have to look at an important variable – the factor of cultural diversity, and then comes the question – to what extent does European Community law harmonize member state laws by allowing for differentiation?

5. Can we assume that the general process of cultural diffusion would ultimately lead to a unified world culture, differentiated only by regional accents? And here is a difference of views and expectations. Adherents of cultural convergence expect a mutual enrichment of the various cultures, opponents however, perceive a threat to cultural identity, diversity and uniqueness. Underlying this is the belief that an excessive communication of foreign cultural products can damage or even destroy an indigenous culture.

Problems of cultural identity are very closely linked with "National Identity", but in no way can they be treated identically.

The feeling of belonging to European culture does not necessarily mean a link with "Eurocracy", but usually means that a significant part of national culture has characteristics in common with European culture as a whole, and in addition to this certain elements are maintained which are characteristic and unique solely for that specific national culture.

Identity is usually defined as an individual self-concept and self-social identity. This includes values, beliefs, "feelings to belong" and reasoning which define one's subjective sense of national identity. Pursuing these problems will lead to a better understanding of the complex ways national identity and attitudes merge with and reconstitute ideas of selfdetermination and society.

National identity is shaped by history and very deeply rooted in tradition, including a historically determined attachment to specific values and institutions passed on from generation to generation. However, tradition is obviously changing. It is always a choice of certain values, norms and institutions from the past. The term "progressive tradition", often used and even abused in the former, socialist system, seems relative. Current research trends point out that tradition can be falsified to include some phenomena which have never occurred. What is more, previously held views and norms are interpreted in such a specific way to meet current requirements and support ideas and institutions which are being created or proposed. Even history can be intentionally falsified and manipulated to evoke specific feelings and attitudes, which are typical sources of nationalism.

Nationalism is based on the divisions of "ours" and "theirs" (or if you prefer "we" and "they") and the formation of social identity through the delineation of different interests, customs, and values, which divide one's own national group from other and not searching for that which could unite them. A division between "ours" and "theirs" aids the formation of an ethical dualism (M. Marody 1991, p. 261–264), which is based on the supposition that certain norms and principles are obligatory in one's own national group, and others in contacts with members of other groups.

By the same token, the growing tendency of a renascent nationalism, often linked with separatist tendencies in multi-national states, is difficult to reconcile with the concept of a "global village" and European integration. However, the problem of preserving national identity and allaying fears of loosing this value in face of "Eurocracy" can be solved in accordance with the postulate presented in the first part of this report "the integration of diversity" and the "global-national and regional interplay".

6. In the wide range of problems concerning the political, social and economic changes in Eastern and Central Europe, we cannot disregard changes in social consciousness since they determine the scope of transformations and the effectiveness of reform that are taken up.

This is the consciousness of the breakthrough period, the period of transition from one system to another. This is why elements of the old system occur side by side with those of the new system (the proportion differs from individual to individual and from social group to social group) and most often result in incoherent and contradictory opinions.

The fact that people accept a market economy and private property does not necessarily mean that they accept the inequalities which result from resourcefulness, initiative, ability, diligence, and success. The acceptance is often very general and idealistic and results from the conviction that the market economy is a social necessity and a condition for obtaining a Western European standard of life. The old centrally planned system combined with "shortage economy" replaced the free market with the distribution of goods as privileges. The lack of criteria for this distribution led to growing differences between particular groups as well as great attachment to privileges. The emerging egalitarian concepts refer to the idea of justice whereby everybody gets an equal share of privileges, subsidies are distributed according to clearly defined criteria and groups are made equal by state interventionism. The growing demand for subsidies for particular branches of industries, services, and farming, coexist with a declared dislike and fear of state interventionism associated with the rejected system which led to the collapse of the country's economy.

The deeply rooted attachment to the protective role of the state (however poor the protection might have been) cannot be treated only as a residue of the former system. The problem can be seen in terms of rights achieved in the process of the shaping labor law and its traditions, and also in terms of the protection of economic and social human rights which have become the subject of the Council of Europe debates. The countries from Central Europe were expected to make contributions to those rights. However, discussions in both the Hungarian and Polish parliaments showed that social and economic rights were treated with obvious reserve. (Z. Kędzia, 1990, p. 11–12)

It's difficult to separate what type of society most people would like to live in from the inconsistency of their opinions regarding political and economic problems. National identity plays an essential role in this vision, coexisting with aspirations of "entering Europe"; in the day-to-day language of our cultural circles, the term "real European" has a positive connotation, however this doesn't necessarily mean that other cultural circles have a similar acceptance. European integration may be perceived by the man in the street as something which will broaden his sphere of activity, but also he may be afraid of economic and political links which are too strong. Some inconsistencies in the social consciousness are characteristic not only for the ordinary people of Central and Eastern Europe but are also emerging in Western European countries, for example certain nationalistic and separatistic currents.

The coexistence of conflicting views in the social consciousness can be perceived as an obstacle to integration. However it can also be seen as a factor that is bound to lead to new solutions at lower levels and as the beginning of the shaping of a new social order in Europe.

I would like ro finish my paper with a reference to a statement mady by Joseph Brodsky – Nobel prize winner in 1987:

"The end of a century – and even more so the end of a millennium – is always accompanied by the idea of a change in the world order. The more incoherent this idea is, the more arresting it becomes." (From the "Tenant's Monologue")

Notes

1 My report is largely based on material from the International Congresses of the last two years, exactly because the most up to date approaches and viewpoints regarding the subject of this report were found there.
2 Joint Meeting of the Law and Society Association and Research Committee on the Sociology of Law of the International Sociological Association (ISA), Amsterdam, June 1991.
3 M. Marody uses these concepts dealing with the process of atomization of Polish society and the resulting consequences. A feeling of identity is connected with emotional links with those persons, who are closest to oneself, like family, friends, acquaintances, a lack of intermediate links or allegiance to any kind of formal institutions; there results a tendency to defend one's interests, selfishness, and a lack of confidence in formal institutions. This attitude results from past experience and attitudes to the political-legal system. (M. Marody, 1991)
4 Dealt with this subject in a broader scale – L. Kotlarska-Bobińska and A. Rychard 1990, M. Mokrzycki 1990.

References

Archer, M., 1990, "Sociology for One World: Unity and Diversity", Presidential Address at the 12th World Congress of Sociology, Madrid, July 1990.

Kędzia, Z., "An East-European Perspective towards an All-European System of Human Rights Protection", the paper presented at the International Conference "All-European System of the Human Rights Protection", Poznań, October 1990.

Kotlarska-Bobińska, L., and Rychard, A., 1990, Polityka i Gospodarka w Świadomości Społecznej (Politics and Economy in Social Consciousness), Warszawa.

Marody, M., 1991, "Jednostka w systemie Realnego Socjalizmu" (Individual in the System of Real Socialism), in: Co nam zostało z tych lat. Społeczeństwo Polskie u Progu Zmiany Społecznej (What's Left of These Years. Polish Society at the Threshold of a New Political System); ed. M. Marody, London.

Mokrzycki, M., 1990, "Dziedzictwo Realnego Socjalizmu. Poszukiwanie Nowej Utopii" (The Legacy of Real Socialism. The Search for a New Utopia), the paper presented at the Congress of Polish Sociological Association, Toruń 1990.

National Science Foundation (ed.), 1990, "Law Beyond the Nation State: Global Perspectives on Sociolegal Studies", Belmont Conference, July 1990, Conference Papers.

Röhl, K. F., 1991, "The Globalization of Legal Phenomena", the paper presented at the International Conference "Law and Society in the Global Village", organized by Law and Society Association and Research Committee on the Sociology of Law of the International Association, Amsterdam, June 1991.

Sztompka, P., 1988, "Conceptual Framework in Comparative Inquiry: Divergent or Convergent", International Sociology, vol 3. No 3, p. 207–218.

Stanisław Gebethner

Stages of Decay and Failure of Real Socialism in Central and Eastern Europe

Comparative Perspectives

Since the beginning of 1989, when the Round Table negotiations had started in Poland, significant and rapid revolutionary changes took place in the whole region of Central and Eastern Europe. This process of radical social, political and institutional (as well as constitutional) changes is still under way. It has not been finished yet. But we can say that the old constitutional, political, social and economic order known previously as real socialism, or the Communist regime, collapsed. Each country or region is now struggling to construct its own version of the future. The ultimate goal may be democracy and capitalism, but there is no consensus on how to get there. The process on institutional and systemic changes in the political sphere is in these countries really impressive and spectacular. But there is no certainty what will be the final outcome of this process. The imposition of an authoritarian post-communist political system – with a right wing and nationalistic oriented dictatorship – is possible as well as the installation of democratic institutions and the development of a democratic political system may be predicted. The character of the eventual future economic system in these countries is not clear, too.

There are widespread opinions in the West that the only way of a future development for these countries – and especially for Central European ones, like Czechoslovakia, Hungary and Poland – is a parliamentary democracy. Politicians, political scientists, journalists seem to be convinced that pressures and incentives coming from the West European governments are strong enough and effective means to secure the establishment of a democratic political system in the post-communist countries in this region of Europe. However, there are not so easy and simple consequences of the collapse of communist authoritarian (or totalitarian) regimes that they should be automatically and spontaneously replaced by democratic political institutions and procedures. It is possible that one authoritarian regime could be replaced by another authoritarian system of government.

In the 1989 peaceful, or revolutionary, radical political changes swept away one ideology in Central and Eastern Europe without replacing it with another as clearly defined one. Democracy based on free elections and a multiparty system as a free market economy may be common and desirable goals, but history (and especially the last forty years), geography and citizens' consciousness (or national psyche) will be influential factors and obstacles in determining how quickly, if at all, they are achieved. The only exception is East Germany (former German Democratic Republic) where the West German type of political system and economic system is a clear goal of changes being performed although not without difficulties.

This process of fundamental changes was initiated in Poland and spread over the whole Central and Eastern Europe. When Timothy Garton Ash arrived to Prague in the middle of the velvet revolution he said: "In Poland it took ten years, in Hungary ten months, in East Germany ten weeks: perhaps in Czechoslovakia it will take ten days!"[1] This accurate observation reflects both the tremendous acceleration of political process which took place in 1989 in Central and Eastern Europe and the pioneering role of the Polish experiences of the last decade.

The whole world was shocked by the events in Central and Eastern Europe in 1989 when one communist regime collapsed after another. The question arises, however, why all these events had happened almost at the same time and just in 1989 and 1990 and why it happened at all?

I would like to focus on the following seven specified factors which conduced to the cumulative effect creating favorable conditions for the outbreak of the chain of weighty events which have been called the Autumn of Nations of the XXth century. There were several reasons of the failure of real socialism and of such cumulative effects of such a course of events.

First, it was a dramatic economic decline caused by inefficient centrally planned national economy, with bureaucratic command and administrative management of industry, trade and agriculture, which produced hardship of daily life and deepening a gap between the socialist block and Western countries.

Second, it was a deteriorating standard of living of the population at large, including a devastation of the ecological environment. The decreasing life expectancy in these countries is one evidence of the deteriorating standard of living

Third, it was a dramatically growing technological gap between the Western countries and socialist block countries.

Fourth, it was a vanishing legitimization of political systems and growing aspirations of the general public for liberty and civic rights and for free elections.

Fifth, it was an erosion of a hegemonic position of the Communist parties which were loosing a capability both to control the monocentric political system and to directing national economy (or – as in cases of Poland, Hungary and Yugoslavia – to perform economic reforms). They had lost effective influence upon public activities of crucial groups of society (and especially the working class) as well.

Sixth, it was a complete decline of Marxist-Leninist ideology and total failure – especially within the younger generation – of the indoctrination of the Communist ideals and values.

Seventh, it is – last but not least – the change of the Soviet concept of relationships between the Kremlin and Central and Eastern European countries, i. e. the formal and practical denunciation of the Brezhnev's doctrine.

The year 1989 is sometimes compared with 1789, 1848 or 1917. It is true that authoritarian political systems in Central and Eastern Europe have collapsed in 1989 and 1990 like a house of cards. In consequence, a pattern that kept Europe for forty years secure, if immobile, was replaced a by future full of unprecedented changes and unimagined possibilities.[2]

What happened in recent years in Central and Eastern European countries is a product of a long process of invisible internal transformations of the system and changes of its environment.

This impressive – and for someone maybe surprising – peaceful revolution in Central and Eastern Europe is a result of the multi-dimensional – economic, social, political, ideological and moral – long lasting structural crises of the formation known as the real socialism or communism. But before the first significant signals of this structural and institutional crisis appeared in the end of the 1960's (in Czechoslovakia the Prague Spring in 1968 and in Poland the workers rebellion in Baltic Coast cities in 1970) the Soviet pattern of government and of economic regime, which were installed after the World War Two, had been initially performed not without some achievements and success in the field of the economy and of social relationships.

Before I will try to discuss the circumstances of the collapse of the real socialism I would like to focus the conditions which ensured the existence of this formation for 45 years in this region.

The soviet pattern of economic system was based on centrally planned economic domination of state's ownership and liquidation of private property, the command-administrative way of management of national economy with its huge bureaucratic governmental apparatus. This economic system was logically synchronized with monocentric political system. The core of this system had been the monopolistic position of the Communist party with elimination of political opposition and civic participation in governing on local level.

In Central and Eastern Europe countries the installation of this political system – as well as of the economic system – was mainly the result of the Communist take-over of power inspired and supported by Kremlin acting through its political agents and directly aided by NKVD. However, this historical process of Communist take-over and installation of new regimes were associated with attractive ideology promising – in line with egalitarian ideals – a quick economic development, full employment, universal social benefits and promotion of broad handicapped strata of a population.

At the beginning the effectiveness of the new regimes had been based on economic and social achievements albeit they were accomanied with the terror of secrete police eliminating any political opposition.

In the late 1960's and in the 1970's the centrally planned economic system had started up to lose its capacity to satisfy growing demands for further and quicker improvement of standard of living of population. The half-hearted economic reforms failed and produced the deterioration of standard of living accompanied by devastation of natural resources and ecological environment at large. The Chernobyl disaster is a tragic symbol of this crucial political issue strengthening the vast dissatisfaction and frustration of a general public at large in the Central and Eastern European countries.

The economic and social performance of the system lost its force to legitimize the authoritarian political regimes. The revolutionary source of legitimization vanished earlier. Of course, owing to the character of their installation in the late 1940's, the post-war political regimes in the Central and Eastern Europe had never been democratically legitimized through fair and free elections. The plebiscite type elections with forced (if not falsified) 99% turnouts were superficial legitimization of existing political system.

At the beginning of the 1980's the dramatically delegitimized political system in Poland was challenged by mass civic protest movement, when the "Solidarity" had emerged. That was the strong and widespread revolt against the existing economic and political system. We may say that the revolution from below had started. Although it was then initiated in one single country, it influenced other Central and Eastern European nations. The virus of "Polish disease" was attracted by the societies of other countries – the Soviet Union including – although in Poland herself the "Solidarity" revolt was for time being "neutralized" by the imposition of martial law. The real conflict, however, was not solved. It was put in dormancy. In fact the final solution was only postponed for nearly one decade.

The monocentric authoritarian political system with a monopolistic position of the Communist party and huge bureaucratic governmental machine was unable to solve the economic and social crises which it had been facing with.

All these factors were coming to a head in a long process for at least 10, or even more, years. In the 1989 all these factors had been cumulated in every single country of this region as well as the region at large ripened to changes at the same time.

Earlier in the past we had witnessed the isolated premature revolt against the Communist regime in 1953 (GDR), 1956 (Poland and Hungary), 1968 (Poland and Czechoslovakia), 1970 (Poland) and 1980–81 (Poland)

What is significant for the characteristics of all these popular revolts, mentioned above, which often had been damned as counter-revolutions and were doomed to failure, that is the fact that, broadly speaking, they were always revolutions spontaneously bursting out from below. Sometimes they met support from above – and were taken over by a part of the ruling elite of native Communist leaders of a given single country – and then they were tamed and eventually betrayed (Gomulka in the late 1950's and Gierek in the 1970's in Poland) or stripped of the leaders who were deposed (Dubcek in 1969 in Czechoslovakia) or physically liquidated (Nagy in 1958 in Hungary).

In Poland in 1980–81 the popular spontaneous revolt, being a revolution from below, had constituted their own leaders against the will of ruling Communist elite. So it turned out of control of the governing establishment. The old scenario so well proved in the past of taking over and taming the popular revolt was inapplicable in this case. This is why eventually the extraordinary measures were undertaken.

The material law was imposed in Poland in December 13, 1981 to halt massive popular revolt led by "Solidarity". Maybe this painful decision saved Poland of a civil war or prevented a direct Soviet military intervention which could have seriously challenged the fragile security system in Europe. But at the same time the martial law saved the existing political system which was the main obstacle to real reforms of economic system. It is true that under the umbrella of martial law the important endeavors to reform economic system were done. They were continued after the martial law was lifted. These reforms were pointed in the right direction, but they generated as many difficulties as they solved. One result had been that a number of state-run enterprises used their independence to exploit their monopoly positions to raise prices, but without elevating either the quality or the availability of goods. The mood of disillusions and frustration of the general public revoked with a new force. This dissatisfaction was articulated in two waves of industrial actions which took place in Poland in May and August 1988. Both the ruling elite and the leaders of opposition gathered around Lech Wałęsa. Chairman of outlawed "Solidarity", realized that the way out from economic, social and political deadlock lies in the initiation of genuine negotiations between the government and the opposition.

Gorbachev's official visit paid to Poland in July 1988, and his declaration of the Pole's right to shape their destiny according to their will and aspirations, enabled General W. Jaruzelski to undertake the bold initiative proclaiming an idea of Round Table talks between the governing Polish United Worker's Party and "Solidatity's" Citizen's Committee headed by Lech Wałęsa. This unique – and then unprecedented in this region of Europe – venture was put into effect in February 1989 and ended successfully with the conclusion of a significant political agreement securing the anti-Communist opposition a power sharing within the frameworks of existing political systems and opened the way to participation in semi-contested free parliamentary elections.

In the Spring 1989 this great political event in Poland seemed to be an isolated fact limited only ot the Polish specific and acute political as well as economic situation. But once again the Polish experiences – this time with the Round Table agreement and its far-reaching consequences – soon sparked off allover the Central and Eastern Europe and produced the collapse of the socialist authoritarian political system (or the Communist regimes) in this region.

What was the real meaning and universal significance of the Polish Round Table? We can point out the four substantial distinctive features which became fairly common for Round Tables arranged in other countries (with the exeption of Romania). Therefore in political terms we may say that the essence of a Round Table in the course of events which took place in the most of the Central and Eastern European countries means:

1. a recognition by the ruling Communist parties of an existence of political opposition, i. e. approbation *de facto* of the fundamental principle of pluralistic democracy;
2. a resignation of the monopoly of one party being the cornerstone of the previous political system in these countries;
3. an acceptance of contested free elections;
4. a commitment to peaceful and gradual transition from an autocratic system of government to a democratic one.

The outcome of the Round Table agreements made up the revolution from above which satisfied a revolutionary mood articulated from below and channeled existing protest feelings of revolted population into democratic procedures of parliamentary elections.

Initially the Polish experience with the Round Table contract seemed to be limited to semi-free – or more to the point, semi-competitive – elections and a slow gradual process of transition from autocratic to democratic system of government. However, the results of parliamentary elections of June 4 1989 have produced a remarkable acceleration of political changes.

The reason of this unexpected acceleration was caused by the will of the Polish electorate which expressed overwhelming support for the "Solidarity" Civic Committee's candidates nominated to both houses of bicameral parliament. At the same time the elections results were devastating for the governing Polish United Worker's Party (PUWP). Extremely humiliating was the defeat of the national list of candidates to the Sejm composed of top leaders of the PUWP, including the Prime Minister at that time, and the two then allied parties: United Peasant's Party (UPP) and Democratic Party (DP).

The majority of Polish voters rejected the old guard leadership of the existing then political establishment, although the party reformers and architects of the Round Table agreement were nominated on the national list. It is true that some candidates (like Prime Minister M. Rakowski) failed to obtain only 2% of votes necessary to required overall majority. Nevertheless the voters' verdict was clear. The overall majority of valid cast votes were against them. What is most significant is the fact that among the voters who rejected the national list were not only the "Solidarity" followers but also the members of the PUWP.

The electoral defeat of the national list in Poland is extremely meaningful in the historical perspective. It anticipated downfalls of the Communist top leaders of older generation in other countries of this region.

Some of them, like I. Pozsgay in Hungary – devoted reformer who two years ago seemed to be unchallenged candidate for the post of the President of Republic – were toppled in 1990 parliamentary elections.

In Czechoslovakia it was not only the whole old guard leadership installed by Brezhniev in Prague after the Soviet military intervention in 1968 which had been deposed, but also A. Dubcek – then the Communist leader of the Prague's Spring of 1968 symbolizing the concept of "socialism with human face" – was overrun in competition to the constitutionally important post of the President of Republic by Vaclav Havel, outstanding spokesman of the long established opposition groupings "Charta 77" – i. e. for a long time, in the late 1970's and in the 1980's, a small group of dissidents which ultimately lead in November 1989 to creation of the massive civic movement, the Civic Forum.

In GRD E. Honecker, for the nearly 20 years an autocratic Communist party leader and in fact an executive State President, and his closest aids were ousted from power under the pressure of massive street protest demonstrations and jailed with charges of corruption. His immediate successor, Egon Krenz, was also quickly toppled by the same revolting population of East Germany, demonstrating on the streets. The post-Communist Party of Democratic Socialism called into existence a completely new leadership recruited from grass-roots (with one exception of a provincial leader, Hans Modrow). They saved their position in the political life of East Germany thanks to the electoral law excluding a personal choice in voting for party lists.

In Bulgaria the situation was somewhat different. Although T. Zhivkow, the oldest pundit in the Eastern Europe being in power since 1954, was ousted in similar conditions to East Germany and jailed with accusations for abuse of power and corruption, the new political leadership emerged from younger generation of the Communist party activists of pro-reforms orientation. For the time being they controlled the situation owing to the weakness of Bulgarian opposition. Eventually – after the June 1990 parliamentary elections, which were formally won by the re-named communist Bulgarian Socialist Party – the ex-Communist leader, Petar Mladenov, who ousted T. Zhivkov, was forced to resign from the post of the President of Republic.

In Romania N. Ceuasescu was overthrown in dramatic conditions of a framed up popular uprising and executed after unfair trail being outside universally accepted standards of due process of law. That was the typical blood feud of the Communist organizers of coup d'état. Up to now it seems be that they still control political system of post-Ceausescu Romania. The situation in Romania is, however, very ambiguous and difficult to predict what will happen in the near future. But the fact is that the old hatred political leadership was ousted in bloody revolution. These circumstances sharply contrasted with democratic procedure of rejection of ancient regime top politicians in Poland during the 1989 parliamentary elections.

The shocking defeat of the national list was a grievous electoral setback of the PUWP which ultimately decided in January 1990 in its self-dissolution. This important fact, however, challenged the fragile Round Table agreement. The very concept of a gradual, evolutionary transition process to a democratic form of parliamentary type of government was overtaken by events. This is the reason why in October 1990 W. Jaruzelsky offered his resignation from the post of President of Republic opening the way to universal and direct free elections of a new State President.

The very essence of the Polish Round Table agreement was the political contract concluded between the PUWP, which had ruled Poland for 45 years, practically as a monopolist (along with subordinate, allied parties: UPP and DP) and the opposition represented by "Solidarity" (or strictly speaking the Civic Committee tied to L. Wałęsa). What the contract in fact said was that the PUWP in coalition with the other parties, was to continue to govern the country, while the independent deputies that would be elected (according to the pre-election contract they could make up no more than 35% of seats in the Sejm) would legally take on the functions of a parliamentary opposition. In the second house of parliament, the Senate – elected without any limitations imposed by pre-election contract – the opposition could attain a majority, but then again, the powers of this newly created house were significantly restricted in the Constitution. The ruling PUWP hoped that it would gain (together with its coalition partners) at least 25% of seats in the Senate. As for the Sejm, the expectations were that the candidates supported by the Civic Committee would get less than 35% of the seats.

The results of the elections on June 4, 1989 completely crossed out these illfounded calculations – leaving everybody surprised, even the opposition leaders too. All the 35% seats in the Sejm allocated to opposition went to candidates of the Civic Committee, i. e. people rallied under the Solidarity banner and blessed by Lech Wałęsa. In the Senate Civic Committee candidates won 99% of seats, while the PUWP and the entire then ruling coalition failed to secure at least one seat in the second chamber of parliament. This was a landslide victory for the opposition – namely for "Solidarity" – and at the same time a devastating defeat for the ruling party and its previous coalition partners.

In effect, the shaky construction of the Round Table agreement broke down – it failed the test of free elections understood as the expression of the nation's unconstrained will passed in the fair procedure of universal voting. If the basic goal of the Round Table was to be maintained – a transition to a pluralistic parliamentary democracy – then it was impossible not to respect the will of the electorate. After some hesitation "Solidarity", as a coalition of oppositional forces, had to take on the burden of responsibility for governing the country. The government dominated by ministers supported by "Solidarity", with the non-Communist Prime Minister in a head, was nominated in Eastern Europe for the first time since the Second World War.

In other words, in the Summer 1989 two crucial events of significant consequences for whole Central and Eastern Europe took place in Poland.

Firstly, for the first time since the Bolshevik Revolution of 1917 the ruling Communist party conceded defeat in elections and acknowledged in this way the essence of rules of the parliamentary democracy.

Secondly, for the first time since the 1948 the Soviet Union recognized the non-Communist government in the region being its sphere of domination and interests. That was the practical test of earlier declared by Gorbachev, during his visit to Poland in 1988, renunciation of the Brezhnev's doctrine. These two crucial events open the way for rapid and significant political as well as institutional and constitutional changes in rest countries in the Central and Eastern Europe.

At the end of the 1980's the very basis of the system of government established on the principle of monopoly of the Communist party backed by the Soviet Union was shaken in this region of Europe from the Baltic (including Estonia, Latvia and Lithuania) to the Balkans (not excluding Albania at least).

That is the beginning of the final stage of collapse of the regime of real socialism not only in given particular country but also in the whole Soviet Block, i. e. in the Russian Empire.

In his book "The Grand Failure" professor Zbigniew Brzezinski has delineated the probable stages of the retreat from communism.[3] According to him this inevitable historical process may be predicted in following phases:

Phase 1: Communist Totalitarianism

In this phase Communist party controls political system and political system controls society and economy. A probable transition to phase 2 could be pursued by succession struggles which divide the ruling Communist party and increase societal pressures for socioeconomic concessions.

Phase 2: Communist Authoritarianism

The Communist party controls the political system but the emerging civil society contests it and political supremacy in the economy is on the defensive. A probable transition to phase 3 could be most likely by top-level coup in response to regime fears of rising social pressures. It is possible, however, that in some exceptional cases there would be direct transition to phase 4 or alternatively, if changed blocked, systemic fragmentation or repressive attempt to return to phase 1.

Phase 3: Post-Communist Authoritarianism

In this phase an autoritarian regime is based largely on national appeal but still the ritualized ideology exists. At the same time civil society becomes political society and political supremacy over economy is in broad retreat. Transition to phase 4 would be most likely turbulent in final stage of phase 3, though peaceful evolution in some exceptional cases may be possible: alternatively, if the change blocked, systemic fragmentation will appear.

Phase 4: Post-Communist Pluralism

In this phase the political system is becoming pluralistic.

This epitome of the phases in the retreat from communism was conceptualized in the summer of 1988, i. e. one year before the Autumn of Nations of 1989 came to being. The course of events in years 1989–1991 in Central and Eastern Europe has verified and corrected this theoretical concept. Looking at the political, social and economic processes which took place in the passed 20–25 years in this region I would like to propose another theoretical concept of phases (or stages) in the retreat from real socialism (or communism) and transition to a new form of government and new economic system. I distinguish the following 5 phases of this historical process:

Phase 1: Stagnation of political and economic systems.

This phase is characterized by stagnation of political life and lack of any institutional changes in the system of government associated with the alienation of ever since old aged Communist party leadership being for decades at the top levels of power. (Only one exception is Poland.) Immobility of political system comes into play accompanied by ritualized ideological rhetoric style of performing power. Destalinization was superficial. The public terror and omnipotence of secrete police were curbed indeed, but ruling Communist party oligarchy was still using instruments of repressions.

There was a lack of economic achievement being a consequence of the exhaustion of the sources of extensive strategy of development as well as of the highly bureaucratic system of management of national economy. Lack of substantial records in running a national economy halted the economic growth and social progress as well as stopped the process of improvement of standard of living of population. The social peace, however, was still maintained owing to the allowance of wide strata of the population being beneficiaries of social and economic promotion offered by socialist revolution. The general passivity of population was also strengthened by strong layers of the subservient (or paternalistic) type of political culture. At the same time the citizen's political passivity was coerced by a lack of real alternatives as well as by hopeless active resistance and unsuccsessful rebellion against existing regime. No signs of effective support from Western governments (respecting Yalta's post-war order in Europe) to revolting people (GRD in 1953, Hungary in 1956 and Czechoslovakia in 1968) consolidated Eastern Europians in their submission to the existing system.

This relative social peace was also the product of some kind of social contract according to which employees accepted very low wages for low productive work and employer (the State authorities) approved low productivity and tolerated corruption in return for passive political attitudes of employees and citizens. Polish sociologists named this phenomenon as "trained passivity". This widespread "trained passivity" conduced to public climate favorable for social pathologies and weakening popular engagement in political and economic changes.

In this phase, however, first signals of the population's disillusionment were coming into play with the existing socio-economic system articulated in mostly spontaneous social unrest (mainly of vindictive character). Tiny dissidents groups were at that time rather isolated in inspiring political protest actions.

Visible atrophy of the revolutionary legitimization of political system and decline of the legitimization, based on economic records and social progress of the system, had started in this phase.

Phase 2: Half hearted and ineffective reforms of the system

Deepening stagnation and immobility of the political system made impossible any real and effective reforms of economy and political life being a response to growing challenges from the social and economic environment. Abortive or/and half-hearted attempts to reform economic system within frameworks of the political system of real socialism were ineffective. They were boycotted by the bureaucracy of State and Communist party apparatus as well as ignored by general public. At the same time these reforms generated more social and economic problems and difficulties than they solved.

However, these half-hearted economic reforms and inconsistency in their implementation, had splitted the internal logic of the socio-economic system from inside and increased its inefficiency. Concessions made under pressure from vindictive worker's demands for higher wages winded up invisible spiral of inflation. But once concession was made in one economic field it generated further social pressure for new concessions which were not only limited to socio-economic sphere, but also dealing with political area.

Accruing structural economic crises provoked discords (although invisible for general public) within the ruling Communist party establishment: pragmatic reformers versus conservative dogmatists. The latter defended status quo and were usually strongly backed by the hardliners and dogmatists within the Soviet leadership.

The widespread public dissatisfaction with the existing socio-economic system became more visible as the standard of living and quality of life had been deteriorating, when at the same time aspirations for better life were growing. Symptoms of structural economic crisis were justified by ruling leaders as "objective difficulties of the growth" and caused by a lack of elaborateness of workers, disintegration of societal bonds as well as by negative effects of speculation and black market.

The activity of dissidents had become more and better organized. But anti-systemic oppostion still lacked broad support in the society. There were yet tiny groups of intellectuals. This nucleus opposition was intensively intimidated and persecuted by the secret police, which did not provoke, however, wide societal protests at that time. That was only the beginning of the creation of political alternatives and of self-emancipation of the society. The young generation ever since was rejecting the system of values of the real socialism.

In official propaganda appeared clearly dysfunctional character of revolutionary rhetorics. Dying official revolutionary Marxist-Leninist ideology has been substituted by appeals to nationalism (or by stimulation of ethnical chauvinism) and to the opportunistic necessity of acceptance of the post-war Yalta's order in Europe.

Phase 3: Full stalemate of political system

This phase is characterized by deepening decay of national economy and sharp decline of the standard of living and quality of life of the population. Half-hearted and abortive economic reforms were generating as many new difficulties as they solved. The old economic system had not been working already, but a new one was not yet introduced, too. Aggravating afflictions of a devastation of the ecological environment became more and more visible. This conduced to increasing discontent of general public and open broad popular protest actions. A stronger wave of protests against corruption and privileges of ruling Communist elite was articulated. Dissidents' activity became intensified and better organized: so, institutionalized anti-systematic opposition came to existence on the political scene.

In the ruling establishment came to a head an increasing pressure for changes articulated by reformers within the Communist party elite provoking at the same time a growing resistance from conservatives' and hardliners' circles. Failure of making reprisals against growing anti-systemic opposition as well as unsuccessful use of coercion became evident. The martial law imposed in Poland in 1981 is a one example and the abortive coup d'état in the Soviet Union in 1991 is another case of these hopeless efforts to restore the old regime. The organized and institutional anti-systemic opposition came out stronger and had obtained ever since forceful support in the society.

All sources of legitimization of regime of the real socialism disappeared. Reformers within the Communist party establishment came to conclusions that their efforts to reform the system are fruitless because the system of real socialism, as such, is unreformable.

In an ultimate result the final and complete stalemate became inevitable. In practice both the economic system and political system were totally blocked: the Communist party lost ability to govern and the anti-systemic opposition was not yet ready to take power.

Phase 4: Resignation of the Communist party hegemony and negotiation with the opposition for power-sharing

Within the Communist party power elite the hardliners are forced to give up their position, and pragmatic reformers had accepted the necessity of negotiations with leaders on institutionalized opposition on ways and means of peaceful and gradual transition from the old authoritarian system to a parliamentary democracy and free-market economy. Communist party leaders were looking for agreement on power-sharing with the opposition. That was in practice a crucial decision of the resignation of the dogma of the leading (hegemonic) role of the Communist party both in the political system and in the economic system. This in fact meant the acceptance of the free elections and of the creation of a multiparty system (multipartisan politics).

The society at large was generally not prepared to such radical changes. The long established "trained passivity" was strongly dominating. In free elections, however, were articulated attitudes and voting behaviors of protest, but also some groups were frightened of unpredicted changes. This part of the electorate was voting for the Communist, or post-Communist, party. In its majority, people are not used to the mechanisms of free market-economy. At the same time the old system of centrally planned and command economy became in complete disarray causing a disastrous situation in daily life of the population. The opposition resolutely blamed the old regime for this state of affairs gaining the overwhelming support in parliamentary elections.

Phase 5: The Communist party is pull out from power in democratic procedure

In free parliamentary elections the Communist (or post-Communist) party was defeated and has been pushed down to the role of a parliamentary opposition and forced to accept a transfer of power to non-Communist government (GDR, Hungary, Czechoslovakia and to some extent in Poland) or to approve various models of transitional cohabitation with former opposition (Bulgaria and to some extent Poland). Romania, where the post-Communists saved their power, is an exception in this field.

Substantial constitutional and institutional political reforms started to be performed. These reforms are directed into building up the foundations of multiparty parliamentary democracy. Parliament being elected in free elections is treated as a constitutional convention and is charged with preparation of fundamentally new Constitution.

The first stage of consolidation of new post-authoritarian multiparty system is coming to a head.

A lot of new political parties have been spontaneously created. Majority of them are rather fringe tiny meaningless groupings.

The most important of them are civic movements organized by former anti-systemic opposition, like the Civic Committees "Solidarity" in Poland, Civic Forum and Public against Violence in Czechoslovakia, Hungarian Democratic Forum, Free Democrats and Young Fee Democrats in Hungary, Union of Democratic Forces in Bulgaria. All of them are the rainbow coalition of former oppositional groupings from the ex-Communist dissidents to the resolute liberal and conservative devoted adversaries of the communist regime. The National Salvation Front in Romania is a similar rainbow coalition, but dominated by the former Communists. Only in GRD such a civic movement was rather weak and performed without significant electoral successes. These civic movements came into being as result of the popular protest against the political parties, as such, what is nowadays a characteristic feature of political life in Central and Eastern Europe.

With the only exceptions of the Smallholders in Hungary and the Polish Peasant Party in Poland, the old historical political parties are rather weak and meaningless in the political scene in these countries.

The right-wing nationalistic parties have appeared, especially in Yugoslav republics and in Slovakia. The green, or ecological parties are evidently weak.

The former Communist parties are in process of transformation to socialdemocratic one. They are proclaiming an abandonment of Marxist-Leninist ideology and are declaring their accommodation to multiparty democracy and free-market (or mixed) economy.

In this phase reforms and changes in political and constitutional dimensions seem to be more impressive than in the economy and social relationships.

In the constitutional (or rather institutional) dimension we have to mention following important changes wich were performed in the past recent months in Central and Eastern Europe.

1. resignation in the constitutions of clauses guaranteeing in legal terms the hegemonic position of a one party (i. e. leading and guiding role of the Communist party);
2. proclamation in the constitutions of a multiparty system patterned on the Western-style democracy;
3. introduction of a new electoral laws based, by and large, on proportional representation;
4. deletion from constitutions of socialist symbols (official names of the state, national emblems or flags);
5. change of constitutional provisions concerning the domination of state ownership;
6. introduction of a presidency instead of a formal collegiate head of state;
7. dissolution of the old and omnipotent secret police;
8. introduction for new institutional guarantees of civil rights;
9. reform of local government and performing of free elections to local councils;
10. in multinational states (Yugoslavia and Czechoslovakia as well as latter on) the very concept of the old highly centralized structure of State is at stake and searching for a new form of confederation is on an agenda.

All of these political and constitutional changes are reflecting the process of profound and rapid acceleration in transformation of the political system and their institutional frameworks.

The most important constitutional change of crucial significance is the deletion of articles which proclaimed a leading position of the ruling Communist party. That was in the past a cornerstone of monocentric authoritarian political system. This principle, named as an imperturbable foundation of the whole socio-political system of real socialism, led up to totalitarian deviations. In nearly all constitutions of the Central and Eastern countries the legal principle of one party monopoly has been dropped out.

It is not only that the constitutional clauses sanctioned the monopolistic position of Communist party were deleted from the constitution. What is more, the new constitutional provisions proclaiming a multiparty system have been enacted. So the cornerstone of the democratic system of government was formally declared in all of these countries. The realities, however, are more complicated.

After forty years of one party rule there is a vacuum in an organized multiparty political infrastructure. Although a lot of new political parties has been created, most of them are in fact nucleus political groupings at least. It is difficult to treat them as real modern political parties which are well established in society and with clear programs and ideological foundations. Particularly this is the case of Poland. However the latest parliamentary elections in Poland have produced a clearer picture of the differentiated identity of the main political parties and scale – although very weak yet – of their influence and support in the Polish electorate.

In Poland old communist Polish United Worker's Party disappeared from the political scene in 1990. In place of it initially two post-communist parties were created: the Socialdemocracy of the Republic of Poland and the Polish Union of Socialdemocracy. The latter one disappeared from the political arena after one year and her leader has been defeated in the last parliamentary elections. The post-Communist social democrats (i. e. the Socialdemocracy of the Republic Poland) are desperately fighting for their existence in the public life in this country. Their fairly well performance in the latest parliamentary elections can not be treated as a success. They got only 1,3 million of votes, which is 5,2% of the electorate at large and 300.000 votes less than gained the year before as the candidate of the post-Communist Left Alliance in the presidential elections.

But at the same time in the second half of 1990 the civic movement "Solidarity" had been splitted. The parliamentary representation of "Solidarity" – the Parliamentary Civic Club – had been fragmented on at least 8 separate fractions. In the latest parliamentary elections participated 6 post-Solidarity political parties: Democratic Union, Center Alliance, Liberal Democratic Congress, Party of Christian Democrats, "Solidarity" of Labor, and Democratic Social Movement. The non-Solidarity anti-Communist opposition was represented in the elections by two political parties: national conservative Catholic Action and more populistic right-wing Confederation of Independent Poland.

In the Autumn 1990 the fiercely contested electoral campaign for Presidency and political struggle between Prime Minister T. Mazowiecki (who created afterwards the Democratic Union) and L. Wałęsa (supported by Center Alliance and Christian Civic Movement, i. e. the predecessor of the Catholic Action) was a clear evidence of the end of the united "Solidarity" movement. That was an inevitable and expected event. In Poland the fragmentation of a new party system is visible evidence of a new phase of the development of the period of post-Communist transition to a future stable political system.

This new phase seems to be characterized by splits within the former anti-

Communist opposition movements and fragmentation of political scene. This is proved not only by the outcome of the latest parliamentary elections in Poland.

In Bulgaria in the second free elections indeed the anti-Communist Union of Democratic Forces has won, but with the very narrow margin and has no overall majority in the parliament. This lack of success is caused to a large extent by splitting groups which left the UDF and run for elections separately.

In Czechoslovakia the Czech Civic Forum has been splitted into two separate parties as well the Slovak former protest movement the Public Against Violence, is divided also into two hostile political groupings. These splits are aggravated by the serious national conflict between Czechs ans Slovaks, which put the very existence of the one federal state in jeopardy. It is very likely that the forthcoming parliamentary elections scheduled for the Summer 1992 will bring a fragmentation of the party system similar to the current Polish case.

In Hungary for time being the situation seems to be fairly stable. But the former anti-Communist opposition had splitted earlier. Although the governing coalition is still based on the solid parliamentary majority, the cleavages within this coalition are visible.

In Romania the ruling post-Communist Front of National Salvation is facing more serious internal conflicts reflecting the dangerous social and economic tensions in this country.

The tragic course of current events in Yugoslavia produced real civil war and disastrous economic chaos with gloomy perspectives for the quick solution.

The politics in the former GDR is exceptional owing to the unique situation of the East territory of Germany. In fact the new party system which emerged during electoral campaign and has been confirmed in parliamentary, local and regional elections – and at least after the all-German parliamentary elections – is a copy of the West German party system.

Of course this new phase of transition from the socialist authoritarian regime to the post-Communist political system is characterized by weakness of the party systems and political fragile stability or even lack of stability. But the main feature of this phase is the general disillusion of the lack of visible progress and improvement of the standard of living. This mood of disillusion is strengthened by anxiety of social insecurity. So, some kind of nostalgia of former real socialism is arising. At the same time the early stage of capitalist economy is producing enormous corruption combined with the alienation and arrogance of the new political elite.

The privatization is producing the inequalities when the majority of the people are used to the socialist concept of social justice and egalitarianism. Also people are not metnally prepared to accept the restriction on the social benefits developed under previous regime.

In another words there is a problem of choice between the concept of "Sozialmarktwirtschaft" or classical liberal free-market economy.

Another legacy of history – and strengthened by Communist period – is a nationalism and populism which may be the main threat to the fragile yet democratic structures of political life and a great obstacle for successful performance of bold economic reforms.

But the main legacy of the authoritarian political system of the last four decades is a lack of an established genuine multiparty system which would be a solid guarantee of a working parliamentary democracy.

Generally speaking the whole process of transition to the democratic political system and way of life is in jeopardy.

Notes

1 Garton Ash, Timothy: "We The People. The Revolution of 89 witnessed in Warsaw, Budapest, Berlin and Prague", Granta Books, Cambridge 1990, p. 78.
2 Tearing Down the Curtain. The People's Revolution Europe (reported) by a team from The Observer. Ed. by Nigel Hawkes, Hodder & Stoughton, London – Sydney – Auckland – Toronto 1990 (Preface).
3 Brzezinski, Zbigniew: "The Grand Failure. The Birth and Death of Communism in the Twentieth Century", Macdonald & Co. (publishers) Ltd, London & Sydney 1990, p. 225.

Contribution to the edited volumes

The recognition and putting into effects of economic and social rights in Poland, in: "La reconnaissance et la mise en œuvre des droits économiques et sociaux. Actes du Colloque internationale de droit comparé. Bruxelles, 14–17 septembre 1967". Centre Interuniversitaire de Droit Comparé, Bruxelles 1972, s. 29.

Political and institutional changes in the management of the socialist economy – the Polish case, in: "East-West relations and future of Eastern Europe – Politics and Economics", eds. M. Bornstein, Z. Gitelman & W. Zimmermana, Allan & Unwin, London 1981, s. 31.

Il sistema dei Partiti. La dinamica delle transformazioni, in: "La societa parallela. Religione, resistenza e opposizione nella Polonia contemporanea", pod. red. Enzo Pace, Milano 1984, s. 56.

Demokracja i wybory, Raport z badań "Opinie Polaków: Jesień '85", Koncepcja i redakcja tomu oraz autorstwo 6 ciu rozdziałów (113 stron) i współautorstwo jednego rozdziału (85 stron), Uniwersytet Warszawski, Warszawa 1989.

Przesłanki ustanowienia Rzecznika Praw Obywatelskich w Polsce, w: "Rzecznik Praw Obywatelskich", pod. red. Leszka Garlickiego, Instytut Wydawniczy Związków Zawodowych, Warszawa 1989, s. 16.

States of Emergency in the Polish Constitutional Law, in: Rapports polonais présentés au treizième Congrès international de Droit comparé. Ossolineum 1990, s. 12.

Polish Party System in Making in Poland of the 1990's, in: Democracy and the Rule of Law (Demokrati & rettsstat: Innlegg pa norsk-polsk seminar i Warszawa, 4. Juni 1990), Royal Norwegian Ministry of Foreign Affairs, Oslo 1991, s. 10.

Articles in professional journals and papers

Wybory do Sejmu i Senatu 1989 r. (Wstępne refleksje), "Państwo i Prawo" 1989, nr. 8., s. 12.

La nouvelle institution du Défenseur de Droits civiques en Pologne, w: Droit polonais contemporain, nr. 1/2 (77/78), Ossolineum 1988, s. 14.

The Polish Transitional Constitution of 1989/90, referat na Conference on Constitutionalism and the Transition to Democracy in Eastern Europe, in: Pécs, czerwiec 18–20, 1990, s. 18.

Stages of retreat from real socialism in Central and Eastern Europe, referat na międzynarodową konferencję październik 26–27, 1990, s. 27.

Imperfect or Foundation Free Elections – referat na III Polsko-Jugosłowiańskie Seminarium Politologiczne, Zakopane, 11–16 listopada 1990, s. 8.

Political Parties and the Electoral System. The Polish Perspective, Paper prepared for the Norwegian-Polish conference: "The Role of the Constitution in Changing Society", Oslo, 14–16 May, 1991, s. 23.

A New Party System in the Making in Poland of the 1990's – in: "Politische Partizipation und Demokratie in Polen und Westdeutschland", hrsg. v. G. Meyer & F. Ryszka, Warsaw/Warschau 1991.

Ludmiła Dziewięcka-Bokun

From Communism to Democracy: the Polish Revolution of 1989 and its Aftermath

A model reconstruction of the situation which the postsocialist societies have to face at present, in view of the lack of a theory, explaining the transformations in the direction of a parliamentary democracy and a market economy, requires framing generalizing hypotheses. Their starting point and verification basis is an analysis of the situation in particular countries in Mid- and Eastern Europe. The subject of this paper is the presentation of the most important consequences of the 1989 revolution for the process of transformations in the Polish political system. The processes and phenomena of the Polish political life which seem to be common (or similar) to other postsocialist European countries were recognized to be of more importance than others.

The common characteristics of political systems and structures emerging in the countries of the Eastern bloc is their instability. It assumes different forms: reshuffles of leaders, changeability of alliances and transitoriness for legal solutions. In some countries it overlaps with a complex of nationalistic issues, which only strengthen the instability, but often undermine the progress achieved in transformations.

In Poland of the nineties the strongest indication of this instability is the course of the fight for power, which takes place in a personal, rather than in a systemic context. Personal rivalry dominates over the endeavour to adjust and establish basic structures and rules of the system. The personalization of the Polish political scene led to a sequence of political and systemic actions: presidential elections – parliamentary elections – the passing of Constitution; which further remove the prospect of obtaining a relatively permanent political stability.

The Polish political system, after the historical changes in 1989, entered a stage of unsteady balance, for which the greatest danger is posed by increasing manifestations of a political chaos. A noticeable erosion of all authorities and norms, and even of the whole legal system can be observed. The inefficiency of the administrative state apparatus increases, which (not only for financial reasons) is unable to cope with solving basic social problems. Thus favourable conditions are created for anarchistic behaviour and populist demagogy. In a situation where the material conditions are getting worse and conflicts within the Solidarity are growing, many organizations and groups resort to demagogical devices. This tendency was particularly strongly manifested during the campaign preceding the presidential elections. The example of Tymińsky forcibly indicated the political chances of a populist orientation.

The use made of the populist attitudes of various social groups speeded up the decline of the authority, not only of the government, but of the political power as such. Currently one also notices the undermining of governmental programmes from populist standpoints. Before the approaching parliamentary elections many groups are trying to turn social discontent to their profit, formulating visions of an easy improvement in the people's material conditions.

Another feature characterizing the changes in postsocialist societies is a lack of new strong political structures. Their non-existence is, in a way, natural stage of the transition period. However, in Poland's present situation, it acquires a special meaning. The accomplished variant of a "revolution from the top" resulted in a state of "systemic void", that is, a relatively permanent situation, where the basic structures of the existing system had disintegrated, but this disintegration was not followed by an emergence of such social forces, which could, in a short time, create the structures of a new system. As a result, the postsocialist system lacks many constructional elements in the spheres of controlling production (property relations), political relations and ideological consensus. According to P. Marciniak, the "systemic void" emerged in the wake of the disintegration, and not, as it is often presented in political science studies, of the overthrow of socialism.[1] In Poland the opposition took over the power from the representatives of the socialist regime, who were no longer able to perform their functions efficiently, rather than overthrew them.[2]

An important element of this void was created by the international context. Socialist societies, as constituent parts of a sub-global system, were heavily dependent on the Soviet Union. A breaking of this dependence on the one hand afforded possibilities to start a process of changes in the system, but on the other hand, made it necessary for the postsocialist countries to find their place anew in the system of international relations. This strongly determines the adoption of a distinctly West-oriented development strategy.

One of the factors hindering the creation of a new political order is the lack of efficient and sufficiently numerous managing elites. There is also the unsolved problem, to what extent can and should the old administrative apparatus of the former elites be used in creating a new state- and self-government system. No general recipes are available in this respect, and no experiences to rely on. It might be probably helpful to take an unemotional look at a similar process which took place in the fifties in West Germany.

Another increasingly significant obstacle to the process of systemic transformations in Poland is a continuous decline of collective activity and a growing social frustration. A characteristic symptom of the former was the low turn-out at the self-governmental elections (42%) and at the presidential elections in 1990 (1st round – 60%, 2nd round – 53%). Confidence in institutions of political life is also decreasing. Opinion polls from the first quarter of 1991 indicate only some growth in confidence towards the military forces and the police, which is sometimes interpreted as an expression of feelings of insecurity. Studies conducted by the Public Opinion Polls Centre on June, 17th an 18th this year showed a decline of sympathies for President Lech Wałęsa by much as 14%, and a corresponding rise by 10% for his opponents. These results placed Wałęsa on the seventh place in the Polish political scene.[3]

A substitute object of social aggression became the "communist nomenclature", and particularly the so called "nomenclature companies". The actual extent of the illegal amassing of wealth by the "nomenclature" managing staff at the cost of State property, harmful to the social interest, bears no relation to the society's strong feelings on the subject.[4] It is a typical example of a substitute theme, prompted by politicians, which, however, finds its breeding ground in public feelings and attitudes shaped by material inconveniences connected with transformations in the system.

The costs of transforming a socialist economy into a market economy are much higher than was thought at the beginning. A rapid deterioration of the material conditions of life of the majority of the population resulted in directing social energy and activity to defend the living standards.

The social frustration is all the more acute, as the objective lowering of the level of material life conditions overlapped with unfulfilled hopes concerning the economic transformations. Therefore it must be stressed that public support for the first non-communist government was mainly based on symbols, not on definite social interests, and it reflected hopes and notions, not attitudes resulting from knowledge and experience. Support built on such fragile foundations was bound to dwindle. Its reconstruction is hindered by conflicts within the "Solidarity" which are for the most part obscure and incomprehensible for the majority of Poles, and which entail inevitable loss of authority of all concerned.

I would like to supplement the above remarks presenting selected aspects of transformations in the Polish system in the beginning of the nineties with a description of the state of the postsocialist social consciousness – a structure rarely taken into account in political science analyses examining the effects of systemic revolutions in countries of Mideastern Europe.

The democratic, free-market social order emerging in East Europe took over from the previous formation the heritage of peoples consciousness. This heritage, shaped by functioning many years in the totalitarian system, constitutes an important obstacle to the process of changes – an obstacle mostly ignored by politicians.

One of the main differences between a totalitarian and a democratic system is that the former requires the individual to be conformist, whereas the latter demands activity and initiative. In the former, a centrally programmed scenario of everybody's life prevents the individual from assuming responsibility. The essence of the latter is the individual's freedom to realize himself on personal and social planes. To achieve this freedom one has to possess certain abilities and skills, such as the ability to negotiate, to foresee the consequences of one's actions and the ability to think in rational terms.

The rebuilding of social mentality – the unconscious and the hardest to change – is a problem in itself in the process of democratization in post-communist countries. The main characteristics of totalitarian mentality are:

1. involuntary treatment of reality as dependent on external factors, which is at present accompanied by feelings of insecurity and anxiety, fear of changes and aggression for the sake of protecting a secure status quo (which lie at the roots of opposition against all radical initiative);

2. an understanding of freedom as a state with no discipline and no regulations, which for some people constitutes the ultimate value of democracy: "If changes do not bring a feeling of security they should at least ensure freedom, in which there are no limitations." (A. Świda-Zięba)[5]

3. A dichotomous picture of the world based on a clear–cut distinction between good and bad, which makes it impossible to formulate heterogeneous opinions, and reflects an inability to accept qualitative differentiation.

The consciousness of being a significant member of society, and a sense of rationality are slowly evolving from new experiences. At the moment, in the process of building a democracy, the post-totalitarian mentality is an important factor in creating a new social reality. It is all the more paradoxical, because just now, freed from the shackles of the system which created it, this mentality has all the possibilities of unrestrained expansion. Thus the problems of the transition period are not only connected with institutional reconstruction, but with creating facts by the mentality.

The changes which started in 1989 under the banner of pluralization of the political system aim at remodelling the institutions in the spheres of articulation and mediation of class- and group interests. Dissimilarity of interests between peasantry, the working class and the newborn middle class, beside the interests of other social and professional groups, in an unquestionable social fact. There can be no doubt about the political importance of the fact that this dissimilarity inevitably generates conflicts.

Democracy – one of the best verified methods of controlling social conflicts – together with market economy, which prevents the "politization" of conflicts emerging from economic discrepancies, is the object of all national revolutions in Central Europe. The shape of democracy in Poland will be determined by the formative process of a system of articulation, representation and negotiation of interests, among other factors. The process is not far advanced yet, and additionally hindered by personal rivalry among the members of the present political elite over positions in the future parliament and central administration. There is a growing number of small political parties, representing mainly the political ambitions of their leaders and of a narrow circle of related persons. An average Pole does not trust in any those parties and prefers to be an observer rather than a participant. The lack of any social willingness to undertake local party work bears witness to that. A well-developed staging of democratic politics is an element in the complicated game for public opinion.[6]

The electoral campaign struggle favours pluralization, and as such is a natural and desirable process. Its outcome is, firstly a number of political programmes, and, secondly, their adherents. A peculiarity of the present Polish political scene is the multitude and weakness of parties and the similarity of their programmes, such as for instance a universal acceptance of the general goals of the present revolution (freedom, democracy, market economy), and a lack of differentiated outlines specifying how to accomplish these goals.

Meanwhile there is an urgent, objective need to create and stimulate the development of structural relations between the articulation of economic interests and their representation within the framework of the political system. When this relation is missing, the process of democratic transformations is seriously impeded, as A. Rychard maintains. At present, as the governmental programme is being implemented, it seems to mobilize and structuralize the interests which are antagonistic to it, instead of animating those interest groups which benefit from its implementation.[7]

The weak and inadequate representation system of social interests – one of the most significant causes of the defeat of socialism – remains a valid structural reason for widespread attitudes of passive expectation (wait-and-see policy) and anarchic defensive behaviour in Polish society. It also poses a major threat to the "Polish way from totalitarianism to democracy".

The state of consciousness and social attitudes, and the lack of institutional changes in the sphere of interest mediation adequate to the adopted direction of the transformation may uncontrollably lead a variety of populist autocracy.[8]

This threat is all the more real, as in the transition period between the old and the new system the discrepancy between the necessity of stabilizing actions and the indispensability of the transformation movement manifests itself most dramatically. Changes in the system are accompanied by mutually overlapping changes due to the existing state of affairs. The above-mentioned discrepancy is often overlooked when discussing the comparative merits of a shock-strategy versus a strategy of gradual changes.[9]

Unawareness of its existence is the reason why many actions which aim at accelerating the changes, in fact slow them down.

In view of the underdevelopment of political system infrastructure in all post-socialist countries, there is an urgent need to create an efficient negotiational mechanism. Experiences made in the previous system and mechanically transferred to present conditions bring about a situation in which the society forces the government to intervene in real processes. Thus the government inevitably has to take sides in conflicts of interests, instead of being an arbitrator who helps to solve them.

The situation is further complicated by the fact, that the government receives no backing from the Polish Parliament. The balance of parliamentary forces is fluid and it has not been reflected in the constitution of the government. At the same time, the arrangement of economic interests is poorly reflected by the composition and actions of the current Parliament. As a result many groups still prefer exerting pressure directly on the government by protest actions instead of subjecting their demands to parliamentary mechanism.[10] This fact can be partially explained by a peculiar structure and status of the "contract-Parliament". In the fundamentally changed political circumstances of 1991 the Parliament, which emerged as a result of the "round table agreement" became, in a way, a "prisoner" of the government and of the governmental elites. Its social legitimacy was too weak for it to oppose the government. Thus it passed the bills exactly as they were presented by the government, confining itself to a public expression of criticism. This became the basic reason for such strange cases, when a bill disapproved of was finally passed with a vast majority voting in its favour (e. g. 1991 budget bill).

Relations between central government organs became even more complicated after the general elections, when Lech Wałęsa was elected President. His electoral campaign was directed against the previous government's policies, but once in office, he appointed a Cabinet whose economic programme is a continuation rather than a basic alteration.

Those and other examples of political phenomena in Poland prove the necessity of a specific kind of political book-keeping where the balance of social gains and losses will be the subject of negotiations between the basic of political forces.

Maybe the drawing of this balance ought to become the subject of a next social contract, as A. Michnik postulates.[11] The historic compromise reached by the basic political forces in Poland in April 1989 has already lost its social legitimacy. A new one seems unattainable, mainly because of the persistent political struggles. However, when the actors and the onlookers get more tired, they might want to establish their own rules of the game in the difficult art of democracy, or else someone might impose his own scenario, called dictatorship. In a transition period both elements are usually present, in periodically changing proportions.

Notes

1 Marciniak, P., Niestabilność i warianty rozwoju sytuacji (Instability and Variants of Situational Development), in: Rola i funkcjonowanie instytucji samorządowych w systemie politycznym (Role and Functioning of Self-government Institutions in the Political System), U. W. COM SNP, TWWP, Warszawa 1989, ch. 6, p. 231.

2 See: Łagodna agonia socjalizmu. Mechanizmy polityczne życia społecznego w Polsce w latach 80 (The Gentle Agony of Socialism. Political Mechanisms of Polish Social Life in the Eighties), ed. by Hausner, J., and Klementowicz, T. (xeroxed tapescript).
See also: Dziewięcka-Bokun, L., The Reform of Political System in Poland in the Eighties; paper presented at the XIVth IPSA World Congress, Washington D. C. 1988.

3 After: Janowski, Andrzej: Czy Lech Wałęsa rozwiąże Sejm? (Is Lech Wałęsa Going to Dissolve the Parliament?), in: Prawo i Życie, N° 26/1991.

4 Skalski, E., Para w gwizdek czyli panorama polityczna przed wyborami (Full Steam into the Whistle, or a Pre-electoral Political Panorama), in: Gazeta Wyborcza 1991, N° 87 A.

5 Swida-Zięba, H., Mentalność posttotalitarna (Post-totalitarian Mentality), in: Społeczeństwo otwarte N° 2/1991, p. 9.

6 Krzemiński, A., Władyka, W., Władza. Atlas ptaków polskich (Political Power. An Atlas of Polish Birds), in: Polityka N° 20/1991, p. 5.

7 See: Rychard, A., Start nowego ładu (The Onset of the New Order), in: Studia nad ładem społecznym (Studies in Social Order), ed. by Nieciuński, W., Żukowski, T., U. W. Warszawa 1990, ch. 2, p. 22–23.

8 Rychard, A., Co może się zdarzyć (What Might Happen), in: Rola i funkcjonowanie instytucji . . ., op. cit., p. 374.

9 W systemowej próżni? Dylematy procesu transformacji? (In a "systemic void"? Dilemmas of the Transformation Process), ed. by Hausner, J., Kraków 1991, p. 97.

10 W systemowej próżni . . . (as above), p. 92.

11 Michnik, A., Etyka a polityka (Ethics Versus Politics), in: Tygodnik Powszechny, 1990, N° 18.

Bogusława Bednarczyk

National Conflicts in the Second Republic and Some Suggestions of their Solution

To discuss this problem the following basic question should be asked: What did the situation of national minorities look like in Poland then? In "ethnographic Poland" German settlers founded cities and were their dominating power before, in course of the time, they became nationalized Poles. Jews, persecuted in the West, found refuge in Poland and were protected by its law. Thus, it is not surprising that they arrived in crowds and gradually took over Polish trade. After Red Ruthenia had been regained and the eastern territories had been incorporated in Poland due to its Union with Lithuania, both Lithuanians and Ruthenians, who in the future were to share the destiny of Poland, became a part of the Polish State.[1]

The Polish Republic before its partitions and then the Second Republic (1918–1939) were inhabited by ethnic minorities. Before the partitions they constituted a rather large percentage of the population. After 1918 when the areas around Vilnius had been annexed to Poland and when new eastern frontiers of Poland had been demarcated due to the Riga Treaty, the reborn Polish State was constituted not only by the ethnic Polish territories but also by the Borderlands with their native Ruthenian and Byelorussian populations, who, in many cases, were an ethnic majority in Poland.[2]

At the same moment when the new Polish State was born after 123 years of captivity and the Second Republic was proclaimed, its situation, in comparison with the period before the partition, underwent some decisive changes: most national minorities and the most important centres of political and cultural life (Kiev, Minsk) were no longer in Poland. These changes led to some decentralizing tendencies, even to the danger of irredentism.

It must, however, be borne in mind that the 19th century, the period of captivity for Poland, also saw the awakening and taking shape of national ideas, of national and cultural identity which, in turn, resulted in creating new political ambitions among these ethnic groups who had not been fully confident of themselves before. At the same time the government of Russia fought against Polishness in Lithuania and Ruthenia without mercy, using schools, churches and offices for this purpose, it encouraged the borderland population to hate any manifestation of Polish life.[3] This is the reason why the process of creating national identity was set against a background of mistrust and ill-will towards Poland, its past (often misinterpreted on purpose) and its culture. Thus it is no wonder that the feeling of suspicion, ill-disposition or even hostility were transferred to the new Polish State.

On the territory of the ex-Austrian partition the Russian and Ukrainian irredentism backed by a dissolving emperor army, led to a civil war. These qualitative changes on the eastern Borderlands were counterbalanced by quantitative changes on the western Borderlands. On the territory of the Prussian partition, for nearly 150 years, there was a very strong colonization aiming at Germanizing the country. This policy seriously increased the number of German settlers in the region of Poznań, West Prussia and Pomerania. Thus, the Second Republic was inhabited by a large and strong, although artificially created, German population on its western territories. This group which was privileged in the past assumed a special attitude towards the new economic conditions.[4]

Considering the situation of the Jewish minority, it should be pointed out that some decisive changes took place in the 19th century and at the beginning of the 20th century. In addition to a traditional racial and religious differences isolating the Jewish from the Polish among whom they lived, Zionism and together with it a growing feeling of national identity appeared. The number of Jews coming to the eastern Borderlands from central Russia increased because the Tsar's government regulation limited their settlement.[5]

Such were the conditions under which nations began their co-existence in the reborn Poland. Generally speaking, feelings and attitudes of these national minorities or at least of some of them were not very positive and together with the Polish they were to decide the future of the whole of Poland. Thus both the quantity and the distribution of particular ethnic groups living in Poland became very important. The census from 1921 showed that although Poles made up ⅔ of the whole population of Poland, Ukrainians, Jews and Byelorussians were in the majority in some eastern regions. The Polish prevailed in the ancient Kingdom of Poland, in West Galicia to the San River and in the territories of the Prussian partition, in the region of Białystok and Vilnius. Other big Polish centres were in Podole, Galicia (Lvov) and Volhynia.[6]

Jews constituted 8–9% of the whole population. They lived in towns and villages in the Kingdom of Poland, in Galicia and in the Eastern Borderlands. Only a few inhabited Silesia, Little Poland and Pomerania. Warsaw was a big Jewish centre, where more than 300 thousand Jews lived (in 1921 they constituted nearly 30% of the whole population of the capital). With regard to their number, Byelorussians were second (after the Ukrainian Slavonic minority constituting 5% of the population of Poland). They lived in the regions of Nowogródek, Vilnius and Białystok. Germans (2–3% of the population) were mainly in Pomerania, Great Poland and Upper and Cieszyn Silesia. Apart from these very numerous ethnic groups enumerated above, Poland was inhabited by much smaller national communities such as: Russians, Lithuanians, Armenians, Tatars, Czechs and Slovaks.[7]

As a result of the demarcation of new Polish borders after the World War I, the problems of national minorities became if not of primary importance, at least one of the most crucial matters for the Second Republic which was then being created. It undoubtedly served as one of the basic factors of economic, social and political integration of the reborn Poland. However, it was also a source of endless social and class tensions which increased during economic crises.

National conflicts broke out although the Constitution of the Second Republic guaranteed the political freedom of minorities: they could develop their political activities, they could form political associations which would represent their interests and, in addition to that, they could possess press and publishing houses to propagate their political, cultural and economic programmes. While formulating their programmes and criticising successive Polish governments, national minorities referred to three basic problems:

1. the restriction of democratic liberties of national minorities and the denial to grant them both linguistic and cultural autonomy (at least for the most numerous minorities);
2. the decrease of the number of schools for national minorities and their replacement with the so-called utraquist schools where Polish was used together with the language of the respective minority;
3. the serious limitation of the number of representatives of these minorities in both the Sejm and the Senate (in the thirties).

Now the question arises which documents regulated the legal status of these minorities in Poland. These legal acts were: the constitution of Poland, instructions of central authorities, regulations of the international system of national minorities' protection. As far as the chronology of these documents is concerned, it must be stressed that, first of all, the status of national minorities was regulated by the provisions of the so-called Little Versailles Treaty signed by Poland on 28 June 1919, which mentions the protection of life and freedom, religious tolerance, citizenship, civil an political rights, free usage of mother tongue, education, religious, charity and social institutions. Some special articles referred to the rights of Jews. All the aforementioned regulations were given under the surveillance of the League of Nations. In spite of the opposition of the extreme nationalists, on 31 august 1919 the Sejm validated the minority treaty.[8] The Constitution of the Second Republic of 17 March 1921 defined, with full details, the rights of minorities. Its basic Article 95 stated that: "On its territory, the Polish Republic will fully protect life, freedom and private property of all its citizens independently of their origin, nationality, language, race and religion."[9]

Moreover, the Slavonic and German minorities in Upper Silesia got some additional warranty as far as the protection of their language, religion, freedom to act in their own organization, rights to develop their national culture were concerned. Russians, Ukrainians and Byelorussians were protected by the regulations in the Article 7 of the Treaty of Riga, and Germans, by virtue of the provisions of the Convention of Geneva from May 1922 which concerned Upper Silesia and which was signed for the duration of 15 years.[10]

However, from the mid-twenties onwards, Polish legislation restricted, little by little, the democratic rights guaranteed to national minorities by the March Constitution and the regulations from the inter-war period. Such a policy led to resistance. At the same time, the regulation act of 31 August 1924 hindered seriously the development of education for minorities. Mixed schools were founded, which served as a pretext to Polonize the minority youth.[11]

Although the April Constitution from 1935 confirmed the equality of all citizens in the eye of the law, it also gave priority to the principle of loyalty to the

State and thus prompted intolerance of any group or minority organization which would, in any way, endanger or injure the State's interests.[12]

The right of vote (to the Sejm, the Senate and local authorities) worked to the detriment of national minorities, as well.

The policy of the Polish government towards national minorities was influenced by many factors, e. g. the number and the role played by these minorities in the economic life of the country, international treaties, etc. The attitude of parties and other political organizations towards the question of national minorities was also one of the most influential determinants. Every government had to consider the opinions about this matter presented by them to the Sejm.

Generally speaking, in Polish society, four trends may be distinguished as far as the question of minorities was concerned:

1. The most extreme attitude was assumed by the "Endecja" or the National Democracy (till 1928 the People's National Union) and other social organizations under its influence. The main slogan of this group was to Polonize the eastern and western territories of Poland by means of a gradual process of denationalization of Slavonic minorities and by forcing the German and Jewish minorities to emigrate. The National Democracy was the most radical party as far as the Jewish question is concerned. Economic anti-Semitism rooted in its programme gave rise to sometimes very cruel anti-semitic actions committed by the extreme fractions of the party: the National Radical Camp, the Falanga group and the Youth National Camp. Taking into consideration the fact that 45% of the bourgeoisie was of Jewish origin, it was rather easy to blame the Jews and to make them responsible for the extremely bad economic and social situation of the Second Republic.[14] In the years 1930–1935 when home affairs became worse in Poland, it happened that fighting squads attacked Jewish merchants and craftsmen in some villages. It was the National Democracy who demanded to increase the "numerus clausus" in high schools. In some high schools and universities there followed riots the target of which were students and those members of the teaching stuff whose ideas were progressive.[15]

2. Józef Piłsudski and his followers created a different programme concerning the question of national minorities. At the beginning of the inter-war period this was the so-called federalist programme. According to its principles, the objective was to create a federal state respecting the rights of all its minorities. This programme aimed at annexing the biggest possible territory to Poland. The Polish-Russian war and the Riga Treaty prompted this trend. Then, the idea of "prometheism" became very popular. Its role was to prevent the Byelorussian and Ukrainian population from having pro-Russian tendencies. It was to be achieved by creating proper conditions for the economic, cultural and national development of these minorities. The most difficult task to fulfill was to convince them that their indissoluble connection with Poland was necessary.[16]

After the May coup d'état in 1926, the followers of Piłsudski united in the Non-Party Block for Cooperation with the Government advocated the principle of the State integration of national minorities. It consisted in granting some, mainly economic privileges, to loyal members of these minorities. After the death of Marshal Piłsudski the programme was changed and the National Unity Camp aimed at an active Polonization of both the eastern and western Borderlands.[17]

3. The third trend was represented by the Polish Socialist Party, the National Workers Union, the Polish Peasant Party "Piast", the Polish Peasant Party "Wyzwolenie" and the Left Wing of Piłsudski's followers. They declared tolerance for national minorities, cooperation with them, respect of their cultural aspirations and observance of the rights to which they were entitled. They somehow backed the aspiration for the territorial autonomy of the Byelorussian and Ukrainian minorities. They also fought against any manifestations of anti-Semitism and chauvinism.[18]

4. The attitude of the Polish Communist Party and its semi-legal fractions differed, in a decisive way, from the three preceding approaches. It was also in strong opposition to the programmes of successive governments of the Second Republic.

The basic principles of the Polish Communist Party were that class interests should go before national problems. This Party always criticised the policy of the Polish government (discrimination) and it backed the minorities' rights of selfdetermination and even their right to detach the territory on which they lived from Poland. It is obvious that such an understanding of the question of Upper Silesia, Danzig (till 1934), Eastern Borderlands and Ukrainia and Byelorussia must have given rise to conflicts.[19]

Lack of a uniform policy towards the question of national minorities hindered any attempt of the Polish government to work out a homogeneous programme dealing with this problem in the years 1919–1939. This task turned out to be even more difficult, even impossible to fulfill because after many long years of captivity there revived the tradition of the Polish power politics advertising the idea of creating a strong Poland "spreading from one sea to another".

As follows from the above, there were several suggestions of how to solve the question of national minorities. Apart from the main trends, in conflict with each other, and propagated by the National Democracy and the Piłsudski's Camp, nearly any government, ministry, office and province office tried to put forward its own programme.

In 1924 the Cabinet of Grabski worked out the most cunning programme consisting in the assimilation of minorities, which was to be achieved by emphasising the point in favour of their education, language, religion, land property (Eastern Borderlands – Ukrainian and Byelorussian minorities). The projects of Grabski were, however, never put into effect.[20]

After the May coup d'état various political tendencies co-existed, e. g. an attempt was made to gain the minorities' favour by promising them the foundation of their own "Russian University", raising hopes of elections to local self-governments, protesting against any anti-Semitic acts together with backing the idea of creating a Jewish State in Palestine and giving up annual school plebiscites. Most of these promises were never kept; the Ukrainian University was never founded in Lvov, a military settlement developed in the Eastern Borderlands and Little Poland was pacified in 1930.[21]

After 1926, successive governments, using different means, tried to make national minorities loyal and create a feeling of their responsibility for the future of the State they lived in. The programme of Piłsudski meant as a gradual process of integration of national minorities gained more and more followers. In March 1934 the National Minorities Committee transformed into the Committee for the National Minorities' Affairs (December 1935) was founded. It was directed by S. Paprocki. Its existence proves that the government was very anxious about a strong link between national minorities and the Polish State. In one of the memorials to this committee the following can be read: "This objective cannot be realized by the policy of denationalization by force . . . much better, stronger, durable and important effects can be achieved by the policy which can warrant an independent social and cultural development of national minorities and which, at the same time, emphasizing cultural achievements of the main nation decisively opposes the misuse any manifestation of socio-cultural activity for political interests other than the interests of the State."[22]

Civil and military authorities executed this policy by various means: the Ministry of Foreign Affairs tried to gain the favour of some Ukrainians with the promise of a great and independent Ukrainia built on the ruins of Soviet Ukrainia; the Ministry of Military Affairs applied the method of forced Polonization and practised the policy of "iron hand". Thus, there were expulsions of the indigenous population, members of Polish "petty gentry" were sought among the Ukrainian population, cultural differences were stressed between Huculs and Lemks, old uniat Orthodox churches were claimed back. It also happened that some drastic steps followed, e. g. in 1939 military authorities eradicated orthodox churches in Volhynia and around Lublin.

In Upper Silesia, the voivode Michał Grażyński tried to stop German cultural and political expansion and he also made efforts to set restrictions on the spreading economic domination of the German middle class.[23] He was against the autonomy of the voivode of Upper Silesia and he stood out against the German education system. The Polish-German conflict about minority schools was brought up before the League of Nations.[24] Fearing a further worsening of relations between the Polish and the Germans, the government tried to make up for the actions of the voivode who wanted to limit the rights of German minority organizations. It was only on the threshold of the World War II and as a result of growing wave of German irredentism in Upper Silesia that Polish authorities decided to restrain the freedom of different German organizations.

As far as the Jewish question is concerned, successive Polish governments did not manage to work out any satisfying programme, either. In the thirties, the Jewish question, already socially and economically discredited, was to be solved by arranging Jewish emigration to Palestine.

It is obvious that political parties and national minorities' organizations both created and helped to solve various national conflicts. Among the four major minority groups, the Germans, although the least numerous, were the best organized ones. They were economically strong and they created a high level of civilisation. They had their own and powerful state across the west border. For these reasons, it was rather easy for them to defend their rights and interests. On the territory of the ancient Russian and Austrian partitions there were their centres in villages and some big cities (Łódź). Although in the ancient partition they were in the minority, they were still owners of big land estates and enterprises. They could support their compatriots (better jobs, higher positions), which, of course, resulted in conflicts. Many Germans emigrated from Pomerania and the region of Poznań, but those who remained there defended, by different means, their property and preserved nationalistic traditions and ideas teaching them to the young generation. The Poles fought against being expropriated from big land estates.

In Upper Silesia the Poles faced a much more difficult situation because they were under economic, political and cultural domination by the Germans. Germans had many representatives in the Silesian Sejm. Their schools were very well equipped, which attracted Polish students.[25] Nationalism was getting stronger. The Polish organizations such as the Union for Defence of the Western Borderlands and the Society of Silesian Insurgents fought against Germanization of Silesia. It is interesting to observe that the Nazis did not succeed in uniting the German movement in Poland. The following German parties were active in Poland: the German Party, the nationalistic German Union (Pomerania and Poznań), the German Peasants Union (Upper Silesia), the nationalistic German Peasants Union (Łódź). The Jungdeutsche Partei supported the Nazi movement in Poland.[26] All these parties encouraged separatist tendencies and backed the attitude of, at first, the Weimar Republic and then of the Third Reich towards the conflicts with Poland. They attempted to bring discredit upon Poland in the area of international politics (schools). In 1933 these parties became the national and socialist movement.

The Jewish community showed many political differences. Three major orientations corresponded with various political trends:

1. conservative Jews – the Union of Israel – preservation of religious traditions, protection against foreign influences, full loyalty to the Polish State;
2. semitic movements objecting to any form of assimilation and promoting the return of Jews to the land of their ancestors where they would build a national State; there were many Semitic organizations;
3. some Jews were members of the Polish Communist Party; socialists belonged to the "Bund" (the Jewish Workers' Union); they fought against Jewish conservatism and the idea of Jewish emigration to Palestine; their most important task was to push for radical social reforms in the country.[27]

In spite of their origin, many Jews grew into one with the Polish society and contributed to the development of Polish science and culture. This fact could not, however, stop a growing wave of anti-Semitism, which became one of the most important social problems leading to many national conflicts. Influenced by nationalism spreading all over Europe, in Poland, though, anti-Semitism had a different nature as it was deeply rooted in the economic situation of the country.

Universities became a stage for very frequent anti-Semitic excesses, the press connected with the nationalistic orientation spread anti-Semitic propaganda and walls were covered with inflammatory slogans. Propaganda treated Jews as strangers ignoring the fact that they had lived in Poland for ages. No wonder that there were pogroms. Anti-Semitic riots started in Lvov in 1929 when students damaged a Jewish secondary school. It was obvious that in such a situation the Polish government encouraged Jews to emigrate. In 1927–1938 twenty four thousand Jews emigrated to Palestine.[28] Nearly at the same time, Poland was forced to give refuge to several thousands of Jews with Polish citizenship who had been expelled by Hitler. Generally speaking, the Jewish population did not create very difficult political problems to the Polish government.

The question of the so-called Slavonic minorities was quite a different matter. Ukrainians were the most numerous. They felt like a defeated nation dominated by an external power. According to them the territory on which they lived was divided among and annexed to different countries such as the Soviet Union, Poland and Czechoslovakia. A great majority of Ukrainians were against communism and they did not want to exist as the Ukrainian Soviet Republic. The Communist Ukrainian Party founded in 1919 did not have many members, either. Fought against by the Polish authorities (the famous "proces świętojurski" 1922–1923)[29], it was dissolved together with the Polish Communist Party. The Ukrainian National-Democratic Union founded in 1925 became the strongest political organization. Its objective was to create an independent state embodying the whole Ukrainian territory. Its activity was legal and it stressed the importance of "organic work". Quite a different programme was promoted by the Ukrainian Nationalists who were for an armed fight, even terrorism.

The Polish were not very enthusiastic about the national ambitions of Ukrainians. The idea to revive the tradition of a Jagiellonian Kingdom where many nations could co–exist failed prompted by a failure of federalist tendencies. The nationalist concept won: Poland was to be a State for the Poles, which meant that Slavonic minorities were to be assimilated, and as a result of this, denationalized. Any attempt of a more conciliatory way by the government was objected by both the Polish society and the local administration.

Responding to it, Ukrainians founded cultural and educational institutions ("Prosvita"), youth associations and cooperatives. Their activity was assisted by the Greek Catholic church. In Lvov, a clandestine Ukrainian University was functioning (the Polish did not put into effect the bill passed to the Sejm about such a university).

Agrarian reforms were in favour of the Polish population. Ukrainian peasants treated Polish colonisation as their expulsion from their own land (many Ukrainian villages were overcrowded). Military settlers were a target of their most vivid hatred. The number of the state-owned schools with the Ukrainian language decreased and they were replaced by utraquist schools. Some attempts were made to break the Ukrainian society into parts by stressing ethnic differences between the Huculs, the mountaineers from the Eastern Beskidy and the western groups of Lemks and Boiks. Polish authorities aimed also at keeping Volhynia from the influence of Lvov.[30]

All the aforementioned steps increased mutual hostility. Both sides were against any attempt of reconciliation or only cooperation with more moderate Ukrainian nationalists. The Organizations of Ukrainian Nationalists encouraged terrorist operations advocating the idea of fighting against all the enemies of the country: setting fire to Polish houses, raiding Polish manors and farms, especially if they belonged to settlers, damaging offices and other acts of sabotage.

The slogan "Poles go back over the San!" became very meaningful. Terrorists and the members of the Organizations of Ukrainian Nationalists killed T. Hołówka, a Polish socialist leader (1931), the minister Pieracki (1934) and Ivan Babija, the director of an Ukrainian school who did not approve of terrorism (1935). The Greek Catholic Church episcopacy objected to it but it also happened that the clergy backed the Organization of Ukrainian Nationalists. The Polish hit back: in the autumn of 1930 they expelled, showing no mercy, Ukrainians from their villages (using the police and the army). They applied the principle of a "collective responsibility" resulting in repressions, mass arrests, closing down some Ukrainian institutions and organizations. The most tragic was the religious persecution of the Orthodox Church believers in Podlasie, Chełmszczyzna and Volhynia. All these incidents deepened the mutual hatred of both nations and bore a feeling of ill-will towards Poland. Byelorussians, the second Slavonic minority, were in a particularly difficult situation. Most of them were Catholics (descendants of units) and poor peasants. A rather small number of intellectuals and bourgeoisie developed, fairly late, a feeling of national identity. Contrary to the Ukrainians, they did not manifest strong nationalist tendencies. After 1918 many Byelorussians were in favour of creating an independent or only autonomous, but always united with Poland, Byelorussia. The Treaty of Riga put an end to such a concept.[31]

Polish authorities wanted to polonize Byelorussians, which was to be rather easy because of their low level of cultural development. They also promoted the "pretty gentry", Catholics and Polish settlers after having lotted out land estates. The activity of cultural and educational institutions was made difficult. The Byelorussian education was restrained. In the period 1937–1938 there were not any schools with the Byelorussian language as the language of instruction. There existed 5 bilingual schools and about 40 schools where the Byelorussian language was taught as one of many matters. During the whole inter-war period (20 years) there was only one Byelorussian secondary school in Radoszkowice. Only a few Byelorussians studied in Vilnius.

As far as politics are concerned, there were many different organizations – parties were founded and dissolved and they represented various political orientations: pro-Soviet, pro-Polish ans pro-Lithuanian. The most important one was the Byelorussian Christian Democracy transformed towards the end of the thirties into the Byelorussian Peasants' Union. The main principle of their programme was to create a democratic and bourgeois republic embodying all the areas inhabited by Byelorussians. The Polish settlers were fought against as harmful to the Byelorussian population. The party tended to develop national culture and education in the Byelorussian language, which was important because nearly all centres of Byelorussian education stopped existing. The Christian Democracy took in many other organizations and supervised the activity of the Byelorussian National Committee. It cannot be forgotten that the peasants living on these poor areas expected, first of all, agrarian reforms, which resulted in Byelorussian political groups, not only the leftists, having radical social programmes. The party "Hromada" (the Byelorussian Peasants' and Workers' Party) founded in 1925 was the strongest and the most influential one. Independence, social reforms, pro-Soviet attitude, the Byelorussian Republic governed by workers and peasants – these slogans appealed to the poor Byelorussian peasant.[33]

As it follows, school, church and land held the balance in the policy of the Polish government and population on the one hand, and the Byelorussian parties on the other. At the same time they were a source of conflicts. Towards the end of the thirties the situation of the Byelorussian movement became tragic because of repressions by Polish authorities. In August 1937 the Byelorussian Union of Teachers was dissolved, the last Byelorussian secondary school was closed down and at the beginning of 1939 the Byelorussian Museum of Ethnography stopped receiving allocations.

Lithuanians (more than 100 thousand) played also an important role among other national minorities. They lived in the regions of Vilnius and Suwałki. They had a science society and a secondary school in Vilnius. They could learn in more than 20 primary schools.[34] The relations between Poland and the Lithuanian Republic were sometimes unsatisfactory and they had a negative influence on the policy of Poland towards the Lithuanian minority. Lithuanians were Catholics and used the same churches as the Polish, which caused sometimes tensions or even fights. The language of sermons and church services was often a reason for these conflicts. Lithuanians belonged to two organizations: the Saint Casimir Society and the Rytas Society, both of them were devoted to educational activities of an anti-Polish character, though. The Lithuanian Committee in Vilnius supervised and coordinated political activities.[35] Its programme was obvious – its main aim was to boycott the Polish State. The question of the Lithuanian national minority played an important role in the conflict over the Polish-Lithuanian borders. Polish authorities restricted the activity of Lithuanian societies in Poland, which was immediately reciprocated by Lithuanians. Those who wanted to work and co-exist peacefully cultivating their mother tongue and their own traditions were afflicted by the most acute suffering. The Polish-Lithuanian conflict had a very negative influence on the situation of the Lithuanian population in Poland. These quarrels and conflicts came to an end only during the World War II. Then, the extreme nationalist Lithuanian groups persecuting Poles, stood on the side of the Third Reich.

Russians were a small national minority. The revolution in Russia prevented them from returning to their country. They did not play an important political role and they did not mix with other minorities and Poles. They might have been Polish allies because they also wanted to overthrow the Soviet government. However, they caused some troubles, as well. Their anti-Soviet emigration gave birth to terrorism. Their acts against the representatives of the Soviet Union in Poland were troublesome for Polish international relationships.[36]

Czechs should be mentioned as well because at the beginning of the thirties 31,1 thousand people declared Czech as their mother tongue. Most of them (31 thousand) lived in Volhynia and 4,1 thousand in the region of Łódź. As far as the region of Cieszyn Silesia is concerned, many Czechs emigrated from its Polish part. They were somehow forced to do so because of, among many other reasons, open hostility of the Poles.

The centre of the Czech in Zelowo near Łódź was very interesting. They arrived in Poland in 1803 escaping religious persecution in their own country. Many tradesmen and workers, specialists in the textile industry, became native there. There situation was quite different in Volhyna where the Czech population was mainly composed of peasants who cultivated national traditions and were interested in social and economic issues. Their assimilation was very slow there. They did not create great problems for the Polish authorities. It must be stressed that the Czechs were loyal citizens of the Polish Republic.

The Slovak minority, according to the census from 1931, counted a little more than 1000 people. The regions of Spisz and Orava were a controversial question. There were no plebiscites there and following the decisions of the allies this area was divided but nobody was satisfied with such a solution. Both sides manifested hostility or even hatred towards each other.[37]

Finally, one more national minority should be mentioned – the Gipsies. In 1930 they might have been about 30 thousand. Their language, different traditions, culture, occupations and life-style stressed their different character. They lived in the background of the Polish society. They did not inspire confidence, they very often stirred up reluctance and fear. The conflicts between the Gipsies and the Polish were caused by their different customs and social isolation.[38]

This short study does not present all the problems of national minorities in the Second Republic. It must be realized that more than 30% of the whole population of Poland was constituted by national minorities.[39] This was a very big percentage. We should also bear in mind another important fact: the Second Republic was a young political system, which made both its internal and foreign policy difficult. The multi-national character of the state served as a pretext to interfere in the internal matters of Poland while settling the problems of national minorities.

Now, I would like to draw some general conclusions. A multi-national structure of the Second Republic hindered the process of integration. There existed no principles of a minority policy which would reconcile the interests of the Polish State and those of minorities. The fact that there were many minorities led to growing, often nationalist, class conflicts and social frictions. Minorities were often unjustly blamed for a difficult economic situation.[40] Apart from the Jews, all other minorities showed strong irredentist tendencies, which endangered the independence of Poland. Successive governments of the Second Republic did not work out any homogeneous programme in this matter and they did not solve the question of national minorities, either, which had a very negative impact on the future of the Polish State.

Contemporary Poland is neither a multi-national nor an ethnically homogeneous country. Most minorities have their own social and cultural organizations.

A special Committee for National Minorities functioning within the Ministry of Culture and Art was founded to cooperate with them. Its workers defend the interests of minorities in conflicts with the local administration. They also pass judgement on various documents concerning ethnic groups. The data about the size of particular minorities are only approximative as they are based on the information given by members of ethnic groups. They are as follows:

- Ukrainians – 300-350 thousand,
- Germans – 200–250 thousand (according to the latest data given by the Society of the German Minority in Śląsk Opolski their number has reached 350 thousand),
- Czechs and Slovaks – 25 thousand (Slovaks are in majority; they live in Spisz and Orava; most Czechs live in the region of Piotrków and in the Kłodzko Valley),
- Byelorussians – 250 thousand,
- Lithuanians – 25 thousand,
- Gipsies and Jews – 15 thousand each,
- Polish Tatars – 2,5 thousand (they live in the region of Białystok)41

A growing activity of national minorities is a new phenomenon, undoubtedly, closely connected with and resulting from the process of democratization of political life in Poland towards the end of the eighties. The most active are the following minorities: the German minority in Silesia, the Byelorussian minority in the region of Białystok, the Ukrainian minority whose members are scattered all over the country. Both the religious and the professional structures have not changed in any decisive way but political changes led to social changes (a class of small and middle businessmen has been joined by some emigrants with their own pecuniary resources). Social and political organizations have also got modified (foundation of parties). Generally speaking, all these changes are positive, but we cannot leave unnoticed the fact that the process of democratization has revived old conflicts (even those ones from the Second Republic). Although it may sound like a paradox it has also created new problems typical of the process of revival of the whole country.

Looking at the Third Republic from the point of view of the national minorities question, the most conspicuous seems to be the problems of Germans, Lithuanians, Slovaks and Gipsies.

Discussing the situations of Germans in Silesia the following question should be asked: Who are they? It is a well known fact that the fight against the identity of the Silesians did not stop in 1975 when as a result of an administrative reform two extremely Silesian districts of Olesko and Lubin became dependent of the voivode of Częstochowa and, in the South, Cieszyn given to Bielsko lost its importance it had always had for Upper Silesia. In such a situation trips to West Germany have become an escape. At this very moment the German question in Silesia gets a very special status. In many cases, after having received the status of a national minority Germans do not know what to do, which leads to conflicts and frictions. These tensions have their roots in the past when, for example, the German language could not be taught in Silesian schools.

At the same time the Society of the German Minority in Śląsk Opolski (approximately 200 thousand members) promotes the idea that Silesia should be a "bridge" connecting Poland with Europe, but it had better be an autonomous "bridge". The Union of Upper Silesia which contained various groups from the whole area of Upper Silesia backed the concept of self-government, too. Silesia has become a "melting pot" and the following slogans serve as a convincing evidence in favour of this statement: "Germans go away!", "Polacken raus!", "Silesia for the Silesians!", "Silesia separated from the Basin!" All of them demand autonomy but with Poland. They also insist on a new plebiscite. For the moment nothing else but chaos results from these suppressed and artificial nationalist tendencies.

The problem is difficult, it concerns many matters and it cannot be passed over in silence. Politics cannot be led by emotions but it should be pragmatic while dealing with the German question. The same statement can be applied to the Lithuanian problem.

No secret is made of the fact that, in spite of many hundred years of neighbourhood and co-existence, the relationships between the Polish and the Lithuanians have not always been satisfactory. These contacts have become particularly painful, violent or even tragic for the last period of ten years when Lithuanians have become conscious of their national identity, ethnic differences and their language hardly ever used by anybody else but peasants has received the status of a national language and has become a literary norm. Apart from many historical determinants disintegration resulting from a strong fear of being absorbed by a more numerous Polish society, has come into prominence. This factor has always been typical of the national minorities' questions. The latest political events – free Lithuania – and the situation of Poles in Lithuania have contributed to conflicts breaking out here and there.

Similarly, the process of democratization in Czechoslovakia has resulted in an international interest in the situation of the Slovak minority in Poland. The question concerns 13 communes in the North of Orawa and 12 communes in Upper Spisz which were annexed to Poland in 1920. It is known that towards the end of the Second Republic some attempts were made to colonize this area (the role of the Roman Catholic Church – there were no services in Slavonic). In 1945, a plebiscite helped by Russian soldiers was held. Although 98% of the inhabitants wanted this territory to be annexed to Czechoslovakia it became a part of Poland.

The next question is wether the Slovaks have been able to act in cultural, social and religious organizations according to the accords of Helsinki.

Gipsies are even less numerous than Slovaks in Poland and no government is going to defend their rights. Their economic status is rather high in some districts, which is a reason of conflicts. Mława can serve to illustrate this thesis. At the same time it points at negative effects of intolerance and doggedness.

The examples chosen by us show that a legal recognition of minorities leads to their subjectivity, which means cooperation for the welfare of the whole nation and country.

The history of national minorities and conflicts in the Second Republic and at the beginning of the nineties are too intricate to be presented, with full details, in such a short study. However, one thing has always been obvious: only tolerance, mutual understanding and elements of law can guarantee a peaceful co–existence of various ethnic groups in one country.

Notes and sources

1 On this, see Jerzy Smolenski, Geografia, historia i ustrój Polski Odrodzonej, in: Piotr Lat (ed.), Dziesi, ęciolecie Polski Nie podległej 1918–1920, p. 43.
2 Ibid, p. 43.
3 Ibid, p. 43–44.
4 Ibid, p. 44 and next.
5 Ibid, p. 50 and next.
6 Ibid, p. 51–52.
7 Ibid, p. 51–52.
8 Z. Urbański, Mniejszosci narodowe w Polsce, Warszawa 1932.
9 Konstytucje Polski: Studia monograficzne z dziejów polskiego konstytucjonalizmu, M. Kollasa (ed.), vol. 2, Warszawa 1990, p. 109.
10 W. Roszkowski, Historia Polski 1914–1990, Warszawa, p. 4, 28, 30.
11 J. Tomaszewski, Rzeczpopolita wielu narodów, Warszawa 1985, p. 93.
12 Konstytucje Polski, op. cit., p. 179.
13 Ibid., p. 211 and next.
14 See, e. g. J. Orlicki, Szkice z dziejów stosunków polsko-żydowskich 1918–1948, Szczecin 1983.
15 Ibid.
16 W. T. Kulesza, Koncepcje ideowo-polityczne obozu rządzącego w Polsce w latach 1926–1935, Ossolineum, Wrocław, Warszawa – Kraków 1985; chapter III, Założenia K. Bartla wobec mniejszóści narodowych.
17 W. Roszkowski, op. cit., chapter 7.6.: Ostatnie lata II Rzeczpospolitej 1935–1939.
18 W. Michowicz, Problemy mniejszości narodowych; stosunki polskich partii do mniejszości narodowych i polityka mniejszościowa panstwa polskiego.
19 Ibid.
20 A. Czubiński, Okres demokracji parlamentarnej 1922–1926, in: J. Topolski (ed.), Dzieje Polski, Warszawa 1977, chapter II, p. 681.
21 Orlicki, op. cit., p. 333.
22 Tomaszewski, op. cit., p. 97 and next.
23 Tomicki (ed.), op. cit. p. 330.
24 See e. g. J. M. Małecki, Zarys dziejów Polski 1864–1939, Kraków 1991.
25 Ibid.
26 See e. g. S. Mauersberg, Szkolnictwo powszechne dla mniejszości narodowych w Polsce w latach 1918–1939, Wrocław 1968, p. 60, 63, 69, 70, 78.
27 Małecki, op. cit., p. 356 and next.
28 Tomaszewski, op. cit., p. 176 and next.
29 Małecki, op. cit., p. 361 and next.
30 Ibid., 362 and next.
31 On this, see e. g. M. Papieżyńska-Turek, Sprawa Ukraińska w II Rzeczpospolitej 1922–1926, Kraków 1979.
32 Tomaszewski, op. cit. p. 149 and next.
33 Ibid.

34 Ibid.
35 Ibid.
36 H. Połujan, Litwini w woj. wileńskim, Warszawa 1936, p. 137.
37 Tomaszewski, op. cit., p. 242.
38 Ibid.
39 Ibid.
40 Tomicki (ed.), op. cit., p. 310.

Janina Czapska

Nationalistische Haltungen der Polen

1. Es ist kaum zu leugnen, daß wir in einer Zeit erhitzter und immer wieder aufflammender Nationalgefühle leben. Fast ununterbrochen erreichen uns Informationen über gewaltsame, nicht selten blutige Auseinandersetzungen, deren Ursachen in nationalen Konflikten zu suchen sind. In den Gesellschaften, die plötzlich an einem schwierigen Wendepunkt ihrer Geschichte angelangt sind, in einer tiefen Krise stecken, aus der einen Ausweg zu finden gar nicht so einfach ist, die kaum noch abzuwendenden Niederlagen entgegensehen, in einer Zeit, in der die alten Strukturen noch nicht zerfallen, neue aber noch nicht entstanden bzw. nicht stark genug sind, wenn zwischen den alten und neuen Eliten ein Machtkampf ausbricht, gewinnen Emotionen der Angst, des Hasses, Fanatismus, Rassismus und Feindschaft gegenüber allem, was schwach, anders oder wehrlos ist, an Stärke und Intensität. In einer solchen Zeit wird die Frage nach Anzeichen, Stärke und Konsequenzen des Nationalismus besonders wichtig.

Ich will hier ein „empirisches Bild" des Nationalismus bei der polnischen Bevölkerung darstellen, über die wichtigsten Ursachen dieses Phänomens nachdenken und Konsequenzen erwägen, die das Vorhandensein solcher Einstellungen nach sich zieht bzw. ziehen kann. Zuerst aber wende ich mich dem Begriff des Nationalismus kurz zu.

2. Der Begriff des Nationalismus ist keineswegs homogen, er bezieht sich auf verschiedene Erscheinungen, von denen zwei mir am wichtigsten erscheinen:

- die entsprechende Ideologie, in der – um es möglichst kurz zu formulieren – der Kategorie der Nation die führende Rolle zukommt, und
- die Bestimmung einer Einstellung.

Ich will mich vor allem auf die Bestimmung des Nationalismus als eine Einstellung konzentrieren. Ihre wichtigsten inhaltlichen Merkmale festzustellen, ist eine schwierige und komplizierte Aufgabe, da sie eine komplizierte Synthese von religiösen, kulturellen, staatlich-politischen und sonstigen Vorbildern/Mustern darstellt (Laswell, 1966,S. 35). Nehmen wir in unserer Analyse eine strukturelle Konzeption der Einstellung an, so müssen wir in ihr drei Arten von Elementen unterscheiden: Überzeugungen, Emotionen und Wertungen sowie ein Handlungsprogramm – mit anderen Worten kognitive, affektive und behavioristische Komponenten. Im Schnittpunkt dieser beiden Kriterien (d. h. des Inhalts- und des ontologischen Kriteriums) entsteht ein kompliziertes Mosaik von Elementen und Bestandteilen nationalistischer Einstellungen. In dieser Situation will ich mich, angesichts der Mannigfaltigkeit und der komplizierten Beschaffenheit der analysierten Objekte, nur auf eine Aufzählung der wichtigsten Anzeichen nationalistischer Einstellungen beschränken, um dann die Antwort auf die Frage zu riskieren, mit welcher Intensität sie bei der polnischen Bevölkerung tatsächlich vertreten ist. Ist nämlich von einer nationalistischen Einstellung der Einzelperson oder einer Menschengruppe die Rede, so darf man dabei nicht vergessen, daß einzelne Elemente dieser Einstellung sich in konkreten Fällen als ungleich intensiv erweisen können. Somit sollte man die Einstellungen eher als ein Kontinuum darstellen, als daß bei ihrer Qualifizierung eine dichotomische Einteilung angewendet wird (nationalistische und nichtnationalistische Einstellungen).

Zu den wichtigsten Symptomen nationalistischer Einstellungen zählen meines Erachtens folgende:

1. stark emotional gekennzeichnete Gegenüberstellung der eigenen Bürger und der Fremden. Dieser unterschiedlichen Darstellung zugrundeliegende Kriterien können sich aus der Überzeugung von der gemeinsamen Herkunft, Sprache, Religion, Territorium, Geschichte usw. ergeben.
2. Überzeugung von der Vollkommenheit seiner eigenen Nation, unkritische Apotheose derselben, Forderung von besonderen Privilegien;
3. die Tatsache, daß man den Interessen der eigenen Nation vor allen anderen Werten den Vorzug gibt;
4. die Neigung, sämtliche politischen und sozialen Probleme dem Kampf um nationale Interessen (die den Interessen anderer Nationen gegenübergestellt werden) unterzuordnen;
5. die Überzeugung davon, daß die Verpflichtungen der Menschen gegenüber der eigenen Nation sie von sämtlichen moralischen Verpflichtungen gegenüber den Mitgliedern anderer Nationen und ethnischer Gruppen befreien;
6. Verachtung und Intoleranz gegenüber den Mitgliedern anderer Nationen und ethnischer Gruppen;
7. extrem negative Emotionen und negative Bewertung von denjenigen Mitgliedern der eigenen Nation, die – in welcher Weise auch immer – sich zu den Banden zu dieser Nation nicht bekennen.

Die aus solchen Elementen bestehende Einstellung „erzwingt" einerseits didaktisch-moralisierende, andererseits autoritäre Haltungen (vgl. J. Kurczewska, 1988, S. 85). Verallgemeinernd kann man sagen, daß das Wesen des Nationalismus in einer rücksichtslosen Absolutisierung der eigenen Nation steckt, was sich wie folgt beschreiben läßt: „Ein Nationalist bedenkt die eigene Nation mit der Größe seltener Attribute, welche diese Nation einmalig und einzigartig erscheinen lassen, sowohl im freudigen Heroismus wie auch im Mut zum Leiden und Opfern: Er kreiert sie, indem er die Merkmale des Vollkommenseins nicht nur den Nationen zuteil werden läßt, die von der sozialen Welt erwählt worden sind, um in ihr eine außergewöhnliche Rolle zu spielen, sondern auch denjenigen, die im Hinblick auf diese Mission für den Zustand größerer und kleinerer Nationalwelten zuständig sind" (J. Kurczewska, 1988, S. 82). Aus diesem Zitat geht klar hervor, daß eins der Elemente einer nationalistischen Einstellung auch die Überzeugung von dem Messianismus der eigenen Nation sein kann und das damit zusammenhängende Bedürfnis, sich für die Randgebiete der eigenen Nation und ihrer Auswirkung auf die Nachbarn zu interessieren.

3. Die emotionale Haltung gegenüber der eigenen und den fremden Nationen bildet seit langer Zeit den Untersuchungsgegenstand der Meinungsforschung in verschiedenen Ländern. Viele Zentren der Meinungsforschung verfügen derzeit über umfangreiche Sammlungen von diesbezüglichen Informationen. Im Zusammenhang damit werden bereits Versuche gestartet, diese theoretisch zu analysieren und zu interpretieren.

In Polen hat man bisher verhältnismäßig wenige Untersuchungen dieser Art durchgeführt. Ich möchte hier auf die gesamtpolnischen, an einem repräsentativen Querschnitt der erwachsenen Bevölkerung durchgeführten Umfragen hinweisen. Bemerkenswert erscheinen unter ihnen die seit 1975 durch das Zentrum für Meinungsforschung OBOP (Zentrum für die Untersuchung der öffentlichen Meinung) veranstalteten Untersuchungen über das Verhältnis der Polen zu anderen Nationen. Seit 1978 werden im Zentrum für Presseforschung Untersuchungen über die polnische Nationalkultur durchgeführt. In der letzten Etappe dieser Forschungen untersuchte und analysierte man die Bedeutung von fremden Nationalkulturen im Bewußtsein der Polen, und an die Resultate dieser Untersuchungen möchte ich im weiteren Teil meiner Erwägungen anknüpfen. Besonders interessant erscheinen von unserem Standpunkt aus die im dritten polnischen Zentrum für Meinungsforschung CBOS (Zentrum für die Untersuchung der gesellschaftlichen Meinung) veranstalteten Untersuchungen zum Thema der positiven und negativen Eigenschaften der Polen.

Prof. W. Pisarek vom Zentrum für Presseforschung ist der Meinung, daß im Bewußtsein der Polen zwei völlig verschiedene, ja gar gegensätzliche Tendenzen zu beobachten sind. Die erstere bezeichnet er als polonozentrisch, die andere sei der westorientierte Eskapismus jeder Art. (W. Pisarek,1990,S. 17) Meiner Meinung nach handelt es sich dabei um zwei verschiedene Arten des Eskapismus, „nach innen" und „nach außen". Sie haben natürlich andere Quellen. Die Ursachen für die polonozentrische Einstellung im Bewußtsein der polnischen Bevölkerung sieht der Autor in einer planmäßigen Gestaltung eines bestimmten Bewußtseinsmodells in den europäischen Staaten des Realsozialismus. Als Zentrum galt hier seit jeher die Sowjetunion, aber die politischen Machthaber in den einzelnen Ländern waren um eine möglichst originalgetreue Nachbildung redlich bemüht. In jedem von diesen Ländern konzentrierte sich die Aufmerksamkeit der Massenmedien lange Jahre auf die innerstaatlichen Geschehnisse, und die Informationen über die übrige Welt wurden wahlweise nur dann serviert, wenn sie der Exemplifizierung ideologisch programmierter Vorstellungen von ihr dienen konnten. In den 80er Jahren hat sich in dieser Hinsicht wenig geändert; das Hauptinteresse der Massenmedien galt nach wie vor dem eigenen Land, und über seine Grenzen hinaus wagten sie sich nur, wenn die Ereignisse außerhalb des Landes mit der inneren Situation im Zusammenhang standen.

Das eskapistische Bewußtsein „nach außen" ist jüngeren Datums. Zurückzuführen ist es meistens auf das Gefühl der drohenden wirtschaftlich-politischen Katastrophe (vorwiegend bei älteren Leuten) oder auf die Gleichgültigkeit gegenüber den – zumindest im Vergleich zu westlichen Maßstäben – wenig ernstzunehmenden Möglichkeiten, sich hierzulande auch einrichten zu können (vor allem bei der jüngeren Generation). Die Relation zwischen Zloty und Dollar, dem technischen Fortschritt und industrieller Entwicklung hüben und drüben, den Zukunftsperspektiven hierzulande und anderswo, scheinen die Überzeugung, daß das wahre Leben nicht hier, sonders woanders, nur in einer anderen Welt möglich ist, nur zu bekräftigen.

4. Aus den Untersuchungen über den Stellenwert fremder Kulturen im Bewußtsein der Polen geht hervor, daß hier eine polonozentrische Orientierung die Oberhand gewinnt (W. Pisarek, 1990, S. 18 ff., 56 ff.). Sie drückt sich unter anderem in einem entschieden größeren Interesse für die politische Entwicklung im Lande als für das, was in der Welt passiert, aus; in der Überzeugung, daß alles, was in Polen geschieht, von den Polen selbst abhängig ist, in der Vorstellung, daß z. B. mit dem Nobelpreis vor allem die Polen geehrt werden. Mit der polonozentrischen Einstellung geht aber keineswegs ein unkritischer Nationalstolz einher. Jede zweite untersuchte Person gab zu, sich mindestens einmal geschämt zu haben, ein Pole zu sein.Von den anderen Nationalitäten schätzt der Pole die US-Amerikaner wohl am höchsten, ihnen folgen Franzosen, Schweden und Engländer. Weniger attraktiv erscheint im Vergleich zu ihnen die tschechische, ungarische und russische Nationalität. An dieser Stelle ist zu betonen, daß ähnliche Präferenzen auch in der alten BRD und in Großbritannien registriert wurden (Untersuchungen aus den Jahren 1967–1980). Und obwohl nach Meinung von 47,6% die Entwicklung in Polen von den Polen selbst abhängig ist, so weist ein beträchtlicher Teil der Antworten doch auf die Überzeugung hin, daß die polnische Kultur heutzutage verschiedenen fremden Einflüssen ausgesetzt ist (43,9%). Nur die Hälfte davon (19%) war überzeugt, daß sich die polnische Kultur jetzt selbständiger entwickeln kann, als es früher der Fall war.

Wie in den bereits erwähnten Untersuchungen finden die stereotypen Vorstellungen von der polnischen Megalomanie auch in den Forschungsergebnissen des CBOS keine Bestätigung. Die Liste der negativen Eigenschaften und die der positiven waren gleich lang. Die Analyse der Antworten hat ergeben, daß in 94,4% der Fälle bei den Polen sowohl positive als auch negative Eigenschaften genannt wurden, in 5% nur positive, und in 0,4% ausschließlich negative. Auf Grund der Ergebnisse gelangen die Autoren zur Ansicht, daß die Polen ziemlich realistisch über sich selbst urteilen, daß sowohl unsere Stärken wie auch unsere Schwächen ziemlich klar gesehen werden. Wie ich bereits festgestellt habe, ist die These von der polnischen Megalomanie empirisch recht schwach untermauert.

Seit 1975 führte das Zentrum für Meinungsforschung OBOP Untersuchungen zum Thema der Einstellung sich selbst und den anderen Nationen gegenüber durch (vgl. Jasińska-Kania,1988, und spätere Berichte des OBOP). Den Probanden wurden Nationalitätenlisten in alphabetischer Ordnung präsentiert, um festzustellen, ob sie ihnen gegenüber Sympathie, Abneigung oder Gleichgültigkeit empfinden. Diese systematisch geführten Untersuchungen ließen mit ziemlicher Zuverlässigkeit verfolgen, wie das Verhältnis der Polen gegenüber der eigenen und den fremden Nationen im Laufe der letzten 16 Jahre variierte. Von ziemlicher

Selbstverständlichkeit ist die Tatsache, daß die Polen der eigenen Nation die höchste Sympathie zukommen lassen; nur wenige empfinden hier eine generalisierte Abneigung. Der Prozentsatz derer, die in der besprochenen Zeitspanne der eigenen Nation Sympathie bekundet haben, ist allerdings sichtbar gesunken (von 95% im Jahre 1979 über 91% 1981 auf 81% im Jahre 1988 und 85% 1991). Dieser Sympathieschwund kann durch die Krisensituation und die zunehmend pessimistischeren Erwartungen der Polen im Bereich der materiellen Lebensbedingungen erklärt werden. Dies scheinen auch die Untersuchungen über die Autostereotype der Polen zu bestätigen (vgl. z. B. J. Szacki, 1966; A. Jasińska, R. Siemieńska 1978, 1983). Im Jahre 1966 war die positive Einschätzung dominant – die Durchschnittsbewertung der positiven Eigenschaften der Stereotypen lag bei 3,6; im Jahre 1975 stieg sie bereits auf 4,6. Bei einer anderen Formulierung der Frage (offene Frage, bei der die Feststellung der Durchschnittsbewertung nicht möglich ist) war im Jahre 1972 die Gruppe derer, die ihre eigene Nation nur im positiven Licht sahen, mit denen vergleichbar, die ihr auch nur negative Eigenschaften zuschrieben, wie auch mit denen, die in ihr sowohl positive als auch negative Eigenschaften orteten. Nach dem Krisenjahr 1981 aber fielen die Proportionen grundsätzlich anders aus: 56% wiesen ausschließlich auf schlechte Eigenschaften der Polen hin, 14% nannten nur gute, und 19% maßen den Polen sowohl positive wie auch negative Eigenschaften bei. Aus dem Vergleich dieser Ergebnisse und denen der früher erwähnten Untersuchungen des CBOS aus dem Jahre 1990 geht deutlich hervor, was für ein empfindliches Barometer der sozialen Stimmung eben die Meinung über die eigene Nation sein kann und wie stark diese auf Krisensituationen reagiert.

Die Ergebnisse erlauben es, die Hypothese von einer starken Abhängigkeit zwischen dem Indikator der positiven Stereotypeigenschaften der Nation und der ihr gegenüber deklarierten Sympathie zumindest vorläufig zu verifizieren (nach D. Katz und K. W. Braly). Nach Meinung von A. Jasińska-Kania erlaubt solch ein Vergleich, noch eine These aufzustellen, nach der die Abnahme der positiven Einschätzung der eigenen Nation mit dem Rückgang von optimistischen Erwartungen hinsichtlich der wirtschaftlichen Zukunft des Landes einhergeht (1988, S. 151).

5. Wird das Verhältnis der Polen zu anderen Nationen untersucht, so zeigt es sich, daß in der 2. Hälfte der 80er Jahre die Sympathie für die meisten Nationen erheblich gesunken ist. In den Umfragen aus den Jahren 1986 und 1987 ist keine Nation (bis auf die eigene) von wenigstens 50% der untersuchten Personen positiv eingeschätzt worden. Dies korrespondiert aber nicht mir einem Anstieg von negativen Werturteilen. Im Gegenteil – der Prozentsatz derer, die ihre Abneigung gegenüber anderen Nationen deutlich artikulierten, ist erheblich gesunken. Es ist hier zu betonen, daß in der besprochenen Zeitspanne auch die antisemitischen Gefühle deutlich an Intensität eingebüßt haben.

Die Differenz zwischen den positiv und den negativ gegenüber der jüdischen Nation gesinnten Personen sank von –37% im Jahre 1975 auf –5% 1987 und –2% im Jahre 1991. Am deutlichsten schwankten aber die Einstellungen der

Polen gegenüber den Russen und den Amerikanern, worauf die sich stets verändernde politische Lage und die sie begleitenden Propagandaaktionen nicht ohne Einfluß geblieben sind. Im allgemeinen aber lassen die Ergebnisse der durch das Zentrum für Meinungsforschung OBOP veranstalteten Untersuchungen die Feststellung zu, daß die Einstellungen der Polen gegenüber sich selbst und anderen Nationen in den 80er Jahren dahin tendierten, daß das emotionale Engagement immer schwächer wurde und die Gleichgültigkeit wuchs. Im Jahre 1975 waren es über 50%, die irgendwelche emotionalen Beziehungen zu 6 Nationen (die eigene ausgenommen) deklarierten. In den nächsten Jahren wurden die Emotionen immer schwächer, bis endlich im Jahre 1987 keine andere Nation, bis auf die eigene, irgendwelche emotionale Beziehung bei mehr als 50% der Probanden hervorgerufen hat (weder Sympathie noch Antipathie).

6. Mit den hier dargestellten Untersuchungsergebnissen sind die stereotypen Vorstellungen vom Nationalismus oder der nationalen Megalomanie der Polen keineswegs aufrechtzuerhalten. Man müßte sich aber die Frage stellen nach den Ursachen der anhaltenden Gleichgültigkeit der Polen gegenüber anderen Nationen. Es ist somit eine Frage nach der Erklärung für typische Einstellungen, die in den Erhebungen gefunden wurden. Vor diesem Hintergrund klingt die wichtige Frage nach den Quellen der immer wieder registrierten Akte des Antisemitismus oder der Intoleranz gegenüber anderen Nationalgruppen (z. B. Zigeuner) besonders dramatisch. Es wäre auch wichtig, die Ursachen einer Haltung zu nennen, die sehr zum Unterschied von dem Gefühl, ein Pole zu sein (polskość-Polentum), manchmal als „polactwo" – eine abartige Form des Patriotismus – bezeichnet wird (J. Sosnowski, 1991). Erwägenswert wäre auch, in welchem Grad die Antworten auf die hier gestellten Fragen universellen Charakters sind und in welchem Ausmaß sie nur auf die spezifisch polnische Situation bezogen sind, und schließlich, in welchem Zusammenhang sie mit den Veränderungen in allen Ländern Osteuropas stehen werden.

Die Einstellungen der Bevölkerung gegenüber der eigenen und anderen Nationen können von einem ganzen Komplex verschiedenartiger Faktoren, die kulturellen, ideologischen, politischen und ökonomischen Charakter haben, bestimmt werden. Eine interessante Hypothese versuchte dieses Phänomen durch den Prozeß einer „Bleichung" von Stereotypen infolge der sozialen Beweglichkeit und des immer höheren Bildungsgrades zu erklären. Man lernt die Mitglieder anderer Nationen durch eigene Erfahrungen und nicht mittels überkommenen Stereotypen kennen (D. Katz, K. W. Braly, G. M. Gilbert). Diese These hat allerdings nur einen begrenzten Umfang. Spätere Erhebungen (Karlins, Coffman, Walters) erbrachten nämlich keinen Beweis dafür, daß das Schwinden von Stereotypen eine Regelmäßigkeit mit Dauercharakter aufweist.

In der polnischen Situation würde ich den politischen und ökonomischen Faktoren die entscheidende Bedeutung zukommen lassen. Will man nämlich für die wachsende Gleichgültigkeit in den 80er Jahren eine Erklärung finden, so muß man vor allem den Einfluß einer recht komplizierten und langanhaltenden Krisensituation mitberücksichtigen – die Polen haben sich fast ununterbrochen mit wirtschaftlichen Schwierigkeiten und den damit verbundenen Problemen des Alltags und des politisch-gesellschaftlichen Lebens auseinanderzusetzen. Dazu gesellt sich in letzter Zeit noch die Bedrohung des Sicherheitsgefühls, die sich aus der Unfähigkeit ergibt, mit der neuen Situation fertig zu werden, wie auch aus einer beträchtlichen Abschwächung der Schutzfunktion des Staates. Auch die internationale Lage wirkt sich ungünstig auf die Einstellungen der Bürger aus – vor allem sind die wachsende Spannung in internationalen Beziehungen und die hiermit verbundenen Gefahren dafür verantwortlich. Die Hypothese von der wichtigen Bedeutung ökonomischer Faktoren scheint in den zur Zeit gültigen Meinungen der Polen über andere Nationen ihre Bestätigung zu finden (gemeint sind hier Untersuchungen aus den 90er Jahren). Gegenüber den meisten Nationen hielt sich die Tendenz eines schwachen emotionalen Engagements aufrecht; in einigen Fällen aber wurden bestimmte Veränderungen registriert. In der ersten Hälfte des Jahres 1991 haben 4 Nationen die Sympathie von mehr als 50% der Probanden gewonnen. Es waren dies Amerikaner, denen gegenüber die Sympathie in den letzten 3 Jahren ständig wuchs, dann Franzosen, Italiener und Engländer. Gleichzeitig aber hatten 5 Gruppen (Araber, Russen, Bulgaren, Rumänen und Zigeuner) große Sympathieverluste zu verbuchen. Im laufenden Jahr wurden die Russen und die Rumänen viel häufiger negativ eingeschätzt (seit dem Jahr 1975 zum ersten Mal mehr negative Hinweise als positive). Zunehmend negative Einstellungen registrierte man auch in bezug auf Zigeuner (47%). Es kam zu einem generellen Antipathieanstieg gegenüber den Nationen, die als ursächlich für die wirtschaftliche Katastrophe Polens gesehen werden (Russen) bzw. schwach oder wehrlos sind (Zigeuner), obwohl es bei den letzteren auch ihr Lebensstil sein könnte oder die Wahrnehmung ihrer Verhaltensweisen. Ich bin der Meinung, daß die abneigende Einstellung gegenüber manchen Nationen und ethnischen Gruppen vor allem durch die zunehmende, aus der Bedrohung des Sicherheitsgefühls in nahezu allen Lebensbereichen resultierende Frustration der Bevölkerung erklärt werden kann, die angesichts der fast aussichtslosen Lage krampfhaft nach Sündenböcken sucht. Es ist hier zu betonen, daß die Verbreitung von solchen Stimmungen in der Zukunft bei der Bevölkerung bestimmte stereotype Vorstellungen nur bekräftigen kann. Wie W. Lippmann behauptet: „Stereotype sind unsere Hochburg . . ., hinter deren Mauern wir uns auf unseren Positionen sicher fühlen können" (zitiert nach J. Wiatr, S. 401).

Eine andere Erscheinung, die Anlaß zur Beunruhigung geben kann, ist der neurotische, fremdenfeindliche, autoritäre Patriotismus, der dazu noch seinen streng katholischen Charakter exponiert. Er stellt ohne Frage eine polnische Abart des in ganz Europa ausbrechenden Nationalismus dar. Er bringt allerlei Gefahren mit sich (vgl. J. Sosnowski, 1991, S. 11),

- allen voran die Gefahr eines Staates der Intoleranz, auch wenn diese Gefahr heute noch wenig wahrscheinlich erscheint. Die Erfahrungen und Ergebnisse vieler Umfragen zeigen eher, daß die öffentliche Meinung wirksam jene Lösungen abzuwehren versteht, die grob gegen die Grundsätze der Demokratie verstoßen. Die Befürchtungen, die nationalen Gruppierungen könnten eine Mehrheit im Sejm bilden, haben sich nicht bestätigt.

■ Zweitens besteht eine Gefahr sozialen Charakters, die sich wie folgt charakterisieren läßt: „In einer unstabilen ökonomischen Situation des Landes muß jeder Bürger und jede Gruppe all ihre Kräfte und das Maximum an Energie der Aufgabe widmen, den stets wandelnden Lebensbedingungen gerecht zu werden. Nationalistische Stimmungen dagegen leiten einen Teil dieser Energie in eine andere Richtung ab, indem sie die Menschen nach Feinden suchen lassen. Es ist zu befürchten, daß diese unfruchtbare Beschäftigung zu der letzten Aktivität von Versagern aller Art werden kann".

■ Die dritte Gefahr ist kultureller Natur. Neben der neuen wirtschaftlichen Ordnung wird jetzt auch ein modernes Modell der nationalen Gemeinschaft ausgearbeitet. Die junge Generation tritt eine Revision unserer Traditionen und Wertsysteme an. Extreme Haltungen können den Nationalismus wirksam fördern oder auch – was in gleicher Weise unerwünscht wäre – zur Ausbreitung einer gewissen Distanzierung beitragen: einer generalisierten Abneigung nicht nur gegen das, was mit „polactwo", d. h. mit extremen polonozentrischen Einstellungen im Zusammenhang steht, sondern auch gegen das, was wir im Rahmen der patriotischen Einstellungen unbedingt erhalten wollen.

In meinem Beitrag wollte ich auf Grund der angenommenen Indikatoren nationalistischer Einstellungen und der Ergebnisse empirischer Untersuchungen zeigen, daß solche Einstellungen in Polen doch als eine Randerscheinung zu betrachten sind, auch wenn manche Erscheinungen dieses Bild potentiell stören könnten. Als die wichtigste Aufgabe für die Zukunft erscheint die Beantwortung der Frage, ob Menschen, die auf nationale Gefühle pochen und nationalistische Parolen verbreiten, sich zu gesellschaftlich wichtigen Bezugsgruppen entwickeln und für ihre Theorien einen nahrhaften Boden finden können.

Literaturverzeichnis

1 R. Inglehart, J. R. Rabier, Trust between Nations: Primordial Ties, Societal Learning and Economic Development, Ann Arbor, Brussels 1984.

2 A. Jasińska-Kania, Postawy Polaków wobec róznych narodów (Einstellungen der Polen gegenüber verschiedenen Nationen): Kultura i Społeczeństwo, 1988, Nr. 4.

3 A. Jasińska, R. Siemieńska, Wzory osobowe socjalizmu (Persönlichkeitsmuster des Sozialismus), Warszawa 1978.

4 A. Jasińska, R. Siemieńska, The Socialist Personality: A Case Study of Poland, International Journal of Sociology, Vol. 13, Nr. 1, 1983.

5 J. Kurczewska, Etnocentryzm a ideologia narodowa (Ethnozentrismus und nationale Ideologie): Kultura i Społeczeństwo, 1988, Nr. 4.

6 H. O. Laswell, Nations and Classes. The Symbols of Identification, in: Reader in Public Opinion and Communication, hrsg. von B. Berelson und M. Janowitz.

7 W. Pisarek, Obce kultury narodowe w świadomości Polaków (Fremde Nationalkulturen im Bewußtsein der Polen), Kraków 1990.

8 Polacy sami o sobie (Polen über sich selbst), ein Bericht des CBOS vom Februar 1990; Biuletyn CBOS, 1990, Nr. 5.

9 Berichte des OBOP über die in den Jahren 1988, 1989, 1990, 1991 durchgeführten Untersuchungen.

10 J. Sosnowski, Polskość i polactwo (Polentum und „Polactwo"): gazeta Wyborcza vom 5. August 1991.
11 J. Szacki, Polacy o sobie i innych narodach (Die Polen über sich selbst und andere Nationen), OBOPiSP; Warszawa 1969.
12 Jerzy Wiatr, Naród i Państwo (Nation und Staat), Warszawa 1969.

Tabelle 1: Sympathie gegenüber anderen Nationen

Prozentsatz der untersuchten Personen, die gegenüber den gegebenen Nationen Sympathie deklarierten (in einzelnen Jahren)

	V 1975	IV 1977	II 1981	IV 1982	II 1983	V 1984	V 1985	V 1986	X 1986	V 1987	V 1988	IV 1989	IV 1990	III 1991
Polen	95	-	91	91	92	91	91	91	88	88	81	84	89	85
Russen	59	52	32	32	36	37	45	31	39	33	30	28	24	16
Ungarn	54	64	56	58	58	53	66	52	46	45	39	44	49	44
Franzosen	54	60	54	56	51	45	47	42	42	41	35	46	62	61
Tschechen	42	46	36	36	38	43	51	42	40	36	37	45	41	36
Slowaken	41	-	43	42	42	42	52	43	39	38	36	39	46	35
Amerikaner	37	44	43	37	29	26	27	25	26	32	37	51	67	68
Italiener	34	-	37	42	40	37	46	45	37	39	37	49	57	59
Vietnamesen	33	-	25	23	26	22	31	23	23	17	16	20	12	16
Bulgaren	30	-	32	34	31	32	44	32	30	25	23	24	23	19
Engländer	28	29	31	29	28	27	32	28	26	27	26	40	48	50
Rumänen	26	-	27	25	26	24	33	24	24	18	20	21	27	17
Spanier	24	-	24	25	28	26	31	30	27	23	22	29	36	37
Schweden	24	-	24	28	26	23	31	31	28	21	21	30	37	38
Neger	18	-	20	17	17	15	21	15	14	12	13	15	14	16
Portugiesen	15	-	12	11	11	-	-	15	-	-	-	-	-	-
Japaner	14	-	13	30	33	27	41	33	34	31	36	41	42	39
Chilenen	14	-	12	11	12	11	-	12	-	-	-	-	-	-
Zigeuner	12	-	12	11	9	10	9	8	7	8	6	10	7	8
Araber	12	11	6	7	8	7	10	9	10	7	6	9	7	7
Deutsche/DDR	8	7	13	23	19	22	28	21	21	17	18	20	13	23
Deutsche/BRD			9	15	9	12	10	12	13	13	16	23		
Türken	6	-	7	8	8	-	-	8	-	-	8	12	12	11
Chinesen	4	6	6	8	9	9	21	16	20	16	17	22	12	14
Juden	4	5	7	6	8	9	13	9	10	11	11	14	15	17

Quelle: A. Jasinska-Kania, 1988, und spätere Berichte CBOP.

Tabelle 2: Abneigung gegenüber anderen Nationen

	Prozentsatz der untersuchten Personen, die gegenüber den gegebenen Nationen Abneigung deklarierten (in einzelnen Jahren)													
	V 1975	IV 1977	II 1981	IV 1982	II 1983	V 1984	V 1985	V 1986	X 1986	V 1987	V 1988	IV 1989	IV 1990	III 1991
Deutsche/BRD	60	61	49	32	46	36	48	35	34	35	29	27	44	34
Deutsche/DDR			37	23	28	23	25	21	22	24	23	28		
Juden	41	38	25	23	24	20	23	18	18	16	19	21	20	19
Zigeuner	39	-	34	29	33	32	38	32	33	29	34	41	44	47
Chinesen	23	27	15	14	12	11	10	6	6	5	6	7	19	11
Neger	14	-	12	12	12	16	17	12	15	15	15	19	21	21
Türken	12	-	12	11	13	-	-	9	-	-	13	14	17	17
Araber	11	14	15	13	14	15	15	14	16	14	20	23	27	32
Tschechen	11	11	17	12	13	9	12	9	7	8	8	15	16	16
Russen	7	12	23	16	14	15	14	12	11	13	13	20	24	32
Japaner	7	-	6	4	3	4	5	4	3	4	4	3	6	5
Chilenen	6	-	3	4	3	5	-	3	-	-	-	-	-	-
Schweden	6	-	5	5	3	4	5	3	3	4	5	4	6	4
Engländer	5	6	4	6	6	5	7	7	7	3	6	5	6	3
Rumänen	5	-	7	7	5	6	8	5	6	7	12	14	17	29
Vietnamesen	5	-	4	4	3	4	6	3	3	3	7	8	12	9
Amerikaner	4	3	5	11	16	14	25	17	13	8	5	3	1	1
Portugiesen	4	-	3	2	3	-	-	1	-	-	-	-	-	-
Italiener	4	-	4	4	4	3	5	2	2	2	3	3	3	1
Bulgaren	3	-	3	3	5	5	6	4	4	4	6	8	11	13
Franzosen	3	2	2	2	2	3	8	3	3	2	3	3	3	2
Spanier	3	-	2	2	1	2	3	1	1	2	2	4	4	2
Slowaken	3	-	4	4	5	2	3	2	3	3	4	6	7	8
Ungarn	2	2	2	2	2	2	1	2	2	1	4	4	5	4
Polen	0	-	1	1	1	0	1	0	1	1	2	2	2	2

Quelle: A. Jasinska-Kania, 1988, und spätere Berichte CBOP.

Tabelle 3: Gleichgültiges Verhältnis zu verschiedenen Nationen

Prozentsatz der untersuchten Personen, die gegenüber anderen Nationen ihre Gleichgültigkeit deklarierten oder keine Meinung hatten

	V 1975	IV 1977	II 1981	IV 1982	II 1983	V 1984	V 1985	V 1986	X 1986	V 1987	V 1988	IV 1989	IV 1990	III 1991
Türken	82	-	81	81	79	-	-	83	-	-	79	74	71	72
Portugiesen	81	-	86	87	86	-	-	84	-	-	-	-	-	-
Chilenen	80	-	83	85	85	84	-	85	-	-	-	-	-	-
Japaner	79	-	71	66	64	69	54	63	63	65	60	56	52	56
Araber	77	75	78	80	78	78	75	77	74	79	74	68	66	61
Chinesen	73	67	70	78	79	80	69	78	74	79	77	71	69	75
Spanier	73	-	73	73	71	72	66	69	72	75	76	67	60	61
Schweden	70	-	70	67	71	73	64	66	69	75	74	66	67	58
Rumänen	69	-	66	68	69	70	59	71	70	75	68	65	56	54
Neger	68	-	68	71	71	69	62	73	71	73	72	66	65	63
Engländer	67	65	65	65	66	68	61	65	67	70	68	55	46	47
Bulgaren	67	-	65	63	64	63	50	64	66	71	71	68	66	68
Vietnamesen	62	-	71	73	71	74	63	74	74	80	77	72	76	75
Italiener	62	-	59	54	56	60	49	53	61	59	60	48	40	40
Amerikaner	59	53	52	52	55	60	48	58	61	60	58	46	32	31
Slowaken	56	-	53	54	53	56	45	55	58	59	60	55	47	57
Juden	54	57	67	71	68	71	64	73	72	73	70	65	65	64
Zigeuner	49	-	57	60	58	57	53	60	60	63	60	49	49	45
Tschechen	47	43	47	52	49	48	37	49	53	56	55	50	43	48
Ungarn	44	34	42	40	40	45	33	46	52	54	57	52	46	52
Franzosen	43	38	40	43	47	52	45	55	55	57	62	51	35	37
Russen	34	36	44	52	50	48	41	57	50	54	57	52	52	52
Deutsche/DDR	32	32	50	54	53	55	47	58	57	59	59	52	43	43
Deutsche/BRD			42	53	45	52	42	53	53	52	55	50		
Polen	5	-	7	8	7	9	8	9	11	10	17	14	9	13

Quelle: A. Jasinska-Kania, 1988, und spätere Berichte OBOP.

Tabelle 4:
Indikatoren der Einstellungsorientierung gegenüber verschiedenen Nationen

	Differenz zwischen den positiven und negativen Einstellungen													
	V 1975	IV 1977	II 1981	IV 1982	II 1983	V 1984	V 1985	V 1986	X 1986	V 1987	V 1988	IV 1989	IV 1990	III 1991
Engländer	+23	+23	+27	+23	+22	+22	+25	+21	+19	+24	+20	+35	+42	+47
Amerikaner	+33	+41	+38	+26	+13	+12	+2	+8	+13	+24	+32	+48	+66	+67
Araber	+1	-3	-9	-6	-6	-8	-5	-5	-6	-7	-12	-23	-27	-32
Bulgaren	+27	-	+29	+31	+26	+27	+38	+28	+26	+21	+17	+16	+12	+6
Chilenen	+8	-	+7	+7	+8	+6	-	+9	-	-	-	-	-	-
Chinesen	-19	-21	-9	-6	-3	-2	+11	+10	+14	+11	+11	+15	-7	+3
Zigeuner	-27	-	-22	-18	-24	-22	-29	-24	-26	-21	-28	-31	-37	-39
Tschechen	+31	+35	+19	+24	+25	+34	+39	+33	+33	+28	+29	+20	+25	+20
Franzosen	+51	+58	+52	+54	+49	+42	+39	+39	+39	+39	+32	+43	+59	+59
Spanier	+21	-	+22	+23	+27	+24	+29	+29	+26	+21	+19	+25	+32	+36
Japaner	+7	-	+17	+26	+30	+23	+36	+29	+31	+27	+32	+38	+36	+34
Neger	+4	-	+78	+5	+5	-1	+4	+3	-1	-3	-5	-4	-7	-5
Deutsche/DDR	-52	-54	-24	0	-9	-1	+3	0	-1	-7	-5	-8	-31	-11
Deutsche/BRD			-40	-16	-37	-24	-38	-23	-21	-23	-13	-4		
Portugiesen	+11	-	+9	+9	+8	-	-	+14	-	-	-	-	-	-
Russen	+52	+40	+9	+16	+22	+22	+31	+19	+28	+20	+17	+8	0	-16
Rumänen	+21	-	+20	+18	+21	+18	+25	+19	+18	+11	+8	+7	+10	-12
Slowaken	+38	-	+39	+38	+37	+40	+48	+41	+36	+34	+32	+33	+39	+27
Schweden	+18	-	+19	+23	+23	+19	+26	+28	+25	+17	+16	+26	+29	+34
Türken	-6	-	-5	-3	-5	-	-	-1	-	-	-5	-2	-5	-6
Vietnamesen	-29	-	+21	+19	+23	+18	+25	+20	+20	+14	+9	+2	0	+7
Ungarn	+52	+62	+54	+56	+56	+51	+65	+51	+44	+44	+35	+40	+44	+40
Italiener	+30	-	+33	+38	+36	+34	+41	+43	+35	+37	+34	+46	+54	+58
Juden	+37	-33	-18	-17	-16	-11	-10	-9	-8	-5	-8	-7	-5	-2
Polen	+95	-	+90	+90	+91	+91	+90	+90	+87	+87	+79	+82	+87	+83

Quelle: A. Jasinska-Kania, 1988, und spätere Berichte OBOP.

Teresa Sasińska-Klas

Die Revitalisierungsfrage der sozialdemokratischen Ideale im heutigen Polen

Wider alle Erwartungen ist in den post-kommunistischen Ländern die Einteilung in linke und rechte Parteiorientierungen nicht verschwunden. Im Gegenteil, heute stehen diese Länder vor dem grundsätzlichen Problem der Entscheidung für die eine oder andere Seite.

Seit den letzten Wahlen zum Sejm am 27. Oktober 1991 ist dies nun auch ein Problem für Polen geworden. Die Wahlergebnisse (siehe Aufstellung auf S. 151) zeigen deutlich die politische Spaltung in der polnischen Bevölkerung. Der alte Konflikt, unterteilt in „Linke – Rechte", existiert auch weiterhin, ist aber nun in bezug auf die Kriterien und den generellen Charakter dieser Aufspaltung anders geworden.

Was ist nun das Wesentliche in den politischen Hauptströmungen in Polen heute, Ende 1991? Die Beantwortung dieser Frage ist nicht einfach. Sie ist jedoch wichtig für das Unterfangen, zu verstehen, was die polnische Gesellschaft teilt, was sie verbindet, wo Übereinstimmung zu erreichen ist und wo die Interessenkonflikte liegen. In diesen Erwägungen wollen wir hier besonders den linken Gruppen unsere Aufmerksamkeit schenken, denn sie sind bei den demokratischen Parlamentswahlen wieder einmal, wenn auch in veränderter politischer Konstellation, zu einem Element des politischen Spieles geworden. Zuerst aber müssen wir uns fragen, was die neuen Richtungslinien der heutigen linken Orientierungen sind, wie sich ihre Schwächen und Stärken darstellen und wie die politischen und institutionellen Interessen – nach zwei Jahren nichtkommunistischer Regierung in Polen – artikuliert sind. In sich selbst ist die politische Linke jetzt sehr unterschiedlich gefärbt: Die verschiedenen Rottöne erstrecken sich vom zarten Rosa über Karminrot bis zu einem tiefen Lila. Jedoch alle diese Farbnuancen treffen sich auf einer gemeinsamen Gedanken- und Gefühlsebene, trotz der recht differenzierten Intensität.[1] Die negativen Erfahrungen des Kommunismus haben bewirkt, daß die Linke heute nicht mehr mit der Bewegung identifiziert werden kann, deren Ziel es war, die Vision einer glücklichen Gesellschaft der siegreichen Revolution zu verwirklichen mit dem Motto „es wird besser werden".[2]

Was sie neue polnische Linke, Anfang der 90er Jahre charakterisiert, ist Kritizismus. Die Menschen, die aus den linken politischen Richtungen hervorgegangen sind, präsentieren einen kritischen Scharfblick: Sie sehen in der sie umgebenden wirtschaftspolitischen Wirklichkeit ein Übel – das Werk anderer Menschen mit anderer Färbung –, welches sie brandmarken. Die postkommunistischen Linken (zahlenmäßig die stärkste Gruppe) sehen der politischen Wirklichkeit, in der sie nach den Wahlen 1989 und der Machtabgabe funktionieren müssen, nicht nur kritisch, sondern auch mißtrauisch entgegen. Sie fordern Veränderungen, sind aber allein nicht stark genug, um sie selbständig realisieren zu können.[3]

Was jedoch bewirkt, daß diese Menschen und die Parteien der politischen Linken im Jahre 1991 mit Determination Änderungen anstreben und daß ihre Kritik momentan den Anschein von Utopie zu haben scheint? Welche Weltanschauung gibt ihnen den Glauben, daß ein ständiger Regierungs- bzw. Staatsordnungswechsel die Wirklichkeit zu bessern vermag? Wie kommt es, daß sowohl der Philosoph Leszek Kołakowski als auch Adam Michnik – ein Politiker der Demokratischen Union – und Włodzimierz Cimoszewicz, der Fraktionsvorsitzende der sozialdemokratischen Linken, sich in vielen Fragen einig sind, auch wenn man sie dessen – dem Anschein nach – kaum verdächtigen sollte?

Auf der linken Seite der politischen Szene in Polen steht die Sozialdemokratie der Republik Polen, die mit den ehemaligen Gewerkschaften der OPZZ den Kern des Bündnisses der Demokratischen Linken im Sejm bildet. (Ihre Wahlliste umfaßte den Parteileiter Aleksander Kwiaśniewski, den Generalsekretär der Partei, Leszek Miller, den Fraktionsvorsitzenden Włodzimierz Cimoszewicz und die Mitglieder Józef Oleksy, Jerzy Wiatr, Longin Pastusiak, Danuta Waniek und andere.) Bei den Wahlen nahm diese Partei mit 11,98% der Stimmen und 60 Mandaten den zweiten Platz im neu gewählten Sejm ein. Knapp gewonnen hatte Tadeusz Mazowiecki's Demokratische Union mit nur 0,33% mehr als die Linken und insgesamt 62 Mandaten.[4] Die anderen linken Splitterparteien, aus der Solidaritätsbewegung hervorgegangen, sind a) Zbigniew Bujaks' Demokratisch-Soziale Bewegung (mit 0,46% Stimmenanteil und einem Mandat)[5] und b) „Solidarität der Arbeit", geleitet von Ryszard Rugaj und Karol Modzelewski, mit 2,05% der Stimmen und 4 Mandaten im Sejm.[6] Links gerichtet sind auch einzelne Mitglieder der Gewerkschaft „Solidarität", die zum neuen Sejm gewählt wurden, wie Bogdan Borusewicz und Jan Rulewski. „Solidarność" gewann 5,05% und 27 Mandate.

Zur linken Richtung im heutigen Polen gehören nicht nur die Exkommunisten, sondern zum Teil auch Mitglieder von „Solidarität" und anderen politischen Konstellationen. Dies ist eine Widerspiegelung der Tatsache, daß es für die meisten Polen schwierig ist, ihre persönliche Verbundenheit zu einer politischen Orientierung klar zu beschreiben – die Ergebnisse der letzten Wahlen dürfen hier wohl als Beweis dessen erwähnt werden. Es liegt doch auf der Hand, daß man nicht von heute auf morgen Sozialdemokrat werden kann, nachdem man 41 Jahre lang Erfahrungen, in enger emotionaler und formaler Verbundenheit, mit der kommunistischen Partei gemacht hatte. Wie bereits erwähnt, sind die heutigen linken Strömungen in Polen sehr differenziert. Aber alle berufen sich, mehr oder weniger offen, auf die Parolen der linken Richtung.[7] Die Teilung jedoch zwischen linker und rechter Politik in Polen, direkt nach den Wahlen zum Sejm, führt keinesfalls zu einer klaren Aufgabenstellung. Angesichts der angestrebten und bevorstehenden Eingliederung in das vereinigte Europa jedoch müssen aber klare Richtlinien ausgearbeitet werden.

Nun wirft sich, nach den unerwarteten Wahlergebnissen zum Sejm, die Frage auf, ob denn eine Revitalisierung der sozialdemokratischen Ideale im heutigen

Polen möglich ist. Die Antwort ist von ausschlaggebender Bedeutung für Polen, aber auch für Osteuropa und auch auf der Weltskala. Politologen, Soziologen, Philosophen, Juristen und Politiker machen sich darüber Gedanken. Warum hat bei diesen ersten völlig demokratischen Wahlen „Solidarność" nicht gewonnen? Weshalb mußte die Präsidentenpartei, aber auch die katholische Religionspartei eine Niederlage einstecken? Wieso haben sich an den demokratischen Wahlen nur 43,2% der Wahlberechtigten beteiligt? Weshalb enthielt sich der Rest der Bevölkerung der Stimme? Wer wählte und wer blieb zu Hause? Gerade diese letzten Fragen sind von großer Wichtigkeit, denn bei den Durchbruchswahlen 1989, nach den Juni-Gesprächen am „Runden Tisch" und der Unterzeichnung des Gesellschaftsvertrages zwischen „Solidarność" und der kommunistischen Regierung und Partei, lag die Wahlbeteiligung bei 62%. Dieses Ergebnis machte damals schon klar, wie hoch die Grenze der gesellschaftlichen Mobilisierung liegt; das spätere Wahlverhalten der polnischen Wähler muß daran gemessen und interpretiert werden. Bei den letzten Wahlen ist das politische Interesse erheblich gesunken – etwa um 20%. 1989 wurde nicht nur *gegen* die Kommunisten gestimmt, sondern auch *für* das Programm der damals noch oppositionellen Seite „Solidarność, d. h. das Programm des Bürgerkomitees. In diesem Programm stand u. a., daß „wir danach streben werden, daß die Landwirtschaft den ihr gebührenden Platz einnehmen kann . . ., wir unterstützen die Politik der Vollbeschäftigung; Hungerrenten betrachten wir als eine Verletzung der Versicherungsverträge; wir wollen den Mitarbeitern des Gesundheitswesens entsprechende Verdienstmöglichkeiten und Bedingungen für die richtige Krankenpflege gewährleisten; wir fordern eine größere finanzielle Unterstützung für das Schul- und Hochschulwesen" etc.[8]

Diese Versprechungen wurden aber nicht eingehalten, und das durch postkommunistische Regierungen geleitete Reformprogramm stand zu ihnen in krassem Widerspruch. Das im Frühjahr 1989 von den Bürgerkomitees der „Solidarność" vorbereitete Programm sollte ein Instrument der Opposition im Wahlkampf werden. Der Wahlsieg der Opposition im Juni 1989 führte dann dazu, daß sie die Macht übernahm. Jedoch war sie außerstande, mit diesem Programm die ökonomische und politische Macht wirksam auszuüben.

Im Mai 1990 fanden in Polen die Kommunalwahlen statt unter dem Motto der vollen Autonomie für die Lokalmacht: „Die Übernahme der eigenen Probleme in die eigenen Hände".[9] Es zeigte sich jedoch nach den Wahlen recht schnell, daß die Lokalmacht nach wie vor entmündigt ist, in diesem Fall nun durch die neue Konstellation der politischen Macht. Die Hoffnung auf territoriale Selbstverwaltung ist sehr ungewiß. Wieder einmal bekam die Wählerschaft zu spüren, daß die Ergebnisse nach den Wahlen die gesellschaftlichen Erwartungen bei weitem verfehlt haben.

Bei den Präsidentenwahlen, die im November und Dezember 1990 stattfanden, war die Mehrheit der Bevölkerung Polens für Lech Wałęsa und für sein Programm der Beschleunigung; und sie war gegen das von dem damaligen Premierminister Tadeusz Mazowiecki realisierte gemäßigte Reformprogramm. Als Kandidat für das Amt des Präsidenten kündigte Lech Wałęsa im Herbst 1990 an, daß er nach seiner Wahl das Postulat der Vollbeschäftigung erfüllen, das Tempo von ökonomischen und politischen Reformen im Lande beschleunigen und die „Kommunisten allesamt nach Sibirien schicken" werde.[10] Es ist nun knapp ein Jahr vergangen, und die politischen Wähler müssen erkennen, daß sie schon wieder einmal nicht das bekamen, wofür sie ihre Stimmen abgegeben hatten. Statt den im Herbst angekündigten Durchbruch zu verwirklichen, setzte die Regierung Premier Mazowieckis Politik fort.

In diesem Licht gesehen erscheinen die Wahlergebnisse weniger überraschend.

Die Revitalisierung der sozialdemokratischen Parolen benötige eine tiefe Reflexion und eingehende Analyse.[11] Diese Parolen wurden von dem Bündnis der Demokratischen Linken verkündet, das aus den Reihen der ehemals kommunistischen PVAP hervorgegangen war.[12] Diese Gruppe erfährt nun wachsende Popularität – knapp zwei Jahre nach der Selbstauflösung der kommunistischen Partei, d. h. seit dem 27. Januar 1990 – mit einem offensichtlichen Wahlsieg der alten kommunistischen Kräfte, die jetzt einen sozialdemokratischen Weg ansteuern. Eine überraschende Wende, denn es waren nicht mehr „vertragliche" Wahlen, wie es noch im Jahre 1989 – nach den Gesprächen am Runden Tisch – der Fall gewesen war. Hatte doch die sozialdemokratische Linke im Sejm der 10. Kadenz, im Bündnis die Demokratischen Linken vertretend, bei den Präsidentenwahlen im Herbst 1990 grundsätzliche Probleme mit der Gewinnung neuer Wähler. Sie konnte nur knapp 10% der Stimmen auf das Konto ihres Kandidaten, Włodzimierz Cimoszewicz, verbuchen. Damals schien es angemessen, die Stärke und den politischen Einfluß der unter sozialdemokratischen Parolen antretenden post-kommunistischen Linken gerade so hoch einzuschätzen.

Bei den letzten Wahlen gewannen sie zusätzlich 2,5%. Dieser Zuwachs, so darf wohl angenommen werden, kam aus den Kreisen derjenigen, die mit der bisherigen Art der Machtausübung durch nicht-kommunistische Eliten unzufrieden waren. Darüber hinaus bezeugt der Anstieg der Wählerstimmen die Attraktivität ihres Programmes, was als ein Ausdruck der demokratischen Legitimisierung der sozialdemokratischen Richtung in der aktuellen Konstellation politischer Kräfte in Polen anzusehen ist.

In den neuesten Wahlanalysen taucht das Argument auf, daß für das Bündnis der Demokratischen Linken ausschließlich die alte Nomenklatur stimmte. Das ist, politisch gesehen, eine recht bequeme These; jedoch scheint sie nicht aufrecht zu erhalten sein. Das scheint auch der Kommentator der einflußreichsten politischen Zeitung Polens, der „Gazeta Wyborcza" (Wahlzeitung), Dawid Warszawski, eingesehen zu haben,[13] wenn er schreibt, daß bei den letzten Präsidentenwahlen der Kandidat der Linken, Włodzimierz Cimoszewicz, 23% der Stimmen in der Region gewonnen hat, der er entstammt (das Gebiet um Białystok herum im Norden Polens). So kann man es also eher als einen Ausdruck der politischen Sympathie dem Kandidaten gegenüber betrachten, ganz unabhängig von seiner politischen Affiliation. (Im politischen Sinne haben sich diese Gebiete bisher nicht besonders hervorgetan, und sie galten auch niemals als ein Zentrum kommunistischer politischer Einflüsse.) 22% der Stimmen jedoch, die bei den letzten Wahlen in Sosnowiec – einem typischen Industriegebiet mit der größten Stahlhütte Polens, Huta Katowice – der Linken zugeteilt wurden , drücken eine tiefe wirtschaftliche Krise aus und bezeugen eine mangelnde politische Unterstützung für den Präsidenten Wałęsa und der von ihm vertretenen politischen Richtung.

Eine zusätzliche Erklärung für die wachsende politische Unterstützung der linken Kräfte Polens liefert die politische Aktivität eines anderen Schauspielers auf der politischen Szene Polens unter einer nicht-kommunistischen Regierung: nämlich der Katholischen Kirche. Das starke politische Engagement der katholischen Priester und ihre beratende Funktion zugunsten christlicher Parteien brachte der katholischen Partei nicht den erhofften Erfolg. Trotz allgemeiner Aufrufe, wie z. B. das Motto „ein Katholik den Katholiken, ein Jude den Juden und ein Kommunist den Kommunisten"[14], gewannen sie nur 8,73% der Stimmen und damit den 3. Platz. Das ist nur ein Bruchteil der ca. 92% Katholiken in Polen. Die Wähler, die für die Linken stimmten, taten das trotz historischer Tatsachen und der Bewertung der kommunistischen Machtausübung der Jahre 1945–1989.

Die letzten Wahlergebnisse geben Anlaß zur Aufstellung einer These über die politische Legitimisierung des Bündnisses der Demokratischen Linken (und somit auch der ehemaligen Kommunisten). Die Gründe sind folgendermaßen:

1. Das Lager „Solidarność" hat nach der Machtübernahme im Sommer 1989 nicht nur die Postulate der sozialen Linken gänzlich verworfen, sondern ist auch von den Idealen und Werten abgegangen, die dem politischen Programm von „Solidarność" zugrunde lagen. Dies hat allmählich zu seiner Delegitimisierung in den Augen des politisch aktiven Teils der polnischen Bevölkerung geführt.

2. Dem linken Flügel der „Solidarność"-Wähler wurde die Chance ihrer eigenen politischen Repräsentation im Rahmen der institutionellen Struktur geraubt, und sie unterstützt nun die Linke.

3. Das Bündnis der sozialdemokratischen Linken führte vor den Wahlen zu Sejm und Senat einen politisch offensiven, argumentativ zielsicheren und, im Endeffekt, wirksamen Wahlkampf. Er erinnerte an die nicht realisierten Versprechungen des „Solidarność"-Lagers aus der Zeit der Sejm-, Kommunal- und Präsidentenwahlen.

4. In der Woche vor den Wahlen wurden im ersten Fernsehprogramm, zur Zeit der höchsten Einschaltquoten, zwei Interviews mit dem Präsidenten Lech Wałęsa ausgestrahlt. Drei Tage vor den Wahlen, am 23. Oktober 1991, kündigte er an, daß er sofort nach den Wahlen dafür sorgen werde, daß die „Kommune fertig gemacht wird", denn „sonst tun es die Leute selbst, und zwar so, daß eine Obduktion not tut". Er sagte auch: „Meine Herren Kommunisten, ihr habt das Recht beraubt, Polen beraubt, Geld ausgeführt. Wir machen uns daran, wenn Polen zu den Wahlen gehen wird." Gleichzeitig aber sagte er auch: „Wenn die Kommunisten gewinnen, werde ich abtreten."[15]

Die Drohungen des Präsidenten, so kurz vor den Wahlen, haben ohne Zweifel die linken Wähler mobilisiert; auch diejenigen, die aus anderen politischen Richtungen hervorgegangen sind, aber dem Bündnis ihre Stimmen gaben, weil sie keine andere Wahl sahen. Die Fragen, die sich infolge des offensichtlichen Wahl-erfolges der linken Kräfte bei den demokratischen Wahlen zum Sejm Ende des Jahres 1991 nun aufwerfen, lauten: Was nun? Wie wird sich die neue Kräftekonstellation jetzt auf der polnischen politischen Szene gestalten? Welche Wege werden jetzt eingeschlagen werden?

Das Ergebnis der Wahlen brachte keine endgültige Entscheidung. Gewonnen hat die Demokratische Union Mazowieckis mit 0,33% mehr Stimmen als die Linke, die aus der „Solidarność"-Bewegung hervorgegangen ist. Die ehemaligen Kommunisten, seit zwei Jahren unter dem Schild der Sozialdemokratie, sitzen ihr jedoch auf „auf den Fersen" – als ein Ergebnis vollkommen demokratischer politischer Entscheidungen der polnischen Wähler.

Dieses Wahlergebnis deutet darauf hin, daß im post-kommunistischen Polen das Vertrauen in die Politik schwächer wird und daß die Leute nicht mehr an den Zusammenhang zwischen dem Urnengang und dem täglichen Leben glauben wollen.

Das sind die politisch denkenden Polen Anno Domini 1991. Dies ist eine äußerst beunruhigende Tatsache, denn die politisch schweigende Mehrheit der polnischen Wähler ist eine politisch unbekannte Größe. Welche Energien in ihr gespeichert sind und in welche Richtung sie freigesetzt werden, ist heute noch schwer abzuschätzen.

Doch die Parlamentswahlen haben gezeigt, wie die Polen heute, nach zwei Jahren nicht-kommunistischer Regierung, denken. Es lohnt sich, dieser Wahrheit ins Auge zu sehen, auch wenn sie die politischen Kräfte der „Solidarność" – bis vor kurzem die größte moralische Autorität – bloßgestellt und das gesellschaftliche Bedürfnis nach den für sozialdemokratische Richtungen typischen Ideale und Werte offenbart hat.

Schlußbemerkungen

Es wäre noch verfrüht zu prognostizieren, ob sich die Attraktivität der sozialdemokratischen Ideale und Werte als eine beständiger Größe erweisen wird. Nichtsdestoweniger ist es bereits jetzt klar, daß die neue, nach den Wahlen 1989 entstandene post-kommunistische politische Konstellation zerfallen ist. Die Zersplitterung der politischen Parlamentslandschaft ist bereits Tatsache geworden.[16] In den demokratischen politischen Systemen ist es das Recht der stärksten Partei, unter dem Mangel einer entscheidenden Mehrheit eine Regierungskoalition zu bilden. In Polen fehlt es jetzt an starken politischen Gruppen. Eine Koalition politischer Kräfte, die die meisten Stimmen erhalten haben, erscheint jedoch unwahrscheinlich. Gemeint ist hier eine Koalition der zentrum-orientierten Demokratischen Union, der post-kommunistischen Linken (die sozialdemokratische Werte lanciert), der konservativen Katholiken der Bauernpartei, der anti-kommunistischen Konföderation „Unabhängiges Polen", der Zentrums-Allianz und der liberalen Partei des Premierministers Bielecki. So stehen also die Linke, das Zentrum und die Rechte vor der Herausforderung, nun auf zivilisierte Art nebeneinander zu existieren und zusammen zu wirken, das Existenzrecht der Gegenseite anzuerkennen und ihren politischen Willen zu berücksichtigen. Die Bereitschaft zu einem Kompromiß ist nicht in Sicht.

Es ist auf den ersten Blick zu erkennen, daß sie Zusammensetzung des Parlaments keine Stabilität der Exekutivgewalt gewährleistet. Die Chance, von einer kommunistisch-nichtdemokratischen zu einer postkommunistisch-demokratischen Ordnung überzugehen, hat nur einen geringen Wahrscheinlichkeitsgrad.[17] Der Wahlerfolg der Sozialdemokratischen Linken zeigt, daß dies keine leichte Aufgabe sein wird. Desto wahrscheinlicher erscheint dagegen die Möglichkeit einer autoritären Regierungsform und Verstärkung des Präsidialsystems. Eine solche Form der Regierung wird allerdings sehr aufmerksam beobachtet und einer politischen Bewertung durch die sich erneuernde sozialdemokratische Richtung unterzogen werden.

Wahlergebnisse vom 27. Oktober 1991

1. Demokratische Union
2. Bündnis der Demokratischen Linken
3. Katholische Wahlaktion
4. Polnische Bauernpartei – Programmbündnis
5. Konföderation „Unabhängiges Polen"
6. Zentrums-Allianz
7. Liberaldemokratischer Kongreß
8. Bauernallianz
9. „Solidarność"
10. Polnische Partei der Bierfreunde
11. Deutsche Minderheit
12. Christliche Demokratie
13. Polnischer Westbund
14. Partei der Christlichen Demokraten
15. Solidarität der Arbeit
16. Union der Realpolitik
17. X-Partei
18. Bewegung für die Autonomie Schlesiens
19. Demokratische Partei
20. Demokratisch-soziale Bewegung
21. Union der Großpolen
22. Bauerneinheit
23. „Für Großpolen und Polen"
24. Solidarität 80
25. Bauernwahl-Allianz „Piast"
26. Wahlkomitee der Orthodoxen
27. Krakauer Präsidentenpartei

28. Podhale-Verband
29. Frauenbündnis für die Probleme des alltäglichen schweren Lebens

Anmerkungen

1 Wojciech Chudy, Istota lewicy. In: „Spotkania" Nr. 40, 16. Oktober 1991, S. 20.
2 Ibidem, S. 20.
3 Ein Interview mit Leszek Kołakowski; Oko za oczy. In: „Wprost" Nr. 42, 20. Oktober 1991, S. 13–14.
4 Ostateczne wyniki wyborów do Sejmu. In: Gazeta Wyborcza, Nr. 256, 2./3. November 1991, S. 1.
5 Ibidem, S. 1.
6 Ibidem, S. 1.
7 Teresa Sasińska-Klas, Changes on the Polish Left: Exit the Communist Party, Enter the Social-democratic. In: Teresa Sasińska-Klas (ed.), From Eastern to Central Europe, University of Guelph, Guelph 1990, S. 198–221.
8 Op. cit. Dawid Warszawski, Pasztet z 27 października. In: „Gazeta Wyborcza", Nr. 256, 2./3. November 1991, S. 8.
9 Ibidem, S. 8.
10 Teresa Sasińska-Klas, Polskie wybory prezydenckie z amerykańskiej i kanadyjskiej perspektywy. Manuskript, Polnische Gesellschaft für Politologen, Kraków, Januar 1991.
11 „Deklaracja Socjaldemokracji Rzeczypospolitej Polskiej uchwalona 29 stycznia 1990 r." und „Statut SDRP przyjęty przez Kongres Założycielski w dniu 28 stycznia 1990".
12 Aleksander Hall, Klatka chorych na socjalizm. In: „Wprost", Nr. 43, 27. Oktober 1991, S. 22–23.
13 Dawid Warszawski, Pasztet . . ., S. 8–9.
14 Op. cit., „The European", 27. Oktober 1991, S. 6.
15 K. L. „Dokończę Komunę" (Lech Wałęsa w telewizji). In: „Czas Krakowski", Nr. 236, 24. Oktober 1991, S. 1.
16 Marian Turski, Wiesław Władyka, Lekcja pokory. In: „Polityka" Nr. 44, 2. November 1991, S. 1 und 4.
17 Mirosław Cielemecki, Smak bąbelków. In: „Przegląd Tygodniowy", Nr. 44, 3. November 1991, S. 7.

Krystyna Daniel

The Role of Schools and the Catholic Church in the Shaping of Xenophobic, Nationalistic and Anti-semitic Attitudes Among Polish Youth

The changes currently taking place in Poland, and in the other countries which were formerly part of the Communist Bloc, raise our interest in questions of nationalism, intolerance and xenophobia. These problems have many aspects and are complex. Focusing on the processes taking place in Poland, which in comparison to such countries as the USSR, Yugoslavia, Czechoslovakia or Romania, has a homogeneous ethnic character, the issue of Polish-Jewish relations comes to the fore. The ease with which it is possible in certain segments of Polish society to arouse dislike, or even animosity, towards Jews is especially disquieting. It is all the more disturbing in light of the fact that the entire Jewish population currently living in Poland numbers only 5,000 to 10,000.[1] This makes us pose questions regarding the processes and source of "Polish anti-semitism sans Jews", which is a peculiar phenomenon as compared to anti-semitism occurring in other countries.

Empirical research conducted in Poland in recent years allows us to formulate a hypothesis, through which a good foundation for the formulation of unfavorable attitudes toward Jews is created during the process of primary and secondary socialization, thereby transmitting negative stereotypes of Jews to the youth, and are additionally reinforced by the formation of nationalistic attitudes. This hypothesis was fully confirmed by the research I did in 1988, among a group of 138 students and pupils of secondary schools.[2] It turned out that a clearly negative attitude towards Jews is closely connected with an extended negative stereotype of Jews and with a definite nationalistic orientation. In the research group almost every fourth person represented this type of attitude. At the same time, it was found that having a positive stereotype and lack of nationalistic orientation is conducive to open and friendly attitudes towards Jews. This was true for 1–8.0% of the research group.

This research also showed that the family plays an important role in the process of forming certain attitudes towards Jews, as does school, literature, the media and the Catholic Church. What is most interesting is that this research allows us to say that there is no difference when we speak about stereotypes and attitudes towards Jews among 17-year-olds and students 4 years older.

The results presented prompted me to do further research on the attitude of Polish youths towards Jews among 14-year-old pupils of some Kraków primary schools. This research was done in the Spring of 1991, using a questionnaire and it included 102 pupils. The questionnaire used consisted of 32 questions and was filled in by pupils during their lessons.

We need to mention at the outset that the topic created a lot of interest among the fourteen-year-olds. The pupils not only filled in the questionnaire clearly and neatly but also asked questions and added comments.

The results are of course not representative of the majority of Polish youths at the age of fourteen, the analysis, however, allows us to notice important tendencies.

First of all, we need to state that Jews are present in the awareness of the pupils studied. What is more, the presence of Jews in Poland is very real for a majority of the people interviewed, for only 12 pupils claim that they know a person of Jewish origin (usually it is a neighbor or an acquaintance of their enumerates Jews parents). A clear majority of the subjects enumerates Jews as an ethnic minority living in Poland (88). What is more, for 40 students Jews create the biggest minority group.

Independently of this result, 42 pupils claim that the number of Jews living in Poland is growing as they came to Poland to use the shops and homes which belong to them. Consequently, answering the question about the number of Jews in Poland the pupils more often choose the answer 500,000 than 5000 (62).

Relatively often the pupils point out that many politicians in Poland are of Jewish origin. And so, answering the question about famous people of Jewish origin, 47 pupils enumerated Tadeusz Mazowiecki – the first prime minister in the noncommunist government. Apart from him, there are several of his coworkers enumerated like Jacek Kuroń (9), Małgorzata Niezabitowska (16), Adam Michnik (5). We can also find answers claiming that the whole government and the whole party led by Tadeusz Mazowiecki "is Jewish". I found 5 such answers.

For comparison, it is worth knowing that 40 pupils cannot enumerate any person of Jewish origin and only 15 of the pupils did not enumerate Mazowiecki, pointing other persons, such as Albert Einstein (9), Korczak (2), Penderecki (3), Kantor (1), Anne Frank (1), Kirk Douglas (6), Roman Polański (1), Jasir Arafat (1), Itzak Schamir (1).

These answers are interesting due to the fact that they clearly point to the media as an important factor in forming the views of the youths. During the election campaign (presidential and parliamentary elections) there were some attempts to discredit Tadeusz Mazowiecki and other politicians on the basis of being Jewish. A campaign was undertaken by some priests claiming that Poles who are Catholics should vote only for a Catholic Pole not for a Jew or a communist.[3]

The results discussed above point out that Jews are not only present in the consciousness of the youth but also show how limited this awareness is. Additionally, other answers support this, too. And so, all the knowledge about the past of Jews is limited to the holocaust (68) and to chosen fragments of the biblical history of Jews (41). The pupils who write about the holocaust choose the camps in Auschwitz and Birkenau and the uprising in the Warsaw ghetto.

On the basis of the knowledge acquired during religious classes, the pupils mention the Jewish flight from Egypt under Moses and the fact that Jesus Christ was a Jew but that he was rejected and crucified by the Jews. Only six pupils see the Polish-Jewish connections, writing that Jews lived in Poland for ages and through trade they gave some input to its development; also they mentioned that they were bankers and doctors of Polish kings.

We need to underline that knowledge, or rather a lack of it is instrumental in the creation of stereotypes and superstitions and prejudice. What is remarkable youths quite often are aware of their limitations and express a willingness to get acquainted with Jewish customs, religion, and history. Every third pupil writes about it explicitly, at the same time expressing disappointment in history, Polish literature and religious classes, during which this topic was completely omitted.

Regarding their lack of knowledge, the pupils also speak of the difficulties which they have with pointing out the district of Kraków traditionally inhabited by Jews. In this district, there are even now some pieces of architecture, among them 8 synagogues, a museum of Jewish history and culture, and 2 cemeteries. This district was properly enumerated by almost 40 of the pupils.

In the search for stereotypical thinking of fourteen-year-olds, they were asked a question concerning typical features characterizing Jews. The answers clearly show that, contrary to the older youths, pupils use stereotypes rather rarely.[4] The majority of the subjects says that Jews are not different from other nations (42) or they point out a different religion and customs. However, 30 pupils give the Jews specific features. Such positive features like godliness, religiosity, tolerance, patience, and wisdom are enumerated by 16 persons. Among the negative features there are some like: ambitious for power, miserly, greedy, insincere. Three persons define Jews as "Judases". The pejorative terms correspond clearly with the conviction that part of the politicians in Poland are of Jewish origin and with the conviction that Jews are coming back to Poland to take back houses and shops which belong to them, raising rent, and thus doing harm to Poles. The terms "Judases" and "insincere" find their justification in the knowledge acquired during religion lessons.

Defining their attitude toward Jews, most of the subjects talk about a positive or rather positive attitude. Only 7 of the pupils wrote that their attitude is rather negative. Those who have a negative attitude have at the same time a tendency towards a negative, stereotyped view of Jews. This tendency is analogous in the case of older youths.

According to the assumptions and the results obtained in the research, among older youth it is connected with nationalistic attitudes. When we talk about fourteen-year-olds, we can point out an analogous tendency. The persons prejudiced against Jews decidedly prefer an ethnically homogeneous country, seeing in a multi-ethnic country a threat to their own national identity, culture and language.

It is worth emphasizing that in the whole study group, we can notice a clear preference for mono-ethnic country (58) as opposed to a multi-ethnic one (28). The rest of the people cannot make a choice. As the argument for the mono-ethnic country shows, the preference can have a clearly nationalistic character, or is connected with the conviction that only in a homogeneous country conflicts and destructive fights for power can be avoided, conflicts, which according to the subjects, comprise an inevitable consequence of joining various national groups into one country. The USSR is given here as an example.

Among the answers pointing to a preference for a multi-national country, the more dominating ones are personal motives, like the possibility of learning foreign languages, other customs and the belief that living in an environment with variety is simply more interesting. Completely sporadically we can find justification showing other positive consequences of close coexistence of various nations like, for example, the growth of tolerance, mutual penetration of the cultures and because of that their mutual enrichment (2).

Finally, the last question is connected with whether or not the pupils notice examples of anti-semitism in Polish society and possible opinions about it. As it turns out, most of the children hold the opinion that lately in Poland we can notice anti-semitism (73). As examples, the pupils point to graffiti and mention conversations with older people, also with parents. Our attention was drawn to the fact that nineteen of the pupils denied the existence of anti-semitism in Poland.[5]

Further analysis of the results presented leads to more general conclusions. Firstly, beyond any doubt, we can say that fourteen-year-olds notice a link between current problems and the presence of Jews in Poland.

Secondly, their entire knowledge about this topic is not only limited and fragmentary but also incoherent or like a jigsaw.

Thirdly, quite clearly there is great interest in deepening their knowledge about Jews.

Fourthly, the pupils rarely use stereotypes and rarely show negative attitudes toward Jews.

And finally, in young people's consciousness a line of attitudes and views is being drawn which in favorable circumstances can comprise fertile ground for the development of various positive and negative attitudes toward Jews (nationalism, the conviction that Poles are not tolerant or open to pluralism, noticing and disapproving of anti-semitism).

When we evaluate the role of the school in the process of shaping the youth's attitude towards Jews in the light of the research discussed, we need to be critical.

First of all, the influence of school is too small, both in giving information about the Jews and in shaping positive attitudes. Such a situation clearly proves the validity of pupils' commentaries that they have not learned anything in school, even though they are interested in getting to know the history and customs of the Jewish nation.

Moreover, it turns out that the schools avoid "Jewish topics" and that they do not fill that important role which would allow the pupils to systematize, to choose and to direct their fragmentary knowledge which they acquire at random in the process of primary (family) and secondary socialization (mass media, other contacts like colleagues, everyday relations, literature, religious education).

A visible effect of lack of the desired influence of school is the large number of pupils who present an incoherent, jigsaw-like picture of Jews. Certainly, the teachers' attitudes have a crucial influence on such state of affairs. The research has been complemented by interviews made with six teachers (of history and Polish). From the interviews, we could draw the conclusion that the teachers themselves do not feel competent in the subject. They think that it is complicated and difficult. What is more, their knowledge about Jews is rather small, sometimes embarrassingly so. And so, for example, only one of the teachers was able to say anything about the events in March 1968, as a result of which the majority of Jews decided to emigrate from Poland.

Independently of this, the teachers are a bit afraid that the subject concerning Jews is controversial and that it is too difficult for primary school pupils. The domineering view is that mentioning Jewish topics can enhance creating anti-semitic attitudes among children; on the other hand, lack of knowledge can protect the children from anti-semitism.

The critical view on school does not, however, concern its passive character. The whole situation is complicated by the impregnation of school programs with concepts which are a good basis for developing nationalistic attitudes. The nationalistic feelings can be easily intensified by making the Polish fight for absolute independence and maintaining cultural identity and by omitting the process of cultural assimilation, the outcome of which is today's Polish culture.

Also, the role of Catholic church in the process of shaping the youth's attitudes towards Jews has to be criticized. The church, just like primary school, seems to prefer a simplified and anachronistic view on the problems concerning Jews. The tendency of priests to concentrate only on biblical themes and Jesus' life proves this. Namely, if a young person knows only that Jews were the chosen people which did not recognize the Saviour and crucified Him, it is hard to expect them to like this nation. It seems much more justified to show aversion and disapproval of such a nation. In this context, it is interesting that the answers of the pupils based on religion classes divided Jews into "good" and "bad".

It seems that for many pupils the church itself is an authority, sometimes greater than school. There are, for example, some commentaries in which the pupils express their interest in getting to know the church's view on problems concerning Polish-Jewish relations. Such expectations are never directed towards school, from which the pupils expect to get knowledge and not opinions or directions. At the same time, it means a lower prestige of school.

Summing up, it is necessary to mention that neither the school nor the church participate in shaping positive attitudes towards Jews; however, they posses such possibilities. As far as the church is concerned, it is sufficient to mention the unprecedented teaching coming from the Bishop's Council, declaration Nostra Aetate No 4, which created a new perception of Judaism.[6] Passivity and lack of openness to pluralism of both institutions may have far-reaching consequences, particularly in the situation where children and youths are completely unprepared to cope with various messages sometimes hostile to Jews.

Notes

1 According to rough estimates. For comparison just before the outbreak of World War II, the Jewish population in Poland amounted to 10% of the total population, i. e., 3.3 million.

2 This research was carried out among 48 students of the Political Science Department of the Jagiellonian University, 46 second form students of a secondary School in Cracow, and 44 second form students of a secondary agricultural school in Czernichów (not far from Cracow). More about this research see: K. Daniel, The Image of the Jews in the Consciousness of Polish Youth, "Europa Ethnica" 1990.

3 For example: Bishop Józef Michalik during his homily in Gorzów Wielkopolski (Sept. 9, 1991) said: ". . . a Catholic is under the obligation to vote for a Catholic, a Christian for a Christian, a Moslem for a Moslem, a Jew for a Jew, a mason for a mason, a communist for a communist." Quote "Gazeta Wyborcza" 1991/230.

4 I assume that important features of stereotype are a strong tendency to a simple, often unjustified, generalized and emotional attitude which manifests itself in a positive or negative opinion about the group to which a given stereotype is referred. Another important feature of a stereotype is its stiffness. This notion of stereotype refers to the classic concept of a stereotype proposed by W. Lippmann, Public Opinion, New York, 1922, Macmillian.

5 For comparison see the questionnaire research carried out in 1991 among second form students of a secondary school in Warsaw: "Res Publica" 1991, vol. 6.

6 This Declaration was dated 28th October 1965.

Petr Mareš, Libor Musil, Ladislav Rabušic

Civic Society and Cultural Change in Czechoslovakia

> The true adversary of the new social movements in the East is not so much the social actor who is determined by his interests and his power as the social actor who is determined by his identification with the "Whole".
> (Alain Touraine: The Birth of Post-Communist Societies, Sociológia 23, 1991, No. 4)

One of the key dimensions of present developments in Czechoslovakia is the process of loss of and/or search for identity under the condition of change. One Dahrendorfs metaphor points to the importance of this process. According to him, it is possible to realize decisive political changes within 6 months and essential economic changes within 6 years. However, cultural changes may require 60 years. Dahrendorf warns against unchecked optimism awakened by the immediacy of the elemental political change in 1991. He points out that the permanency of the political change and of all other related political, economic and other changes – as well as the ability of the society to achieve consensus about their basic direction – will depend on a parallel, and slow, cultural change. Only the cultural change, if it takes place, will become a source of positive legitimacy of various institutional changes that will substitute current negative legitimacy derived from the superficial denial of the past.

Paternalism as a cultural heritage

As many as 9.7 million of current citizens of Czechoslovakia, that is, 62 percent of its population, were born after 1948. Socialization of this part of the population took place under the strong influence of paternalist ideology and practice of the Communist state. Despite the fact that the Communist ideology has not been generally accepted, it has influenced habits of people and encouraged creation of value orientations, strategies and patterns of behavior adopted to the practice of state paternalism. Through these modifications, byproducts of the Communist ideology permeated even those social strata which have been otherwise opposed or inert to the ideology as such.

Values derived from peoples reactions to the practice of state paternalism have grown without competition. Because civic society has not existed, the only milieu capable of resistance against the state ideology was the family. But the family itself has been either helpless or has had no interest in competing with the

Communist values[1]. This penetration of paternalism into the culture of nationalities comprising the population of Communist-ruled Czechoslovakia has been also facilitated by particular historical circumstances.

Above all, it had been the post-war loss of a multi–cultural background (supported until World War Two by German and Jewish elements) and isolation from the wider world after the Communist takeover of 1948. Then it was also the traditional attractiveness of the egalitarian social ideal and related leftist tendencies. In Czechoslovakia, socialist movements have always attracted strong following. Today, potential supporters of Communist involve 10 to 15 percent of the electorate. This proportion roughly corresponds to the long-term support given the Communist Party in all three parliamentary elections conducted in pre-war Czechoslovakia. A substantial part of todays electorate are people who would be willing to vote for other leftist-oriented political groupings. Leftist thinking has always found resonance among the Czechoslovak intelligentsia.

These circumstances paved the way for the indoctrination of state paternalist values into which the Communist regime transposed its ideology or which became a response to the paternalist practice of state institutions ruled by the Communists. These values, widely shared today, found their expression particularly in the beliefs that:

- Society should be as little differentiated as possible, and its members should be as equal as possible, particularly in terms of wealth. Large material inequality is illegitimate because it is not just and suggests illegal sources of wealth. Homogeneity of social structure and lifestyle is desirable.[2]
- People should have a right to work[3] regardless of its productiveness or meaningfulness. The state must guarantee work to every person. People who are unemployed are simply those who avoid work. Society perceives them as asocial persons.
- State institutions know best what is needed and hence should determine and control all activities pursued by individuals outside the most intimate private realm. Individual initiative is not only unimportant but also undesirable because it could conflict with "scientific goals" of state institutions. (Such initiative can be meaningful only if it is directly demanded by these institutions.) Not the citizens but the state institutions know best what the citizens need.
- Society should be stable, change is a dangerous disturbance of the desirable order, a negative deviation[4]. Such attitude stems from the conviction that the living standard does not have to be too high and lifestyle too varied. What is important is that living conditions should be stable. Social certainty has greater value than uncertain chance.

These beliefs have been rooted in the subconsciousness of the Czechoslovak population despite the existence of substantial inequality based on differentiated political and social capital. There is a remarkable hypothesis that the political changes of 1989 had been so easy because a part of the Communist elite decided to legitimize its previously accumulated economic capital and use it legally in the conditions of market economics (see e. g. Mon, 1991). Despite of these circumstances, paternalist values of social homogeneity and social certainty have created cultural framework for social behavior in the majority of the population. Remarkable is also a supposition that a substantial number of people who demonstrated in the streets in November 1989 did so because they believed that the powers-that-be could no longer guarantee the social certainties on which the citizenry based their life strategies. The powers thus broke the unwritten social contract and, in the absence of the compensatory effect of the social certainties, became an unacceptable burden. Therefore, they had to bow out.

Identity in doubt

Bělohradský (1991) says that post-Communist societies are characteristically panic-ridden because the societies have become unfathomable. Values of social homogenization and social certainties have been put to doubt and virtually threatened. Substantial part of the population believes (or wants to believe) that the current chaos is only a temporary phenomenon, some kind of payment for better organization of societies. The source of uncertainties is lack of clarity concerning what exactly is better.

Paternalist values have been to a great extent rendered doubtful and suppressed by the pathos of revolutionary events. They have been only hidden under the surface and current economic changes and their social consequences are revitalizing them. According to the public opinion polls, some fifty percent of Slovak citizens maintained in June 1991 that the previous regime, compared to the present one, had certain advantages (Bútorová et al, 1991). The resentment, based on the values of homogeneity and certainty, slows down the process of creation of civic society by paradoxically stimulating new expectations of paternalistically oriented initiatives of the state. Such initiatives should, according to some citizens, soften the impact of economic reform even at the cost of state intervention into the nascent market relationships. Creation of the civic society itself is being tied, above all, to the initiative of the state.

People reconciliate themselves to the practical consequences of institutional changes that they verbally demanded and supported only a short time ago. Liberalization of economic conditions which appears to be an automatic and legitimate aspect of social change runs against fixated paternalist values. People do not want to refuse the change but, at the same time, are not capable of accepting it fully. Chaos results, as an empirical research done in the Autumn 1990 (Rabušic, Mareš, Musil, 1991) showed in the symbiotic preference of liberal social order with a strong emphasis on the values of equality and social certainty.

We think that the continuation of the economic reform and the growing intensity of its consequences could lead to the replacement of this chaotic world-view by feelings of destruction and collapse. Probably only a small part of the population perceives current developments as an exchange of disputable certainty for open chances. People who have accepted the philosophy of the paternalist state see the current situation more in terms of losses than as a replacement of one value by another that is perhaps equally meaningful or perhaps even more important.

If the public perceives the transformation from totality to democracy as attractive in political terms, transformation from paternalism to liberalism in economic terms is difficult for the population which has become used to the protective hand of the state[5]. Transfer from totality to democracy offers the option of taking responsibility for ones life into ones own hands. Institutional transformation from paternalism to liberalism changes this attractive possibility into an unpleasant everyday reality. Economic capacities of households are changing abruptly, social structure is losing its homogeneity, culturally fixated strategies for coping with problems of everyday life are not changing, however. They are still permeated by expectations of a facilitative intervention of the state. What to do, though, when the intervention does not take place or is even denied?

Inconsistencies between changing conditions of life and cultural backgrounds of the population cause an insufficient orientation in a new situation. It is a struggle against the identification of individuals with the whole that Touraine calls attention to (1991).

Nationalism as a new source of identity?

A question arises: what can replace the lost identity? We suppose that the emotionally strong identification with the idea of national or regional autonomy which has been strongly voiced in Slovakia and partially also in Moravia, is, to a great extent, the product of search for identity with the "whole". Threatened values of security and social homogeneity have been replaced by values of national or regional togetherness and uniqueness. Paternalistically oriented citizens can hardly turn coats and promptly identify themselves with the individualism of liberal origin. However, they can easily find satisfaction of their need for identity in a collective experience of national or regional togetherness. Although we do not consider this as the only reason for the growth of nationalism in post-Communist countries, it is certainly not an insubstantial reason.

The hypothesis of value vacuum, caused by the threats to and doubts in the paternalist values of social homogeneity and security, can be supported by empirical data concerning identification with national or regional community (Mareš, Musil, Rabušic, 1991) articulated in "Moravian movement". It can be perceived as a specific variant of regional nationalism and in our understanding it has been partly brought about by frustrations of some part of population who lost (for the reasons mentioned above) their existential identity.

The Moravian nationalist movement finds its supporters relatively often among persons without finished high school education, mostly laborers and lower-level clerks. Significantly frequent support can be also found among members of the middle generation. Paternalist elements can be found in their reactions to survey questions more often than among other categories of respondents. Supporters of the Moravian movement are more often represented by those who prefer state ownership to private ownership. These people frequently share the conviction that even highly effective performance does not lend legitimacy to high earnings, and they also often share the opinion that the state should assume responsibility for the fate of individual citizens. The proportion of persons with consistently liberal attitudes, i. e., those who prefer private ownership, income differentiation according to job performance differences, and individual responsibility, is relatively small among citizens of the Moravian capital, Brno. Among supporters of the Moravian movement there is still smaller proportion of respondents with consistently liberal orientation than in the whole survey sample. Inconsistent attitudes, characterized by mixture of liberal elements and paternalist value orientation, on the other hand, are relatively more frequent among them.

Value orientation among supporters of the Moravian movement is typically framed by the conviction that individuals are limited in their activities by external circumstances. This existential feeling of unfreedom apparently breeds unwillingness to rely on ones own strength and gives rise to demands that problems of individuals be solved by the state. Interventions into lives of individuals are legitimized by emphasis on equality among people voiced by supporters of the Moravian movement more strongly than by other respondents who prefer personal freedom.

When supporters of the Moravian movement evaluate social situation in Czechoslovakia, they tend to show worries concerning economic threat, particularly fear of substantial decline of living standard. It is still more fear of lower income than of unemployment. This is probably related to the expectation of forthcoming state intervention in the economy. Such expectation, that the state will be the ultimate provider of employment, reflects their past experiences.

These empirical data suggest that the value of regional togetherness attracts often those people whose notion of economic reform does not correlate with their value orientation. Economic reform awakens fears in them and is perceived as a product of someone elses will. We can offer a hypothesis that priorities of many people who identify themselves with the Moravian version of regional nationalism (with its centre in Brno) are not rooted in civic and political rights but in social rights in Marshall's (1973) sense. The key causal factor of local nationalist movement in Moravia is probably social, or more precisely, cultural stress. This has led to frustrations of the population that has been deprived of certain social certainties on which these people based their life strategies.

It is possible that the need to compensate for this loss contributed more to the growing popularity of the Moravian movement than the consciousness of cultural difference, regional uniqueness and desire of a greater regional autonomy.

Notes

1 Milan Šimečka (a Czech dissident writer) dealt with that in his book "Restoration of Order" (1989) written in 1970s. He showed how the communist regime abused children as hostages by the threat they would be denied of high school or University education if their parents had not behaved loyally to the regime. Another side of reasons why the family was powerless is showed by Mon (1991) who explains how families as social groups colonized successfully the "socialist" state by means of social networks and their social capital. The importance of social networking under Communism in Czechoslovakia was also stressed by Šrubař (1991).

2 Sociology of envy would find rich inspirations for its development in Czechoslovakia. It would also find a number of examples of sophisticated ways of hidden use of real material well-being in supposedly Czechoslovak homogeneous society.

3 The right to work was a part of unwritten social contract between citizenry and the state. Employment was not a personal contract between an employer and an employee but it was something which was guaranteed simply by the fact that a person was born and lived here. In this way the regime managed to present the right to work as the basic human right (Mon, 1991a). Such perception of employment still exists. Also Václav Havel, as the president shortly after his inauguration, has appealed that economic transition was made without substantial unemployment and expressed his hope that it would be so. Mr. Mečiar, the then prime minister of Slovak republic, made a statement in front of workers of industrial plants of a Slovak town Martin in spring 1991, saying: "It is necessary to talk here about our responsibility in terms of your employment".

4 Symptomatically, the central topic of Czechoslovak sociology of work has been personal turnover.

5 The transition from totalitarianism to democracy is difficult due to undeveloped system of relevant institutions, social control, and both norms and values. Civic society as the basis for liberal attitudes does not exist. If there are discussions about democratic traditions in Czechoslovakia now, they are rather resentment than reality. Despite the fact that Czechoslovakia was really an island of democracy among totalitarian and semitotalitarian states of the then Central and Eastern Europe, we have to realize that we are three generations away of that reality now. Also, liberal values, valid and existent in those days, got covered with almost half a century of state paternalism.

References

Bělohradský, V.: Postkomunismus jako panika (Postcommunism as Panic). Mladá fronta dnes, 12 července 1991.

Boguszak, M. et al.: Československo – listopad 1990 (Czechoslovakia – November 1990). AISA, Praha 1990.

Bútorová, Z. et al.: Slovensko – Júl 1991 (Slovakia – July 1991). Ústav pre sociálnu analýzu UK, Bratislava 1991.

Dahrendorf, R.: The Modern Social Conflict. California University Press, Berkeley 1990.

Mareš, P. et al.: Obavy a naděje brněnské populace (Fears and Hopes of Brno Population). Závěrečná zpráva empirického výzkumu, Masarykova univerzita, Brno 1991.

Mareš, P., Musil, L., Rabušic, L.: Fenomén moravanství (Moravian Phenomenon), Sociológia, ročník 28, 1992, ù. 5 (forthcoming).

Marshall, T. H.: Class, Citizenship and Social Development. Greenwood Press, Westport 1973.

Možný, I.: Proč tak pozdě a pro tak snadno (Why So Late and Why So Easy). Slon, Praha 1991.

Možný, I.: Nezaměstnanost v roce nula (Unemployment in Year Zero). In: Možný, I., Mareš, P. (eds).: Nezaměstnanost – nizozemská zkušenost a československá realita (Unemployment – Dutch Experience and Czechoslovak Reality), sborník z ěskoslovensko – nizozemské konference, Masarykova univerzita, Brno 1991).

Rabušic, L., Mareš, P., Musil, L.: Sociální změna očima české veřejnosti (Social Change in Perception of Czech Public), Sociologický asopis, roč. 27, 1991, č. 6.
Radičová, I.: Sociológia je kritické intelektuálne vedomie o událostech okolo nás – R. Dahrendorf (Sociology is Critical Intelectual Knowledge about Events around us). Sociológia, roč. 22, 1990, č. 6.
Ùrubař, I.: Společnost a sítě (Society and its Networks). Přítomnost, 2/1991, pp. 13–15.
Toffler, A., Toffler H.: Socialismus in Crisis: China's Answer. World Monitor., Vol. 2, No. 1, January 1989, pp. 34–43.
Tourain, A.: Zrod postkomunistických společností (The Birth of Post-Communist Societies). Sociológia, roč. 23, 1991, č. 4.

Zora Bútorová

Two Years After November, 17, 1989: The Hard Birth of Democracy in Slovakia

Two years have elapsed since November 1989. The game which is being played for the future of the post-communist Czecho-Slovakia is in full swing. What lies ahead for the fosterlings of the totalitarian regime on their path towards pluralistic democracy and a prosperous economy? Will they succeed in carrying out this extraordinarily complicated transition?

Nothing could bring us closer to understanding the complicated character of the Slovak political scene than the description of one Autumn afternoon. It is Thursday, the 19th of September 1991. In the Square of the Slovak National Uprising in Bratislava a meeting for the sovereignty of Slovakia is taking place, organized by the Slovak National Party, the Movement for a Democratic Slovakia, and the cultural and educational institution Matica slovenská. Not far away from this square, on the Danube riverside, at the monument of the Czecho-Slovak Republic the supporters of the common state have come together at the same time. Apart from the Deputy Prime Minister of the Czech Government, there were also representatives of Public Against Violence, the Democratic Party, the Hungarian Independent Initiative, the Social Democrats, and the Roma.

The same day an oecumenical divine service was held in St. Martin's Cathedral, the ancient Catholic church where Maria Theresia and other kings had been crowned long ago. Václav Havel took part in this recent celebration as well. Representatives of all larger denominations in Slovakia were present, including the two antagonistic ones, the Greek Catholics and the Orthodox Church. Hundreds of believers inside the church, as well as several ten thousands more listening to the radio, were deeply moved by the Jewish litany the singer of which also reminded them the concentration camps during the second World War. Before the divine service V. Havel met the representatives of the Slovak Protestants. "It is necessary to overcome our enemies by Love only", the President was told by one of the priests who had been imprisoned in a Stalinist concentration camp.

At five o'clock there was an opening of the sale of two books in the avant-garde bookshop Artfórum. Both concern such events in Slovak history which had been put under a taboo for decades.

The first one, with the characteristic title "You Will Not Be Able to Eradicate Them", was written by the former Catholic dissident František Mikloško [12]. For the first time the cruel persecution of the Catholic Church under the communist regime has been described in this book. The author, however, has not mentioned the leading role of Slovak Catholicism during the Slovak state.

In the second book the Slovak historian Ivan Kamenec describes the origin of the anti-Jewish policy of the Slovak State and the horrors of deportations [10].

He has descended to the very bottom of the tragedy of the Slovak Jews; nobody in Slovakia has done anything like this before him.

This day carries nearly all typical features of present-day Slovakia: almost 50 years of undemocratic regimes characterized by religious, class and racial intolerance, as well as by a mythologization and falsification of history; the years in which the persecutors became the persecuted and the persecuted changed into persecutors; the still unsolved relations between Czechs and Slovaks deformed by communist centralism; the complicated search for a social consensus.

1. The Painful End of Immobility

The faces of the people in the squares or streets of Slovakia are similar to those of their East European neighbours – the Poles, Hungarians, Czechs or Bulgarians. The euphoria from the "velvet revolution" has faded away; now pessimism and fear of the future are prevailing. Under the pressure of the first steps of the radical economic reform and of the dramatic shifts on the political scene the criticism towards the present regime has become sharper and the evaluation of the former system more benevolent. According to surveys of the Institute for Social Analysis at the Comenius University [2; 3], only one third of the adult people in Slovakia are persuaded that the present regime has more advantages than the communist one. Among the positive traits of the communist regime full employment, a stabilized price level and living standard are appreciated; among the negatives the lack of political and religious freedom, nepotism and privileges of the communists.

The economic reform has had a heavier impact upon the Slovak economy than upon the Czech one: the number of unemployed is approximately twice as large here. That is one of the reasons why the first steps of the economic reform have evoked among the Slovak population more fear and distrust than in Bohemia.[1] Only now it has become evident how efficient was the propaganda stressing the anti-social character of market economy and capitalism. In comparison with the Czechs, but also with the Hungarian minority, the Slovaks take up a more reserved attitude towards privatization and foreign capital [2; 14]. The growing unemployment is considered by the majority of the population as a pathological phenomenon. The tendency is still prevailing to push on to the state the responsibility for every enterprise and every citizen. However, in the last months the first shock induced by the reform has calmed down a little and the support of the economic policy has become stronger [3].

The ups and downs on the political scene have been one of the reasons of a steep decline of the public and political activity.[2] For the majority of the population which has not acquired any experience with parliamentary democracy, real democracy means its direct form.[3] The changes in public opinion are considered to be a sufficient reason for questioning the legitimacy of the parliament and the government. The representatives of the government coalition at both the federal and national level get nowadays less support than the opposition.

Besides the economic fear, the feeling of political threat is wide-spread, too. Among the different reasons prejudices are intermixed with people's ancient and recent historical experience. Several paradoxes are occurring at the same time. Despite the prevalence of believers in Slovakia, 74% of adult persons fear a too great interference of the Church into politics. Despite the almost negligible small extent of the Jewish community in Slovak society (only 3–4000 members), 61% of population are afraid of a too great influence of the Jews upon politics and economics. Despite the recent dependence of Czecho-Slovakia on the Soviet Union, 59% of the Slovaks are afraid of a too high dependence on the USA and only 34% of the inclusion of Slovakia into the Soviet sphere of influence. The activity of the mafias of the old regime (the state security STB, KGB, the communist structures) is considered to be a danger only by 54% of the population.

Strong is the fear of an increase of national and race hatred (69%). This fear reflects the high degree of national tension and intolerance typical of the Slovak society of these days. First of all a high aversion is felt between the Roma (Gipsies) and the rest of the population; in this sense Slovakia has achieved the first place among the countries of Central, or Eastern Europe [13]. There is also a rather high tension in the relations between the Slovak population and the Hungarian minority [l; 2; 14]. A revitalization of anti-Semitism is taking place: the social distance toward Jews has reached almost such a high degree as in Poland [6; 8]. Strong is also the animosity against foreigners, immigrants, and refugees [3].

2. The Divided Slovakia

Two years ago the crowds in Bratislava and in Prague were chanting the slogan "United We Stand, Divided We Fall!" Today the people in Bratislava have to meet separately in two different squares.

People gathering at the monument of the Czecho-Slovak Republic are irritated by the question: What kind of a regime will in the nearest future become the successor of the "real socialism" in Slovakia? Will not the Velvet Revolution result here in a new form of totalitarian, or at least authoritarian regime – this time of a national colouring? How can we prevent it?

In the square of the Slovak National Uprising, however, the problem is formulated in a different way: Will the Slovak nation continue to be the younger brother only, going for the left-overs and doing some patchwork in the shadow of Prague's fame? The appeals are made to proclaim a rather vaguely formulated sovereignty of Slovakia, or an unambiguously required state independence of the Slovak Republic.

The participants of the meeting for the common state are scared by a vision of national socialism connected with isolation and backwardness; whereas those demanding sovereignty of Slovakia, by the vision of an anti-social denationalization neglecting the interests of the rank and file of the Slovak nation.

Mutual labelling has become a typical feature of political discussion: For the latter, the former ones are cosmopolitans similar to the communist internationalists, traitors of their own nation, lackeys of some foreign master (usually in Prague, or in Budapest, but also of the imperialists or the Zionists). The former, on the other hand, see the latter as nationalists who, in their greed for power, strive for replacing one kind of totalitarianism by another one, pushing Slovakia towards the Balkan, into the sphere of political instability and chaos.

For the latter, the present events in Slovakia are the natural expression of the national liberation efforts of the Slovaks; the former consider them a deviation from the universalistic principles of the Velvet Revolution and an inclination towards destructive nationalism.

For the former, the falling apart of the common state would mean the amputation of a part of the vitally important space for the Slovaks, the coming to nothing of the historical efforts of their ancestors, the impairment of family and personal links, but also complications for the Slovak economy; while the latter are lured by the possibility to put an end to the Czech power play, by the possibility to work at long last on one's own patch of earth, just for oneself, by the possibility to choose one's own path respecting the Slovak specificities and to bear the full responsibility for one's own decisions.

The former support the demand to preserve the Czecho-Slovak state by geopolitical arguments; the latter smile indulgently at such "ghost stories"; being inspired by the development in Yugoslavia, they are presuming, however, a possibility "to part in a cultural way", on the base of some agreement.

The supporters of the Declaration of Sovereignty of the Slovak Republic are attracted by several argumentations. The first of them accentuates the plebeian character of the Slovaks from time immemorial, their poverty and the injustice having been done to them.[4] The second one suggests the vision of the Slovak nation as a community of deeply religious People, practically unaffected by decades of the construction of communism, who must be protected from the tricky Western liberalism infiltrating Slovakia also through the Czech Republic.[5] The third argumentation refers to the historical continuity of the efforts of the Slovaks for an independent state of their own and, abstracting from its contents, stresses the achievement of this goal in Tiso's totalitarian Slovak State.[6] According to the fourth version, the Slovaks need an independent state for being able to continue building up reformed socialism, or to find the "third way" between socialism and capitalism[7].

All these different types of argumentation stress the historical and cultural difference between Slovak and Czech society, absolutize them and make conclusions about the irreversible divergence between Czech and Slovak society. In a downright totalitarian spirit they appeal to the Slovaks to unite in their common "national interest", not to miss "their last historical chance": to set off – either in a constitutional, or a less constitutional way – on the irreversible, historically predestined path of building up their own national state.

Why do these arguments seem to be so convincing? To find the answer, we must go back the history.

3. Shadows of the Past

Unlike the Czechs, the Slovaks have never had – with the only exception of the period during World War II – a state of their own. For 1000 years the Slovak nation was seeking a consensus with the Hungarians within the framework of the greater Hungarian state. This coexistence of Slovaks, Hungarians, but also of other nations was more or less satisfactory. This went wrong only in the 19th century when the originally rather broad concept of a Hungarian state was reinterpreted as the dominance of the Hungarian ("Magyar") nation over all the other nations, so that these felt threatened by Hungarian nationalism. For Slovakia an important role in this process was played by the cultural and educational institution called Matica Slovenská which was fiercely suppressed by the former Hungarian government. The struggle of the Slovak nation for its survival achieved an especially cruel form at the end of the 19th and beginning of the 20th century when there was a very strong pressure for "Hungarianization" or "Magyarization".

The foundation of the first Czechoslovak Republic in 1918 from the common will of the Czechs and the Slovaks was the optimal solution for both these nations. For the Slovaks it meant national salvation and it brought them many economic and cultural impulses, too. In this state, however, the idea of "Czechoslovakism" was asserted based upon a paternalistic approach of the more advanced Czech nation towards a younger, more backward partner. And thus the Slovaks even in this first Czechoslovak Republic were not pushed into a situation where they could with full responsibility take their destiny into their own hands, where they would learn to be in charge of their own affairs. This statement is valid also for the 40 years of coexistence of Czechs and Slovaks "building up socialism".

Since the very beginning of the Czecho-Slovak Republic there was a tension between religious Slovak Catholicism represented, first of all, by the charismatic priest A. Hlinka and between the secularized Czech culture and politics. The Catholics, although constituting the majority of the Slovak nation, did not have the feeling of an adequate political representation, in contrast to the Slovak Protestants who have traditionally felt a higher affinity to the Czech culture.

Slovakia achieved its sovereignty as a state only in the year 1939–1945. This state was connected with Catholicism, its leading force was Hlinka's Slovak People's Party (HSLS) and its President the Catholic priest Jozef Tiso. The totalitarian character of Tiso's regime found its most conspicuous expression in the deportations of 70 thousands of Jews. In August 1944 the Slovak National Uprising against the Slovak state broke out. Thanks to this resistance the Slovaks joined the victorious nations of World War II.

After 1948 the Catholics became the object of hard political persecutions. Very soon they created a secret "God's community" which became dominant in the Slovak parallel culture [11; 12]. The period of the Slovak State was put under taboo. The representatives of the Slovak State were condemned, first of all, for their clericalism and anti-communism. Antisemitism was not formulated as the moral problem of the whole society. The totalitarian character of this state was, for easily understandable reasons, not mentioned by the communist regime.

As a consequence of this misinterpretation, a loss of the historical memory has taken place, as well as a tendency to idealize the Slovak State. At present [1; 2] only one third of the Slovak population has assumed a critical attitude towards that period of Slovak history. The second third has taken up no clear-cut position, while the third one even glorifies it for the sole fact that this was the first "independent" Slovak state, as well as for the relatively high standard of material consumption of its population, ignoring or deliberately neglecting the tragedy of Jews in this period.

4. Jobs and Bread

While the basic processes of industrialization and urbanization had taken place in Bohemia before the foundation of Czechoslovakia in 1918, feudalism came to a close very slowly in Slovakia. During the first Republic, Slovakia was partly in a semi-colonial position, the living standard was lower than in Bohemia and emigration did not stop. After the second World War the massive industrialization began; in the 70s intensive urbanization succeeded. Both processes substantially changed the face of Slovakia and were connected with a growth of prosperity as well.

Of course, Slovakia could not avoid the typical negative social effects of rapid industrialization, with the destruction of traditional relations and bonds, the release of social control, social pathology, and an abrupt deterioration of the environment among them. Moreover, the industrialization has brought a low proportion of final production, a strong dependence of Slovak industry upon the import of raw materials and energy and a high proportion of the arms industry. That is why the Slovak economy has to cope with a heavier package of problems than the Czech one.

Nevertheless, the experience in rapid industrialization is still well remembered in Slovakia; it was and still is broadly used in communist propaganda ("we have given the people jobs and bread"). It is present, for instance, in a more positive attitude of the Slovaks towards manual work, in a certain depreciation of human inventiveness and creativity; and also in a less critical approach to the period of the "construction of socialism".

After the Prague Spring, in the period of the so-called normalization (1968–1989) Slovakia was a more pacified part of the humiliated Czecho-Slovakia. The processes of "consolidation" in Slovakia were not of such a dramatic character and the polarization of society was not so deep [11; 15; 16]. Due to the differences in social and economic development, the feeling of general social decay was less intense in Slovakia than in Bohemia. The resistance to the regime was dispersed among several centres: the small group representing civil dissent, the much broader circles of Catholic dissent, the environmentalists, independent artists, scientists and researchers [4; 15]. In comparison with the opposition in Bohemia, the Slovak one was weaker and more atomized. The networking among these groups became more intensive only in the last months before November 1989. The events in Prague in November 1989 speeded up the overcoming of isolation; they became a signal for their unification on the basis of the movement Public Against Violence – the sister organization of the Civic Forum in Bohemia.

5. After the Big Bang

The Velvet Revolution has brought the birth of political pluralism to Slovakia. Since then a considerable mobility and instability was characteristic of the development of the political scene. The shifts on the political scene had the form of waves [15]. The first, anti-totalitarian wave reached its peak at the end of November and beginning of December 1989. The culminating point of the second one, connected with a revival of spiritual and religious life, was recorded at the end of April 1990. The partly clerical character of this wave provoked a reaction which at the beginning of June 1990 was reflected by the victory of the movement Public Against Violence (PAV) proclaiming a civic-liberal orientation.

Development of political preferences in Slovakia during 1990/91

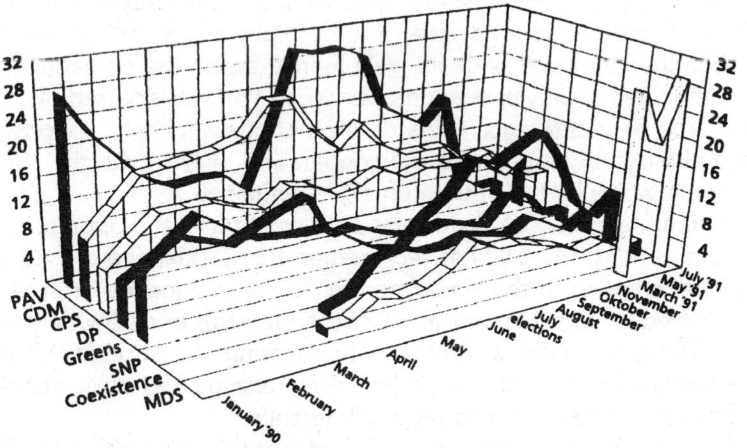

In October and November the nationalist wave reached its culmination. After several manifestations of national intolerance and aggression which this wave brought at its culminating point, the public responded by another shift to PAV, though less conspicuously than in June. After January 1991, in connection with the first steps of the economic reform and the preparation of the constitutions, a new, nationally tinged wave, this time a primarily social one, began to rise. This wave is still dominating (see graph). An important role in escalating the national and social tension was played by the mass media.

Let us describe the play of political parties which has stood in the background of these waves.

1st Act: Bringing The National Question on the Public Agenda

In the last years of the communist regime criticism increased of the unequal relations between Czechs and Slovaks. The interest in the Slovak minority in Hungary has been revived: the unsuitable conditions for the development of their national identity were criticized, as well as the too great broad-mindedness of the Slovaks towards the Hungarian minority in Slovakia. Right after the Velvet Revolution in November 1989 it was the newly created Slovak National Party which followed in the wake of these efforts.

The tensions between Czechs and Slovaks broke out fully with the controversy about the official name of the Czecho-Slovak state (the so-called "hyphen war"). It was Slovak National Party (SNP) which organized massive demonstrations in order to emphasize the existence of Slovakia in the name of the Republic. Already here the leaders of the SNP cast doubt upon the legitimacy of the federative arrangement of Czecho-Slovakia, although before the elections only some of them supported the idea of the total independence of Slovakia.

Quite opposite was the style of argumentation of Public Against Violence whose representatives took the stand of adherents of the Czecho-Slovak coexistence. They underestimated, however, the necessity of repeatedly assuring the Slovak public that they will with full vehemence assert the demand for a just solution of the Czecho-Slovak relations. Very soon PAV was accused of "Czecho-Slovakism" and of indifference towards the national interests. A considerable part of the public condemned also the cooperation of PAV with the Hungarian Independent Initiative and with the Roma Civic Initiative.

By describing the history of Slovakia as a series of tricks and oppression by the neighbouring nations, the SNP has represented the Czechs and the Hungarians as the greatest enemies of the Slovak nation. The search for the external enemy has been connected with a glorification of the merits of one's own nation, with a pathetic appeal for national pride,[8] with stressing the necessity of national unity. The meetings of the SNP have been characterized by a hostile atmosphere, by manifestations of national and racial intolerance.

The representatives of the SNP have stressed that their separatism matches the effort to liberate the nations of the Soviet empire and similar efforts of the nations in Yugoslavia. They have tried to play down the fact that foreign investments into the economy are dependent upon the political stability of the country. On the opposite, the SNP has aroused in its supporters the alluring belief that the Slovak emigrants abroad will render Slovakia an efficient economic assistance, provided that the Slovak Republic becomes a sovereign state.

Playing the role of a defender of the common people the SNP has applied elements of social demagogy and pointed up the feelings of social insecurity and frustration in the working people. The SNP has not stressed the necessity of defending people against the former communist structures, against the still powerful mafias or intrigues of the former secret police. On the contrary, with special vehemence it played the role of an irreconcilable enemy of Public Against Violence. It has made use of the customary distrust of the power elite and tried to replace in the minds of common people the communist bosses by those who have dethroned them.

The aims of the SNP have attracted people frustrated by the loss of the old stereotypes of their everyday existence and perspectives of life who have been seeking simple explanations and solutions; they brought 14% of votes for the SNP in the parliamentary elections in June 1990.

2nd Act: The First Challenge to the Slovak Parliamentarism and National Tolerance

In this period the confrontation between the civic and the nationalist line went on. The representative of the former was, above all, Public Against Violence, the latter was represented by the so-called National Bloc whose most influential part was the SNP. In the shadow of a duel between these two main actors, the coalition partners of PAV – the Christian Democratic Movement (CDM) and the Democratic Party (DP), as well as the oppositionist Communist Party of Slovakia – took up a wait-and-see attitude.

The increasing popularity of the SNP was enabled by the on-going inability of the representatives of the victorious PAV to present their programme of radical economic reform and democratization as a programme which suits the national interests of the Slovaks. As time went on, the communication gap between the public and the leadership of this movement represented by a group of intellectuals became greater.

On the other hand, the SNP created in the eyes of many people the impression of being a real alternative to the government coalition. Although its economic programme was fragmentary, it still was attractive: it promised social securities. The solutions proposed by the SNP in the sphere of economy were even closer to the state-paternalistic practices of real socialism than the economic programme of the new leadership of the Communist Party.

The SNP met with a positive acceptance of the public by supporting vigorously the demand of legalizing Slovak as the only official language in Slovakia. The proposal of the language law presented in the Slovak National Council by the MPs of the SNP had a clearly discriminating character with regard to the national minorities. Against this proposal a group of MPs belonging to the government coalition brought in a bill which was more in accordance with the international standards. However, its propagation met with the barrier of public opinion and with the irritated tone of the mass media which interpreted the Coalition Bill as anti-Slovak. The instigation of anti-Hungarian attitudes fell on a fertile soil: a considerable part of the Slovak population, mainly people living in the purely Slovak regions, without any personal contacts with Hungarians in every-day life, accepted the idea that the interests of the Slovak nation were threatened [1; 2]. The Slovak National Council, however, decided in favour of the coalition proposal.

After the unsuccessful attempt of the SNP to organize a coup against the parliament and the government, the political prestige of the SNP decreased. An important contribution to the loss of popularity of the SNP was the fascist-like behaviour of its supporters during the meeting organized on the day of the first anniversary of the Velvet Revolution. In the local elections in November the SNP suffered a failure.

Since January 1991 when the economic transformation started, the SNP concentrated upon a disqualification of this transformation as being anti-Slovak; its propaganda against the "Federals" met with considerable success. At this time the SNP already openly raised the demand of an independent Slovak state. The number of its followers stabilized at the level of approximately 10%.

Characteristic of them is an anti-Parliament radicalism, a rejection of the economic transformation, an increased national intolerance. In the last months, several new smaller nationalist parties emerged, typical of which are loud meetings and an aggressive tone.

3rd Act: Sovereignties, Competences, Constitutions

In the period of the growing tension between Slovaks and Hungarians, the Czecho-Slovak relations became more complicated as well. Under the pressure of the Slovak government, especially its Prime Minister V. Mečar, negotiations were initiated about a redistribution of the competences between the federal bodies and those of both republics. The complicated process resulted in the so-called Law about Competences accepted by the Federal Parliament in December 1990, which meant a breakthrough into the practices of centralist decision-making.

The vigour and endurance with which Prime Minister V. Mečiar pushed through the decentralization of competences carried him to the very top of political popularity in Slovakia. In the eyes of the public this politician, inclining to populistic manoeuvring, became a charismatic leader, a defender of the interests of the Slovak nation and a guarantee of building up an authentic federation.

At the beginning of the radical economic reform V. Meùiar, however, turned away from the original programme of the coalition government and started to proclaim the necessity of the preservation of social securities, even if the reform ought to be slowed down, and to take up a less cooperative attitude towards the federal and the Czech government. This change of Meùiar's orientation, combined with the autocratic style of his leadership, led to a split in PAV in Spring 1991. After V. Meùar had been recalled from his post of Prime Minister of the Slovak Republic, his populistic wing founded an independent Movement for a Democratic Slovakia (MfDS). The passing over of this movement to the opposition led to an essential change in the lay-out of forces on the Slovak political scene. The MfDS has soon become the strongest political party in Slovakia. In a short time, in the Slovak as well as in the Federal Parliament an "ad hoc alliance" was created by the deputies of MFDS, SNP and PDL. According to empirical surveys [2; 31] the adherents of all these three parties have some common features which situate them on the same pole of the political spectrum of Slovakia: anti-parliamentary radicalism (mainly MfDS and SNP), a strong pro-socialist economic orientation (mainly PDL and MfDS) and national intolerance (mainly MfDS and SNP).

V. Mečar himself turned away from the originally proclaimed concept of an authentic federation, favouring a confederative arrangement based on the so-called "inter-state treaty" between the Czech Republic and the Slovak Republic. At present he tries to play an integrating role in the creation of a "unified national Slovak bloc" which would push through the proclamation of the sovereignty of the Slovak Republic. However, the MfDS itself is not united; there are indices of a possible split of this movement in the coming months.

After the split in PAV, the Christiam Democratic Movement (CDM) is represented in the Slovak and federal parliament by the greatest number of deputies. Its attitude towards Czech-Slovak coexistence is rather ambivalent. Although it is proclaiming the will to preserve the common state, at the same time it claims for Slovakia some attributes typical of any completely sovereign and independent state.

On the one hand, in comparison with the separatism of the SNP and other smaller nationalist parties, the CDM is the more moderate alternative because it does not demand the immediate separation of Slovakia from Bohemia. For months the leader of CDM, at present the Prime Minister of the Slovak Government, Ján Čarnogurský, has repeatedly stated that Slovakia ought to remain in the common state until the year 2000 when it gains its own seat in the European Parliament and its own star on the European firmament. On the other hand, however, by constantly stressing of the temporary character of the common state, the CDM weakens the motivation towards coexistence on the Czech side and thus supports disintegrative tendencies.

Within the CDM itself, there is a struggle between two streams. The former is more radical, confederative or even separatist; some of its adherents are following the traditions of the Slovak State. The latter, the more moderate line, represented by Ján Čarnogurský, is seeking for a compromise with his clearly pro-federatively oriented coalition partners – the PAV (in October 1991 transformed into Civic Democratic Union – PAV), the Democratic Party and the Hungarian Independent Initiative. Both of these streams inside the CDM, however, share the idea that maximal decentralization of competences between the federal and republic representation is the optimal division of competences, whereas the coalition partners of the CDM are supporting the idea of a rational division of power. The differences among the coalition partners do not concern only their ideas about the form of Czecho-Slovak coexistence, but also different ideological premises: the openly anti-liberal orientation of the CDM clashes with the liberal orientation of its coalition partners. Serious disparities are also to be found in the approach toward the economic reform where the CDM, in contrast to its coalition partners, pushes through a "socially more sensitive" programme containing clear-cut elements of a state paternalism.

The Party of the Democratic Left, following the tactics used during the controversy around the Language Law, has taken up a wait-and-see attitude also in the controversy about the Czecho-Slovak coexistence. In contrast to its Czech partner – The Communist Party of Bohemia and Moravia, the PDL supports in a higher degree the Slovak demands. The social and class demagogy of this party contains national elements: the criticism of the "unitarian" approach of the federal and the Czech bodies which, allegedly, do not respect the interests of Slovakia. The PDL is misusing the nervous discussion on Czecho-Slovak relations for an overall criticism of the government coalition on both the federal and the republic level. The representation of the PDL interprets the complications in the negotiations about the legal arrangement of the state only as a proof of the incompetence of the new power elite.

6. Dilemmas of Czecho-Slovak Coexistence in the Public opinion

Let us leave the squares and political negotiations and have an insight into the attitudes of the "average people" forming the "silent majority" of the population of Slovakia. How do they respond to this intricate situation?

First of all the fact has to be stressed that in the population of Slovakia the feeling is prevailing of belonging together with the Czech nation.[9] Contrary to the impression which might be gained especially by following the mass media, the majority of the people do not place their national identity above their civic one.[10] The will to preserve one common state is constantly prevailing: about one fifth of the people prefers the unitarian state or the status quo; approximately one half prefer the federation of two equal republics; in spite of a moderate increase in their number, the supporters of the secession of Czecho-Slovakia do not constitute more than one fifth of the population, and the supporters of a confederation another one tenth. For the time being it can be stated that the secession of Czecho-Slovakia could take place only against the will of the prevailing majority of the citizens of the Slovak Republic and would be enabled only by a failure of the democratic mechanisms allowing the citizens to manifest their will.

However, the attitude of the Slovaks towards the Czechs is characterized by a strong distrust, by the frustration of "the younger brother" who feels to be underestimated and disadvantaged.[11] In the eyes of one third of all adult citizens of the Slovak Republic, the Czechs appear in an unambiguously negative light; the most frequent stereotype of the Czech is that of a calculating egoist who, in contrast to the hard-working Slovak, prefers useless sophistry to an honest piece of work and who feels to be superior to him [9].

In this feeling of being the loser, the argumentation is reflected about the old historical wrongs, as well as an interpretation of the economic transformation being Prague's instrument for suppressing the national interests of the Slovaks which has become rather wide-spread in Slovakia.[12]

It is this fear of the unequal position of Slovakia by which the attractivity of the rather vague slogans about the sovereignty of Slovakia may be interpreted. However, the notion of sovereignty is rather unclear to a considerable part of the population. Wide-spread are also incorrect ideas about the attributes of different forms of a legal arrangement of the state [2]. One third of the people who proclaim the support of the federation, for instance, demand the superiority of the laws of the Slovak Republic to those of the federation. On the other hand, almost one quarter of the supporters of an independent state refuses the independence of the Slovak army. There could be mentioned more such examples of such inconsistent thinking which is typical of about one half of the Slovak population. Needless to say, this state of legal knowledge and political culture opens the door for demagogy and political manipulation.

7. Connections under the Surface

When looking at the problem of a further coexistence of the Czechs and the Slovaks through the prism of the future prospects of a pluralistic democracy and economic prosperity in Slovakia, the question must be posed whether the attitude towards the legal arrangement of the state is connected with people's broader value orientations.The analysis of empirical findings [2; 7] give us a positive answer.

A loosening of the links between the Czech and the Slovak Republic is preferred to the greatest extent by people who support the principles of socialist economy and direct democracy and who are characterized by a high degree of intolerance not only against the Czechs, but against other national and ethnic minorities (Hungarians, Jews, Roma). This group (approximately one fourth of the population) consists of two different types – the radical anti-liberals and the nationalistic anti-parliamentarians.

The opposite value stream, with approximately the same number of adherents, is represented by nationally tolerant people who accept the principles of parliamentary democracy and are convinced supporters of a federation, or a unitarian state. This stream consists of two types of people: of those of a liberal orientation, supporting the principles of market economy and an elimination of the influence of the state upon social life, as well as of people of a social democratic orientation who assume an ambivalent attitude towards the radical economic reform.

About one half of the citizens of the Slovak Republic are situated between these two poles: although these people, in most of the cases, proclaim to be supporters of the common state, they do not consistently reject the attributes of independence. In this broad ambivalent middle two different types can be found. The first of them consists of people with no sharp outline, mostly older and with the lowest education, who have the greatest troubles with orientating themselves in the current political situation. The second category are the so-called Slovak patriots: they are rather distrustful against other nations or nationalities, they find the Slovak nation permanently disadvantaged and take up a reserved attitude towards the economic reform. They are, however, no extreme nationalists; their attitudes are not deeply anchored, but rather influenced by the nationalist campaign misusing the feelings of social uncertainty.

The fact that questioning or even openly rejecting the common state finds the loudest echo among intolerant people of an anti-parliamentarian, anti-reform, pro-communist orientation, suggests the probability of a catastrophic scenario of the development in Slovakia after a possible falling apart of the common state – the pushing of Slovakia into the realm of political instability, economic retardation, the violation of human rights and moral chaos [5].

Nobody is able to answer the question how things will turn out in the end. At the present moment we can only hope that the imperfect mechanisms of political democracy which are still in the making and which are operating under the conditions of a low political culture and a lack of experience with parliamentarism, will prevent this catastrophic scenario to come true.

Notes

1 In May 1991, 90% of the adult persons were afraid of unemployment and social insecurity, 80% of a long-lasting economic decrease of the country, 79% of the economic retardation of Slovakia within the ČSFR, 78% of a deterioration of human relations as a consequence of the economic reform [2].

2 In May 1991 only 17% of the respondents considered their political and public activity to be higher in comparison with that before November 1989 [2].

3 According to 66% of the respondents, the government officials should be directly responsible to the people, and not to the parliament or a political party [2].

4 This argumentation is often used e. g. by the Leader of Matica slovenská, Jozef Markuš.

5 Recently this vision has been repeatedly expressed e. g. by Ján Čarnogurský, former Catholic

dissident, now Prime Minister of the Slovak Government and leader of the Christian Democratic Movement.

6 This argumentation is typical of some of Slovak emigrants who are ideologically related to Tiso's state, e. g. of František Vnuk.

7 This argumentation is being asserted e. g. by the NEZES (group of economists of a reformed communist orientation) or by Vladimír Mináč, one of the prominent novelists and party officials, nowadays member of the Federal Parliament.

8 This glorification has found a fertile soil in Slovakia. A comparison of auto–stereotypes among the Czech and the Slovak population has revealed that a lower self-criticism is typical of the Slovaks [1].

9 The conviction that "in spite of all misunderstandings, the Czechs and Slovaks are linked together by friendly bonds which must be preserved" has been expressed by approximately 80% of all citizens of the Slovak Republic [1; 2].

10 According to almost 80% of population in Slovakia, people should be as proud of being citizens of the ČSFR as they are proud of their nationality [1; 2].

11 75% of the respondents from the Slovak Republic suspect the Czechs of not handling them as equal partners; 60% are convinced that the Slovaks are disadvantaged by the Czechs [2].

12 44% of the respondents in Slovakia expressed their conviction that one of the consequences of the economic reform would be the suppression of the national interests of Slovakia, and 77% were afraid of an underprivileged position of Slovakia within the framework of the ČSFR [2].

Literature

[1] Aktuálne problémy Česko-Slovenska – november 1990. Správa zo sociologického v skumu.. (Topical Problems of Czecho-Slovakia). Bratislava, CVSP 1990.

[2] Aktuálne prob1émy slovenskej spoloùnosti – máj 1991. Správa zo sociologického v skumu. (Topical Problems of Slovakia). Bratislava, ÚSA UK 1991.

[3] Aktuálne problémy slovenskej spoloùnosti – júl 1991. Správa zo sociologického v skumu. (Topical Problems of Slovakia). Bratislava, ÚSA UK 1991.

[4] Bútora, M.: Ochranárstvo ako prejav obùianskej spoloùnosti. (Environment Protection as a Feature of Civic Society). In: Sociológia 1990/3.

[5] Bútora, M.: Už Nie, ešte nie! (is it time already? Not, not yet!) In: Smena, 10. 1991.

[6] Bútorová, Z.: Antisemitizmus na Slovensku: marginálny jav, alebo vrcholùek æadovca? (Antisemitism in Slovakia: A marginal Phenomenon, or the Tip of an Iceberg?) In: Kultúrny život 1991 (in print).

[7] Bútorová, Z./Rosová, T.: Samostatné demokratické Slovensko? (An Independent Democratic Slovakia?) In: Kultúrny život 1991 (in print).

[8] Chceme Západ (We want to go West). Sociologick v skum AISA, In: Lidové noviny, 24. 5. 1991.

[9] Friù, P. – Bútorová, Z. – Rosová, T.: Ùesko-slovenské vzûahy v zrkadle v skumu. (Czecho-Slovak Relations in the Mirror of Research). In: Sociológia 1992/1 (in print).

[10] Kamenec, I.: po stopách tragédie. (on the Track of a Tragedy). Bratislava, Archa 1991.

[11] Kus , M.: Slovensk fenomén. (The Slovak Phenomenon). In: Fragment K 1990/3.

[12] Mikloško, F.: Nebudete ich môcû rozvrátiû. (You Will Not Be Able to Erradicate Them). Bratislava, Archa 1991.

[13] The Pulse of Europe: A Survey of Political and Social Values and Attitudes. Times Mirror Center for The People & The Press. Washington 1991.

[14] Rosová, T. – Bútorová, Z.: Hungarian Minority in Slovakia in Public Opinion, A Paper at the International Conference on Slovak-Hungarian Relations. Budapest, September 1991.

[15] Szomolányiová, S.: The Repolitization of the Slovak Society. World Congress of Soviet and East European Studies. Harrogate, 1990.

[16] Šimeùka, M.: Obnovenie poriadku. (Restoring the Order). Bratislava, Archa 1990.

Helga Matuschek

Nationalismus und Universalismus in der Behandlung von Ausländern in Österreich

Einleitung

Die Migration von Ausländern nach Österreich hat in den letzten drei Jahren eine prominente Stelle in der öffentlichen und politischen Diskussion eingenommen. Dazu trug auch die steigende Zahl von AsylwerberInnen (1989: 21.882; 1990: 22.789) und ausländischen Arbeitskräften (1989: 167.381; 1990: 217.611) bei. Die mit diesem Prozeß verbundenen Veränderungen der österreichischen Gesellschaft wurden als problematisch für den Zusammenhang der Nation gesehen. Hinweise wie „Österreich ist keine Einwanderungsland" oder „das Boot ist voll" dienten als Legitimation, den Ausschluß der Ausländer zu fordern und die Stabilität der Nation wiederherzustellen.

Diese nationalistische Idee der Problemlösung steht im Widerspruch nicht nur zur Internationalisierung von Wirtschaft, Waren- und Arbeitsmärkten, sondern auch zu den Menschenrechten.

Es ist ein Widerspruch, der nicht nur die österreichische Republik und Demokratie kennzeichnet, sondern die meisten Nationalstaaten.

Ziel dieses Beitrages ist es, sich mit diesen zwei Normensystemen, dem republikanischem Universalismus und dem Nationalismus, auseinanderzusetzen und darzustellen, in welchem Umfang sie die Teilhabemöglichkeiten von Ausländern in verschiedenen gesellschaftlichen Bereichen bestimmen.

Nationalismus und Menschenrechte

Die modernen Staaten sind Nationalstaaten und sowohl dem republikanischen Universalismus als auch dem Nationalismus verpflichtet. Während die liberale Demokratie die Rechte ihrer Bürger aus den universalen Menschenrechten ableitet, geschieht dies im Nationalismus durch Überlieferung und Berufung auf gemeinsame Abstammung und Tradition. (Heckmann 1991: 63).

Universalistische Prinzipien wie Menschenrechte, Leistungen, Qualifikationen gelten im Nationalstaat eingeschränkt oder werden außer Kraft gesetzt. Dadurch wird eine Unterscheidung von Staatsbürgern und Nichtstaatsbürgern geschaffen und somit ihre Lebens- und Teilhabechancen beeinflußt.

Im Nationalstaat können nur Bürger politische, soziale und bürgerliche Rechte erwerben. Für Nichtbürger gelten die universalen Menschenrechte und liberale Prinzipien, daß Menschen ihr Handeln selbständig im Rahmen der Gesetze gestalten können, nicht. Über den rechtlichen Status „Staatsbürgerschaft" werden Beziehungen geschaffen, die von sozialer Ausschließung und Einschließung,

Ehrerbietung und Herabsetzung getragen sind und durch konventionelle Sanktionen aufrechterhalten werden (Lockwood 1987: 31)

Die Anwesenheit von Fremden im Zusammenhang mit der internationalen Migration oder der raschen und intensiven sozio-ökonomischen Veränderungen (Habsbawm 1991: 197) stellt demnach eine Verletzung des nationalistischen Prinzips dar.

Durch rechtliche Segregation zwischen den auf einem Staatsgebiet lebenden Menschen wird daher versucht, diese Verletzung abzustellen und eine Homogenisierung von politischen und nationalen Einheiten herbeizuführen (Gellner 1991: 8).

Die Stellung der Ausländer zwischen Universalismus und Nationalismus in Österreich

Universalismus und Nationalismus sind in der österreichischen Bundesverfassung gemeinsam institutionalisiert und bestimmen den Umgang mit Ausländern. Diese entgegengesetzten Normensysteme stehen sich auf einem Kontinuum gegenüber. Bei Auftreten von gesellschaftlichen Problemlagen können diese Prinzipien in zeitlicher, sachlicher, räumlicher und auch personeller Hinsicht (Ermacora 1988: 10) flexibel zur Behandlung von Nichtstaatsbürgern eingesetzt werden und damit auch für diese unterschiedliche Teilhabechancen schaffen.

Die Teilhabe von Ausländern an den universalen Menschenrechten ist in Österreich begrenzt und im Vergleich zu anderen europäischen Ländern begrenzter.

Das republikanische Verfassungsverständnis von Freiheit und Gleichheit findet keine Anwendung bei den Ausländern. Liberale „Jedermann"-Rechte, die als allgemeingültige Menschenrechte verankert sind, gelten nur eingeschränkt. Die Gleichheit vor dem Gesetz ist ein Bürgerrecht und schließt Ausländer aus (Ermacora 1988: 68). Die Freiheit der Berufswahl und Berufsausbildung ist zwar als Menschenrecht für „jedermann" konzipiert, doch schließt dieses nicht Ausländer ein, da sie kein Recht auf Freizügigkeit und Wohnsitznahme haben. (Ermacora 1988: 335).

Auch das Recht auf Freizügigkeit wird Ausländern nur eingeschränkt gewährt, da der rechtmäßige Aufenthalt verfassungsmäßig nur den Staatsbürgern zusteht (Ermacora 1988: 443)

Nicht ausgeschlossen sind Ausländer hingegen von jenen Grundrechten, die ein „faires Verfahren" vor dem gesetzlichen Richter, die Achtung des Privat- u. Familienlebens, Recht auf Glaubens- u. Gewissensfreiheit (Ermacora 1988: 135 ff.) bedingen.

Ein Recht auf Asyl gewährt Österreich nicht. Doch für die Dauer des Asylverfahrens wird Asylwerbern ein zeitlich befristetes Recht zum Aufenthalt gewährt.

Der geringe Umfang der Inklusion von Ausländern in die universalen Rechte hebt die nationalistische Behandlung der Ausländer in Österreich hervor. Diese Tatsache kann bereits als Abwehr gegenüber der gesellschaftlichen Teilhabe von Ausländern klassifiziert werden.

Doch ihr Umfang hat sie sich auch unter dem Einfluß gesellschaftlicher Veränderungen gewandelt.

Die Entwicklung der politischen und rechtlichen Behandlung der Ausländer zeigt, daß Österreich einen Weg beschreitet, der immer stärker nationalistische Prinzipien gegenüber universalistischen betont. Dies kommt besonders deutlich gegenüber den AsylwerberInnen zum Ausdruck, deren Behandlung sich immer weniger an universalen Werten wie Freizügigkeit und Humanität orientiert. Diese Entwicklung zeigt sich auch an der Stellung der Ausländer im österreichischen Arbeits- u. Bildungsbereich.

Der zugeschriebene Status „Ausländer" steht im deutlichem Gegensatz zu jenem des „Staatsbürgers", der ein mehr an Rechten, aber auch Pflichten gegenüber dem Staat beinhaltet.

Die Nichtstaatsbürger sind generell stärker staatlicher Verfügungsmacht ausgesetzt. Demokratische Rechte von Freiheit, Gleichheit und Liberalität bleiben nur Österreichern vorbehalten oder werden Ausländern weniger gewährt. Ihre Teilhabemöglichkeiten sind in Einzelregelungen festgelegt, sie stellen Ausnahmen dar und zeigen wenig Verhältnismäßigkeit (Ermacora 1988: 327).

Ihre Teilhabemöglichkeiten in verschiedenen gesellschaftlichen Bereichen, insbesondere dem zentralen Lebensbereich Arbeitsmarkt, werden von nationalistischen Prinzipien und Zielsetzungen begrenzt, wie weiter unten dargestellt wird.

Zentrale Normen zur Durchsetzung nationalistischer Ausgrenzung

Der österreichische Nationalstaat versucht seine innere Ordnung mittels zentraler Normen – „öffentliche Ruhe, Ordnung und Sicherheit" – zu schützen. Durch deren Anwendung gegenüber bestimmten Ausländerkategorien sollen allgemeine Gefahren für Leben, Gesundheit und Sicherheit des Volkes und für die innerstaatliche Ruhe und Ordnung abgewehrt werden (Thienel 1990: II: 182). In anderen gesellschaftlichen Bereichen, wie z. B. dem Arbeitsmarkt, können noch andere Normen wirken, doch werden diese immer mit den zentralen Normen verkoppelt. So darf eine Beschäftigung von Ausländern nur gewährt werden, wenn keine fremdenpolizeiliche Bedenken dagegen sprechen.

Die Bedeutung dieser handlungsrelevanten Normen ist darin zu sehen, daß sie zu einer Vereinheitlichung von Bürgern und Territorium beitragen können und sollen.

Sie finden daher besondere Anwendung beim Zugang zum und beim Abgang vom Staatsgebiet, aber auch bei der Einbürgerung, bei der es um die Erlangung der vollen Bürgerrechte geht.

Kennzeichen dieser zentralen Normen ist der politische Interpretationsspielraum, der es ermöglicht, die jeweiligen nationalen Interessen zu erreichen.

Grenzziehungen gegenüber Ausländerkategorien

Alle gesellschaftlichen Bereiche, in denen nationalistische Prinzipien die Teilhabemöglichkeiten von AusländerInnen begrenzen, können hier nicht erfaßt werden. Auch sollen nur begrenzte Aussagen über ihre historische Veränderbarkeit erfolgen.

Dargestellt werden sollen die Teilhabechancen von zwei Ausländerkategorien, den Arbeitsmigranten und den AsylwerberInnen, da ihre Migration als besonderes Problem für die innere Ordnung und Stabilität Österreichs angesehen wird. Die Darstellung konzentriert sich dabei auf einige gesellschaftliche Bereiche wie Territorium, Arbeitsmarkt, Politik, soziale Sicherheit und Einbürgerung.

Grenzziehung nach Außen

Der Verlust Österreichs als Transitland für Asylwerber und Flüchtlinge und die fehlende politische Akzeptanz als Einwanderungsland haben in den letzten drei Jahren zur Abschottung der territorialen Grenzen gegenüber einer weiteren Migration von Ausländern und damit zur Betonung der nationalen Einheit geführt.

Mit zahlreiche Maßnahmen wurde versucht, eine weitere Migration von Ausländern in das Staatsgebiet zu behindern oder zu verunmöglichen.

Zu diesen Maßnahmen zählen insbesondere jene, die die Kontrolle der Staatsgrenze zum Ziel haben.

Die Kontrolle der Staatsgrenzen

Die Gewährung des Zutritts zum Staatsgebiet ist kein Menschenrecht, sondern eine Ermessenssache des Staates. Asylwerber haben in Österreich kein verfassungsmäßig gewährleistetes Zutrittsrecht zum Territorium wie in Deutschland. Asyl ist demnach in Österreich eine humanitäres und kein politisches Institut (Ermacora 1988: 124).

Nationale Interessen und gesetzliche Regelungen bestimmen daher, wer und wie lange ein Fremder Zutritt zum Staatsgebiet hat.

Seit drei Jahren werden verschiedene legistisch-administrative Maßnahmen gesetzt, um den Zugang zum Staatsgebiet zu erschweren und um eine Homogenisierung von Volk und Territorium herbeizuführen. Diese installierten Maßnahmen sind mit folgenden Auswirkungen gegenüber Asylwerbern, aber auch anderen Fremden verbunden.

Das Erfordernis, Identitätspapiere und eine Einreiseerlaubnis zu besitzen, wehrt jene ab, die auf illegale Migration angewiesen sind. Die Einführung der Visapflicht richtet sich gegen bestimmte Nationalitäten (Türken) und verneint die politische Verfolgung in diesen Ländern. Das Vorweisen von finanziellen Mitteln

(Bulgaren, Türken, Rumänen) dient ebenfalls dem Ausschluß derjenigen, die diese Mittel nicht besitzen.

Die verschärfte Kontrolle der Grenze durch das Militär, die Sanktionierung von Fluglinien, die Ausländer ohne Papiere nach Österreich transportieren sind ebenfalls Maßnahmen, die humanitäre Normen reduzieren und die nationalistische Praxis betonen.

Dieses System von Kontrollen und Barrieren gegenüber Ausländern, das zur nationalistischen Stabilität und Sicherheit beitragen soll, hat folgende quantifizierbaren Effekte:

Im Jahr 1990 wurden ca. 110.000 Fremde an den Bundesgrenzen zurückgewiesen und vom Betreten des österreichischen Staatsgebietes abgehalten. (Amnesty International 1991: 71).

Erteilung und Beendigung des Aufenthaltes

Das universale Recht auf Freiheit und Sicherheit steht Ausländern nicht zu, da sie kein Recht auf Aufenthalt und Wohnsitz haben. Der Aufenthaltsstatus von Ausländern ist daher an Zweckmäßigkeitsüberlegungen orientiert (Asyl, Arbeit, Studium etc.) und somit prinzipiell unsicher, zeitlich befristet und verfassungsmäßig nicht gewährleistet (Ermacora 1988: 120). Durch zwischenstaatliche Vereinbarungen können auch abgestufte Regelungen für bestimmte Nationalitäten festgelegt werden.

Die gewährte Dauer des Aufenthaltes beträgt bei AsylwerberInnen 3–6 Monate (Österreichisches Helsinki Komitee 1990: 39), bei Studierenden ein Studienjahr, und bei ausländischen Arbeitskräften kann sie sich von mehreren Monaten auch bis zu einer zeitlichen Unbefristetheit erstrecken.

Der Aufenthaltsstatus wird individuell und nicht familienbezogenen gewährt, wodurch sich auch innerhalb von Familien rechtliche Differenzierungen ergeben können.

Der Aufenthaltsstatus kann daher Ausländern auch entzogen werden, wenn ihre Anwesenheit nicht mehr im Einklang mit den nationalen Interessen steht.

Ausgrenzung aus dem innerstaatlichen Bereich

Zur Reduktion der Zahl der Ausländer im innerstaatlichen Bereich und damit auch zur Homogenisierung von Territorium und Volk wurden seit 1990 neue und abgestufte Mittel (Zurückweisung, Ausweisung, Abschiebung, Schubhaft) zur Ausschließung von Ausländern aus dem Staatsgebiet geschaffen.

Die Fremdenpolizei hat nun rechtliche Möglichkeiten, öffentliche Plätze und Straßen, Flüchtlingspensionen und Wohnheime zu kontrollieren und bei Gefährdung von oder Verstoß gegen zentrale nationale Interessen Fremde zwangsweise in ihre Herkunftsländer zurückzuführen.

Verstoß gegen die Rechtsordnung (Straßenverkehrsordnung, Ausländerbeschäftigungsgesetz, Steuer-, Abgaben-, Zollgesetze, Verurteilung durch Gerichte, u. a.), Verstoß gegen die ökonomischen Interessen des Staates (Leben in schlechten wirtschaftlichen Verhältnissen oder Beanspruchung von Sozialhilfe als Basis des Lebensunterhaltes), Verstoß gegen eine angenommene Qualität des Volkes (Gesundheit, Moral) und politische Betätigung sind solche Ausschließungsgründe (Hermann, Hackauf, Sellner 1986: 73).

Besonders eingeschränkt wird das humane Prinzip österreichischer Asylpolitik durch den Ausschluß bestimmter Nationalitäten (Bulgaren, Rumänen, Türken aus bestimmten Provinzen) von der Bundesbetreuung. Dies trifft auch auf jene zu, die keine Identitätspapiere vorweisen können. Für die davon betroffenen Ausländerkategorien übernimmt der österreichische Staat keine Sicherung eines minimalen Lebensunterhaltes (Unterkunft, Essen, Taschengeld, Gesundheitsversorgung). Diese nationalistische Maßnahme produziert präventiv einen Notstand bei diesen Ausländerkategorien und ermöglicht dadurch mittels fremdenpolizeilichen Handelns ihren Ausschluß aus dem Territorium.

Der Erfolg dieser nationalistischen Maßnahmen läßt sich nicht abschätzten, da neben freiwilliger auch eine unfreiwillige Rückkehr möglich ist. Amnesty wies darauf hin, daß 1990 mehrere tausend Fremde, die sich bereits im Staatsgebiet befanden, in Schubhaft genommen und zwangsweise zurückgeschoben wurden. (Amnesty 1991: 77). Unter ihnen befanden sich nicht nur Erwachsene, sondern auch Kinder (Matuschek 1991: 94)

Grenzziehung im Inneren: Kontrolle der Arbeitsmarktprozesse

Die Rechtmäßigkeit des Aufenthaltes ist eine unabdingbare Voraussetzung für Ausländer, um in anderen gesellschaftlichen Bereichen teilhaben zu können.

Als zentraler Bereich erweist sich hier der Arbeitsmarkt.

Die Teilhabechancen der Ausländer am Arbeitsmarkt sind vor allem an nationalistisch-partikularen und weniger an universalistischen Interessen orientiert.

Nationale Kategorien (Lage und Entwicklung des Arbeitsmarktes, wichtige öffentliche und gesamt-wirtschaftliche Interessen) bestimmen die Teilhabechancen von Ausländern am Arbeitsmarkt und reduzieren die Wirkung universaler Kriterien (Sprache und Qualifikation), die die Ausländer begrenzt besitzen.

Nach 30 Jahren Ausländerbeschäftigung wird den Ausländern noch immer ein zeitlich befristeter Rechtsstatus und kaum Freizügigkeit innerhalb des Arbeitsmarktes gewährt.

Ihr Zugang zum und ihr Abgang vom Arbeitsmarkt wird nationalistisch gehandhabt. Die Beschäftigung von Ausländern hat Nachrang gegenüber jener von Österreichern, jedoch Vorrang bei der Kündigung.

Ziel des Ausschlusses von universalen Rechten ist es, gesellschaftliche Umverteilungen aufgrund von Marktmechanismen zu begrenzen und damit sozio-ökonomische Probleme innerhalb der Gesellschaft zu bewältigen.

In den letzten drei Jahrzehnten wurde mittels mehrerer rechtlicher und administrativer Maßnahmen versucht, die jeweiligen nationalen Ziele zu erreichen. (Matuschek 1985)

Diese bestanden Anfang der 60er Jahre darin, Arbeitsmarktlücken zu schließen und Wohlfahrt für die Bürger und Wirtschaftswachstum zu steigern. Seit 1973 wird dieses Ziel in der Reduktion der Zahl der beschäftigten Ausländer im Bundesgebiet gesehen.

Stabilisierung der Zahl der Ausländer am Arbeitsmarkt und innerhalb der Gesellschaft wird seit 1988 angestrebt.

Die Zuwanderung von Ausländern nach Österreich soll auch politisch durch das Eingreifen in die Arbeitsmarktprozesse gesteuert werden.

Ziel nationalistischer Überlegungen ist es, das Überangebot an ausländischen Arbeitskräften, ihre illegale Beschäftigung und die Substitution von längerfristig beschäftigten Ausländern durch billige neu eingewanderte (Nowotny 1991: 43) zu reduzieren.

Die installierten Maßnahmen dienen der Aufrechterhaltung nationalistischer Prinzipien und nationalstaatlicher Abgrenzung. Zu diesen Maßnahmen zählen insbesondere die Fixierung der Angebotsmenge an ausländischen Arbeitskräften in der Höhe von 10% des Arbeitskräftepotentials und die Beschränkung der Freizügigkeit der ausländischen Arbeitskräfte in regionaler und zeitlicher Hinsicht.

Die meisten der ausländischen Arbeitskräfte besitzen nur eine einjährige Arbeitsbewilligung und keine regionale Freizügigkeit. Nur rund 33% der Arbeitsmigranten (September 1991: 88.327 gegenüber 267.890) wird eine auf 5 Jahren befristete Freizügigkeit gewährt, wenn sie bestimmte Aufenthalts- u. Beschäftigungsbedingungen erfüllt haben oder mit einem österreichischen Staatsbürger verheiratet sind.

Die Beachtung von Beschäftigungs- und Aufenthaltsdauer in Österreich führt zwar zur Verbesserung des Rechtsstatus einiger Ausländerkategorien und damit zur Abstufung ihrer Teilhaberechte am Arbeitsmarkt und an der sozialen Sicherheit.

Doch bieten diese Maßnahmen den Ausländern keinen Schutz. Denn durch das politisch gezielte Eingreifen in die Marktprozesse, wie es durch das Inländerprimat, die Mengenrationierung, die zeitlich befristeten Teilhaberechte erfolgt, hat der Staat die Möglichkeit, zwischen Angebot und Nachfrage auszugleichen und Arbeitsplätze für Inländer freizumachen.

Von 1973 bis 1984 wurden durch diese nationalistische Politik über 100.000 Ausländer aus dem Arbeitsmarkt freigesetzt.

Grenzen dieser nationalistischen Arbeitsmarktpolitik

Eine Ausgrenzung der im Staatsgebiet lebenden Arbeitsmigranten ist jedoch aus folgenden Gründen nur begrenzt möglich.

Die Wirtschaft hat ein Interesse an der Beschäftigung von ausländischen Arbeitskräften.

Die zunehmende Überalterung insbesondere von Wien, die sinkenden Geburtenraten schaffen Versorgungs-, Renten- und Bevölkerungsprobleme, die durch Zuwanderung gelöst werden sollen. (Faßmann, Münz 1990: 23)

Der Status der ausländischen Wohnbevölkerung hat sich aufgrund von zwischenstaatlichen und internationalen Vereinbarungen gefestigt. Österreich muß seit 1985 die Familieneinheit der Ausländer beachten (Weh 1986: 305). Arbeitslosigkeit oder Verstoß gegen die zentralen Normen ist kein territorialer Ausgrenzungsgrund.

Die nationalistische Politik der Freisetzung von Ausländern aus dem Arbeitsmarkt ist begrenzt, da Ausländer die unqualifizierten Tätigkeiten verrichten und eine Substitution durch Österreicher kaum möglich ist.

Für den österreichischen Staat ist diese nationalistische Arbeitsmarktpolitik ein Gewinn. Ungerechtigkeiten in den Lebensbedingungen zwischen Österreichern und Ausländern müssen nicht ausgeglichen, sondern nur stabilisiert werden. Ausländer können in den unqualifizierten, gesundheitsgefährdenden, schlecht bezahlten, mit starken Belastungen versehenen Arbeitsplätzen verbleiben (rund 90% sind noch immer als unqualifizierte Arbeitskräfte tätig). Maßnahmen zur Förderung ihrer sozialen Mobilität oder beruflichen Qualifizierung müssen über das notwendige nationale Interesse hinaus nicht gewährt werden.

Der Staat kann durch sein Eingreifen in die Arbeitsmarktprozesse Ausländer um ihre Erwerbstätigkeit bringen und sie schneller und auch länger arbeitslos machen. (BMAS 1990: 42). Der Ausschluß von Arbeit ist mit kürzeren sozialversicherungsrechtlichen Leistungsfristen, mit einem Verarmungsrisiko verbunden (Bauböck 1986: 403 ff.) und kann zur territorialen Ausgrenzung führen.

Zugang zur selbständigen Erwerbstätigkeit

Auch der Zugang zur selbständigen Erwerbstätigkeit ist an nationalen Interessen ausgerichtet und daher Ausländern nur in abgestufter Form möglich. Neben einem generellen Ausschluß von bestimmten Erwerbsarten (Waffen, Rohrleitungen) können Ausländer jedoch bei Vorweisen von Qualifikationen selbständig erwerbstätig werden. Dabei stellt die Nationalität ein wichtiges Selektionskriterium dar. So besteht eine Gleichstellung für Staatsangehörige aus Belgien, der BRD, aus Holland, Italien und den USA, eine beschränkte für Angehörige von EFTA-Staaten. Die geringsten Chancen haben hingegen die Arbeitsmigranten aus Jugoslawien und der Türkei. (Matuschek 1989: 74 f.)

Soziale Rechte

Auch im sozialstaatlichen Bereich werden nationalistisch-partikulare Interessen zur rechtlichen und auch faktischen Begrenzung der Teilhabemöglichkeiten von Ausländern eingesetzt. Soziale Rechte, die in der Bundesverfassung nicht explizit verankert sind, werden den Ausländern kaum und in Abhängigkeit zum Aufenthaltszweck gewährt.

Die Reziprozität staatlicher Leistungsverpflichtungen grenzt bereits Nationalitäten aus, für die keine bilateralen Abkommen geschlossen wurden. Die in den Abkommen über soziale Sicherheit festgelegte formale Gleichheit von Lohnbedingungen und sozialen Rechten von Arbeitsmigranten aus Jugoslawien und der Türkei inkludiert sie gleichwertig in die Leistungspflichten des Staates. Es besteht daher keine rechtliche Segregation in ihren Beitragspflichten (Lohn, Wohnbauförderung, Sozialversicherung etc.) Diese tritt jedoch in ihren Anspruchsrechten auf soziale Leistungen auf. Diese werden ihnen nur abgestuft gewährt, da der Staat der Sicherung ihres Lebensstandards, der Gewährung von Schutz und Hilfe in Notlagen eine geringere Priorität als bei Staatsbürgern einräumt. Ausländer, die ein größeres Lebensrisiko tragen müssen, werden somit in geringerem Umfang in die nationale Solidaritätsgemeinschaft aufgenommen. An den fiskalischen Gewinnen, die der Staat durch die Arbeitsmigranten erzielt hat, werden sie nur begrenzt beteiligt. Diese betrugen 1990 1,2 Milliarden Schilling alleine bei der Arbeitslosenversicherung. (Köppl u. Ziniel 1984; 1991).

Asylwerber, denen ein Zugang zum Arbeitsmarkt wie jedem neu Eingereisten gewährt werden kann, haben keinen Anspruch auf Deckung von Minimalbedürfnissen. Es liegt im Ermessen des Staates, welche Nationalitäten und in welchem Umfange er in seine Betreuungsleistungen einbezieht. Ausgeschlossen sind derzeit Bulgaren, Rumänen sowie Türken aus bestimmten Provinzen. Die Grundversorgung, die Österreich Asylwerbern gewährt, besteht in Unterkunft, Essen, Gesundheitsmaßnahmen und einem monatlichen Taschengeld von öS 400.–.

Die Entwicklung von Einzel- zur Familienwanderung Mitte der 70er Jahre und die Finanzkrise des Staates führten zur Betonung von nationalistischen Kriterien am Arbeitsmarkt und auch im Bereich der sozialen Sicherheit. Sozialstaatliche Einrichtungen und Leistungen wurden reduziert oder werden Ausländern erst ab einer bestimmten Anwesenheits- oder Leistungsdauer gewährt. Ausgeschlossen sind Ausländer vom sozialen Wohnungsbau, wodurch sie auf den privaten Wohnungsmarkt als Nachfrager verwiesen werden.

Einige familienbezogene Beihilfen oder Leistungen aus der Arbeitslosenversicherung werden ihnen erst nach einer oder nur für eine bestimmte Dauer gewährt. Die Reduktion der Familienbeihilfe für die im Ausland lebenden Kinder, die zeitliche Staffelung von Anspruchsfristen für familienbezogene Leistungen, um nur einige zu nennen (Matuschek 1989: 555 ff.), sind als nationalistische Maßnahmen zur Abwehr von ausländischen Ansprüchen zu sehen.

Denn ihre Ansprüche auf Teilhabe an sozialen Leistungen können weiter als jene der Österreicher zurückgedrängt werden. Ihr Rechtsstatus bietet ihnen geringe Möglichkeiten, sich gegen die staatlichen Eingriffe in ihre Lebens- und Handlungsbereiche zu wehren.

Eine soziale Absicherung über das zweite Netz ist nur im geringem Umfang gegeben. Eingeschlossen werden alle jene Ausländer, denen eine zeitlich befristete Freizügigkeit von 5 Jahren am Arbeitsmarkt zugestanden wurde. Es handelt sich dabei um rund ein Drittel der ausländischen Arbeitnehmer einschließlich der

2. Generation, die für die Dauer von 39 Wochen in die Subsidiaritätsleistungen der Notstandshilfe einbezogen werden.

Bei allen anderen ausländischen Arbeitskräften wird das erhöhte Lebensrisiko, das sie in Österreich haben (Arbeitslosigkeit, Unfall, Gesundheit), nicht durch ihre Einbeziehung in die sozialen Rechte ausgeglichen.

Die nationalistische Politik ist nur begrenzt auf Schutz und Sicherung eines Lebensminimums der Ausländer ausgerichtet, da immer ihre Alternativrolle „Ausländer" mitbeachtet wird. Ausländer sind daher weniger vor Armut und damit auch vor sozialer bis zur territorialen Ausgrenzung geschützt. Denn die Beanspruchung von Sozialhilfe, die den Ausländern nur in einigen Bundesländern (ausgenommen Wien, Vorarlberg, Kärnten) gewährt (Pfeil 1990: 35) wird, ist verknüpft diese mit der Ausweisungsdrohung. Es läuft dem nationalen Interesse zuwider, für Fremde den Lebensunterhalt sicherzustellen. (Hermann, Hackauf u. Sellner 1988: 78).

Bildungsrechte

In die Bildungsrechte als universale Menschenrechte sind die Ausländer einbezogen, und es besteht auch für die Kinder eine Schulpflicht. Der Staat ist jedoch zu keiner positiven Leistung verpflichtet (Ermacora 1988: 224). Durch Betonung der Territorialsprache „Deutsch" führt er eine Ungleichheit von Sprache und Kultur der ausländischen Kinder herbei und gestaltet damit die Schul- und Unterrichtskonzepte nationalistisch. (Gstettner 1989: 42). Die Kinder haben keinen Anspruch auf Unterricht in ihrer Sprache, was ihren Spracherhalt weder schützt noch fördert. (Österreichische Rektorenkonferenz 1989: 147). Trotz vieler Maßnahmen, die im Zusammenhang mit dem neuen Bildungsziel „interkulturelles Lernen" gesetzt wurden, ist es fraglich, wie weit diese die Bildungschancen der ausländischen Kinder erhöhen.

Die Universalisierung von Sprache und Leistungsbeurteilung wirkt sich noch immer in einem hohen Schulversagen und Überweisungsverhalten in die Sonderschule aus. (Matuschek 1982). Förderungsmaßnahmen zu Spracherwerb und Spracherhalt wurden gesetzt, doch individualisierten sie damit die schulischen Probleme der Kinder. Der muttersprachliche Zusatzunterricht wird nur jugoslawischen und türkischen Kindern, nicht aber anderen Nationalitäten erteilt. Er ist zeitlich begrenzt, nicht mehr obligatorisch und kann auch nicht in seiner Konzeption den Spracherhalt der ausländischen Kinder sicherstellen.

Ausschluß von den politischen Rechten

Das demokratische Prinzip, daß alle jene, die von politischen Entscheidungen betroffen sind, die Möglichkeit haben, sich daran zu beteiligen (Hammar 1990: 2), trifft auf die Ausländer kaum zu. Sie werden in größerem Umfang als in anderen Ländern von den politischen Rechten ausgeschlossen (Rosenmayr 1986: 102). Die demokratische Idee der Freiheit vom Staat wird auf sie kaum angewendet. Ihre Handlungsmöglichkeiten sind sehr eingeschränkt, und ihre Behandlung unterliegt Zweckmäßigkeitsüberlegungen. Das Recht auf freie Meinungsäußerung gilt eingeschränkt (Ermacora 1988: 188), Vereins- u. Versammlungsfreiheit kommt nur österreichischen Staatsbürgern zu (Ermacora 1988: 206 ff.) genauso wie das passive und aktive Wahlrecht zu den allgemeinen Vertretungskörpern (Ermacora 1988: 233).

Das aktive Wahlrecht steht ihnen bei den Wahlen des Betriebsrates, der Arbeiterkammer, der Handelskammer und der Hochschülerschaft zu. Auch die plebiszitären demokratischen Stimmrechte stehen ihnen nicht zu, da diese an die Staatsbürgerrolle gebunden sind. (Volksbegehren, Volksabstimmung)

Politisches Engagement kann mit der Ausgrenzung geahndet werden, da sie öffentlichem (nationalem) Interesse zuwiderläuft (Hermann, Hackauf, Sellner 1988: 75)

Die Einbürgerung

Dem Erwerb der österreichischen Staatsbürgerschaft liegen vor allem nationalistisch völkische Kriterien, aber auch universalistische zugrunde. Oberstes Erwerbsprinzip ist die Abstammung, die eine Verbindung von Volk und Staatsbürgern herstellt (Pernthaler 1982: 37 ff.). Die Einbürgerung ist auf die bürgerliche Gleichstellung von „Ausländern" und „Österreichern" und auf Aufnahme in den Loyalitätsverband des Staates ausgerichtet. Die Staatsbürgerschaft erstreckt sich auf die Republik, wird jedoch von den Bundesländern verliehen.

Universalistische Prinzipien haben Vorrang gegenüber völkischen bei der Einbürgerung bestimmter Ausländerkategorien (Wissenschaftler, Künstler, Sportler und Wirtschaftsleute), die durch ihre erbrachten und zukünftig noch zu erwartenden „Leistungen" zum nationalen Wohle beitragen sollen.

Abgestufte Möglichkeiten des Erwerbs werden an Aufenthaltsfristen gebunden, die zwischen 10 und 3 Jahren liegen können. In diesen kommen universalistische und nationalistische Ideen zum Ausdruck. Nach 4 Jahren können anerkannte Flüchtlinge, aber auch Ausländer mit den erforderlichen beruflichen Qualifikationen die vollen Bürgerrechte erhalten, aber auch jene, die sich an die österreichische Lebensart angepaßt und besondere Bindungen entwickelt haben (Thienel 1990: 207). Nach 30 Jahren ununterbrochenem Aufenthalt erhalten die Ausländer einen Rechtsanspruch auf Staatsbürgerschaft (in Deutschland liegt diese Grenze bei 15 Jahren).

Wie weit diese rechtliche Möglichkeit von den Arbeitsmigranten und ihren Familienangehörigen ausgeschöpft wird, kann derzeit noch nicht festgestellt werden.

Eine Studie aus dem Jahre 1985 zeigt, daß die Bereitschaft von Jugoslawen und Türken zur Annahme der österreichischen Staatsbürgerschaft gering (4,8%

der befragten Jugoslawen und 2,5% der Türken) ist, hingegen die der Annahme einer Doppelstaatsbürgerschaft höher (6,8% zu 10,5%) (Bundesministerium für soziale Verwaltung 1985: 218).

Wesentlich für die Einbürgerung ist die Identifikation der Bewerber mit den zentralen nationalen Werten. Diese werden an ihren vergangenen und zukünftigen Handlungsmöglichkeiten in rechtlicher, sozialer, wirtschaftlicher und politischer Hinsicht geprüft. (Thienel 1990: II: 187) Bejahung der Republik Österreich gehört genauso dazu wie die Verläßlichkeit der Bewerber. Diese wird an ihren Handlungsmöglichkeiten gemessen. Dazu zählen folgende normativen Erfordernisse: Ausländer müssen ihren eigenen Lebensunterhalt bestreiten, Gesetze einhalten, zur öffentlichen Ruhe, Ordnung und Sicherheit beitragen und gesicherte Lebensverhältnisse in Form von Arbeit, Pension etc. vorweisen.

Wie weit die Einbürgerungsbehörden diesem Mythos von der Homogenität und Qualität von Volk, Kultur und Nation Handlungsrelevanz zumessen, steht empirisch nicht fest. Die Behördenpraxis ist in den Bundesländern unterschiedlich. (Edtstadler 1988: 601 ff.).

Doch offensichtlich ist, daß die jährlichen Einbürgerungsraten nur rund 1‰ (absolut rund 8000 Menschen) betragen und sich vor allem auf Deutsche und weniger auf Jugoslawen und Türken konzentrieren.

Zusammenfassung

Österreich schließt Ausländer nur in einem geringem Umfang in universalistische Rechte ein und ermöglicht ihnen daher nur zeitlich befristete Teilhabemöglichkeiten an der österreichischen Gesellschaft. Nationalismus als Ordnungsprinzip ist nicht mehr zeitgemäß. Es ist von der Dynamik der technischen, ökonomischen Entwicklung überholt und kann die politische Integrations- u. Funktionsfähigkeit der Gesellschaft beeinträchtigen (Radtke 1988: 117).

Durch Kontrolle der Staatsgrenzen, durch Mengenbegrenzung der Zahl der Ausländer (Arbeitskräfte, betreuende Asylwerber) wird politisch versucht, eine Stabilisierung der österreichischen Gesellschaft zu erreichen und den Nationalstaat zu festigen.

Doch sind diesen Maßnahmen Grenzen gesetzt.

Der Staat kann seine nationalen Interessen gegenüber den Ausländern jedoch nicht durchsetzen. Dies liegt in internationalen Vereinbarungen, den Interessen der Wirtschaft ebenso begründet wie in demographischen Entwicklungen. Außerdem setzen sich Kirche und andere Bevölkerungsgruppen für die Rechte der Ausländer ein.

Die nationalistischen Maßnahmen, die auf Homogenisierung von Territorium und Volk abzielen, bieten Österreich keine Zukunftsperspektive an.

Literatur

Amnesty International: Keine Mauern gegen Flüchtlinge, Wien 1991.

Bauböck, R.: Ausländerpolitik und Ausländerarmut, in: Zeitschrift für Politikwissenschaft 4/1986, S. 403–423.

Bundesministerium für Soziales und Arbeit (Hg): Die Arbeitsmarktlage 1990, Wien 1991 (Eigenverlag).

Bundesministerium für soziale Verwaltung: Ausländische Arbeitnehmer in Österreich, Wien 1985.

Edtstadler, K.: Die Verleihungspraxis der österreichischen Staatsbürgerschaft im Land Salzburg, in: Khol, A., Ofner, G., Stirnemann, A. (Hg.): Österreichisches Jahrbuch für Politik 1987, Wien – München 1988, S. 601–619.

Ermacora, F.: Grundriß der Menschenrechte in Österreich, Wien 1988 (Manz).

Faßmann, H., Münz, R.: Einwanderungsland Österreich? Wien 1990.

Gellner, E.: Nationalismus und Moderne, Berlin 1991 (Rotbuch Verlag).

Hammar, T.: Democracy and the Nation State. Aldershot 1990.

Heckmann, F.: Ethnos, Demos und Nation, oder: Woher stammt die Intoleranz des Nationalstaats gegenüber ethnischen Minderheiten?, in: Bielefeld, U. (Hg.): Das Eigene und das Fremde, Hamburg 1991, S. 51–78.

Hermann, A., Hackauf, F., Sellner, E.: Paß-, Fremdenpolizei- und Asylrecht, 3. Aufl., Wien 1986 (Juridica).

Hobsbawm, E.: Nationen und Nationalismus, Frankfurt/Main, New York 1991 (Campus).

Lockwood, D.: Schichtung in der Staatsbürgergesellschaft, in: Giesen, B., Haferkamp, H. (Hg.): Soziologie der sozialen Ungleichheit, Opladen 1987, S. 31–48.

Köppl, F., Ziniel, G.: Probleme ausländischer Arbeitnehmer am Beispiel Wien, Wien 1984.

Gstettner, P.: Das „Interkulturelle Lernen" ist der Maßstab, in: Soziales Förderungs- und Forschungsinstitut (Hg.): Soziales Europa? Wien 1989 (Falter) S. 39–44.

Matuschek, H.: Ausländerpolitik von 1960–1982, in: Journal für Sozialforschung 2/1985, S. 159–198.

Matuschek, H.: Selbständige Erwerbstätigkeit von Ausländern in Wien, in: Österreichisches Institut für Raumplanung: Aktionen zur Integration von Ausländern, Wien 1989, S. 71–80.

Matuschek, H.: Die Auswirkungen der „Ausländerpolitik" auf Schul- und Berufsausbildung der jugoslawischen und türkischen Jugendlichen in Wien und Niederösterreich. Situation und Lösungsmöglichkeiten, Wien 1982.

Matuschek, H.: Familien von ArbeitsmigrantInnen und AsylwerberInnen in Österreich, in: Bundesministerium für Umwelt, Jugend und Familie (Hg.): Lebenswelt Familie, Familienbericht 1989, Wien 1989, S. 545–568.

Matuschek, H., u. a.: Minderjährige auf der Flucht. Situation und Probleme unbegleiteter minderjähriger AsylwerberInnen in Österreich, Wien 1991.

Nowotny, I.: Ausländerbeschäftigung in Österreich, in: WISO – Wirtschafts- und sozialpolitische Zeitschrift 1/91, S. 38 –63.

Österreichische Liga für Menschenrechte: Menschenrechtlicher Befund für Österreich 1990 (Manu), Wien 1990.

Österreichisches Helsinki Komitee: Asylland Österreich: Zutritt verboten? Wien 1990.

Österreichische Rektorenkonferenz: Lage und Perspektiven der Volksgruppen in Österreich, Wien 1989.

Pernthaler, P.: Land, Volk und Heimat als Kategorien des österreichischen Verfassungsrechts, Wien 1982 (Braumüller).

Pfeil, W.: Aktuelle Auswirkungen der Trennung zwischen Sozialversicherung und Sozialhilfe, in: Dimmel, N., u. a. (Hg): Sozialhilfe, Strukturen, Mängel, Vorschläge, Wien 1989 (Verlag des ÖGB), S. 111–132.

Rosenmayer, St.: Die öffentlich-rechtliche Stellung von Gastarbeitern, insbesondere das Aufenthaltsrecht, in: Institut für Höhere Studien (Hg.): Untersuchung über die ausländischen Arbeitskräfte in Österreich, Bd. II, Wien 1984, S. 349–430.

Thienel, R.: Österreichische Staatsbürgerschaft, 2 Bde. Wien 1990.
Weh, W. L.: Aufenthaltsverbot und „Familienleben", in: Zeitschrift für Verwaltung 1986/3, S. 303–310.

Ernst Bruckmüller

Die gespaltene Mythologie

Hintergründe eines uneinheitlichen Nationalbewußtseins

Der vorliegende Text möchte die Frage diskutieren, inwiefern die kollektiven Befindlichkeiten der Österreicher „zwischen Nationalismus und Universalismus" Auswirkungen auf die Offenheit (oder Verschlossenheit) gegenüber den Nachbarstaaten Mitteleuropas signalisieren. Die Folgen solcher Befindlichkeiten können selbstverständlich durchaus unterschiedliche Auswirkungen im Hinblick auf unsere Zukunft haben.

Meine zentrale These lautet folgendermaßen: „Nationalbewußtsein" als ein Grundkonsens einer bestimmten Population ist nicht von objektiven Kriterien bestimmt, sondern ist eine subjektive Kategorie, die durchaus Ähnlichkeiten mit religiösen Empfindungen besitzt, in der historischen Perspektive zum Teil auch als säkularisierte Ablösung religiöser Vorstellungen gelten kann. Es ist daher sehr sinnvoll, jenes Paket von „Mythologie" zu untersuchen, das hinter jedem „Nationalbewußtsein" steht. *Im Falle des österreichischen Nationalbewußtseins vermute ich, daß eine einheitliche Mythologie nicht oder nur rudimentär existiert.*

Auf den ersten Blick wird dieser Befund scheinbar nicht bestätigt, die Umfragedaten scheinen im Gegenteil eine Befestigung der nationalen Identität der Österreicher nachzuweisen:

Tabelle 1
Die Österreicher als Nation (in % der Befragten)[1]

Österreicher	1964	1970	1972	1980	1987	1990
sind Nation	47	66	62	67	75	74
beginnen sich als Nation zu fühlen	23	16	12	19	16	20
zusammen	70	82	74	86	91	94

Diese allgemeinen Aussagen sind nicht unerheblich nach Alter und sozialer Position zu differenzieren.

Von 1956 bis 1985 durchgehend zeigt sich eine stärkere, wohl auch unreflektiertere, Österreich-Identifikation bei Bauern und Arbeitern.

Schon 1956, im Rahmen der ersten Befragung zum (National-)Bewußtsein der Österreicher, ließen die Höhergebildeten eine deutlich größere Neigung erkennen, sich „deutsch" zu fühlen. Damals erklärten 49% der Befragten, Österreich sei ein „eigenes Volk" (gegen 46% – „Teil des deutschen Volkes"). Arbeiter sahen hingegen zu 62% und Bauern zu 56% Österreich als eigenständig an. Ganz ähnliche Schlüsse lassen die Ergebnisse einer Gallup-Studie zu, die 1966 für William T. Bluhm durchgeführt und 1973 in seinem Buch „Building an Austrian Nation" veröffentlicht wurden: Auf die Behauptung „Österreich ist eine völlig eigenständige Nation" antworteten 39% der Arbeiter und 33% der Bauern mit „Ja", aber nur 16% der Beamten. Dagegen wurde die Feststellung: „Obwohl Österreich ein unabhängiger Staat ist, gehört Österreich zur deutschen Nation" nur von 8% der Arbeiter und 12% der Bauern, jedoch von 19% der Beamten bejaht (nach politischen Parteipräferenzen bejahten 30% der FPÖ-, 12% der ÖVP- und 6% der SPÖ-Anhänger diese Formulierung).[2] Auch die Ergebnisse der Umfrage zum österreichischen Nationalbewußtsein 1979 veranlaßten die Herausgeber zur Feststellung: „Bauern und Arbeiter fühlen sich Österreich als ihrer unmittelbar erlebten Heimat in umfassender Emotionalität verbunden. Die höher Gebildeten machen noch eher feinere Unterschiede und sind gegen Kultur und Lebensmuster kritischer."[3] Eine ORF-Umfrage vom Herbst 1985 erhob Landes- und Bundespatriotismus. Dabei waren nach dem Berufsstatus selbständige Landwirte vor Fach- und sonstigen Arbeitern die ausgeprägtesten Patrioten, gefolgt von Arbeitslosen, Gewerbetreibenden (ganz knapp unter dem Durchschnitt!), Angestellten/Beamten, Freiberuflern, Großunternehmern, Schülern und Studenten. Nach dem Kriterium „Schulabschluß" wiesen Akademiker den geringsten, Menschen ohne abgeschlossene Schulbildung und Pflichtschulabsolventen den höchsten Grad an „Patriotismus" auf.[4] Es können diese Zahlen verschieden interpretiert werden und natürlich *auch* bedeuten, daß erhöhte Bildungschancen verminderte Lokalborniertheit und größere Bereitschaft zu Weltbürgerlichkeit nach sich ziehen. Doch wird man auch deutschnationale Denkmuster als Hintergrund solcher Abstufungen nicht ausschließen können.

Die Umfrage von 1987[5] gestattet aber noch eine Reihe weiterer Aussagen:

1. „Nation" wird ganz überwiegend als auf einen Staat bezogene Gruppierung mit einem besonderen Selbstbewußtsein gesehen; nur eine Minderheit von etwa 21% führt nationales Bewußtsein auf gemeinsame Sprache zurück.
2. Hinsichtlich der Generationenabfolge ist bei den Sechzigjährigen 1987 (anders als 1980) die Österreich-Skepsis stärker ausgeprägt – „alt" sind heute die 1938 „jung" Gewesenen, während nur mehr sehr wenige Menschen noch von der Monarchie geprägt sind.
3. Die stärkste Österreich-Bejahung ist bei den Zwanzig- bis Fünfzigjährigen vorhanden.
4. Überraschend ist eine erhebliche Skepsis gegenüber einem österreichischen Nationalbewußtsein bei den ganz Jungen; die Unter-Neunzehn-Jährigen lagen mit 9% „keine Nation" bzw. 62% „Nation" erheblich über bzw. unter dem Durchschnitt. Läßt sich *hierin* eine zunehmende Brüchigkeit des für die Mittelgeneration bei allen Problemen an und in diesem Österreich doch selbstverständlichen nationalen Grundkonsens ablesen, gegründet in Waldheim-Problemen, Proksch-, AKH- und sonstigen Skandalen, genährt von sensationshungrigen Medien, hinter deren (an sich notwendiger) Kritik und Destruktion keinerlei integratives Wertsystem erkennbar ist, begünstigt von einer Kulturpolitik, die diesen Zerfall des österreichischen Selbstbewußtseins massiv fördert?[6]
5. Nach Partei-Präferenzen ist bei der Gefolgschaft der „Grünen" die „reinste" „Österreich"-Gesinnung, praktisch ohne jedwede „deutsche" Färbung, zu

finden. Etwas stärkere deutsch-orientierte Minderheiten gibt es bei SPÖ (ca. 6%) und ÖVP (ca. 6%); die bloß 5%ige deutsche Konfession der FPÖ-Anhänger wird freilich dadurch korrigiert, daß sich 23% dieser Gruppe durch die deutsche Wiedervereinigung „angesprochen" fühlen (SPÖ: 10%, ÖVP 12%, Grüne 5%). Und diese Ergebnisse sind recht gut vergleichbar mit einer Fessel- Umfrage vom Dezember 1989, die in Ostösterreich (Niederösterreich und Wien) veranstaltet wurde – danach haben 7% der Befragten insgesamt, aber 21% der FPÖ-Sympathisanten den Wunsch, Österreich möge sich einem wiedervereinigten Deutschland anschließen; immerhin noch 7% der ÖVP- und 5% der SPÖ-Sympathisanten äußerten analoge Bedürfnisse; nur die Grünen sind dagegen gänzlich immun.[7] Innere Verwandtschaft mit Deutschland wird in bestimmten Teilen der Bevölkerung noch deutlicher ausgedrückt, wenn etwa 1980 34% (!) der Befragten die Aussage unterstützten: „Der Anschluß (1938) brachte endlich wieder die natürliche Verbindung mit dem deutschen Volk" – dieser Anteil sank freilich bis 1987 auf 20%.[8] Ganz deutlich ausgeschlossen wird ein „Anschluß" in der Zukunft 1980 nur von 55% (darüber liegen Maturanten, Akademiker, Wiener, Niederösterreicher und Burgenländer, darunter Pflichtschulabsolventen sowie die Einwohner aller anderen sechs Bundesländer).[9]

Mögliche Erklärungen für diese Identitätsprobleme

Eine ausführliche Erklärung für diverse Brüche und Probleme im österreichischen Selbstbewußtsein steht hier nicht zur Debatte. Was ich hier anbiete, ist der begrenzte Versuch, einen bestimmten Erklärungsweg zu beschreiten, jenen über die Frage nach einer *verbindenden nationalen Mythologie.* Mythenbegründend können zahlreiche einzelne Ereignisse, Revolutionen, Siege, Persönlichkeiten, aber auch bestimmte kollektive Vorstellungen sein.

Im folgenden gehe ich auf folgende ein:

a) Der Abstammungsmythos

Ein Klagenfurter Sprachwissenschaftler hat in einer vielfach sehr interessanten kritischen Äußerung zum Sprachgruppenbericht der österreichischen Rektorenkonferenz[10] u. a. folgendes festgehalten:

„Die Frage, wie österreichische Identität und Bekenntnis zum Deutschtum vereinbar sind, wird nicht gestellt, vielmehr sind die Verfasser bemüht, die deutsche Abstammung der Österreicher tunlichst auszublenden . . . *Abstammungsmäßig sind die deutschsprachigen Österreicher zum größten Teil Baiern, zu einem kleinen Teil Alemannen, und niemand wird daran zweifeln, daß Baiern und Alemannen Deutsche sind.* Daher kann man jedem Österreicher die Entscheidung selbst überlassen, was er ist, inklusive der Minderheiten, und man hat *jedes* Bekenntnis zu achten und auch zu akzeptieren . . ."

Dieser Mythos der deutschen Abstammung der Österreicher ist weit verbreitet. Es existiert aber auch ein Konkurrenzmythos, der an die Stelle des Glaubens an die deutsche Abstammung den Glauben an die vielfältige Abstammung als Folge der intensiven mitteleuropäischen, ja europäischen Vernetzung Österreichs in seiner Geschichte setzt.[11]

Damit ergibt sich eine recht deutliche Gegensätzlichkeit.

Auf der einen Seite wird „Österreich" mit ethnischem Pluralismus umschrieben, auf der anderen die „deutsche Abstammung" beschworen. Wie sind nun diese verschiedenen Ansichten zu bewerten?

1. Wir sollten uns darüber klar werden, daß für gegenwärtiges Nationalbewußtsein weniger die *tatsächliche Abstammung wichtig ist, als vielmehr ein bestimmter Abstammungsglaube.* Diesen eigentümlichen Sachverhalt haben moderne ethnische Gruppen mit alten Ethnien durchaus gemeinsam. Immer hat man sich selbst über Abstammung von Göttern oder Heroen ein besonderes Bild von sich selbst bzw. von der eigenen ethnischen Gruppe gemacht. Mit der fortschreitenden Säkularisierung und damit der Entfernung von solchen Bildern durch die Christianisierung gewann die Abstammung von älteren und hoch bewerteten Völkerschaften an Bedeutung.

2. Diese *geglaubte* Abstammung hat mit den realen genealogischen Zusammenhängen unterschiedlich viel gemeinsam. Hieb- und stichfeste „Beweise" für Abstammungslinien ganzer Volks- oder Sprachgruppen sind für die Zeit vor der Anlegung der Matriken (17. Jahrhundert) wohl kaum zu führen.

3. Als faktische sozialhistorische Prozesse lassen sich für die Zeit, da uns einigermaßen verläßliche Unterlagen zur Verfügung stehen, für Stadt und Land unterschiedliche Entwicklungen nachweisen. Die Population von *Städten* ist eher überregional zusammengesetzt – wobei die Weite des Einzugsbereiches mit der Reichweite der zentralörtlichen Funktionen positiv korreliert: Wien hat daher wahrscheinlich einen weiteren Einzugsbereich als Klagenfurt. Die *ländliche Bevölkerung* weist hingegen eher beharrende Tendenzen auf. Wir wissen natürlich nicht, ob diese aus der frühen Neuzeit gewonnenen Aussagen auf das Mittelalter zurückprojiziert werden können. Immerhin gab es im Hochmittelalter beträchtliche Wanderungsbewegungen, die als „deutsche Ostkolonisation" – wahrscheinlich nicht ganz richtig, aber immerhin – bekannt sind.[12]

4. Damit läßt sich für das Wien des 18. bis frühen 20. Jahrhunderts ethnische Pluralität der Herkunft mit einiger Sicherheit begründen, obgleich es auch hier zahlreiche methodische Probleme gibt. Aber die ethnische Pluralität der Abstammung hat es in Wien sicher gegeben, ebenso wie in anderen Großstädten Mitteleuropas (Triest, Prag, Budapest).

5. Damit ist die Frage der „deutschen Abstammung der Österreicher" jedoch keineswegs erledigt, da es hier primär um die hochmittelalterliche Kolonisationsbewegung geht. Es ist nun die Frage, wie die Ausbreitung des Bairischen bzw. Alemannischen (in Vorarlberg) vor sich ging: Durch Besiedlung menschenleerer Räume bzw. Ausrottung der alpenromanischen, alpen- und alpenvorlandslawi-

schen bzw. norddanubischen slawischen Population und nachfolgende Ansiedlung von Baiern *oder* durch Machtübernahme seitens bairischer Bischöfe und Adelige, feudale Landausstattung bairischer Vasallen und Ministerialen, teilweise Neusiedlung und *sprachliche Assimilationsvorgänge* der einheimischen Bevölkerung? Für Kärnten sind uns relativ früh (im 9./10. Jahrhundert) Beispiele für solche Assimilationsvorgänge genauer bekannt, in deren Folge Mitglieder der karantanischen Oberschicht bairische Namen annahmen – wie auch Mitglieder des bairischen Adels karantanische (Zwentibold). Diese Ergebnisse mahnen uns zu noch größerer Vorsicht gegenüber jeder Vereinfachung: Nachdem das Namengut ein primäres Indiz der Siedlungsgeschichte ist, bedeutet nun offenkundig das Auftauchen bairischer Namen nicht unbedingt eine *neue* Oberschicht, genauso umgekehrt. Das heißt nicht, daß es nicht auch Eroberungs-, Ausrottungs- und Neubesiedlungsphasen gegeben haben kann. Die Eroberung von „Gars" (Holzwiese ob Thunau am Kamp), die Neuansiedlung der überlebenden Unterlegenen im Talboden und die Neuerrichtung der riesigen Burganlage Gars deutet schon in eine solche Richtung. Umgekehrt spricht die Übernahme zahlreicher Berg- und Flußnamen aus slawischen Sprachen ins Bairische gegen eine Tabula rasa – wer hätte denn die Namen noch mitteilen können, und warum hätte man dann im Bairischen etwa den hier ja völlig unverständlichen Namen „Ötscher" (oče) noch weiterführen sollen? Realistischer ist also die Annahme, es habe mehr oder minder gewaltsame Assimilationsvorgänge gegeben, und es habe sich die Sprache der Unterworfenen den neuen Gegebenheiten angepaßt. Dabei können auch Führungsgruppen der überwiegend slawischen Bevölkerung als Vasallen oder Ministerialen der neuen Herren aufgetreten sein (in Niederösterreich sprechen für diese Annahmen zahlreiche Ortsnamen, in denen der Gründername überliefert wird – hier sind neben bairischen durchaus auch slawische Namen enthalten: Aber zur Vorsicht sei auf das oben aus Kärnten Berichtete verwiesen!).[13]

6. Wir könnten dieses Spiel natürlich bis zu Urvater Adam zurückspielen: Auch die Slawen waren keine Urbevölkerung, auch sie haben zuvor eine ältere Population zur Assimilation bewogen. Immer sind es die politischen Verhältnisse, denen Sprache und ethnisches Bewußtsein folgten. Das heißt letztendlich: Eine klare und eindeutige Aussage, von wem denn die deutschsprachige Mehrheitsbevölkerung Österreichs „abstamme", gibt es nicht und kann es nicht geben. Das ändert freilich nichts an der Tatsache, daß mit Ausnahme von Kärnten die im Mittelalter neu entstehenden „Länder", deren Bevölkerung man zumindest in den führenden Schichten als „Neustämme" ansprechen kann, ganz überwiegend deutschsprachig wurden, mit fortlaufender Zurückdrängung der alpenromanischen und slawischen Sprachen.

Soweit also der historische Befund, in aphoristischer Kürze. Das Überwiegen der deutschen Sprache im heutigen Österreich ist also nicht auf biologische Vorgänge zurückzuführen, sondern auf politische. Aber auch die ethnische Pluralität der späten Monarchie in ihren zentralen (und anderen Teilen) ist keine „naturwüchsige" Angelegenheit, sondern Folge der zentralen Funktionen Wiens, die eben Zuwanderer aus allen Überschußgebieten der Monarchie, vorwiegend aber aus den böhmischen Ländern, nach Wien gebracht haben. Die zentrale Frage ist aber gar nicht die, ob und in welcher Form der Raum des heutigen Österreich multiethnisch zusammengesetzt war oder ist. Die zentrale Frage ist viel eher, ob irgendein „Abstammungsglaube" für unsere gegenwärtige Identität eine Rolle spielt. Sind solche Annahmen (irgendwelcher Art) auch in großen Teilen der Bevölkerung wirksam?

Bedauerlicherweise lassen uns diesbezüglich die Gurus der Sozialforschung im Stich. Genaue Antworten auf unsere hier gestellten Fragen erhalten wir nicht. Immerhin können wir uns mit dem vorhandenen Material einigermaßen indirekt an unser Problem annähern. So stellt uns die Österreich-Umfrage von 1987 einigermaßen zuverlässige Antworten auf die Frage zur Verfügung, wie sich Österreicher selbst in „nationaler" Hinsicht sehen. Natürlich können wir nicht unbedingt schließen, daß etwa „deutsches" Nationalbewußtsein „deutschen" Abstammungsglauben automatisch einschließt oder daß „österreichisches" Nationalbewußtsein ein unbedingt multiethnisches sein müsse. Erste Anhaltspunkte gibt es immerhin. So wurde etwa nach der „größten inneren Verwandtschaft" mit Nachbarländern gefragt. In den Antworten könnte nun so etwas wie ein unterbewußtes Abstammungsbewußtsein mitschwingen. Das sieht dann so aus:[14]

Tabelle 2
Innere Verwandtschaft der Österreicher

Es sind der Meinung, daß Österreich die größte innere Verwandtschaft hat mit	Rangzahl		Prozent		Veränderung 1980–87
	1980	1987	1980	1987	
BRD	1	1	70	64	–6
Ungarn	2	2	10	16	+6
Schweiz	2	3	10	10	0
Italien	6	4	0	3	+3
Liechtenstein	5	5	1	2	+1
ČSSR	4	5	5	2	–3
Jugoslawien	5	7	1	1	0
keine Angabe	–	–	3	4	+1

Nach Bundesländern aufgeschlüsselt (in %)

	Wien	NÖ	Bgld	Stmk	OÖ	Sbg	Ktn	Tirol	Vlbg
BRD	52	64	60	66	71	71	69	65	59
andere Länder	42	32	35	33	31	25	31	34	39
darunter:									
Ungarn, ČSSR, Jugoslawien	34	20	21	16	14	11	11	8	7
Schweiz	6	11	14	15	15	12	11	16	31
Italien	2	1	–	2	2	2	9	10	1

Fragt man nach der Sympathie für Nationen (1980 und 1987), also nicht nur für

Nachbarn, so erhält man folgende Rangreihenfolge:

Tabelle 3
Sympathie für Nationen[15]

	Rangzahl 1980	Rangzahl 1987	Prozent 1987
Deutschland	1	1	29
Schweiz	2	2	22
Italien/Südtirol	7	3	11
Griechenland	10	4	4
Amerika, USA	3	5	3
Frankreich	4	5	3
Jugoslawien/Türkei	–	5	3
Ungarn/ČSSR	7	5	3
Großbritannien	7	9	2
Kanada/Australien	11	9	2
skandinavische Länder	4	9	2
andere westeuropäische Länder	4	12	3

Nun, wie auch immer diese Zahlen zu interpretieren sind – sie signalisieren jedenfalls, daß 1. die Verwandtschaftsannahmen durchaus Veränderungen unterliegen, daß aber 2. jene Länder, deren Populationen historisch zur beschworenen kulturellen und sonstigen österreichischen Vielfalt ja in der Tat beigetragen haben, keineswegs sehr hoch in der Sympathie der Österreicher rangieren.

Nicht einmal in Ostösterreich ist die Sympathie für jene Nationen, denen nicht wenige Vorfahren heutiger Wiener entstammen, besonders ausgeprägt („Presse" vom 16./17. 12. 1989 und vom 19. 12. 1989). Bei der Ermittlung von „Sympathie" kamen die Ungarn am Besten davon: Nur 6% erklärten sie für unsympathisch oder eher unsympathisch. Gefolgt wurden sie von der DDR: Deren Bewohner erhielten 87% Sympathie-Stimmen, die Russen 76, die Tschechen nur 73, Slowenen 58 und Polen 62% Zustimmung. Bei den Polen war auch die Ablehnung am ausgeprägtesten: 32% Negativstimmen. Die zweitmeisten Negativstimmen erhielten die Slowenen (27%), aber auch die Tschechen, die sich gerade erst aus jahrzehntelanger Unterdrückung bravourös befreit hatten, erhielten 24% Antipathiestimmen. Die Antipathie gegen die Tschechen resultiert aus der Vertreibung der Sudetendeutschen, negativer Kriegserfahrung, Ärgernis wegen der vielen Besucher, persönlich negativer Erfahrung, negativ eingestelltem Elternhaus, aus der angeblichen Unehrlichkeit der Tschechen. Natürlich traten alle diese Motive bei jungen Leuten stärker in den Hintergrund. Die Jungen traten auch am stärksten dafür ein, eine slawische Sprache unterrichten zu lassen. Höhere Schulbildung und selbständige Tätigkeit korrespondieren ebenfalls positiv mit der Höherbewertung der Sprachen der Nachbarn.

Für den Abstammungsglauben spielt also, soweit sich diese Daten in aller Vorsicht interpretieren lassen, die tatsächliche Vielschichtigkeit der Herkunft wenig Rolle. Unsere Vorfahren, soweit sie Deutsch sprachen, verstanden sich als „Deutsche", und sie taten dies während des 19. Jahrhunderts in einem Sinne, der schon mehrfältig, mindestens doppelsinnig war, nämlich „deutsch" *und* „österreichisch". Es entstand im Zuge der Ausbildung der Sprachnationen, wie ich glaube, eine deutsche Nation in Österreich, mit deutlicher Abgrenzung zu den nichtdeutschen Nationen (aber auch mit einer gewissen Abgrenzung zu den Deutschen in Deutschland, den „Reichsdeutschen"). Diese Selbstdefinition unserer Vorfahren lag auch der Staatsgründung von 1918 zugrunde, die keinen multiethnischen Staat, sondern einen deutschen Nationalstaat wollte – jeder Beamte, den dieser neue Staat anstellte, mußte seine deutsche Nationszugehörigkeit nachweisen![16] Im rezenten Bewußtsein wirken solche Befindlichkeiten nach, auch wenn die historischen Ursachen für den Glauben unserer Großväter (nämlich die Nationsbildungsprozesse und Nationalitätenkämpfe im alten Österreich) heute für uns nicht mehr relevant sind.

b) Nationale Symbole

Brüche im österreichischen Selbstbewußtsein zeigen sich auch in den nationalen Mythen und Symbolen. Nationale Feiertage sind häufig dem Mythos revolutionärer und militärischer Erfolge verpflichtet. Fahnen und Hymnen verherrlichen die Siege der Vorväter mit dem Zweck, in der Gegenwart Gemeinschaft herzustellen und zu sichern. Wie sieht es mit solchen kollektiven Identifikationszeichen in Österreich aus?

Wenig Kontinuität zeigt der Nationalfeiertag. In der ersten Republik galt der 12. November, der Tag, an dem 1918 offiziell die Republik ausgerufen worden war, als Staatsfeiertag. Die politische Rechte, die sich dadurch Jahr für Jahr neuerlich an ihre damals recht bescheidene Rolle und an die (wenn auch nicht langlebige) Macht der Sozialdemokratie erinnert sah, liebte diesen Feiertag nicht. 1934 wurde er abgeschafft. – Nach 1945 knüpfte man an die Tradition von 1918 nicht an. Erst 1965 wurde der seit 1957 gefeierte „Tag der Fahne" als Nationalfeiertag deklariert. Es ist der 26. Oktober. Das war jener Tag im Jahre 1955, an dem der österreichische Nationalrat den Beschluß über die immerwährende Neutralität Österreichs gefaßt hat. Damit war die in Moskau eingegangene Verpflichtung der Österreicher, nach Abschluß und Inkrafttreten des Vertrages von sich aus die immerwährende Neutralität nach Schweizer Muster anzunehmen, erfüllt worden, und zwar genau am ersten Tag nach dem Ende jener 90-Tage-Frist, die vom Inkrafttreten des Staatsvertrages an (27. Juli 1955) den Alliierten ihrerseits für den Abzug ihrer Truppen zur Verfügung stand.[17]

Im Unterschied zu anderen Feiertagen dieser Art wird an diesem Tag weder eines besonderen militärischen Sieges noch einer erfolgreichen Revolution oder der Erringung bzw. Behauptung der Unabhängigkeit gedacht. Sicher steht der Tag in einer engen Beziehung zur Erlangung der vollen staatlichen Selbständigkeit und Souveränität, gewissermaßen als Abschluß jenes langen Prozesses, der im April 1945 begonnen und am 15. Mai 1955 mit der Unterzeichnung des Staatsvertrages seinen vielumjubelten Höhepunkt erreicht hatte. Aber stark emotional besetzt ist der Tag nicht (und es ist auch bezeichnend, daß für ihn regierungsamtlich eher triviale Aktivitäten, wie Wanderungen, propagiert werden). Ins Positive gewendet könnte man auch sagen: Der österreichische Nationalfeiertag bietet ganz sicher keinerlei Anlaß für nationalistischen oder chauvinistischen Überschwang.

Auch die Geschichte der österreichischen Hymnen ist ein Beispiel für gespaltene bzw. mehrdeutige Identität. Die von Haydn 1797 vertonte Kaiserhymne wurde bis 1918 als das bekannte „Gott erhalte . . ." gesungen, danach mit dem Kernstock -Text („Sei gesegnet . . ."), der seit 1929 als offizielle Hymne galt, wodurch die Renner-Kienzl-Hymne von 1920 („Deutschösterreich, du herrliches Land . . .") abgelöst wurde. Bei offiziellen Anlässen der 1930er Jahre konnte es daher passieren, daß zu ein und derselben Haydn-Melodie drei verschiedene Texte gesungen wurden: Von Legitimisten das „Gott erhalte . . .", von braven Christlichsozialen das „Sei gesegnet . . ." und von Nationalsozialisten (aber auch Sozialdemokraten) das ebenfalls auf diese Melodie passende Deutschland-Lied („Deutschland, Deutschland über alles . . ."). Die Verwirrung war perfekt, die schöne Melodie Haydns daher 1945 rettungslos diskreditiert. Seit 1946 ist Paula von Preradovic' „Land der Berge" unsere Bundeshymne, zu einer Melodie, die leider nicht ganz von Mozart stammt.[18]

Etwas einfacher ist es schon mit der Fahne – das Rot-weiß-rot steht immerhin schon mit einem legendenhaften Vorfall des späten 12. Jahrhunderts in Zusammenhang und taucht als Bindenschild-Wappen seit dem 13. Jahrhundert auf. Als Flagge wurde das Rot-weiß-rot (mit einer heraldischen Krone) erst unter Joseph II. für die österreichische Marine verwendet. Als Flagge der Kriegsmarine blieb sie bis 1918 in Gebrauch. Der neue Staat von 1918 griff hier also durchaus auf ein älteres Symbol zurück – genau genommen auf das Wappen von „Neu-Österreich" (das heute niederösterreichische Fünf-Adler-Wappen wurde unter Rudolf IV. als „Alt-Österreich" als Beweis älterer, höherer Würde forciert), das als Hauswappen des Hauses Österreich weitum im ehemaligen Habsburgerreich aufzufinden ist.[19]

Anders der Adler: Der kaiserliche, letztlich auf Byzanz zurückgehende Doppeladler war 1918 obsolet geworden. Dennoch glaubte man ohne ein entsprechendes Tier nicht auskommen zu können. Gefunden wurde ein Adler, dessen Symbole (Hammer, Sichel, Bürgerkrone) die drei hauptsächlichen Klassen (oder Stände) der Bevölkerung symbolisieren sollen: Bauern, Arbeiter und Bürger. Es handelt sich also keineswegs um eine „kommunistische" Symbolik, wie heute immer wieder zu hören ist. 1934 kam eine neue Version des Doppeladlers, 1938 der deutsche Reichsadler mit Hakenkreuz und 1945 wieder der Adler der ersten Republik, freilich ergänzt mit den gesprengten Ketten als Symbol der wiedergewonnen Unabhängigkeit von Deutschland.[20] – Es ist aber interessant, daß bei Umfragen immer wieder auch der Doppeladler als österreichisches Symbol (*auch* als „richtiges" Staatswappen!) genannt wird.[21]

Auch einzelne Personen können als nationale Identifikationsfiguren dienen.

Die Umfrage von 1980 ergab im Hinblick auf verstorbene politische Führungspersönlichkeiten einen deutlichen Vorsprung von Maria Theresia vor Karl Renner, dem Kaiser Franz Joseph und Julius Raab. Aber dieses Quartett wurde nach Bekanntheit und Einschätzung der Bedeutung (bzw. Charakteristik für Österreich) klar von zwei Musikern geschlagen: Johann Strauß und Wolfgang Amadeus Mozart. Unter den lebenden Österreichern wurde Bruno Kreisky mit noch größerer Eindeutigkeit Bekanntheit, Bedeutung und Charakteristik für Österreich zugeschrieben – noch vor zwei so wichtigen Persönlichkeiten aus der Unterhaltungsbranche wie der Skiläuferin Annemarie Moser-Pröll und dem (inzwischen verstorbenen) Schauspieler Heinz Conrads.[22] Interessanter (und überraschender) ist die überragende Rolle Bruno Kreiskys für die österreichische Identität der jüngsten Vergangenheit. Albert F. Reiterer hat in seinem Buch „Die unvermeidbare Nation" die zeitliche Koinzidenz der Befestigung des österreichischen Nationalbewußtseins mit der Regierungsperiode Kreiskys dargestellt. Kreisky sei, als Symbol der von der SPÖ 1970 angekündigten „Modernisierung" Österreichs und ebenso auf Grund seiner starken internationalen Präsenz für die Österreicher (weit über die SPÖ hinaus) zur nationalen Identifikations- und Integrationsfigur geworden. In gewisser Weise könne er daher als „charismatischer Führer" interpretiert werden.[23] Im übrigen war Kreisky wohl auch das Symbol für ein neues, säkularisiertes, republikanisches, für Sozialisten und andere Linke und Liberale stärker akzeptables und nicht mehr mit den alten Assoziationen, wie „katholisch", habsburgisch usw., verbundenes Österreichbewußtsein. – 1987 aber sucht das österreichische Selbstbewußtsein Identifikation kaum mehr bei Politikern, eher bei Künstlern und Musikern. Die gerade von Kreisky so forcierte „Rolle Österreichs in der Welt" verlor ihren Glanz, Stolz auf die österreichische Staatspolitik waren 1980 72%, 1987 nur mehr 27% – die Politik scheidet als nationaler Identifikationsfaktor aus.[24]

c) Anknüpfungspunkte für identitäre Erinnerung

Hält man sich die bedeutende Rolle vor Augen, die in vielen Fällen eine gemeinsame Krone, ein heiliger König, aber auch das Erinnern an erfolgreiche Schlachten und Kriege, an erfolgreiche Unabhängigkeitsbewegungen und Revolutionen für die nationale Identität spielten (also altertümliche und moderne Versatzstücke einer „origo gentis", eines nationalen Entstehungsmythos), dann läßt sich für Österreich ein gewisser Mangel feststellen:

- In der Schatzkammer zu Wien werden zwar bis heute zwei hochbedeutsame Kronen ausgestellt, keine aber ist eigentlich ein Symbol für ein Gebiet, das irgendwie mit dem heutigen Österreich identisch ist: Die Krone des heiligen Römischen Reiches, aus dem 11. Jahrhundert, war die Kaiserkrone und damit eigentlich ein europäisches Symbol, das zuletzt ein römisch-deutsches Reich repräsentierte. Die herrliche Krone Rudolfs II., die Krone des Hauses Österreich, war zwar in der offiziellen Staatssymbolik des Kaisertums Österreich als offizielle Krone präsent, verwendet wurde sie bei Krönungen aber nicht. Und natürlich war sie niemals das gemeinsame Symbol für die althabsburgischen „deutschen" (oder „österreichischen") Erbländer – jener Mythos, der heute noch (etwa) die Stephanskrone umgibt, verband sich niemals mit ihr. – Konkurrenz zu diesen überregionalen Kronen ist noch in diverse Herzogshüten zu sehen, von denen jener des Erzherzogtums Österreich zu Klosterneuburg der bekannteste ist: Ausdruck nicht so sehr eines gesamtstaatlichen, sondern des niederösterreichischen Landesbewußtseins.[25]

■ Als „heiliger Spitzenahn" (wenigstens) Ober- und Niederösterreichs löste im 17. Jahrhundert der heilige Leopold, Mitglied eines ehrwürdigen Herrschergeschlechts, den vorher amtierenden heiligen Koloman ab – ein interessanter Versuch, eine gemeinsame Verehrungsfigur aus der frühen Geschichte zu popularisieren, was ganz gut gelang. Freilich konnte er schon die Landesheiligen der anderen Länder nicht verdrängen, geschweige denn den heiligen Wenzel oder Stephan.[26]

■ Die Revolutionen in den österreichischen Ländern sind immer gescheitert. Sowohl die ständische Revolte von 1519 wie die soziale, bürgerliche, bäuerliche und nationale Revolution von 1848. Infolge des Scheiterns der ständischen Bewegung des 16. und frühen 17. Jahrhunderts fehlt auch die Tradition eines Generallandtages als Anknüpfungspunkt für eine genuine parlamentarische Tradition.[27]

■ Gerade das 20. Jahrhunderts, als jener Zeitraum, der (gerade noch) auch von realen Erinnerungsresten überblickt wird, ist außerordentlich arm an kollektiven gemeinsamen Erfolgserlebnissen. Ganz im Gegenteil: Das Erinnern und Ge- bzw. Bedenken rekonstruiert immer wieder ganz widersprüchliche und feindselige Erinnerungen: 1918 war für die Linken „Revolution", für die Rechten Zerfall und Niederlage. 1938 bedeutete für alle Nationalsozialisten, Deutschnationalen und Deutschbewußten Erfolg und Triumph, für alle Österreichbewußten, Juden und politischen (rechten und linken) Gegner des Nationalsozialismus Katastrophe. 1945 brachte ebendiese Katastrophe für die großen Scharen der deutschbewußten und nationalsozialistischen Österreicher, Freude über das Wiedererstehen Österreichs bei den Unterlegenen von 1938 (freilich konnte auch bei vielen „Ehemaligen" sukzessive ein positives Bewußtsein gegenüber dem neuen Österreich wachsen). Erst 1955 konnte sich tatsächlich ganz Österreich gemeinsam über den Abzug der vier Besatzungsmächte freuen. Hierin liegt der „kollektive Erfolg", den ein gemeinsames kollektives Bewußtsein wohl ebenso braucht wie die kollektive Erfahrung gemeinsamer gesicherter Existenz innerhalb gewisser Grenzen. In der Tat ist es dieses Jahr, das jenes kollektive Erfolgserlebnis enthält, das zur Basis eines Konsenses der österreichischen „Konsensualnation"[28] wurde – interessanterweise inzwischen zur Mythisierung nur eines Bestandteiles jenes „annus mirabilis" verschoben, der Neutralitätserklärung. Gerade am 8. 11. 1991 wurden Umfragedaten veröffentlicht, die sehr deutlich den hohen Wert der Neutralität im Bewußtsein der Österreicher signalisieren – eine Mehrheit würde lieber diese Neutralität beibehalten, als um den Preis ihrer Aufgabe (oder Veränderung) der EG beitreten.[29]

Es existiert also ein „verbindlicher" nationaler Mythos Österreichs heute nicht, abgesehen vom Staatsvertrags- und Neutralitäts-Mythos. Es ist dieses Manko auf die Geschichte der letzten drei bis vier Generationen von Österreichern zurückzuführen, die eben, bis zum Staatsvertrag von 1955, kein historisches Ereignis als integrativ und identitätsstiftend erfahren konnten. Erst mit 1955 wird eine Basis erreicht, die relativ wenig bezweifelt wird. Aber wird diese Basis ausreichen, um die älteren Schichten einer gespaltenen kollektiven Mythologie zu überlagern? Stellen wir abschließend die Frage, ob diese gespaltene Mythologie für ein (mittel-)europäisch offenes Verhalten, ohne Minderwertigkeitsgefühle und ohne Überheblichkeiten, eine günstige Voraussetzung bietet. Die jüngsten Umfragen scheinen eher Angst vor Europa (genauso wie Angst vor Fremden, Nachbarn usw.) zu signalisieren. Es könnte dies mit der gespaltenen Mythologie zusammenhängen: Nationaler Mythos vermittelt ja nicht nur grausliche nationale Überheblichkeiten, sondern auch Identität, Geborgenheit. Ob aus dem Fehlen der letzteren automatisch Weltbürgerlichkeit entsteht, darf bezweifelt werden.

Weltbürgerlichkeit ist daher nicht erreichbar als Flucht vor eigenen Identitätsproblemen – nur wer sich seiner selbst sicher ist (also, um es klar zu sagen, wer die Frage „österreichisch" oder „deutsch" ein für allemal geklärt hat), gibt einen unverkrampften Weltbürger ab. Nur wer seine lokalen, regionalen und überregionalen Identitäten in sich verarbeitet und gesichert hat, kann daher sinnvoll den Anspruch auf eine Identität erheben, die sich an der gesamten Menschheit orientiert.

Anmerkungen

1 Gerald Stourzh, Vom Reich zur Republik. Studien zum Österreichbewußtsein im 20. Jahrhundert, Wien 1990, S. 102. Ferner vgl. Felix Kreissler, Der Österreicher und seine Nation. Ein Lernprozeß mit Hindernissen. Wien 1984; Georg Wagner, Von der Staatsidee zum Nationalbewußtsein (I) – Die Meinungsumfragen über die österreichische Nation 1956–1980 (II), in idem (Hg.), Österreich. Von der Staatsidee zum Nationalbewußtsein, Wien 1982, S. 109 ff; Peter A. Ulram, Österreichbewußtsein 1987, Wien 1988 (Datenband eines von Gerald Stourzh und Peter A. Ulram durchgeführten Projektes des Jubiläumsfonds der österreichischen Nationalbank). Zur Problematik vgl. ferner Peter Gerlich, Nationalbewußtsein und nationale Identität in Österreich. Ein Beitrag zur politischen Kultur des Parteiensystems, in: Anton Pelinka, Fritz Plasser, Hg., Das österreichische Parteiensystem (Studien zu Politik und Verwaltung 22), Wien – Köln – Graz 1988, S. 235–270; Anton Pelinka, Zur österreichischen Identität. Zwischen deutscher Vereinigung udn Mitteleuropa, Wien 1990, und Oliver Rathkolb, Georg Schmid, Gernot Heiß, Hg., Österreich und Deutschlands Größe. Ein schlampiges Verhältnis, Salzburg 1990.

2 William T. Bluhm, Building An Austrian Nation. New Haven – London, 1973, S. 224 ff.

3 Das österreichische Nationalbewußtsein in der öffentlichen Meinung und im Urteil der Experten, Wien 1980, S. 26.

4 Für die Überlassung der Daten habe ich Herrn Dr. Peter Diem vom ORF herzlichst zu danken.

5 Ulram, Österreichbewußtsein, passim.

6 Zu dieser Kulturpolitik nur ein paar Hinweise: Die von der SPÖ installierte Vorherrschaft des bundesdeutschen Elements im Burgtheater, stete Berieselung auch noch durch den ärgsten bundesdeutschen Schwachsinn im „nationalen" ORF, prinzipielle Heranziehung (meist) bundesdeutscher Fachleute (Wissenschaftler) auch bei den trivialsten Dingen usw. Ich führe dies letztlich auf den ungebrochenen Glauben der österreichischen Linken zurück, daß sich der

„Fortschritt" eben nur westlich des Inn bzw. nördlich des Main abspiele – eine (unbewußte?) Fortsetzung Bauerscher Vorstellungen?

7 Die Presse, 16./17. Dezember 1989, S. 4.

8 Ulram, Österreichbewußtsein, S. 53.

9 Gerlich, Nationalbewußtsein, S. 256 f.

10 Heinz Dieter Pohl, Die Diskussion läuft so in falschen Bahnen, in: Carinthia I, 179, 1989, S. 389–402, hier insbes. 393.

11 Der multiethnische Abstammungsmythos etwa bei Oskar A. H. Schmitz, Der österreichische Mensch, Wien 1924.

12 Zuwanderung nach Wien bei Gustav Otruba, Wiens Bevölkerung – nationale Herkunft und soziale Entwicklung, in: Donauraum 13. 1968, S. 12–42; ein Fallbeispiel für die kleinräumige Ergänzung der ländlichen Bevölkerung: Hermine Loderer, Bockfließ – Heimatkundliche Beiträge, Bockfließ 1978; zur Ostkolonisation vgl. Richard Koebner, The Settlement and Colonization auf Europe (The Cambridge Economic History of Europe, vol. 1, 1966), S. 1–91; Walter Schlesinger, Hg., Die deutsche Ostsiedlung als Problem der europäischen Geschichte (Vorträge und Forschungen XVIII), Sigmaringen 1974.

13 Zu diesem Problemkreis vgl. Michael Mitterauer, Karolingische Markgrafen im Südosten (Archiv für österreichische Geschichte 123), Wien 1963; zu Gars: ders., Zur räumlichen Ordnung Österreichs in der frühen Babenbergerzeit, in: Mitteilungen des Instituts für österreichische Geschichtsforschung LXXVIII, 1970, insbes. S. 115.

14 Ulram, Österreichbewußtsein, S. 32.

15 Ebd., S. 33.

16 Herta Hafner, Die öffentlich Bediensteten 1918–1920, Geisteswiss. Diss. (Ms.) Wien 1989.

17 Zum Nationalfeiertag vgl. Wagner, Staatsidee, S. 265.

18 Zu den Hymnen vgl. Eckart Früh, Gott erhalte? Gott bewahre! Zur Geschichte der österreichischen Hymnen und des Nationalbewußtseins zwischen 1918 und 1938, in: Österreich in Geschichte und Literatur 32, 1988, Heft 5, S. 280–315.

19 Zur Staatsflagge vgl. Wagner, Staatsidee, S. 257 ff.; zu Alt- und Neu-Österreich vgl. Erich Zöllner, Der Österreichbegriff. Formen und Wandlungen in der Geschichte, Wien 1988, S. 45 ff.

20 Zum Wappen vgl. Wagner, ebd., S. 260–264.

21 Das österreichische Nationalbewußtsein in der öffentlichen Meinung und im Urteil der Experten. Eine Studie der Paul-Lazarsfeld-Gesellschaft für Sozialforschung, Wien 1980, S. 7.

22 Ebd., S. 39 f.

23 Albert F. Reiterer, Die unvermeidbare Nation. Ethnizität, Nation und nachnationale Gesellschaft, Frankfurt – New York 1988, S. 262.

24 Ulram, Österreichbewußtsein, S. 26–29.

25 Ob der Klosterneuburger Erzherzogshut tatsächlich ein Symbol für die österreichischen Länder des Generallandtages von 1518 war, wie Georg Wagner (Staatsidee, S. 113) meint, bedürfte wohl noch gründlicher Forschung – hier läge, gemeinsam mit dem Generallandtag, ein ebenso interessanter Ansatz für eine besondere *österreichische*, auf einen dem heutigen Österreich wenigstens vergleichbaren (wenn auch nicht deckungsgleichen) Raum bezogene Staatsbildung der Frühneuzeit vor wie in den diversen Königreichsplänen für ebendiese Erblande (vgl. Wagner, in diesem Band, S. 394 bis 432); freilich wurden sie nicht weiterverfolgt! Über die beiden Kaiserkronen vgl. Hermann Fillitz, Die Insignien und Kleinodien des Heiligen Römischen Reiches, Wien – München 1954; ders., Die österreichische Kaiserkrone, Wien – München 1959.

26 Über den heiligen Leopold als „Spitzenahn" und zentralen österreichischen Heiligen vgl. Floridus Röhrig, Leopold III. der Heilige, Markgraf von Österreich, Wien – München 1985; Elisabeth Kovács, Der heilige Leopold – Rex perpetuus Austria? in: Jahrbuch des Stiftes Klosterneuburg NF 13, 1985, S. 159–211.

27 Zu diesem Themenkomplex zusammenfassend Ernst Bruckmüller, Nation Österreich. Sozialhistorische Aspekte ihrer Entwicklung (Studien zu Politik und Verwaltung 4), Wien – Köln – Graz 1984, S. 164–199.

28 Dieser Begriff bei Stourzh, Reich, S. 105 (nach Anton Burghardt).

29 Die Presse vom 9./10. 1991, S. 5: Laut einer Umfrage der Sozialwissenschaftlichen Studiengesellschaft (SWS) mit einem Sample von mehr als 1700 Österreicherinnen und Österreichern lehnten es 57% ab, die Neutralität abzuändern, um zur EG zu gelangen. Bei der Präsentation verbalisierte der SWS-Vizepräsident Heinz Kienzl ganz klar den „mythologisierten" Charakter der Neutralität (ebd.) – sie wird als möglicher Schutzschild vor Angriffen verstanden (von 39%!), also als Sicherheits- und damit Identitätsspender.

Karl Stuhlpfarrer

Der alpenländische Mensch. Oder: Deutsch sein. Die Geschichte einer Verführung

Als schon vor vielen Wochen das Thema zu formulieren war, da konnte noch niemand ahnen, daß wir gerade heute durch eine Zeit gehen, die uns so plastisch vor Augen führt, wie der alpenländische Mensch die Weite des Raumes und die Ferne der Zeiten durchmißt. Und dieses Gefühl der Erhabenheit hätte mich fast übermannt, mich bewogen, mein Thema zu fliehen, mich weniger bedrängenden Fragen zuzuwenden. Aber wie Peter Rosegger in einem Billet vom 1. Juli 1899 so treffend sagte: „Im Selbsterhaltungskampf gibt es nur eine Tugend, die der unbegrenzten Treue zum eigenen Volke."[1]

So steht der alpenländische Mensch auch 1930 im Joppe und Krachlederner, mit Spielhahnfeder auf dem Hut und Bergstock in der Linken aufrecht vor der ihn überragenden, burgengekrönten Germania und hält ihre Rechte in festem Griff. Die Grenzbalken zwischen Deutschland, Deutschösterreich und den Abgetrennten Deutschen ist niedergeworfen, den schwarzen einköpfigen Adler schützt die mächtige Krone der Eiche.

Unter dieses Gemälde von Prof. H. Bergmeister, da passen so recht die Verse:

„Gib uns deine Mutterhände
Königin Germania!
Doch um keine Gnadenspende
Bettelnd steht Deutschöstreich da.

Reich an Erbgut wackrer Väter
Kommen wir, und wären eins,
Deiner Kinder, auch beredter,
Tatbereiter, Frau, ist keins." (Ottokar Kernstock)[2]

Was Ottokar Kernstock treuen Muts hier antönt, ist keineswegs dem ganzen Alpenland gemein gewesen. Nicht einmal ganz Österreich konnte er meinen, wie uns das Reisebuch aus den österreichischen Alpen von Ernst Krenek überzeugt, das 1929 in seinem elften Lied die Alpenbewohner charakterisiert:

> „Die Alpen werden von wilden Nomaden bewohnt. Mit ungeheurem Lärm kommen sie hergebraust, Sommer und Winter spei'n die geduldigen Züge ihre Scharen aus. Heuschrecken gleich bedecken sie das Land. Mit unsäglicher Banalität schreien sie laut und deutlich in die Landschaft, als wollten sie den Berggeist wecken. Selten sieht man Urbewohner stumpf und mürrisch den Greu'l betrachten und im Stillen den Gewinn berechnen, den sie den Fremden aus Norden, sie so seltsam sprechen, obgleich es deutsch sein soll, aus der Tasche ziehen werden. . . ."

„So muß Weltuntergang sein!" So schließt das Lied. Nun, wissen Sie, Krenek konnte nicht mehr lange in Österreich bleiben und setzte dann, als die schwere Zeit nach Österreich kam, seine Arbeit in den USA fort.

Aber wie schon der voralpenländische Mensch, der in der inneralpinen Beckenlandschaft seinen Aufstieg fortsetzte, sagte, es ginge „ja nicht darum, ob Österreich ein Teil des deutschen Volkes oder sonst was war, sondern welchen Beitrag Österreich im Rahmen der deutschen Geschichte geschrieben hat, getragen hat und zu dem man sich auch bekennen kann."[3]

Jörg Haider sagte einmal bei anderer passender Gelegenheit, es gebe keine deutsche oder slowenische Wahrheit. Wer wollte ihm widersprechen? Es gibt sie nicht, auch nicht einmal eine kärntnerische oder österreichische.[4] Wir müssen ihm recht geben. Aber wie soll der alpenländische Mensch damit fertigwerden? Das wollen wir in den folgenden Minuten ein wenig erproben.

Martin Wutte war der früheste Zeithistoriker Österreichs, das sagen die einen. Die anderen aber kennen ihn als den berüchtigten Erfinder der Windischen. Noch bevor er diesen windischen Bewohner des Alpenlandes ersann, wußte aber Wutte: „Die Deutschen sind ohne Zweifel die Schöpfer aller höheren Kultur . . ." Wutte scheint apodiktisch, aber es fehlt ihm jeder Größenwahn. Er beschränkte sich bescheiden auf Kärnten, fügte aber dann doch noch hinzu: Kein Wunder, daß viele Slowenen „ihre Sprache verlernten und mit der deutschen Kultur auch die deutsche Sprache annahmen".[5] Wutte schrieb das 1918, ein ereignisreiches Jahr für Kärnten, und hatte sicher wenig Zeit, zu lesen. Er hätte das schmale Heft studieren können, das im gleichen Jahr erschienen und mit der rot gedruckten Widmung „Dem Kärntner Heimatdienst" versehen war. Herausgegeben von der Österreichischen Waffenbrüderlichen Vereinigung, berichtete darin der Direktor des k. k. Kaiser-Karl-Museums für österreichische Volkskunde, M. Haberlandt, über die nationale Kultur der österreichischen Volksstämme. Und Haberlandt gibt uns weiteren Stoff zum Nachdenken über den Unterschied zwischen der Bevölkerung im Alpenlande – wir greifen jetzt schon ein wenig über Kärnten hinaus –, wenn er schrieb: „Von den benachbarten Deutschen in Steiermark und Kärnten unterscheiden sich die Slowenen durch dunklere und reine Typen. Ihre von Haus aus günstige Volkskonstitution wird durch starken Alkoholismus beeinträchtigt."[6]

Assimilatorische Kraft und geschwächter Widerstand. Aber die Bestimmungsfaktoren der beschleunigten Akkulturation der Slowenen nach Haberlandt/Wutte bleiben sonderbar ambivalent. Hätten die Slowenen nun abstinenter leben oder noch mehr trinken sollen? Ach wüßten wir doch, was Wutte dazu gesagt hätte. Wir werden es leider nie erfahren. Wir müssen schweigen und zugeben: Es bleibt dabei, der alpenländische Eindeutschungsvorgang – jener von oben her – bleibt unzweifelhaft bewiesen nur in romanisch-keltischen Tälern durch die Walser – ein Erfolg der Milch-, der Almwirtschaft.[7]

Aber haben wir deshalb das Recht, aufzugeben? Wir bleiben in den Ostalpen und seinem Deutschtum. Heinz Scheibenpflug: „Berge um uns. Ein Buch vom deutschen Alpenland." Erschienen zuerst in Berlin 1939, meine Ausgabe aus 1941 oder später. „Den Bergen, die im Süden des deutschen Siedlungsraumes aufragen, die unsre Heimat im Mittag begrenzen, gilt dieses Buch."[8] So heißt es im Vorwort. Dann folgt eine Photographie mit der markanten Silhouette der Drei Zinnen. Erstaunlich, wie mutig der Autor oder wie schlampig die deutsche Zensur damals gewesen ist. Südtirol und deutsch? Das zu behaupten, war damals schon verboten in Deutschland. Alloglotti oder Allogeni, d. h. Anderssprachige oder Andersstämmige lebten dort nach damaliger italienischer Diktion. Die deutsch-italienischen Umsiedlungsabkommen von 1939 hatten diese Allogeni in deutscher Version zu „Volksdeutschen" gemacht, zu Optionsberechtigten, zu Wählern für oder gegen deutsche Staatsangehörigkeit. Die meisten von ihnen waren fasziniert von den Erfolgen NS-Deutschlands im Kriege. Aber da gab es auch noch andere Volksdeutsche dem Buchstaben der Verträge nach. Sie sprachen ladinisch und slowenisch und wurden doch, zuerst gegen den Widerstand, dann mit italienischer Zustimmung zur Option zugelassen.[9]

Heftig entbrannte der Streit um die Kunst – und nicht allein aus immateriellen Gründen. Als deutsch markierte Kunst- und Kulturwerke konnten mitgenommen werden – andere nicht. Südtirol und Kultur oder Kunst, das war den einen mit deutsch identisch, den anderen italienisch oder gar auch Teil einer übergreifenden alpenländischen Kultur. Da ging es um Flügelaltäre und Kachelöfen, um wertvolle Handschriften und Hausrat. Wir wissen nicht, wie der Konflikt ausging. Das Ende des Krieges bewahrte die Südtiroler vor der Entscheidung der Wissenschaftler und politischen Experten.[10] Denn nicht überall war es scheinbar so einfach wie bei den zwei Denkmälern: Walther von der Vogelweide deutsch und deshalb als Denkmal in Bozen schon lange entfernt. Dante italienisch, deshalb in Trient unberührt seit den Tagen der Habsburgermonarchie.[11]

Heinz Scheibenpflugs Alpen reichen weit, bis zu seinem südlichsten Punkt des Großdeutschen Reiches, noch südlicher als Görz im „wieder zum Reich heimgekehrten Unterland", wo die alte deutsche „Markburg" liegt.[12] „Markburg", das ist Marburg.

Dort lag die Sache ganz anders als in Südtirol. Dort galt das in der Rede Hitlers vom 20. Februar 1938 formulierte völkerrechtliche Großraumprinzip. Es beanspruchte – es klingt noch heute wie eine Drohung – das „deutsche Schutzrecht für die deutschen Volksgruppen fremder Staatsangehörigkeit".[13] Und die slowenische Steiermark erhielt, wie Helmut Carstanjen schrieb, ihr „deutsches Gesicht" aufgeprägt. Die Argumente sind die tirolischen – aber mit ganz anderem Ergebnis: altes deutsches Land, Identität des Landes in Haus- und Siedlungsformen, Tracht und enger Verbundenheit mit dem Gesamtdeutschtum. Jetzt Wolfram statt Walther, dazu „deutscher Liederfürst Hugo Wolf" – aber hatte der nicht slowenische Großeltern? – und erster „Verfechter deutscher Seegeltung" Tegetthoff. Romako sah das noch anders.

„Jeder, der die Untersteiermark bereist", behauptete Helmut Carstanjen vom Südostdeutschen Institut in Graz, „empfindet die Landschaft unbedingt als zum deutschen Siedlungsbereich gehörig. Organisch ist sie den angrenzenden Alpenländern eingegliedert. Das Deutschtum hat sie geformt und ihr das Antlitz gegeben, das sie uns heute zeigt."[14]

Und die Sprache? Nicht einmal ein Prozent der Schulkinder sprach deutsch, gab selbst Carstanjen zu.[15] Kein Problem: Gemeinsames Blut schlägt verschiedene Sprache, galt da die Parole – nicht ohne sophistisches Auswahlprinzip.

Die Ausländer wurden erfaßt, besonders die Juden und die Emigranten. Da nützte das Blut dann nichts mehr. Den Zigeunern – für die Nazi-Rassisten voll ganz anderen Bluts – ging es, Sprache hin, Sprache her, nicht viel besser.[16]

Es war nicht wenig gleichgültig, wer von den Slowenen in welcher Kategorie gelandet war. Die römischen Rassenziffern und politischen Verhaltensbuchstaben verrieten, wer Intellektueller oder gar kein Steirer war, wer die richtige Frau, den richtigen Mann geheiratet oder wer gar in einem Gebiet, in einem Haus lebte, auf das schon andere, höherer rassistischer und politischer Kategorisierung Anspruch erhoben hatten. Römisch IVe – eine Lebenskatastrophe, römisch IIa – das zweifelhafte Eindeutschungsglück, römisch III mit wenig Chancen. Integration und Ausgrenzung machte – o verräterische Sprache – jene, die den Nazis der Eindeutschung wert schienen, zu Eindeutschungsfähigen im Steirischen Heimatbund und die von ihnen ausgegrenzten Verfolgten zu Schutzangehörigen, von deren Kennzeichnung S für Slowenen, wie J für Juden und P für Polen, gerade noch abgesehen wurde.[17] Ostarbeiterinnen durften deutsche Tracht nicht tragen. Denn auch solche Distinktionen entschieden über Lebens- oder Überlebenschancen.[18]

Deutsch sein bedeutete, sich an der Spitze der Hierarchie zu fühlen, an der Spitze der Hierarchie der Völkergemeinschaft, wenn man so sagen will, auch oder gerade wenn man innerhalb der deutschen Volksgemeinschaft nur wenig von der sozialen Spitze zu sehen bekam, im sozialen Raum – gemessen an den materiellen, ideellen und symbolischen Gütern, über die persönlich verfügt werden konnte – nur an sehr minderwertigen Positionen verortet war.

Deutsch sein bedeutete im Extremfall Leben, nicht deutsch sein konnte bedeuten Unterdrückung, Abschließung und Tod. Aber deutsch sein hieß nicht immer Überleben. Es starben auch die deutschen KZ-Häftlinge, Renitenten und die deutsche Zivilbevölkerung und deutsche Soldaten im Krieg oder im Kampf, und je nach sozialem oder militärischem Rang gelegentlich auch schneller als manche Nichtdeutsche.

Heute ist alles wieder ein wenig anders geworden und doch gleich geblieben. Auf der Reise von Maribor zurück nach Graz kann es 1990 schon passieren, von einem Grenzbeamten – Sie wissen, das sind diese Leute, die der Gruppe II/C des Innenministeriums unterstehen – gefragt zu werden, wie man zu einer Bestätigung komme, daß jemand Mitglied des Steirischen Heimatbundes gewesen wäre. Nun ja, mit solchen Vorfahren wird man auch heute schneller Deutscher.

Österreichs Geographen entwickelten seit den zwanziger Jahren das Konzept vom deutschen Volks- und Kulturboden, zuerst Penck, dann Hassinger. Auf diesem Boden siedelten „Tschechen, Slowenen, Wenden und ein Teil der Polen"[19], die Hassinger 1931 für Mitteleuropa noch nicht reif sein mochten. Dann sollte doch zumindest der Anschluß Österreichs an Deutschland die gewünschte mitteleuropäische Verständigung in einem ersten Schritt erreichen. Sechs Jahr später, im Jahr vor dem „Anschluß" Österreichs an Deutschland, faßte der Wiener Historiker Heinrich Srbik nur mehr lapidar zusammen: „Dieser mitteleuropäische Raum ist ganz überwiegend deutscher Volks- und Kulturboden."[20] Srbik versprach zwar noch ein Mitteleuropa, das kein Verlangen nach Entnationalisierung kenne, aber seiner Meinung nach sollte „sich an die deutsche Lebensgemeinschaft des Reichs und Österreichs eine lose politische Gemeinschaft ostmitteleuropäischer Staaten angliedern, deren Deutsche eine Bluts- und Herzensgemeinschaft mit dem staatlich getrennten Hauptkörper ihres Volkes bilden".[21]

Mitteleuropa wird in dieser Form nicht wiedererstehen können. Es fehlen ihm die Deutschen, die überall in seinen Ländern lebten, und die heute noch dort lebenden haben die Trennung der Österreicher weg vom Deutschtum verpaßt.

Mehr aber noch fehlen, wie Peter Hanák erinnerte, die Juden. Sie vor allem bestimmten und förderten - gewiß, auch die andern – den fruchtbaren Kulturaustausch von fünfzehn Nationen.[22]

Die Juden in Österreich, die zur Jahrhundertwende der Moderne den Weg bereiteten, hatten ihr Deutschsein bald zu verlernen. „Die Juden waren deutsch, weil ihnen das deutsche Volk in Österreich ein Symbol für Freiheit und Fortschritt war", erinnerte sich der Wiener Zionist Isidor Schalit in seinen Erinnerungen.[23] Aber „Die Wahrheit" hatte den Einstellungswandel der Wiener Juden schon früher kundgemacht: noch 1925 eindeutige Zuordnung zur deutschen Kulturgemeinschaft, elf Jahre später Distanzierung von der ausschließlichen Zurückführung des Begriffs der Nation auf die Sprache, zu einer Zeit also, als das austrofaschistische Regime seinen Weg an NS-Deutschland anzunähern begann.[24] Was deutsch war, wollte Schuschnigg damals nicht allein Hitlers Bestimmung überlassen, den indessen weniger Skrupel plagten, deutsches Blut zu vergießen.

Deutsch ist uralt, wenn es gilt, Ansprüche zu legitimieren. Immer schon saßen die Deutschen wo, bevor andere kamen.[25] Deutsch ist frei und herrisch – nicht den Awaren knechtisch, slawisch.[26]

Deutsch ist heilsam wie die Medizin, es heilt von der slawischen Krankheit: „Warum ist der Anschluß die einzige nationale Rettung für unser Volk?" fragten die Nationaldemokratischen Flugschriften 1919. Und antworteten selbst: „Weil wir sonst im Slawentum untergehen. Wir sind unserer ganzen Anlage nach der wenigst widerstandskräftige Teil des deutschen Volkes und haben stets eines Blutzuschusses aus dem Reiche bedurft, um den Kampf um unser Dasein bestehen zu können. Uns fehlt es nicht an Fähigkeiten, wohl aber an gesunder Ordnung und Zucht. . . . Nur der Anschluß kann unserem Gemeinwesen innere Gesundung, kann uns die Beseitigung der zum Teil durch slawische Einflüsse bedingten Schlamperei, Korruption und Disziplinlosigkeit bringen."[27] Verslawt und magyarisiert zu werden – ein Schrecken. „Jeder selbstbewußte Deutsche, der weiß, daß er dem größten, dem edelsten Volk Europas angehört, wird diese Zumutung stolz und entrüstet abweisen, er wird jetzt die im Blute liegende Treue zum deutschen Volke halten und sich diesem anschließen."[28] Das schrieb der alte General Krauß, um seine Offizierskameraden zu überzeugen, daß der Eid auf Kaiser Karl obsolet geworden sei.

Deutsch ist harmonisierend und integrativ. Es nützt konzeptionell die gleiche Strategie wie der Antisemitismus. „Der Jude ist an allem schuld", beteuern fortwährend die judenfeindlichen Agitatoren. Und die Leute blicken um sich –

und siehe da – es gibt wirklich Juden. Die Deutschen brachten die Kultur, beteuern fortwährend die Germanomanen. Und die Leute blickten um sich. Und siehe da – da wurden alle, die nicht als kulturlos gelten wollten – zu Deutschen.

Denn deutsch ist gefräßig, manchmal schier unersättlich – eine lange Periode der Magersucht ging eben gerade vorbei. Eben hat die deutsche Küche Österreich noch verschont und sich auf Brandenburg und Pommern, aber auch schon auf Schlesien und Ostpreußen geworfen.[29] Doch die Deutsche Seele von 1988 zieht Beethoven noch Mozart vor, „hat immer wieder auch mit Sigmund Freud zu tun"; und sie will neben Rembrandt und Dürer nicht auf Böcklin und Breughel und Hodler verzichten.[30]

Was „Die Deutsche Seele" satirisch vermeldet, will deutsche Kunstwissenschaft heute auch ernst noch nicht missen. Leichtfertig vermengt sie alte mit neuen, immer aber zu deutschen Räumen. „Der Begriff der deutschen Kunst", schreibt Werner Hager in seinem 1989 erschienenen Band über Historienmalerei im 19. Jahrhundert, „deckt sich damals noch mit dem Umfang des Alten Reiches, schließt also Österreich mit ein. Die Schweiz geht ihre eigenen Wege . . ."[31] So darf ich mich also identifizieren mit diesem kleinen tapferen Jungen an der Hand Thusneldens im Triumphzug des Germanicus? Oder sollte ich es besser tun mit seiner Darstellung durch Karl von Piloty. Am besten ist natürlich beides durcheinander. „Die nationale Traditionsstiftung", beobachtet Hanns Haas ganz richtig, „durchforstet also die tausendjährige Geschichte ziemlich willkürlich nach brauchbaren Elementen, um sich je nachdem in Großmachtallüren oder Opferphantasien zu gefallen."[32]

Wer wird sich aufregen, wenn in Deutschland über die deutschen Kaiser von Karl dem Großen bis Karl I. von – nota bene noch dazu – Österreich-Ungarn publiziert wird?[33] Die deutschen Professoren! Karl Dietrich Erdmann will die ununterbrochene Parallelität der deutschen und der österreichischen Geschichte, und er bekommt sie, auch wenn die Daten sich biegen. In arroganter Größe legt er den Siedlungsraum des deutschen Volkes auch nach Österreich, ohne die Eingeborenen zu fragen; im „Stil eines aufgeklärten, wohlmeinenden wilhelminischen Kolonialoffiziers in Deutsch-Südwest um 1910", wie Anton Pelinka pointiert feststellte.[34]

Wohlwollend auch Wolfgang Mommsen, der uns unlängst mahnte, doch von der künstlichen Schaffung einer österreichischen Nationsidee und künstlicher neuer nationaler Identitätsstiftung abzulassen, nicht anachronistisch und sachlich unangebracht einen spezifisch österreichischen Menschen oder eine österreichische Kultur zu beschwören, von intellektuellen Gedankenspielen und artifiziellen Identitätsstiftungen dieser Art abzustehen, vernünftig zu sein, denn Österreich gehört der deutschen Kulturnation. Da schlägt Natur und Zeitgeist zu. Auf der langen Suche nach ihrer Identität[35] haben aber viele andere Deutsche zum Leidwesen wieder mancher Österreicher, die „die Alpendeutschen" noch immer für den konstantesten und stabilsten Bevölkerungsanteil Österreichs halten, keine Phantasien über ein deutsches Österreich mehr.[36]

Auch die Österreicher haben, wenn die Angaben von 1985 sich nicht allzu sehr verändert haben, ganz andere Präferenzen als die deutschen Professoren und manche österreichische Ideologen. Sie finden ihre Identität lieber in der Zuordnung zu Mensch (45%), Österreicher (20%), dem jeweiligen Wohnort oder der Wohngegend (19%) und dem jeweiligen Bundesland (12%). Unabhängig von der Bildungsstufe identifizieren sich nur 1% als Deutsche. Und dazu kommt, daß Gruppenidentifikationen über Sprache erst an vierter Stelle stehen. Die Rangordnung des Zugehörigkeitsgefühls geht ganz anders: Österreicher, Weltanschauungsgemeinschaft und Berufsgemeinschaft. Vor allem für die meisten jungen Österreicher ist das Konstrukt eines deutschen Volkes, dem sie angehören sollen, eine inhaltliche Leerformel.[37]

Volk kann in diesem Bewußtsein nicht mehr die Aufmerksamkeit beanspruchen, die sie über eine Rechtskategorie hinaushebt. Volk mag ideologische Kategorie, ja sogar Sozialisationsprodukt einer Gesellschaft vorstellen, aber gewiß kein Naturprodukt ausmachen. Die Natur schafft keine Völker, auch nicht das deutsche, immer nur Mädchen und Buben.

Volk kann aber, wie wir aus unserer Geschichte erfahren haben, wenn wir es nur wissen wollen und uns nicht gegen sie absperren, auch operative Prämisse für ein Herrschaftsprogramm und ein diktatorisches politisches System sein.

Ist es also nur schwierig oder gar unmöglich festzustellen, was deutsch ist? Deutsch ist nicht gleich deutsch, weil zur gleichen Zeit Verschiedenes deutsch genannt wird, und deutsch ist nicht gleich deutsch, weil zu verschiedenen Zeiten deutsch verschiedenes bedeutet. Das ist weiter nicht schlimm. Deutsch ist nichts Außergewöhnliches. Als Begriff teilt es dieses Schicksal mit vielen.

Aber wie die Geschichte zeigt, gibt es immer einmal die Tendenz zur zwangsweisen Homologisierung von Deutschen. Eine Homogenese besteht nicht. Was aber bestehen kann, ist ein Identitäts- und gleichzeitig Kontinuitätskonstrukt, das unzulässig verallgemeinert, manchmal ein wenig schwindelt und sich selbst zum Fetisch macht.

Nehmen wir ein Beispiel. Da sagt mir ein bedeutender Regionalhistoriker und Archivdirektor, daß schon – in ich weiß nicht in welchem Jahrhundert – die kaiserlichen Soldaten in Ungarn Deutsche genannt wurden. Alle zusammen, die Steirer und Tiroler, die Schwaben und Sachsen. Einverstanden. Gab es deshalb damals eine deutsche Nation, die ihre Soldaten ausschickte? Ich glaube nicht. Denn was gesagt ist, ist gesagt. Steirer und Tiroler, Schwaben und Sachsen werden damals und dort in ihrer Funktion als kaiserliche Truppe zu Deutschen. Sonst nichts, und nichts anderes.

Zwanghaft Deutsch? hat Peter Gstettner gefragt, als er „Über falschen Abwehrkampf und verkehrten Heimatdienst" schrieb.[38]

Die Frage wird erst zu beantworten sein, wenn wir doppelte oder mehrfache Identitäten ermöglichen, zulassen, akzeptieren, wenn wir gelernt haben, wie Haberlandt 1918 gemeint hatte, auch die diesem durchmengten „Boden entwachsene Kulturarbeit vorurteilslos zu beachten und entsprechend zu werten."[39]

Was verführt also den alpenländischen Menschen, deutsch sein zu wollen? Zuerst einmal die Begierde nach Größe. Die engen Täler zwingen ihn hinauf in die Berge. Ihnen gegenüber ist er winzig und klein. Aber der erhabene Blick in die Welt vom Gipfel zieht ihn hinaus. So sind die Schweizer in die Welt hinaus gezogen, um Krieg zu führen oder um den Papst zu schützen. Auch die Österreicher sind hinausgezogen in das Elbrusgebirge, um ihre Heimat zu verteidigen, und nach Narvik, um den Engländern zu zeigen, was Gebirge heißt. Noch heute künden in allen Orten die Kriegerdenkmäler davon, daß der alpenländische Mensch weltoffen ist und weit in die Lande zieht – um dort zu sterben.

Aber der alpenländische Mensch holt auch die Welt nach Österreich herein. Und diese Welt ist immer deutsch. In allen unseren Filmen spricht alle Welt deutsch. Wer Bush und Arafat, wer James Bond und Terminator in ihrer Sprache sprechen hören will – na ja, warum denn nicht. Man lernt auf diese Weise viele Sprachen. Von Geiselgasteig bis Wenzel-Lüdecke-Synchron. Denn der alpenländische Mensch ist voll des Mißtrauens gegen fremde, er ist aber auch voll der Unsicherheit gegen seine eigene Sprache. Besonders Rundfunk und Fernsehen haben in Österreich Pate gestanden beim Verlassen des Seins, dieser Mensch hat gestanden, auch als er gestanden ist, wo nichts zu gestehen war.[40]

Aber der alpenländische Mensch wird auch verführt durch seinen Wunsch, zu helfen. Wir wissen es ja. Deutschland ist ohne Österreich nicht imstande, mit anderen Völkern umzugehen. Wir hingegen haben eine jahrhundertelange Begabung für diesen Umgang, Die Kommandosprache der k. u. k. Armee als Vorbild: Habt Acht und Ruht. Und öfter auch ewig.

Den alpenländischen Menschen verführt aber auch die Sehnsucht, geliebt zu werden. Alles Nichtdeutsche erniedrigt, und so will er erhöht bleiben. Auch der Tourismus lehrt es ihn:

„Oft saß Jakob schweigend in ihrer Mitte oder sagte bewußt Dummheiten, über denen sie gewöhnlich nicht einen Augenblick innehielten und fortfuhren in ungebrochener Begeisterung. Er mußte schon sehr beharrlich sein, und dann konnten sie es nicht glauben, wenn der Bedenken äußerte, starrten ihn erstaunt an oder lallten betrunkenes Zeug, und nicht nur einmal habe man ihm einen Arm um die Schultern gelegt und ganz nah, viel zu nah vor seinem Gesicht mit ein paar Worten alles gutzumachen versucht: komm, warum er sich aufrege, wir sind doch alle deutsch, und Jakob roch den Alkohol und sah wortlos den Mann an, oder er sah die Frau an, die den ganzen Abend schon von der anderen Seite ihren Schenkel an seinem rieb und jetzt schaute, als wäre sie nicht mehr zu halten und wollte ihn auffressen mit Haut und Haar."[41] Alpenländische Männerphantasien von Norbert Gstrein, in denen die Einheimischen „die Deutschen Leute" nannten, „als wären sie selbst keine, und dann wieder Piefke und mit Spott belegten und den übelsten Schimpfworten".[42]

Denn der alpenländische Mensch ist auch verführt in seinem innersten Drang, er möchte kultiviert werden. Und das geschieht seit vielen Jahrzehnten. Schon im Jahre 1919 schrieb Julius Mayr vom Deutschen und Österreichischen Alpenverein:

> „Seit Jahrhunderten durch die Pflege der Antike mit dem Verständnis von Schönheit und Größe durchtränkt, noch im Nachklang der naturfreudigen Goethe-Periode lebend, war der Deutsche wie kein anderer Mensch der

Welt geeignet, die aus Furcht und Vorurteil gewebte Hecke zu durchbrechen, die die Alpen umzäunte, und seinem Volke, ja der Welt das Märchenschloß zu öffnen. Und wieder fügte es ein günstiges Geschick, daß dies nicht von innen heraus geschah, nicht aus dem Beweggrund enger heimischer Interessen, sondern daß der Drang von außen kam, von Männern, die weit draußen in den Städten des flachen Landes wohnten. Dadurch allein ward dem Unterfangen schon von vornherein der Stempel der Uneigennützigkeit aufgedrückt, dadurch allein die reine Idee zum werbenden Wahrzeichen erhoben."[43]

Da schweigt nunmehr der alpenländische Mensch und wendet sich – nach innen.

Und zurück. Zurück zu jenen Beteiligten und Betroffenen der deutsch-sehnsüchtigen alpenländischen Menschen. „Weil sich dieses leicht entflammbare Wesen (Österreichs) vor Anfechtung nicht zu schützen wußte, weil es ihnen nicht selten in einer kindhaften Unbefangenheit und vertrauensseligen Torheit von selber zutrieb, erlag es Gefahren, vor denen seine ahnungslose Phantasie blind geblieben war. Ja sie selber hat ihm den Traum vom Deutschen Reich eingeredet, an dem es dann zuschanden gehen sollte. Vielleicht war freilich gerade diese verführbare Phantasie einer der Handlanger des Schicksals, das Österreich zweimal zerschlagen wollte, um es in einer vollendeten Gestalt auferstehen zu lassen, wahrscheinlich sollte es erst von seinen Irrtümern befreit werden, ehe es wieder seinen ehrwürdigen Namen empfangen durfte."[44] „Wir brauchen wieder die Ruhe des ersten Österreich, die keine tatenlose Stille war . . . es war vielmehr eine wohltemperierte Lebensart der hastlosen Menschen, ein unausgesprochener Einklang mit der Natur und dem Natürlichen . . ."[45]

„Und wir brauchen wieder die Inbrunst des zweiten Österreich, die nach Untergang und Zerstreuung, nach Verlust und Verschwendung keine besessene Hysterie war. . . ."[46]

„Die gesellige Neigung des wahren Österreichs, nun erkennen es viele, und es werden ihrer immer mehr werden, gehört der Welt . . . und eines Tages wird dann die Meinung, Österreich müßte ein Teil des Deutschen Reiches sein, die sich an den Nachfolgern von nicht mehr erreichbaren Urhebern so sehr rächte, nur mehr eine historische Episode sein."[47]

„So haben wir über dem einen ‚Anschluß an Deutschland' den Anschluß an die Welt versäumt."[48]

„So ist der Geist Österreichs: Weltbescheidenheit. Er ist: Überwindung der Lebensunrast."[49]

So gut konnte 1946 Josef Friedrich Perkonig über seine und die Verführung des alpenländischen Menschen hinwegschreiben. Heute, Sie hörten es, ist schon mehr Anstrengung vonnöten.

Anmerkungen

1 Gedrucktes Motto auf einem Billet mit Bild und handschriftlichen Grußworten Roseggers, 1. 4. 1899. Antiquariat Löcker, Wien.
2 Landbund-Kalender 1930 für Steiermark, S. 40.
3 Jörg Haider, ORF, Inlandsreport, 18. 8. 1988.
4 Der Standard, 21./22. 7. 1990, S. 6.
5 Martin Wutte, Deutsche und Slowenen in Kärnten, Klagenfurt 1918, S. 4 und 5.
6 M. Haberlandt, Die nationale Kultur der österreichischen Volksstämme. Wien 1918 (Österreichische Bücherei 2), S. 75.
7 Josef Birkenhauer, Die Alpen. Paderborn 1980 (Uni-Taschenbücher 995), S. 26 ff.
8 Heinz Scheibenpflug, Berge um uns. Ein Buch vom deutschen Alpenland. Berlin 1939, S. 5.
9 Vgl. Karl Stuhlpfarrer, Umsiedlung Südtirol, 1939–1940, 2 Bde. Wien – München 1985.
10 Option – Heimat – Opzioni. Eine Geschichte Südtirols. Una storia dell'Alto Adige. Katalog zur Ausstellung des Tiroler Geschichtsvereins, Bozen. Bozen 1989, S. 275–277.
11 Oswald Egger und Hermann Gummerer (Hrsg.), Walther. Dichter und Denkmal. Wien – Lana 1990.
12 Scheibenpflug 1939, S. 51.
13 Aus dem Vortrag von Carl Schmitt „Völkerrechtliche Großraumordnung mit Interventionsverbot für raumfremde Mächte", 1. 4. 1939, Opitz, Europastrategien Nr. 85, S. 641–648; 643.
14 Helmut Carstanjen, Die Untersteiermark. Eine politische Aufgabe an der Südostgrenze des Grossdeutschen Reiches. Marburg (1941), S. 5.
15 Carstanjen 1941, S. 13.
16 IZDG, Ljubljana, Oroznistvo Stajersko, 91/I/6. Kommandeur der Gendarmerie beim Chef der Zivilverwaltung in der Untersteiermark an alle Gendarmeriedienststellen in der Untersteiermark, 28. 5. 1941.
17 Vgl. Tone Ferenc, Quellen zur nationalsozialistischen Entnationalisierungspolitik in Slowenien 1941–1945. Viri o nacisticni raznarodovalni politik v Sloveniji 1941–1945. Maribor 1980, Nr. 171 und 315.
18 IZDG, Der Landrat des Kreises Völkermarkt, F 57/III/1. Der Landrat des Kreises Völkermarkt an alle Bürgermeister, 22. 6. 1943.
19 Hugo Hassinger, Geographische Grundlagen der Geschichte. Freiburg im Breisgau 1931, S. 197.
20 Heinrich von Srbik, Mitteleuropa. Das Problem und die Versuche seiner Lösung in der deutschen Geschichte. Weimar 1937, S. 5.
21 Srbik 1937, S. 38 f.
22 Peter Hanák, Diskussionsbeitrag bei der Tagung der RAI Bozen „Verfolgt, verfemt, vertrieben", Bozen, November 1989.
23 Zitiert nach Marsha L. Rozenblit, Die Juden Wiens 1867–1914. Assimilation und Identität. Wien – Köln – Graz 1988 (Forschungen zur Geschichte des Donauraumes II), S. 42.
24 Die Wahrheit, 13. 11. 1925, S. 7. Zitiert nach Jens Budischowski, Assimilation, Zionismus und Orthodoxie in Österreich 1918–1938. Jüdisch-politische Organisationen in der Ersten Republik. Diss. Wien 1990, S. 36.
25 Adam Müller-Guttenbrunn, Wohin gehört Westungarn? Wien 1919, S. 3.
26 Günther Berka, Slawen in den österreichischen Donauländern. Graz 1923.
27 Nationaldemokratische Flugschriften Nr. 3, Wien 1919.
28 Alfred Krauß, Der Treueeid des alten österreichisch-ungarischen Soldaten. München o. J., S. 4.
29 Rotraud Degner, So kocht Deutschland. Klassische und neue Rezepte aus allen Regionen. München 1985.
30 Eckart Hachfeld, Die Deutsche Seele. München 1988.
31 Werner Hager, Geschichte in Bildern. Studien zur Historienmalerei des 19. Jahrhunderts. Hildesheim, Zürich – New York 1989.

32 Hanns Haas, Zur österreichischen Nation – eine Spätlese. In: Zeitgeschichte 18 (1990/91), S. 304–313, S. 306.
33 Gerhard Jaeckel, Die deutschen Kaiser. Eine illustrierte Geschichte der deutschen Herrscher von Karl dem Großen bis Wilhelm II und Karl I von Österreich-Ungarn. Oldenburg – Hamburg – München 1980.
34 Anton Pelinka, Die Arroganz der Größe. Zu Karl Dietrich Ermanns „Die Spuren Österreichs in der deutschen Geschichte", in: Informationen der Gesellschaft für politische Aufklärung Nr. 25, Juni 1990, S. 11.
35 Karen Schönwälder, Auf der Suche nach der „deutschen Identität". Ein Literaturbericht, in: Blätter für deutsche und internationale Politik 12/1985, S. 1450–1465.
36 Vgl. Andreas Mölzer, Und wo bleibt Österreich. Berg am See 1991, S. 102 und 121. Vgl. . . . Der Standard.
37 Vgl. Albert F. Reiterer, Nation und Nationalbewußtsein in Österreich. Ergebnisse einer empirischen Untersuchung. Wien 1988.
38 Peter Gstettner, Zwanghaft deutsch? Klagenfurt 1988.
39 Haberlandt 1918, S. 78.
40 Vgl. Georg Schmid, . . . Sagen die Deutschen. Annäherung an eine Geschichte des Sprachimperialismus, in: Oliver Rathkolb/Georg Schmid/Gernot Heiß (Hrsg.), Österreich und Deutschlands Größe. Ein schlampiges Verhältnis. Salzburg 1990, S. 23–34.
41 Norbert Gstrein, Einer. Frankfurt/M. 1988 (edition suhrkamp), S. 56.
42 Norbert Gstrein 1988, S. 57.
43 Julius Mayr, Ein Halbjahrhundert Alpenverein. In: Zeitschrift des Deutschen und Österreichischen Alpen-Vereines, Bd. 50, 1919. Wien 1919, S. 1.
44 Josef Friedrich Perkonig, Wir Österreicher, in: Kärntner Almanach 1946. Klagenfurt 1946, S. 15–21, S. 16.
45 Perkonig 1946, S. 16.
46 Perkonig 1946, S. 17.
47 Perkonig 1946, S. 17.
48 Perkonig 1946, S. 18.
49 Perkonig 1946, S. 21, zitierend: Inon, Neu-Österreich. Ein Aufruf an alle Österreicher, 1923.

Krzysztof Glass

Die Wiederentdeckung Mitteleuropas: Alte Kleider und neue Gelüste

Einleitung

In den letzten zwei Jahren veränderte sich einiges in Mitteleuropa, das mitten in der Phase der Installierung einer gesamteuropäischen wirtschaftlichen Einheit und der endgültigen Aufhebung der Nachkriegsteilung recht unterschiedliche Signale setzte. Einige dieser Signale verursachten kurzfristig eine gewisse Verstimmung, andere führten zu innenpolitischen Irritationen, weil sie zumindest als Fauxpas angesehen wurden. So war es z. B. mit dem deutsch-sowjetischen Treffen am östlichen Ufer des Bug-Flusses in Brest-Litowsk[1], d. h. direkt an der polnisch-sowjetischen Grenze. In gewisser Weise bedeutete das eine Wiederholung des Szenarios aus der letzten Phase des Ersten Weltkrieges und ebenso aus dem Zeitraum 1939/1940[2]. Man könnte die Legitimität des Vergleichs anzweifeln und dies als ein reines Zufallsprodukt eines eng gedrängten Politkalenders bewerten. Trotzdem bleibt die Geschichtsträchtigkeit des Ortes im Raum stehen. Für einen Teil der geschichtsbewußten Öffentlichkeit Polens hat dieser Dialog direkt vor den eigenen Türen einen unangenehmen Beigeschmack.

Ein ähnliches Unbehagen verursachte ein anderes Treffen in Sachen Entspannung und eines bewußt konzipierten neuen Anfangs. Es ist die Rede von Václav Havels Reise nach München[3], die als Signal für eine qualitativ neue Nachbarschaftspolitik verstanden sein sollte. Das Echo der Begegnung mit dem deutschen Bundespräsidenten Richard von Weizsäcker ist unterschiedlich ausgefallen, wobei in den westlichen Massenmedien die Reaktionen viel positiver formuliert wurden als in den ehemaligen Ostblockländern. Für viele hat das Münchner Treffen an einem unglücklich gewählten Ort und zu einem nicht minder falsch gewählten Zeitpunkt stattgefunden.

Im deutsch dominierten Westeuropa wurde Havels Mut zu spektakulären Schritten und die Fähigkeit des europareifen Denkens unterstrichen. östlicher erinnerte man sich an München '38 bzw. an die Jahre danach.[4] Diesem Schritt folgten bald nächste, die in gewisser Weise einen ahistorischen Standpunkt der neuen Eliten des Ostens ergänzten. Der slowakische Nationalismus entdeckte z. B. Pater Tisos Verdienste um „die nationale Eigenständigkeit" in der gerade ansetzenden Diskussion über die Selbstbestimmungsrechte im mitteleuropäischen Raum.

Entsprechend dem Motto „Was zusammengehört . . .", das vom Denkmal der deutschen Sozialdemokratie – Willy Brandt – den DM-gläubigen Massen der Ex-DDR zum „Anheften" auf die gesamtdeutschen Fahnen gebracht wurde, unternahm man den Versuch, den Prozeß der Restauration zu perfektionieren. Es kam zu bewußt beschlossenen Entscheidungen, deren flüchtige Analyse schon über die Verschiebung der außenpolitischen Gewichte der BRD gewisse Schlußfolgerungen erlaubte. Das Übersiedeln des Macht- und Politzentrums nach Berlin ist, unabhängig von dem relativ unwesentlichen Zeitraum für die Neuinstallierung der Hauptstadt, eine Tatsache, die den westlichen Partnern in der EG früher oder später zu denken geben müßte.

Zu der zu wenig beachteten Optik des Wiedervereinigungsprozesses gehören auch Entscheidungen, die im Zusammenhang mit der Reaktivierung des alten Reichstags als Parlamentsgebäude stehen. Ebenso wurde im Ausland Helmut Kohls Teilnahme an der Überführung der sterblichen Überreste Friedrichs des Großen beinahe übergangen. Zur Erinnerung: Auch ein anderer deutscher Kanzler nahm in der Vergangenheit an der Überführung der „heiligen Überreste" der großen Väter der preußischen Expansionspolitik teil – sein Name war Adolf Hitler.

Viele dieser – rein symbolisch gedachten – politischen Akte haben gegenüber der Öffentlichkeit ihren Zweck erfüllt. Trotz der vielerorts unternommenen Bestrebungen, diese Akte als Zeichen der Verbeugung vor der Geschichte oder der Verbundenheit mit der Vergangenheit darzustellen, konnte man die aufkommenden Zweifel am demokratischen Charakter der politisch-wirtschaftlichen Wende in Mitteleuropa nicht überhören.

Zur Vorsicht in der Einschätzung des mitteleuropäischen Veränderungsprozesses mahnen außerdem partikulare Tendenzen wie z. B. in der Tschechoslowakei oder gewaltvolle Entladungen der zwischennationalen Konflikte wie z. B. in Jugoslawien.

Das Auftreten der staatlich gesteuerten bzw. spontan entstandenen nationalistischen Manifestationen in einem so sensiblen Teil Europas gibt zu denken. Daher wäre es legitim, zu behaupten, daß das Umbaustadium im ehemaligen Osteuropa mehr destabilisierende Momente und Ansätze unvorhersehbarer Konflikte als Anzeichen einer positiven und in den Grundzügen demokratischen Entwicklung in sich birgt.

Hier stellt sich die Frage, was sich hinter dem schon viel zitierten Begriff „Mitteleuropa" verbirgt? Sicherlich haben nicht nur die Vorgeschichte und der Ablauf der letzten zwei Weltkriege, sondern auch eine ganze Reihe politisch-wirtschaftlicher und kultureller Probleme die Vergangenheit dieses Teils des Okzidents bestimmt und geprägt. Vor allem ist hier von einem Gebiet die Rede, das von vielen Staaten der Gegenwart in unterschiedlicher Weise und im unterschiedlichen Ausmaß beansprucht wurde und wird, d. h. vom Gebiet der Bundesrepublik Deutschland, Polens, der Tschechoslowakei und Österreichs. Das ist der Kern des traditionellen Mitteleuropas. Verschiedentlich werden zu diesem Gebiet noch die Benelux-Länder, nördliche Teile Italiens und Jugoslawiens und Ungarn dazugezählt.

Mitteleuropa im politischen Sinne bedeutet angesichts der historischen – bis heute nicht abgetragenen – Lasten ein Aufmarschgebiet der zwei deutschen Nationalismen, von denen der eine den kompromißlosen preußischen Expansionismus (Großdeutschnationalismus) darstellte und der andere die K. u. K.Habsburger Missionierungs- und Kolonisierungspolitik verkörperte.[5]

In den letzten 150 Jahren wurden verschiedene Spielvarianten des gleichen

„Drangs nach Osten" und Süden ausprobiert. Dazu ist der Mitteleuropagedanke, der mit der deutsch-österreichischen Blockbindung verbunden war, zu zählen. Der Mitteleuropagedanke entwickelte sich aus der Auseinandersetzung mit der Idee des Nationalstaates und hatte vorwiegend einen antinationalen und antirevolutionären Charakter. Er reifte in der Periode Metternichs und fand ebenso bei Bismarck als Grundlage seiner außenpolitischen Bündniskonzepte großes Interesse.[6] Sehr stark wurde der Mitteleuropagedanke von den Alldeutschen forciert und in Ansätzen von den Nationalsozialisten übernommen.

Die praktische Umsetzung dieser Idee läßt sich durch die Analyse der Schwarzenberg-Bruckschen Pläne oder der C. Frantzschen föderalistischen Konzepte nachvollziehen. Mit der Verwirklichung der Mitteleuropapläne sollten erstens hegemonial-wirtschaftliche Ambitionen Deutschlands erfüllt werden und zweitens bestimmte Ordnungsmodelle auf den südost-europäischen Raum ausgeweitet werden. Genauer gesagt, das eigentliche Hauptstoßgebiet lag nördlicher, d. h. im Bereich des preußischen Expansionismus und betraf die polnischen Gebiete.

Der südöstliche Raum sollte zusätzliche Siedlungsmöglichkeiten und eine beträchtliche Ausweitung der wirtschaftlichen deutschen Einflußsphäre bieten. Trotz der vielen unterschiedlich gewichteten Mitteleuropapläne hat das Prinzip des unheilvollen Verbindens einer wirtschaftlichen Integration mit der politischen Dominanz Deutschlands immer wieder zum Grundriß dieser Strategien gehört.

Grundsätzlich wiesen diese Ausrichtungen die Pläne der deutsch-österreichischen Union und die nationalsozialistischen Vorstellungen von der vollen Integration der besetzten Gebiete auf.

Beim Vergleich der Habsburger Missionierungs- und Kolonisierungspolitik mit dem preußischen großdeutsch-nationalen „Drang nach Osten" kann man feststellen, daß die österreichische Variante eine liberalere und weniger tiefgreifende Form der Bevormundung und Unterdrückung der besetzen Länder war.

Ungleich massiver und militanter zeigte sich die Politik des „Eisernen Kanzlers" und seiner Nachfolger im Umgang mit polnischen Minderheiten oder Mehrheiten in den Gebieten Großpolens, Pommerns, Schlesiens, Masowiens etc. Die vollkommene Verkörperung des Geistes dieser Politik bietet der 1894 gegründete Ostmarken-Verein, der in Polen unter der Bezeichnung HAKATA (von den Namen Hansemann. Kennemann, Tiedemann) besser bekannt war.

Heute, in Zeiten, die von politischer Destabilität und wirtschaftlicher Schwäche der ČSFR, Polens etc. gekennzeichnet sind, sollten gewisse Signale der verstärkten deutschen Präsenz mehr Aufmerksamkeit finden. Und das obwohl die neuen Eliten ausländische Investoren willkommen heißen und sich die nötigen Impulse z. B. seitens der deutschen Treuhandgesellschaft erhoffen. Eine Pikanterie am Rande: Eine namensgleiche Organisation hatte in den Jahren 1940–1944 die Enteignung und Ankäufe zu Spottpreisen auf dem Gebiet des Generalgouvernements durchgeführt.

Da einerseits die Länder des ehemaligen Ostblocks einer übermächtigen und expandierenden Volkswirtschaft des westlichen Nachbarns keine stabilen wirtschaftlichen Strukturen entgegensetzen können und andererseits die BRD und

Österreich ihre alten Interessen im Osten und Südosten Europas nicht aufgegeben haben, kann man annehmen, daß eine weitere Demontage der mitteleuropäischen Nachkriegsordnung zur Entstehung einer ähnlichen Machtteilung wie in der ersten Hälfte des 20. Jh. führen kann. Obwohl die Bestandsaufnahme des Konsolidierungs- und Unifizierungsprozesses zu einem relativen Optimismus verleitet und die wirtschaftlichen Daten noch keine beunruhigenden Werte erreicht haben, ist zu befürchten, daß sich im neu entstandenen Machtvakuum Mitteleuropas alte politische Ambitionen bemerkbar machen werden. In der Vergangenheit waren sie meistens deutscher Provenienz.

Das Ende des alten Traums und die neue Wirklichkeit

1945, als – nach 6 Jahren einer in der Geschichte beispiellosen Periode der totalen und industriellen Vernichtung und Ausbeutung aller „rassisch Minderwertigen" – der Zwischenkriegszeittraum von einem Mitteleuropa – der im Jahre 1939 vorläufig ausgeträumt war – endgültig zu Ende ging, konnte niemand eine Entwicklung voraus ahnen, die in den letzten zwei Jahren zu einer beinahe völligen Negation[7] der politisch-wirtschaftlichen Folgen des 2. Weltkrieges wurde. Was damals mit Mitteleuropa als historischer, geographischer und kultureller Begriff von der europäischen Karte scheinbar spurlos verschwand, das waren nicht nur die traditionellen Trenn- und Einflußlinien oder die Formen der multikulturellen Koexistenz und nicht selten Konfrontation, sondern auch die kleine Welt der unzähligen jüdischen Gemeinden, die in den letzten zwei Jahrhunderten zur Bereicherung des gesellschaftlichen, wirtschaftlichen und kulturellen Lebens Wesentliches beigetragen haben. Die versunkene Multiwelt der Stetls war nicht der einzige Teil der verlorengegangenen Vorkriegswirklichkeit Mitteleuropas. Der physischen Extermination der Kriegsjahre, denen 6 Millionen polnische StaatsbürgerInnen (darunter ca. 3 Millionen Juden, einige tausend Zigeuner und beinahe die gesamte polnische Intelligenz) 3 Mio. west-, ost- und südost-europäische Juden zum Opfer fielen, folgte zu Kriegsende und in den ersten Monaten und Jahren danach eine zweite Flucht-, Zwangs- und Umsiedlungswelle. Die erste wurde in diesem Raum bekanntlich von den Deutschen organisiert und durchgeführt. Die zweite von der Goebbelsschen Propaganda in den Monaten Jänner und Februar 1945 initiiert.

Das Werk der mehr oder weniger planmäßigen Vernichtung der dörflichen, kleinstädtischen und städtischen Gemeinschaften wurde mit der freiwilligen Flucht der Deutschen (vor dem Eintreten der Roten Armee) aus Pommern, Masuren, Schlesien oder dem sogenannten Warteland fortgesetzt.

Nach dem geschichtlichen Abgang des preußischen Junkertums (aus den Gebieten: Warmland, Masuren, Schlesien, Warteland) bzw. der pommerschen Gutsbesitzer kam die große, zum Teil freiwillige und zum Teil erzwungene Migrationswelle[8]. So endete vorläufig die Geschichte Mitteleuropas, ihre kulturelle Tradition und ihre sprachliche, nationale und soziale Vielfalt. Obwohl auf den Ruinen völlig entvölkerter Städte und auf den Fundamenten vernichteter Dörfer neues Leben entstand und in der sehr widersprüchlichen stalinistischen Periode der Versuch der Reaktivierung der Vorkriegstopographie und urbanen Identität unternommen wurde, hatte die mit großer Pietät erbaute Normalität nur den „alten" Glanz der Fassaden und der Straßenzüge, aber nicht die besondere Atmosphäre mit sich gebracht.

Die Wirklichkeit der vierziger und fünfziger Jahre erlaubte den Wiederaufbau bzw. die Lösung elementarer existentieller Fragen, aber nicht die Entstehung von Strukturen, die ein dynamisches und kreatives Bürgertum hervorbringen könnten. Statt urbaner Zentren mit einer pulsierenden Vielfalt entstanden Schlafstätten für Millionen eines uniformierten Systems. In der veränderten Gesellschaft des ehemaligen Mitteleuropas entstand in den Nachkriegsjahren eine paradoxe Situation der horizontalen Überlagerung zweier sehr unterschiedlicher Wertvorstellungen und Auffassungen von der Beschaffenheit der Beziehungen zwischen dem Individuum und der Gemeinschaft.

Unter der oktroyierten Totalität der Volksdemokratie mit ihren massiven Versuchen der grundsätzlichen Umwandlung der Gesellschaft in Richtung eines dirigistischen Systems des Denkens, Agierens und Gestaltens lebte die alte – zum Teil amputierte – Vorstellungswelt und die Tradition der christlich orientierten Kultur weiter. So war der Verlust der christlich–bürgerlichen Identität nur eine rein oberflächliche Erscheinung, die sich mehr in der Wunschvorstellungswelt der neuen politischen Eliten als in der Realität der nur zeitweise vollständig überwachten Refugien der gesellschaftlichen Basis abspielte.

Während sich östlich des Eisernen Vorhangs die Auseinandersetzung mit der eigenen Vergangenheit und der Vorkriegsgeschichte auf einen ritualisierten Umgang mit der Tradition und den Aufbau künstlicher Identifikationsmodelle beschränkte, war westlich dieser Trennlinie das Festhalten am geschichtlichen Anspruch auf das natürliche Recht der Revision der neuentstandenen Ordnung und somit die Restauration der alten Machtverhältnisse tonangebend.

Natürlich waren auch die im Westen erfolgten Veränderungen des gesellschaftlichen Systems nicht frei von dualistischen Zügen. Unter der schützenden Glocke des Wirtschaftswunders fanden sich neben der zum Teil zwangsweise eingeführten Demokratie alle Vorzeichen der alten preußisch-deutschnationalen politischen Kultur, die in zwei Bereichen des westdeutschen Systems konsequent kultiviert wurde. Einerseits wurde sie durch das offizielle Bonn de facto verwaltet und andererseits in den „Heimatvertriebenen-Verbänden" innen- und außenpolitisch vertreten.

Der – Ende der vierziger und Anfang der fünfziger Jahre – einsetzende Prozeß der Eingliederung der sogenannten „Heimatvertriebenen" in die westdeutsche Gesellschaft ließ nicht, wie Heinrich A. Winkler meint, „das größte Reservoir nationaler Ressentiments kontinuierlich schrumpfen"[9], sondern – im Gegenteil – wachsen. Die gemäßigte Rechte, also die Unionsparteien, stellte sich gerne in den Dienst der großdeutsch-nationalen Ideologie, die sie zum wichtigsten Element der neuen Staatsraison erhoben hatte. Das Bonn der Wirtschaftsprosperität konservierte und festigte all das, das ein solides Fundament für eine beständige

Politik der Revision garantierte. Gleichzeitig verfolgte man jedoch parallel dazu das Ziel der supranationalen Integration. Diese Doppelstrategie bedeutete kein Novum, und beide praktizierten Konzepte gehörten zu einer gemeinschaftlich, d. h. durch alle parlamentarischen Kräfte (inklusive Sozialdemokraten) getragenen Politik.

Derselbe Konrad Adenauer, der nach Ansicht von Heinrich A. Winkler ein überzeugter „Anti-Nationalist"[10] war, vertrat zugleich beide „Handlungsstränge" des Nachkriegsdeutschlands, d. h. im Westen mit der Überzeugung eines aufrichtigen Demokraten die Idee der Westintegration und im Osten den unverrückbaren monolithartigen Anspruch auf die Wiederherstellung des Deutschen Reiches und mindestens in den Grenzen des Jahres 1937. Bemerkenswert war dabei, daß dieses „Monument" der deutschen Christdemokratie immer wieder deutliche Signale Richtung Osteuropa setzte, deren Sprache eindeutig mit dem geschichtlich belasteten „Drang nach Osten" im Zusammenhang stand. So war es z. B. mit dem bekannten Auftreten in der Öffentlichkeit im Mantel des Großmeisters des Deutschen Ritterordens und bei vielen Anlässen, die der politischen Aufwertung der Vertriebenen-Verbände galten.

Diese Doppelzüngigkeit der westdeutschen Außenpolitik, also das demokratische Gesicht für die Westeuropäer und der bismarcksche Schatten für den Osten bedeutete keine nennenswerte Kursänderung und keinen Bruch in der Tradition des preußisch-wilhelminischen Machtdenkens.

Golo Manns Meinung: „Schlesien und Preußen, das waren Landschaften von ausgeprägter Kultur und Eigenart gewesen; in ihrem deutschen Charakter um tausend Jahre jünger zwar als Rheinland und Schwaben, aber um dessentwillen nicht weniger deutsch"[11] markierte den offiziellen Standpunkt der westdeutschen Demokratie ohne der extrem ausfallenden Haltungen, die so typisch für revanchistische Kreise waren und sind. Abseits der zurückhaltenden Sachlichkeit Golo Manns existierte bereits die sich deutlich artikulierende Welt einer ungestümen Deutschtümelei mit dem ganzen Reichtum der „völkischen Phraseologie".

In den Ländern des damaligen Ostblocks war die Öffentlichkeit ständig mit uniformierten, gleichklingenden und oft indifferent-oberflächlichen Meinungen über die deutsche innenpolitische Szenen konfrontiert. Der verheerende Einfluß des Monopolisierungsprozesses im Informationsbereich zeigte erst nach dem Fall des Eisernen Vorhangs die tiefen Spuren einer zu lange andauernden Ritualisierung im Bereich der Meinungsbildung. In den 50er, 60er, 70er Jahren genügte es, dank der Existenz des gut geschützten Monopols des Staates auf die Gestaltung und Weitergabe der Information, eine oberflächliche Darstellung der westdeutschen Wirklichkeit für das Aufrechterhalten der stereotypen Feindbilder zu nützen. Dies führte zur Immunisierung der Gesellschaft gegen alle Inhalte, die vom Propagandaapparat zu bestimmten Anlässen verfaßt wurden. Mit der Zeit entfernte man sich immer mehr von den Grundsätzen der Rationalität und den Geboten der Sachlichkeit im Bereich der Wiedergabe der politischen Vorgänge in der BRD. Man schuf eine künstliche Realität und begünstigte die Entstehung kontraproduktiver Reaktionen im informellen gesellschaftlichen Bereich. Dadurch kam es einerseits zu einer gewissen Abstumpfung gegenüber bestimmten außenpolitischer Themen, wie z. B. Rechtsradikalismus und Revisionismus in der BRD, und andererseits zum Ansteigen politisch nicht mehr verantwortbarer Informationsdefizite in der Rezeption des westdeutschen Alltags.

Das Fehlen pluralistischer Freiräume in den Massenmedien erzeugte entweder eine totale Ablehnung und Abstumpfung oder eine automatisierte Identifikation mit dem propagandistisch aufgearbeiteten Inhalten. Dabei wuchs die Entfernung zwischen dem tatsächlichen Bild der westdeutschen Gesellschaft und ihrem Abbild in den Massenmedien des Ostblocks ständig.

Dank dieser mangelhaften Informationspolitik der Ostblockstaaten entstand ein gefährliches Vakuum, eine Situation, in der nur einige wenige von den tatsächlichen Vorgängen innerhalb der westdeutschen Polit- und Wirtschaftseliten Bescheid wußten. Der Großteil der Bevölkerung baute seine Vorstellungen von der Außenpolitik der BRD auf den klischeehaften Bildern, die vom Propagandaapparat aufbereitet wurden, auf. Da sowohl die Erinnerung an Kriegsgeschehnisse weiterhin wirksam war als auch die Monopolisierung des Informationswesens den herrschenden Parteien die manipulative Arbeit vereinfachte, war es nicht schwer, dieselben Inhalte jahrzehntelang anzuwenden. Das Fehlen der nötigen Sachlichkeit und Seriosität bei der Erstellung außenpolitischer Analysen erlaubte eine partielle Wahrnehmung der Wirklichkeit ohne einen tieferen Einblick in die innenpolitische Atmosphäre der westdeutschen Demokratie, in den 70er oder 80er Jahren waren seriöse und fundierte außenpolitische Analysen nicht gefragt. Nach dem Fall des Eisernen Vorhangs war es schon zu spät.

Die diskreditierten Politeliten des auseinanderfallenden Ostblocks sind nach unterschiedlichen, mehr oder weniger friedlichen Machtübergabemustern abgetreten. Nach und nach änderte sich die politische Landschaft des östlichen Teils Mitteleuropas, aber die Lücke, die die alten Machteliten hinterlassen haben, konnte nur provisorisch geschlossen werden. Das neue Bild des wiederentstehenden demokratischen Lebens bietet dem Betrachter trotz der sehr gegensätzlichen Signale eigentlich ein einheitliches und ein sehnsüchtiges Zurückblicken auf die „guten alten Zeiten".

Außer den restaurativen Sehnsüchten existieren zur Zeit viele andere Gemeinsamkeiten des Wandels, die von einer totalen Absage gegenüber dem Kommunismus und allem, was mit linkem Gedankengut identifizierbar ist, beherrscht sind. Gemeinsam sind die Länder des östlichen Mitteleuropas mit schwer bewältigbaren Lasten der Umstrukturierung der Wirtschaft und der Schulden konfrontiert, wobei das Ende einer langen Durststrecke nicht absehbar ist.

Gemeinsam ist ihnen auch die Frustration der Desillusionierten, die nach dem anfänglichen Enthusiasmus die Tiefen einer enttäuschenden Realität zur Kenntnis nehmen müssen.

Mitten in der Phase des unsicheren Prozesses des Improvisierens stehend, der immer noch die vermeintlichen oder echten Gefahren der Rückkehr zu den alten Zuständen in sich birgt, versuchen sie einerseits zu einer Identität und zu einem zeitgemäßen Selbstbewußtsein zu finden und andererseits all das, was eine vordergründige Ideologisierung signalisiert, von Anfang an zu unterbinden. Ersteres führte zu paradoxen Rückgriffen auf schon längst diskreditierte Denk-

und Verhaltensweisen wie z. B. Nationalismus, Klerikalismus, Fremdenhaß mit allen xenophobischen Spielvarianten. Die ideologische Lücke muß eben gefüllt werden. Das zweite bedeutet einen sich langsam andeutenden Prozeß der Verdrängung der geschichtlichen Vorgänge, die direkt zur Machtübernahme nach 1945 durch die sogenannten Kommunisten führten. Es ist nicht schwer zu erraten, daß die enttäuschten und durch den Alltag überlasteten Gesellschaften des östlichen Mitteleuropas die Zeiten der deutschen Okkupation und Dominanz vergessen machen möchten.

In den westlichen Gegenden Mitteleuropas weiß man über die allgemeine Stimmung Bescheid. Daher wird emsigst an Strategien der friedlichen Rückgewinnung gearbeitet.

Machtpolitisch gesehen kann es nicht schaden, wenn im westlichen Ausland die schon plakative Bejahung der EG mit der Idee „Europa der Regionen" untermauert wird. Es ist also kein Wunder, daß in den Reihen der Proponenten dieser Idee vor allem deutsche Politiker vom Schlag Theo Weigels, Max Streibls oder Lothar Späts zu finden sind.[12]

Schon während der letzten Konferenz, die dieser Problematik gewidmet war, präsentierten sie nicht nur zwei unterschiedliche politische Gruppierungen, sondern auch Konzepte, die einmal größere Autonomie den Regionen und ein anderes Mal die dominierende Rolle des Überregionalen akzentuierten. Bereits vor ca. 3 Jahren wurde die „Gemeinschaftscharta" der Regionalisierung vom Europäischen Parlament verabschiedet. Dieses wage Konzept einer Minimallösung beinhaltete – nach dem Prinzip des kleinsten gemeinsamen Nenners – solche Forderungen an den Status der zukünftigen Regionen, die bei allen Beteiligten Akzeptanz finden würden.

Natürlich fand sie in der BRD eine breite Zustimmung im Wissen von der „repräsentativen Bedeutungslosigkeit" des Europäischen Parlaments.

Es scheint den politischen und wirtschaftlichen Eliten wichtig zu sein, sich gleichzeitig mehrere Optionen offen zu halten und zeitweilig auf die atlantische, gesamteuropäische oder osteuropäische Karte – je nach Bedarf – zu setzen.

Zugleich fehlt es nicht an distanzierten Betrachtungen der Idee „Europa der Regionen". Gisela Müller-Brandeck-Boquet schrieb vor kurzem: „Wie sehr jede Region innerhalb dieses ‚Europas der Regionen' ihr eigenes Süppchen kocht, läßt sich auch daran ablesen, daß sich die autonome Region Südtirol von einem EG-Beitritt Österreichs und einer föderalistischen Gliederung der EG an erster Stelle ein Ende der ‚künstlichen Grenze am Brenner' erhofft"[13].

Das Zugeben der politischen Gefahren, die aus einer Installierung der neuen Ordnung resultieren könnten, zeigt, daß eine kritische Öffentlichkeit über mögliche Entwicklungen nachzudenken scheint. Was in Westeuropa in Betracht gezogen wird, daß sollte auch für Osteuropa gelten. Wenn also die Vertreter der deutschen Minderheit in Polen laut über die mögliche Regionalisierung Polens nachdenken und der Öffentlichkeit die Demontage der staatlichen Eigenständigkeit schmackhaft zu machen versuchen, dann ist das auch eine der vielen Facetten der Vorstellung vom „Europa der Regionen".

Schlußwort

Während auf der politisch-formellen Ebene die konservativen Protagonisten der „Zusammenlegungsidee" im westlichen Ausland am Werk sind, versuchen ihre CDU/CSU-Parteifreunde die notwendige Basisarbeit für die Unterstützung der deutschen Minderheit zu leisten. Die immer stärker werdende Präsenz der BdV-Funktionäre in Schlesien, Pommern, Masuren etc. wird damit begründet, daß man seitens der Vertriebenen-Verbände eine kulturelle und wirtschaftliche Entwicklungshilfe an die Deutschstämmigen leisten möchte.

Bei näherer Betrachtung zeigt sich, daß die Aktivitäten wenig mit den vorgegebenen Zielen gemeinsam haben und in vielem Ähnlichkeiten mit altbekannten Methoden des Unterwanderns aufweisen. Schon im direkten Umfeld einer ganzen Reihe von sogenannten „Privatinitiativen" werden die Parallelitäten zwischen den Vorgangsweisen bzw. Schwerpunktsetzungen der 20er und des Anfangs der 90er Jahre sichtbar.

Während in der Mitte der 20er Jahre der deutsche Agrarkreditapparat die Funktion der „Steuerung" des reichsdeutschen Einflusses übernommen hatte, haben 1991 die gezielten Gründungen von Joint-Venture-Firmen eine ähnliche Rolle gespielt. Diese Formen der politisch-wirtschaftlichen Einflußnahme werden durch eine ganze Reihe legaler Maßnahmen ergänzt. Mit Hilfe von „Strohmännern" kauft man Boden, Landwirtschaftsbetriebe und andere Unternehmen. Alles passiert scheinbar unkoordiniert und augenscheinlich nach dem Prinzip des Zufalls, aber der Großteil dieser Aktivitäten konzentriert sich zur Zeit auf die – zumindest inoffiziell – beanspruchten Gebiete West- und Nordpolens. Der desolate Zustand des polnischen Staates, seiner Wirtschaft und auch der Gesellschaft einerseits und die Korrumpierbarkeit, Apathie und eine steigende Illoyalitätsbereitschaft seiner Bürger andererseits erlauben den anonymen Konsortien ein ungestörtes Wirken im gesetzlosen Raum.

Währenddessen ist man in Polen selbst bemüht, den anhaltenden „Ausverkauf" der polnischen Souveränität zu übersehen und in der Öffentlichkeit zumindest als einen Sachzwang der Geschichte den besorgten Teilen der Bevölkerung darzustellen. Anders ist es im vereinten Deutschland, wo man zur Zeit neben „Großmachtuntertönen" und einer gewissen Umorientierung der Ostpolitik auch kritische Stellungnahmen wahrnehmen kann. Obwohl diese Stimmen z. T. im informellen Bereich, wie z. B. der Presse, artikuliert werden, zeugen sie doch von Bedenken, die angesichts der geschichtlichen Erfahrungen eine realpolitische Dimension bekommen.

Bei einer nüchternen Bestandsaufnahme der wirtschaftspolitischen Vorgänge im ehemaligen Ost-, Mitteleuropa kann die langsam vor sich gehende Ausbreitung des deutschen Einflusses nicht übersehen werden, und darum scheint es zulässig zu sein, all diesen Stimmen recht zu geben, die vor die Stabilität in dieser Region gefährdenden Aktivitäten warnen.

Anmerkungen

1 Vgl. Golo Mann, „Deutsche Geschichte des 19. und 20. Jahrhunderts", Frankfurt/Main 1958, S. 635 ff; Karl-Heinz Ruffmann, „Schlüsseljahre im Verhältnis zwischen dem Deutschen Reich und der Sowjetunion", in: „Aus Politik und Zeitgeschichte" B 24/91.
2 Vgl. Jürgen Förster, „Fünfzig Jahre danach: Ein historischer Rückblick auf das ‚Unternehmen Barbarossa'", in: „Aus Politik und Zeitgeschichte" B24/91.
3 Vgl. Ernst Bloch, „Politische Messungen, Pestzeit, Vormärz", Frankfurt/Main 1985, S. 266 ff.
4 Vgl. Franz Neumann, „Behemoth", Frankfurt/Main 1984, S. 591 f.; Ernst Bloch a. a. O., S. 269 ff.
5 Vgl. Johannes Willms, „Nationalismus ohne Nation", Frankfurt/Main 1985, S. 425 ff. und 475 ff.; Anton Staudinger, „Austrofaschistische ‚Österreich'-Ideologie", in: Talos/Neugebauer (Hg.), „Austrofaschismus", Wien 1985, S. 297 ff.
6 Vgl. Golo Mann, a. a. O., S. 443 ff. und 451 ff.; Lothar Gall (Hg.), „Bismarck: Die großen Reden", Frankfurt/Main 1984, S. 329 ff.
7 Vgl. Erwin Oberländer, „Hitler-Stalin-Pakt 1939. Das Ende Ostmitteleuropas?", Frankfurt/Main 1989.
8 Die hier angesprochene Fluchtwelle und die spätere, d. h. nach dem Ende des 2.Weltkrieges erfolgte, Zwangsausweisung der deutschstämmigen Bevölkerung aus den ehemals gemischtsprachigen oder polnischen Gebieten unterscheidet sich von der Politik der tschechoslowakischen Behörden, die nach der Befreiung gegenüber der deutschen Minderheit angewandt wurde.
9 Heinrich August Winkler, „Nationalismus, Nationalstaat und nationale Frage in Deutschland seit 1945", in: „Aus Politik und Zeitgeschichte" B 40/91, S. 14.
10 Vgl. Heinrich August Winkler, a. a. 0., S. 14.
11 Golo Mann, a. a. O., S. 1019.
12 Vgl. Gisela Müller-Brandeck-Boquet, „Ein föderalistisches Europa?", in: „Aus Politik und Zeitgeschichte" B 45/91, S. 21.
13 Gisela Müller-Brandeck-Bocquet, a. a. O., S. 21.

Literatur

Bloch, Ernst, „Politische Messungen, Pestzeit, Vormärz", Frankfurt/Main 1985.
Eichholz/Pätzold, „Der Weg in den Krieg", Berlin 1989.
Feuchtwanger, Joseph Edgar (Hrsg.), „Deutschland – Wandel und Bestand", Frankfurt/Main 1976.
Focke/Reimer (Hrsg.), „Alltag der Entrechteten", Hamburg 1980.
Glaser, Hermann (Hrsg.), „Bundesrepublikanisches Lesebuch", Frankfurt/Main 1980.
Greiffenhagen, Martin und Sylvia, „Ein schwieriges Vaterland", Frankfurt/Main 1981.
Herzfeld, Hans, „Die Weimarer Republik", Frankfurt/Main – Berlin 1966.
Mann, Golo, „Deutsche Geschichte des 19. und 20. Jahrhunderts", Frankfurt/Main 1958.
Mosse, Georg L., „Die Nationalisierung der Massen", Frankfurt/Main 1976.
Neumann, Franz, „Behemoth", Frankfurt/Main 1984.
Oberländer, Erwin (Hrsg.), „Hitler-Stalin-Pakt 1939", Frankfurt/Main 1989.
Olszewski, Henryk, „Zwischen Begeisterung und Widerstand", Poznań 1989.
Willms, Johannes, „Nationalismus ohne Nation", Frankfurt/Main 1985.
Tálos/Neugebauer (Hrsg.), „Austrofaschismus", Wien 1985.

Peter Malina

„Der besonderen Obhut der österreichischen Gesellschaft anvertraut?"

Nationale Minderheiten in österreichischen Geschichtslehrbüchern

1.

Geschichtslehrbücher sind (auch) ein Ergebnis öffentlichen Geschichtsbewußtseins. Es ist daher legitim, sich zu fragen, welcher Stellenwert „nationalen" Minderheiten in diesen offiziellen, von der staatlichen österreichischen Schulverwaltung approbierten Lehr- und Lernmittel eingeräumt wird. Diese Frage ist um so berechtigter, als sich gegenwärtig deutlich zeigt, daß sich auch die österreichische Gesellschaft tendenziell zu einer multikulturellen Gesellschaft wandelt. Es interessierte also die Frage, wie das österreichische Geschichtslehrbuch mit den Österreichern/Österreicherinnen umgeht, die nicht die Sprache der Mehrheit sprechen und deswegen als „Minderheit" diagnostiziert werden.[1] Wenn im folgenden von „dem" österreichischen Geschichtslehrbuch und seinen Inhalten gesprochen wird, so ist festzuhalten, daß es sich hier nur um tendenzielle Aussagen handeln kann. Gewiß gibt es „das" österreichische Geschichtslehrbuch so nicht, wohl aber lassen sich Schwerpunkte, Haltungen und Einstellungen generalisierend feststellen, die für den Umgang österreichischer Schulbuchtexte mit Minderheiten charakteristisch sind. Es ist nicht die Intention dieses Beitrags, Schulbuchtexte schulmeisterlich zu korrigieren oder leichthin zu sagen, wie es besser gemacht werden sollte; es geht vielmehr darum, an einigen ausgewählten Beispielen das historische Bewußtsein österreichischer Geschichtslehrbücher und ihr Verständnis von Minderheit und Mehrheit zu skizzieren und sich nach möglichen Ursachen zu fragen.[2]

Entsprechend dem in der Öffentlichkeit immer wieder beschworenen Bild eines gesprächsbereiten und vermittelnden Österreich wäre zu erwarten, daß Geschichtslehrbücher am Beispiel der österreichischen Minderheiten Verständnis für Gegensätzlichkeiten und Unterschiede zur Sprache bringen und anhand der historischen Entwicklung in Österreich aufarbeiten. Tatsächlich jedoch – dies sei vorweggenommen – nimmt die Annäherung an die verschiedenen „Österreicher" im österreichischen Geschichtslehrbuch nur einen höchst marginalen Platz ein. Daß dieses Österreich ein Österreich der slowenisch, kroatisch und deutsch sprechenden Österreicher ist, wird im österreichischen Geschichtslehrbuch bestenfalls dann zur Kenntnis genommen, wenn der „Staat" in Gefahr oder die öffentliche Ruhe gefährdet ist.

2.

Im Gegensatz zu diesem ersten Befund ist zunächst festzuhalten, daß – und dies scheint zunächst ein Widerspruch zu sein – die Schutzwürdigkeit von Minderheiten für das österreichische Geschichtslehrbuch außer Zweifel steht. Der Thematisierung der Rechte der Minderheiten geht kaum ein Schulbuch aus dem Wege.[3] Toleranz, Akzeptanz auch anderer Formen (nationaler) Lebensverwirklichung gehören zu den immer wieder beschworenen Absichten des Geschichtslehrbuchs. Insbesondere in den Büchern, die den Bereich der „Sozialkunde" abdecken, wird deutlich die Verschiedenheit von Menschen und ihr Recht auf diese Verschiedenheit angesprochen – denn: „Jeder ist anders."[4] Es werden auch Fragen an die Schüler/Schülerinnen gestellt, die diese Erfahrung mit dem Anderssein in die konkrete Lebensrealität einbringen sollen. Zum Beispiel heißt es in einem Lehrbuch zur Sozialkunde, Wirtschaftskunde und Zeitgeschichte für den Polytechnischen Lehrgang:

> „Warum kommt es so häufig zu Konflikten zwischen den Menschen? Welche Konflikte gibt es bei euch in der Klasse, in der Schule, zu Hause? . . . Mögliche Ursachen für Meinungsverschiedenheiten und Konflikte liegen auch darin, daß jeder anders ist. Wir kommen aus verschiedenen Familien, sind unter verschiedenen Umständen aufgewachsen und waren verschiedenen Einflüssen ausgesetzt. Was macht die Unterschiede aus? Wodurch unterscheiden sich die Menschen?"[5]

Die Schwierigkeiten eines tatsächlich entspannten Umgangs mit den Konflikten, die sich aus diesen Unterschieden ergeben, illustriert dasselbe Lehrbuch im Kapitel „Die Republik Österreich entsteht". Hier reduziert sich die Darstellung wieder auf die traditionellen Muster der Schulbuchgeschichte, für die die Aufarbeitung von Konflikten einen deutlich geringeren Stellenwert als die Darstellung der Ereignisse hat. Nun geht es im (durchaus zurückhaltend und distanziert formulierten) Text nur mehr um die österreichische Perspektive – von den Erfahrungen und Problemen der „anderen" (die Österreich verließen und in eigenen Staaten leben wollten) ist nicht mehr die Rede.[6]

Als „Lehrstoff" haben die Minderheiten jedenfalls im Schulbuch ihren Platz gefunden. Daß die Auseinandersetzung mit der prinzipiellen Frage des Verhältnisses von „Minderheit" und „Mehrheit" damit keinesfalls gelöst ist, wird dann deutlich, wenn es konkret darum geht, die österreichischen Minderheiten zu ihrem historischen Recht kommen zu lassen. Die Nationalitäten der Donaumonarchie sind für die tendenziell immer noch (groß-)österreichisch ausgerichteten Geschichtslehrbücher eine Verlegenheit, manchmal auch ein Ärgernis. Auf jeden Fall sind die Nationalitäten verantwortlich für den Zerfall der „österreichischen" kaiserlichen und königlichen Monarchie, deren Herrschaftssystem nach den Schulbuchtexten zu schließen nur sehr wenig oder gar nichts mit der Eskalation des Nationalitätenkonfliktes zu tun hat.[7]

Die Orientierung an einem normativen Verständnis von Politik macht es dem

Lehrbuch für Politische Bildung an Berufsschulen „Du in der Gemeinschaft" möglich, auf mehr als einer Seite die „Grund- und Freiheitsrechte" in Österreich im Detail aufzulisten und zum Schluß – zunächst noch ohne Einschränkung – unter dem Titel „Gleichheit vor dem Gesetz" festzustellen: „Es gibt jedenfalls keine Vorrechte der Geburt, des Geschlechtes, des Standes, der Klasse und des Bekenntnisses." Für dieses an Zielvorstellungen, nicht aber an der gegenwärtigen Realität und schon gar nicht an den historischen Entwicklungen ausgerichtete Verständnis politischer Bildung ist der Schutz der Minderheiten in Österreich durch eine volle Gleichberechtigung und insbesondere durch „besondere Vorrechte der Slowenen und Kroaten (z. B. eigene Schulen, Gerichts- und Amtssprache, zweisprachige Ortstafeln)" gekennzeichnet.[8]

Als „Grundlage der Freiheit"[9] stehen Menschenrechte für das österreichische Geschichtslehrbuch außer Diskussion. Daß hinter diesen Rechtsnormen eine durchaus widersprüchliche Wirklichkeit steht, erschließt sich vielfach nur anhand der widersprüchlichen Aussagen des Schulbuchs selbst: So ist für „Sozial- und Wirtschaftskunde" die „pluralistische Gesellschaft" eine Tatsache, die er erforderlich mache, „tolerant" (das heißt: duldsam, nachsichtig, weitherzig, versöhnlich, verständnisvoll) zu sein.[10] Freilich kann sich das Lehrbuch im Kapitel „Europa" mit dieser Pluralität nicht recht abfinden. Die Attraktivität eines geeinten Europa ist für die Autoren offenkundig so stark, daß an dieser Stelle nun Unterschiede als störend und hemmend empfunden werden. Unter einem Bild einer Gruppe in Gailtaler Tracht findet sich nun überraschenderweise der Text: „Vielfalt der Sprachen, Kulturen und Völker erschwert die europäische Einigung".[11]

3.

Ausgerichtet auf einen nicht weiter hinterfragten Begriff von Österreich, behalten österreichische Geschichtslehrbücher auch bei der Behandlung des Zusammenbruchs der Donaumonarchie im Jahre 1918 die Sicht der herrschenden (deutschen) Mehrheit weiter bei: Das Staatsgebiet „wurde zerschlagen" und auf sieben Nachfolge-Staaten verteilt; die Volksabstimmung im Kärnten vom Oktober 1920 ist eine Entscheidung für ein „ungeteiltes Kärnten und somit für Österreich",[12] und bedauernd-wehmütig wird festgestellt, daß weite Gebiete der alten Monarchie nicht dem „neuen österreichischen Staat" zugesprochen worden waren.[13] Die Bildung neuer Staaten wird als Ergebnis eines Zerfalls und als ein Verlust gedeutet, der „Österreich" Gebietsabtretungen brachte.[14] Aus der Sicht der Mehrheit sind die Selbständigkeitsbestrebungen der Nationalitäten Österreich-Ungarns nur als Infragestellung des „Staates" zu verstehen:

> „Der Bestand des Staates war äußerst gefährdet, da ein Teil der slawischen Völker, allen voran die Tschechen, eine größere staatliche Selbständigkeit verlangte. Öfters kam es auch dazu, daß tschechische und andere slawische Soldaten an der russischen Front zum Feinde übergingen."

Aus dieser deutsch-österreichischen Perspektive kann dann die Auflösung der Donaumonarchie nur mehr als „Abfall der Völker" und das Selbstbestimmungsrecht als im Grunde unverständliche Forderung interpretiert werden:

> „Die meisten Nationalitäten wollten am Ende des verlorenen Krieges keinen gemeinsamen Staat mehr. Sie beriefen sich auf das Selbstbestimmungsrecht der Völker und beschlossen den Abfall."[16]

Teil verständnislos, teils resignierend stehen österreichische Geschichtslehrbücher vor der Tatsache, daß die Nationalitäten Österreich-Ungarns den Staatsverband verlassen wollten. Letzte „Rettungsversuche" wie das Oktobermanifest Kaiser Karls 1918 kamen zu spät. „Die Völker gingen bereits ihre eigenen Wege, und die Donaumonarchie löste sich auf."[17] Ein nicht weiter problematisierter, vereinnahmender Österreich-Begriff, der die historisch gewordene Donaumonarchie als notwendig gegeben akzeptiert, wirkt sich insbesondere dort aus, wo es darum geht, die Nachkriegsordnung 1918–1919 zu beschreiben. Beklagt wird nun, daß sudetendeutsche Gebiete noch 1918 von tschechischen Truppen „besetzt" und 1919 endgültig an die Tschechoslowakei abgegeben wurden. Ähnliches gilt für die Kärntner Volksabstimmung, die immer noch als Ergebnis des „Abwehrkampfes" dargestellt wird:

> „Obwohl zeitweise sogar Klagenfurt und Villach von den Jugoslawen besetzt wurde, machten die Abwehrkämpfe auf die Pariser Friedenskonferenz einen so großen Eindruck, daß Jugoslawien seine Ansprüche nicht durchsetzen konnte und statt dessen eine Volksabstimmung angeordnet wurde. Dabei stimmten am 10. Oktober 1920 in Südkärnten 59% der Einwohner (also auch Slowenen) für Österreich. Südkärnten blieb bei Österreich".[18]

Die Bestimmungen des Friedensvertrages von Saint-Germain sind aus dieser Sicht nichts anderes als die aufgezwungene Reduzierung des „großen" auf ein „kleines" Österreich, wobei die Existenz der neuen (Nachfolge-)Staaten und ihre Ansprüche nach wie vor aus der Perspektive der ehemals bestimmenden (deutschen) Österreicher beurteilt werden:

> Auch von Österreich wurden verschiedene Gebiete abgetrennt, die nicht mehr zu dem neuen Kleinstaat der Republik Österreich gehören sollten, sondern den Nachbarstaaten gegeben wurde, So marschierten italienische Truppen nach dem Zusammenbruch der österreichischen Front bereits schnell in Südtirol, im Kanaltal, in Görz, Triest und Istrien ein. Diese Gebiete waren dem Königreich Italien ja heimlich versprochen worden, und Italien wollte sie gleich in Besitz nehmen und vollendete Tatsachen schaffen."[19]

In der Tradition des alten Österreich stehend, kann sich so manches Schulbuch noch immer nicht von dem „großen", alten Österreich trennen und trauert um die verlorenen Gebiete:

> „Die Abtretung Südtirols an Italien war ein schwerer Verlust. 230.000

deutschsprachige Südtiroler gerieten unter italienische Herrschaft. Ihnen wurde das Selbstbestimmungsrecht verweigert."[20]

Im Vordergrund des historischen Interesses steht immer noch die Bewahrung des „Staates" und seiner (deutschen) nationalen Integrität. Verhaftet einem österreichisch-„nationalen" Denken, das in diesem Zusammenhang freilich ein „deutsch-österreichisches" ist, wird einerseits der Zusammenbruch der österreichischen (das heißt deutsch-österreichisch dominierten) multinationalen Donaumonarchie bedauert, andererseits aber die Multinationalität in den Nachfolgestaaten als Unrecht interpretiert. Als selbstverständlich hingenommen wird sie hingegen dort, wo es um die nationalen Volksgruppen innerhalb des neuen kleinen Österreich geht.

Das Denken in Grenzen und Begrenzungen läßt beispielsweise ein Schulbuch recht vordergründig bei der Darstellung der Nachkriegsverhältnisse fragen: „Was soll zu Österreich gehören?" und gleichzeitig mit einem Unterton des Bedauerns feststellen, daß die meisten umstrittenen Gebiete an die Nachbarstaaten abgetreten werden mußten.[21] Ein anderes Schulbuch regt seine Leser dazu an, die Nachfolgestaaten zu benennen und darauf zu achten, daß sich die politischen Grenzen und die Sprachgrenzen keineswegs decken.[22]

Es überrascht nicht, daß auch bei der Darstellung der Geschichte der Ersten Republik Österreich diese „anderen" Österreicher dem Vergessen anheim fallen. Dasselbe trifft auch für die Zeit der deutschen Okkupation Österreichs zu. Die Aggression der Okkupanten richtete sich für das österreichische Geschichtslehrbuch gegen „Österreicher". Vergessen bleibt, daß zu diesen Österreichern auch die in den übrigen Kapiteln meist von „den" Österreichern unterschiedenen Angehörigen österreichischer Minderheiten gehörten. Daß slowenische Österreicher diesem Terror extrem ausgesetzt gewesen waren, geht den meisten Schulbüchern ebenso verloren wie die Tatsache, daß österreichische Slowenen einen wesentlichen Teil des österreichischen Widerstandes getragen haben.[23]

Bei der Behandlung der österreichischen Geschichte nach 1945 ist von österreichischen Minderheiten dann die Rede, wenn es Schwierigkeiten gibt, wobei die Konflikte um die slowenische Volksgruppe in Kärnten in den 70er Jahren einen deutlichen Schwerpunkt bilden. Der „Ortstafelkrieg" 1972 bleibt in keinem Geschichtslehrbuch unerwähnt. Das heißt allerdings nicht, daß damit die Perspektive der Mehrheit verlassen ist. Selbst jene Bücher, die einen deutlich kritischen Anspruch erheben, haben weiterhin ihre Probleme, Ursachen und Wirkungen auseinanderzuhalten und Argumente für eine kritische Auseinandersetzung bereitzustellen. So interpretiert ein Lehrbuch die Ereignisse in Kärnten 1972 als Zeichen von „Unmutsäußerungen" in „weiten Teilen" der deutschsprachigen Bevölkerung, die dann schließlich in einem „Ortstafelsturm" gipfelten. Seither allerdings sei es in Kärnten wieder ruhiger geworden, denn: „Sowohl bei den Slowenen als auch bei der deutschsprachigen Bevölkerung hat man erkannt, daß Gewalt keine geeignete Lösung verspricht."[24] Als Unruhestifter werden Kräfte von außen (Jugoslawien) oder die nicht einsichtigen Betroffenen selbst geortet:

„Eine amtlich durchgeführte Erhebung der muttersprachlichen Zugehörigkeit (‚Minderheitenfeststellung') erbrachte wegen des passiven Widerstandes der Slowenen ein kaum brauchbares Ergebnis, doch führten Verhandlungen zur Beruhigung des Konflikts."[25]

Unbehagen verursacht offenkundig nicht so sehr der Anlaß des Konflikts – die ungenügende Berücksichtigung der berechtigten Forderungen der Kärntner Slowenen –, sondern die möglichen außenpolitischen Konsequenzen, da – so ein anderer Text – mit den diplomatischen Interventionen Jugoslawiens eine internationale Diskussion der anstehenden Probleme – das heißt: die „Gefahr außenpolitischer Verwicklungen"[26] – nicht zu vermeiden ist.

4.

Für die Darstellung der Minderheiten in Österreich gelten in etwa ähnliche Kriterien, wie sie auch für andere Untersuchungen zu Teilbereichen der Geschichte festgestellt worden sind.[27] Personalisierung, Ereignisgeschichte und Reduzierung historischer Prozesse auf Fakten und Daten ergeben ein Bild der historischen Wirklichkeit, das die Komplexität der Vergangenheit nicht wiederzugeben vermag. Dazu komme (selbst bei sozialwissenschaftlich orientierten, durchaus kritischen Büchern) ein geradezu unwiderstehlicher Zwang zur Harmonisierung, der gesellschaftliche und politische Widersprüche nicht offenlegen möchte. Am Ende einer umfangreichen Passage über „Österreich als Asylland" halten „Zeiten, Völker und Kulturen" (Bd. 3) beispielsweise lediglich fest:

„Zwischen 1945 und 1983 flüchteten 1,942.700 Menschen nach Österreich. Davon blieben etwa 590.000, das sind 7,8 Prozent der Gesamtbevölkerung, in Österreich . . . Sie fanden alle in Österreich Aufnahme, und viele konnten sich integrieren."[28]

Sozialpsychologische und gesellschaftspolitische Fragen stehen trotz mancher Ansätze immer noch im Hintergrund. Die Ereignisgeschichte hingegen bietet die Möglichkeit, gesellschaftliche Spannungen zu harmonisieren und Widersprüche und Gegensätzlichkeiten mit dem Hinweis auf die „Fakten" abzuschieben. So schildert „Zeitgeschichte" (3. Aufl.) den Ortstafelkonflikt 1972 als eine Abfolge von Ereignissen, die mit der Einführung zweisprachiger Ortstafeln in Kärnten begannen und mit der teilweisen Wiederaufstellung wieder ins Lot kamen:

„Als im Sommer 1972 die Einführung zweisprachiger Ortstafeln im südlichen Kärnten nur mit den Stimmen der Sozialisten beschlossen wurde, kam es kurze Zeit darauf zu schwerwiegenden Demonstrationen und Gegendemonstrationen . . . Inzwischen ist durch die Wiederaufstellung von zweisprachigen Ortstafeln in einigen Gemeinden Südkärntens Beruhigung auf beiden Seiten eingetreten."[29]

Immerhin finden sich vereinzelt Ansätze, den immer noch prägenden, gesellschaftlich „leeren" Begriff von Geschichte zu verlassen. Das Lehrbuch „Politische Bildung" (Teil 1) spricht beispielsweise davon, daß auch in der österreichischen Gesellschaft Vorurteile tagtäglich eingeübt und „Feindbilder" für politische und wirtschaftliche Interessen eingesetzt werden.[30] Insbesondere schwächere Gruppen der Gesellschaft sind davon betroffen. Vorurteile gegen sie werden bewußt geschürt, um von den eigenen Problemen abzulenken: „Minderheiten dienten und dienen oft als ‚Sündenböcke' einer Gesellschaft."[31]

Es wäre verfehlt, pauschal zu behaupten, die gegenwärtig im Gebrauch stehenden Schulbücher für die Bereiche Geschichte und Sozialkunde gingen am Problem der Minderheiten in Österreich vollkommen vorbei. Tatsächlich finden sich in einigen Büchern redliche Versuche, eindringlich auf die Frage von Vorurteilen und den Umgang mit unterschiedlichen anderen einzugehen.[32] Im Detail zeigt sich allerdings, daß diese Toleranz nicht so grenzenlos ist. Minderheiten wird in den österreichischen Geschichtslehrbüchern immer noch ein relativ geringer Raum zugemessen, in dem sie vor allem als geduldete Minderheiten oder als schutzbedürftige Objekte, nicht aber als eigenständige gesellschaftliche Realitäten präsent sind:

> „Neben den Angehörigen der ungarischen und der kroatischen Minderheit im Burgenland sind aus allgemeinmenschlichen Erwägungen und wegen der Bestimmungen des Staatsvertrages auch die Slowenen Kärntens der besonderen Obhut der österreichischen Gesellschaft anvertraut."[33]

Minderheiten sind vor allem das Problem der „Mehrheit", die nicht imstande ist, andere Lebensformen neben sich zu akzeptieren. Minderheiten stellen daher notwendigerweise auch die Identität der Mehrheit in Frage. Im österreichischen Geschichtslehrbuch wird dieser Aspekt allerdings nur in Ausnahmefällen berücksichtigt. Dort, wo keine Fragen gestellt werden, sind auch keine Antworten notwendig. Dies gilt teilweise auch für die Vergangenheit, denn – so ein Lehrbuch der Geschichte für Fachschulen:

> „Trotz aller ungelöster Probleme gewährte die Donaumonarchie den Angehörigen von 12 Nationen ein Zusammenleben, wie es später niemals möglich war. Geistig, kulturell und wirtschaftlich war es ein gegenseitiges Geben und Nehmen, das alle Beteiligten förderte. Die Vielheit Europas fand hier in kleinem Rahmen ihr Spiegelbild."[34]

Minderheiten in Österreich sind für das österreichische Schulbuch nicht zuletzt auch deswegen kein besonderes Problem, weil für sie Minderheiten per Definition nur einen kleinen Teil der österreichischen Gesellschaft abdecken. Geübt wird dies beispielsweise mit einer sicherlich gut gemeinten Aufgabe, in der dazu aufgefordert wird, den Prozentanteil der „Fremdsprachigen" in den einzelnen Bundesländern zu berechnen. Fazit für das Schulbuch: „Das Einvernehmen der Minderheiten zu den anderen österreichischen Staatsbürgern ist im großen und ganzen nicht von schwerwiegenden Problemen belastet. Trotzdem kam es immer wieder zu Reibereien."[35]

Karl Stuhlpfarrer hat 1978 zur Präsenz Kärntner Slowenen in österreichischen Geschichtslehrbüchern gemeint: „Die Kärntner Slowenen haben keine eigene Geschichte in den österreichischen Geschichtslehrbüchern . . . Ihre Geschichte bildet nur ein Derivat österreichisch-deutscher Herrschaftsgeschichte, sie wird nur in Konfliktfällen aktualisiert und als Konflikt präsentiert."[36] An diesem Befund hat sich trotz der 1984 von Stuhlpfarrer festgestellten leichten und vielversprechenden, aber insgesamt „noch nicht ausreichenden Entwicklung zum Besseren"[37] nicht viel geändert. Österreicher/Österreicherinnen, die einer Minderheit angehören, haben im österreichischen Geschichtslehrbuch noch immer nur wenig Platz. Wenn von ihnen die Rede ist, dann wird über sie gesprochen, sie selbst kommen nicht zu Wort. Die gut gemeinten Absichten, die einem Großteil der untersuchten Bücher gewiß nicht abgesprochen werden können, verfehlen daher so lange ihre Wirkung, als nicht ernsthaft darangegangen wird, mit einem „anderen Blick" an die Vergangenheit heranzugehen. Denken in historischen Alternativen, die Abwendung von einer Geschichte der Erfolgreichen und das Ernstnehmen der Geschichte auch als historischer Sozialwissenschaft werden notwendig sein, um auch die Geschichte der Kleinen, der Unterdrückten und der an den Rand Gedrängten in den Blick zu bekommen.

Anmerkungen

1 Zur Minderheitenproblematik in Österreich liegt ein umfangreiches Schrifttum vor, das von den Schulbuchautoren offenkundig nur in Ausnahmefällen rezipiert wurde. Verwiesen sei beispielhaft auf einige ältere Arbeiten, die den untersuchten Schulbüchern (von denen mehr als die Hälfte vor 1990 erschienen sind) jedenfalls zur Verfügung gestanden wären: Theodor Veiter, Das Recht der Volksgruppen und Sprachminderheiten in Österreich. Mit einer ethnosoziologischen Grundlegung und einem Anhang. Wien, 1970; Hanns Haas/Karl Stuhlpfarrer, Österreich und seine Slowenen, Wien 1977; Die rechtliche Stellung der Volksgruppen in Österreich. Eine Dokumentation, Wien 1977; Karl M. Brousek, Wien und seine Tschechen. Integration und Assimilation einer Minderheit im 20. Jahrhundert, Wien 1980; Minderheiten und Regionalkultur, Wien 1981; Ethnische Gruppen in der Bundeshauptstadt Wien, Wien 1982; Wilhelm Filla/Ludwig Flaschberger/Franz Pachner/Albert F. Reiterer, Am Rande Österreichs. Ein Beitrag zur Soziologie der österreichischen Volksgruppen, Wien 1982; Kein einzig Volk von Brüdern. Studien zum Minderheiten-Mehrheiten-Problem am Beispiel Kärnten, Wien 1982; Arnold Suppan, Die österreichischen Volksgruppen. Tendenzen ihrer gesellschaftlichen Entwicklung im 20. Jahrhundert, Wien 1983. Zur aktuellen Diskussion über die Problematik der ethnischen/nationalen Identität siehe neuerdings: Österreichische Zeitschrift für Politikwissenschaft, 1991, 4 (Themenschwerpunkt: „Ethnische Identität und transnationaler Staat"), dort auch weiterführende Literaturhinweise. Zur Begriffsklärung siehe auch: Wolfgang Holzinger, „Volksgruppen" und „Minderheiten". Eine Begriffsklärung aus soziologischer Sicht, T. 1–2, in: Informationen der Gesellschaft für Politische Aufklärung, 1991, 28, 5 ff.; 1991, 29, 6 ff.

2 Überlegungen zur Problematik inhaltsanalytischer Schulbuchanalyse bei Walter Kissling, Beiträge zur Weiterentwicklung der Schulbuchforschung in Österreich. Grund- und integrativwiss. Diss., Wien 1989, 22 ff. („Aufmerksamkeitsrichtungen und Desiderate der Schulbuchforschung in Österreich"). Kissling spricht hier von einer „autoritären" Inhaltsanalyse, die entweder den Schulbüchern vorwirft, zu schreiben, „was ist" oder „was sein soll".

3 Ein beträchtlicher Teil der untersuchten Schulbücher widmet der Minderheitenproblematik jeweils ein spezielles Kapitel: Aigner/Bachl, Geschichte, Sozialkunde, Politische Bildung,

114 ff.; Aspernig/Atzl/Volker/Winkler, Gestaltete Welt, 3, 187 ff.; Atschko/Dusek/Rauch, Sozial- und Wirtschaftskunde (inkl. Zeitgeschichte), 5 ff., 22 ff., 114 ff.; Draxler/Elser/Eder/Zoller/Reinberg, Du in der Gemeinschaft, 83 ff.; Ebner/Glaser/Majdan, Österreich und das Weltgeschehen, 197 ff.; Eisl/Thonhauser, Wir, 153 ff.; Lernpeiss/Schmid/Trummer, Politische Bildung, T. 1, 57 ff.; Mentschl/Hieber/Lauer/Schausberger/Schindl/Waas, Rechtskundliche Beiträge zur Politischen Bildung, 50 ff.; Rettinger/Weissensteiner, Zeitbilder, 4, 106 ff.; Schausberger/Oberländer/Strotzka, Wie? Woher? Warum?, 118 ff.; Schödl/Forstner, Sozialkunde, Wirtschaftskunde, Zeitgeschichte, 5; Stecher, Staatsbürgerkunde, 5; Tscherne/Krampl, Spuren der Zeit, 134 ff; Tscherne/Scheipl/Scheithauer/Machacek, Geschichte und Sozialkunde, 4. Kl., 128 ff.

4 Schödl/Forstner, Sozialkunde, Wirtschaftskunde, Zeitgeschichte, 5.

5 Ebenda, 5.

6 Immerhin werden die Schüler/Schülerinnen in einer Frage angeregt, darüber nachzudenken, warum die Völker der Monarchie nicht mehr bereit waren, in diesem Staat zu leben: Schödl/Forstner, Sozialkunde, Wirtschaftskunde, Zeitgeschehen, 96.

7 Eine Diagnose, die schon Anfang der 80er Jahre gestellt worden ist: „Eine gut strukturierte Verknüpfung der Nationalitätenfrage mit dem Herrschaftssystem der Habsburgermonarchie ist immer noch ein Desiderat. Es fehlen die anschaulichen Angaben über Zahl und Verhältniszahl der Nationalitäten, die rechtlichen Grundlagen der Nationalitätenpolitik und ihrer praktischen Realisierung und der sozioökonomisch und soziokulturell begründeten Konflikte im zentralen und vor allem im regionalen Rahmen der österreichischen Reichshälfte, und sei es auch nur als Vorgeschichte der Länder des heutigen Österreich." Stuhlpfarrer, Die Kärntner Slowenen im österreichischen Geschichtslehrbuch, in: Zeitgeschichte, 11 (1983/1984), 395.

8 Draxler/Elser/Eder/Zoller/Reinberg, Du in der Gemeinschaft, 85.

9 Tscherne/Krampl, Spuren der Zeit, 134.

10 Schödl/Forstner, Sozial- und Wirtschaftskunde, 9.

11 Ebenda, 124.

12 Draxler/Elser/Eder/Zoller/Zoller/Reinberg, Du in der Gemeinschaft, 60.

13 Ebenda, 60.

14 Schödl/Forstner, Sozial- und Wirtschaftskunde, 107.

15 Göhring/Hasenmayer, Zeitgeschichte (3. Aufl.), 20; gleichlautend auch Göhring/Hasenmayer, Zeitgeschichte (2. Aufl.), 14.

16 Göhring/Hasenmayer, Zeitgeschichte (3. Aufl.), 20; gleichlautend auch Göhring/Hasenmayer, Zeitgeschichte (2. Aufl.), 14.

17 Tscherne/Krampl, Spuren der Zeit, 125.

18 Absenger/Knarr/Pfeifer/Speiser, Der Mensch im Wandel der Zeiten, 3, 227.

19 Maderner/Walzl/Sitte, Zeitgeschichte. Lehr- und Arbeitsbuch für die 2. Klasse Handelsschule, 52.

20 Zeiten, Völker und Kulturen, 3, 54.

21 Schimper/Hitz/Hasenmayer/Göhring/Tuschel, Geschichte miterlebt, 4. Kl., 29 f.

22 Rettinger/Weissensteiner, Zeitbilder, 4. 19.

23 Auch dies wurde – offenkundig ohne entscheidende Wirkung – schon vor mehreren Jahren bei Stuhlpfarrer, Die Kärntner Slowenen im österreichischen Geschichtslehrbuch, 395 f., moniert.

24 Atschko/Dusek/Rauch, Sozial- und Wirtschaftskunde (inkl. Zeitgeschichte) für den Polytechnischen Lehrgang, 115.

25 Aspernig/Atzl/Volker/Winkler, Gestaltete Welt, 3, 150.

26 Ebenda, 150.

27 Von den am Institut für Zeitgeschichte der Universität Wien durchgeführten Untersuchungen zum Geschichtsbewußtsein österreichischer Geschichtslehrbücher sein in Auswahl verwiesen auf: Karl Haas/Manfred Hahn/Gustav Spann/Wilfried Aichinger, Österreichische Schulbuchwirklichkeit. Zeitgeschichtliche Aspekte im österreichischen Geschichtslehrbuch, in: Die Republik, 13 (1977), 3, 16–50; Peter Malina/Gustav Spann, Faschismus in Österreich: hilflose Schulbücher, in: Emmerich Talos/Wolfgang Neugebauer (Hrsg.), „Austrofaschismus". Beiträge

über Politik, Ökonomie und Kultur 1934–1938, 4. Aufl., 1988, 247–266; Peter Malina, Geschichte ohne Vergangenheit? Überlegungen zum Umgang mit Geschichte im österreichischen Geschichtslehrbuch, in: Schulheft, 1986, 43, 121–127; Eduard Fuchs, Schule und Zeitgeschichte oder Wie kommen Jugendliche zu politischen Klischeevorstellungen, Wien – Salzburg 1986; Peter Malina/Gustav Spann, Der Nationalsozialismus im österreichischen Geschichtslehrbuch, in: Emmerich Talos/Ernst Hanisch/Wolfgang Neugebauer (Hrsg.), NS-Herrschaft in Österreich 1938–1945, Wien 1988, 577–599. Zur Darstellung österreichischer Minderheiten siehe insbesondere: Karl Stuhlpfarrer, Die Kärntner Slowenen im österreichischen Geschichtslehrbuch, in: Zeitgeschichte, 11 (1983/1984), 390–399. Ein annotierter Überblick über die Schulbuchforschung in Österreich ist neuerdings zu finden bei Kissling, Beiträge zur Weiterentwicklung der Schulbuchforschung in Österreich, 145 ff.

28 Zeiten, Völker und Kulturen, 3, 161.

29 Göhring/Hasenmayer, Zeitgeschichte (3. Aufl.), 133; gleichlautend auch Göhring/Hasenmayer, Zeitgeschichte (2. Aufl.), 152.

30 Lernpeiss/Schmid/Trummer, Politische Bildung, T. 1, 54 f.

31 Ebenda, 57.

32 So zum Beispiel das Kapitel „Alle Menschen sind gleich – sind sie's wirklich?", in: Atschko/Dusek/Rauch, Sozial- und Wirtschaftskunde (inkl. Zeitgeschichte) für den Polytechnischen Lehrgang, 5–6; „Probleme des Zusammenlebens durch Vorurteile", in: Eisl/Thonhauser, Wir, 83.

33 Maderner/Walzl/Sitte, Zeitgeschichte. Lehr- und Arbeitsbuch für die 2. Klasse der Handelsschule, 131.

34 Absenger/Pfeifer, Geschichte für Fachschulen, 2, 35.

35 Ebner/Glaser/Majdan, Österreich und das Weltgeschehen, 197.

36 Stuhlpfarrer, Die Kärntner Slowenen im österreichischen Geschichtslehrbuch, 395.

37 Ebenda, 395.

Als Grundlage für die zur Analyse herangezogenen Schulbuchtexte diente die vom Bundesministerium für Unterricht und Kunst herausgegebene Schulbuchliste für das Schuljahr 1991/92. Ausgewählt wurden 25 Schulbücher verschiedenster Schultypen und Schulstufen für die Fachbereiche Geschichte, Sozialkunde und Politische Bildung. Falls aus dem Titel nicht ersichtlich, ist in Klammer jeweils die entsprechende Einstufung (Schulstufe/Fach) angegeben. Um den Anmerkungsapparat nicht zu sehr zu belasten, wird zum Nachweis der Zitate lediglich der Kurztitel zitiert.

Albert G. Absenger/Walter Knarr/Herbert Pfeifer/Irmfried Speiser: Der Mensch im Wandel der Zeiten. Lehr- und Arbeitsbuch für Geschichte und Sozialkunde, T. 3, Wien 1990.

Albert G. Absenger/Herbert Pfeifer: Geschichte für Fachschulen, T. 2, Wien 1989.

Manfred Aigner/Irmgard Bachl: Geschichte. Sozialkunde. Politische Bildung, 8. Schulstufe, Linz 1988.

Walter Aspernig/Albert Atzl/Klaus Volker/Gerhard Winkler: Gestaltete Welt, 3: Von der Neuzeit zur Gegenwart. Ein approbiertes Arbeits- und Lehrbuch für Geschichte und Sozialkunde, Wien 1984 (4. Jg. HTL, 3. Kl. Gewerbliche, technische und kunstgewerbliche Fachschulen).

Gerhard Atschko/Peter Dusek, Helmut Rauch: Sozial- und Wirtschaftskunde (inkl. Zeitgeschichte) für den Polytechnischen Lehrgang, 4. Aufl., Wien 1984.

Josef Draxler/Manfred Elser/Josef Eder/Alois Zoller/Elisabeth Zoller/Peter Reinberg: Du in der Gemeinschaft. Politische Bildung. Wien 1990 (Berufsschulen/Politische Bildung).

Anton Ebner/Herbert Glaser/Harald Majdan: Österreich und das Weltgeschehen. Zeitgeschichte, Wien 1989 (2. Kl. Handelsschulen/Zeitgeschichte).

Franz Eisl/Fritz Thonhauser: Wir. Lehr- und Arbeitsbuch für Politische Bildung an Berufsschulen, Wien 1991.

Edgar Fuhry/Ernst Hochrainer/Christian Sitte: Geschichte. Kultur und Gesellschaft 1848 bis zur Gegenwart. Lehr- und Arbeitsbuch. Wien 1989 (3. Kl. Fachschulen für wirtschaftliche Berufe, 2. Kl. Fachschule für Mode- und Bekleidungstechnik, 3. Jg. der höheren Lehranstalt für Mode und Bekleidungstechnik).

Franz Göbhart/Erwin Chvojka: Zeitbilder. Geschichte und Sozialkunde, 8. Vom ersten Weltkrieg bis zur Gegenwart, Wien 1990 (8. Kl. AHS/Geschichte und Sozialkunde).

Walter Göhring/Herbert Hasenmayer: Zeitgeschichte. Ein approbiertes Lehr- und Arbeitsbuch für Geschichte und Sozialkunde, 2. Aufl., Wien 1979 (8. Kl AHS, 4. Jg. BHS).

Walter Göhring/Herbert Hasenmayer: Zeitgeschichte. Ein Lehr- und Arbeitsbuch für Sozialkunde, 3. Aufl., Wien 1986 (8. Kl. AHS).

Angela Lernpeiss/Franz Schmid/Uwe Trummer (Hrsg.): Politische Bildung, Teil 1, Wien 1990 (Berufsschulen).

Josef Maderner/August Walzl/Christian Sitte: Zeitgeschichte für Handelsschulen, Wien 1989 (2. Kl./Zeitgeschichte).

Josef Mentschl/Margarete Hieber/Ingrid Lauer/Norbert Schausberger/Ludwig Schindl/Elfriede Waas: Rechtskundliche Beiträge zur politischen Bildung, 4. Aufl., Wien 1986 (6.–8. Kl. AHS).

Leopold Rettinger/Friedrich Weissensteiner: Zeitbilder. Geschichte und Sozialkunde, 4. Wien 1990 (4. Kl. HS und AHS).

Norbert Schausberger/Erich Oberländer/Heinz Strotzka: Wie? Woher? Warum? 3: Geschichte und Sozialkunde. 4. Klasse, Wien 1988.

Arnold Schimper/Harald Hitz/Herbert Hasenmayer/Senta Göhring/Manfred Tuschel: Geschichte miterlebt. Ein Lehr- und Arbeitsbuch für Geschichte und Sozialkunde. 8. Schulstufe, Wien 1989 (4. Kl. AHS).

A. Schödl/R. Forstner: Sozialkunde, Wirtschaftskunde, Zeitgeschichte, SWZ, 7. Aufl, Wien 1991 (Polytechnischer Lehrgang/Sozial- und Wirtschaftskunde).

Albert Stecher: Staatsbürgerkunde. Ausgabe für Haushaltungsschulen und Hauswirtschaftsschulen. 8. Aufl., Bregenz 1989.

Hannelore Tscherne/Silvia Krampl: Spuren der Zeit, Wien 1990 (3. Kl. HS und AHS/Geschichte und Sozialkunde).

Werner Tscherne/Josef Scheipl/Erich Scheithauer/Robert Machacek: Geschichte und Sozialkunde, 4. Klasse, 2. Auflage, Wien 1990.

Werner Tscherne/Erich Scheithauer/Manfred Gartler: Weg durch die Zeiten, 4. Arbeits und Lehrbuch für Geschichte und Sozialkunde für die 8. Klasse Oberstufe, Graz 1982.

Reinhard Wagner: Sozial- und Wirtschaftskunde mit Zeitgeschichte. Für den Polytechnischen Lehrgang, 4. Aufl., Wien 1991.

Zeiten, Völker und Kulturen. Lehr- und Arbeitsbuch für Geschichte und Sozialkunde, 3, Wien 1989 (4. Kl. HS und AHS).

Robert Menasse

Der dritte Nationsbegriff

Die Aporien der nationalen Identität Österreichs

Kein Land der Welt hat sich selbst öffentlich so wenig problematisiert und grundsätzlich reflektiert wie die zweite österreichische Republik. Selbst die Nationalfeiertage, anderswo Gelegenheit für programmatische Überlegungen der politischen Repräsentanten, wurden hierzulande bald nur noch für Aufrufe zu Fit-Märschen genützt, während weitgehend sogar vergessen wurde, woran der Nationalfeiertag erinnern sollte, ganz zu schweigen von den Konnotationen, die es gerade in Österreich hat, wenn das Volk aufgerufen wird, zu marschieren. Intellektuelle und Künstler, die sich kritisch mit der politischen und gesellschaftlichen Verfaßtheit Österreichs auseinandersetzten, wurden von den Gerichten verfolgt bzw. später, im Zuge einer Liberalisierung oder zumindest einer Erosion der versteinerten Verhältnisse, dazu aufgefordert, sich psychiatrieren zu lassen. Auch die schließliche Aufdeckung von politischen Skandalen befriedigte in keiner Weise das Bedürfnis nach wenigstens einem Minimum von politischer Aufklärung, sondern übersättigte mit einem Maximum an Aufklärung über das Fehlverhalten einzelner Menschen, was zu einer Moralisierung der Republik führte, statt zu ihrer Aufklärung.

Diese Abwehr gegenüber jeder grundsätzlichen Problematisierung der Republik wird gerne mit der traumatischen Erfahrung begründet, die mit der ersten Republik gemacht wurde: daß ein Staat untergehen kann, wenn nicht an ihn geglaubt wird. An die zweite Republik mußte daher bedingungslos und ohne Widerspruch geglaubt werden. Das programmatische „Nie wieder!" der Nachkriegspolitiker bezog sich nicht so sehr auf den Faschismus als auf die Konflikte, Widersprüche, Auseinandersetzungen und die Kritik, die erfahrungsgemäß einen Staat existentiell bedrohen können. Die Gründerväter der 2. Republik, die erlebt hatten, daß Menschen wegen ihrer Gesinnung verfolgt worden sind, beschlossen, damit dies nie wieder geschehe, ein System zu errichten, in dem man sich ohne Gesinnung zusammensetzen kann.

Dieses System, die Sozialpartnerschaft, bewirkte, daß alle gesellschaftlichen und politischen Widersprüche und Gegensätze identisch wurden, wodurch österreichische Identität bald nichts anderes mehr bedeutete, als daß hier jegliche konkrete Identität obsolet geworden ist.

Erst in letzter Zeit begann sich das zu ändern. Die Erfolge österreichischer Schriftsteller, die sich konsequent mit der österreichischen Realität kritisch auseinandersetzten (wie etwa Bernhard, Turrini, Haslinger), sind ein Indiz dafür, daß ein gesellschaftliches Bedürfnis nach Selbstreflexion wuchs, die jüngste Entwicklung in Europa machte die Frage nach der Selbsteinschätzung Österreichs und seiner Stellung im nun völlig geänderten Kontext virulent, und die Perspektive, daß Österreich relativ bald wieder in einem größeren wirtschaftlichen und politischen Zusammenhang, dem der EG, aufgehen wird, verstärkte noch zusätzlich die aufkommende Diskussion um Österreichs Identität. Ich weiß nicht, wie sehr dieser allzu späte Beginn einer breiteren Auseinandersetzung über die Verfaßtheit Österreichs nicht schon a priori nostalgisch ist, das heißt, wie sehr es womöglich nur noch darum geht, daß wir, wenn wir auf Knien in Brüssel angekommen sein werden, wissen wollen, wer wir gewesen sind. Tatsache allerdings ist, daß sich bei dieser Diskussion das historische Defizit, der Mangel an Tradition einer entsprechenden Auseinandersetzung und das Fehlen eines gewachsenen reflexiven Selbstverständnisses und daraus folgender Parameter allzu deutlich bemerkbar macht. Die Beschreibung österreichischer Verhältnisse wird ja heute gleich als Parodie oder zumindest als Übertreibung empfunden, eine einfache analytische Ableitung als zweifelhafte Spekulation und das Denken in historischen Zusammenhängen, die manches an der eigentümlichen Gewordenheit der Zweiten Republik verständlich machen, gilt als Provokation, als „Aufreißen alter Wunden". Diese Wunden muß man natürlich mitdenken, um die vollständige Bedeutung des Satzes zu ermessen, daß Österreich ein Verbändestaat ist.

Die Art, wie von offizieller Seite mit österreichischer Geschichte und österreichischer Identität umgegangen wird, schlägt allerdings immer neue Wunden – Wunden in jedes denkende Gemüt. Dazu zwei Beispiele:

Bundespräsident Waldheim bat am letzten Nationalfeiertag um Entschuldigung für seinen Satz, er habe als Leutnant der deutschen Wehrmacht nur seine Pflicht getan. Ist ihm also die inhaltliche Tragweite dieses Satzes doch noch zu Bewußtsein gekommen, hat er zu einem späten, aber letztlich doch noch akzeptablen Einsehen gefunden, was er mit diesem Satz eigentlich gesagt hatte? Nein. Er entschuldigte sich, sinngemäß zusammengefaßt, vielmehr dafür, daß er nach vielen Jahren im Ausland nicht wissen habe können, daß sich mittlerweile das geistige Klima in Österreich dahingehend verändert habe, daß ein solcher Satz nicht mehr selbstverständlich von allen akzeptiert werde. Wäre ihm dies bekannt gewesen, hätte er diesen Satz gewiß nicht gesagt. Mit anderen Worten: Der Präsident, der einen Großteil seiner Amtszeit mit dem Dementieren des Vorwurfes, daß er gelogen habe, zugebracht hat, erklärt am Ende seiner Amtszeit, daß er auch in diesem Punkt liebend gerne gelogen hätte, wenn er nur besser darüber informiert gewesen wäre, was die Öffentlichkeit in dieser Frage zu hören wünscht.

Unlängst erklärte Bundeskanzler Vranitzky im Parlament, daß es eine österreichische Mitschuld an den Nazi-Verbrechen gegeben habe. Sechsundvierzig Jahre nach Kriegsende und drei Jahre nach dem sogenannten „Bedenkjahr" kommt ein solches Eingeständnis eigentümlich spät. Wer wollte Vranitzky dafür tadeln? Man könnte ja auch sagen: endlich ein Regierungschef, der ein jahrzehntelanges Versäumnis ausräumt, endlich eine offizielle Anerkennung der bekannten Tatsache, daß diese Republik auf einer Geschichtslüge begründet wurde, auf der Lüge, daß Österreich ausschließlich ein Opfer der Nazi-Aggression gewesen sei. Spät, könnte man sagen, aber endlich doch!

Nun war aber Vranitzkys Erklärung leider keine grundsätzliche Erklärung zu Österreichs Geschichte und Verfaßtheit, sondern gewissermaßen nur eine Fußnote zu einer Erklärung über die Situation in Slowenien. Und die „österreichische Mitschuld an den Nazi-Verbrechen" wurde in einer Weise zugegeben, die sie gleichzeitig einmal mehr dementierte: Es habe eine Mitschuld gegeben – aber nur von seiten einzelner, jedoch nicht von Seiten des Staates. Mit anderen Worten, es bleibt dabei: Der Staat war ein Opfer. Weil ihn keiner wollte und weil es ihn dann auch gar nicht mehr gab. Nur die Staatsbürger waren Täter. Nicht einmal die Staatsbürger, da es ja den Staat nicht mehr gab, sondern die einzelnen, die da lebten, in dieser Gegend, in diesem Raum, wo erst später, als der Nazi-Spuk vorbei war, wieder ein Staat gegründet wurde, der daher, als Staat, auch weiterhin als unschuldig zu gelten habe.

Es gäbe unzählige solche Beispiele. Aber schon diese beiden zeigen symptomatisch das Dilemma jeglicher österreichischer Selbstreflexion. Ihr Prinzip ist das Entweder-und-Oder, eine unerträglich sich spreizende Verrenkung, mit der versucht wird, von jeder Seite des Widerspruchs ein Zipfelchen zu erhaschen, von den historischen Notlügen einerseits, die man nicht wegdiskutiert haben will, und von der historischen Wahrheit andererseits, die man nicht mehr ganz wegdiskutieren kann. Es wäre ein Irrtum zu glauben, daß diese strukturelle Homologie in den Argumentationen zweier so unterschiedlicher Charaktere wie Waldheim und Vranitzky ein Zufall ist. Beide Äußerungen sind logische Konsequenz einer Systemlogik, die jede offizielle oder offiziöse Äußerung der Repräsentanten dieser Republik affiziert. Österreich *ist* das Land des Entweder-und-Oder und dies ist bereits in der Gründung der Zweiten Republik und in der Begründung ihres nationalen Selbstverständnisses angelegt. Die Geschichte von den traumatischen Erfahrungen mit der ersten Republik, aus denen die Gründer der Zweiten Republik ihre Lehren gezogen haben, ist ja nur ein Teil der Wahrheit. Tatsache ist, daß die Gründer der Zweiten Republik Repräsentanten einer Generation waren, die, in der Geschichte höchst ungewöhnlich, um nicht zu sagen: einmalig, fünf Mal ihre politische und staatliche Identität wechseln mußte: Habsburger-Monarchie – erste Republik – Ständestaat – Nationalsozialismus – Zweite Republik. Diese Erfahrung mußte natürlich zu einem tiefen Mißtrauen gegenüber jeglicher eindeutigen, positiv formulierten Identität führen, weshalb alle Gründungspostulate der Zweiten Republik wesentlich negativ abgeleitet waren: Dies soll nie wieder möglich sein und jenes nie wieder passieren können! Und überall dort, wo doch inhaltlich konkrete, positiv bestimmbare Beschlüsse getroffen wurden, wurden sie auch sofort in der Praxis in ihrem Gegenteil aufgehoben: Man behielt die nationalsozialistische Legislation weitgehend in Kraft, während man entnazifizierte. Man entnazifizierte und buhlte gleichzeitig unverhohlen um die Stimmen der ehemaligen Nazis. Man stellte die Widerstandstätigkeit österreichischer Kommunisten gegen den Nationalsozialismus gegenüber den Alliierten aus, während man gleichzeitig die Kommunistische Partei innenpolitisch ächtete, Man rekurrierte auf die Leistungen der Habsburgermonarchie als identitätsstiftenden Faktor und beschloß die Habsburgergesetze. Und so weiter.

Der Staat war gegründet, und man könnte diese Politik des Entweder-und-Oder für eine konjunkturelle politische Pragmatik halten. Aber der Staat war noch nicht souverän. Und wenn man nun untersucht, wie Österreich seine staatliche Souveränität erlangte, wird man feststellen, daß dieses Lavieren zwischen Gegensätzlichem, dieses eklektizistische Verhältnis zu historischen Widersprüchen, diese Angst vor eindeutiger politischer Selbstdefinition aus tief verwurzelter Angst vor den Wechselfällen der Geschichte zum Fundament der Unabhängigkeit Österreichs wurde und damit zur Basis jeder weiteren politischen Praxis bis heute. Die Politik des Entweder-und-Oder hatte System und wurde systembegründend.

Zur Erlangung der staatlichen Unabhängigkeit war der Nachweis unabdingbar, daß Österreich eine eigene Nation sei. Nur dadurch nämlich war der Wunsch nach staatlicher Souveränität wohlbegründet und jeder Verdacht auf weitere Anschlußgelüste an Deutschland ausgeräumt.

Meines Wissens ist die Zweite Republik Österreich der einzige Nationalstaat, der sich zu seiner Nationswerdung *entschlossen* hat, und, das ist gewiß einmalig, der einzige, dessen Nationswerdung wesentlich *außenpolitische* Gründe hatte. Innenpolitisch gab es keine zwingende Tendenz zur Selbstdefinition als eigene Nation. Noch 1956 waren bei einer Meinungsumfrage 46% der Bevölkerung der Meinung, daß Österreicher „zum deutschen Volk gehören". Man kann sich vorstellen, wieviel höher der Prozentsatz zehn Jahre vorher, noch vor Einsetzen der massiven Nations-Propaganda, gewesen ist. Am Beispiel der Nationswerdung Österreichs nach 45 lassen sich wie in einem Brennspiegel die ungelösten Widersprüche Österreichs studieren, besser gesagt, wie gerade das Nicht-Lösen von Widersprüchen, das Oszillieren zwischen den Widersprüchen und das Vermeiden jeder eindeutigen Position zur genuinen „österreichischen Lösung" wurde.

Es gab und gibt bekanntlich zwei „klassische" Nationsbegriffe: den aus der deutschen romantischen Tradition, der Nation wesentlich als Sprach- und Kulturgemeinschaft versteht, und den im Sinne der französischen revolutionären Tradition, derzufolge eine Nation nichts anderes ist als ein Staat, der vom kollektiven Wunsch gebildet wird, jedem einzelnen die bürgerlichen Freiheiten und Rechte zu garantieren.

Außenpolitisch verbot sich der deutsche Nationsbegriff natürlich von selbst. Man setzte also zunächst massiv auf den französischen Nationsbegriff und propagierte die Idee einer österreichischen Nation, die wesentlich durch den kollektiven Willen der Bevölkerung zu Freiheit und Unabhängigkeit gebildet werde. Zugleich rekurrierte man, in Hinblick auf die Bundesrepublik Deutschland, von der man sich propagandistisch doch klarer unterscheiden wollte, auch wieder auf den deutschen Nations-Begriff: Es wurden kulturelle Besonderheiten Österreichs im Unterschied zu Deutschland geltend gemacht, ein Argument, das innenpolitisch als „Mentalitätsunterschiede" wiederkehrte und durch die Anti-„Piefke"-Ressentiments, die es in Österreich nach 45 gab, verstärkt wurde.

Man spielte mit diesen Anti-„Piefke"-Ressentiments und propagierte die Idee einer österreichischen Nation, deren kulturelle Eigenart sich historisch aus dem Verschmelzen mannigfachster Einflüsse aus den ehemaligen österreichischen Kronländern entwickelt habe, und bestand gleichzeitig gegenüber den nun in Österreich lebenden Minderheiten auf der deutschen Sprachgemeinschaft als Basis für nationale Identität. Man gestand Sprache und Geschichte als konstitutiv für nationales Selbstgefühl zu und mußte das forcierte nationale Selbstgefühl ununterbrochen von sprachlichen Fallen und historischen Verbindlichkeiten reinigen: Die Propagierung der „österreichischen Nation" vermied tunlichst das Adjektiv „national", um nicht irrtümlich in den Anruch großdeutscher Propaganda zu kommen (es ist überaus lehrreich, die diesbezüglichen sprachlichen Windungen und Wendungen im „Neuen Österreich", der damaligen Regierungszeitung, nachzulesen), und die Verweise auf die große österreichische Geschichte umgingen konsequent jegliche Auseinandersetzung mit den personellen und strukturellen Kontinuitäten aus der NS-Zeit.

Heute, post festum, kann man sagen: Die Idee hat funktioniert. Österreich hat seine Souveränität erhalten. Daß Österreich eine Nation sei, steht heute innenpolitisch noch weniger in Frage als außenpolitisch. Der Frage, ob Österreich eine eigene Nation sei, stimmen laut Meinungsforschern mittlerweile fast 90% der Österreicher zu – womit die Österreicher sogar die Franzosen übertreffen, für die „nation" ja bekanntlich ein Synonym für ihren Staatsnamen ist. Zugleich zeigen die Meinungsumfragen, daß niemand in Österreich verbindlich zu sagen wüßte, was eine Nation eigentlich sei beziehungsweise worin die nationalen Eigenheiten Österreichs bestünden. Das ist, wenn wir die Genese des österreichischen Nationalgefühls untersuchen, nicht verwunderlich: Es besteht ja tatsächlich aus nichts Bestimmten, besser gesagt, es besteht aus der wechselseitigen Aufhebung der klassischen Nationsbestimmungen. Es besteht aus Entweder-und-Oder. Wir sind eine deutsche Sprachgemeinschaft, die sich von der deutschen Sprachgemeinschaft distanziert. Wenn wir im Ausland deutsch sprechen, weisen wir darauf hin, daß wir Österreicher sind, und erwarten, daß wir daraufhin besser behandelt werden, als die Deutschen. Wir definieren uns über unseren Willen zu bürgerlichen Freiheitsrechten, die wir aber selbst nicht allen zugestehen wollen. Wir sind daher solidarisch mit allen, die sie haben, wir sind also zum Beispiel solidarisch mit Weiß-Afrika und bieten Grenzschutz auf gegen Rumänen. Wir definieren uns über unsere Kultur und unsere Geschichte, und unsere Kultur besteht aus einem selektiven Umgang mit Geschichte, und Geschichte ist für uns die herzeigbare geerbte Kultur. Wir sind neutral, aber wir haben unsere Verpflichtungen, weshalb wir über Nacht Gesetze ändern, um die Durchfuhr von Kriegsmaterialen durch unser Land zu ermöglichen, ohne unsere Neutralität zu verletzen. Wir sind ganz was Eigenes, aber wir rutschen auf Knien nach Brüssel, um wieder einmal um unsere Selbstaufgabe zu bitten. Wir sitzen vor dem Fernsehgerät und sehen im „Club 2" eine Diskussion, in der Jörg Haider unwidersprochen den Nations-Begriff so lange in Richtung „Sprach- und Kulturgemeinschaft" uminterpretiert, bis er schließlich sogar einen sich natürlich windenden Simon Wiesenthal dazu bringt „zuzugeben", daß er der „deutschen Nation" angehöre, und wir wissen, hier sind wir zu Hause. Wir halten Jörg Haider wegen seiner Aussagen zur österreichischen Nation und zum Nationalsozialismus als Landeshauptmann von Kärnten untragbar, aber wir halten ihn als Landeshauptmannstellvertreter für tragbar. Kurz gesagt, Österreich ist die Verwirklichung der Hegelschen Definition von Identität, derzufolge Identität nichts anderes sei als die Identität mit der

Nicht-Identität. Mit anderen Worten: Wir sind ehrlich davon überzeugt, nicht zu lügen, solange wenigstens das Gegenteil wahr ist.

Man kann mit Fug und Recht sagen, daß im Spannungsfeld der außenpolitischen Notwendigkeit, Österreich zur Nation zu erklären, und der innenpolitischen Unsicherheit, zu erklären, worin die nationale Identität Österreichs bestehe, Österreich zu einer Nation neuen Typs wurde: Österreich hat durch die Amalgamierung von Elementen der beiden „klassischen" Nations-Begriffe einen dritten Nations-Begriff herausgebildet, der letztendlich zu einer sehr diffusen, aber doch auch sehr deutlichen eigenen österreichischen Identität beitrug. Daß diese sich selbst nicht eindeutig definieren kann, entspricht ihrem Wesen, ist logische Konsequenz ihrer Genese.

In ihr war immer schon beides angelegt: die großzügige Asylantenpolitik 1956 und 1968, und der Rassismus und Fremdenhaß, den wir heute erleben. Die weltoffene Außenpolitik Kreiskys und ihre innenpolitische Konsequenz, die sich von der Welt abschottende Präsidentschaft Waldheims. Und die Synthese von allem in der Außenpolitik Mocks: der eine umfassende Intensivierung der Zusammenarbeit mit den osteuropäischen Ländern zurückweist, mit der Begründung, daß unsere eindeutige Präferenz die EG sei – und der Österreich der EG andient, mit der Begründung, mit uns hätte die EG einen besseren Zugang zu den osteuropäischen Ländern.

Es ist eine eigentümliche Ironie der Geschichte, daß die so spät begonnene, aber letztlich doch gesellschaftspolitisch real wirksame Nationswerdung Österreichs zu einer Identität führte, die sich in der wechselseitigen Aufhebung ihrer Bestimmungen, und letztlich in der Aufhebung ihrer selbst erfüllt – die also ihr Heil erst recht in einem Anschluß an einen größeren Zusammenhang, im Aufgehen in der EG sieht. Aber vielleicht ist Österreich so etwas wie ein trojanisches Pferd vor den Toren der EG. Die Konterbande, die es mit sich führt, heißt: „Neutralitätsvorbehalt". Und „Neutralitätsvorbehalt" heißt, wie wir aus der österreichischen Geschichte wissen: wir wollen mitreiten, im Zweifelsfalle aber wollen wir nicht dabei gewesen sein.

Ich weiß nicht, ob das noch einmal klappen wird. Ich weiß auch nicht, ob es eine größere Katastrophe wäre, wenn Österreich der EG beitritt oder wenn Österreich draußen bleibt. Aber eines weiß ich ganz gewiß: Bei der Wahl zwischen Katastrophen entscheiden wir uns für jene, die uns nachträgliche Verklärung und Idealisierung ermöglicht. *Das* haben wir aus der Geschichte gelernt.

Erich Fröschl

Das Alte am neuen Konservativismus

Der politische Konservativismus war eine bedeutende geistige und politische Strömung der beiden letzten Jahrhunderte. Er ist uns dabei in verschiedenen Varianten entgegengetreten. Wir haben ihn als wirtschaftsliberalen Konservativismus kennengelernt, aber auch als einen Konservativismus, der – von der christlichen Soziallehre beeinflußt – die soziale Komponente stärker in den Vordergrund gerückt hat, und wir haben ihn schließlich, zu Beginn dieses Jahrhunderts, auch in einer radikalautoritären Variante fundamentalistischer Art kennengelernt.

Der politische Konservativismus hat das politische Spektrum der modernen demokratischen Industriegesellschaften zusammen mit Liberalismus und Sozialdemokratie entscheidend mitgeprägt. Er hat auch immer wieder eine Herausforderung geliefert für die anderen geistigen und politischen Strömungen in der Konkurrenz der Ideen um die Gestaltung der Gesellschaft. Auch dies eine unbestrittene Aufgabe, da wir doch alle bis zu einem gewissen Grad Gefangene unserer jeweils eigenen Ideensysteme sind und uns die Herausforderung durch andere Ideen dazu zwingt, auch über die Glaubwürdigkeit der eigenen Ideen jeweils aufs neue nachzudenken.

Der Konservativismus spielt schließlich eine nicht unbedeutende Rolle innerhalb der industriellen Gesellschaft, die von einer sehr starken Dynamik, starkem sozialen Wandel und heftigen Veränderungsschüben geprägt ist und in der nicht von vornherein jede Änderung per se schon vernünftig und gut ist. Es gibt innerhalb dieses Veränderungsprozesses durchaus Dinge, deren Bewahrung über den Tag hinaus wünschenswert und notwendig ist. Hier hat der Konservativismus die Aufgabe übernommen, eine mahnende Rolle zu spielen.

Man könnte also grob formuliert folgendes sagen: Der *Liberalismus* stellt innerhalb der industriellen Gesellschaft die dynamisch entfesselnde Kraft dar, die jedoch ohne Rücksicht auf soziale Verluste agiert und den Sieger privilegiert. Der *Konservativismus* spielt innerhalb dieses Änderungsprozesses eine die traditionellen Werte betonende Rolle, wenn auch z. T. mit dem Ziel des Bewahrens von Vorteilen für gesellschaftliche Schichten, die schon eine dominante und privilegierte Position in der Gesellschaft haben. Die *Sozialdemokratie* steht in der Frage der industriellen Dynamik dem Liberalismus wesentlich näher. Sie liegt mit dem Konservativismus dort im Konflikt, wo dieser Veränderungen ablehnt, um historisch dominanten gesellschaftlichen Schichten weiterhin überproportionalen Einfluß im Macht- und Verteilungsprozeß der Gesellschaft zu sichern. Sie betont gegenüber beiden Richtungen in der politischen Diskussion die demokratische und egalitäre Komponente, mit dem Ziel, ihre Grundwertekombination „Freiheit & Gleichheit & Gerechtigkeit & Solidarität & Demokratie" für möglichst viele Menschen auch im Alltag Wirklichkeit werden zu lassen.

In jüngster Zeit spielte der Konservativismus auch eine Rolle bei der Diskussion über das jeweils optimale Mischungsverhältnis zwischen der Anarchie des sich selbst überlassenen Marktes und den notwendigen gesellschaftlichen Regulationen durch staatliche Rahmenbedingungen und Institutionen. Die Sozialdemokratie tendiert hier seit ihrer Frühzeit, nachdem die Debatte zwischen Selbsthilflern und Staatshilflern deutlich zugunsten der Staatshilfler entschieden war, zum deutlichen Einsatz staatlicher Instrumentarien im Rahmen des marktwirtschaftlichen Wirtschaftsprozesses mit dem Ziel des sozialen Ausgleichs und der Chancengleichheit für alle Mitglieder der Gesellschaft. Der Konservativismus hält ideologisch zwar die Fahne der freien Marktwirtschaft hoch, scheut sich aber in der Praxis ebenfalls nicht, den Staat als Umverteilungsinstrument vor allem nach oben zu nützen.

Es ist allerdings in dieser Frage „Markt & Staat" zwischen der christdemokratischen Variante des Konservativismus und sozialdemokratischen wirtschaftspolitischen Ansätzen in den letzten Jahrzehnten eine gewisse Konvergenz festzustellen. Die Christdemokraten haben stärker als früher erkannt, daß der Wirtschaftsprozeß von entsprechenden sozialpolitischen Begleitmaßnahmen gestützt werden muß, um gesellschaftliche und ökonomische Anarchie zu verhindern. Die Sozialdemokratie stellt, stärker als früher, positive Auswirkungen marktwirtschaftlicher Prozesse auf den notwendigen industriellen Wandlungsprozeß in Rechnung.

In den späten 70er Jahren kam es zu einem *Pendelschwung* von keynesianischen Wirtschaftsauffassungen, in denen der Staatsinterventionismus als Korrektur des Marktversagens seinen fixen Platz hatte und die seit der Nachkriegszeit tonangebend waren, zu *neokonservativen Wirtschaftsauffassungen*, die die Markt- und Angebotsseite dogmatisch in den Vordergrund rückten. Die Verheißung von neuer Dynamik der Gesellschaft, Job-creation und allgemeiner Wohlstandsmehrung durch Steuersenkungen und Zurückdrängung des staatlichen Einflusses auf die Wirtschaft war der Kern dieser neokonservativen Wirtschaftsideologie, die zu Beginn der 80er Jahre – insbesondere in den USA und England – auch mit großer politischer Konsequenz in die Praxis umgesetzt wurde.

Ronald Reagan beispielsweise versprach die „shining city on the hill", Metapher für eine neokonservative gesellschaftliche und wirtschaftliche Revolution, an deren Ende sich alle Amerikanerinnen und Amerikaner in einem wesentlich besseren ökonomischen und gesellschaftlichen Zustand befinden würden als vorher. Dies war – speziell für die Mittelklasse – eine attraktive Aufstiegsutopie.

Sie war aber auch mit einem bestimmten Gesellschaftsbild verbunden, in dem die Konkurrenzphilosophie des Ellbogenkapitalismus verabsolutiert wurde und ein sozialdarwinistisches Menschenbild in den Vordergrund trat. Anstelle der wohlfahrtsstaatlichen Philosophie der Existenzsicherung und Riskenminderung für den einzelnen tritt das Recht des Stärkeren. Dementsprechend wird von Neokonservativen den Verlierern in diesem sozialen Kampf die Schuld für ihr individuelles Versagen zugeschoben, und sie werden auch sehr schnell zu Schmarotzern an der Gesellschaft gestempelt, wenn sie das soziale Netz der Gesellschaft in Anspruch nehmen wollen, bzw. es wird dieses Netz auch zielstrebig zerschnitten.

Diese neokonservative Wirtschafts- und Gesellschaftsphilosophie war ein beherrschendes Paradigma der 80er Jahre in der westlichen industriellen Welt. Besonders ausgeprägt in den USA sowie in Großbritannien, in abgeschwächter Form auch in einigen kontinentaleuropäischen Ländern, die in dieser Zeit konservativ regiert wurden.

Exemplarisch durchexerziert wurde das Modell in den USA und Großbritannien, wo es mehrmals auch von der Bevölkerung bei Wahlen mit Mehrheiten ausgestattet wurde. Kontinentaleuropa unterschied sich tendenziell dadurch, daß sich diese Ideen mit einer gewissen Verspätung und auch in Modifikationen als Paradigma der Politik ausbreiteten. Die wohlfahrtsstaatliche Tradition und ihre institutionelle Verankerung sind in Kontinentaleuropa wesentlich stärker ausgeprägt als etwa in Großbritannien und vor allem in den USA. Sie erwies sich daher gegenüber den Attacken des Neokonservativismus als wesentlich stabiler.

Es ist nun – zu Beginn der 90er Jahre – nach zehn Jahren Neokonservativismus legitim, nach den konkreten Resultaten dieser Wirtschafts- und Gesellschafts„revolution" zu fragen. Betrachtet man die Situation der Gesellschaften in den neokonservativen Musterländern zu Beginn der 90er Jahre, so sieht man, daß *dieser Rückfall in den Fundamentalismus der wirtschaftsliberalen Frühphase des Konservativismus die entscheidende Schwäche des neuen Konservativismus* offenbart hat. Sie liegt im ökonomischen Bereich. Es ist der *alte Irrglaube* an die Selbstregulierungskräfte des Marktes und die Annahme, daß der Mensch prinzipiell und ausschließlich als Homo economicus konstruiert ist und auch dementsprechend reagiert, dem der neue Konservativismus wieder verfallen ist.

Die USA befinden sich in einer tiefen Rezession. Sie sind eine kaputte und gespaltene Gesellschaft mit einer hohen und weiter steigenden Armutsrate, steigendem Drogenmißbrauch und zunehmender Kriminalität sowie einer Devastierung der öffentlichen Einrichtungen (Kindergärten, Schulen, Hochschulen, Spitäler), die sich in einer Weise dramatisch verschärft hat, daß sie selbst die Konkurrenzfähigkeit der USA am Weltmarkt immer mehr gefährdet. Dazu kam eine Welle der Zentralisation und Konzentration im Finanz- und Industriesektor, die zur Herausbildung neuer Oligopole und Monopole geführt hat. Dieser Prozeß war begleitet von hysterischer Spekulation und einer Welle von Firmenzusammenbrüchen. Dieser wirtschaftliche Niedergang hatte auch seine Auswirkungen auf beträchtliche Teile der Mittelschichten, die zu Beginn begeisterte Anhänger dieser neokonservativen Gesellschaftsauffassung waren und sich – angesichts der Pleite und Rezession – nun in zunehmendem Maße von ihr abwenden. Das zeigen nicht zuletzt eine Reihe von Nachwahlergebnissen in den USA und in Großbritannien. Anstelle der von Reagan versprochenen Illusion von der „shining city on the hill" sind die „burning slums" Realität geworden.

Die Entwicklung in Großbritannien ist ähnlich verlaufen. Dieses ist heute ein zutiefst gespaltenes Land mit immer wieder aufflackernden heftigen sozialen Konflikten. Viele der von finanziellen Abenteurern in den 70er und 80er Jahre ins Leben gerufenen Prestigeprojekte einer vielgepriesenen neuen industriellen Gründerzeit, wie beispielsweise die Londoner Docklands, werden heutzutage als Spekulationsruinen wieder fluchtartig verlassen.

Positiv ist festzuhalten, daß am europäischen Festland diese neokonservativen Wirtschafts- und Gesellschaftsphilosophien nicht im vollen Maße zum Tragen kamen. Auch die christdemokratischen Parteien haben in Kontinentaleuropa eine moderatere Politik eingeschlagen, innerhalb des Europäischen Parlaments dominiert eine große Koalition aus Sozialdemokraten und Christdemokraten, und wir haben uns in weiten Teilen Europas bisher zumindest die radikalen Experimente der Neokonservativen ersparen können. Auch in Österreich war dies der Fall, wenngleich auch hier die öffentliche Debatte in den 80er Jahren von Elementen der neokonservativen Ideologie mitgeprägt wurde. In Österreich vertritt derzeit weniger die christdemokratische Partei als vielmehr die rechtspopulistische Freiheitliche Partei wesentliche Kernelemente der neokonservativen Wirtschafts- und Gesellschaftsphilosophie. Sie ist durch die Dominanz von Versatzstücken der wirtschaftsliberalen Ideologie des 19. Jahrhunderts und eines sozialdarwinistischen Geschichts- und Menschenbildes in ihrer Programmatik auch wesentlich besser dafür geeignet als die auch von katholischer Soziallehre und korporatistischen Überlegungen mitgeprägte österreichische Christdemokratie.

Was haben diese Überlegungen nun im Kontext dieser Tagung über die weitere Entwicklung Mittel- und Osteuropas zu tun? Was kann für die zukünftige wirtschaftliche und gesellschaftliche Entwicklung in diesem anderen Teil Europas aus den Experimenten der neokonservativen Art der 80er Jahre gelernt werden?

Wir sehen, daß gerade in manchen Ländern Mittel- und Osteuropas nun ein Wettlauf eingesetzt hat, neokonservative Sanierungsmodelle, wie sie vom Währungsfonds und von der Weltbank propagiert wurden, an Radikalität noch zu überholen. Dies gilt vor allem für die Länder Polen und ČSFR. Wie die bisherige Entwicklung zeigt, hat dieser radikale Kurswechsel nicht die gewünschten Erfolge gezeitigt. Im Gegenteil, die durch die kommunistische Planwirtschaft ohnedies stark demolierten Systeme wurden noch weiter zerrüttet. In Ländern, in denen moderater vorgegangen wird – wie beispielsweise in Ungarn –, ist gleichzeitig ein ruhigerer Umwandlungsprozeß zu beobachten.

Nun ist der rasche und radikale wirtschaftsprogrammatische Paradigmenwechsel in Osteuropa durchaus verständlich. Es herrscht große Orientierungslosigkeit. Es gibt keine Rezepte und keine Analysen der Situation. Es gibt auch keine vergleichbaren historischen Beispiele, an denen man sich orientieren könnte. Es ist eine nachrevolutionäre Situation, in ihrem qualitativen Sprung durchaus vergleichbar mit den großen Zeitenwenden 1789, 1848 und 1918. Es ist politisch auch ein zutiefst positiver und erfreulicher Prozeß der Befreiung von kommunistischen Diktaturen durch demokratische Revolutionen, die vor allem ein Werk der Bevölkerungen in den Ländern Mittel- und Osteuropas selbst waren.

In dem nun bestehenden Hunger nach neuen Ideen, Theorien und Konzepten, die der kommunistischen Doktrin diametral gegenüberstehen, ist die Hinwendung zu neokonservativen Vorstellungen verständlich. Es werden sehr große Hoffnungen mit Privatisierung, Entfesselung marktwirtschaftlicher Kräfte sowie einer marktwirtschaftlichen Akkumulation verknüpft. Sie ist im hohen Maße auch notwendig. Es erhebt sich nur die Frage, ob es sinnvoll ist, sich statt des alten staatsmonopolistischen Fundamentalismus, der gerade in einem bewunderungswürdigen Freiheitskampf abgeschüttelt wurde, einen neuen ökonomistischen Fundamentalismus der Wirtschaftsanarchie einzuhandeln.

Die wirtschaftlichen und sozialen Verhältnisse in den Ländern Mittel- und Osteuropas sind äußerst schlecht. Die Rezession grassiert, die Arbeitslosigkeit steigt, die Inflation nimmt zu, das soziale Netz wird immer brüchiger. Diese Hoffnungslosigkeit der Situation ist natürlich eine gute Voraussetzung für die gläubige Orientierung an der Wundertätigkeit neuer Ideologien. Es erhebt sich jedoch die Frage, ob die Sanierung dieser Situation durch einen kostspieligen neokonservativen Umweg nicht doch vermeidbar ist. Ob die Orientierung an Gesellschaftsmodellen, die anderswo bereits wieder Auslaufmodelle geworden sind, noch sinnvoll ist.

In diesem Zusammenhang ist abschließend noch die konkrete Frage zu stellen, inwieweit österreichische Erfahrungen der unmittelbaren Nachkriegszeit und der wirtschaftlichen Rekonstruktionsperiode bis 1960 doch auch als Modellbeispiele dafür herangezogen werden könnten, wie aus einer geschickten Kombination von marktwirtschaftlicher Entwicklung, staatlicher Intervention und internationaler Hilfe von außen ein relativ rascher und auch erfolgreicher Rekonstruktionsprozeß in Gang gesetzt werden kann. Es ist eben nicht alles von vornherein gut, was privat ist, und es ist nicht alles von vornherein schlecht, was staatlich organisiert wird. Es wird z. B. auch gerne vergessen, daß Osterreich und die BRD in der Phase ihrer Rekonstruktion von 1945 bis 1955 erst schrittweise zu frei konvertierbaren Währungen übergegangen sind und daß für die Rekonstruktionsphase in beiden Ländern staatliche Regelungen und soziale Absicherung des gesellschaftlichen Wandels eine große Rolle spielten.

Ich sehe hier auch eine Aufgabe der Zusammenarbeit sozialdemokratischer und christdemokratischer Politik in österreich. Sie sollten, gestützt auf diese österreichischen Erfahrungen, gemeinsam diese noch stärker als bisher auch in Mittel- und Osteuropa propagieren, ausgehend von der Grundüberlegung, daß die Entfaltung der Marktkräfte von einer gleichzeitigen sozialen Absicherung des notwendigen Wandels begleitet werden muß, um explosive gesellschaftliche Spannungen zu verhindern und damit auch ein Anwachsen rechtspopulistischer, nationalistischer und rassistischer Strömungen in Mittel- und Osteuropa zu verhindern. Eine Aufgabe, die sich übrigens auch in „Westeuropa" stellt.

Ich meine, daß das Einschlagen dieses Weges in mehrerer Hinsicht für alle Beteiligten in Mittel- und Osteuropa lukrativer wäre. Es sind weniger soziale Unruhen und Spannungen zu erwarten, weniger Radikalismus und Nationalismus, weniger Wanderungsbewegungen. Es ist andererseits mit einem rascheren ökonomischen Wachstum zu rechnen, das die Länder Mittel- und Osteuropas auch rascher zu gleichwertigen ökonomischen Partnern macht. Letztlich ist dieser Weg ein besserer Weg der Modernisierung, der mehr Lebensqualität in Freiheit und Demokratie für die einzelnen Menschen in diesen Ländern verspricht.

Literatur

A. Crawford: Thunder on the Right, New York 1980.
M. Harrington: The Other America. Poverty in the United States, Harmondsworth 1983.
R. Lekachman: Die Reichen reicher machen – Reagonomics oder wie Ronald Reagan den Sozialstaat abbaut, Reinbek 1982.
M. Gordon/Th. E. Weißkopf: Beyond the Waste Land. A Democratic Alternative to Economic Decline, New York 1983.
C. M. Aho/M. Levinson: The Economy After Reagan, in: Foreign Affairs, vol. 67, no. 2, 1988, p. 10 ff.
H. Schmidt: Wer zahlt Reagans Rechnung?, in: Die Zeit, Nr. 47, 1988, S. 27 ff.
J. K. Galbraith: The Rush to Capitalism, in: International Herald Tribune, 23. 11. 1988, p. 4.
K. Philips: The Confident Smile Has Left Bush's Lips, in: International Herald Tribune, 12. 10. 1990, p. 4.
J. Eastwell: Whatever Happened to Britain. The Economics of Decline, London 1982.
L. Fagin/M. Little: The Forsaken Families. A Timely and Disturbing Report on the Effects of Unemployment in Family Life in Britain, Harmondsworth 1984.
Th. Noetzel: Die Revolution der Konservativen. England in der Ära Thatcher, Hamburg 1987.
A. Fuchs: Geistige Strömungen in Österreich 1867–1918, Wien 1978.
F. L. Carsten: Faschismus in Österreich, München 1988.
W. Abendroth/K. Lenk: Einführung in die politische Wissenschaft, Bern – München 1968.
C. E. Schorske: Fin-de-Siècle Vienna, Politics and Culture. New York 1980.
F. Butschek: Die österreichische Wirtschaft im 20. Jahrhundert, Wien 1985.
B. Kreisky (Hrsg.): Zwanzig Millionen suchen Arbeit. Ein Programm für Vollbeschäftigung in den 90er Jahren, Wien 1989.
K. M. Gauss: Die Vernichtung Mitteleuropas, Salzburg 1991.
W. Mantl (Hrsg.): Neue Architektur Europas. Reflexion in einer bedrohten Welt, Graz 1991.
E. J. Hobsbawm: Nationen und Nationalismus. Mythos und Realität seit 1780, Frankfurt – New York 1990.
K. Duffek/E. Fröschl (Hrsg.): Die demokratischen Revolutionen in Mittel- und Osteuropa, Wien 1991.
J. K. Calbraith: The Machine Need Not Run Full, in: International Herald Tribune, 23. 11. 1989, p. 4.
V. Komarek: Economic Shock Theory Endangers the Patients, in: International Herald Tribune, 8. 1. 1992, p. 4.
C. Offe: Das Dilemma der Gleichzeitigkeit. Demokratisierung und Marktwirtschaft in Osteuropa, in: Merkur, 45. Jg., H. 4, 1991, S. 279 ff.
L. Volkow: Curing the Madhouse Effect. The UdSSR on the Way to a Social Market Economy, in: EWF – UdSSR, Moskau 1990.

Klaus Unterberger

Moderner Konservatismus und Systemintegration – Positionen und Perspektiven der aktuellen Konservatismus-Debatte

Keine politische Etikettierung der 80er Jahre hat so viele Assoziationen, Stellungnahmen und Interpretationen hervorgerufen wie der in variantenreicher Darstellung präsentierte „Neokonservatismus". Standen die 70er Jahre noch unter dem deutlichen Einfluß einer wohlfahrtsstaatlichen Entwicklung, die im politischen Szenario Westeuropas maßgeblich durch Regierungsmehrheiten sozialdemokratischer Parteien gestützt wurde, schien sich Anfang bis Mitte der 80er Jahre das politische Kräfteverhältnis umzukehren. In der Diktion der konservativen Opposition, die sich nicht nur auf die Mandatsverteilung in den Parlamenten beschränkte, waren die „Versäumnisse und Defizite" sozialstaatlicher Entwicklung offensichtlich geworden, die Zielsetzung weitgehender Unabhängigkeit von den Krisenzyklen marktwirtschaftlicher ökonomischer Dominanz ebenso zerbrochen wie ein allgemeiner „Emanzipationsoptimismus", der noch ein Jahrzehnt zuvor einem weitgehenden Demokratisierungsprozeß „aller Lebensbereiche" zu einem attraktiven Symbol sozialdemokratischer Reformpolitik verholfen hatte. Eine deutliche Zunahme traditionell konservativer Werte im politischen Diskurs stand am Anfang einer Entwicklung, die sehr rasch das Ausmaß eines in der politikwissenschaftlichen Betrachtung formulierten „Paradigmenwechsels" annahm.

Die „konservative Revolution" stützte sich demnach sehr stark auf den einsetzenden Wertewandel, der in Folge zu einem der wesentlichsten Indikatoren gesellschaftlicher Veränderungen wurde. Die Erkenntnis, daß der – die politische Tagesordnung bestimmende – (Zeit-)Geist der 80er Jahre nunmehr „rechts" stand, fand sehr rasch ein geeignetes Schlagwort: „Neokonservatismus" schien auf den Punkt zu bringen, was als umfassende politische Tendenz die gesamtgesellschaftliche Entwicklung zu prägen imstande war.

„Thatcherism" und „Reaganomics" kennzeichnen dabei den pragmatischen Charakter einer „konservativen Revolution", die sich auf die gesellschaftlichen und sozialen Defizite stützt, die – nach konservativer Lesart – von staatsinterventionistischen Maßnahmen verursacht eine wachstumsorientierte Wirtschaftsplanung verhindert haben. Vor allem die wirtschafts- und sozialpolitischen Prinzipien des – die wohlfahrtsstaatliche Entwicklung bestimmenden – keynesianischen Grundkonsenses, also einer antizyklischen Stabilisierungspolitik, einer staatlichen Organisation und rechtlichen Absicherung des Sozialgefüges sowie der Einbindung der Gewerkschaften in die gesamtwirtschaftliche Verantwortung, gelten der konservativen Programmatik folgend als unzulängliche Instrumentarien zur Bewältigung der im Zuge der Wachstumskrise der westlichen

Industrienationen entstandenen ökonomischen und sozialen Folgeprobleme. Breite gesellschaftliche Akzeptanz findet die Krisenregulierungspolitik unter konservativem Vorzeichen aufgrund politisch-restriktiver Entwicklungen innerhalb der sozialstaatlich orientierten Gesellschaften. Bürokratisierung sowie eine Reihe den persönlichen Freiraum der Staatsbürger einschränkende Maßnahmen, die die rechtlich-administrative Umsetzung sozialstaatlicher Zielvorstellungen gewährleisten sollen, unterstützen die zentrale konservative Forderung, die einen Rückzug des Staates aus der Wirtschaft sowie einen Ausbau des privatwirtschaftlichen Sektors vorsieht.

Die massive Betonung neoliberaler Elemente in der Wirtschaftspolitik beschreibt jedoch nur unzureichend den Bedeutungsumfang der konservativen Wende, deren wesentliche Bestandteile von traditionellen Merkmalen konservativen Politikverständnisses getragen sind. Neu an diesem mit der „Wende" assoziierten „Neo"konservatismus wäre dabei ausschließlich eine zwar markante aber – wie die Entwicklung der späten 80er Jahre zeigt – vorübergehende Verschiebung im politischen Machtgefüge zugunsten der bürgerlich-konservativen Parteien.

Doch bereits wenige Jahre nach der euphorisch proklamierten „konservativen Revolution", die eine beachtliche Aufbruchsstimmung vermitteln konnte, erklärt eine Reihe ihrer ursprünglichen Wortführer das vorläufige Scheitern einer umfassenden Neuorientierung in der Politik. Eine nur bruchstückhafte Verwirklichung der angestrebten gesellschaftspolitischen Veränderungen – gemessen an der Regierungstätigkeit der konservativen Parteien – hinterläßt bereits Mitte der 80er Jahre eine nur mäßig erfolgreiche Bilanz der „konservativen Offensive". Der „Eintritt in ein neues Zeitalter" fand nicht statt.

Der leitbildhafte Charakter des „Neokonservatismus" in Gestalt der proklamierten „Wende" reduzierte sich somit auf einen sehr unterschiedlich rezipierten gesellschaftlichen Wandel, dem angesichts der realen politischen Durchsetzungsfähigkeit kaum weltanschauliche Perspektiven zugeordnet werden konnten. Doch während selbst konservative politische Beobachter bereits das Scheitern der Politik der Wende zum Gegenstand ihrer Analysen wählten und – zumeist parteigebundene – Kritiker erleichtert das Ende des „konservativen Roll back" festhielten, standen längst neue Umbrüche und Neuorientierungen auf der Tagesordnung der gesellschaftspolitischen Veränderungen. Die „postindustrielle Gesellschaft", das „Zeitalter des Posthistoire" und schließlich der Begriff der „Postmoderne" lieferten in zunehmenden Ausmaß die Stichwörter für eine umfassende gesellschaftspolitische Debatte, die nahtlos an jenen aktuellen Zeitdiagnosen ansetzten, die auch konservative Theoretiker zum Anlaß ihrer Krisenbefunde nahmen.

Denn die im Zuge des „Wertewandels" und des „Paradigmenwechsels" stattgefundenen Veränderungen erreichen in ihrem Bedeutungsumfang weit mehr als die Entscheidung über die Frage, wer die bessere „konservative" Politik (also eine Politik der Wende im Sinne eines gesellschafts- und wirtschaftspolitischen Adaptions- und Regulierungsprozesses) in der Alltagspraxis durchsetzt: die konservativen Parteien, die mit ihrem traditionell konservativen „Erneuerungsanspruch" an die Grenzen der Systemregulierung stoßen, oder die an die Modifikationen innerhalb eines entwickelten kapitalistischen Systems – durch Jahre praktizierter Regierungstätigkeit an diese Adaptionsprozesse gewöhnten – sozialdemokratischen Parteien. Beide in ihren (Wahl-)Erfolgen unterschiedlichen Akteure behandeln die Politik der Wende als – dringend erforderliche – Neu-Justierung, die es nachzuvollziehen gilt. Nur teilweise betroffen ist davon die Neu-Orientierung , die sich aufgrund der veränderten gesellschaftlichen Bedingungen ergibt und über den Konkurrenzkampf um Parlamentsmehrheiten hinweg einen neuen Anforderungskatalog legitimationsstiftender Maßnahmen entwickelt.

Im Gegensatz zu den am historischen Konservatismus angelehnten Interpretationsversuchen steht im folgenden der Versuch, Neokonservatismus als eigenständiges reaktionsfähiges Instrumentarium politischer Mechanismen zu definieren, die an der Funktionalität eines herrschenden politischen Systems orientiert sind. Grundgelegt ist dabei die Anpassungsfähigkeit der Formen politischer Herrschaft im Rahmen eines gesellschaftspolitischen Systems sowie die Notwendigkeit systemregulierender Reformen, die einen politisch dynamischen Charakter annehmen können und somit keinesfalls in dem Sinne „konservativ" sind, als daß sie an den jeweils überlieferten Traditionen und Werten festhalten müssen. Dabei können es, wie sich zeigt, unterschiedliche gesellschaftliche Gruppen, Schichten oder Institutionen sein, die als effizienteste Vertreter eines geforderten Regulierungsinteresses auftreten. Gerade in gesellschaftlichen Umbruchphasen, in denen Systemregulierung zum notwendigen Überlebensmechanismus wird, ist es wahrscheinlich, daß sich diese Aufgabe mehrere politische Handlungsträger in verschiedenartiger Art und Weise teilen. Der latente Konkurrenzkampf der in der aktuellen Situation präsenten politischen Kontrahenten kann somit zum Regulativ gesteigerter Systemeffizienz werden – das allerdings nur, wenn die grundsätzlichen Bedingungen des Systemcharakters bestehen bleiben und in den Forderungen der politischen Akteure unangetastet bleiben.

Eben das scheint einer derzeitig realistischen Beurteilung der politischen Lage zu entsprechen: Das System ist nach dem Zusammenbruch der Länder des „real existierenden Sozialismus" unbestritten – wenn auch nicht ohne Kritik – die kapitalistische Wirtschafts- und Sozialordnung auf der Basis des Privateigentums und der Profitmaximierung. Die politische Herrschaft innerhalb dieses Systems ist offensichtlich verschiedenartig und den jeweils aktuellen politischen Bedingungen mehr oder weniger angepaßt.

Die aktuelle Lage ist instabil, d. h. durch eine Vielzahl latenter Krisenerscheinungen gekennzeichnet, die sich regional unterschiedlich entweder als ökonomische Überlebensfragen (wie in den Entwicklungsländern) oder als kulturell dominierte Identitätsfragen (wie in den hochindustrialisierten Ländern Westeuropas und den USA) darstellen. Augenscheinlich ist, daß sich das Kriterium der Überlebensfähigkeit des politischen Systems des entwickelten Kapitalismus nicht an der Dominanz eines bestimmenden Modus an politischer Herrschaft orientiert, sondern in einer Vielzahl verschiedener angepaßter Regulationsprozesse besteht. Mechanismen, die sich in Konkurrenz bewähren und von verschiedenen Handlungsträgern entwickelt und durchgesetzt werden.

Tatsache ist weiters, daß die Komplexität hochentwickelter Gesellschaften ein Ausmaß erreicht hat, das die Erhaltung grundsätzlicher Systemstabilität durch ein sinnstiftendes Moment allein nicht ermöglicht. Im Gegensatz etwa zu den dem religiösen Fundamentalismus verpflichteten Ländern im Nahen Osten kann die Herrschaftslegitimierung in Ländern der 1. Welt weder durch eine prägende religiöse Option noch durch ein (einziges und bestimmendes) Ideologieelement hergestellt werden. Auch der soziologische Befund hochindustrialisierter Gesellschaften schließt eine ähnlich einfache Legitimationsstrategie aus: So sind die unterschiedlichen Bedürfnisse ausdifferenzierter gesellschaftlicher Gruppen nicht durch ein bestimmendes Element gesellschaftlicher Vorgaben, Zielsetzungen und Optionen im Rahmen der grundsätzlichen Beibehaltung des Systemcharakters zu befriedigen. Notwendig ist vielmehr ein System – zwangsläufig – unterschiedlicher Leistungen, die die Einbindung der verschiedenen sozialen und kulturellen Gruppen in den Gesamtzusammenhang des Systems – unter der Bedingung der Reproduktion systemkonformer Situationen – herstellen können. Notwendig dafür sind Systeme zur Integration unter der Voraussetzung hochgradiger Komplexität.

Unter diesen Gesichtspunkten integrativer Leistungen und systemstabilisierender Funktionen soll im folgenden der Begriff „Neokonservatismus" untersucht werden.

Als „konservativ" ist dabei die grundsätzliche Systemkonformität zu einer kapitalistischen Wirtschafts- und Sozialordnung zu verstehen. Das Präfix „neo" beschreibt die Anforderungen, auf veränderte gesellschaftliche Bedingungen zu reagieren. „Moderner Konservatismus" als weltanschauliche Perspektive beinhaltet damit, was gesellschaftlicher Entwicklung insgesamt zugrunde liegt: ständige Anpassungs- und Reaktionsfähigkeit, innovative Stärke zu adäquaten Veränderungsmaßnahmen und Reformbereitschaft.

Neokonservativ kann somit nicht die Erhaltung des unveränderten Status quo historisch festgeschriebener traditionell konservativer Forderungen sein, sondern erstreckt sich vielmehr auf das Terrain gesellschaftlicher Evolution auf der Grundlage kapitalistischer Dominanz.

Dieser sehr umfassende Erklärungsansatz widerspricht dem Begriff von „Neokonservatismus" als historisch definierter und an bestimmte Handlungsträger gebundener Weltanschauung. Vielmehr stehen Fragen der Funktionalität politischer Prozesse im Vordergrund. Ein wesentliches Bestimmungsmerkmal dabei ist es, die jeweils systemintegrative Wirkung der zu untersuchenden Phänomene zu klären und ihre auch die politische Lagerbildung überschreitende Wirksamkeit darzustellen.

„Neokonservatismus" kann in diesem Sinn nur dann ein für die Analyse relevanter, eigenständiger und sinnvoller Begriff sein, wenn festgehalten wird, daß es neben den Adaptionsversuchen von traditionellem konservativen Politikverständnis vor allem um Entwicklungen geht, die aufgrund der Wahrnehmung ihrer unmittelbar politisch-dynamischen, gesellschaftlich innovativen und in bestimmter Hinsicht sogar utopieträchtigen Politikinhalte auf den ersten Blick nichts oder nur wenig mit dem Konservatismus alter Prägung zu tun haben. Die Frage-stellung ist daher weniger, „wie erfolgreich sind die (traditionell) Konservativen", sondern „wie (auf welche Art) konservativ sind die zur Zeit erfolgreichen politischen Entwicklungen und Strömungen"?

Die Wirtschaftspolitik der „Wende"

Eine – naheliegende – Bezugnahme auf das aktuelle Zeitgeschehen in wirtschaftspolitischer Hinsicht ist geprägt von der – regionalen – Expansion kapitalistisch-marktwirtschaftlicher Dominanz. Noch im Verlauf des Zusammenbruches des kollektivistisch-zentralistischen Modelles sozialistischer Planwirtschaft stellt sich die unbestrittene „Vorherrschaft" einer kapitalistischen Wirtschaftsordnung als tagespolitische Selbstverständlichkeit dar. Tatsächlich ist mit der beobachtbaren Auflösung des „real existierenden Sozialismus" auch auf wirtschaftspolitischem Terrain die einzige – politische Funktionalität erreichende – Alternative zu kapitalistisch-marktwirtschaftlicher Initiative gegenstandslos. Die uneingeschränkte Geltung von Strukturen und Regeln kapitalistischer Prägung scheinen damit bestätigt und geraten in der – medialen – Reflexion sogar zu einer Art „Naturgesetzlichkeit", die – im konservativen Sinn – das Marktdogma als „natürliche" wirtschaftliche Entsprechung gesellschaftlicher Entwicklung versteht.

Das Tempo sowie das Ausmaß des Zusammenbruches des politischen Ostens hält dabei nicht nur einen „historischen Sieg" über die marxistisch-leninistischen Konzeptionen fest, sondern unterstellt eine universelle Geltung der „amerikanischen Internationalen", die sich vor allem durch wirtschaftspolitische Dominanz ausdrückt.

Kapitalismus-kritische Einwände entsprechen in dieser auf die rasche Erschließung des – vorerst – osteuropäischen Raumes orientierten Entwicklung nicht dem aktuell vorherrschenden „Zeitgeist".

Weitgehend unberücksichtigt bleibt dabei, welche Bedeutung die gesellschafts- und wirtschaftspolitischen Veränderungen in den kommunistischen Ländern hinsichtlich der sozialen Absicherung und des sich darauf beziehenden Legitimationscharakters im Westen haben. Der euphorisch gefeierte Prozeß der sukzessiven „Einbeziehung" des gesamten Ostblocks in den „gemeinsamen Markt" verdrängt zumindest vorübergehend die systemimmanenten Strukturkrisen und kompensiert die ökonomischen wie gesellschaftlichen Konfliktkonstellationen durch eine Konzentration auf den „Schauplatz Osteuropa".

Die faktische Außer-Frage-Stellung der ökonomisch vorherrschenden Paradigmen des „freien Marktes" unterstützt die Krisentheorien der konservativen Sozialwissenschafter, die sich in ihrer Diagnose der gesellschaftlichen Umbrüche und Strukturschwächen auf den Bereich der kulturellen (Wert-)Wandelprozesse beschränken. „Ökonomisch" ist ihr Erklärungsansatz nur dahingehend, daß sie die gesellschaftlichen Bedürfnisse im Rahmen der massendemokratischen Wohlfahrtsstaaten für nicht mehr einlösbar erachten und den Rückzug von einem von der grundsätzlichen staatlichen Regulation abhängigen Wirtschaftsprogramm als adäquate Reaktion auf die Problemlasten entwickelter kapitalistischer Länder einfordern.

Tatsächlich ist der Begriff der „Wende" in erster Linie mit der monetaristischen und angebotsorientierten Wirtschaftspolitik der konservativen Parteien Anfang der 80er Jahre verbunden. Ihr Konzept stützt sich auf die Kritik der sozialstaatlichen Reformpolitik, die vor allem in Westeuropa den Charakter wirtschaftspolitischer Entwicklung geprägt hat. Voraussetzung für die umfassende „Wende" in den wirtschaftspolitischen Perspektiven war die Erkenntnis der mangelnden Krisenbewältigungskapazität des „keynesianischen Konsensus" (Galbraith, 1980), der die Nachkriegszeit paradigmatisch beeinflußt hat.

Als Reaktion auf die sichtbaren Krisenerscheinungen dieses Wirtschaftskonzeptes formierte sich noch im Verlauf der 70er Jahre eine offensiv ausgerichtete Kritik der Konservativen. „Neu" ist an den wirtschaftspolitischen Konzeptionen dieser „Wende" allerdings nur wenig. Sie bestehen im wesentlichen in einer Zurücknahme staatlicher interventionistischer Maßnahmen, die die Entwicklung des Marktes behindern, sowie in einer Entinstitutionalisierung sozialstaatlicher Strukturen.

Steuersenkungen für die Unternehmen, eine Reduktion der Sozialleistungen und eine weitgehende Deregulierung bestimmen das Programm der „Wende", das in zentralen Passagen ein vom technokratischen Konservatismus geprägtes Paradigma darstellt. Die „Redynamisierung der Wirtschaft" (Grande,1987) zielt auf eine Offensive marktwirtschaftlicher Initiative, die einen neuen Ordnungsrahmen für wirtschaftspolitische Entwicklungen bringen soll. Sie stützt sich auf

- den weitgehenden Abbau von Subventionen,
- eine Einschränkung der Sozialpolitik,
- eine forcierte Technologiepolitik sowie
- eine umfassende Privatisierung.

Obwohl die wirtschaftspolitischen Maßnahmen der „konservativen Wende" bis heute unvermittelte Wirkung behalten haben, sind die – ersten – euphorischen Erwartungen nicht erfüllt worden. Die enge Verknüpfung der Unternehmen im sozialstaatlichem Verband sowie die Komplexität wohlfahrtsstaatlicher Strukturen hat der „konservativen Revolution" nur unzureichenden Gestaltungsfreiraum gelassen. Mit der Ausnahme von Großbritannien ist in keinem Land Westeuropas der konzipierte – konservative – Gegenentwurf zum Sozialstaat verwirklicht worden. Gerade die radikalen wirtschaftlichen Strukturveränderungen des britischen „Thatcherismus" und seine sozialen Folgewirkungen haben dazu beigetragen, daß das konservative „Roll back" viel von seiner leitbildhaften Funktion verloren hat.

Nicht geglückt ist der prognostizierte Erfolg neoliberaler Wirtschaftspolitik in Form seiner ideologisch besetzten Ankündigung. Von besonderer Tragweite sind jedoch die grundlegenden Motivationsstrukturen der „Wende", die mittlerweile von allen politischen Institutionen und Parteien in unterschiedlicher Weise aufgegriffen und modifiziert worden sind. Dabei differenziert sich – in Übereinstimmung mit der Arbeitshypothese – das grundsätzlich systemstabilisierende Moment in eine Vielzahl von Interessen und Handlungsträgern. Der Gehalt dieser „Wende" kann in diesem Verlauf auch von anderen als traditionell konservativen Akteuren im politischen Spektrum instrumentalisiert werden. So mußte beispielsweise in Österreich die konservative Partei miterleben, daß sowohl am internationalen Höhepunkt der „konservativen Renaissance" Mitte der 80er Jahre als auch bei der Wahlentscheidung 1990 das von der Sozialdemokratie angeführte konventionelle Krisenmanagement – inhaltlich durchaus auf der Basis der konservativen Wende in der Wirtschaftspolitik stehend – größeren Anklang bei der Bevölkerung gefunden hat als der eigentliche und naheliegende Vertreter der „Wende" auf politisch institutioneller Ebene, die konservative Partei. Ein typisches Beispiel dafür, daß der Erfolg des grundsätzlichen Anliegens des Neokonservatismus weniger von der Durchsetzungsfähigkeit der im politischen Alltag auftretenden Konservativen (Parteien, Interessen, Motive etc.) abhängig ist, sondern in der innovativen Ausdifferenzierung und Adaption einer systemregulierend wirksamen Perspektive liegt. Dabei gewinnt eine Unterscheidung zwischen der realpolitischen Wirkung der Konservativen und der Funktion neokonservativen Politikverständnisses an Bedeutung. Unbestritten ist der wesentliche Anteil der konservativen Initiative am Projekt der Wende und den daraus resultierenden gesellschaftlichen und wirtschaftlichen Reformen. Wie bereits ausgeführt, vermittelt die konservative Krisentheorie wesentliche Kriterien der aktuellen gesellschaftspolitischen Entwicklung. Der Komplexitätsgrad der industrialisierten kapitalistischen Länder sowie der Stand der Produktivkraftentwicklung verteilt jedoch die „Lasten der Systemregulation" auf mehrere Handlungsträger, die sich – einem immanenten Prinzip entsprechend – einer Konkurrenzsituation um den jeweiligen Grad des tatsächlichen politischen Einflusses stellen müssen.

Welche beschränkte Wirkung die wirtschaftspolitischen Zielsetzungen einer weitgehenden Liberalisierung des Marktes erzeugen, zeigt sich gegenwärtig sehr deutlich im Zusammenhang mit den Integrationsbestrebungen in die Europäische Gemeinschaft . Vor allem der in der Landwirtschaft tätige Teil der Bevölkerung wehrt sich vehement gegen den Abbau der bestehenden Subventionspolitik und hält „konservativ" an sozialstaatlichen wirtschaftspolitischen Regulierungsmaßnahmen fest. Auch hier erweist sich die leitbildhafte Trendumkehr der Wende als unzureichendes Krisenmanagement.

Die Werterenaissance der Wende

Neokonservatismus als Reaktion auf die Defizite einer langjährigen Etappe wohlfahrtsstaatlich orientierter Politik: Das war – übereinstimmend – der erste Befund über die gesellschaftspolitischen Veränderungen Mitte der 80er Jahre. Eine Renaissance konservativer Werte, die ein fundamentales Unbehagen im Umgang mit der Natur, der Umwelt und den einengenden Maßnahmen staatlicher Verwaltung zum Ausdruck bringt, dient als Ausgangspunkt für eine Analyse, die sich auf veränderte soziale Bedingungen und deren Auswirkungen bezieht. Die Erwartungen und Hoffnungen, die einen dynamischen Veränderungsprozeß getragen haben, zerbrechen an den restriktiven Erfahrungen mit einem bürokratischen Verwaltungsapparat und schwerwiegenden Defiziten im unmittelbaren – privaten – Alltag. Demgegenüber profiliert sich eine Bedeutungszunahme traditionell konservativer Werte, die sich durch die Attraktivität der „Besinnung", des „Wiederentdeckens" und des „Empfindens" auszeichnet. „Man kann wieder darüber sprechen" (Klett, 1971), „Konservativ Chance und Zukunft" (Buchtitel, 1979), „Ich bin konservativ – mir gefällt's" (Slogan der JES-Studentenorganisation Anfang der 80er Jahre): Parolen und Appelle wie diese sind kennzeichnend für eine Umkehrung der politischen Meinungsbildung zum Begriff „konservativ".

Die grundlegenden Strukturen kultureller Bestimmungen stellen einen wesentlichen Impuls bei der Konstitution neokonservativen Politikverständnisses dar. Fragen der Modernität, der traditionellen Moral und den kulturellen Erosionen im Wertgefüge sind der Kernpunkt der Kritik der Neokonservativen am aktuellen Zeitgeschehen.

Bereits 1955 problematisierte Hans Freyer den Zusammenhang der Anforderungen einer modernen Industriegesellschaft mit der traditionsgebundenen Moral. Im Mittelpunkt stehen dabei Fragen der Technikbewertung, der Auswirkungen der technologischen industriellen Kapazitäten auf die Wertdisposition der Bevölkerung.

Vor allem die schwerwiegenden Folgeprobleme der industriell-wissenschaftlichen Entwicklung sowie der steigende Legitimationsdruck, der durch das teilweise Versagen des „technischen Staates" entstanden ist, haben den konservativen Ruf nach einem Wertbewußtsein, das die Sinnfrage gegenüber systemgefährdenden Alternativoptionen absichern soll, verstärkt. Für konservative Autoren, wie etwa Hermann Lübbe, entsteht dabei ein Bedarf an wertsichernden Traditionen, denen vorwiegend entlastende Funktion zukommt.

Die erforderliche Sinnproduktion stützt sich dabei auf die traditionellen Tugenden, die dem konservativen Wertereservoir entnommen werden und identitäts- und legitimitätsstiftende Wirkung ausüben.

Traditionelle „Besinnung" auf konservative Werte sollten jene sinnvermittelnde Orientierung erzeugen, deren Fehlen als prägendes Defizit in der lebensweltlichen Praxis der wohlfahrtsstaatlichen Gesellschaften wahrgenommen wurde. „Leistung", „Treue", „Heimat", „Ordnung" oder der erneut als zentrale Bestimmung aufgenommene Begriff der „Privatheit" sollten jenes Wertevakuum füllen, das durch den Zusammenbruch der Entwicklungsoptionen einer sozialstaatlich organisierten Arbeitsgesellschaft und den damit verbundenen individuellen und kollektiven Krisen entstanden war.

Dabei wird deutlich, daß die Frage nach den bürgerlichen Werten, die zur Entlastung und Absicherung in einer vom Industrialismus geprägten Welt von vorrangiger Bedeutung sind, auf der Ebene der Kultur erörtert werden muß. „Kultur" wird somit zum zentralen Feld, auf dem sich der Gehalt zivilisatorischer Entwicklung fokussiert.

Rückblickend kann festgehalten werden, daß die Renaissance traditionell konservativer Werte einen Aufschwung erlebte, der als geradezu idealtypisch für die Zukunftsentwürfe konservativer Autoren gelten kann.

Einem „neuen Zeitalter" nach konservativer Prägung standen allerdings nicht nur die vielfältigen sozialökonomischen Verbindlichkeiten des Wohlfahrtsstaates im Weg, sondern auch die Tatsache, daß die radikale marktwirtschaftliche Initiative an die Grenzen der Verträglichkeit gesellschaftspolitischer Veränderungen gestoßen war. Hinsichtlich der Funktion kapitalistischer Produktion und den entsprechenden Reproduktionsmechanismen erwiesen sich die am traditionellen Konservatismus orientierten Problemlösungskonzepte als ungeeignet, eine dynamische, systemintegrative Wirkung auf der Basis des hohen Komplexitätsgrades der – kapitalistisch – entwickelten Staaten zu erzeugen. Neben der „suboptimalen" Effizienz der wirtschaftspolitischen „Wende", stellte sich auch die Werterenaissance traditionell konservativer Einstellungen als unzureichendes Legitimationskonzept heraus. Die zunehmende Segmentierung der Gesellschaft in eine Vielzahl an Gruppen, Schichten und Interessenlagen verhinderte, daß ein universalistisches, sich auf die „ewigen Werte" des Konservatismus berufendes Paradigma ausreichend „sinnstiftende" Motive zur Lebensbewältigung und damit zur – weitgehend konfliktfreien – Integration herstellen konnte. Das als „Orientierungswissen" konzipierte „Roll back" in den persönlichen Werten und Einstellungen erfüllte somit nicht die ihm zugedachte Aufgabe, als Legitimationsgrundlage die Einbindung der Gesellschaftsmitglieder in den Gesamtzusammenhang der Funktionsanforderungen der technisch-industriellen Entwicklung zu bewerkstelligen.

Die innovatorische Kompetenz der konservativen Traditionalismen reichte nicht aus, ein funktionierendes Legitmationskonzept der postindustriellen Gesellschaft beizustellen.

Tendenziell richtig – d. h. den beobachtbaren Entwicklungen entsprechend – thematisieren Lübbe, Forsthoff, Schelsky und ihre amerikanischen Kollegen den Bedarf einer Legitimationsstrategie für eine postindustriell ausgerichtete Gesellschaft. Deutlich aber überschätzten sie die Bedeutung, die der traditionelle Konservatismus dabei spielt.

Während die „alten Konservativen" daran festhalten, nur die Wiederbelebung ihrer Wertmuster könne zur aktuellen Krisenbewältigung beitragen, entwickelt sich weit über das traditionell konservative Lager hinaus eine tatsächlich moderne und damit neue, also neokonservative Perspektive. Sie nimmt den Beitrag systemstabilisierender Effekte, die durch den Einsatz eines bürgerlichen Normenkataloges zustande kommen, gerne an, entwickelt daraus aber ein wesentlich breiteres – und der gesellschaftlichen Realität der Differenzierung der sozialen Schichten angepaßtes – Spektrum legitimationsstiftender Sinngehalte.

Die Kulturkritik der Konservativen thematisiert also einen zentralen Bereich aktueller Konfliktkonstellationen. Indem sie aber auf eine Analyse der Abhängigkeiten der Wert- und Einstellungsmuster von dem ökonomischen Organisationsgrad der Gesellschaften verzichtet, überschätzt sie die Wirkung konservativer Motivationsstrukturen.

So richtet sich etwa die Trendumkehr im Meinungsbild der Bevölkerung in den entwickelten Ländern – der kapitalistischen Produktionslogik folgend – gegen eine strenge Arbeitsmoral, die noch die bürgerliche Gesellschaft im Aufbau ihrer industriellen Kapazität ausgezeichnet hat. Demnach geraten autoritäre wie religiös inspirierte Motivationsstrukturen an die Grenzen der geforderten Systemfunktionalität. Den Vertretern eines traditionell konservativen – auf Bewahrung der fundamentalen konservativen Werte ausgerichteten – Modells einer bürgerlichen Gesellschaft werden die grundlegenden Argumente schrittweise entzogen.

Der Wertepluralismus ist somit zwar subversiv gegen die vorherrschenden industriellen Hierarchien und deren Absicherungsstrukturen, stellt jedoch als Reaktion kapitalistischer Entwicklungsdynamik nur ein neues Anforderungsprofil sowohl an die wirtschaftliche als auch an die gesellschaftspolitische Produktionslogik.

Deutlich wird der reaktive Veränderungsablauf von einer industriellen hin zu einer nachindustriellen Gesellschaft an den zur Zeit bereits beobachtbaren Entwicklungsschritten, die ein – den Kriterien ausdifferenzierter Bevölkerungsschichten gerecht werdendes – Netz neuer Verwertungsbedingungen entwickeln. Zerfallen die großen sozialen Schichtungen in eine Vielzahl segmentierter Einheiten, die sich durch unterschiedliche soziale Verhältnisse und – dementsprechend – unterschiedliche Interessenlagen auszeichnen, kann auch die legitimationsstiftende Kraft nicht länger durch ein zentrales moralisches Motiv – etwa der protestantischen Arbeitsethik – hergestellt werden. Die Funktionalität der Produktionslogik und der Verwertungsstruktur muß dem Grad der Ausdifferenzierung im Sozialgefüge entsprechen und statt kollektiven Motivations- und Legitimationsleistungen spezifische, individuelle Anreize und Verbindlichkeiten schaffen.

Die produktionstechnischen und gesellschaftlich legitimatorischen Forderungen der „konservativen Tendenzwende" erreichen eben in diesem Grad der Ausdifferenzierung der Gesellschaften und der – für einzelne Bevölkerungsschichten geltenden – „moralischen Unverbindlichkeit" gegenüber traditionell konservativen Werten die Grenze ihrer realpolitischen Umsetzbarkeit. Der universelle Geltungsanspruch einer an der bürgerlichen Rationalität ausgerichteten konservativen Wertestruktur zerbricht an dem gesellschaftspolitischen Tatbestand der „pluralistischen Gesellschaft". Der legitimatorische „Handlungsbedarf" in dieser Phase gesellschaftlicher Ausdifferenzierung besteht in der Herstellung adäquater, d. h. den einzelnen Gruppen angepaßter Reproduktionsstrategien, die entsprechende soziale wie ökonomische „Angebote" (Dienstleistungen, Privilegien etc.) und „sinnstiftende" Wertmuster beinhalten müssen. Eben das entspricht der politischen Funktionalität des Neokonservatismus, der über das Projekt der „Wende" hinausgeht. „Gewendet" mußten die Bedingungen werden, um die Voraussetzungen marktwirtschaftlicher Dominanz sicherzustellen. Die von Alternativoptionen besetzten „ideologischen" Ansprüche mußten relativiert und von ihrer gesellschaftspolitischen Verbindlichkeit „befreit" werden. Erst das bereitet die Basis für einen „neuen" und „modernen" Konservatismus, der als wesentliches Kriterium ein ausgeprägtes Innovationsbewußtsein entwickelt.

Die Wertekultur im Neokonservatismus ist „mobil" und dynamisch. Ihre moralische Kapazität wird der Produktionslogik angepaßt und damit systemimmanent. Jeder – auch traditionell konservative – Universalitätsanspruch muß ausgegrenzt werden und den ausdifferenzierten, reaktiven Legitimationsprozessen Platz machen.

Diese „Managementstrukturen" betreffen unmittelbar die Konfliktbewältigung im politischen Szenario, indem sie die Austragung divergierender Interessen zu einem verwaltungstechnischen Problemlösungsmechanismus machten. Aktuelle Szenarien einer derartigen Konfliktregulation könnten sein:

Ausdifferenzierter Konsum statt Bedürfnisbefriedigung

Die Palette der konsumistischen Nachfrage ist entsprechend der Vielzahl an sozialen Gruppen unterschiedlich. Nicht mehr gilt, daß der Massenandrang der Bevölkerung auf die Wohlstandsdurchschnittsware die Konsumgüterindustrie stimuliert. Spezifikation im Angebot heißt: spezifische Bedarfsabdeckung, die zwar den wirtschaftlichen Schwung garantiert, aber auch ein soziales Kriterium darstellt.

Demnach stellt nicht mehr der Anteil an der allgemeinen materialistischen Bedürfnisbefriedigung den Preis für aktive Leistungsbereitschaft dar, sondern spezielle Dienstleistungen ersetzen den allgemeinen Konsum und versprechen individuellen Profit.

Entsprechend differenziert streichen auch die Leistungsanforderungen immer deutlicher die individuelle Komponente hervor: Mobilität und Privatinitiative verstärken den latenten Konkurrenzkampf mit dem Resultat steigender Produktivität.

Das Problem: Die sozialen und auch allgemein persönlichen Bedürfnisse müssen sowohl in ihrer Stimulierung als auch in ihrer Abdeckung streng kalkulatorischen Kriterien folgen.

Segmentierte Identität statt Emanzipation

Die auftretenden Identitätskonflikte, die für die einzelnen Mitglieder in den ausdifferenzierten Gruppen entstehen, werden nicht mehr anhand eines emanzipatorischen Anspruches thematisiert, sondern durch spezielle individuelle und gruppenspezifische Leistungs- und Profitoptionen realisiert. Jeweils entsprechend der sozialen Schicht stehen dafür unterschiedliche sinnvermittelnde „Produktidentitäten" zur Verfügung, die jeweils unterschiedliche Selbstverwirklichungsszenarien möglich machen. Das Angebot dafür ist vielfältig: Es reicht von der Schulung zum ganzheitlichen Manager über die privatfinanzierte psychologische Selbstfindung bis hin zu etwas billigeren esoterischen Welt- und Selbstversicherungen.

Neokonservative Wirkung erzeugen dabei die bereits im politischen Alltag beobachtbaren Prozesse der Entideologisierung, der Individualisierung und Personalisierung sowie die Psychologisierung und die Konzentration auf intrapersonale Abläufe. Eine zunehmende Beeinflussung durch irrationale Wertmuster unterstützt zusätzlich den Bedeutungsverlust kollektiver – auf die Wahrnehmung übergeordneter, systemkritisch ausgerichteter – Kategorien und verhindert zugleich die konzeptionelle Erfassung politischer Realität, welche über die regionalisierten, den spezifischen Gruppen und Bevölkerungsteilen angepaßten Interessenlagen hinausgeht.

Das Problem dabei: Als Kriterium für diese Sinnstiftungen gelten nicht mehr Veränderungsprozesse, die eine Befreiung aus der Umklammerung bestehender Abhängigkeiten bedeuten, sondern die Übereinstimmung mit dem Rollenverständnis der jeweiligen Gruppe oder Schicht.

So ersetzt ein „psychedelischer Bazar" (Dubiel, 1985) alle universalen religiösen wie politisch ideologischen Ansprüche.

Kompensation statt Interessenausgleich

Die in den einzelnen Gruppen entstehenden sozialen Defizite werden sozialverwalterisch kategorisiert. Individualistische oder gruppenspezifische Betreuungsmodelle schaffen ebensolche, nämlich individualistische und gruppenspezifische Konfliktlösungen, die systemgefährdende Reaktionen ausschließen. Potentielle Konflikte werden durch Maßnahmen der sozialen Kontrolle vermieden.

Das Problem dabei: Die Angebote dieser administrativen Betreuung, die im übrigen in zunehmenden Ausmaß durch private Dienstleistungen ersetzt werden (z. B. im Bereich der Pflege alter und kranken Menschen), führen nicht zur Lösung der beanstandeten Probleme und deren Ursachen, sondern nur zu kompensatorischen Beschäftigungs- und Reparatureffekten.

Besinnung statt Kritik

Auch im Bereich der „gegenkulturellen Bewegungen" lassen sich Entwicklungen beobachten, die eine erhöhte Verwertungskapazität einer „Integrationsspirale" ausweisen. So entsprechen verschiedene „Fundamentalismen", die den Charakter einzelner „Protestbewegungen" bestimmen, den dargelegten neokonservativen Anforderungen. Exemplarisch kann etwa die im Zuge des Feminismus ausgeprägte gynozentrische Orientierung auf die typisch weiblichen Bestimmungsmerkmale in den Wertvorstellungen für eine Entwicklung herangezogen werden, in der eine Eigensphäre politischer Beurteilung aufgebaut wird, die sich den Kategorien der traditionellen, emanzipatorischen Kritik entzieht. Die Betonung der „weiblichen Natur", die moralische Instanz der „Mütterlichkeit", die Konstitution einer eigenen „Frauengeschichte" basiert auf anthropologischen Grundlagen und verbindet sich mit Formen weiblicher Spiritualität, die den Einfluß irrationaler Indikatoren auf die Meinungsbildung ausweist. Eine auf sozialökonomische Unterscheidungen ausgerichtete Gesellschaftsanalyse wird durch die Definition einer „phallokratischen Kultur" (Irigaray, 1979) ersetzt. Der radikale Ansatz des feministischen Gynozentrismus formuliert eine globale Kritik am Patriarchat und den an der Moderne orientierten Denktraditionen. Diskursive Rationalität wird als abzulehnendes „männliches Merkmal" bestimmt, das der weiblichen Sinnlichkeit und der unmittelbaren Naturverbundenheit der Frau gegenübersteht. Hinsichtlich der angesprochenen – neokonservativen – Integrationsleistung stellt sich das „subversive Element" des gynozentrischen Weltbildes als Position dar, die sich vergleichbar mit den postmodernen Konzepten außerhalb von bestimmenden Machtkonstellationen ansiedelt und die emanzipatorischen Anliegen in einer Reihe globaler, klassenneutraler und spirituell aufgelöster Selbstverwirklichungsstrategien kanalisiert. Die darauf aufbauende Gesellschaftskritik entwickelt autonome Wertsphären, die sich von kapitalismus-kritischen Positionen abwenden und zu fundamentalen Neuorientierungen führen, „die im Zuge der antifeministischen Reaktion eine Anpassung an vorhandene Gesellschaftsstrukturen zur Folge haben könnten." (List, 1989)

Auch die fundamentalistischen Perspektiven der Ökologiebewegung beinhalten neben ihrem ausgewiesenen Protestpotential Elemente, die systemimmanenten Kompensationstrategien entsprechen. So führt etwa die naturrechtliche Positionierung der Kritik an der kulturtechnischen Zivilisation zu Gesellschaftsentwürfen, die vor-moderne – ökonomische wie soziale – Machtverhältnisse als Entwicklungsoption präsentieren. Die als „Irrwege des Rationalismus" bezeichneten Resultate der technisch-industriellen Welt sind der Ausgangspunkt für eine konservative „Wiederbelebung des Verlorenen" (Mühlenfeld, 1959), die anthropologische Kategorien als bestimmendes Politikelement einsetzt.

Charakteristisch ist auch der Stellenwert des Individuums im Rahmen grünfundamentalistischer Orientierung. Die Konzentration auf das „Praktisch-Konkrete" verlangt als Kriterium immer die einzelne Person, die von einem unmittelbaren – und persönlichen – Erfahrungshintergrund abhängig ist. Politisch-ideologische Lebenszusammenhänge, die über die Betroffenheit des einzelnen hinausgehen, verlieren entsprechend dem Attraktivitätszuwachs von individuellen Werten an Bedeutung. Auch die im Zuge ihres Orientierungswandels einsetzende Regionalisierung politischer Prozesse führt dazu, daß spezifische Einzelinteressen den Vorrang gegenüber Problemlösungen gewinnen, die sich auf überregionale Aspekte beziehen. Ein weitgehender Verlust einer strukturpolitischen Dimension ist die Folge dieser Beschränkung auf örtliche Gegebenheiten. Die Konzentration auf einzelne Personen als Handlungs- und Verantwortungsträger, die in der aktuellen politischen Auseinandersetzung die Debatte zu „Persönlichkeitswahlrecht" prägt, unterstützt die Formen demokratiepolitischer Partizipation, die sich auf individualistische Wertmuster und Kriterien stützt und system-kritische Veränderungstendenzen aufgrund der eingeengten Auswahl der Objekte der – politischen – Wahrnehmung verhindert.

Ein zynischer Kreislauf an Integrationsleistungen, dessen Funktionalität um so reibungsloser verläuft, als er individuellen „Sinn" herstellt und damit Entfremdungswahrnehmungen kompensiert, wäre die Konsequenz solcher Szenarien, deren Charakteristik darin besteht, daß nichts an den sich innovativ regulierenden Machtdispositionen verändert werden müßte. Der aus den einheitlichen, „großen" sozialen Strukturen entlassene Bürger verliert den Bezug zu den übergeordneten „großen" Zusammenhängen und kann nur mehr isoliert, dafür aber individuell seine Rechte geltend machen und – als Gegenleistung – seine Individualität als Produktivkraft anbieten.

Ein neues Regelsystem gesellschaftlicher Leistungen und Anforderungen integriert auf diese Art auch postmaterialistische Werthaltungen und setzt Marktfunktionen dort ein, wo systemgefährdende Konstellationen zu möglichen Konflikten führen könnten.

Letzteres deutet an, daß die postmaterialistische Wertkultur keineswegs eine „neokonservative Erfindung" ist oder ausschließlich im Dienst einer konformitätssteigernden Strategie steht. Im Gegenteil zeigt sich, daß wesentliche kapitalismus-kritische Aspekte aus der der materialistischen Entwicklungsdynamik abgewandten „Gegenkultur" stammen. Hingewiesen soll an dieser Stelle nur darauf sein, welche Perspektiven die Veränderungsprozesse systemintegrativer Regulierung hinsichtlich der Reaktion auf den beschriebenen Wertewandel haben können.

Während also die Befürworter einer konservativen Renaissance in dem Zerfall traditioneller Wertsysteme und dem Aufbau neuer, pluraler Wertschichten – zu Recht – eine Gefahr für den traditionellen Konservatismus sowie einen wirtschaftspolitischen Liberalismus, der von der hierarchisierten Arbeitsethik der bürgerlichen Gesellschaft abhängig ist, sehen, entwickelt der tatsächlich neue und in besonderem Sinne moderne Konservatismus längst schon Integrationsmodelle, die an den veränderten wirtschaftlichen und gesellschaftspolitischen Bedingungen ansetzen.

Eine derartige, neue Struktur systemlegitimierender Maßnahmen, die neokonservativer Funktionalität entspricht, existiert heute – als einheitliches Konstrukt – noch nicht. Anzunehmen ist, daß die Komplexität der industrialisierten Staaten auch in Zukunft verhindert, daß sich dieser an der Effizienz orientierte Regulationsprozeß institutionalisiert. Neokonservatismus bleibt damit abstrakt, selbst wenn sich die realen politischen Auswirkungen dieses Konzeptes im ständigen Ablauf der gesellschaftlichen Entwicklung konkretisieren. Die „gewendeten" Bedingungen auf der ökonomischen und sozialen Ebene, die eine Voraussetzung für marktwirtschaftliche Dominanz darstellen, schaffen ebenso wie ein erfolgreicher Meinungsbildungs- und Wertewandelprozeß, in dem allgemein verbindliche emanzipatorische Ansprüche relativiert werden, die Basis für einen Fortschrittsbegriff, der den Anforderungen des Pluralismus und der Flexibilität entspricht. „Neokonservativ" ist damit ein interaktives Regelsystem von Anpassungsprozessen, die eine systematische Relativierung und Ausgrenzung systemkritischer Ansätze durchführen und jene gesellschaftlichen Strukturen schaffen, die erforderlich sind, um eine – weitgehend konfliktfreie – Integration ebenso wie eine erfolgreiche Kompensation differenzierter Legitimationsdefizite zu ermöglichen.

Die Renaissance traditioneller Konservatismen unter dem Schlagwort der „Wende" hat ebenso wie eine radikale Vernunftkritik ihren Beitrag dazu geleistet und trotz unterschiedlicher Akzentsetzungen die Beschäftigung mit den Veränderungstendenzen in den gesellschaftlich wirksamen Paradigmen angeregt.

Neokonservative – im Sinne der Arbeitshypothese – reagieren also auf die zwingend erscheinenden Regulationsschritte, die mehr oder weniger liberal oder der sozialdemokratischen Programmatik verpflichtet das sozialstaatliche Erbe verwalten, und entwickeln Vorschläge, die die Legitimationsstrategien auf Grundlage veränderter Sozial- und Meinungsbildungskonstellationen innovativ ausrichten und im Sinne gesteigerter Systemeffizienz die sich abzeichnenden gesellschaftlichen Veränderungen berücksichtigen.

Daß dabei nicht so sehr politiktheoretisches Neuland betreten wird und – wie anzunehmen wäre – spekulative Utopien den Gegenstand dieser neokonservativen Gesellschaftslehre bestimmen, belegen sowohl die in den geistes- und sozialwissenschaftlichen Brain tanks laufenden Projekte, die sich intensiv mit den langfristigen Konsequenzen der Kommunikations- und Technologieentwicklung beschäftigen als auch die Erfahrungswerte mit legitimationsstiftenden Maßnahmen in dem entwickelsten kapitalistischen Staat, den USA, deren internationale Vormachtstellung nach dem Ende einer „real existierenden sozialistischen Alternative" wohl unbestritten ist.

Gerade die in den letzten Monaten stattgefundenen Zerfallsprozesse in diesen Ländern haben kurzzeitig von den internen Steuerungsproblemen der westlichen Industriegesellschaften abgelenkt und das Interesse auf die Auflösungsprozesse der politischen Strukturen des „Ostblocks" gelenkt.

Zweifellos wird die darauf folgende – kapitalistische – Expansion, die regional unterschiedlich bereits eingesetzt hat, den Themenkatalog der nächsten Jahre bestimmen. Weder die strukturpolitischen Maßnahmen im Bereich der Wirtschaft und der administrativen – staatlichen – Verwaltung noch die darauf Bezug nehmende (politik)wissenschaftliche Forschung wird jedoch die auftretenden Legitimationsdefizite unberücksichtigt lassen können, die den Entwicklungsstand jener Gesellschaften charakterisieren, die auch gegenüber den „Entwicklungsländern" des Ostens „an der Spitze des Fortschrittes" marschieren. Daß damit weniger eine Position traditioneller „Stabilisierungen", sondern innovative Effizienzreflexe nachgefragt sind, beschreibt nicht nur eine Aufgabenstellung im Bereich der tagespolitischen „Neuorientierungen", sondern auch den Handlungsbedarf einer neokonservativen Entlastungsstrategie.

Literatur (Auswahl)

Beck, Ulrich, Risikogesellschaft, Frankfurt, 1986.
Bell, Daniel, Die nachindustrielle Gesellschaft, Frankfurt,1975.
Bell, Daniel, Die Zukunft der westlichen Welt, Frankfurt, 1976.
Dahrendorf, Ralf, Homo Sociologicus, Köln, 1961.
Dubiel, Helmut, Neue soziale Bewegungen im Spiegel neokonservativer Kritik, in: Journal für Sozialforschung 2, Frankfurt, 1984.
Dubiel, Helmut, Populismus und Aufklärung, Frankfurt, 1986.
Dubiel, Helmut, Was ist Neokonservatismus, Frankfurt, 1985.
Fetscher, Iring (Hg.), Neokonservative und Neue Rechte, München, 1983.
Forsthoff, Ernst, Der totale Staat, Hamburg, 1933.
Freyer, Hans, Theorie des gegenwärtigen Zeitalter, Stuttgart, 1955.
Fritsche, Klaus, Konservatismus im gesellschaftlich-geschichtlichen Prozeß, in: Neue politische Literatur 1979/80.
Gehlen, Arnold, Studien zur Anthropologie und Soziologie, Neuwied, 1963.
Grande, Edgar, Schwierigkeiten mit der Wende, in: ÖZP 3/1987; Wien, 1987.
Greiffenhagen, Martin, Das Dilemma des Konservatismus in Deutschland, Frankfurt, 1986.
Habermas, Jürgen, Die neue Unübersichtlichkeit, Frankfurt/Main, 1985.
Huyssen, Andreas/Scherpe, Klaus (Hg.), Postmoderne – Zeichen eines kulturellen Wandels, Hamburg, 1986.
Irigaray, Luce, Das Geschlecht, das nicht eins ist, Berlin, 1979.
Kaltenbrunner, Gerd-Klaus (Hg.), Initiative (fortlaufende Reihe), München.
Kaltenbrunner, Gerd-Klaus (Hg.), Rekonstruktion des Konservatismus, Bern/Stuttgart, 1974.
Kaltenbrunner, Gerd-Klaus, Prospektiver Konservatismus, in: Konservativ – Chance und Zukunft, Innsbruck, 1979.
König, Helmut, Von der Masse zur Individualisierung, in: Leviathan 2/1988.
Kreuder, Th./H. Loewy, Konservatismus in der Strukturkrise, Frankfurt, 1987.
List, Elisabeth/Studer, Herlinde, Denkverhältnisse. Feminismus und Kritik, Frankfurt, 1989.
Lübbe, Hermann, Säkularisierung. Geschichte eines ideenpolitischen Begriffes, München, 1965.
Mannheim, Karl, Konservatismus, Frankfurt, 1984.
Schäfer, Wolf (Hg.), Neue Soziale Bewegungen , Frankfurt, 1983.
Schelsky, Helmut, Auf der Suche nach Wirklichkeit, Köln, 1965.
Schumann, Hans Gerd, Konservatismus, Köln, 1974.
Szopo, P., Deregulierung in Österreich, Wien, 1986.

IV.
Zeitsignale

Volkmar Lauber

Demokratisierung und Wirtschaft in West- und Ostmitteleuropa (1945–1991)

In der europäischen Geschichte gab es mehrere Demokratisierungsphasen. Am wichtigsten für die folgenden Überlegungen sind die Demokratisierungsschübe, die seit dem 2. Weltkrieg erfolgten: im (politisch definierten) Westeuropa in den späten vierziger Jahren, in Südeuropa in den siebziger Jahren und in Ostmitteleuropa (Polen, Tschechoslowakei, Ungarn) seit 1988/89. Demokratisierung in West- und Südeuropa bedeutete nicht nur die Einführung formaler demokratischer Institutionen, sondern auch die materielle Einbeziehung von bis dahin mehr oder weniger marginalisierten Bevölkerungsgruppen (insbesondere der Industriearbeiterschaft und der politischen Linken). In Ostmitteleuropa ist die Ausgangslage anders; es erhebt sich die Frage, wieweit die Entwicklungen vergleichbar sind und zu einem vergleichbaren Ergebnis führen können.

Im folgenden Beitrag wird vor allem der Zusammenhang zwischen Demokratie und Wirtschaft thematisiert. Im Zug des Demokratisierungsschubs in Westeuropa sind diesbezüglich drei grundlegende Positionen zu unterscheiden.

Die erste Tradition soll die „formaldemokratische" (im amerikanischen Verständnis liberale) genannt werden und findet sich in ihrer klassischen Formulierung schon im amerikanischen Denken zu Ende des 18. Jahrhunderts. In dieser Tradition wird ein weit verbreitetes, vor staatlicher Willkür geschütztes Privateigentum als Grundlage aller anderen Freiheitsrechte und somit auch als Grundlage für die liberale Demokratie empfunden. Privateigentum verleiht die Mittel, sich gegen die Staatsmacht zu wehren, und die Grundlage dafür, am grundsätzlich offenen Wettbewerb um die Macht teilzunehmen. Diese Position war im Westeuropa der Zwischenkriegszeit bei den demokratisch gesinnten Konservativen klar dominant.

Gewissermaßen als Gegenstück bildete sich eine zweite Position heraus, die das Prinzip allgemeiner und freier Wahlen mit der politischen Einbeziehung der Arbeiterschaft und einem starken Einfluß der Politik auf die Grundsätze des Wirtschaftslebens zu verbinden bestrebt war. Erst eine solche Mitsprache im Sinn eines historischen Kompromisses zwischen den großen gesellschaftlichen Gruppen und Klassen könne, so diese Position, Demokratie auch materiell verwirklichen. Hier geht es vor allem um eine bestimmte Auffassung von Gerechtigkeit. Diese Position soll in der Folge die „demokratisch-sozialistische" genannt werden, obwohl sie gerade in der unmittelbaren Nachkriegszeit auch von anderen politischen Kräften vertreten wurde (z. B. in Mitteleuropa von manchen katholischen oder protestantischen Kreisen, in Frankreich von den Gaullisten, in England von einem Teil der Konservativen).

Eine dritte Position ist mehr pragmatisch und betont die Bedeutung eines breiten Wohlstands für demokratische Stabilität. Sie beruht zum Teil auf US-amerikanischen Erfahrungen (New Deal, Fordismus), zum Teil auf keynesianischen und technokratischen Zukunftsvisionen von einer Entpolitisierung durch Wirtschaftswachstum, zum Teil auch auf einer ganz bestimmten Interpretation der Erfolgsbedingungen für die Ausbreitung des Faschismus. In dieser Position – am besten ausformuliert ist sie vielleicht in den Schriften von Seymour Martin Lipset (1965) – stellen Privateigentum, wirtschaftliche Stabilität und ein gewisses Ausmaß an Entpolitisierung die wesentlichen gesellschaftlichen Voraussetzungen für den Bestand der Demokratie dar; ohne diese können weder formaldemokratische Normen noch soziale Gerechtigkeit bei gleichzeitiger Armut zu effektiv demokratischen Verhältnissen führen. Demokratisierung besteht also in der Schaffung jener sozialen und wirtschaftlichen Bedingungen, die die formaldemokratischen Normen erst mit Leben erfüllen. Diese Position soll in der Folge die „liberal-apolitische" genannt werden. Liberal wegen der Verwandtschaft mit grundlegenden Ideen des Pluralismus, die hier allerdings zur Inspiration von Reformen und nicht zur Konservierung und Legitimation alter Machtverhältnisse herangezogen werden; apolitisch deshalb, weil in diesem Verständnis Politik weitgehend durch Wirtschaftswachstum ersetzt wird.

Diese Positionen sollen nun als Raster für die Entwicklung in Europa seit dem Zweiten Weltkrieg herangezogen werden, mit dem Ziel, grobe Muster herauszuarbeiten und Vergleiche zwischen Zeitperioden einerseits und West- bzw. Ostmitteleuropa andererseits herzustellen. Dabei läßt sich aus jeder Position auch ein Modell der Demokratisierung ableiten.

In Westeuropa kamen die zweite und die dritte Position schon relativ bald nach dem Krieg (und in kurzem Abstand voneinander) zum Tragen. Das „demokratisch-sozialistische" Modell der Demokratisierung bezog seine Unterstützung aus dem intellektuellen Milieu und den Machtverhältnissen der Jahre unmittelbar nach dem Weltkrieg. Das „liberal-apolitische" Modell wiederum erhielt wahrscheinlich den stärksten Auftrieb durch den Marshallplan. Beide Modelle inspirierten die praktische Politik und waren in einem Komplex miteinander verbunden, der später – zur Zeit seines Niedergangs – der „sozialdemokratische Konsens" genannt wurde. Erosionserscheinungen zeigten sich schon in den siebziger Jahren, aber erst mit der neo-konservativen Wende wird das „demokratisch-sozialistische" Modell bzw. der davon inspirierte Strang von Reformen heftig in Frage gestellt und teilweise abgebaut, während das „liberal-apolitische" Modell eine neue Ausformung erhält.

In Osteuropa gab es ähnliche historische Zäsuren. Dort waren es die Ablehnung des Marshallplans und der Kampf gegen die US-Hegemonie, die zur wirtschaftlichen Integration im Rahmen des Rats für Gegenseitige Wirtschaftshilfe und in der Folge zur Stalinisierung der osteuropäischen Volkswirtschaften führten – zu einer Extremvariante der politischen Kontrolle über Wirtschaftstätigkeit, die allerdings (mangels demokratischer politischer Institutionen) keine Demokratisierung darstellte; Ansätze formaldemokratischer Institutionen wurden beseitigt, bei Neubildung in kurzer Zeit wieder niedergeschlagen. Auch hier gibt es – vor allem in den siebziger und achtziger Jahren – Erosionserscheinungen: Die Durchsetzung der politischen Kontrolle wird wenigstens in einzelnen Ländern zusehends schwieriger, einzelne Sektoren der Wirtschaft und Gesellschaft entziehen sich mehr und mehr dieser Kontrolle bzw. erzwingen ein teilweises Eingehen des Staats auf ihre Wünsche. Der Stalinismus weicht einem zunehmend apolitischen Verhalten der kommunistischen Eliten, die durch Wirtschaftswachstum und teilweise auch durch Lockerung der Freiheitsbeschränkungen ihre Legitimation zu retten suchen.

Mit dem Umsturz 1989 kommt auch hier eine Art neokonservative Wende, allerdings viel massiver und radikaler. Das „formaldemokratische" Modell scheint die Hauptinspirationsquelle für die neuen Eliten dieser Länder darzustellen. Die Umstände sind wesentlich weniger günstig als in Westeuropa vier Jahrzehnte vorher; vorläufig zeichnen sich keine Gegenstücke zu den beiden anderen Modellen ab, die wahrscheinlich für die progressive Verankerung und Stabilisierung der Demokratie in Westeuropa ganz wesentlich waren. So wird es harte Übergänge geben, die erfahrungsgemäß zu gesellschaftlicher Destabilisierung, oft auch zu Radikalisierung führen und die in der Vergangenheit wiederholt die Demokratie gefährdeten oder gar zerstören halfen. Die Gefahr einer derartigen Entwicklung darf auch im heutigen Ostmitteleuropa nicht übersehen werden.

I. Die Entwicklung bis Ende der sechziger Jahre

A. Westeuropa

1. Der „demokratisch-sozialistische" Entwicklungsstrang

Bisher war von einem Modell die Rede; genaugenommen geht es aber um eine Reihe von Maßnahmen, die am besten als Entwicklungsstrang aufgefaßt werden können. Die grundlegendsten Neuerungen wurden in den Jahren nach dem Zweiten Weltkrieg anfänglich von einem breiten politischen Spektrum getragen, doch das Modell blieb auch noch später Inspirationsquelle für konkrete Maßnahmen, so daß von seiner allmählichen Entfaltung über mehr als zwei Jahrzehnte gesprochen werden kann. Die Ausgangslage nach dem Krieg war gekennzeichnet durch die ausgeprägte Diskreditierung des Kapitalismus, wie man ihn in der Wirtschaftskrise erfahren hatte; nie wieder – so eine weitverbreitete Ansicht – sollte das Wohl ganzer Gesellschaften oder Nationen von einer kleinen Zahl von Privateigentümern abhängen, die sich von ihren finanziellen Eigeninteressen leiten ließen. Und nie wieder sollte die arbeitende Bevölkerung schutzlos dem Wirken des Arbeitsmarktes preisgegeben werden. Der Staat sollte Verantwortung für die Wohlfahrt der Bevölkerung übernehmen. Der Gedanke einer durchgehend verstaatlichen Planwirtschaft nach sowjetischem Muster wurde aber (außer von den Kommunisten) abgelehnt, und das „demokratisch-sozialistische" Modell erfuhr in den verschiedenen Ländern Westeuropas durchaus verschiedene Ausprägungen.

Dennoch gab es gewisse Gemeinsamkeiten. Fast überall findet man die

Schwerpunkte soziale Sicherung, verstärkten staatlichen Einfluß auf die Wirtschaft und Neuverteilung der Macht zugunsten einer größeren Einflußnahme von Arbeitnehmerorganisationen, die nun verschiedentlich in die wirtschaftlichen und politischen Machtstrukturen miteinbezogen werden sollten. Verstärkte soziale Sicherheit bedeutete einerseits den Ausbau des zumeist noch recht rudimentären Sozialversicherungssystems, Arbeitnehmer- und Mieterschutz und die Subventionierung lebensnotwendiger Güter und Dienstleistungen. Verstärkter staatlicher Einfluß auf die Wirtschaft erfolgte über Verstaatlichungen (zur Sicherung der „Kommandohöhen der Wirtschaft", aber auch aus anderen Gründen wie etwa Mangel an Privatkapital oder Kollaboration der früheren Eigentümer mit den nationalsozialistischen Machthabern; verstaatlicht wurde hauptsächlich in den klassischen Industriebereichen Stahl, Energie, außerdem bei Banken und im Versicherungswesen), über Elemente der Wirtschaftsplanung (eine Notwendigkeit in Zeiten der Bewirtschaftung; später zunehmend „indikativ" und über Anreize abgewickelt) und über eine mehr oder weniger keynesianische Vollbeschäftigungspolitik. Die neue Macht der Gewerkschaften fand ihren Niederschlag in verschiedenen Formen der betrieblichen oder überbetrieblichen Mitbestimmung (bis hin zum Tripartismus etwa in Institutionen der Wirtschaftsplanung) sowie in einer privilegierten Stellung im öffentlichen Sektor (Shonfield 1969). Mit diesen Maßnahmen sollte der Markt nicht ersetzt, sondern nur zivilisiert, die Wirtschaft „demokratisiert" werden; die Politik und mittelbar die Bevölkerung sollten die Möglichkeit erhalten, die wirtschaftliche Entwicklung in Richtung eines pluralistisch definierten Gemeinwohls zu lenken.

2. Der „liberal-apolitische" Entwicklungsstrang in Westeuropa

Die Inspiration für die Maßnahmen, die dieses Modell umsetzten, kam zunächst aus den USA. Am Ende des Zweiten Weltkriegs wollten diese die Weltwirtschaft auf der Basis des Freihandels gestalten, um so – aus ihrer Sicht – den Frieden zu sichern. Für das wirtschaftlich geschwächte Europa bedeutete das eine große Härte. Unter dem Eindruck dieser Schwäche und des sich verstärkenden Kalten Krieges schwenkte die US-Außenpolitik um. Das Ergebnis war die weitgehende Suspendierung des GATT und sein Ersatz durch ein neues Konzept: den Marshall-Plan.

Die (vor allem im US-amerikanischen, New-Deal-Sinn) „liberalen" Vorstellungen vom Zusammenhang zwischen Wirtschaft und Demokratie erfuhren ihren größten Auftrieb mit diesem Hilfsplan. Demokratie war hier gleichzeitig ideologisch und geopolitisch definiert und wurde gleichgesetzt mit einem pluralistischen System (Wettbewerb der Parteien), einer leistungsfähigen Marktwirtschaft, weitverbreitetem Wohlstand auf dieser Basis und der Zugehörigkeit zur atlantischen Staatengemeinschaft. Ein solcher Zustand existierte zwar in Ansätzen in Westeuropa, doch sahen ihn die USA noch als sehr gebrechlich an – einerseits bedroht durch kommunistische Subversion von innen und sowjetische

Expansion von außen, andererseits gefährdet durch innere Schwächen von europäischer Politik und Wirtschaft, die es zu überwinden galt (Calleo und Rowland 1973, Calleo in Skidelski 1977). Der Marshall-Plan sollte diese Situation stabilisieren. Insbesondere wollte man eine Wiederholung der Fehler der Zwischenkriegszeit (vor allem in der Frage der deutschen Reparationen) vermeiden.

Die Marshall-Plan-Technokraten, die nun nach Westeuropa kamen, hatten durchwegs eine missionarische Vorstellung von ihrer Aufgabe. Ihnen schwebte ein moderner, leistungsfähiger, aber auch ein durch Gewerkschaften und Staat zivilisierter Kapitalismus nach dem Modell des New Deal vor. Ihr wichtigster Kritikpunkt betraf die Antiquiertheit und Kleinkariertheit der europäischen Ordnung: die Aufsplitterung in viele Staaten mit getrennten Wirtschaftsräumen, dazu in jedem Land wieder die Präsenz relativ vieler Unternehmen selbst in Branchen, in denen sie einen hohen Grad an Unternehmenskonzentration längst als zeitgemäß ansahen (etwa Stahl, Automobilindustrie u. dgl.). Jedes dieser wenig dynamischen Unternehmen pflegte einen kleinen, geschützten Markt, war wenig aggressiv bei der Marktdurchdringung (Konsumgüterproduzenten peilten oft nur die Oberschicht als Abnehmer an) und zahlte dementsprechend dürftige Löhne, was wiederum die Absatzchancen für die Industrieproduktion insgesamt verminderte und den Arbeitnehmern wenig Grund zu Zufriedenheit gab. Ein moderner Kapitalismus sollte mit großen Einheiten Massenproduktion für Massenkonsum betreiben. Der Weg dazu bestand in einem größeren Markt (daher auch die amerikanischen Bemühungen um ein westeuropäisches Wirtschaftsgebiet mit entsprechendem Abbau von Handelshemmnissen und anderen staatlichen Behinderungen), in einer hohen Investitionsquote und in einem Umbruch der unternehmerischen Landschaft; aggressive Kapitalgesellschaften sollten Familienbetriebe und ihr restriktives Denken ersetzen (Maier 1978).

Die Liberalisierungswelle, die durch den Marshall-Plan eingeleitet wurde, war zwar schwerpunktmäßig durchaus verschieden von den „demokratisch-sozialistischen" Reformvorstellungen der unmittelbaren Nachkriegszeit, die eher einen „dritten Weg" zwischen Privatkapitalismus und Planwirtschaft anstrebten als einen modernisierten, dynamischen Kapitalismus. Andererseits war der Marshall-Plan mit großen Bereichen der „demokratisch-sozialistischen" Reformen durchaus vereinbar. Ein großer Teil der Marshall-Plan-Gelder etwa ging in jene strategisch wichtigen Industriesektoren, die eben erst verstaatlicht worden waren. In Österreich floß der größte Teil der Marshall-Plan-Hilfe (etwa drei Viertel) in die verstaatlichen Bereiche Elektrizitätswirtschaft, Kohlebergbau und Grundstoffindustrie. Die den Regierungen zur Verfügung gestellten Hilfsmittel (Güter, Kapital) stellten außerdem eine wichtige Grundlage für die damalige Wirtschaftsplanung dar.

Die Marshall-Plan-Manager hatten auch nichts gegen starke Gewerkschaften einzuwenden, solange diese nicht kommunistisch waren; sozialdemokratische oder christliche (oder am besten überhaupt weitgehend entpolitisierte) Gewerkschaften paßten gut in ihr Gesellschaftsbild und wurden auch entsprechend gefördert. Wirtschaftswachstum und gewerkschaftlicher Druck in Richtung höherer Löhne wurden nicht als unvereinbar angesehen, solange Gewinne und

Investitionstätigkeit dadurch nicht beeinträchtigt wurden; höhere Löhne waren schließlich entscheidend für den Aufbau einer Massenkonsumgesellschaft, bei der alle Beteiligten gleichzeitig gewinnen konnten. Für die Stärkung der Funktionsfähigkeit des Marktes sollte vor allem die Liberalisierung des Handels sorgen. Wenn gleichzeitig der Abbau von Subventionen für Güter des grundlegenden Bedarfs eingefordert wurde, so geschah das, um sicherzustellen, daß die Marshallplan-Hilfe tatsächlich für Investitionszwecke verwendet und nicht bei der Stützung des Konsums versickern würde. In Österreich gab das Anlaß zur größten Streikwelle der Nachkriegsgeschichte anläßlich des vierten Lohn-Preis-Abkommens; die Beendigung des Streiks leitete gleichzeitig die Entpolitisierung der Gewerkschaften und die Disziplinierung ihrer Aktivisten ein (Prader 1974).

Marshall-Plan(European Recovery Program)-Mittel bedeuteten unter anderem niedrigverzinsliche Kredite für Unternehmen und damit eine Förderung der Kapitalbildung in Unternehmerhand; das war eine der Voraussetzungen für den Expansionsschub durch verstärkte Investitionstätigkeit. Der Abbau der Subventionen diente dem gleichen Zweck. Hand in Hand damit ging eine tendenzielle Umverteilung nach oben, wobei das „trickle-down"-Prinzip, das im allgemeinen Aufschwung auch weitgehend effektiv wurde, die Rechtfertigung abgab.

Die beiden Modelle oder Stränge konnten also durchaus neben- und miteinander fortbestehen. Sie führten zu einem neuen wirtschafts- und sozialpolitischen Konsens und dadurch zur weitgehenden Entpolitisierung dieses in früheren Zeiten so sensiblen Bereichs. Jahrzehntelang konnte sich dieser „sozialdemokratische Konsens" entfalten und brachte eine stete Erhöhung der Wirtschaftsleistung und der Reallöhne, aber auch ständig zunehmende Verbesserungen bei der sozialen Sicherheit und bei Schutzbestimmungen für Arbeitnehmer und Konsumenten. Die dadurch steigende Staatsquote wurde als Nebenerscheinung angesehen und zum Teil sogar positiv bewertet, weil sich so für den Staat zusätzliche Steuerungsmöglichkeiten im wirtschaftlichen Bereich ergaben. Der mit dieser Entwicklung einhergehende Strukturwandel brachte zwar Härten für einzelne Gruppen der Bevölkerung, die sich in schrumpfenden Sektoren befanden (etwa Bauern, Bergarbeiter usw.); diese Härten wurden aber gedämpft durch das allgemeine Wachstum der Beschäftigung vor allem im tertiären Sektor, durch die Einrichtungen des sozialen Netzes und zum Teil auch durch großzügige Übergangsregelungen. Wirtschaftswachstum erschien als das Grundrezept zur Lösung fast aller gesellschaftlichen Probleme. (Lauber 1983)

B. Ostmitteleuropa bis Ende der sechziger Jahre

Bis zum Ausbruch des Kalten Krieges scheint die Entwicklung in Ostmitteleuropa nicht völlig unterschiedlich von der in Westeuropa zu verlaufen, was Gestaltung und Struktur der Wirtschaft betrifft. Natürlich gab es teilweise größere Probleme durch größere Kriegsschäden, Bevölkerungsverluste, Vertreibungen, zum Teil auch durch die Präsenz der Roten Armee. Wie in Westeuropa gab es auch hier einen allgemeinen Ausschlag des Pendels nach links, in Richtung erhöhter politischer Kontrolle über die Wirtschaft, u. a. durch die Verstaatlichung insbesondere von deutschem oder von Kollaborateurs-Eigentum. Das war kein speziell kommunistischer Gedanke. Im übrigen waren die kommunistischen Parteien seit der Kominform-Deklaration von 1943 zunächst auf die Akzeptanz „nationaler Wege zum Sozialismus" eingeschworen.

In Polen wurde ein solches System von einem KP-Regime unter Gomulka praktiziert und bedeutete effektiv die (oft widerwillige) Duldung eines signifikanten privaten Sektors, nicht nur in der Landwirtschaft. In der Tschechoslowakei wurde – zwar unter kommunistischem Druck, aber mit Zustimmung anderer Parteien, die damals noch Selbständigkeit besaßen – unter einem sozialdemokratischen Premier und von einem sozialdemokratischen Industrieminister 1945 ein verstaatlichter Sektor geschaffen, der knapp über 60 Prozent der Industriearbeiter beschäftigte. Im Jahr darauf wurde (inzwischen unter KP-Premier Gottwald) ein erster Wirtschaftsplan formuliert, der von einem Nebeneinander von öffentlichem und privatem Sektor unter Fortsetzung eines traditionell westorientierten Außenhandels der Tschechoslowakei ausging (Luža 1978, 1988 und 1992). In Ungarn hatten die Wahlen von 1945 eine nicht-kommunistische Mehrheit erbracht, mit den Kleinbauern als stärkste Partei. In Ungarn und der Tschechoslowakei waren die Kommunisten also nur über Koalitionen mit anderen Parteien an der Macht beteiligt und stellten eine Minderheit dar, die allerdings über Polizei, Armee und Gewerkschaften immer mehr Machtpositionen besetzte. Pluralistische Demokratie existierte aber durchaus in Ansätzen (in Ungarn bis Jänner 1947, in der Tschechoslowakei bis Februar 1947). Interessant ist in diesem Zusammenhang auch, daß im Sommer 1947 die inzwischen von Kommunisten angeführten Regierungen Polens und der Tschechoslowakei lebhaft an der Teilnahme am Marshall-Plan interessiert waren (Yergin 1978, 119–120, Luža 1978, 93).

Der Kalte Krieg und der Marshall-Plan brachten hier die Wende. Die Sowjetunion, die zunächst noch selbst eine Teilnahme erwogen hatte, verurteilte diesen Plan am 2. Juli 1947 als Akt des amerikanischen Imperialismus, mit dem Europa unter amerikanische Hegemonie gebracht werden sollte. Die Regierungen Polens und der Tschechoslowakei wurden am 9. Juli von Moskau dazu gezwungen, ihre Teilnahmeabsichten ebenfalls zurückzuziehen. Kurz darauf begann die effektive Gleichschaltung Osteuropas im Sinn einer Stalinisierung, einer Ausrichtung auf das sowjetische Modell in wirtschaftlicher und politischer Hinsicht und die Integration in einen gemeinsamen Wirtschaftsraum (Molotow-Plan, vor allem Kominform-Konferenz vom September 1947). Gomulkas polnischer Weg zum Sozialismus wurde verurteilt, ebenso jener der DDR. Kollektivierung nach dem sowjetischen Modell wurde zur einzig legitimen Form sozialistischer Wirtschaftsentwicklung erklärt und für alle osteuropäischen Länder verbindlich gemacht (Yergin 1978, 127–129).

Das stalinistische Modell bedeutete eine fast vollständige Kontrolle der Zentralen des Staats bzw. der KP über Wirtschaft und Gesellschaft. Die Wirtschaft wurde aus ideologischen und politischen Erwägungen sowie für die Zwecke der

Zentralverwaltung in große Einheiten gegliedert. Diese Kontrolle durch die Zentrale erhob nicht den Anspruch auf Demokratisierung der Wirtschaft im Sinn einer pluralistisch vermittelten Kontrolle durch die Wählerschaft (die Verstaatlichungen in der Tschechoslowakei 1945 konnten noch in diesem Sinn aufgefaßt werden); dafür fehlten sowohl die freien Wahlen wie auch die Beschränkung der Staatsgewalt. Und das stalinistische Modell führte eher zum Gegenteil einer „Demokratisierung der Gesellschaft" im liberal-apolitischen Sinn, also zu einer Zivilisierung der Machtkampfs zwischen verschiedenen gesellschaftlichen Gruppen auf der Basis wohletablierter pluralistischer Regeln und als Ergebnis der materiellen Sicherheit und relativen Zufriedenheit der betroffenen Gruppen. Schon die Absicht dazu war nicht gegeben, außer vielleicht langfristig (in der Utopie der sozialistischen Überflußgesellschaft gäbe es ja auch keine Klassenkämpfe mehr). Kurz- und mittelfristig sollte das stalinistische Wirtschaftsmodell einerseits Aufstieg und Herrschaft einer KP-nahen Industriearbeiterschaft sowie einer KP-Nomenklatura sichern, gleichzeitig aber auch den zwangsweisen Abstieg der bisherigen Eigentümer der Produktionsmittel bzw. überhaupt der bisherigen Ober- und Mittelschichten organisieren (durch Kollektivierung von Landwirtschaft und Industrie, niedrige Einkommen für Angestellte und frühere Freiberufler wie etwa Ärzte).

Während also das liberal-apolitische Wachstumsmodell eine größere Kohäsion der Gesellschaft durch Befriedung der wirtschaftlichen Spannungen anstrebt, führt das stalinistische Modell zunächst zur gegenteiligen Entwicklung; es führt zu Spannungen, die vermutlich ihren Niederschlag in radikalen Massenbewegungen gefunden hätten, wenn die Ausdrucksmöglichkeiten dafür bestanden hätten (immerhin kam es zu wiederholten Ausbrüchen). Die westeuropäische Erfahrung insbesondere der Zwischenkriegszeit zeigt ja, daß der plötzliche Abstieg des kleinen und mittleren Bürgertums – absolut gemessen an Wohlstandskriterien, aber vor allem im Vergleich zur aufstrebenden und durch ihre gewerkschaftliche Organisation als übermächtig empfundenen Arbeiterschaft – die Entstehung und Ausbreitung des Faschismus stark begünstigte. In Osteuropa wurden derartige soziale Veränderungen von den kommunistischen Machthabern sogar gezielt herbeigeführt (was normalerweise für noch stärkere Emotionen sorgt), allerdings wurde die politische Organisation der negativ betroffenen Gruppen durch den Charakter des bestehenden politischen Systems verhindert. Es ist aber wahrscheinlich, daß derartige Spannungen, wenn sie keinen Ausdruck finden können und auch nicht abgebaut werden, lange weiterbestehen und tiefe Spuren hinterlassen.

Stalinistische Wirtschaftsentwicklung bedeutete Spannungen nicht nur durch die gezielte Herbeiführung des Auf- und Abstiegs einzelner Gruppen, sondern auch durch die im Lauf der Jahre immer deutlicher hervortretende geringe wirtschaftliche Leistungsfähigkeit des Systems. Die Kollektivierung der Landwirtschaft war dabei ein Faktor; aber auch das Wachstum im industriellen Bereich, das hauptsächlich extensiver Natur war (Einbeziehung neuer Ressourcen an Arbeitskraft, Kapital, Rohstoffen usw. [Tardos 1989, 34; Valenta 1989, 20–22]), erreichte seine Grenzen längstens innerhalb von zwei Jahrzehnten. Die aus politischen Gründen angestrebten großen Einheiten waren ökonomisch schwerfällig, es fehlte der ständige Strukturwandel als Anpassung an wechselnde Marktbedingungen. Sowohl die Politik wie auch die materielle Produktion waren immer weniger in der Lage, die gesellschaftlichen Ansprüche zufriedenzustellen.

Ausbruchsversuche aus diesem Muster (DDR und Tschechoslowakei 1953, Ungarn und Polen 1956, Tschechoslowakei 1968, Polen 1970) wurden mit massivem Gewalteinsatz unterbunden.

C. Fazit der ersten zwei Jahrzehnte

In Westeuropa war die „demokratisch-sozialistisch" inspirierte „Demokratisierung der Wirtschaft" von Anfang an von pluralistisch-demokratischen Strukturen getragen und besiegelte den historischen Kompromiß mit der Arbeiterschaft sowie die Verpflichtung des Staates zur sozialen Gerechtigkeit; zum Teil mag es sich dabei letzten Endes um symbolische Politik gehandelt haben. Das dadurch geschaffene soziale Netz hat aber auch dazu beigetragen, die „schöpferischen Zerstörungen" des neuen dynamischen Kapitalismus in Grenzen zu halten, die als akzeptabel empfunden wurden. Der Kompromiß zwischen diesem und dem im Lauf der Zeit an Gewicht gewinnenden, liberal-apolitischen Modell brachte zwei Jahrzehnte lang ein die Gesellschaft stark harmonisierendes Wirtschaftswachstum, führte zur Verringerung der großen wirtschaftlichen und sozialen Konflikte (Entpolitisierung) und zu hoher Legitimität eines pluralistisch gesteuerten Kapitalismus.

Die Entwicklung in Osteuropa steht in scharfem Gegensatz dazu. Die erste Phase einer sozialistisch inspirierten Demokratisierung der Wirtschaft (soweit eine solche existierte) wurde ab 1947 ersetzt durch das stalinistische Modell einer zentralen Kontrolle ohne (pluralistische) Demokratie. Die Verwirklichung des Modells brachte die Expansion von Industriearbeiterschaft und Nomenklatur, alte Mittel- und Oberschichten dagegen wurden wirtschaftlich degradiert. Die damit verbundene schlechte wirtschaftliche Leistung produzierte Unzufriedenheit, zunehmend sogar bei den angeblichen Nutznießern des Systems selbst. Insgesamt brachten zwei Jahrzehnte extensiven Wachstums (mit teilweise durchaus hohen Zuwachsraten) für diese Gesellschaften hohe interne Spannungen, die nur durch das sich zwischen Autoritarismus und Totalitarismus bewegende politische System unterdrückt werden konnten – und auch das nicht zur Gänze, wie die wiederholten Ausbrüche zeigen. Auch die kommunistischen Eliten wußten um diese Mängel; sie reagierten mit einer Reihe von Stabilisierungsversuchen, die in der zweiten Hälfte der sechziger Jahre ein neues Muster einleiteten.

II. Europa seit Ende der sechziger Jahre

A. Westeuropa: Wirtschaftskrisen und Neokonservativismus

Der jahrzehntelange Nachkriegsboom zeigte schon Ende der sechziger/Anfang der siebziger Jahre deutliche Krisenerscheinungen (Inflationsdruck und dadurch bedingte Austeritätsprogramme; Zerfall des Systems von Bretton Woods). Die Liberalisierung des Welthandels wurde stärker wirksam, und die verschärfte Konkurrenz durch die Industrie aus den Schwellenländern, vor allem in Südostasien, führte zu Druck auf ganze Branchen (Textil, Stahl . . .) und zu vereinzelten Schutzmaßnahmen. Vor allem die beiden Ölkrisen von 1974 und 1979 stellen eine neue Herausforderung dar: Um die verteuerten Importe zu bezahlen, mußten westeuropäische Länder ihre wirtschaftliche Leistung erhöhen. Andererseits stiegen die Sozialausgaben als Folge der neuen Arbeitslosigkeit.

Die Konflikte über die Bewältigung dieses Problems führten zu einer kurzfristigen Repolitisierung. Die Linke forderte eine Belebung der Wirtschaft durch Konsum über Beibehaltung des hohen Lohnniveaus (keynesianische Stützung), verstärkten Schutz für Arbeitnehmer durch Ausbau des sozialen Netzes und Ausweitung des staatlichen Einflusses über die Wirtschaft bis hin zu neuen Verstaatlichungen. Im übrigen forderte nicht nur die Linke eine Ausweitung des „demokratisch-sozialistischen" Modells. Ähnliche Initiativen gab es bis Mitte der siebziger Jahre auch von konservativer Seite (in Großbritannien unter Heath 1972, in Frankreich unter Giscard und Chirac 1975; Lauber 1985).

Gleichzeitig begann ein Teil der Rechten, den Status quo der bisher verwirklichten „sozialistischen" Maßnahmen radikal in Frage zu stellen. In ihrer Sicht war es genau die exzessive Einflußnahme des Staats, die an der geringen Leistungsfähigkeit der Wirtschaft die Hauptschuld trug. Der Sozialstaat behindere die rechtzeitige Anpassung von Wirtschaft und Gesellschaft an neue Bedingungen und schaffe parasitäre Gruppen auf Kosten des Allgemeinwohls: etwa Arbeitnehmer, die durch gesetzliche Schutzbestimmungen oder politische Patronage künstlich vor Entlassung geschützt würden, ohne ihre alte wirtschaftliche Funktion zu erfüllen oder eine neue zu erlernen; oder Unternehmen, die durch restriktive Regulierung oder Subventionen vor Wettbewerb geschützt würden; oder gar verstaatlichte Unternehmen, die die Tendenz entwickelten, statt Gewinn ihre Kosten (insbesondere die Lohnkosten) zu maximieren. Staatliche Regulierung und exzessive Steuerbelastung (eine unvermeidliche Folge der staatlichen Sozialprogramme) behinderten außerdem die schöpferischen Kräfte der Wirtschaft in ihrer Entfaltung.

Die neokonservative Antwort auf diese Analyse hieß: mehr Markt und weniger Staat – also Deregulierung (z. B. bei Entlassungsschutz), Privatisierung, Abbau bei Sozialprogrammen und Subventionen und schließlich Senkung der Steuerquote; außerdem entscheidende Reduktion gewerkschaftlicher Macht. Nach anfänglichem Widerstand schwenkten auch die meisten sozialdemokratischen Parteien auf diesen Kurs ein, allerdings mit Mäßigung und etwas anderen Akzenten

(Merkel 1990). Abgesehen von der kurzen Phase der Reideologisierung blieb es also im großen und ganzen bei der Entpolitisierung der Wirtschafts- und Sozialpolitik. Wirtschaft und Gesellschaft wurden in stärkerem Maß dem Markt ausgesetzt, was eine neue Welle von Strukturwandel und entsprechenden Anpassungsleistungen auslöste.

Das „demokratisch-sozialistische" Element hat dadurch ganz klar an Bedeutung verloren. Markt und Kapitalismus sind weniger staatlichen Kontrollen und Steuerungen unterworfen als früher; allerdings hatten sich eben auch starke Zweifel bezüglich der Sinnhaftigkeit derartiger Maßnahmen ausgebreitet. Die verstärkte Dynamik des Marktes brachte neue Spannungen, einige davon kurzfristig (Entlassungswellen), andere längerfristig wirksam: Das soziale Problem der Zweidrittelgesellschaft stellte sich mit größerer Intensität, die Konkurrenz am unteren Ende des Arbeitsmarkts schürte die Gastarbeiterproblematik und schuf günstige Verhältnisse für die Neue Rechte. Insgesamt schienen diese Spannungen die Verarbeitungsmechanismen demokratischer Gesellschaften – und die politischen Grundprinzipien dieser Gesellschaften – aber noch nicht übermäßig zu belasten.

B. Ostmitteleuropa

1. Bis 1989: Reformversuche in Polen und Ungarn, Verhärtung in der Tschechoslowakei und der DDR

Noch während des großen Nachkriegsbooms in den westeuropäischen Ländern (bis Mitte der siebziger Jahre) hatte es in Ostmitteleuropa wiederholt Zeiten sehr schwacher wirtschaftlicher Leistung gegeben. Die dortigen Ökonomen sahen die Ursache dafür in einzelnen Einrichtungen des planwirtschaftlichen Systems, das es daher mit Hilfe marktwirtschaftlicher Elemente zu verbessern galt. Zur bis dahin größten Reformwelle kam es in der zweiten Hälfte der sechziger Jahre, insbesondere in der Tschechoslowakei und in Ungarn (Jeffries 1990). Die Reformen gediehen in Ungarn zwar weiter als in der Tschechoslowakei, doch fiel der reformerische Impuls in beiden Ländern der Stagnationsphase zum Opfer, die nach der Militärintervention gegen den „Prager Frühling" den gesamten Ostblock ergriff. Das planwirtschaftliche System wurde wieder installiert, allerdings mit einer bedeutenden Veränderung. Hier teilt sich die Entwicklung in zwei Pfade. In Polen und Ungarn kam es durch die Einführung marktwirtschaftlicher Elemente zur Verstärkung der Macht der „Großreiche" (Heinrich 1991), also jener industriellen und agrarischen Großunternehmen, die für Planungszwecke geschaffen und seither noch durch Fusionen vergrößert worden waren. In der DDR und der Tschechoslowakei dagegen wurden die dort eingeleiteten Reformen in Richtung Marktwirtschaft wieder rückgängig gemacht. Die dortigen Regime setzten nicht auf erhöhte Akzeptanz durch verbesserte Wirtschaftsleistung, sondern auf Rezentralisierung und verstärkte Repression.

In Polen und Ungarn emanzipierten sich die Großunternehmen nicht nur von den zentralen Kommandostellen; sie verhinderten auch eine Disziplinierung durch den Markt. Die zentralen Verteilungsinstitutionen wurden auch nicht abgeschafft, sondern immer mehr von den „Großreichen" kolonisiert: durch die Präsenz von Vertretern dieser Betriebe in der Zentralverwaltung oder in den obersten Parteigremien selbst. Dadurch sicherten sich die Großreiche ihre Vorteile auf Kosten der übrigen Betriebe (und der Substanz der Volkswirtschaft) in Form von Kapitalzuweisungen, Subventionen, höheren Löhnen, geringerem Innovationsdruck, bequemeren Produktionsquoten usw. Insgesamt ging es dabei um den Schutz vor der gesamtwirtschaftlich wünschenswerten Anpassung. Die zentralen Organe Planer und Partei, die ihre (d. h. aus ihrer Sicht die gesellschaftlichen) Prioritäten mangels der dafür notwendigen Legitimation nicht mehr durchsetzen können, sichern sich die politische Loyalität der Großreiche und ihrer Arbeitnehmer; im Austausch für diese Unterstützung wird von ihnen allerdings die Gewährung von Sonderkonditionen erwartet. Diese schwache Position der KP-Zentralen gegenüber den wirtschaftlichen Großorganisationen und gegenüber der Bevölkerung (Legitimitätsschwäche) führt nicht ganz unerwartet zu zwei weiteren Entwicklungen: der Kapitulation vor steigendem Lohndruck und – daraus resultierend – der zunehmenden Auslandsverschuldung zu Zwecken der gesellschaftlichen und politischen Stabilisierung (Heinrich 1991, 249; Ickes 1990; Kaminski 1991; Machowski 1990).

Für die zentralen Stellen von Partei und Staat stellt diese Entwicklung eine deutliche Auflösungstendenz dar. Die Großreiche entziehen sich jeder Disziplin – der des Marktes ebenso wie jener des Plans, den sie jetzt verstärkt mitgestalten oder auch umgehen können. Die Arbeiterschaft bekommt ebenfalls große Anreize, sich volkswirtschaftlich problematisch zu verhalten. Wegen ihrer kleinen Privilegien sind die Arbeitsplätze in den oft parasitären Großreichen die erstrebenswertesten, so daß paradoxerweise die Beschäftigung dort zunimmt, wo sie am wenigsten sinnvoll ist. Andererseits sind durch die größere De-facto-Autonomie der quasi-monopolistischen Einzelbetriebe und durch die Verschuldungspolitik der Regierung naheliegende Grenzen für Lohndisziplin abgebaut. Austerität wird immer weniger geduldet; die Betriebe können die Forderungen auf die Preise überwälzen, die Regierung nimmt ihrerseits Zuflucht zu Budgetdefiziten, Notenpresse und Auslandsverschuldung. Hier zeigt sich auch, wie der Anspruch dieser KP-Regime auf Alleinherrschaft effektive Machtlosigkeit im wirtschaftlichen Bereich zur Folge hatte. Die kommunistisch geführten Gewerkschaften waren mangels Legitimation nicht mehr in der Lage, den zentrifugalen Tendenzen des Lohndrucks entgegenzuwirken, und eine Gruppe wie Solidarność konnte wiederum nicht mäßigend wirken, solange sie nicht über politischen Einfluß verfügte. Ohne eigenen Einfluß bestand aber kein Anlaß dazu, Verantwortung für das Gesamtwohl zu übernehmen. Die Wirtschaftsreformen in Polen und Ungarn führten also zur Notwendigkeit einer immer wieder aufgeschobenen Sanierung, die mangels ausreichend starker Regierungsmacht nicht durchgeführt werden konnte.

In der Tschechoslowakei und der DDR verlief die Entwicklung anders. Auch hier hatten Reformen zur Einführung marktwirtschaftlicher Elemente geführt. In beiden Ländern setzten sich aber in der KP jene Elemente durch, die derartige Reformen als staatsgefährdend betrachteten und daher ablehnten. In der Tschechoslowakei erfolgte eine Rezentralisierung der wirtschaftlichen Entscheidungen; gleichzeitig entging das Land auch der steigenden Auslandsverschuldung. In der DDR verfolgte die Sowjetunion die unter Ulbricht eingeführten Wirtschaftsreformen mit Mißtrauen, was schließlich (zusammen mit Ulbrichts Ablehnung der sowjetischen Entspannungspolitik) zu dessen Sturz und der Einsetzung Honeckers führte. Beide Regime lehnten sich verstärkt an die Sowjetunion an und konzentrierten sich auf den Ausbau der Repression (Batt 1991).

Insgesamt nahmen also die wirtschaftlichen Spannungen in den ostmitteleuropäischen Ländern in diesem Zeitraum zu (mit der teilweisen Ausnahme Ungarn, wo sich in den achtziger Jahren ein zwar noch bescheidener, aber doch recht beachtlicher privater Sektor entwickelte). Vor allem in den achtziger Jahren wird die wirtschaftliche Stagnation immer ausgeprägter. Die Bevölkerung fordert den versprochenen steigenden Lebensstandard ein; die politische Elite ist sich der zunehmend prekären Situation (steigende Auslandsverschuldung, stagnierende Produktion, Sanierungsbedarf bei gleichzeitig schwindender ideologischen Legitimation) wohl bewußt und verliert mehr und mehr den Glauben an die alten Rezepte.

Zusätzlich schwindet noch eine weitere Stütze ihrer Macht. Die „sozialistische Solidarität" – die Kontrolle der Beibehaltung einer orthodoxen KP-Linie durch die Androhung militärischer Intervention seitens der Länder des Warschauer Pakts – verlor schon seit Gorbatschows eigenen Reformbestrebungen an Gewicht, noch mehr aber mit der Entmachtung Ligatschows 1988. Zunehmend gab es seitens Gorbatschows Aufforderungen an die KP-Regime zu größerer Flexibilität. Wollten die herrschenden Eliten ihr Überleben sichern, so mußten sie einen Weg beschreiten, den autoritäre Regime in der Vergangenheit oft genommen hatten: die Bevölkerung bzw. die oppositionellen Kräfte einladen, an der Macht – und vor allem an der Verantwortung für unvermeidliche, aber unpopuläre Maßnahmen – teilzunehmen (Frankreich 1789, Deutschland 1918). Mit Glück konnten sie dann hoffen, ihre zunehmend gebrechlichere Alleinherrschaft durch eine stabilere Hegemonie zu ersetzen. Für die Reformer unter den KP-Eliten bot sich dabei gleichzeitig die Möglichkeit, ihre Position in der eigenen Partei zu stärken.

Das war der Weg, den Gorbatschow selbst beschritt, als er 1987 die Erneuerung der Nomenklatura von unten durch Wahlen mit mehreren Kandidaten (aber nicht mehreren Parteien) durchsetzte (Hill/Löwenhardt 1991). In Ungarn erfolgte dieser Schritt schon 1983 bzw. 1985, als die ersten Wahlen nach diesem System abgehalten wurden, und auch die Verhandlungen am Runden Tisch (zwischen Regime und inzwischen legalisierten Oppositionsparteien) im Sommer 1989 hatten im Grunde ein ähnliches Ziel, auch wenn die Bereitschaft zur Abgabe der Alleinherrschaft inzwischen gewachsen war (Tökes 1990, 55–57). Im Prinzip ähnlich verliefen auch die Verhandlungen des polnischen Regimes mit Solidarność im Frühjahr 1989. Die großen Streiks vom Vorjahr konnten nur durch

Gespräche zwischen Walesa und der KP-Führung und durch die Ankündigung von Verhandlungen am Runden Tisch über grundlegende wirtschaftliche und politische Fragen zu Ende gebracht werden. Das Verhandlungsergebnis sollte die Hegemonie der KP wenigstens für eine weitere Legislaturperiode (bis 1993) garantieren (Lewis 1990).

In der Tschechoslowakei und der DDR dagegen waren die Reformkräfte innerhalb der KP dem orthodoxen Flügel gegenüber zu schwach, um einen solchen Prozeß rechtzeitig einleiten zu können. Dort waren bis zum Schluß ausgeprägte Hardliner an der Macht, die das Tienanmen-Massaker ausdrücklich gebilligt hatten und auch innenpolitisch zu ähnlicher Gewaltanwendung bereit schienen. Erst unter dem Eindruck überwältigender Massendemonstrationen und Loyalitätsverlusten in den eigenen Reihen waren sie zu Verhandlungen bereit – zu einem Zeitpunkt, als ihre Niederlage schon besiegelt war und die Opposition das Regime auch ohne Runden Tisch zum Einsturz bringen konnte (Batt 1991). Diesbezügliche Angebote von Ministerpräsident Adamec im November 1989 oder von der Regierung Modrow Anfang 1990 kamen zu spät, um noch Wirksamkeit entfalten zu können.

2. Nach 1989: Welche Demokratisierung?

In den Umstürzen von 1989 wurde die politische Macht auf Regierungsebene neu verteilt. Selbst dort, wo die Reformkommunisten Chancen für einen für sie selbst sanften Übergang ausgehandelt hatten (Polen und Ungarn), führten die Wahlen zu anderen Ergebnissen. 1990 waren in Polen, Ungarn und der Tschechoslowakei Regierungen an der Macht, die Demokratie und Marktwirtschaft nach westlichem Muster anstrebten. Was aber bedeutet Demokratisierung nach westlichem Muster?

Westeuropa (oder auch Südeuropa) kann bestenfalls für das mittel- oder langfristige Ergebnis der angestrebten Entwicklung als Vorbild dienen, nicht aber für den Pfad der Entwicklung selbst. Zu groß sind die Unterschiede in der jeweiligen Ausgangslage. Ostmitteleuropa hat in seiner Geschichte wenig Erfahrung mit der Demokratie schon im formalen Sinn; selbst in diesem Bereich sind Probleme vorstellbar. Und während in West- oder Südeuropa Demokratisierung die Einbeziehung bislang marginalisierter Schichten in den grundlegenden politischen Konsens (vor allem bei der Wirtschafts- und Sozialpolitik) bedeutete, gehen die Erfordernisse der wirtschaftlichen Sanierung und der Eingliederung in eine weitgehend liberalisierte Weltwirtschaft in die Richtung der Einschränkung politischer Partizipation. Diese Entwicklung wird durch jene konservativen Ideologien noch verstärkt, die als Reaktion auf den Kommunismus derzeit das Feld beherrschen. Schließlich werden durch die Einführung der Marktwirtschaft soziale Spannungen entfesselt, die erst später durch wirtschaftlichen Erfolg und Hilfe von außen begrenzt werden können. Osteuropa wird also seinen eigenen Weg der Demokratisierung finden müssen.

Bei der geringen Erfahrung mit pluralistischer Demokratie geht es nicht nur um die fehlende Praxis beim Umgang mit Institutionen wie freien Wahlen und Grundrechten. Die „zivile Gesellschaft" selbst ist erst im Entstehen begriffen und wird sich erst mit der neuen Eigentumsordnung ganz ausbilden, welche selbst wieder nur allmählich entstehen kann. Die Privatisierung und Umgestaltung vor allem der parasitären „Großreiche" ist eine so große Aufgabe, daß sie die in Westeuropa im Zug der neokonservativen Welle durchgeführten Privatisierungsmaßnahmen gänzlich in den Schatten stellt. Im Bereich der politischen Kultur wiederum sind plötzliche Veränderungen erfahrungsgemäß nicht zu erwarten; und Antikommunismus bedeutet noch keine Unterstützung für demokratische Normen. Das Auftauchen autoritärer Elemente in allen drei Ländern (Agh 1991, 147–150) kann diesbezüglich als Warnzeichen gesehen werden. Die Tendenz zur Stärkung der Exekutive ergibt sich dabei zum Teil aus der Aufsplitterung der Parteienszene, zum Teil kann sie auch als unbewußte Fortsetzung früherer Praktiken gesehen werden (Stojanov 1991); in diese Richtung zeigt auch das Verbot des Kommunismus in der ČSFR Ende 1991.

In West- und Südeuropa bedeutete Demokratisierung ganz wesentlich die Einbeziehung bis dahin politisch marginalisierter Schichten. In Ostmitteleuropa gibt es zwar durch die formaldemokratischen Institutionen eine Einbeziehung, die für den Großteil der Bevölkerung neu ist; gleichzeitig werden aber vor allem Arbeitnehmer tendenziell ausgeschlossen. Zum einen ist das die Folge einer antikommunistischen Reaktion auf die frühere Privilegierung des „Proletariats", auch haben die vorherrschenden konservativen Strömungen traditionell wenig Platz für Arbeitnehmerpartizipation. Das galt schon für die neue Solidarność; es gilt auch für die neokonservative Wirtschaftspolitik eines Vaclav Klaus oder den traditionellen Konservativismus des Demokratischen Forums in Ungarn (Schöpflin 1991).

Die heutige konservative Hegemonie und die Restriktion der Partizipation resultiert aber auch aus den scheinbar unvermeidbaren Erfordernissen der Wirtschafts- und Finanzpolitik. Dort liegt der Akzent notgedrungen auf Sanierung von Budget und Betrieben, auf Stabilisierung der Währung und auf Austerität – insgesamt also auf einer Politik der Deflation, die den Schaden wiedergutmachen soll, den das jahrelange Versagen der KP-Regime bei der Bewältigung dieser Aufgaben angerichtet hat. Deflationspolitik bedeutet so gut wie immer eine Einschränkung der Partizipation für Arbeitnehmer; aber eben dieses Phänomen behindert auch den Aufbau neuer Loyalitäten jener Art, wie sie das „demokratisch-sozialistische" Modell in Westeuropa hervorbrachte.

Die Einführung der Marktwirtschaft bringt zusätzliche Probleme durch die Entfesselung von sozialen Spannungen, die die sozialen Folgen der Sanierung noch verschärfen. Hier geht es nicht bloß (wie im Westeuropa der Nachkriegszeit) um die Umwandlung eines kleinkarierten und traditionellen Kapitalismus in einen modernen und leistungsfähigen. In Ostmitteleuropa müssen Marktwirtschaft und Marktdisziplin nach einem halben Jahrhundert von ganzen Gesellschaften wieder neu erlernt werden. Zur Beschleunigung dieses Prozesses wird es notwendig sein, die Bildung von Risikokapital und den Status der Unternehmer zu privilegieren, im Sinn einer Umverteilung der Ressourcen von unten nach oben. Das Nebeneinander von traditionellen Arbeitnehmern (oder Pensionisten) mit einer neuen, finanziell erfolgreichen Unternehmerschicht muß zu sozialen Spannungen führen, die „wirtschaftlich Zurückgebliebenen" könnten leicht für radikale Ideologien verfügbar werden (auch wenn die „Impfung gegen den Kommunismus" von Dauer sein dürfte).

In Westeuropa wurde eine solche Entwicklung (die im übrigen nicht annähernd so radikal war) durch großzügige Hilfe von außen und rasche Erfolge entschärft. Heute aber gibt es keinen Kalten Krieg und keine Sowjetunion, aus deren Einflußbereich die osteuropäischen Staaten durch Wirtschaftshilfe herausgelöst werden sollen. Der Zusammenbruch der Sowjetunion schafft auch noch andere Probleme (durch den teilweisen Zusammenbruch der Handelsbeziehungen mit Osteuropa). Gleichzeitig ist die internationale Wirtschaft durch einen Grad an Liberalisierung und Wettbewerb gekennzeichnet, die Westeuropa in der unmittelbaren Nachkriegszeit erspart blieben. Das haben auch die Verhandlungen um die Assoziierungsabkommen zwischen der EG und Polen, Tschechoslowakei und Ungarn Ende 1991 gezeigt. Das „liberal-apolitische" Modell wird also in Mitteleuropa vermutlich nicht vor einigen Jahren zum Tragen kommen.

Die Tatsache, daß die in Westeuropa angewandten Modelle (demokratisch-sozialistisch und liberal-apolitisch) nicht anwendbar erscheinen, bedeutet natürlich nicht, daß nicht andere Formen der Demokratie im Sinn einer Teilnahme an der Gemeinschaft verwirklicht werden könnten. Großes Potential liegt diesbezüglich bei den Privatisierungen und der dabei diskutierten Lösung, den Bürgern dieser Länder einen Anteil an der wirtschaftlichen Entwicklung zu sichern. De Gaulle schwebte eine derartige Lösung vor; er wollte sie mit Hilfe der berühmten „participation" verwirklichen (diese sollte für Arbeitnehmer jene Funktion erfüllen, welche das Privateigentum für die Bourgeoisie hatte; es blieb aber beim Projekt). Die Ausgabe von Gutscheinen an alle Bürger, mit denen später Aktien an privatisierten Betrieben erworben werden können, stellt eine solche Möglichkeit konservativer Demokratisierung dar; viel hängt hier von der konkreten Ausgestaltung ab (Fink 1990).

Es ist absehbar, daß der Prozeß der Demokratisierung in Ostmitteleuropa voller Gefahren steckt. Eine Phase hoher sozialer Spannungen und starker psychischer Desorientierung ist als Folge der gesellschaftlichen Umwandlungen zu erwarten. Politisches Desinteresse – wie bei den jüngsten Wahlen in diesen Ländern ersichtlich (Barany und Vinton 1990) – wäre eine naheliegende Folge; von da zur Verfügbarkeit für antidemokratische, radikale Bewegungen mag es nur mehr ein Schritt sein.

Westeuropäische Rezepte erscheinen fürs erste nicht anwendbar. Viel wird also auf die Initiative und Kreativität der Ostmitteleuropäer selbst ankommen; und die Gefahr eines Abgleitens in autoritäre Verhältnisse wird wohl noch für einige Zeit bestehen.

Literatur

Agh, Attila, The Transition to Democracy in Central Europe: A Comparative View, in: Journal of Public Policy 11:2 (1991), 133–151.

Barany, Zoltan D., und Louisa Vinton, Breakthrough to Democracy: Elections in Poland and Hungary, in: Studies in Comparative Communism 23:2 (1990), 191–212.

Batt, Judy, The End of Communist Rule in East-Central Europe: A Four-Country Comparison, in: Government and Opposition 26:3 (1991), 368–390.

Calleo, David P., Keynes and the Pax Americana, in: Skidelski 1977, 95–103.

Calleo, David P., und Benjamin M. Rowland, America and the World Political Economy. Bloomington, 1973.

Fink, Gerhard, Zur Diskussion „Wirtschaftsreformen und Systemänderungen in Osteuropa", in: Wirtschaftspolitische Blätter 37:5 (1990), 531–539.

Heinrich, Hans-Georg, Was bleibt vom „realen Sozialismus"?, in: Österreichische Zeitschrift für Politikwissenschaft 20:3 (1991), 245–256.

Hill, Ronald J., und John Löwenhardt, Nomenklatura and Perestroika, in: Government and Opposition, 1991, 229–243.

Holzer, Jerzy, Polens Weg aus dem Kommunismus, in: Aus Politik und Zeitgeschichte, Nr. 12–13 (16. 3.1990), 17–28.

Ickes, Barry W., Obstacles to Economic Reform of Socialism: An Institutional-Choice Approach, in: Annals of the American Academy of Political and Social Science, Jänner 1990, 53–64.

Jeffries, Ian, A Guide to the Socialists Economies. London, 1990.

Kaminski, Bartlomiej, Systemic Underpinnings of the Transition in Poland: The Shadow of the Round-table Agreement, in: Studies in Comparative Communism 24:2 (1991), 173–190.

Lauber, Volkmar, From Growth Consensus to Fragmentation in Western Europe, in: Comparative Politics 15:3 (1983), 329–349.

Lauber, Volkmar, Die Krise in Politik und Wirtschaft: Großbritannien und Frankreich, in: Österreichische Zeitschrift für Politikwissenschaft 14:3 (1985), 325–341.

Lewis, Paul, Non-Competitive Election and Regime Change: Poland 1989, in: Parliamentary Affairs 43:1 (1990), 90–107.

Lipset, Seymour Martin, Political Man. The Social Basis of Politics (Garden City, 1960).

Luža, Radomir, Czechoslovakia Between Democracy and Communism, 1945–1948, in: Maier (1978), 73–106.

Machowski, Heinrich, Polens schwieriger Weg in die Marktwirtschaft, in: Aus Politik und Zeitgeschichte, 16. März 1990, 29–38.

Maier, Charles S., The Origins of the Cold War and Contemporary Europe. New York, 1978.

Merkel, Wolfgang, Niedergang der Sozialdemokratie?, in: Leviathan 18:1 (1990), 106–133.

Prader, Hans, Ziele und Resultate kooperativer Gewerkschaftspolitik im Wiederaufbau nach 1945, in: ÖZP 3:3 (1974), 347–366.

Schöpflin, George, Conservatism and Hungary's Tradition, in: Problems of Communism 40:1 (1991), 60–68.

Shonfield, Andrew, Modern Capitalism. Oxford 1969.

Skidelsky, Robert, The End of the Keynesian Era. New York 1977.

Stojanov, Christo, Das „Immunsystem" des „real existierenden Sozialismus", in: Aus Politik und Zeitgeschichte, 3. 5.1991, 36–46.

Tardos, Martin, The Blueprint of Economic Reforms in Hungary, in: Economic Commission for Europe: Economic Reforms in the European Centrally Planned Economies. New York 1989, 34–41.

Tökes, Rudolf L., Hungary's New Political Elites: Adaptation and Change, 1989–90, in: Problems of Communism 39:6 (1990), 44–65.

Valenta, Frantisek, Framework of Economic Reform in Czechoslovakia, 34–41, 20–27, in: Economic Commission for Europe: Economic Reforms in the European Centrally Planned Economies.New York 1989. 34–41.

Yergin, Daniel, Shattered Peace: The Origins of the Cold War and the National Security State, in: Maier 1978, 107–142.

Literatur

Anton Pelinka

Ethnische Konflikte und Konfliktlösungen in Mittel- und Osteuropa

Die Veränderungen in Europa, die wir seit 1985 beobachten können, können nur mit dem Umbruch des Kontinents zwischen 1945 und 1948 verglichen werden. Seit dem Beginn der Amtszeit Michael Gorbatschows als Generalsekretär der UdSSR und dem dramatischen Zusammenbruch der kommunistischen Regime in Europa 1989 und 1990 ist die 1945 und danach etablierte Nachkriegsordnung zu Ende – die Ordnung der Stabilisierung durch Satelliten, des Gleichgewichts zwischen Ost und West, des Kalten Krieges; die Ordnung also, die Europa vier Jahrzehnte hindurch dominierte. Das Ende der kommunistischen Regime hat verschiedene Aspekte:

- Demokratisierung. Einparteiensysteme sind zusammengebrochen und haben mehr oder weniger westlichen, kompetitiven Mehrparteiensystemen Platz gemacht.
- Marktwirtschaft. An Stelle zentral geplanter, sogenannter sozialistischer Wirtschaftsordnungen werden kapitalistische Ökonomien errichtet.
- Ethnische Konflikte. Ethnische Gegensätze, viele Jahre hindurch von einem politischen System unterdrückt, das für sich den endgültigen Sieg über solche Gegensätze beansprucht hat, erleben eine Renaissance.

Dieser dritte Aspekt gleicht einem Prozeß des Auftauens. Nationale Gegensätze, ethnischer Haß, kollektives Vorurteil – alles das scheint wiederum, wie schon am Beginn dieses Jahrhunderts, lebendig zu werden; wiedergeboren und bereit, die Gesellschaften des östlichen Mitteleuropas und Osteuropas durch die letzten Jahre dieses Jahrhunderts abermals zu bestimmen. Der Zusammenbruch der kommunistischen Diktatur ist wie das Öffnen der Büchse der Pandora. Die Völker Mittel- und Osteuropas haben Demokratie gewollt – und sie erhalten soziale Bedingungen, die offenkundig denen des Balkans des Jahres 1901 gleichen. Haben die europäischen Völker auch die Balkankriege zu fürchten, als Ergebnis dieser sozialen Bedingungen?

Ein Indikator dieser Entwicklung, der eine solche Furcht rechtfertigt, ist der offensichtliche Verlust von historischer Erinnerung. Viele der nunmehr Demokratie genießenden Völker neigen dazu, bestimmte, besonders schmerzvolle Etappen ihrer vorkommunistischen Geschichte einfach aus ihrem Gedächtnis zu streichen. Slowakische Nationalisten beanspruchen Josef Tiso als nationalen Helden – denselben Tiso, der nicht nur für den Eintritt der Slowakei in den 2. Weltkrieg auf deutscher Seite die Verantwortung trägt, sondern auch für die Diktatur und für die Durchführung des Holocaust auf dem Boden der Slowakei. Einige ungarische Nationalisten scheinen zu vergessen, daß Ungarn zwischen den beiden Weltkriegen keineswegs eine westliche Demokratie war, sondern eine halbfaschistische Diktatur mit antijüdischen Gesetzen. Und die Pilsudski-Renaissance im heutigen Polen übersieht anscheinend den entschieden antidemokratischen und ebenso antisemitischen Charakter des polnischen Regimes, bevor dieses Opfer der Aggression des Großdeutschen Reiches wurde. Wenn es einen besonders tragischen Fehlschlag der Erziehung gibt, die die kommunistischen Parteien für sich in Anspruch genommen haben, dann ist es der Mißerfolg im Umgang mit ethnischen Konflikten. In dieser Hinsicht haben diese Länder viel zu lernen – insbesondere von Westeuropa.

Ethnische Konflikte als „vormoderne" Konfliktlinien

In der vergleichenden Politikwissenschaft wird zwischen verschiedenen Konfliktlinien unterschieden, die für Konflikte verantwortlich sind, die wiederum ein bestimmtes politisches System dominieren. Nach den Analysen, die Politikwissenschafter wie z. B. Ronald Inglehart vorgelegt haben, kann man drei Typen von Konfliktlinien unterscheiden:

- Die vormaterialistischen Konfliktlinien, die für sich industrialisierende Gesellschaften typisch sind, noch von der Landwirtschaft beherrscht, verbunden mit schwergewichtig nicht-ökonomischen Gesichtspunkten und auch artikuliert als nicht-ökonomische Interessen. Die beiden wichtigsten Fälle dieser Konfliktlinien sind Religion und Ethnizität.
- Die materialistischen Konfliktlinien, typisch für industrialisierte Gesellschaften, charakterisiert durch die Dominanz von Schwerindustrie und Industriearbeiterschaft, verbunden mit wirtschaftlichen Gesichtspunkten und als wirtschaftliche Interessen artikuliert. Der wichtigste Fall dieser Konfliktlinien ist Klasse.
- Die postmaterialistischen Konfliktlinien, typisch für hochindustrialisierte und spätindustrialisierte Gesellschaften, charakterisiert durch bestimmte soziale Indikatoren – wie etwa den Rückgang der Industriearbeiterschaft und den Zuwachs von Dienstleistung und Erziehung, mit Faktoren verbunden, die nicht mehr, zumindest nicht mehr vordergründig, ökonomisch sind. Die wichtigsten Fälle dieser Konfliktlinien sind Ökologie, Geschlecht und Generation.

Unter den Voraussetzungen eines liberalen politischen Systems – eines Systems, das auf dem freien Wettbewerb zwischen mehreren politischen Parteien um Wählerstimmen aufbaut – ist die wichtigste Konsequenz solcher Konfliktlinien das Parteiensystem. Die Existenz und die Dominanz von Parteien, die auf ethnischen und (oder) religiösen Interessen bauen, ist für früh industrialisierte Gesellschaften typisch. Politische Parteien in Asien und Afrika sind die besten Beispiele für dieses Entwicklungsniveau – Parteien, die religiöse oder ethnische Interessen artikulieren. Die Folge der Industrialisierung auf der Ebene des Parteiensystems war, zumindest in Europa, der Aufstieg der Klassenparteien – insbesondere in der Dichotomie zwischen „bürgerlichen" Parteien (konservativ oder liberal) und Arbeiterparteien (sozialistisch, sozialdemokratisch oder kommunistisch) ausgedrückt. Als ein Ergebnis der sozialen Entwicklungen nach der Stabilisierung eines sozialen Systems, charakterisiert durch die Kombination von kapitalistischer Marktwirtschaft und pluralistischer liberaler Demokratie, beginnen nun die Klassenparteien abzusteigen oder ihre Eigenschaften zu verändern – entsprechend der Bedeutung postmaterialistischer Konfliktlinien.

Die Verbindung zwischen sozialer Entwicklung, sozialen Konfliktlinien und politischen Parteien bedeutet selbstverständlich nicht, daß es immer nur eine einzige Ebene der Artikulation von Interessen gibt, verantwortlich für den Konflikt, der ein politisches System dominiert. In der realen Welt der Politik gibt es immer eine Kombination von Interessen. Sogar in den entwickeltsten Industriegesellschaften spielen religiöse und ethnische Interessen eine bestimmte Rolle; und der wirtschaftliche Aspekt des Klasseninteresses hört nicht einfach nur deshalb auf, weil der Postmaterialismus im Aufschwung ist.

Die Erfahrungen Westeuropas

Die politischen Systeme Westeuropas waren nach 1945 sehr stark vom Muster des „Materialismus" beeinflußt. Die Parteiensysteme folgten im wesentlichen dem traditionellen Links-Rechts-Spektrum, das Wahlverhalten war sehr stark vom Faktor Klasse bestimmt. Und in Ergänzung zum Parteiensystem entwickelte sich ein Netz von korporatistischen Entscheidungsmustern aufbauend auf einer Parität zwischen Kapital und Arbeit – wesentlich und hilfreich bei der Stabilisierung der politischen Systeme im Westen Europas, ebenfalls den materialistischen Charakter unterstreichend. Stabilisierung wurde definiert als ein Kompromiß zwischen Klasseninteressen. Die Interessen, die als „vormaterialistisch" galten, waren „sekundär" – mit ihnen wurde in relativ erfolgreicher Form umgegangen. Beispiele dafür sind die Lösungen vieler ethnischer Konflikte durch die Garantie einer Autonomie für die Minderheit: Wie in Italien für das Aosta-Tal und für Südtirol; wie in Deutschland für die dänischsprechende Minderheit in Schleswig-Holstein; wie in der Schweiz durch die Machtbalance zwischen den drei Sprachgruppen, schon Ende des 19. Jahrhunderts etabliert und erneuert durch die Lösung des schwierigen Jura-Problems 1974; wie in Spanien, nach dem Ende des Franco-Regimes, in den Fällen des Baskenlandes und Kataloniens.

Die Regeln, die bei der erfolgreichen Lösung ethnischer Konflikte in Westeuropa nach 1945 angewandt wurden, folgten immer der Idee der Machtteilung. Alle ethnischen Interessen, die stark genug für die Bildung einer Fragmentierung waren, wurden eingeladen, sich an den Machtstrukturen des politischen Systems zu beteiligen. Entsprechend dem Modell der „Konkordanzdemokratie", das Lijphart beschreibt, ist die Lösung ethnischer Konflikte möglich entweder als „Separation" innerhalb eines föderalen Systems (wie in den Fällen des französischsprechenden Teiles des Kantons Bern, der der neue Kanton Jura wurde) oder als ethnische Machtteilung auf regionaler Ebene (wie im Fall Südtirols). Diese zweite Variante ist freilich nur dann erfolgreich, wenn die ethnische Gruppe, die als Minderheit auf nationaler Ebene gilt (wie die Deutschsprechenden in Südtirol), die Rolle der Mehrheit auf regionaler Ebene eingeräumt bekommt – das ist innerhalb der autonomen Provinz Südtirol (Bozen) der Fall. Unter „Lösung" ethnischer Konflikte ist aber niemals die Aufhebung solcher Konflikte, sondern ihre Stabilisierung innerhalb eines politischen Systems zu verstehen.

Der Fall der Schweiz unterstreicht auch besonders, wie wichtig ein bestimmter Faktor für die erfolgreiche Integration verschiedener ethnischer Gruppen in das politische System ist: das Vorhandensein von sich überlagernder Konfliktlinien. Die Schweiz ist ein Land, das nicht nur durch sprachliche, sondern auch durch religiöse Gegensätze bestimmt ist. Die Fragmentierung zwischen Katholiken und Protestanten, in der Vergangenheit – wie zuletzt 1847 – für Gewalt, Krieg und explosive Auseinandersetzungen verantwortlich, ist eben nicht parallel mit der ethnischen Fragmentierung. Die größten ethnischen Gruppen, die Deutsch- und die Französisch-Schweizer, verteilen sich ungefähr gleichmäßig auf Katholiken und Protestanten. Das bedeutet, daß ein religiöser Konflikt zwischen Protestanten und Katholiken nicht identisch ist mit einem ethnischen Konflikt. Indirekt hilft die ethnische Fragmentierung, die religiösen Spannungen zu integrieren – und die religiöse Fragmentierung bedeutet die Aufweichung ethnischer Spannungen.

Die westeuropäischen ethnischen Konflikte sind jedoch nicht immer erfolgreich gelöst. Belgien, trotz vieler Verbesserungen, die die neue Verfassung brachte, ist weiterhin tief geteilt in einer sehr feindseligen Weise – geteilt entsprechend den sprachlichen Gegensätzen. Nordirland ist überhaupt die dramatische Ausnahme: In diesem Fall war die westeuropäische Demokratie nicht fähig, irgendein Modell zur Lösung des Konfliktes zu finden – ein besonders explosiver Fall einer vormaterialistischen Konfliktlinie zwischen Protestanten und Katholiken. Dennoch – verglichen mit der Vergangenheit ist die Bilanz Westeuropas im Umgang mit vormaterialistischen und materialistischen Konflikten erfolgreich. Westeuropa war und ist daher in der Lage, sich mehr und mehr auf die Konfliktlinien zu konzentrieren, die für diesen hochindustrialisierten Kontinent typisch sind: auf die Umwelt, auf das Geschlecht und auf die Generation.

Freilich: Im Umgang mit ethnischen Konflikten neuen Typs ist auch Westeuropa keineswegs erfolgreich. Gegenüber nicht traditionell ansässigen ethnischen Gruppen, wie Migranten und Einwanderer, entwickelt sich in Westeuropa eine feindselige Abwehr. Diese ethnischen Konflikte neuen Typs stellen für Westeuropa eine neue Herausforderung dar. Allerdings sind, durch die Wanderungsströme, von diesen ethnischen Konflikten neuen Typs die neuen Demokratien in Mittel- und Osteuropa nicht unmittelbar betroffen.

Zur Typologie ethnischer Konflikte in Mittel- und Osteuropa

Die ethnischen Konflikte in Mittel- und Osteuropa können in zwei Gruppen geteilt werden: in internationale und in intranationale ethnische Konflikte.

Internationale ethnische Konflikte sind Konflikte, die bestehende internationale Grenzen überschreiten. Die ethnische Fragmentierung in diesen Fällen schließt die Möglichkeit oder auch Wahrscheinlichkeit von Konflikten zwischen souveränen Staaten ein – wie auch die Möglichkeit oder Wahrscheinlichkeit von politischen Absichten, die auf die (mehr oder weniger friedfertige) Umverteilung von Territorien zwischen solchen souveränen Staaten zielen. Das übliche Muster der internationalen ethnischen Konflikte ist, daß ein Staat die Rolle des Anwaltes für eine ethnische Gruppe innerhalb der Grenzen eines anderen Staates übernimmt.

In Mittel- und Osteuropa gibt es viele Beispiele für solche Konflikte: der bereits artikulierte Konflikt zwischen Ungarn und Rumänien bezüglich der ungarischen Minderheit in Siebenbürgen; der mögliche Konflikt zwischen Ungarn und der ČSFR (oder der Slowakei) bezüglich der ungarischen Minderheit in der Slowakei, ein Konflikt, der noch nicht offiziell artikuliert ist; der Konflikt zwischen der Türkei und Bulgarien bezüglich der türkischen Minderheit in Südbulgarien, ein Konflikt, der in der Schlußphase des kommunistischen Regimes in Bulgarien bereits heftige Formen angenommen hat; der traditionelle Konflikt zwischen Bulgarien und Jugoslawien (oder Mazedonien) bezüglich des ethnischen Status von Mazedonien und der Mazedonier, eines Volkes, das – dem traditionellen bulgarischen Verständnis entsprechend – eigentlich Teil des bulgarischen Volkes ist; der Konflikt zwischen Albanien und Serbien bezüglich der albanischen Bevölkerung im Kosovo, eine Bevölkerung, die in dieser autonomen serbischen Provinz die deutliche Mehrheit bildet; der Konflikt zwischen Rumänien, der Ukraine, Moldawien und – soweit als politischer Akteur überhaupt noch vorhanden – der UdSSR über die komplexen ethnischen Verhältnisse im Grenzgebiet; der Konflikt zwischen Polen und Litauen bezüglich der polnischen Minderheit in Litauen bezüglich der polnischen Minderheit in Litauen.

Intranationale ethnische Konflikte sind Konflikte zwischen ethnischen Gruppen innerhalb bestehender, international anerkannter Grenzen – ohne die Möglichkeit des Eingreifens von außen durch einen anderen souveränen Staat, der die Rolle des ethnischen Anwalts spielt. Intranationale ethnische Konflikte beinhalten die Möglichkeit, daß die Existenz eines souveränen Staates durch das Aufbrechen dieses Konfliktes bedroht wird; daß ein solcher Staat letztlich in mehrere Staaten zerfällt, wie etwa nach dem Zusammenbruch Österreich-Ungarns 1918.

Diese Konflikte sind in der Region Mitteleuropas und Osteuropas zahlreich. Die bloße Existenz von Bundesstaaten, die für die europäische Ordnung nach 1945 so wichtig waren, wurde durch solche Konflikte bedroht und schließlich zerstört – die Existenz der UdSSR und Jugoslawiens, beide als multiethnische Föderationen gegründet; beide auf einem Verfassungskompromiß zwischen den verschiedenen ethnischen Gruppen (oder Nationen) aufbauend, beide mit einer Nation, die traditionell eine Führungsrolle beansprucht – die Russen und die Serben. Aber auch ein anderer Staat ist massiv von intranationalen ethnischen Konflikten betroffen – die Republik der Tschechen und Slowaken, die auf dem mühsam arrangierten Kompromiß zwischen den beiden Völkern aufbaut; einem Kompromiß, der von slowakischen Nationalisten bereits wieder in Frage gestellt wird. Der Zerfall Jugoslawiens, begleitet von kriegerischer Gewalt, und der Zerfall der

UdSSR sind in erster Linie die Folgen solcher intraethnischer Konflikte. Der Zerfall bedeutet die Umwandlung intraethnischer in interethnische Konflikte – etwa bezüglich der serbischen Minderheit in Kroatien, bezüglich der russischen Minderheit in der Ukraine, bezüglich der ukrainischen Minderheit in Moldawien.

Auf der Suche nach Lösungen

Die Fälle intranationaler ethnischer Konflikte zeigen deutlich, daß es keine einfache Lösung für die ethnischen Konflikte in Mittel- und Osteuropa gibt. Die Neuziehung von Grenzen und die Unabhängigkeit bestimmter Regionen löst die ethnischen Konflikte nicht. Es gibt überhaupt keine einfache Lösung – weil es keine klaren, übereinstimmend akzeptierten ethnischen Grenzen in dieser Region Europas gibt. Überall in Mittel- und Osteuropa gibt es das Phänomen der „Minderheit in der Minderheit". So waren z. B. für die UdSSR die Letten eine ethnische Minderheit – konfrontiert mit der Mehrheit der Russen. Aber in Lettland selbst sind nun die Russen eine ethnische Minderheit, konfrontiert mit den Letten, die eine knappe Mehrheit in Lettland sind. Die Russen haben nun, gemeinsam mit Litauern und Esten, Ukrainern und Weißrussen, Deutschen und Juden, den Status einer Minderheit. Und innerhalb Lettlands gibt es keine Region, die einfach nur von Russen bewohnt würde. Die Russen sind über Lettland verstreut, in einigen Teilen – wie etwa in Riga – sind die Russen sogar die stärkste ethnische Gruppe.

Lettland ist nur ein Beispiel – die volle Unabhängigkeit Lettlands kann als Konsequenz demokratischer Prinzipien gerechtfertigt werden, auch als eine historische Wiedergutmachung angesichts des Schicksals, das Lettland (wie auch die beiden anderen baltischen Staaten) 1940 zu erleiden hatte. Aber die lettische Unabhängigkeit bedeutet überhaupt nicht die Lösung der ethnischen Konflikte. Sie bedeutet nur, daß diese Konflikte von der Ebene einer riesigen Föderation auf die Ebene eines vergleichsweise kleinen Staates verschoben wurden.

Der Konflikt zwischen den Georgiern und den Osseten in der Republik Georgien demonstriert einen anderen Aspekt möglicher ethnischer Explosionen: Am 31. März 1991 und am 26. Mai 1991 sprach sich eine überwältigende Mehrheit der Wähler Georgiens für die Unabhängigkeit des Landes aus. Zur selben Zeit aber beschloß das georgische Parlament in Tbilissi, die Autonomie der Region Südossetien aufzuheben – eine Autonomie, die diese Region innerhalb der Verfassung der UdSSR genießen konnte. Georgischer Nationalismus, der – verständlich – für sich die Werte der Demokratie und des Selbstbestimmungsrechtes in Anspruch nahm, um die Unabhängigkeit zu rechtfertigen, verwehrte einer nichtgeorgischen Minderheit die Selbstverwaltung innerhalb Georgiens.

Ein anderer Fall ist der des serbischen Nationalismus: Dieser nimmt die Rolle des ethnischen Advokaten für die serbische Minderheit innerhalb Kroatiens in Anspruch; gleichzeitig aber hat Serbien die Autonomie der Albaner im Kosovo aufgekündigt, eine Autonomie, die dieses Volk innerhalb der (Tito-)Verfassung von 1972 in Anspruch nehmen konnte. In beiden Fällen berief sich der Nationalismus auf demokratische Werte, um die kommunistische Ordnung herauszufordern – aber derselbe Nationalismus war und ist nicht bereit, bestimmte Rechte anderer ethnischer Gruppen zu respektieren.

Die ethnischen Konflikte in Mittel- und Osteuropa sind um so explosiver, als sie nicht, wie in der Schweiz, von überlagernden religiösen Faktoren relativiert und gemäßigt werden. Nahezu alle Serben sind orthodoxe Christen – es gibt keine signifikante katholische Minderheit innerhalb Serbiens. Die Kroaten sind wiederum in ihrer überwältigenden Mehrheit Katholiken – es gibt keine signifikante Zahl von orthodoxen Kroaten. Die Ungarn in Rumänien sind entweder Protestanten oder Katholiken – sie sind aber nicht orthodox wie die große Mehrzahl der (ethnischen) Rumänen. Die Fragmentierung zwischen Türken und (ethnischen) Bulgaren in Bulgarien ist durch die Tatsache verhärtet, daß diese Fragmentierung auch eine zwischen Moslems und Christen ist. Der faktische Bürgerkrieg zwischen Azeris und Armeniern in Aserbaidschan ist durch die parallele religiöse Fragmentierung um so bedrohlicher – die Azeris sind traditionell Moslems, die Armenier ebenso traditionell Christen. Ethnizität und Religion in Mittel- und Osteuropa sind üblicherweise parallel – die Religion spielte und spielt eine entscheidende Rolle bei der Schaffung von ethnischer Identität.

Zurück ins 19. Jahrhundert?

Diese Entwicklung ethnischer Konflikte ist verantwortlich für die wichtigsten Probleme, mit denen die Region nach dem Zusammenbruch der kommunistischen Regime konfrontiert ist. Es gibt keine Anzeichen, daß der postmaterialistische Faktor die politischen Parteien und den Parteienwettbewerb in Mittel- und Osteuropa dominieren wird. Und es gibt auch keine Anzeichen, daß der materialistische Faktor die politischen Strukturen herausbilden wird, die Mittel- und Osteuropa bestimmen werden. Es ist nicht der Klassenkonflikt, der die politische Landschaft in Mittel- und Osteuropa heute beherrscht; das ist, beispielsweise, der Grund, warum – vielen Voraussagen zum Trotz – sozialdemokratische Parteien bei den ersten Wahlen in diesen Ländern so wenig erfolgreich waren. Es sind der ethnische Konflikt und, in einem gewissen Ausmaß, der religiöse Konflikt, die die entscheidenden Faktoren für die Erklärung des Ergebnisses der ersten Wahlen unter den Rahmenbedingungen eines Mehrparteiensystems sind. Während Westeuropa mehr und mehr vom Postmaterialismus bestimmt wird, erleben Mittel- und Osteuropa die Demokratie in Verbindung mit der Wiederkehr des Vormaterialismus.

Natürlich gibt es dafür auch Erklärungen – ein Klassenkonflikt, jedenfalls im marxistischen Sinn, kann nicht ohne (sozioökonomisch definierte) Klassen stattfinden. Und eine „bürgerliche" Klasse in diesem Sinn besteht in den vormals kommunistischen Ländern eben nicht. Das allein kann aber noch nicht den

Rückfall in den Vormaterialismus erklären; ein Rückfall, der vormoderne Züge trägt.

Es ist wie in einem Spiel, in dem die Spieler zurück auf das Anfangsfeld müssen. Das gilt freilich auch für Westeuropa – die ethnischen Konflikte neuen Typs, repräsentiert durch Migranten und Einwanderer, werden von den erfolgreich erprobten Konfliktlösungsmustern im Umgang mit traditionellen ethnischen Konflikten nicht erfaßt. Das gilt aber auch und vor allem für die politischen Systeme Mittel- und Osteuropas.

Nach der Lähmung, in die die kommunistischen Regime gemündet haben, entdecken die Gesellschaften Mittel- und Osteuropas nun die Demokratie westlichen Stils. Sie beginnen, die Abwesenheit politischer Unterdrückung und die Abwesenheit eines Machtmonopols zu genießen. Aber statt ihre politischen Systeme entsprechend den Erfahrungen zu gestalten, die Westeuropa nach 1945 gemacht hat, scheinen Mittel- und Osteuropa in Zustände zurückzufallen, die für den Anfang unseres Jahrhunderts charakteristisch waren. Dies war ein Europa, das durch Nationalismus und ethnische Spannungen bestimmt war; durch Kriege, die mit nationalen Interessen gerechtfertigt wurden; ein Europa, das einen erschreckenden Mangel an ethnischer und religiöser Toleranz aufwies. Die neuen Demokratien scheinen viel mehr von einem Europa der Balkankriege und der traditionellen deutsch-französischen Rivalitäten beeinflußt – und viel weniger von einem Europa, das Adenauer und de Gaulle, De Gasperi und Churchill erfolgreich aufgebaut haben.

Mittel- und Osteuropa müssen nicht nur die Demokratie, sondern auch die Geschichte wiederentdecken. Sie müssen die einfache Tatsache zur Kenntnis nehmen, daß es keinen Stillstand in der sozialen Entwicklung gibt; daß der europäische Friede und die europäische Demokratie es notwendig machen, aus der europäischen Erfahrung zu lernen. Wenn Europa ein Kontinent des Friedens und der Demokratie sein soll, dann muß sich die Geschichte vorwärts entwickeln – und nicht rückwärts.

Ryszard Skarzyński

Erschöpfung einer Gedankenwelt. Das klassische Paradigma des Konservatismus im 20. Jahrhundert

Der Konservatismus des 20. Jahrhundert ist keine tote Denkströmung. Im Gegenteil. Wir beobachten das Aufblühen von verschiedenen Richtungen des Konservatismus, was mit den Krisen unserer Gesellschaft verbunden ist. Eine genaue Analyse dieser Gedankenwelt im 20. Jahrhundert zeigt jedoch, wie unterschiedlich diese Richtungen sind. Ihre Vertreter deuten und beurteilen sehr oft auf eigene Weise die Vergangenheit, die Tradition des Konservatismus und, was besonders wichtig ist, die Wirklichkeit der gegenwärtigen Gesellschaft. Sie denken manchmal ganz im Sinne von Edmund Burke, manchmal aber lehnen sie seine Ideen ab. Das stellt uns die wichtige Frage nach dem Wesen des Konservatismus in der Zeit der großen Umwälzungen des 20. Jahrhunderts und nach der Aktualität des klassischen Paradigmas dieser Denkstruktur.

1. Das klassische Paradigma des konservativen politischen Denkens

Es wird zwar nach den Wurzeln des Konservatismus in den Gedanken von Richard Hooker gesucht,[1] jedoch das reife Paradigma dieser Strömung findet man bei Edmund Burke, der als erster großer Vertreter der konservativen Denktradition anerkannt ist. In seinem Werk *Betrachtungen über die französische Revolution* skizzierte er die Struktur einer Gedankenwelt, die wir als konservative bezeichnen. Später versuchten verschiedene Denker diese Tradition zu modernisieren und zu verändern, trotzdem blieb sie in den Werken anderer Autoren erhalten. Deswegen können wir von einem Paradigma des Konservatismus sprechen, das auch im 20. Jahrhundert lebendig ist, obwohl diese Ideenwelt zahlreichen Spaltungen unterlag, die mit ihrer Erneuerung und Anpassung an die neuen Gesellschaftsverhältnisse verbunden waren.

Das Hauptziel des politischen Denkens von Burke und anderen Ideologen der Gegenrevolution war die Erhaltung des Bestehenden, der Wirklichkeit der vorhandenen Welt, die gegen freie Aktivität des Menschen geschützt werden sollte. Er kritisierte die französische Revolution und versuchte diejenigen natürlichen Kräfte der Gesellschaft aufzuzeigen, die über ihre Vitalität entscheiden. Burke bekämpfte nicht alle Veränderungen, wollte jedoch beweisen, daß eine große Umwälzung der Gesellschaftsstruktur auf keinen Fall durch Menschen geleitet werden könnte. Sie ist nicht zu beherrschen und bringt mit sich nur eine Zerstörung der bisherigen Errungenschaften.

Das Hauptziel des Konservatismus bestimmt seine Denkstruktur, die in drei Ideengruppen gegliedert werden soll: 1. in einen politischen Skeptizismus: 2. eine pessimistische politische Anthropologie; und 3. eine organische Gesellschaftstheorie.

1. Der Konservatismus war eine Antwort auf die hoffnungsfreudige Philosophie der Aufklärung und optimistische politische Visionen des Liberalismus. Burke und andere Vertreter der gegenrevolutionären Strömung kritisierten den Glauben an die menschliche Vernunft, die angesichts der ungeheuren Probleme der modernen Gesellschaft machtlos ist. Sie waren der Ansicht, daß eine für die Beherrschung dieser Probleme und eine erfolgreiche Leitung der menschlichen Gemeinschaft erforderliche Vision durch die theoretischen Spekulationen nicht zu erreichen sei.

In dieser Überzeugung wurzelt die negative Haltung gegenüber allen Vorschlägen einer radikalen Gesellschaftsveränderung, die jedoch nicht nur mit der Beurteilung der menschlichen Vernunft, sondern auch mit einer besonderen Deutung der politischen Aktivität der Massen verbunden ist. Die Konservativen sind gegen die Ausdehnung des politischen Bereiches, in dem verschiedene Kräfte um die Macht kämpfen. Der Mensch ist nicht nur auf intellektueller Ebene schwach, sondern auch auf dem Gebiet des Moralischen unvollkommen und deswegen nicht reif zur freien Handlung. Die politische Freiheit, die mit einer Loslösung von Tradition und ethischen Werten verknüpft ist, bringt Unsicherheit und Destabilisierung der Gesellschaft mit sich.

2. Der politische Skeptizismus der konservativen Schriftsteller war eine Reaktion auf die Modernisierungsversuche der feudalen Gesellschaft und verursachte eine Ablehnung der Selbständigkeit des einzelnen Individuums, die nicht nur in den Ideen der intellektuellen und moralischen Unvollkommenheit des Menschen gipfelt, sondern auch die Quelle der pessimistischen politischen Anthropologie ist. Die Grundlage dieser Anthropologie schafft die Überzeugung, daß der Mensch von Natur aus böse ist, d. h., er wird als gefährliches und dynamisches Wesen betrachtet. Bei den Schriftstellern der Gegenrevolution verbindet sich diese Idee mit dem theologischen Dogma von der Sünde, wo sie eine besonders evidente Rechtfertigung erreicht.

3. Die konservative Gesellschaftstheorie stützt sich auf den politischen Skeptizismus und die pessimistische politische Anthropologie. Diese Ideen begründen eine wichtige Behauptung: Weil der Mensch zur autonomen Tätigkeit nicht fähig ist, müssen Faktoren gefunden werden, die seine Handlungswege bestimmen und die Überwindung seiner moralischen und intellektuellen Schwächen ermöglichen. Als die drei wichtigsten Faktoren betrachten die Konservativen Gemeinschaft, Tradition und Religion.

Burke schrieb, daß die Gesellschaft auf einem Vertrag beruhe, den man jedoch nicht auflösen könne, weil er eine Partnerschaft bedeute, und zwar zwischen den Verstorbenen, den Lebenden und denjenigen, die in Zukunft geboren werden.[2] Diese Idee von den aufeinanderfolgenden Generationen gibt uns die richtige Vorstellung von der großen Bedeutung der Gemeinschaft, der Tradition und der Religion im konservativen politischen Denken. Alle diese Faktoren spielen wichtige Funktionen in der Erhaltung von stabilen Gesellschaftsverhältnissen.

Die Gemeinschaft bildet einen Teil der Gesellschaft. Sie besteht nicht aus einzelnen, isolierten Individuen, sondern aus Personen, die untereinander in besonderen Verhältnissen stehen. Diese Beziehungen werden durch Sitten, Hierarchie, Tradition und Religion bestimmt. Auf diese Weise ist die Gemeinschaft so etwas wie ein klar abgegrenzter Organismus mit eigener Struktur. Jeder Mensch besitzt Vorrechte und Aufgaben, die von seiner Stellung in der Gemeinschaft abhängig sind. Religion und Tradition liefern für diese Gesellschaft oberste Werte und üben eine wichtige Integrationsfunktion aus. Die Religion, festgesetzte Normen und Sitten bilden die Grundlage der Zivilisation und ermöglichen eine wirksame Übernahme und Fortsetzung der Errungenschaften der aufeinanderfolgenden Generationen.

Bei einzelnen Schriftstellern der Gegenrevolution, besonders in den Werken von Joseph de Maistre, rechtfertigt die pessimistische politische Anthropologie die Vision einer absoluten Macht. Der König ist, wie der allmächtige Gott, ein omnipotenter Gesetzgeber, zu dem die letzte Entscheidung gehört. Er ist ein Hüter des Staates, von dem die ganze Wirklichkeit abhängig ist.

Burke und andere Denker der Gegenrevolution verteidigten die Idee der ewigen Wirklichkeit, die sich zwar auf einzelnen Gebieten langsam verändert, ihr Wesen bleibt jedoch für immer erhalten. Die ewige und unentbehrliche Ordnung war damals die Ordnung der feudalen Gesellschaft, mit ihrer Hierarchie, Tradition, ihren Sitten und ihrer geschlossenen politischen Elite. Die Konservativen haben diese Gesellschaft als einen Teil der von Gott geschaffenen Weltordnung gesehen. Es war eine natürliche Haltung, die man als Folge des Willens zur Verteidigung des Bestehenden betrachten muß.

2. Konservative Antwort auf die Krisen des 20. Jahrhunderts

Zahlreiche Gesellschaftskrisen im 20. Jahrhunderts verursachten eine entsprechende Entwicklung des Konservatismus. Besonders die Krise der zwanziger Jahre und dann die Jahrzehnte nach dem Zweiten Weltkrieg sind mit dem Aufblühen von verschiedenen Strömungen dieser Ideologie verbunden. Die Antwort der konservativen Intellektuellen auf die Veränderungen der gegenwärtigen Gesellschaft war uneinheitlich, weil diese nicht nur in sehr unterschiedlichen Milieus lebten, sondern auch an verschiedene Denktraditionen dieser Richtung angeknüpft und Ideen aus anderen Gedankenwelten übernommen hatten.

Der Wiederaufbau des klassischen Konservatismus war jedoch ein überwiegend europäisches Phänomen. Amerikanische Neokonservative interessierten sich viel mehr für die gegenwärtige Politik als für die alten Denkstrukturen. Sie respektierten die Tradition, die Religion und die durch die Vorfahren hinterlassenen Sitten, aber sie verstanden auch wichtige Probleme, die mit den Gesellschaftsveränderungen verbunden waren. Deswegen akzeptierten sie oft liberale Ideen, beschäftigten sich mit der Entwicklung der Marktwirtschaft, anerkannten die liberale Demokratie und wollten nicht nach den metaphysischen Wahrheiten oder Faktoren, die die Gesellschaft in einer unveränderten Gestalt erhalten könnten, suchen.[3]

Den europäischen Konservatismus des 20. Jahrhunderts kennzeichnet dagegen ein einzigartiger Radikalismus, der mit der Ablehnung der gegenwärtigen Wirklichkeit verbunden ist. In den zwanziger Jahren war die konservative Reaktion auf die Gesellschaftskrise besonders in Deutschland kräftig. Der revolutionäre Konservatismus bildet als Beispiel dieses Radikalismus eine höchst interessante Erscheinung. Er hat jedoch nicht viel mit der Rückkehr zum klassischen Paradigma des Konservatismus zu tun. Die Gedankenwelt der revolutionären Konservativen ist eine Mischung von links- und rechtsradikalen Ideen, die man gegenüber anderen Strömungen nicht genau abgrenzen kann.[4] Erst im politischen Denken der deutschsprachigen Emigration und von anderen europäischen Konservativen, besonders den englischen, finden wir einige Erinnerungsversuche an das klassische Paradigma dieser Strömung.

Der Radikalismus des gegenwärtigen Konservatismus bringt uns noch einmal eine wichtige Frage zum Bewußtsein: Was bedeutet heute Konservatismus? Ist er nur eine politische Haltung, die auf der Verteidigung des Bestehenden beruht? Oder ist das eine Lehre, die mit der Gesellschaftswirklichkeit wenig zu tun hat? Im ersten Fall ist die Erschöpfung des klassischen Paradigmas dieser Richtung sichtbar. Im zweiten Fall bleibt zwar dieses Paradigma erhalten, scheint jedoch politisch bedeutungslos zu sein.

3. Gegenwärtige Versuche des Wiederaufbaus des klassischen Konservatismus

Der Wiederaufbau des klassischen Konservatismus im 20. Jahrhundert bildet eine interessante Erscheinung. Diese Versuche führten jedoch zu keiner Entstehung einer eigenständigen Strömung im Rahmen der konservativen Ideologie. Es sind eher Ideen, die von einzelnen Intellektuellen kommen, als politische Programme, die mit den Interessen von bestimmten Gruppen verbunden wären. Deswegen ist es sinnvoll, sich auf die Analyse ausgewählter Beispiele zu beschränken, die uns das Wesen dieses Phänomens zeigen könnten.

Einer der interessantesten Versuche eines Wiederaufbaus der klassischen konservativen Gedankenwelt ist das Werk von Eric Voegelin. Er gehört zu den deutsch-jüdischen Intellektuellen, die nach Hitlers Machtübernahme nach Amerika gingen und dorthin die europäischen Denkstrukturen übertrugen. Seine Auseinandersetzung mit der Gesellschaftskrise der modernen Welt führte zur Entwicklung einer politischen Philosophie, die sich auf klassische Ideen des Konservatismus stützte.

Voegelin war ein Kritiker der modernen Gesellschaft, in der er nur die Entwicklung des Gnostizismus gesehen hat, d. h. einer Strömung, die auf die Veränderung der bestehenden Welt ausgerichtet ist. Zu den führenden Gnostikern gehören, nach Voegelin, nicht nur Hegel und Marx, sondern z. B. auch Sorel, Nietzsche, Comte und Heidegger. Der Gnostizismus verursachte eine Atomisierung der Gesellschaft und eine Säkularisierung der westlichen Zivilisation.[5] Deswegen wollte Voegelin die Wurzeln der Tradition, die der Erneuerung der Gesellschaft dienen könnten, sichtbar machen, verdammte den Rationalismus und seine utopischen Versuche eines Aufbaus einer menschlichen Gemeinschaft.

Den Kern Voegelins politischer Philosophie bildet die Verteidigung der transzendenten Grundlagen des gesellschaftlichen Daseins. Er meinte: „Ewiges Sein verwirklicht sich in der Zeit. (. . .) Der Ort der Verwirklichung ist im gegebenen Fall die Seele des Philosophen, des *amator sapientiae*, die nach dem ewiges Sein begehrt und seinem Eindringen liebend sich öffnet. (. . .) Wenn also Geschichte der Prozeß ist, in dem ewigen Sein sich in der Zeit verwirklicht, dann ist Philosophie ein geschichtliches Ereignis in dem prägnanten Sinne, daß in der Responsio des Philosophen ewiges Sein in der Zeit wirklich wird."[6]

So wurde Philosophie zur Lieferantin der Wahrheit über das ewige Sein. Krise jeder Gesellschaft ist eine geistige Krise. Ihre Überwindung ist nur von einem Denker möglich, der zur Entdeckung der wahren geistigen Grundlagen einer Gesellschaftsordnung fähig ist, und zwar „durch realistische Verwendung (. . .) von Bestandteilen, die in dem Gesellschaftskörper ständig anwesend sind"[7]. Was in der Geschichte wichtig ist, ist nur die Suche nach den ewigen Wahrheiten, die das gesellschaftliche Leben bestimmen. Jede Epoche hat eigene Wahrheiten, die das Wesen der göttlichen Ordnung und den Sinn der menschlichen Existenz besser zeigen.

Voegelin konnte sich kaum auf die Tradition der bestehenden Gesellschaft berufen, weil diese durch den Gnostizismus beherrscht worden war. Deshalb mußte er eine neue Tradition finden. Er fand sie in einer Strömung der Philosophie, die sich nicht auf das Bilden einer Utopie, sondern auf Entdeckung von ewigen Wahrheiten konzentriert. Die Tradition der richtigen politischen Philosophie fängt mit den Werken der israelischen Propheten und griechischen Philosophen an. Sie widersetzten sich der Zerstörung der Ordnung und schufen Visionen eines richtigen Staates. So ist die Tradition, nach Voegelin, keine Tradition, die durch das menschliche Zusammenleben entsteht, sondern eine Tradition des menschlichen Denkens, das nach ewigen Wahrheiten sucht.

Dieses mußte wesentliche Spuren an der Auffassung der Gemeinschaft hinterlassen, die im politischen Denken von Voegelin eine geistige Gemeinschaft ist. Sie existiert, weil sie eine gemeinsame Symbolik besitzt, die durch Propheten oder Philosophen geschaffen worden war, und drückt durch die gemeinsame Erfahrung des Ewigen aus. Gesellschaftsstruktur und Machtsystem sind hier nicht so wichtig; sie sind einfach von dem Ewigen abhängig.

Etwas anders sah diese Probleme Hermann Rauschning, der auch zum Kreis der deutschsprachigen Emigranten gehörte. Er stand unter dem Eindruck des Nihilismus, der – seiner Meinung nach – zur Zerstörung der geistigen Grundlagen der Zivilisation und der traditionellen Normen führt.[8] Der moderne Mensch setzte sich auf Gottes Thron und machte sich selbst zum Zentrum des Daseins. Er war jedoch nicht in der Lage, die geistigen Grundlagen der Zivilisation zu schützen, und konnte sich dem Verfall der obersten Werte nicht widersetzen. „Wenn sich die obersten Werte entwerten", schrieb Rauschning in einem Buch, das Mitte der fünfziger Jahre veröffentlicht wurde, „so wird alles fraglich, was der Mensch als Norm, Recht, Gerechtigkeit entwickelt. Dann steht der Mensch nicht in einer objektiven Ordnung, sondern jede Ordnung ist nur auf relativen Werten und Wahrheiten begründet. Dann waltet nicht eine absolut geltende Gesetzmäßigkeit, sondern willkürliche Regelungen bestimmen das menschliche Verhalten. Sie verpflichten nicht innerlich, sind ohne bindende Autorität."[9]

Die Gemeinschaft, deren Vorstellung man in den Werken von Rauschning findet, ist keine ausschließlich geistige. Er suchte in der mittelalterlichen Gesellschaft die Wurzeln der richtigen Tradition. Der moderne Mensch macht sich selbst zur alleinigen Quelle von Werten und Wahrheit. Mit dem autonomen Menschen ist jedoch ein organisches Ganzes, ein Volk, eine Gemeinde, sogar eine Familie unvereinbar. Jede Gemeinschaft erfordert Solidarität und ein Verhältnis wechselseitigen Dienstes füreinander. Die menschliche Vernunft ist kein Instrument der Integration. Die Gemeinschaft braucht andere Faktoren, die eine wirksame Identifizierung des einzelnen mit dem Ganzen ermöglichen. Ein Wunschbild war für Rauschning die mittelalterliche Menschheitsordnung. Sie war „ein gliedhaftes Ganzes, das auf ein einziges Zentrum hin bezogen war. Dieses Zentrum war Gottes Wille. (. . .) Die Institutionen, die ‚Gerechtigkeit' der weltlichen Ordnungen waren trotz aller ihrer Schäden und Schwächen sanktioniert, weil einem ständigen Gericht, einer immerwährenden Korrektur unterworfen"[10].

Der wichtigste Teil der Gedankenwelt von Rauschning ist die Idee der Gemeinschaft, die das ganze menschliche Leben erfaßt. Sie ist zugleich, mit ihren obersten Werten und Sitten, so etwas wie eine Tradition, deren Anfang die mittelalterliche Gemeinde bildet. Diese Tradition kann der modernen atomisierten Gesellschaft entgegengestellt werden. Sie bringt als Vorbild eine Vision der stabilen Gesellschaft mit sich, die der Erneuerung der gegenwärtigen Welt dienen könnte.

So finden wir in den Werken von Voegelin und Rauschning wichtigste Ideen des klassischen Konservatismus. Der politische Skeptizismus ist bei den beiden Verfassern sehr deutlich: Der Mensch soll auf keinen Fall die bestehende Welt verändern, weil dieses nur zu eine Katastrophe führt. Die Wirklichkeit ist autonom, und sie muß autonom bleiben, damit die Gesellschaft erhalten bleiben könnte. Die pessimistische Anthropologie scheint auf den ersten Blick abwesend zu sein, wenn wir jedoch die wichtigsten Arbeiten von Voegelin und Rauschning genauer lesen, wird auch sie sichtbar. Sie steckt nämlich in der These, daß der Mensch im Verhältnis zum Bestehenden passiv bleiben soll. Er ist unvollkommen und deswegen nicht imstande, sie zu verbessern. Die Menschen machen jedoch in dieser Richtung ständig Versuche. Die revolutionäre Neigung ist dauerhaft. Das ist das Gefährlichste im Menschen und verursacht, daß er sich unter ständiger Kontrolle befinden muß. Er braucht unbedingt oberste Werte und Sitten, die sein Leben und Verhalten bestimmen.

Rauschning entwickelte auch eine der klassischen Fassung entsprechende konservative organische Gesellschaftstheorie. Die Gemeinschaft ist – nach ihm – ein gut geordneter Organismus. Er kehrte hier zur richtigen Quelle zurück, nämlich zur feudalen Gemeinschaft des Mittelalters. Bei Voegelin ist es etwas anders. Die organische Gesellschaftstheorie ist hier in ihrer klassischen Darstellung abwesend, weil dieser Denker tiefer gegriffen hat. Er fand die Wurzeln der Tradition im Altertum. Es war ein Versuch, das alte Paradigma in einer neuen Fassung zu zeigen, was eine bessere Rechtfertigung seiner Hauptideen bringen sollte. Im politischen Denken von Voegelin gibt es jedoch auch eine Gemeinschaft, die nicht auf den Sitten, die durch aufeinanderfolgende Generationen übermittelt worden waren, sondern auf obersten Werten und Wahrheiten beruht, die durch Propheten oder Philosophen entdeckt wurden. Sie machen die Gesellschaft zur homogenen politischen Einheit und ermöglichen ihre Erhaltung. Auf diesem Weg ist der Sinn der klassischen Gemeinschaft bewahrt.

4. Zwischen Vergangenheit und Gegenwart. Konservative Ablehnung der Wirklichkeit des 20. Jahrhunderts

Das Problem der bestehenden Wirklichkeit ist so etwas wie die Leitidee des Konservatismus. Das ist kein Zufall, sondern die Folge dessen, daß diese Gedankenwelt eine Antwort auf revolutionäre Versuche der Gesellschaftsveränderung bildet. Angesichts des revolutionären Angriffs auf die existierenden Verhältnisse stellten die konservativen Denker Ende des 18. und Anfang des 19. Jahrhunderts fest, daß die Wirklichkeit gegen die Unwirklichkeit der revolutionären Programme verteidigt werden muß. Utopische Visionen einer besseren Welt, menschliche Träume, bringen die Möglichkeit einer Zerstörung der bestehenden Welt mit sich, weil sie die Massen bewegen und den Glauben an das Erdichtete rechtfertigen.

Die konservativen Intellektuellen verstehen jedoch die Wirklichkeit nicht eindeutig, sondern sie haben mindestens drei unterschiedliche Interpretationen dieses Problems.[11] Sie betrachten die Wirklichkeit als eine ewige Welt, die sich zwar verändert, aber in ihrem Wesen fest bleibt. Alle Umwandlungen betreffen nur sekundäre Gebiete, dagegen werden die obersten Werte und Wahrheiten für immer erhalten, und nur diese bestimmen tatsächlich das menschliche Leben. Sie wurden nicht vom Menschen geschaffen, sondern von ihm ausschließlich entdeckt, deswegen hat er kein Recht, sie zu bestimmen oder zu verändern.

Die zweite Deutung zeigt die Wirklichkeit als Dasein, das durch eine lange Dauer gekennzeichnet ist, d. h., es unterliegt nur sehr langsamen Umwandlungen. Hier möchten die Konservativen auf keinen Fall die Wirklichkeit in ihrer Totalität erfassen. Sie interessieren sich nur für die Zivilisation, für das, was im menschlichen Zusammenleben wesentlich ist und möglichst lang unverändert bleiben soll. Die obersten Werte und Wahrheiten haben für diese Richtung kein absolutes Maß, sie sind einfach ein Ergebnis menschlichen Zusammenlebens, ein Werk der Gemeinschaft.

Die dritte Interpretation betrifft wortwörtlich die existierende Welt, d. h. nicht die Zivilisation, sondern nur die Wirklichkeit des Alltags. In dieser Auffassung ist jede bestehende Ordnung, die schon entsprechend lange dauert, eine richtige und wahre Ordnung. Wenn sie nicht verändert werden muß, soll sie erhalten bleiben.

Im Sinne des klassischen Paradigmas war zuerst nur die erste Deutung möglich. Die bestehende Welt schien ewig zu sein. Die Französische Revolution war jedoch für die konservativen Verfasser eine große Überraschung, die ihre feste Vision der ewigen Welt nicht sofort, aber allmählich zerstörte. Schon Anfang des 19. Jahrhunderts haben die Schriftsteller der Gegenrevolution erkannt, daß die Wirklichkeit sich umwandelt und daß das ein ordnungsgemäßer Prozeß ist. Diese Feststellung brachte die erste bedeutsame Transformation dieser Gedankenwelt mit sich und bildete einen Ausgangspunkt zur Anpassung des Konservatismus an die Bedingungen der existierenden Gesellschaft.

Aber nicht alle Vertreter dieser Richtung wollten eine solche Modifizierung anerkennen. Es war schon ein Grund zur Spaltung und Entstehung von unterschiedlichen Ideenwelten des Konservatismus. Diese Erscheinung kann auch im 20. Jahrhundert beobachtet werden, und sie bildet ein interessantes Phänomen, das eine Grundlage für den Radikalismus in konservativen Kreisen schafft. Die gegenwärtige Wirklichkeit kann nicht mehr als ein ewiges Dasein betrachtet werden. Sie paßt nicht in das alte klassische Paradigma des konservativen Denkens, das als eine Sammlung von obersten Wahrheiten angenommen wird. Im Gegenteil, diese Wirklichkeit macht die Realisierung dieser Wahrheiten und Werte unmöglich. Deswegen muß sie abgelehnt werden.

Das ist die erste und wichtigste Quelle der konservativen Kritik der bestehenden Welt: Diese Welt widersetzt sich ihren Idealen und wird auf diese Weise zu einem fremden Objekt. Ein Teil der Konservativen hat sich entschieden, diese Welt zu opfern und die alte Tradition dieses Denkkreises weiter zu pflegen.

Solche Stellungen findet man besonders leicht in den Werken der konservativen Intellektuellen der deutschsprachigen Emigration, in den Arbeiten von Rauschning, Voegelin und auch von Leo Strauss. Die Ablehnung der gegenwärtigen Wirklichkeit brachte den Wiederaufbau des klassischen Paradigmas mit sich. Für Strauss ist die Geschichte des politischen Denkens eine Geschichte der Verselbständigung des Menschen, was zur Zerstörung der Welt führt, weil der Mensch nicht nach obersten Werten und Wahrheiten sucht, sondern sie selbst schafft.[12] Es ist kein Denkschema, das man auch in den Werken von Voegelin und Rauschning findet. Zum Beispiel: Letzterer sah im Nihilismus die wichtigste Ursache der beiden Weltkriege und der Zerstörung bürgerlicher Gesellschaft.

Ähnliche Visionen der Krise versuchte der englische Konservative Michael Oakeshott zu schaffen. Sein Begriff des „Rationalismus" dient der Kritik und Ablehnung gegenwärtiger Welt. Der Nachrenaissance-Rationalismus ist eine Denkweise, die die Tradition, oberste Werte und anerkannte Sitten, also die Grundlagen der Zivilisation bagatellisiert. Dagegen glaubt der Rationalist bedingungslos an die Macht des eigenen Verstandes, der ihm angeblich die Bestimmung aller Wahrheiten ermöglicht. Tatsächlich bringt der Rationalismus den Sieg der Ideologie über die Tradition, den Glauben an die Fähigkeiten des Menschen zur Verbesserung der Welt wider den Glauben an Gott und die Abweisung der durch vergangene Generationen geschaffenen Sitten.[13]

Der Radikalismus der konservativen politischen Philosophie wurzelt in der Deutung der gegenwärtigen Wirklichkeit. Das klassische Paradigma des konservativen Denkens bildet hier die wichtigste Grundlage ihrer Beurteilung und macht die Annahme dessen, was tatsächlich existiert, unmöglich. Im Gegenteil: Dieses Paradigma regt zur Suche nach einer besseren Welt an. Nur auf diese Weise kann die politische Philosophie des Altertums oder die mittelalterliche Gemeinschaft als richtige Wirklichkeit anerkannt und der gegenwärtigen Unwirklichkeit gegenübergestellt werden. So wird ein Kritiker der Utopie zum Schöpfer der „wahren" Gesellschaft, die zwar keine glückliche Gemeinschaft bildet (persönliches Glück gehört nicht zum Thema der konservativen politischen Philosophie), jedoch nichts mehr oder sehr wenig mit den Realitäten unseres Zusammenlebens zu tun hat.

5. Erschöpfung des konservativen politischen Denkens im 20. Jahrhundert: Ende eines Paradigmas?

Rauschning war sich dessen bewußt, daß die alten Denkstrukturen im 20. Jahrhundert nicht ausreichen. Im Buch über den Nihilismus schrieb er deutlich: „Die Zuspitzung der allgemeinen Krise erweist damit ihren Katastrophencharakter: die Unzulänglichkeit aller bisherigen Kategorien"[14]. Er war jedoch nicht in der Lage, eine Antwort auf die Krise zu geben, die sich auf originelle Ansätze stützen könnte. Die neue Welt war nicht akzeptabel für ihn, deswegen suchte er Grundlagen für sein eigenes politisches Denken im klassischen Paradigma des Konservatismus.

Im gegenwärtigen Konservatismus sind leicht wesentliche Widersprüche zu finden. Der wichtigste Widerspruch ist sein Radikalismus, der in der Ablehnung des Bestehenden gipfelt. Sie entstehen, weil Vertreter dieser Richtung keine einheitliche Wirklichkeitstheorie besitzen. Deswegen befinden sich z. B. in den Werken von Rauschning interessante Analysen der gegenwärtigen Welt, besonders im Buch *Die Zeit des Deliriums*. Dort jedoch, wo er eigene Meinungen verallgemeinern wollte, sieht die Sache ganz anders aus. Rauschning konnte die bestehenden Verhältnisse nicht akzeptieren und deutete sie nur als Zeichen des Nihilismus. Das klassische Paradigma des Konservativismus war für ihn ein wichtiger Stützpunkt, der die Rechtfertigung der Ablehnung gegenwärtiger Wirklichkeit ermöglichte.

Die Erneuerung der klassischen konservativen Denkstrukturen ist auf keinen Fall ein allgemeines Phänomen. Ganz im Gegenteil. Die eingehende Analyse dieser Erscheinung ist jedoch für das richtige Verstehen des Konservatismus des 20. Jahrhunderts unbedingt notwendig. Sein Wesen zeigt sich deutlich in der Vision der Wirklichkeit und im Verhältnis zur bestehenden Gesellschaft. Der Konservativismus kann nämlich ganz unterschiedlich sein, und das hängt in erster Linie von seiner Konzeption der Wirklichkeit und der Gebundenheit an die klassischen Ideen der Gegenrevolution ab.

Die politische Philosophie von Carl Schmitt ist ein gutes Beispiel, wie man das konservative Denken entwickeln kann, ohne sich auf das klassische Paradigma zu berufen. Sein Dezisionismus bildet auch einen Versuch einer Verteidigung menschlichen Zusammenlebens. Es ist jedoch kein ewiges Dasein. Jede Ordnung muß – nach Schmitt – hergestellt werden, und zwar durch einen Souverän, der „die Situation in ihrer Totalität schafft und garantiert. Er hat das Monopol dieser letzten Entscheidung".[15]

Es ist eine neue originelle Idee der Wirklichkeit im konservativen Sinne. Sie findet ihre Rechtfertigung nicht in ewigen Wahrheiten, in der Vergangenheit oder im Ertrag der Kultur, sondern in der Entscheidung des Souveräns, der die höchste, rechtlich unabhängige und nicht abgeleitete Macht besitzt. Sie wurzelt in der Überzeugung, daß es keine Legitimität mehr im alten, traditionellen Sinne gibt. Die obersten Werte und Wahrheiten können die Macht nicht begründen, weil sie eigene Evidenz verloren haben. Deswegen bleibt es nur eine Diktatur.

Eine wichtige Modifizierung des Konservatismus hat auch ein anderer deutscher Denker unternommen. Gert Kaltenbrunner stellte Mitte der siebziger Jahre ein Programm des „neuen Konservatismus" vor. Er forderte damals den Verzicht auf die Ideale der Vergangenheit und die Akzeptierung der Zukunft. Es ging ihm um die liberale Demokratie, Auseinandersetzung mit den tatsächlichen Problemen der gegenwärtigen Welt, d. h. mit der Entwicklung der Zivilisation, Erneuerung der Gesellschaft und Verteidigung der Verfassung. Kaltenbrunner hat offen gesagt, daß Monarchie und ihre theologische Rechtfertigung heute keine Bedeutung mehr haben.

Diese Beispiele zeigen uns, wie unterschiedlich die konservativen Denkstrukturen sein können. Die politischen Ideen von Strauss, Rauschning, Voegelin und Oakeshott sind mit den politischen Visionen von Schmitt und Kaltenbrunner unvereinbar. Sie sahen die Grundlagen des menschlichen Zusammenlebens ganz anders und haben verschiedene Lösungen zur Erhaltung des Staates vorgeschlagen.

Trotz des Wiederaufbaus des klassischen Konservatismus im 20. Jahrhundert muß gesagt werden, daß das Paradigma dieser Denkstruktur eine tiefgreifende Krise erlebt. Es ist nicht möglich, auf dieser Grundlage das Wesen der gegenwärtigen Welt zu verstehen. Das klassische Paradigma kann in seiner Totalität nur als Ausgangspunkt zur Ablehnung der existierenden Gesellschaft dienen, wie in den Werken von Rauschning, Voegelin, Strauss oder Oakeshott. Ein moderner Konservatismus, der nicht in utopischen Visionen gipfeln möchte, darf lediglich einzelne seiner Ideen übernehmen, aber die ganze Denkstruktur muß von den konservativen Intellektuellen neu geschaffen werden. Nur eine solche Haltung ermöglicht eine vernünftige Berücksichtigung aller Phänomene, die der modernen Gesellschaft eigen sind.

Wie gezeigt wurde, können sich mehrere Konservative in der modernen Welt nicht wiederfinden. Sie haben die gegenwärtige Wirklichkeit als Unwirklichkeit erkannt und suchten Grundlagen für ein eigenes Denken, das die Entdeckung der wahren Wirklichkeit ermöglichen würde. Als eine solche Grundlage ist das klassische Paradigma des Konservatismus bezeichnet worden. Das verursachte jedoch die Entwicklung des konservativen Radikalismus, weil für einen Teil der Vertreter dieser Richtung die Suche nach einer idealen Gemeinschaft oder obersten Wahrheit wichtiger war als das wirkliche Zusammenleben der Menschen. So ging das ursprüngliche Wesen des Konservatismus verloren. In der Fassung von Voegelin, Rauschning, Oakeshott und Strauss hörte diese Strömung auf, eine Verteidigung des Bestehenden oder der vergangenen Gemeinschaft zu sein. Träume vom Ewigen brachten nur utopische Visionen einer besseren Welt.

Die Frage nach dem Wesen des heutigen Konservatismus kann nur beantwortet werden, wenn wir diese Phänomene berücksichtigen. Sie erzeugten die Spaltung des Konservatismus und die Radikalisierung eines Teils ihrer Vertreter. Die kritiklose Annahme des klassischen Paradigmas führte unbedingt zum Radikalismus, aber sie war nur dort möglich, wo die konservativen Intellektuellen sich zu einer Ablehnung der Wirklichkeit entschieden haben. Ihr Verhältnis zur gegenwärtigen Gesellschaft war der wichtigste Faktor. Die Verachtung des Wirklichen zwang zur Suche nach dem Ewigen, das Unwirklichkeit gegenübergestellt werden könnte.

Das klassische Paradigma ist als einheitliche Gedankenwelt keine Grundlage mehr des Konservatismus, der noch die bestehende Wirklichkeit erfassen will, weil er in einem solchen Fall im Radikalismus gipfelt. Deswegen berufen sich diese Konservativen, die sich im Rahmen der gegenwärtigen Welt bewegen möchten und auf diese Welt Einfluß auszuüben beabsichtigen, nur auf einzelne Ideen des klassischen Paradigmas oder versuchen sogar neue Paradigmen zu schaffen.

Jedoch bedeutet der realistische Konservatismus heute dasselbe, was er auch Anfang des 19. Jahrhunderts bedeutete: die Verteidigung des Bestehenden, weil das Bestehende bekannt und sicher (obwohl heute nicht mehr ewig) ist, während das, was angeblich besser sein soll, ganz unbekannt und noch nicht überprüft worden ist. Auf jeden Fall ist dieses politische Denken mit der Gefahr einer falschen Einschätzung der Wirklichkeit verbunden. Das Bestehende kann nämlich sehr oft nicht mehr haltbar sein. Aber die Konservativen müssen das Risiko eingehen. Das ist die Folge ihrer politischen Haltung. Zur Rechtfertigung dieser Haltung brauchen sie jedoch ein neues Paradigma, das die einzelnen Ideen der Gegenrevolution enthalten sollte, jedoch als Ganzes von neuem geschaffen werden müßte.

Anmerkungen

1 A. Quinton: The Politics of Imperfection. The Religions and Secular Traditions of Conservative Thought in England from Hooker to Oakeshott. London 1978, S. 28.
2 E. Burke: Reflections on the Revolution in France (1790). London 1964, S. 93.
3 P. Steinfels: The Neoconservatives. The Men Who Are Changing America's Politics. New York 1979, S. 49–69.
4 S. Breuer: Die „Konservative Revolution" – Kritik eines Mythos. Politische Vierteljahresschrift, 1990, H. 4., S. 586, 603.
5 E. Voegelin: The New Science of Politics. Chicago 1952.
6 Ders.: Anamnesis. Zur Theorie der Geschichte und Politik. München 1966, S. 254–255.
7 Ders.: Nietzsche, the Crisis and the War. Journal of Politics, 1944, H. 2, S. 179 und 195.
8 H. Rauschning: Die Revolution des Nihilismus. Kulisse und Wirklichkeit im Dritten Reich. Zürich 1938, S. 8.
9 Ders.: Masken und Metamorphosen des Nihilismus. Frankfurt/M. 1954, S. 15–16.
10 Ebd., S. 125–126.
11 R. Legutko: Konserwatyzm (Konservatismus). Res Publica, 1988, H. 2, S. 145–159.
12 L. Strauss: The Three Waves of Modernity. In: ders.: Political Philosophy: Six Essays. Indianapolis 1975, S. 81–98.
13 M. Oakeshott: Rationalism in Politics (1974). In: ders.: Rationalism in Politics and Other Essays. New York 1962, S. 1–36.
14 H. Rauschning: Masken und Metamorphosen, S. 87.
15 H. Schmitt: Politische Theologie (1922). Berlin 1985, S. 20.

V.
Anhang

Summaries

Bogusława Bednarczyk

National Conflicts in the Second Republic and Some Suggestions of their Solution

The object of this study had been to present in a general outline the national conflicts of the Second Republic and the project of their solutions in relation to the history of the Second Republic, and to the current political problems of inter-war Poland, as well as some reflections concerning contemporary Poland.

Special reference has been made to the spread of national consciousness. The nationality factor in Polish history possessed an immense range of nuances, which are often misrepresented in modern studies. Therefore it has been necessary to set forth the explanation of general term nationalism.

In 1918 the task of integrating the peoples, institutions and traditions of the country's disparate elements was immense. Therefore our main areas of interest in this paper lay in the ethnic issues. There was the whole kaleidoscope of the organizations serving each of the minorities. While formulation their programmes and criticising successive Polish governments, national minorities referred to three basic points which have been presented in this article.

We also deal with the political stance of the leading circles, where there may be distinguished four trends concerning the minorities question.

In our final assumption it has been emphasized that the problems concerning national minorities and conflicts are very intricate, however one conclusion is obvious: only tolerance, mutual understanding and elements of law can guarantee a peaceful co-existence of various ethnic grups in one country.

Maria Borucka-Arctowa

European Integration and National Identity

Is European Integration a danger for national identity or, on the contrary, unity versus diversity constitutes a false dichotomy in social theorizing? Other problems discussed in the paper include: the emergence of "globalization" as a process of growing interconnectedness of structure, culture and agency; the challenge for the social sciences – the search of theoretical assumptions and the multi-level approach to the new problems; how to understand the "alien" beliefs and tradition?; the different ways of self- and social-identity, their historical and cultural conditions; nation, State and "global village" as basis for identity; the role of the law in the process of integration; the way of Central and East European countries to the Common European House, expectations and reality; social consciousness of the breakthrough period, its crucial role in transformations and inevitable inconsistencies.

Zora Bútorová

One Year After Free Elections: The Difficult Birth of Democracy in Slovakia

On first sight, the fall of the communist regime in Slovakia had the same dimension as the revolution in Bohemia. In reality, however, it has occurred in a society which differs from Bohemia in so many historical and political, cultural and intellectual, as well as economic respects that these characteristics cannot be neglected. The present contribution analyses the development of the political scene in Slovakia after November 1989 and interprets it in the context of the major political events and social problems of this period. Particular attention is given to the national question and the reaction of the population towards the first steps of radical economic reform. The present contribution relies on the results of a whole series of empirical investigations of the department of social analysis of Komensky University at Bratislava.

Ernst Bruckmüller

The Divided Mythology. The Backgrounds of a Non-uniform National Identity

National identity as the consensus of a defined population is not based on objective criterions, but it is a subjective category. There are meanings and ideas like religious feelings. We can see them as a package of "mythology".

In Austria an unambigous national identity is not existing. Now we can find an increasing national identity, but quite diverse identification models.

The author discusses the following problems:

The myth of descent: This myth is bringing security of self-consciousness, because men like it to find the "roots" of a group in common descending. Now, in austria a part of the population believes that Austrians are descending from Bavarians, another part believes in descent of Celts, Slaves, Romans, etc.: a divided myth.

The mythology of national symbols: The National Holiday shows little continuity. In the First Republic the 12th of November was designated a National Holiday – observed only until 1933. In 1965 was the "Day of Flag", which had been celebrated since 1957, declared a National Holiday. Belonging the anthem, the beautiful music of Haydns "Kaiserhymne" in 1945 was hopeless compromised. Now there is a new anthem with the text of Paula von Preradovic. The flag and the state coat of arms presented fewer problems.

The referring points of memory building a collective identity. There are existing historical deficits: Austria did not have a common crown for the countries building the state. In Austria also failed revolutions. We cannont find any integrative experience of political or military "success" in the history of the 19th and 20th century, excepting the State Treaty of 1955. Because of this the myth of State Treaty and Neutrality is very important for the national identity of Austria.

Janina Czapska
Nationalistic Attitudes of the Polish People

Our times are full of flared up and easily inflammable national feelings. Many societies go through deep crises. Old social structures and systems of value fall apart. In such times one question becomes substantial – the one questioning the manifestations, the force and the consequences of nationalism. The article, on the basis of indicators of nationalist attitudes pointed out in the introduction, presents an analysis of their "empirical aspect" in the Polish society. The results of research indicate that the empirical foundation of the thesis of Polish megalomania is very frail. Poles look at themselves in a considerably realistic way; they are aware of both the advantages, as well as the disadvantages. A contemptuous attitude towards other nations is the second important indicator of a nationalist attitude. In the second half of the 80's the Polish attitudes towards other nations could have been described as distinctively lacking all emotional engagement and growing indifferent. The reasons of such a situation could be found in long-term economic crisis, which resulted in the concentration for Poles' attention on everyday hardships.

In the beginning of the 90's the situation went through a considerable change; an express, increasing fondness of rich nations of the Western Europe and America, together with a clearly distinguishable decrease of liking for nations determined as the ones responsible for our economics, were observed. The latter nations were usually small and weak. This occurrence was most likely connected with such factors as growing sensation of threat in basic aspects of everyday life and the weakening of safety, caused by the inability to adapt oneself to the changes taking place.

In such a social context the locally appearing examples of intolerance and hostility towards some nations, as well as the emphasis placed on the exceptionality of the Polish nation are very alarming.

The most important task for the future seems to be the determination whether these nationalistic groups have a real chance of becoming a reference group of great consequence.

Krystyna Daniel

The Role of Schools and the Catholic Church in the Shaping of Xenophobic, Nationalistic and Anti-semitic Attitudes Among Polish Youth

There are certain images of Jews in the consciousness of Polish youth. Because of lack of direct contact of Polish young generation with Jews those images are often limited, incoherent and concerning the older youth stereotyped which have been created in the process of primary and secondary socialization. Among the socializing institutions, apart from family, an important role is also played by school and the Catholic Church (in the process of religious education), especially when the content conveyed by them is cohesive with the content internalized in the primary socialization.

According to the presented research the real role of school and the Catholic Church in the process of creation a positive attitude towards Jews among 14–years-old seems to be passive and far away from pluralistic orientation. The whole situation is complicated by the impregnation of school programs with concepts which are a good basis for developing nationalistic attitudes.

Ludmiła Dziewięcka-Bokun

From Communism to Democracy: the Polish Revolution of 1989 and its Aftermath

The paper discusses political phenomena in Poland after the historical changes in 1989 such as: unsteady balance, reshuffles of leaders, changeability of alliances and transitoriness of legal solutions, post-communist mentality, lack of efficient and sufficiently numerous elites, absences of self-representation of competing societal interests. The polish variant of a "revolution from the top" has resulted in a state of "systemic vacuum" which is currently demonstrated by lack of social forces which could create the structures of a new system and by continuous decline of collective activity and a growing social frustration. The alleged author's hypothesis is that not only the Polish but also the East European future is likely to be neither a liberal democracy nor an authoritarian dictatorship but a hybrid that will resemble much to the particular pattern of state-society relations from which it has emerged.

Erich Fröschl

What Is Old About New Conservatism?

In the 19th and 20th century conservatism played an important role together with liberalism and social democracy in developing political theory for modern industrial society.

In the eighties of our century neo-conservatism has established growing influence as an ideology reaching back to the ancient Manchester liberalism and trying to change the societies by a so called neo-conservative revolution. The results can be studied in contemporary British and US-society. From the point of view of welfare-state oriented continental democratic societies this roll back to pure market anarchy is a mess.

Also in Eastern Europe nowadays the neo-conservative fundamentalism has some attractivity as an alternative to the long rule of communist central planning ideology. But the critical question is the high price and the social costs for this radical change.

A clever mixture of market economy, state interventionism and international support – typical for the reconstruction-period of Austria and Germany after 1945 – could be the far better way to build up flourishing democratic societies in Middle and Eastern Europe.

Stanisław Gebethner

Stages of Decay and Failure of Real Socialism in Central and Eastern Europe

Since the beginning of the 1989, when the Round Table negotiations had started in Poland, significant and rapid revolutionary changes took place in the whole region of Central and Eastern Europe. This process of radical social, political and institutional (as well as constitutional) changes is still under way. It has not been finished yet. But we can say that the old constitutional, political, social and economic order known previously as the real socialism, or the Communist regime, collapsed. Each country or this region is now struggling to construct its own version of the future. The ultimate goal may be democracy and capitalism, but there is no consensus on how to get there. The process on institutional and systemic changes in political sphere is in these countries really impressive and spectacular. But there is no certainty what will be a final outcome of this process. The imposition of an authoritarian post-communist political system – with right wing and nationalistic oriented dictatorship – is possible as well as the installation of democratic institutions and development of democratic political systems may be predicted. The character of the eventual future economic system in these countries is not clear, too.

Krzysztof Glass

The Rediscovery of Central Europe: Old Clothes and New Desires

In the last two years Central Europe has changed considerably, while diverse new directions are being set by the establishing of economic unity in Europe and the end of the post-war division of the continent. Some of these signals caused a slight sense of annoyance for a short time, others led to irritations in domestic policy because they were at least regarded as faux pas. That was the case e. g. during the German-Soviet meeting at the eastern bank of the Bug river at Brest-Litowsk, i. e. directly at the Polish-German border. In a certain sense this meant a repetition of the scenario of the last phase of World War I and also of the period 1939/40. One can doubt whether this comparison is legitimate and regard this a pure coincidence of a tight political schedule. Nevertheless the historic significance of the place remains. Among that part of the Polish public which is conscious of history this dialogue immediately in front of their own door step left a slightly bitter taste.

Volkmar Lauber

The Democratiozation of the Economy in Western and Eastern Europe

The democratization under way in East Central Europe since 1989 differs in important respects from that which took place in Western Europe in the years after World War II. In Western Europe a new balance was struck in favour of working class, which was thus drawn into a new political consensus and more effective participation. Also, the building of a dynamic capitalism by the Marshall Plan was well designed to enhance the loyalty of the population towards democratic political institutions.

In East Central Europe by contrast the much harder transition taking place since 1989 is not similarly cushioned. The necessary economic stabilization of public finance and the economy tends to restrict popular and parliamentary participation in politics. The introduction of the market economy is likely to increase social tensions before the produced wealth can diminish them. These are unfavorable conditions for the development of democratic institutions and of political loyalty towards such institutions. East Central Europe needs to invent its own path towards democracy.

Peter Malina

National Minorities in Austrian School-Books

The discussion of the history of ethnic/national minorities in Austrian school–books is principally characterized by two significant approaches. On the one side there is no doubt, that minorities and their specific problems are of great importance: most of the school-books reserve at least one chapter to the description of the rights of minorities in Austria as well as in the world. When historical events are to be discussed, minorities on the other side become rather invisible. As a silent minority they are almost neglected and are only mentioned, when they cause troubles to the (german speaking) majority. Their aims to separate from the multinational Donaumonarchie 1918 are interpreted as desertion; when describing the history of the First Republic of Austria, school-books forget the legal claims of those Austrians, who belonged to an ethnic minority (Slovenes, Croats . . .) and they very seldom mention the part of the Slovenian Austrians in the resistance movement against nazism 1938–1945. Summing up: inspite of some revisions Austrian history school-books still have problems to realize, that Austria is a country inhabited by Austrians of German, Slovenic and Croatic language with their own history.

Helga Matuschek

Nationalism and Universalism

The paper deals with the participation of foreigners in Austria. Their participation is located between two basic principles. The first one is the democratic idea, the second one the nation state principle.

The influence of these principles is discussed on different topics: Regulations of immigrants, the status of foreigners, participation of the labour market, social and political rights and naturalisation.

Robert Menasse

The Third Connotation of Nation Conception. Austria's Problems in Becoming a Nation and its Effects on the Changed Situation in Central Europe

Austria's becoming a nation was put into effect de facto as well a socio-politically quite late, namely after 1945. This had, historically unique in the process of becoming a nation, fundamental policy reasons: to reattain state sovereignty it was indispensable to prove that Austria was an independent nation. Only in this way, could the wish for state sovereignty be well founded and any suspicion as to further desire to join Germany dispelled. Within the area of conflict between foreign policy's necessity to declare Austria a nation and internal political insecurity in explaining what Austria's national identity might be, a new version of both "classical" concepts of a nation came about. A curious amalgamation of elements stemming from both concepts came together to create a third and new concept, which at long last contributed internally in a very nebulous way to a unified austrian identity, however, causing distinct contradictions externally, particularly in Austria's Central European policy.

Petr Mareš/Ladislav Rabušic/ Libor Musil

Bourgeois Society and Cultural Changes in Central Europe

In Central Europe a wide-ranging political turn has occurred, and subsequently further economic changes are taking place. In order to avoid a reversal of these changes, a profound change in the culture of the populations in post-communist countries is essential. About 70% of the population have been socialized by communist ideology and the masses have been imbued with the idea of state paternalism, including those who were enemies of communist ideology. Without cultural changes towards a society based on bourgeois values stability and democracy cannot be maintained. The contradiction between the new social reality and the old values are still regarded as frustrating. Thus, while a new identity is still being searched for, such reactions like e. g. growing nationalism become possible.

Krzysztof Pałecki

The Dynamic of Political Transition: Toward the New Paradigm

The collapse of communism exposed the misery of political theory. At least that important part of it which concerns the politicaL change. What has happened in Central and Eastern Europe in this decade not only had not been predicted – with very few exceptions – but what is much worse, has not been adequately and satisfactorily explained till now.

This situation raises a provocative question as to the capability of existing methods of explanation in political science for the elucidation of such political changes. In spite of numerous works devoted to this task, an unproportionately small step has been made toward our understanding of this historical set of events, labeled sometimes by the internally contradictory term: the peaceful or quiet revolution.

Anton Pelinka

Ethnic Conflicts and Solutions in Central and Eastern Europe

The developments after the break-down of the communist regimes have led to a return of ethnic conflicts, although many believed that such intensive conflicts had already been overcome. This is also a particular aspect of the political defeat of Marxism-Leninism. In solving these conflicts, simple formulae (like the "right of self-determination") would not be of any real help. What is more promising is to resort to experience in Western Europe, which shows how to deal with ethnic conflicts in a democratic way.

Manfred Prisching

Collection Catchwords. Intellectual Currents in the Western Europe Countries

Social groups use catchwords, labels or metaphors in order to express their considerations or sentiments concerning the situation of the society in which they live. There are books which shape these paradigms, and some of them become bestsellers. The catchwords penetrate the feuilletons, they are more and more used in discussions and conferences. In a time when most people recommend to the East European countries to follow the path of Western industrialism it is appropriate to sketch the dimensions and the structure of the Western states by listing up these attempts which shall condense the situation of a social entity in certain terms. Such terms are, e. g., the post-industrial society, the post-materialist revolution, post-modernity, the affluent society, late capitalism, the achieving society, modern narcissism, market society, limits of growth, zero-sum society, civic culture, civil society, corporatism, ungovernability, and many others. The collection of terms shows the intellectual fashions which rise and decline, and it gives an impression of the complexity of modern societies – and of the difficulty to grasp their nature.

Teresa Sasińska-Klas

The Question of Reviving Social-Democratic Ideals in Poland Today

The metamorphosis of the system in Poland in the years 1989–1990 has caused changes among the political left: On the one hand it has led to the dissolution of the communist party and the foundation of social-democratic parties at its place; on the other hand, new "shades of red" and new forms of political articulation emerged, like e. g. the "Social-democratic Union" and the "Social-democracy of the Polish Republic". The strategies of both parties are not very different from each other, although both groups choose different tactics. While the first party wants a true share of power, the second is contented with having just political influence. Two questions arise from the present situation: 1. Why does social-democracy not find a larger acceptance and legitimation among the voters? 2. If the social-democratic movement is not credible enough, then one may ask with which other political alternative this would be the case?

Barbara Serloth

Back to the Present: Old and New Kinds of Irrationalism

The fall of the Iron Curtain was a clear sign of the end of confrontation and the beginning of wide cooperation. It is true that this development in the East and West of Europe has raised certain expectations but it has not in any way influenced the change which was already beginning to emerge but only deepened the negative trends of the 1980s. These trends set by irrationalism (or rather by various kinds of irrationalism) can be called quite probably a by-product of post-modernism.

By looking more closely at the wide spectrum of irrational ways of thinking and acting, one simply cannot help asking which are the off-springs of the traditional views of the world within the wide field of nationalism and conservatism and which are new forms of anti-rational attitudes in communication and consumer society. As a result, the first part of this contribution "Back to the present" suggests that on the one hand restorative tendencies seem to be present again in social politics and culture, and supposed relationships between old and new forms of irrationalism are being discussed.

Ryszard Skarzyński

Exhaustion of an Intellectual World. The Classical Paradigm of Conservatism in the 20th century

Changes of conservativism in the 20th century give rise to the major question of the importance and relevance to the present of the classical paradigm of this movement, which was created in the 18th century. In the intellectual world of the 20th century we find numerous attempts of modernizing this paradigm, which aim at revising and adapting this ideology to the conditions of present-day society. These attempts, however, entail a profound change of the classical paradigm. On the other hand, some attempts at reviving this paradigm ended with a radical rejection of present-day reality and had less political influence. This shows that classical conservatism cannot grasp the conditions of contemporary society with the paradigm created in the 18th century and exhausts its intellectual energy by going back to ideals of the past. This is how the political thinking in the sense of the old conservative paradigm has become impossible. What is important is only the question which aspects of this intellectual world have remained relevant.

Karl Stuhlpfarrer

The Alpine Man. Or: Being German. The History of a Seduction

Many weeks ago, when we had to formulate the topic, nobody could have the faintest idea that we are living through a period which has shown us how the Alpine man traverses the expanse of space and time. The feeling of the sublime almost overcame me to flee from my topic, to turn towards less oppressing questions. But as Peter Rosegger once so aptly said in a note of July 1, 1899

"There is only one virtue in the fight for self-assertion, and that is unbounded loyalty towards one's own people."
Thus the Alpine man of the year 1930 stands erect in his heavy jacket and lederhosen with the feather on his hat and his walking stick in his left. In front of him towering Germania, crowned with castles and holding her right hand firmly. The border barrier between Germany, German-speaking Austria, and the torn-off Germans is thrown down, the black, one-headed eagle is shielded by the mighty crown of the oak-tree.

Klaus Unterberger

The Modern Conservatism and Integrative Functions of the Political System. Perspectives and Positions within the Actual Conservatism-Discussion

The main aspect of this article deals with a political slogan, which has set the tone of the sociological discussion of the eighties: The "New Conservatism" affecting the theory of the industrial civilization.

In the center of the reflections is the amount of the influence of these political conception concerning the actual scientific discourse as well as daily life. Discussed are the economic strategies of the modern conservative theory, its relevance to the status of the welfare system and its change during the last years. How the conservative values affect the forming of opinion is described at different spheres of society.

The "new conservatism" is not restricted to the traditional conservative institutions. Its social significance relate to different political interests. This is why the different types of regulative and integrative functions are the principle criterion for the sociological effiency of the strategies of the modern "conservatism".

How these regulative strategies get realized is part of a description of different social scenarios.

Biographical Notes

Bednarczyk, Bogusława
Dr. Ph. D. , June 1977, Jagiellonian University Cracow, Poland. Dissertation: The History of British Imperial Doctrines in the XIXth century. M. A. Cum Laude, September 1970, Jagiellonian University, Cracow, Poland. Thesis: Clausulas concerning the Enemy Countries after the Second World War enclosed in the Charter of the United Nations. Present post: lecturer at the Faculty of Law, Institute of Political Science, Jagiellonian University, Cracow.
Publications: Some Reflections on British 19th Century Imperial Thought, in: Studia Historica, Jagiellonian University 1981. – "Historic Compromise" – Italian Communist Party During the 70s, in: Occasional Paper Research Institute The John Hopkins University, Bologna Center, no. 28, April 1980. – The Role of the Universal Declaration of Human Rights in the Development of Modern Political Thought in Eastern Europe – paper prepared for the 20th Study Session on Human Rights in Strasbourg, July 1989.

Maria Borucka-Arctowa
Univ. Prof. Dr., is Professor of Sociology of Law and Legal Theory in the Institute of Political Sciences of the Jagiellonian University of Cracow. She received her degree of law from the same university. She was teaching Theory of Law and State, Sociology of Law, Philosophy of Law, Logic, Methodology of Social Sciences and Social Psychology. She is also the Head of the Research Group on Legal Consciousness at the Institute of Legal Sciences of the Polish Academy of Sciences. She was directing many Research Projects and published numerous books and articles on natural law and socio-legal aspects of human rights, legal policy, legal and political consciousness, functions of law, efficiency of administration of justice. Her current research interests include the impediments of transition toward the new democracies, legal socialization, the socio-legal aspects of European Integration.

Bútorowá, Zora
Dr., graduate of the Department of Sociology at the Philosophical Faculty of the Comenius University in Bratislava. Author of more than fifty studies in the field of the sociology of work, standard of living, sociology and ethics of science. Member of the Committee of the Slovak Sociological Society and the editorial board of the journal Sociólogia. In the ISA she concentrates on the nationality problem.

Busek, Erhard
Dr., born in Vienna, Austria, on March 25, 1941, Erhard Busek received his law degree from the University of Vienna in 1963. During his studies, he showed keen interest and organizational talent in student affairs (Chairman of the Austrian Youth Council).
He began his professional career as legal adviser to the association of members of the Austrian People's Party at the Austrian Parliament and, later, as Secretary General of the Austrian Federation for Trade and Commerce. In 1975 he was appointed Secretary General of the Austrian People's Party and elected Member of Parliament in 1975.
In 1976 Dr. Busek entered municipal politics. He was appointed head of the Viennese People's Party and City Councillor. After the municipal elections in 1978, he won the seat of Vice-Mayor of Vienna, a position that he held until 1987. In April 1989 he was appointed Minister of Science an Research.
Dr. Busek was elected Chairman of the Austrian People's party on June 28th, 1991 and appointed Vice Chancellor of Austria on July 2nd, 1991.

In addition to his political career, Dr. Busek has held many lectures on domestic and foreign matters and participated in a great number of historical and political symposia in Austria and abroad. His travels led him to many European countries as well as to the United States, Central America and the Far East. Starting in 1981 Dr. Busek has travelled to Poland frequently to meet with members of the Solidarność movement. He has also travelled to several other neighbouring countries. During these trips he has met representatives of trade unions and Christian social groups, long before the "Silent Revolution" took place.
Over the past twelve years, Dr. Busek has invited many prominent international personalities, including scientists, economists, and people active in the cultural sector to lecture in Vienna, thus promoting international exchange between Austria and international intellectual life.
Publications: "Die unvollendete Republik", 1968. – "Demokratiekritik – Demokratiereform", 1969, together with G. Wilflinger. – "Urbanisierung", 1970, together with other authors. – "Qualitative Marktwirtschaft", 1975, together with Ch. Festa and I. Görner. – "Wien – ein bürgerliches Credo", 1978. – "Mut zum aufrechten Gang", 1983. – "Projekt Mitteleuropa", 1986, together with E. Brix. – "Wissenschaft, Ethik und Politik", 1989, together with M. Peterlik. – "Brücken in die Zukunft – Weltausstellung Wien – Budapest 1995", 1989.

Bruckmüller, Ernst
Univ. Prof. Dr., born in 1945, in St. Leonhard am Forst, Lower Austria; studied history and German philology at the University of Vienna. There he is Extraordinarius Professor and teaches at the Institute of Social and Economic History. Since 1971 publisher of "Beiträge zur historischen Sozialkunde", common with Hannes Stekl and others; since 1991 chairman of the "Institut für Österreichkunde".
Principal publications: Landwirtschaftliche Organsiationen und gesellschaftliche Modernisierung. Vereine, Genossenschaften und politische Mobilisierung der Landwirtschaft Österreichs vom Vormärz bis 1914, Salzburg 1977. – Nation Österreich. Sozialhistorische Aspekte ihrer Entwicklung, Vienna 1984. – Sozialgeschichte Österreichs, Vienna 1985.

Janina Czapska
Dr., born on January 17, 1955 in Jaworzno. Law studies at the Jagiellonian University in Kraków. 1974 diploma thesis "Right of defence". Since 1978 assistant professor at the Jagiellonian University. Empirical investigations, e. g. on private prosecution proceedings, attitudes towards politics among workers, workings of the supreme administrative court. 1987 dissertation "Role conflict and compliance with the law". Since then adjunct professor at same chair. Numerous empirical investigations. Research and publications in the fields of sociology of the law and social psychology of the law, e. g. sense of security, attitudes towards the law and the court, legal socialization, private prosecution proceedings, workings of legal institutions like the supreme administrative court and extraordinary revision of the code of criminal procedure.

Daniel, Krystyna
Dr., 1975 Master of Law, 1980 Master of Sociology, 1983 Doctor of Law, 1985 Judge examination. Scholar at the Institute of State and Law, Polish Academy of Sciences, 1976–1987. Since 1988 lecturer at the Faculty of Law, Jagiellonian University, Kraków.
Selected publications: Farmer's Attitudes on Aim and Results of the Ownership, Law. Monograph., Ossolineum 1987. – Social Attitudes on the Function of Law (co-authored, ed. by M. Borucka-Arctowa), Ossolineum 1982. – The Effectiveness of Dispute Settlement in Civil Proceedings, in: Pracitce and the Partie's Opinions (co-authored, ed. by

M. Borucka-Arctowa), Ossolineum 1989. – The Social Attitudes towards Courts (co-authored, ed. by M. Borucka-Arctowa), Jagiellonian University Press 1990.

Dziewięcka-Bokun, Ludmiła

Dr., studied law and political science at the Wrocław University from where she took her PhD in 1983. She was a visiting Fellow in the Beograd University, St Hilda's College – Oxford and the Leningrad University. She was also awarded a Fellowship at the Heidelberg University by German Academy of Science (DAAD) and a Democratic Institutions Research Fellowship by NATO. She has published several articles on Polish politics and social policy. She is also an active member of Polish Political Association, International Political Science Association and Policy Studies Organizations of Eastern Europe. Her current research interests include the transition towards democracy in East Central Europe and social/public policy – comparative approach.

Fischer, Heinz

Doz. Dr., born Oct., 9, 1938 in Graz, Austria.

Education: Grammar School from 1948 to 1956 (GCE in July 1956, 1957 finishing a course at a Vienna High School for trade and commerce. 1957 to 1961 studies at Vienna University, Faculty of Law, July 1961 graduation as doctor of laws followed by one year of practice at a Vienna court of justice.

Career: 1963 to 1975 Secretary of Socialist group in Austrian Parliament. 1975 to 1983 and since 1987 Speaker of Labour MPs until 5th November 1990, since 1978 venia legendi as university teacher for political sciences at the University of Innsbruck and the University of Vienna. Since 1979 Deputy Chairman of Austrian Socialist Party. 1983 to 1987 Federal Minister for Science and Research. President of the Austrian Parliament since 5th November 1990.

Fröschl, Erich

Dr., born 1944, studies in political sciences and contemporary history of the 19th and 20th century at University of Vienna and University of Salzburg. Ph. D. 1975, thesis on "Science, research and development policy in Austria 1945–1975". 1970–1975 studying assistant, department of political sciences, University of Salzburg. 1975–1980 chief of press and public relations department of the Social Democratic Party of Salzburg, since 1980 director of Dr.-Karl-Renner-Institut, Vienna, the political academy of the Social Democratic Party of Austria.

Publications: co-editor of "State and nation in multi-ethnic societies", Vienna 1991. – "Democratic revolutions in middle and eastern Europe", Vienna 1990. – "The movement-100-years of Social Democracy in Austria", Vienna 1989.

Gebethner, Stanisław

Dr. jur., lecturer at the department of political sciences of the University of Warsaw. Publications on problems of constitutional law, comparative studies on the question of political culture. Editor and contributor to the studies "Demokracja i wybory – raport z badań Opinie Polaków – Jesień '85" (Democracy and elections – report on the investigation 'Opinions of the Polish – autumn '85). Advisor of the commission of constitutional law of the Polish parliament. Author of the electoral law project of the commission.

Publications: Rząd i Opozycja JKM w systemie politycznym Wielkiej Brytanii, Książka i Wiedza, Warszawa 1967, s. 346; Ustrój polityczny Polskiej Rzeczypospolitej Ludowej, Krajowa Agencja Wydawnicza, Warszawa 1976, s. 375; Modele rządów prezydenckich, IZOiDK, Warszawa 1982, s. 85; The reform of electoral system in Poland and the new Election to People's Councils act of February 13, 1984, Wydawnictwa Spółdzielcze,

Warszawa 1984, s. 34; The reform of electoral system in Poland and the new Election to the Seym Act of May 29, 1985, Interpress, Warszawa 1985, s. 40.

Gerlich, Peter
Prof. Dr., born December 17, 1939. Graduation from Grammar School in 1958. 1958–1964 Studies of law at the University of Vienna. Doctorate in 1964. 1961–62 Columbia University, School of Law. 1962 Master of Comparative Law. 1963–64 University of Saarbrücken. 1973 Habilitation at the University of Vienna (Associate Professor of Political Science).
Publications: Helmut Kramer/Peter Gerlich, Members of Parliament in party democracy, Vienna 1969. – Karl Ucakar/Peter Gerlich, Citizen and representation of the people, Salzburg 1981. – W. C. Müller/Peter Gerlich, Between coalition and competition, Vienna 1983. – Herbert Dachs/Peter Gerlich, Handbook of the political system of Austria, Vienna 1991.

Glass, Krzysztof
Mag. Dr., born August 30, 1944 at Kraków, 1958–63 art grammar school, 1964–70 studies of art history and graphic art at the Jagiellonian University and the Academy of Fine Arts at Krakow. 1973–76 Academy of Plastic arts in Vienna, stage set. 1976–79 Academy of Plastic Arts in Vienna, sculpture. 1983–86 Studies of political science and anthropology. 1986 M. A. (Thesis title: "The Gordian knot in the question of German-Polish coexistence"). 1986–1991 doctoral studies of political science, dissertation: "The conservative alliance. The isms of the 1980s".
Publications: 1981 "Ab- und Zufälle" poetry. – 1982 "Ab- und Zufälle" poetry. – Numerous articles in "Wiener Zeitung", "Arbeit und Wirtschaft", "Frauen in den 80er Jahren" (Women in the 1980s), "Metamorphosen der Wirklichkeit in der Gegenwart Ost- und Mitteleuropas" (Metamorphosis of reality in present-day Eastern and Western Europe), etc.

Jagschitz Gerhard
Univ.-Prof. Dr., born October 27, 1940 in Vienna, 1960/61 start of studies of psychology, education, folklore, egyptology, German language and literature, and history at the University of Vienna. 1968 Doctor of philosophy. 1968–1978 assistant at the department of contemporary history at the University of Vienna, December 1978 habilitation as lecturer of modern history with emphasis on contemporary history. Since May 1, 1985 extraordinary professor of modern history with emphasis on contemporary history at the University of Vienna.
Member in numerous scientific committees and institutions, e. g. chairman of the study group of Austrian audio-visual archives, chairman of the society of photography and history, chairman of the scientific council of the Ludwig-Jedlicka-memorial prize, member of the study group of the Austrian film archive.
Publications: "The youth of Federal Chancellor Dr. Engelbert Dollfuss. A contribution to the intellectual and political situation of the so-called war generation of World War I" (Phil. diss., Vienna 1967). – "The Putsch. National-Socialists in Austria in 1934" (Graz 1976). – "Time takings. Austria in pictures from 1945 to today" (2nd ed. Vienna 1985). – Numerous scientific articles on contemporary Austrian history and on the use of audio-visual media in history. More than 150 lectures.

Lauber, Volkmar
Univ.-Prof. Dr., born in 1944, studied law in Vienna, and Harvard and political science in Paris and at the University of North Carolina at Chapel Hill. Taught in the United States

and the Johns Hopkins School of Advanced International Studies in Bologna, Italy; currently Professor of Political Science at the University of Salzburg. Noumerous contributions on economic, environmental and energy policy and politics. *The Political Economy of France* (New York: Praeger 1983).

Malina, Peter
Dr. phil., born 1941, University of Vienna; since 1982 head of the library, Institute of Contemporary History, Vienna.

Mareš, Petr
Dr., born 1947 in Zlin, Czechoslovakia. M. A. (1974) J. E. Purkyně University, Brno (Masaryk University at present), Department of Sociology. PhDr. (1975) J. E. Purkyně University, Brno, Department of Sociology. Since 1990 Assistent Professor, Department of Sociology, Masaryk University, Brno.
Selected Publications: The Dealing with Unemployment, Universitas 1991, together with L. Rabušic. – Interruption – Some Social Consequences, Brno 1988.

Matuschek, Helga
Doz. Dr., sociologist; assistant professor at the department of sociology, University of Vienna. Founder and spokeswoman of the section "migration and ethnic minorities" of the Austrian Sociological Society.
Publications on the following topics: immigration policy, school and employment problems of foreign youths; family situation of work migrants and persons seeking political asylum; situation and problems of minors seeking political asylum.

Menasse, Robert
Dr., born June 21, 1954. Studied German language and literature, philosophy and political science in Vienna, Salzburg and Messina. Doctorate in 1980. 1981–1988 visiting assistant at the department of literary theory of the University S°o Paulo, Brasil. Lives as a writer in Vienna.
Publications (books): Sinnliche Gewißheit (Sensual certainty), novel, Reinbek bei Hamburg 1988. – Die Sozialpartnerschaftliche Ästhetik, Essays zum österreichischen Geist (The esthetics of social partners, essays on the Austrian mind), Vienna 1990. – Selige Zeiten, brüchige Welt (Blessed times, crumbling world), novel, Salzburg 1991.

Musil, Libor
Dr., born 1959 in Brno. Studies of sociology at Brno University (1978–1982). Doctor of Philosophy 1982. Since september 1990 Assistant Professor at the Department of Sociology, Social Policy and Social Work of the Philosophical Faculty, Masaryk University, Brno.
Selected Publications: Principles of Environmentalization of Technologies, EKO 1/90. Activities of State as a Factor of Unemployment, Brno 1991.

Neisser, Heinrich
Hon. Prof. Dr., born 1939 in Vienna, grammar school, studies of Law at the University of Vienna, followed by doctoral studies in Government and the Course in International Studies. 1960 professional training for judges, 1961–1966 secretary at the constitutional court in Vienna, since 1966 at the Federal Chancellor's Office, 1969/70 minister at the Federal Chancellor's Office, from 1975 Member of Parliament (until 1987), again from May 1989, from January 1987 to April 1989 Secretary of Federalism and Administrative Reform.

Scientific activities: since 1985 lecturer at the department of political science of the University of Vienna, since 1989 honorary professor at the same institution.
Publications: The Federal Chancellor in the framework of the Austrian constitution (together with Welan). – Austrian military law, 3 volumes, 1981 (together with Kopf and Ermacora). – How secure is Austria? (together with Windhager). – Federal electoral law and direct democracy. Articles and contributions in particular on parliamentarism, electoral law, fundamental rights politics, reform of bureaucracy, politics of science.

Pałecki, Krzysztof
Univ.-Prof. Dr., is presently professor at the Faculty of Law, Chair of Sociology of Law, Jagiellonian University, Cracow, Poland. He specialises in legal theory, sociology of law and political science and has contributed numerous essays, articles and books in these fields, both in Poland and abroad. Since 1984 elected Director of the Institute of Political Sciences. In 1991 elected President of Polish Association of Political Science. Member of IPSA and ISA.

Pelinka, Anton
Univ. Prof. Dr., born in Vienna in 1941, studied law and political science, after being professor at the University of Essen and the Pedagogical University in Berlin, professor of political science at the University of Innsbruck. Visiting professor at the University of New Orleans (1981) and at Harvard University (1990/91).
Publications of books and articles on questions of political systems in Austria, parties and organizations and the theory of democracy.

Prisching, Manfred
Doz. Dr., born in 1950 in Bruck/Mur (Austria), studies of law (Dr. jur. in 1974) and economics (Mag. rer. soc. oec. in 1974), assitant professor at the departments of philosophy of law, of economics and economic policy, and of sociology. Habilitation in 1985, award Innitzer-Prize, 1978/88 at the Rijksuniversiteit Limburg (Maastrich/NL).
Publications: "Crises. A sociological analysis", 1986. – "Protest of the unemployed and resignation in the economic crisis", 1988. – Numerous articles in economic theory and policy, sociology of politics, cultural sociology, theory of social sciences, history of ideas.

Rabušik, Ladislav
Dr., born 1954 in Uherskě Hradistě. M. A. (1978) J. E. Purkyně University, Brno, Department of Sociology, Department of English and American Studies. PhDr. (1980) J. E. purkyně University, Brno, Department of Sociology. 1985–1987 Visiting Lecturer, Department of Czech Studies, Beijing, China.
Selected Publications: Life Activities of Czechoslovak Youth, SPFFBU 1982.
Scandinavian Marriages – Anticipation of Development of European Family?, Brno 1985.
The Role of Kinship in Aging Chinese Society, vol. 59, No. 1, 1991.

Sasińska-Klas, Teresa
Dr., born 1948. M. A. in Sociology 1970, Jagiellonian University (with distinction). Ph. D. in Political Science 1977, Jagiellonian University (with distinction). Head of the Section on Journalism, Jagielloniean University (1984).

Serloth, Barbara
Mag. Dr., born August 26, 1963 in Vienna. Studies of political science and anthropology. Diploma thesis "Political currents in Switzerland between 1930 and 1950". 1986–1991

doctoral studies of political science, dissertation: "Social passivity as a stabilizing alternative in society".
Publications: Numerous articles in "Wiener Zeitung", "Arbeit und Wirtschaft", "Frauen in den 80er Jahren"(Women in the 1980s), "Metamorphosen der Wirklichkeit in der Gegenwart Ost- und Mitteleuropas" (Metamorphosis of reality in Eastern and Western Europe today), "Zukunft", etc.

Skarzyński, Ryszard
Univ. Prof. Dr., born February 2, 1956. Doctorate 1983, habilitation 1988. Professor at the University of Warsaw, Białystok campus. Head of the department of political science. Lecturer at the institute of political studies at the Polish Academy of Sciences in Warsaw, head of the department of the history of political thinking. Research focuses on the history of political thinking and political theory. In preparation: A book on the political theory of Carl Schmitt. Head of a research programme on the history of liberalism
Major publications: The intellectuals and the crisis. A study of political thinking of the German-speaking emigration (1988, revised edition 1991).

Stuhlpfarrer, Karl
Doz. Dr., born 1941 in vienna, assistant professor of contemporary history at the University of Vienna. Publications on Austrian, German and Italian contemporary history, in particular on questions of minorities.

Unterberger, Klaus
Dr., born 1962, studies of political science, communication science; free-lance journalist at the Austrian Radio.